GEDDES & GROSSET

WELSH-ENGLISH dictionary

GEDDES & GROSSET

WELSH-ENGLISH dictionary

Published 2006 by Geddes & Grosset,
David Dale House, New Lanark, ML11 9DJ, Scotland

Dictionary compiled by D. Geraint Lewis
Phrasebook written by Dr D Islwyn Edwards

ISBN 10: 1 84205 568 2
ISBN 13: 978 1 84205 568 7

Printed and bound in China

Foreword

The *Welsh Dictionary* is an accessible and practical reference book for all those interested in learning the Welsh language. It consists of two sections that combine to provide a comprehensive reference tool: a basic, clearly set-out Welsh–English/English–Welsh dictionary that contains over 20,000 headwords; and a Welsh phrasebook with useful phrases in English and Welsh and easy-to-use pronunciation guides to help learners make themselves understood in everyday situations.

CONTENTS

THE WELSH LANGUAGE TODAY

Welsh is spoken by a total of 508,098[(1)] people in Wales or 18.7 per cent of the population aged three years and over (2,723,623). In fact, 24.6 per cent of the children aged between 5 and 9 and 26.9 per cent of the children aged between 10 and 14 claimed to have knowledge of the language which is quite remarkable in view of its decline during the last hundred years.

The numbers of Welsh speakers who live outside Wales is not known, although it is estimated that there are between 150,000 (extrapolated from Census data) and 450,000 (from a media survey) Welsh speakers in England. In Patagonia, Argentina, it is estimated that there are 1,000 speakers of the language. There are further unknown numbers in Scotland, Ireland and various countries throughout the world.

Between 1800 and 1900 the percentage of Welsh speakers dropped from 80 per cent to 50 per cent, and that was mainly due to the Industrial Revolution that brought an influx of English-speakers into the country. In fact, the proportion of Welsh-speakers has further declined at every Census since 1901:

43.5 per cent spoke Welsh in 1911.
37.1 per cent spoke Welsh in 1921.
36.8 per cent spoke Welsh in 1931.
28.9 per cent spoke Welsh in 1951.
26 per cent spoke Welsh in 1961.

20.8 per cent spoke Welsh in 1971.
18.9 per cent spoke Welsh in 1981.

Then in 1991 only a slight decline was recorded but this time there were also grounds for optimism about the future of the Welsh language. In 1981, 18 per cent of those between the ages of 3 to 15 claimed to be able to speak Welsh, a figure which had risen to 22 per cent by 1991. For the first time since 1891, when the census first concerned itself with the Welsh language, knowledge of Welsh was found to be more widespread among children than among the population as a whole.(2)

Half the population of Wales live in the anglicised regions of Gwent and in the Cardiff area of Wales, where the proportion of Welsh-speakers is down to about a mere 2 per cent in some areas. It is not surprising that the counties of Anglesey, Gwynedd, Ceredigion and Carmarthenshire, where Welsh-speaking percentages in excess of 50 per cent of the population are to be found, and as high as 75 per cent in certain areas, are considered to be the strongholds of the Welsh language, and this is reflected in the culture generally and in the political affiliation to Plaid Cymru – the Party of Wales.

It is estimated that approximately 1 in 5 of the population of Wales speak Welsh and read and write the language with a high degree of fluency. It is the first language of many in the western inland areas of Wales and in some parts of north Wales. It has its own television and radio stations; Welsh-medium schools are more popular than ever before and some 50 publishers publish approximately 600 books annually in Welsh as well as magazines. In addition, around 50 regional newspapers (*papurau bro*), which were established between 1973 and 1988, are published voluntarily in all parts of Wales. Within the context of lesser-used languages in Western Europe, this is an extraordinary achievement.(3)

In many parts of Wales it is deemed a distinct advantage to

possess bilingual skills when applying for a job in the public sector. In fact, throughout Wales, more and more employers in public, private and voluntary sectors, in response to the growing expectations of their customers, are becoming aware of the benefits of using the Welsh language. On the surface the language seems to be resurging and making a comeback after considerable Anglicisation in urban and many rural areas.

Since the 1960s there has been a renaissance of interest in the language, among the younger generation in particular. A new awareness of the Welsh language and its culture has resulted in some positive efforts to secure the future of the vernacular in Wales. There is widespread support across the country for the Welsh language and most people consider it will continue as a living entity for the forseeable future. In a recent survey it was found that only 5 per cent of those surveyed (1,192 interviews) actually opposed the use of Welsh. Even among those who spoke no or very little Welsh, there was a clear majority (61 per cent) supporting the use of the language.[(4)]

Background

The Welsh language has derived from the Indo-European language that was spoken about 6,000 years ago. Speakers of this language migrated across Europe and Western Asia. The Indo-European separated into different languages across the world and this family consists of 9 different branches, which evolved into other languages. The Welsh emerged from the Celtic branch which gave rise to 6 different languages, split into two subgroups: Irish, Scots, Gaelic and Manx belong to the Goidelic group; Welsh, Cornish and Breton to the Britannic group. By the second half of the 6th century the Welsh language had emerged as a distinct tongue. It is therefore by far the oldest language spoken in Britain today and is among the oldest in Europe with its origins dating from at least 2,500 (maybe 4,000) years ago.

Literary background

Very little is known about early Welsh and it has only survived in a few inscriptions and marginal notes or glosses. The succeeding phase of the language extends from about 850 to 1100 but evidence again is limited. There is little beyond marginal notes and a few brief texts and poems. However, a substantial body of literature was composed in the early years of the language. For example, a long poem attributed to the poet Aneirin in a 13th-century manuscript known as the *Book of Aneirin*, commemorates the heroic deeds of a war-band chosen from the Gododdin tribe (the Votadini, who lived on the banks of the Firth of Forth) and its allies, who fell in an assault upon the site of Catraeth (Catterick, Yorkshire) about the year 600. Linguistic evidence suggests that this poem was written much later than the 6th century. Scholars agree that before the poem was ever committed to its written form there must have been a long period during which it was transmitted orally. However, the balance of opinion favours the belief that the original nucleus of this long poem was composed shortly after the event to which it refers.

Twelve early Welsh tales, written around the 12th century but which date back to earlier times, were published in 3 volumes between 1838 and 1849 under the general title *Mabinogion*, meaning 'tales of youth'.

Between 1100 and 1300 there was a class of poets known as *Y Gogynfeirdd* (the Fairly Early Poets) who sang to the Welsh princes. These were professional poets who expressed their learning in ancient diction and intricate forms. The works of about 150 *Beirdd yr Uchwelwyr* (Poets of the Gentry) have also survived and date from around 1330 onwards for 300 years or more. The 14th-century poet Dafydd ap Gwilym (c. 1320–1370) is considered to be one of the finest poets that Wales has ever produced and some of his love and nature poems suggest that he was very much aware of the literary fashions and conventions, which penetrated Wales from the Continent. Approximately 150 of his poems have survived.

The first Welsh book was published in 1546, a collection of religious prose by Sir John Price (1502–55). Between 1546 and 1660, 108 books were published in Welsh. However, during that same period only 4 books were published in Scottish Gaelic and 11 in Irish. During the 16th century a number of Welsh scholars followed the trend set in a number of other European countries by publishing grammars and dictionaries of the Welsh language.

The New Testament and Prayer Book were published in Welsh in 1567 and the Welsh Bible, which was translated in its entirety by Bishop William Morgan (c. 1545–1604), appeared in 1588. William Morgan's Welsh Bible is the foundation stone on which modern Welsh literature has been based. It is a work, too, that probably did more than anything else to ensure the survival of the language. In fact, the Welsh Bible became the sheet anchor of the Welsh language; without it Welsh might have gone the same way as the language of south-west England. This Bible gave an impetus to Welsh writing after the decline of the Bards and the Welsh poetic tradition, at a period when Welsh was in danger of becoming a purely oral language.

The decline of the Welsh language

From 1536, the date of the Act of Annexation of Wales to England under Henry VIII, until 1942, only the English language was used in law and administration throughout Wales and a Welshman who did not speak English could not hold public office. Welsh was actively discouraged in education and governmental establishments, but the Nonconformist religion and other religious movements from the 17th century onwards upheld the language. However, use of the Welsh language was strictly forbidden in schools in the latter half of the 19th and early 20th centuries.

In 1991, of the total resident population in Wales (2,835,073) some 77 per cent were born in Wales, but of the total population able to speak Welsh (508,098) nearly 10 per cent (48,919) were born outside Wales. This demonstrates the degree to which incomers have committed themselves to learning the language.[(5)] At the beginning of the 21st century, there are more than 20,000 adults in Wales who attend classes to learn Welsh, more than at any time previously. There are thousands more learning by following radio or television programmes or on the Internet.

This does not hide the fact that there was a steady decline throughout the last century in the number of Welsh-speakers. There are a number of different reasons for the decline:

a *Migration patterns from rural to urban areas in search of work.* There has been a steady decline in the concentration of employment in the industries, which have previously been the mainstay of many communities in Wales. At the beginning of the 21st century, the quarries of Gwynedd in north Wales and the coalmines of south Wales only employ a few hundred workers compared with many thousands in the early 20th century. As late as 1958, there were 12 major mining pits working in the Rhondda alone; but, by 1969 there was only one, Maerdy, still operational. An average of 10 pits a year closed in the 1960s. In fact, from 1947 to 1972, 150 collieries in south Wales were closed down, and 75,000 jobs disappeared with them.[(6)] The history of steel and tinplate manufacture since 1945 is quite similar to that of the coal-mining industry.

During the 1970s and 1980s, agriculture remained an important industry in the rural areas of Wales employing about 57,000 people as farmers or employees. The sector, as in many industrialised countries, received substantial levels of public support. Changes in mechanisation brought alterations to the structure and pattern of the agricultural industry and this increased productivity but it also brought a reduction in regular full-time employment in favour of a growth in part-time work. Those who were involved in agriculture during the 70s and 80s were in receipt of adequate incomes. Throughout the 90s, however, the industry appeared to be in a perpetual state of crisis.

b *Inward migration of English-speakers to rural areas.* Urban dwellers, especially from the south of England came to Wales in search of rural retreat, tranquillity and scenic alternatives to the modern urban bustle and hurried life. In the mid 1960s, it was estimated that more than 40,000 caravans were located in over 1,000 sites throughout Wales.(7) They came to Wales in search of peace and serenity in the countryside. In demographic terms, Wales has become the most cosmopolitan society among the four home countries. In 1981, over 20 per cent of the population were born outside Wales, with English immigrants as the largest minority, representing 17 per cent of all residents.(8)

With the decline of the farming industry and the number of people working full-time on the land, housing exceeded the requirements of the local community and consequently, many of the houses were bought as holiday homes, and a minority of the owners settled permanently in their second homes on retirement. In 1978 it was estimated that there were 26,000 holiday homes in Wales, 28.6 per cent of which were located in Gwynedd and Anglesey.

By the early 90s, it was found that up to 40 per cent of the total housing stock in some villages in north Wales were second homes. Property was inexpensive in rural Wales compared to England and this accelerated the influx especially in the rural south-west and north-west of the country. In the early 1980s, with 40,000 English people migrating to Wales each year, the fear arose that Welsh-speaking rural communities would be submerged.

Wales is still considered an attractive country to live in and approximately 60,000 people migrate from England to Wales annually. This is in comparison with the 50,000 who migrate to Scotland. In 1998 alone, Wales had an inflow of 59,800 compared to Scotland's 52,600. The outflow for the same period was 56,600 from Wales, 56,400 from Scotland. In some parts of west Wales, the proportion of those born outside Wales rose to almost 50 per cent of the population.[9] This resulted in the gradual fragmentation of the core areas of the Welsh language and the erosion of the Welsh-speaking territorial heartland of Wales.

c *Increased availability of English-language news and entertainment media.* The new prosperity of working-class families in the 1960s and 1970s meant that they were able to afford the luxuries of modern life. Mobility became less of a problem as families purchased cars, which enabled them to enjoy urban amenities. By 1969, 92 per cent of homes in Wales were in possession of a television set, which opened their eyes to a whole new world of consumerism and made cinema-going less of an attraction as every home was transformed into a picture-house. Telephones were installed in most homes and an electricity supply became available to the inhabitants of rural areas. The English culture was the attraction of the day and this resulted in the erosion of local traditions and customs.

However, at the end of the 20th century, tourism had become a key employer in the Welsh-speaking heartland and an essential element of its economy. Referring to the effects of tourism, it has been argued that the increasing use of English in Welsh-speaking areas by tourist's is likely to Anglicise the native culture and undermine Welsh as a living community language.

The brave new world offered new opportunities but also posed new threats to the language. Through the electronic mass media, English influences penetrated deeply into areas where the Welsh language was the natural medium of communication and where English was seldom heard. Rural Wales became a favoured tourist destination as the number of Welsh-speakers fell drastically. The arrival of the telegraph, the telephone and especially the wireless enabled the English language to cross national boundaries and penetrate the homes of people who seldom spoke English. No longer were the mountains of Wales a barrier to the diffusion of English and American culture.

d *General secularisation of society.* This lead to a decline in the chapel attendance on which so many traditional Welsh-medium activities were centred. Perhaps there is little that is different in Wales from England, but to many it is the quality and influence of Nonconformists in Wales that is significant, and so much greater than in England. The Nonconformists reached an all-time peak in the years 1910–1914 in total membership, and as in the case of the Welsh language, has been in decline since then. The Nonconformist background of 'chapel, choir and pulpit' was very much the culture of the majority of the Welsh people until the early 1970s, and it shaped many of their commonest attitudes – to speaking, to music, to authority and government. By the end of the 20th century, however, with only 13 per cent of the inhabitants of Wales regularly attending a place of worship, it was somewhat difficult to claim that the Welsh were a Christian nation – an astonishing volte-face in view of the nation's devotion to religious observance earlier in the 20th century. In a survey conducted in 1995, it was found that 62 per cent of those attending church were aged 45 or over and 35 per cent were 65 or over. At least 67 per cent of those who attended were women. A fall in the proportion of Welsh-speakers from nearly 55 per cent of the population in 1891 to 18.7 per cent in 1991 was a critical factor in the process of decline in attendance(10).

The Welsh language in schools

It is likely that the 2001 Census will demonstrate that the percentage of Welsh-speaking children and young people has increased since the previous Census, and this will be mainly due to the fact that there has been a significant rise in the number of primary school children in Wales who receive their education in Welsh-medium or bilingual schools. In primary school education in Wales, the figures for the year 2000–2001 reveal that:

- Out of the 1,660 primary schools in Wales, 445 have classes where Welsh is the sole or main medium of instruction.
- The number of pupils in classes where Welsh is the sole or main medium of instruction is 51,600.
- Throughout Wales, 227,668 children are taught Welsh as a second language out of a total number of 291,687 primary school pupils.

In addition, secondary education figures for 2000–2001 show that:

- Out of the 229 secondary schools in Wales, 52 have classes where Welsh is the sole or main medium of instruction.
- The number of pupils in classes where Welsh is the sole or main medium of instruction is 36,289.
- Throughout Wales, from a total number of 204,158 pupils, 25,072 were taught Welsh as a first language, and 122,112 as a second language.

Significant also is the fact that 12,954 children attended 935 Welsh-medium playgroups in Wales in the year 2000.[(11)]

Welsh became a compulsory subject for all pupils in Wales at Key Stages 1, 2 and 3 (i.e. up to age 14) in 1990. In 1999, it became a compulsory subject in Key Stage 4. This means that all pupils in Wales will study Welsh either as a first or a second language for 11 years, from the ages of 5 to 16.

The Welsh Language Society

Considerable campaigning took place during the second half of the 20th century to safeguard the interest of the Welsh language. New organisations emerged constantly developing new ways of acting on its behalf. As the long-term trend seemed to point to greater exposure to the English language, decreasing competence in spoken and written Welsh was recorded. By the mid-50s, Welsh monoglots were becoming extinct as the native tongue was viewed by many as a badge of ignorance[(12)]. Then on 13 February 1962, in what turned out to be a celebrated moment in the history of the Welsh language, Saunders Lewis (1893–1985), dramatist and critic, delivered his historic radio lecture, *Tynged yr Iaith* ('The Fate of the Language'), in which he declared that the demise of the language would be imminent if the linguistic status quo were to prevail for much longer. His aim was to awaken the people of Wales to the crisis facing the Welsh language. The lecture brought the plight of the language to the forefront and he called on Plaid Cymru (the Welsh Nationalist Party) to abandon their electoral campaigns and make use of the language as a political weapon. The lecture exerted a profound influence as it engendered a new sense of commitment, especially among the young, to the recovery of the Welsh language. In direct response to the lecture, Cymdeithas yr Iaith Gymraeg (the Welsh Language Society) was formed in October 1962. Its aim was to embark on a programme of public protest designed to promote the use of Welsh. Its founders were aware of the urgent need for an active and direct campaign to safeguard the interests of the language in public life. The methods used were often militant and uncompromising, requiring police intervention, and resulting in prosecution, fines and imprisonment. Court appearances proved to be an effective platform for the Society's members and the publicity was utilised to demand equal status for the Welsh language. Since 1962 approximately 200 activists have been sentenced to periods of imprisonment for their part in various campaigns associated with the Welsh language.

From 1968 there was an increase in militancy especially prior to the investiture of the Prince of Wales in July 1969, and many English-only road signs were damaged. Several hundred activists joined the sign-daubing of the Welsh Language Society and a substantial growth in its membership resulted, although the total number of fully-fledged members has seldom exceeded 2,000. Gradually the Society became a political force in Wales and this was achieved by the militant approach and the use of non-violent civil disobedience. Concessions were achieved grudgingly on issues such as bilingual road signs, car tax discs and official documentation, and then the establishment, after an unwavering campaign, of a fourth channel devoted to Welsh-medium broadcasting.

The Welsh language and the Assembly

The Welsh Assembly constitutes a significant institutional development as it symbolises a degree of power to Wales which will reassert its identity. Its policies and decisions will impact significantly on the language and the lives of the people of Wales in the 21st century.

The Welsh-language protagonists were at the forefront of the campaigns to secure a greater degree of autonomy for Wales, as they believe that the Welsh language is the prime ethnic indicator of Welsh identity – an identity, according to many, that was all but lost following the assimilation of Wales with England some 600 years ago. That identity was undermined and weakened as the Welsh language itself continued to decline. Decentralisation of power, it was argued, was fundamental if Wales was to become an independent force again and reassert its identity.

Yet it seems that Welsh nationalism based on the language will be replaced in the 21st century by a more broad based civic or institutional nationalism. As a result, it appears to many[13] as if the Welsh language has become a marginal indicator of ethnic identity in Wales. The language is seen as a divisive symbol, a barrier to the real unity of Wales based on a common Welshness, and it therefore should be relegated from the political agenda. It has been claimed that Plaid Cymru is a party that represents the interest of the self-indulgent Welsh-speaking minority in Wales.[14] Nationalism has transcended language in Wales and its support has usually been drawn from the rural, Welsh-language strongholds of the west and north of the country.

Scottish nationalism on the other hand is not so dominated by its linguistic pride and has gained acceptance in both urban and rural areas of Scotland.

The National Assembly in Cardiff epitomises and physically represents Welshness in the 21st century. Hence the Welsh language, it seems, has to accept an anachronistic role. The implication of such a development is a matter for debate, but if the language spoken by only a fifth of the population is seen as divisive, then it will ultimately become more and more marginalised as it is sidelined by institutional nationalism with its growing panoply of institutions.

The authors of a recent study(15) concluded that there is a real danger that, like Scotland and Ireland, a Welsh identity could develop that would owe little to the Welsh language. The language and its culture could then be perceived as having performed a function of preserving identity only to become of secondary significance in the 21st century when institutions such as the Welsh Assembly grow in dominance in Welsh life.

The National Assembly for Wales has taken over most of the responsibilities and functions of the Secretary of State for Wales. These include:

- agriculture
- ancient monuments
- culture
- economic development
- education and training
- the environment
- health and health services
- highways
- housing
- industry
- local government
- social services
- sport and recreation
- tourism
- town and country planning
- transport
- water and flood defence
- the Welsh language.

The Assembly will not be responsible for subjects which are handled in Westminster on a common basis throughout the United Kingdom – including taxation, defence, foreign affairs, social security and broadcasting.

The Assembly has 60 elected members; 40 are elected on the first-past-the-post system in the 40 Parliamentary constituencies; 20 are elected by proportional representation on the basis of 4 members for each of the 5 current European constituencies. It contains a balance of power between:

1 the executive committee (cabinet) made up of Assembly Secretaries who are appointed by the First Minister; and
2 the subject committees, whose members are elected by the full Assembly in accordance with party balance, apart from the Assembly Secretaries who are appointed by the First Minister.

Greater participation by women in the Assembly was consciously promoted at the outset and has proved a success as it is one of the most gender-balanced institutions in Europe.[16] Proportional representation has also secured a balance of the major parties in Wales, and a spirit of inclusiveness has been prevalent since its opening by the Queen on 26 May 1999. The voice of every party is heard and this willingness by all to promote democratic debates can only benefit Wales and its future.

Wales has entered the new millennium with its own representative national institution and is eager for it to succeed. It has waited a long time for it to happen, and now that it has, its repeal is inconceivable.

The Welsh Language Act

The status of the Welsh language was enhanced with the passing of the Welsh Language Act in 1993, which confirmed in law the principle of equality between the Welsh and English languages. The Act specifies three things:

1 Welsh and English are to be treated on an equal basis when providing services to the public in Wales;
2 Welsh speakers have an absolute right to speak Welsh in court;
3 the establishment of the Welsh Language Board to oversee the delivery of these promises and to promote and facilitate the use of the Welsh language.

The right for everyone to gain access to public services in Wales through the medium of Welsh has been secured by virtue of the Welsh Language Act. For example, applications for passports and driving licences, income tax, VAT, and local government enquiries can all be conducted in Welsh. Utility bills are available also in the individual's chosen language.

By virtue of this development and the establishment of a National Assembly for Wales, many maintained that the struggle for the language was over and hence there was little need for a Welsh Language Society. There is little doubt that the Welsh Language Society has succeeded in elevating the status of the Welsh language from one of deprivation to official recognition and of equal status with that of English in Wales.

As a result of the Government of Wales Act 1998, Welsh and English are both recognised as the official languages of the National Assembly for Wales. The Assembly is required to treat both languages equally and Assembly Members are free to use either language in debate and correspondence.

The Welsh language is an essential part of the cultural heritage of Wales, which continues to influence and shape its national identity. The Welsh Language Board distributes over £2 million in grants to organisations for activities to increase the use of Welsh and a further £2 million to support the teaching of Welsh in schools.

Conclusion

It is evident that there is a broad base of support for the Welsh language. Recent research carried out among 815 people, Welsh speakers and non-Welsh speakers, reported that 88 per cent of respondents felt that the Welsh language was something to be proud of; 75 per cent believed that Welsh and English should be treated equally, and 71 per cent supported the use of Welsh.[17] Parallel to this is the decline of the language among native Welsh-speakers in the traditional heartlands. Welsh is no longer principally associated with farming, slate quarries, coal mines, chapels and *eisteddfodau*; it is linked more with the middle-class élite who have moved from the Welsh Wales (*Y Fro Gymraeg*) to the Anglicised towns and cities of south-east Wales.[(18)] It is estimated that over 10 per cent of all Welsh speakers in Wales live within a 25-mile radius of Cardiff. In addition, a large proportion of Welsh speakers are linguistically isolated within their households, as 52 per cent of them have only one Welsh speaker and 70 per cent no Welsh-speaking children within them.[(19)] The percentage of Welsh speakers who claim Welsh as their first language was only 56 per cent in 1992, and the number of households where all the adults and children speak Welsh was as low as 2.5 per cent of the population.[(20)] It is also true to maintain at the beginning of the 21st century that the Welsh language rarely impinges on the lives of 80 per cent of the population of Wales. A third of Welsh children acquire the language outside their homes and in fact only a fifth of the children of Wales are fluent in Welsh by the age of11[(21)].

The 20th century witnessed a struggle for the normalisation of the Welsh language as a medium of day-to-day communication in the widest possible range of domains. To some, the struggle for recognition is now over, for the bilingual National Assembly has institutionalised the existence of a Welsh bilingual society.[(22)] To others this is merely the start of a development that will ultimately lead to a fully comprehensive bilingual society in Wales.

(1) 1991 Census
(2) Janet Davies, *The Welsh Language* (Cardiff, 1993)
(3) Glanville Price (ed.) *Encyclopaedia of the Languages of Europe* (Oxford, 1998)
(4) Source: Welsh Language Board, *State of the Welsh Language 2000 – Survey Report*
(5) John Aitcheson and Harold Carter, *A Geography of the Welsh Language* (Cardiff, 1994)
(6) D Gareth Evans, *A History of Wales 1906–2000* (Cardiff, 2000)
(7) The Welsh Office, *Report of the Mobile Homes Review* (London, 1977)
(8) D Gareth Evans, *A History of Wales 1906–2000* (Cardiff, 2000)

(9) Office for National Statistics
(10) Prys Morgan, *Background to Wales* (Llandybïe, 1968)
(11) *The Welsh Language Board*
(12) Geraint H Jenkins and Mari A Williams, (eds.) 'The Fortress of the Welsh Language 1900–2000; Introduction' in *Let's Do Our Best for the Ancient Tongue: The Welsh language in the Twentieth Century* (Cardiff, 2000)
(13) John Aitcheson and Harold Carter, *Language, Economy and Society* (Cardiff, 2000)
(14) John Davies, *History of Wales* (London, 1990)
(15) John Aitcheson and Harold Carter, *Language, Economy and Society* (Cardiff, 2000)
(16) The Wales Yearbook 2000
(17) The Welsh Language Board
(18) Geraint H Jenkins and Mari A Williams, (eds.) 'The Fortress of the Welsh Language 1900–2000; Introduction' in *Let's Do Our Best for the Ancient Tongue: The Welsh language in the Twentieth Century* (Cardiff, 2000)
(19) John Aitcheson and Harold Carter, 'Household Structures and The Welsh Language' *Planet*, 113 (1995)
(20) John Aitcheson and Harold Carter, 'The Welsh Language Today', in David Dunkerley and Andrew Thompson (eds.), *Wales Today* (Cardiff, 1999)
(21) Geraint H Jenkins and Mari A Williams, (eds.) 'The Fortress of the Welsh Language 1900–2000; Introduction' in *Let's Do Our Best for the Ancient Tongue: The Welsh language in the Twentieth Century* (Cardiff, 2000)
(22) Colin H Williams, 'Restoring a Language' in *Let's Do Our Best For The Ancient Tongue: The Welsh language in the Twentieth Century* (Cardiff, 2000), Geraint H Jenkins and Mari A Williams (eds.)

ABOUT WALES

Cymru or Cymry

(Both pronounced kuhm-ri with the emphasis on the first syllable.) Cymru is the Welsh term for Wales, whereas Cymry denotes the Welsh people. The word Cymru dates back to the middle of the 16th century, but Cymry, which was until about 1560 the word used to describe both the country and its people, is a much older term. It was probably used around 635 when the Anglo-Saxons invaded Britain.

The Welsh word for a Welshman is *Cymro*, plural *Cymry*, a compound of *com*, a prefix meaning 'together' or 'jointly', and *bro*, meaning 'land' or 'country'. It seems that it has evolved from the Brittonic word *combrogi* meaning 'fellow-countrymen'. Initially the word referred to Wales as well as the Old North, a name given to the ancestral territories of the Britons, which lay to the south of a line from Stirling to Loch Lomond and extended southwards over Cumbria, much of Lancashire and Yorkshire, and eastwards to the Humber estuary. The word Cymry or Kymry survives today in Cumbria.

The word Cambrian, which is the Latinised form of Cymru, was extensively used until the late half of the 19th century, when it was replaced by the term 'Welsh'. The word 'Wales' has derived from the Old English noun, *walh* or *wealh*, which means a native Briton as distinct from an Anglo-Saxon. The plural forms for these nouns were *walas* or *wealas*, which is very similar to the modern 'Wales'. 'Welsh' is a form derived from the adjective *welisc* or *waelisc* that probably dates back to the Anglo-Saxon period.

Daffodil

(*Cenhinen Bedr* – pronounced ken-hin-en bed-rr.) In the 19th century the daffodil gained in popularity as the national emblem of Wales. One possibility for this is that the same Welsh word is used for daffodil and leek and the confusion could have resulted in both being adopted as emblems. Early in the 20th century, the daffodil was used in preference to the leek in ceremonies and in publications relating to Wales.

Harp

(*Telyn* – pronounced tel-in.) The harp is regarded as the national instrument of Wales. However, no native harp from earlier than 1700 survives today and very little is known about the intervening years. The only surviving music is the manuscript of Robert ap Huw (1580–1665), harpist to King James I. Although this famous manuscript was written about 1613, it was copied in part from another earlier manuscript and has intrigued music scholars since the mid-18th century. Five scales were used, but nobody has yet transcribed the music into modern notation. By the end of the 18th century, the triple harp had become widely popular and named by many as the traditional Welsh harp, its name derived on account of its three rows of strings. The 19th century brought to Wales the classical concert harp, with its large chromatic pedal, that still dominates today.

Leek

(*Cenhinen* – pronounced ken-hin-en.) The leek has been used for centuries by the Welsh as a national emblem. According to legend, Dewi Sant (St David) advised the Britons to wear the plant in their caps to distinguish them from the pagan Saxon enemy on the eve of battle in a field full of leeks. A similar strategy was adopted when Welsh archers fought with Henry V at the battle of Agincourt, and later in his play, *King Henry V*, Shakespeare refers to the custom of wearing the leek as ancient tradition. Leeks are also said to have been part of the frugal diet of Dewi Sant. By the 14th century the colours of green and white, associated with the Welsh Princes, were being used as a primitive form of military uniform. The leek is worn today as a badge-cap by the Welch Regiment, which still adheres to a tradition that the youngest recruit has to eat a raw leek on St David's Day (1 March).

Lovespoons

From the 15th century onwards it has been customary for young Welshmen to carve spoons for their sweethearts as a token of their affection. More often than not, the carving was too elaborately ornamental for the spoons ever to be used, since one of their main functions was to demonstrate how skilfully the suitor could carve. The earliest surviving specimen is dated 1667 but the tradition lives on through the hands of only a few professional carvers in Wales today – craftsmen who still work in the authentic ways by hand carving from a single piece of wood.

Significance has been attached to certain designs: the number of links in a carved wooden chain indicated the number of children the suitor would like; the keyhole that he wished to provide a house; the wheel that he would work for his sweetheart; the captive balls in the cage again represented the number of children he desired; the heart indicating his love for her. Other designs represented good luck, wealth, health and happiness. A variety of objects were added to the original spoon. Knives, forks, anchors, chains were attached as additional decorations, also inset panels, on which the dedication was written, are often found. All these spoons had a ring or a hole for suspending them on a wall as a decoration.

It is always the handle that is decorated as the bowl retained its functional shape. The handle of the spoon was enlarged to form a panel for decoration. Spoons vary in size from three quarters of an inch to as much as 3 feet in length. The giving of a love spoon by a suitor and its acceptance or refusal by the lady of his choice developed into a ritual of betrothal or rejection amongst the country people of Wales.

National anthem 'Hen Wlad Fy Nhadau'

(Pronounced hehn wlahd vuhn had-(eye) – meaning 'Land of My Fathers'.) The words of the national anthem were composed by Evan James (1809–1878), a weaver by trade of Pontypridd, in south Wales:

Mae hen wlad fy nhadau yn annwyl i mi,
  Gwlad beirdd a chantorion, enwogion o fri;
Ei gwrol ryfelwyr, gwladgarwyr tra mad,
  Tros ryddid, collasant eu gwaed.

Cytgan
Gwlad! Gwlad! pleidiol wyf i'm gwlad;
  Tra môr yn fur
  I'r bur hoff bau,
O bydded i'r heniaith barhau.

The land of my fathers is dear to me,
  Land of bards and singers, famous men of distinction;
Its brave warriors, worthy patriots,
  For freedom shed their blood.

Chorus
Wales! Wales! I support thee Wales;
  While the sea remains a bastion
  For this dear country,
Oh may the ancient language endure.

The tune was composed by Evan James' son, James (1833–1902) who assisted his father in the wool factory, and, after 1873, kept public houses in Pontypridd and Mountain Ash. A memorial to both father and son was erected in Ynysangharad Park, Pontypridd, in 1930. The song was sung publicly for the first time in 1856 but it is uncertain when it was adopted as a national anthem. However, it was given much prominence during the Bangor National Eisteddfod in 1874, and from around that time onwards, it became accepted as the national anthem of Wales.

St David, the patron saint of Wales

(*Dewi Sant* – pronounced de-wi sant.) St David is believed to have died on 1 March 589. Little is known for certain concerning his life, but after being educated first in Ceredigion and subsequently in Llanddeusant in Carmarthenshire, he went on an arduous pilgrimage through parts of south Wales and the west of England, where it is alleged that he founded important religious centres such as Glastonbury and Croyland. He then returned to *Glyn Rhosyn* (St David's) in Pembrokeshire and established a community leading a strict ascetic life. Later, he undertook a pilgrimage to Jerusalem, where he was consecrated archbishop.

A large number of feats and miracles were attributed to him. During the 12th century Dewi's fame extended swiftly to Ireland and to Brittany. It was at this time that St David's Cathedral became a popular place of pilgrimage, and it is here that Dewi's remains are buried. St David's, which is totally independent of Canterbury, achieved official city status in 1994 and remains the country's spiritual and ecclesiastical centre. Pope Calixtus II in 1120 decreed that two journeys to St David's amounted to the spiritual equivalent of one pilgrimage to Rome.

The celebration of 1 March is both a religious and patriotic celebration and a leek or a daffodil is worn.

The Prince of Wales feathers

The crest of three ostrich plumes and the *Ich Dien*, which means *Rydw i'n gwasanaethu* ('I serve'), is the motto of the Prince of

Wales and the Royal Welch Fusiliers. In 1346, it was adopted by Edward, the Black Prince, the eldest son of Edward III, at the battle of Crécy, the first major encounter of the Hundred Years War. It was here that some 5,000 Welsh soldiers played a decisive role in the defeat of the French. They were dressed in green and white and this is thought to be the first time that troops wore a uniform on a continental battlefield. Today, the feathers adorn the badge of the national rugby team of Wales.

The Red Dragon

(*Y Ddraig Goch* – pronounced uh thr(eye)g gohch.) The Red Dragon on a green and white background has been the official Welsh flag since 1959 and is seen flying from public and private buildings throughout Wales. The motto *Y Ddraig Goch ddyry cychwyn* ('the Red Dragon gives impetus'), which was added to the royal badge in 1953, was first brought to prominence in a poem written in the 15th century by Deio ab Ieuan Du (1450–1480).

The dragon flag was first introduced into Britain by the Roman legions and when they left in 410 it was brought westwards into Wales. During the Tudor reign between 1485 and 1603, the Red Dragon was part of their standard, but when the Stuarts came to the English throne following the death of Elizabeth 1 in 1603, it was replaced by the unicorn. The Red Dragon made its reappearance as the royal badge for Wales in 1807. Thereafter it has been used in the regalia of Welsh patriotic societies and has become, together with the three white ostrich plumes, the symbol for Wales.

The Welsh costume

The Welsh costume worn by women on special occasions, such as folk dancing competitions and *eisteddfodau* and by children on St David's day, is a product of the 19th century. During this period it became fashionable to use home-spun material or flannel patterned in stripes and checks. The garments worn, though not characteristically Welsh, were prominent among women in many rural parts of Wales.

From about 1834, Lady Llanover (Augusta Hall 1802–1896), a patron of Welsh folk-culture, made it her objective to persuade the women of Wales to wear heavy flannel garments in preference to cotton or calico on public occasions. The Welsh costume, as it is known today, was commercialised by the picture-postcard people and souvenir makers in the latter part of the 19th century. Their main aim was to romanticise and idealise the everyday dress of the common people as it represented a way of life that had become very much part of history in Wales.

The costume, as designed by Lady Llanover, consists mainly of the following garments:

Bedgown: an upper garment made from coloured, stiff flannel material (often a black and red striped pattern), worn over a chemise and an ankle-length petticoat of contrasting colour to the bedgown.

Shawl: a plain shawl, that could also be used to carry a baby.

Apron: an apron worn to protect the front of the petticoat.

Cloak: a red cloak of ample proportions sometimes incorporating a hood; considered to be an essential garment as it was worn in all weathers.

Hat: a tall, black-brimmed hat completes the costume. The steeple hat evolved from headwear fashionable in the late Tudor period, and used to be made from beaver or hard board covered with thin beaver fabric. In the past, a white cotton or muslin cap was worn under the hat, but a white lace frill, sewn to the inner brim of the hat, is employed now to give the impression of a bonnet.

Welsh–English
English–Welsh
DICTIONARY

ABBREVIATIONS

abb	abbreviation
adj	adjective
adv	adverb
conj	conjunction
excl	exclamation
f	feminine noun
m	masculine noun
num	numeral
poss	possessive
prep	preposition
v	verb
v aux	auxiliary verb
vn	verb-noun (i.e. verb infinitive used as a noun, which is characteristic of Welsh)

INTRODUCTION

In the Welsh–English part of the dictionary, the use of the word *see* refers the reader from an irregular plural form to the singular (noun), where gender and meaning will be found, and *from* references give examples of changes to the root of verbs, adjectives and prepositions. While it would be impossible to list all the forms in which these changes occur, it is hoped that such examples will give the reader a possible clue to the meaning of otherwise inexplicable forms he or she might encounter.

If you are using a Welsh dictionary for the first time, there are one or two things of which you need to be aware:

1 The Welsh alphabet does not follow exactly the same order as the English alphabet:

a b c d e f g h i j k l m n o p q r s t u v w x y z
a b c **ch** d **dd** e f **ff** g **ng** h i j l **ll** m n o p **ph** r **rh** s t **th** u w y

The most significant difference is that 'ng' follows 'g' in the Welsh alphabet not 'n'. Welsh words containing the highlighted letters may not appear in the alphabetical sequence you would expect in English.

2 Certain letters in Welsh mutate (i.e change, as in English *wife* changes to *wives*). However, in Welsh these mutations may take place at the beginning of a word, thus *cath* ('cat') may appear as *y gath* ('the cat'), *ei chath* ('her cat'), *fy nghath* ('my cat'). Words in the dictionary are listed in their unmutated form. If you fail to find a word beginning with the following letters, it may be the mutated form of a word, which starts with the listed letter. If the word starts with:

a	it could be a mutation of	**g**
b	it could be a mutation of	**p**
ch	it could be a mutation of	**c**
d	it could be a mutation of	**t**
dd	it is a mutation of	**d**
e	it could be a mutation of	**g**
f	it could be a mutation of	**b**
	or it could be a mutation of	**m**
g	it could be a mutation of	**c**
ng	it is a mutation of	**g**
ngh	it is a mutation of	**c**
h	can appear before any of the vowels (**a e i o u w y**) in Welsh	
l	it could be a mutation of	**ll**
	or it could be a mutation of	**g**
m	it could be a mutation of	**b**
mh	it is a mutation of	**p**
n	it could be a mutation of	**d**
nh	it is a mutation of	**t**
o	it could be a mutation of	**g**
ph	it is a mutation of	**p**
r	it could be a mutation of	**rh**
	or it could be a mutation of	**g**
th	it could be a mutation of	**t**
w	it could be a mutation of	**g**
y	it could be a mutation of	**g**

3 In Welsh, there is a great variety of standard word forms. There are far more ways of forming the plural for example than adding -s; adjectives and numerals have masculine and feminine forms, and verbs too conjugate through a variety of changing forms. It has not been possible to list all possible variations, but one feature of this dictionary is that it includes examples of the main changes, which should give the user a clue as to the likely derivation (and therefore meaning) of a particular word form.

Welsh-English Dictionary

A

a *rel pron* that, which. • *interrogative particle.*
a, ac *conj* and.
â, ag *conj* as. • *prep* with.
â *from* **mynd.**
ab, ap *m* son of.
abad *m* (**·au**) abbot.
abades *f* (**·au**) abbess.
abat·y *m* (**·ai**) abbey.
aber *m* (**·oedd**) mouth of river.
aberth *m/f* (**ebyrth**) sacrifice.
aberthged *f* ceremonial wreath.
aberthu *v* to sacrifice.
abl *adj* able; rich.
absen *m* slander.
absennol *adj* absent.
absenoldeb *m* absence.
abwyd *m* (**·od**) bait.
abwyd·yn *m* (**·od**) worm.
abwydyn y cefn *m* spinal chord.
ac *conj* and.
academaidd *adj* academic.
academ·i *f* (**·ïau**) academy.
acen *f* (**·nau, ·ion**) accent.
acennu *v* to accentuate.
acer, acr *f* (**aceri**) acre.
act *f* (**·au**) act.
actio *v* to act.
actores *f* (**·au**) actress.
acw *adv* there.
acwsteg *f* acoustics.
ach *f* (**·au**) pedigree.
achles *m* manure.
achlod *m* shame.
achlysur *m* (**·on**) occasion.
achlysurol *adj* occasional.
achos *m* (**·ion**) cause; case. • *conj* because.
achosi *v* to cause.
achub *v* to save.
achubiaeth *f* salvation.
achub·wr, achub·ydd *m* (**·wyr**) saviour.
achwyn *v* to complain.
achwyniad *m* (**·au**) complaint.
achwyn·wr, achwyn·ydd *m* (**·wyr**) moaner; plaintiff.
adain *f* (**adenydd**) wing.
adar *see* **aderyn.**
adareg *f* ornithology.
adargraffiad *m* (**·au**) reprint.
adarydd *m* (**·ion**) ornithologist.
adborth *m* (**·ion**) feedback.
ad-daliad *m* (**·au**) repayment.
ad-drefnu *v* to reorganise.
adeilad *m/f* (**·au**) building.

adeiladol *adj* constructive.
adeiladu *v* to build.
adeilad·wr *m* (**·wyr**) builder.
adeiledd *m* (**·au**) structure.
adeiniog *adj* winged.
adennill *v* to regain.
adenydd *see* **adain.**
aderyn *m* (**adar**) bird.
adfach *m* barb.
adfail *m* (**adfeilion**) ruin.
adfeilio *v* to decay.
adfer *v* to restore.
adferf *f* (**·au**) adverb.
adferiad *m* recovery.
adfyd *m* adversity.
adfywiad *m* (**·au**) revival.
adfywio *v* to revive.
adio *v* to add.
adiol·yn *m* (**·ion**) additive.
adladd *m* aftermath.
adlais *m* (**adleisiau**) echo.
adlam *m* rebound.
adlamu *v* to rebound.
adleisio *v* to resound.
adlen *f* (**·ni**) awning.
adlewyrch, adlewyrchiad *m* reflection.
adlewyrchu *v* to reflect.
adlewyrchydd *m* reflector.
adloniadol *adj* entertaining.
adloniant *m* entertainment.
adlunio *v* to remodel.
adlyn *m* (**·ion**) adhesive.
adlynol *adj* adhesive.
adnabod *v* to know.
adnabyddiaeth *f* knowledge.
adnabyddus *adj* well-known.
adnau *m* (**adneuon**) deposit.
adnebydd *from* **adnabod.**
adnewyddu *v* to renovate.
adnod *f* (**·au**) (Bible) verse.
adnodd *m* (**·au**) a resource.
adolygiad *m* (**·au**) review.
adolygu *v* to review.
adolyg·ydd *m* (**·wyr**) reviewer.
adran *f* (**·nau**) department.
adref *adv* homewards.
adrodd *v* to recite.
adroddiad *m* (**·au**) report.
adrodd·wr *m* (**·wyr**) elocutionist, narrator.
aduniad *m* (**·au**) reunion.
aduno *v* to reunite.
adwaen *from* **adnabod.**
adwaith *m* (**adweithiau**) reaction.
adweinir, adweinid *from* **adnabod.**
adweithio *v* to react.
adweithiol *adj* reactionary.
adweithydd *m* (**·ion**) reagent.
adwerthu *v* to retail.
adwy *f* (**·au, ·on**) gap.
adyn *m* scoundrel.
addas *adj* suitable.
addasiad *m* (**·au**) adaptation.
addasrwydd, addaster *m* suitability.
addasu *v* to adapt.
addasydd *m* (**·ion**) adaptor.
addaw(af) *from* **addo.**
addawol *adj* auspicious.
addef *v* to admit.
addew(ais) *from* **addo.**
addewid *m/f* (**·ion**) promise.
addfwyn *adj* gentle, meek.
addfwynder *m* gentleness.
addo *v* to promise.

addod *m* treasure; **wy addod** (*china*) nest-egg.
addol·dy *m* (**·dai**) place of worship.
addolgar *adj* devout.
addoli *v* to worship.
addoliad *m* (**·au**) service.
addol·wr *m* (**·wyr**) worshipper.
adduned *f* (**·au**) vow.
addunedu *v* to vow.
addurn, addurniad *m* decoration.
addurnedig *adj* decorated.
addurniadol *adj* decorative.
addurno *v* to adorn.
addwyn *adj* fine.
addysg *f* education.
addysgiadol *adj* educational.
addysgu *v* to teach, to educate.
aeddfed *adj* mature.
aeddfedrwydd *m* maturity.
aeddfedu *v* to mature.
ael *m* (**·iau**) eyebrow.
aelod *m/f* (**·au**) member.
aelodaeth *f* membership.
aelwyd *f* (**·ydd**) hearth; branch of Urdd.
AEM *abb* HMI.
aer *m* air; heir.
aer-dynn, aerglos *adj* airtight.
aeres *f* (**·au**) heiress.
aeron *pl* berries.
aerwy *m* (**·au, ·on**) yoke.
aeth *from* **mynd**.
aethus *adj* poignant.
af *from* **mynd**.
afal *m* (**·au**) apple.
afallen *f* (**·nau**) apple tree.
afan *pl* raspberries.
afanc *m* (**·od**) beaver.
afiach *adj* unhealthy.
afiaith *m* glee.
afiechyd *m* (**·on**) illness.
afieithus *adj* exuberant.
aflafar *adj* harsh (sound).
aflan *adj* unclean.
aflednais *adj* coarse.
aflem *adj* obtuse (angle).
aflêr *adj* untidy.
aflonydd *adj* restless.
aflonyddu *v* to disturb.
afloyw *adj* opaque.
aflunio *v* to distort.
aflwyddiannus *adj* unsuccessful.
aflywodraethus *adj* uncontrollable.
aflwyddiannus *adj* unsuccessful.
aflwyddian·t *m* (**·nau**) misfortune.
afon *f* (**·ydd**) river.
afonig *f* rivulet.
afradlon *adj* prodigal.
afradu *v* to waste.
afreal *adj* unreal.
afreolaidd *adj* irregular.
afreolus *adj* uncontrollable.
afresymol *adj* unreasonable.
afrifed *adj* innumerable.
afrlladen *f* (**·nau**) wafer (in Mass).
afrosgo *adj* ungainly.
afu *m/f* liver.
afwyn *f* (**·au**) rein.
affliw *m* particle.
affwysol *adj* abysmal.
ag *see* **â, ag**.
agen *f* (**·nau**) gap.
agendor, gagendor *m/f* gap.
ager *m* steam.
agor *v* to open.
agoriad *m* (**·au**) opening; key.

agos *adj* near.
agosatrwydd *m* intimacy.
agosáu *v* to draw near.
agwedd *m/f* (**-au**) attitude.
angau *m* death.
angel *m* (**angylion, engyl**) angel.
angen *m* (**anghenion**) need.
angenfilod *see* **anghenfil.**
angenrheidiau *see* **anghenraid.**
angenrheidiol *adj* necessary.
angerdd *m/f* passion.
angerddol *adj* passionate.
anghaffael *m* mishap.
angharedig *adj* unkind.
anghelfydd *adj* clumsy.
anghenfil *m* (**angenfilod**) monster.
anghenion *see* **angen.**
anghenraid *m* (**angenrheidiau**) necessity.
anghenus *adj* needy.
angheuol *adj* fatal.
anghlywadwy *adj* inaudible.
anghofiedig *adj* forgotten.
anghofio *v* to forget.
anghofus *adj* forgetful.
anghredadun *m* (**anghredinwyr**) infidel.
anghredadwy *adj* incredible.
anghrediniaeth *f* unbelief.
anghwrtais *adj* discourteous.
anghwrteisi *m* discourtesy.
anghydfod *m* disagreement.
anghydffurfiol *adj* nonconformist.
anghydrif *m* (**-au**) odd number.
anghydweld *v* to disagree.
anghyfannedd *adj* uninhabited.
anghyfartal *adj* unequal.
anghyfartaledd *adj* inequality.
anghyfarwydd *adj* unaccustomed.
anghyfeb *adj* barren.
anghyfiaith *adj* alien.
anghyfiawn *adj* unjust.
anghyfiawnder *m* injustice.
anghyflawn *adj* incomplete.
anghyfleus *adj* inconvenient.
anghyfreithlon *adj* illegal, unlawful.
anghyfrifol *adj* irresponsible.
anghyfforddus, anghyffyrddus *adj* uncomfortable.
anghyffredin *adj* uncommon.
anghymedrol *adj* immoderate.
anghymeradwy *adj* unacceptable.
anghymesur *adj* assymetrical.
anghymharol *adj* incomparable.
anghymharus *adj* ill-matched.
anghymwys *adj* unsuitable.
anghynefin *adj* unfamiliar.
anghynnes *adj* odious; cold.
anghysbell *adj* remote.
anghyson *adj* inconsistent.
anghysondeb, anghysonder *m* (**-au**) inconsistency.
anghysurus *adj* uncomfortable.
anghytbwys *adj* unbalanced.
anghytûn *adj* at odds.
anghytundeb *m* disagreement.
anghytuno *v* to disagree.
anghywir *adj* incorrect.
angladd *m/f* (**-au**) funeral.
angladdol *adj* funereal.
angof *m* oblivion.
angor *m/f* (**-au**) anchor.
angorf-a *f* (**-eydd**) anchorage.
angori *v* to anchor.
angyles *f* angel.

angylion *see* **angel**.
ai *conj* is it; either . . . or.
âi *from* **mynd**.
aidd *m* ardour.
aiff *from* **mynd**.
aig *f* shoal.
ail *adj* second.
ail isradd *m* square root.
ailadrodd *v* to repeat.
ailafael *v* to take up again.
aileni *v* to regenerate.
ailennyn *v* to rekindle.
ailgylchu, ailgylchynu *v* to recycle.
ail-law *adj* second-hand.
ailwampio *v* to refashion.
ais *see* **asen**.
ait *from* **mynd**.
alaeth *m* sorrow.
alarch *m* (**elyrch**) swan.
alaru *v* to have a surfeit of.
alaw *f* (**·on**) tune.
alcal·i *m* (**·ïau**) alkali.
alcam *m* tinplate.
alch *f* (**eilch**) grate, grill.
alegor·i *f* (**·ïau**) allegory.
alergedd *m* allergy.
alinio *v* to align.
almon *f* almond.
aloi *m* (**·on**) alloy.
allan *adv* out.
allan·fa *f* (**·feydd**) exit.
allanol *adj* external.
allblyg *adj* extrovert.
allbrint *m* (**·iau**) printout.
allbwn *m* (**allbynnau**) output.
allt, gallt *f* (**elltydd, gelltydd**) slope (wooded).
am *prep* at; for; on.
amaeth *m* agriculture.
amaeth·dy *m* (**·dai**) farmhouse.
amaethu *v* to farm.
amaeth·wr *m* (**·wyr**) farmer.
amaethyddiaeth *f* agriculture.
amaethyddol *adj* agricultural.
amarch *m* disrespect.
amau *v* to doubt.
ambarél *m* umbrella.
ambell *adj* some.
amcan *m/f* (**·ion**) intention; notion.
amcangyfrif *m* (**·on**) estimate. • *v* to estimate.
amcanu *v* to estimate.
amdan(af) *from* **am**.
amd·o *m* (**·oeau**) shroud.
amddifad *adj* destitute.
amddifadu *v* to deprive.
amddiffyn *v* to defend.
amddiffyn·fa *f* (**·feydd**) fortress.
amddiffyniad *m* defence.
amddiffynnol *adj* defensive.
amddiffynnwr *m* (**amddiffynwyr**) defender.
amfesur *m* perimeter.
amffib·iad *m* (**·iaid**) amphibian.
amffibiaidd *adj* amphibious.
amgae(af) *from* **amgáu**.
amgaeedig *adj* enclosed.
amgant *m* periphery.
amgáu *v* to enclose.
amgen, amgenach *adj* other; better.
amgrwm *adj* convex.
amguedd·fa *f* (**·feydd**) museum.
amgyffred *v* to comprehend.
amgylch *m*: **o amgylch** around.
amgylchedd *m/f* environment.

amgylchiad *m* (**·au**) circumstance.
amgylchynu *v* to surround.
amharchu *v* to dishonour.
amharod *adj* not prepared.
amharu *v* to spoil.
amhendant *adj* vague.
amhenodol *adj* indeterminate.
amhêr *adj* bitter.
amherffaith *adj* imperfect.
amhersonol *adj* impersonal.
amherthnasol *adj* irrelevant.
amheuaeth *f* (**amheuon**) suspicion.
amheu(af) *from* **amau**.
amheus *adj* doubtful.
amheuthun *adj* rare.
amhleidiol *adj* impartial.
amhosibl *adj* impossible.
amhriodol *adj* inappropriate.
amhrisiadwy *adj* priceless.
amhrofiadol *adj* inexperienced.
amhûr *adj* impure.
amhuredd *m* impurity.
aml *adv* often.
amlbwrpas *adj* multi-purpose.
amlder, amldra *m* abundance.
amledd *m* frequency.
amleiriog *adj* verbose.
amlen *f* (**·nau, ·ni**) envelope.
amlhau *v* to increase.
amlinelliad *m* outline.
amlinellu *v* to outline.
aml-lawr *adj* multi-storey.
amlochrog *adj* many-sided.
amlosg·fa *f* (**·feydd**) crematorium.
amlwg *adj* obvious.
amlwreigiaeth *f* polygamy.
amlygrwydd *m* prominence.
amlygu *v* to reveal.
amn·aid *f* (**·eidiau**) nod.
amneidio *v* to beckon.
amnest *m* amnesty.
amod *m/f* (**·au**) condition.
amodol *adj* conditional.
amran·t *m* (**·nau**) eyelid.
amrantiad *m* twinkling of an eye.
amrediad *m* range.
amrwd *adj* raw, crude.
amryddawn *adj* versatile.
amryfal *adj* various.
amryfusedd *m* error.
amryliw *adj* multi-coloured.
amryw *adj* various.
amrywiad *m* (**·au**) variant.
amrywiaeth *m/f* (**·au**) variation.
amrywio *v* to differ.
amrywiol *adj* variable.
amser *m* (**·au**) time.
amseriad *m* tempo, timing.
amserlen *f* (**·ni**) timetable.
amserol *adj* timely.
amseru *v* to time.
amsugno *v* to absorb.
amwynderau *pl* amenities.
amwys *adj* ambiguous.
amwysedd *m* ambiguity.
amynedd *m* patience.
amyneddgar *adj* patient.
anabl *adj* disabled.
anabledd *m* disability.
anad *adj*: **yn anad** above all.
anadl *m/f* breath.
anadlu *v* to breathe.
anadnabyddus *adj* unknown.
anaddas *adj* unknown.
anaeddfed *adj* immature, unripe.

anaele *adj* dire.
anaf, anafiad *m* (**-iadau, -au**) wound, blemish.
anafu *v* to injure.
anallu *m* inability.
analluog *adj* incapable.
anamddiffynadwy *adj* indefensible.
anaml *adj* infrequent.
anamlwg *adj* indistinct.
anap, anhap *m* mishap.
anarchiaeth *m* anarchy.
anarchydd *m* anarchist.
anarferol *adj* unusual.
anatomegol *adj* anatomical.
anawsterau *see* **anhawster**.
andwyo *v* to spoil.
andwyol *adj* injurious.
anedifeiriol *adj* impenitent.
aneffeithiol *adj* ineffectual.
aneglur *adj* unclear.
aneiri, aneirod *see* **anner**.
aneirif *adj* innumerable.
anelau, anelion *see* **annel**.
anelu *v* to aim.
anenwog *adj* unrenowned.
anerch(af) *see* **annerch**.
anerchiad *m* (**-au**) address, speech.
anesboniadwy *adj* inexplicable.
anesmwyth *adj* restless.
anesmwythder, anesmwythyd *m* uneasiness.
anfad *adj* wicked.
anfadwaith *m* villainy.
anfaddeuol *adj* unpardonable.
anfant·ais *f* (**·eision**) disadvantage.
anfarwol *adj* immortal.
anfarwoli *v* to immortalise.
anfedrus *adj* unskilful.
anfeidrol *adj* infinite.
anfeidroldeb *m* infinity.
anferth *adj* huge.
anfesuradwy *adj* immeasurable.
anfodlon *adj* unwilling.
anfodlonrwydd *m* discontent.
anfodd *m* unwillingness.
anfoddhaol *adj* unsatisfactory.
anfoddog *adj* dissatisfied.
anfoesgar *adj* impolite.
anfoesol *adj* immoral.
anfoesoldeb *m* immorality.
anfon *v* to send.
anfoneddigaidd *adj* ungentlemanly.
anfri *m* disgrace.
anfuddiol *adj* useless.
anfwriadol *adj* unintentional.
anfwytadwy *adj* inedible.
anfynych *adj* infrequent.
anffaeledig *adj* infallible.
anffafriol *adj* unfavourable.
anffasiynol *adj* unfashionable.
anffawd *f* (**anffodion**) misfortune.
anffodus, anffortunus *adj* unfortunate.
anffurfiol *adj* informal.
anffyddiaeth *f* atheism.
anffydd·iwr *m* (**·wyr**) atheist.
anffyddlon *adj* unfaithful.
anh- *pref* un-. *See also* **annh-**.
anhaeddiannol *adj* unmerited.
anhapus *adj* unhappy.
anhawsed *from* **anodd**.
anhawster *m* (**anawsterau**) difficulty.
anheddau *see* **annedd**.

anhepgor, anhepgorol *adj* essential.
anhraethol *adj* unutterable.
anhrefn *m* anarchy.
anhrefnus *adj* disorganised.
anhreuliedig *adj* undigested.
anhrugarog *adj* merciless.
anhrwyddedig *adj* uncertified.
anhuddo, enhuddo *v* to bank up.
anhunanol *adj* unselfish.
anhunedd *m* insomnia.
anhwyldeb, anhwylder *m* illness.
anhwylus *adj* unwell.
anhwylustod *m* inconvenience.
anhyblyg *adj* inflexible.
anhydawdd *adj* insoluble.
anhyderus *adj* diffident.
anhydraidd *adj* impermeable.
anhydrin *adj* unmanageable.
anhydyn *adj* obstinate.
anhyfrydwch *m* unpleasantness.
anhyglyw *adj* inaudible.
anhygoel *adj* incredible.
anhygyrch *adj* inaccessible.
anhylaw *adj* awkward.
anhysbys *adj* unknown.
anhywaith *adj* intractable.
anial *adj* desolate.
anialwch *m* wilderness.
anian *m/f* (**-au**) nature, temperament.
anifail *m* (**anifeiliaid**) animal.
anifeilaidd *adj* brutish.
anlwc *m* misfortune.
anlwcus *adj* unlucky.
anllad *adj* wanton.
anlladrwydd *m* wantonness.
anllygredig *adj* incorrupt.
anllythrennog *adj* illiterate.
annaearol *adj* eerie.
annarllenadwy *adj* illegible.
annatodadwy *adj* inextricable.
annaturiol *adj* unnatural.
annealladwy *adj* incomprehensible.
annedwydd *adj* discontented.
annedd *f* (**anheddau**) dwelling.
annel *m/f* (**anelau, anelion**) aim.
annelwig *adj* vague.
anner *f* (**aneiri, aneirod**) heifer.
annerbyniol *adj* unacceptable.
annerch *v* to address (speak).
annhebyg *adj* unlike.
annhebygol *adj* unlikely.
annheg *adj* unfair.
annhegwch *m* unfairness.
annheilwng *adj* unworthy.
annherfynol *adj* infinite.
annheyrngar *adj* disloyal.
annhymig *adj* premature.
anniben *adj* untidy.
annibendod *m* untidiness.
annibyniaeth *f* independence.
annibynnol *adj* independent.
Annibynnwr *m* (**Annibynwyr**) Congregationalist.
annichon *adj* impossible.
anniddig *adj* irritable.
anniddigrwydd *m* irritability.
anniddorol *adj* uninteresting.
anniddos *adj* unsheltered.
annifyr *adj* disagreeable.
anniffoddadwy *adj* inextinguishable.
annigonol *adj* inadequate.
annileadwy *adj* indelible.

annilys *adj* invalid.
annillyn *adj* ugly.
annioddefol *adj* unbearable.
anniolchgar *adj* ungrateful.
annirnadwy *adj* incomprehensible.
annisgwyl *adj* unexpected.
anniwair *adj* unfaithful.
anniwall *adj* insatiable.
annoeth *adj* unwise.
annog, annos *v* to urge.
annuwiol *adj* ungodly.
annwfn, annwn *m* fairyland; underworld.
annwyd *m* (**anwydau**) a cold.
annwyl *adj* dear; beloved.
annymunol *adj* unpleasant.
annynol *adj* inhuman.
annysgedig *adj* unlettered.
anobaith *adj* despair.
anobeithio *v* to despair.
anobeithiol *adj* hopeless.
anochel, anocheladwy *adj* inevitable.
anodd *adj* difficult.
anoddefgar *adj* intolerant.
anogaeth *f* exhortation.
anogaf *from* **annog**.
anonest *adj* dishonest.
anonestrwydd *m* dishonesty.
anorchfygol *adj* invincible.
anorfod *adj* inevitable.
anorffenedig *adj* incomplete.
anorthrech *adj* invincible.
anos *from* **anodd**.
anrhaith *f* (**anrheithiau**) destruction; booty.
anrheg *f* (**·ion**) present, gift.
anrheithio *v* to plunder.
anrhydedd *m/f* (**·au**) honour.
anrhydeddu *v* to honour.
anrhydeddus *adj* honourable.
ansad *adj* unsteady.
ansathredig *adj* unfrequented.
ansawdd *m* (**ansoddau**) quality.
ansefydlog *adj* unsettled.
ansicr *adj* uncertain.
ansicrwydd *m* uncertainty.
ansodd·air *m* (**·eiriau**) adjective.
ansoddau *see* **ansawdd**.
answyddogol *adj* unofficial.
ansymudol *adj* immovable.
ânt *from* **mynd**.
anterliwt *m/f* (**·iau**) interlude.
anterth *m* prime.
antur *m* venture.
anturiaeth *f* (**·au**) adventure.
anturiaethus *adj* adventurous.
anturio *v* to venture.
anturus *adj* adventurous.
anudon *m* perjury.
anufudd *adj* disobedient.
anufudd-dod *m* disobedience.
anufuddhau *v* to disobey.
anuniongyrchol *adj* indirect.
anwadadwy *adj* undeniable.
anwadal *adj* fickle.
anwahanadwy *adj* inseparable.
anwar, anwaraidd *adj* uncivilised.
anwariaid *pl* savages.
anwastad *adj* uneven.
anwe *f* woof, weft.
anwedd *m* steam, vapour.
anweddu *v* to evaporate.
anweddus *adj* unseemly.
anweledig *adj* invisible.
anwes *m* fondness.

anwesu *v* to fondle.
anwiredd *m* **(·au)** untruth.
anwybodaeth *m/f* ignorance.
anwybodus *adj* ignorant.
anwybyddu *v* to ignore.
anwydau *see* **annwyd.**
anwydog *adj* chilly.
anwyldeb *m* dearness; fondness.
anwyled *from* **annwyl.**
anwyliaid *pl* loved ones.
anwylo *v* to fondle.
anwylyd *m/f* darling.
anwyl·yn *m* **(·iaid)** favourite.
anymarferol *adj* impracticable.
anymwybodol *adj* unconscious.
anymwybyddiaeth *f* unconsciousness.
anynad *adj* peevish.
anysbrydoledig *adj* uninspired.
anysgrifenedig *adj* unwritten.
anysgrythurol *adj* unscriptural.
anystwyth *adj* inflexible.
anystyriol *adj* thoughtless.
anystywallt *adj* intractable.
ap *see* **ab.**
apêl *m/f* **(apelau, apeliau)** appeal.
apelio *v* to appeal.
apig *m* **(·au)** apex.
apostol *m* **(·ion)** apostle.
apwyntiad *m* **(·au)** appointment.
apwyntio *v* to appoint.
âr *m* tilth.
ar *prep* on, upon.
arabedd *m* wit.
aradr *m/f* **(erydr)** plough.
arad·wr *m* **(·wyr)** ploughman.
araf *adj* slow.
arafu *v* to slow.
arafwch *m* slowness.
araith *f* **(areithiau)** a speech.
arall *adj* **(eraill)** other.
aralleiriad *m* paraphrase.
aralleirio *v* to paraphrase.
araul *adj* sunny.
arbed *v* to save.
arbelydru *v* to irradiate.
arbenigo *v* to specialise.
arbenigrwydd *m* distinction.
arbenig·wr *m* **(·wyr)** specialist.
arbenigwraig *f* expert.
arbennig *adj* special.
arbrawf *m* **(arbrofion)** experiment.
abrofi *v* to experiment.
arbrofol *adj* experimental.
arch *f* **(eirch)** coffin; ark.
arch(af) *from* **erchi.**
archdderwydd *m* archdruid.
archeb *f* **(·ion)** order.
archebu *v* to order.
archesgob *m* **(·ion)** archbishop.
archfarchnad *f* **(·oedd)** supermarket.
archiad *m* bidding.
archif *m* **(·au)** archive.
archif·dy *m* **(·dai)** records office.
archifydd *m* archivist.
archoffeir·iad *m* **(·iaid)** high priest.
archoll *m/f* **(·ion)** wound.
archolli *v* to wound.
archwaeth *m/f* appetite.
archwiliad *m* **(·au)** audit.
archwilio *v* to inspect.
ardal *f* **(·oedd)** region.
ardalydd *m* **(·ion)** marquis.
ardd(af) *from* **aredig.**
arddangos *v* to exhibit.

arddangos·fa *f* (**·feydd**) exhibition.
arddegau *pl* teens.
arddel *v* to own to.
arddeliad *m* conviction.
ardderchog *adj* excellent.
arddod·iad *m* (**·iaid**) preposition.
arddull *f* (**·iau**) style.
ar-ddweud *v* to dictate.
ardd·wr *m* (**·wyr**) ploughman.
arddwrn, garddwrn *m* (**arddyrnau, garddyrnau**) wrist.
aredig *v* to plough.
areithiau *see* **araith**.
areithio *v* to make a speech.
areith·iwr *m* (**·wyr**) public speaker.
aren *f* (**·nau**) kidney.
arf *m/f* (**·au**) weapon; tool.
arfaeth *f* intention.
arfbais *f* (**arfbeisiau**) coat of arms.
arfer *m/f* (**·ion**) custom. • *v* to accustom.
arferiad *m* (**·au**) custom.
arferol *adj* customary.
arfog *adj* armed.
arfogaeth *m* armour.
arfogi *v* to arm.
arfordir *m* (**·oedd**) coast.
arfwisg *f* (**·oedd**) suit of armour.
arffed *f* lap.
argae *m* (**·au**) dam.
argel *adj* hidden.
arglwydd *m* (**·i**) lord.
arglwyddes *f* lady.
arglwyddiaethu *v* to govern.
argoel *f* (**·ion**) sign.
argoeli *v* to portend.
argraff *f* (**·au**) impression.
argraffiad *m* (**·au**) print.
argraffu *v* to print.
argraff·wr *m* (**·wyr**) printer.
argraffydd *m* (**·ion**) printer (machine).
argyfwng *m* (**argyfyngau**) emergency.
argyhoeddi *v* to convince.
argyhoeddiad *m* (**·au**) conviction.
argymell *v* to recommend.
argymhell·iad *m* (**·ion**) recommendation.
arholi *v* to interrogate.
arholiad *m* (**·au**) examination.
arhol·wr *m* (**·wyr**) examiner.
arhos(af) *from* **aros**.
arhosfan *m/f* (**arosfannau**) lay-by.
arhosiad *m* (**arosiadau**) a stay.
arhosol *adj* lasting.
arial *m/f* vigour.
arian *m* silver.
ariangar *adj* covetous.
ariannaid *adj* silver.
ariannaidd *adj* silvery.
ariannog *adj* wealthy.
ariannu *v* to fund.
arlais *f* (**arleisiau**) temple (head).
arloesi *v* to pioneer.
arloesol *adj* pioneering.
arloes·wr *m* (**·wyr**) pioneer.
arlunio *v* to paint.
arlun·ydd *m* (**·wyr**) artist.
arlwy *m/f* (**·on**) feast.
arlwyo *v* to cater.
arlywydd *m* (**·ion**) president.
arlliw *m* (**·iau**) vestige.
arllwys *v* to pour.
arn(af) *from* **ar**.
arnofio *v* to float.

arobryn *adj* prize-winning.
arofal *m* (**·on**) maintenance.
arogl, aroglau *m* (**·au, arogleuon**) smell.
arogldarth *m* incense.
arogli, arogleuo *v* to smell.
arolwg *m* (**arolygon**) survey.
arolygu *v* to supervise.
arolyg·wr *m* (**·wyr**) inspector.
arolygydd *m* (**·ion**) superintendent.
aros *v* to wait.
arosfannau *see* **arhosfan**.
arosiadau *see* **arhosiad**.
arswyd *m* terror.
arswydo *v* to dread.
arswydus *adj* terrible.
arsylwi *v* to observe.
arsyll·fa *f* (**·feydd**) observatory.
artaith *f* (**arteithiau**) torture.
arteithio *v* to torture.
arteithiol *adj* excruciating.
artist *m* (**·iaid**) artist.
arth *f* (**eirth**) bear.
arthio *v* to growl.
aruchel *adj* sublime.
aruthredd *m* amazement.
aruthrol *adj* terrific.
arwain *v* to lead.
arwedd *f* aspect.
arweiniad *m* guidance.
arweinydd *m* (**·ion**) conductor, leader.
arweinyddiaeth *f* leadership.
arwerthian·t *m* (**·nau**) auction.
arwerth·wr *m* (**·wyr**) auctioneer.
arwisgiad *m* investiture.
arwisgo *v* to enrobe.
arwr *m* (**arwyr**) hero.
arwres *f* (**·au**) heroine.
arwriaeth *f* heroism.
arwrol *adj* heroic.
arwydd *m/f* (**·ion**) sign.
arwydd·air *m* (**·eiriau**) motto.
arwyddlun *m* (**·iau**) emblem.
arwyddo *v* to sign.
arwyddocâd *m* significance.
arwyddocaol *adj* significant.
arwyddocáu *v* to signify.
arwynebedd *m* (**·au**) area.
arwynebol *adj* superficial.
arwyr *see* **arwr**.
arysgrif, arysgrif·en *f* (**·au**) inscription.
AS *abb* MP.
as *f* ace.
asbri *m* zest.
asen *f* (**·nau, ais, eis**) rib; (**·nod**) she-ass.
asesu *v* to assess.
asgell *f* (**esgyll**) wing.
asgell·wr *m* (**·wyr**) winger.
asgwrn *m* (**esgyrn**) bone.
asiad *m* (**·au**) joint.
asiant *m* (**·iaid**) agent.
asio *v* to join.
astell *f* (**estyll**) plank.
astrus *adj* complicated.
astud *adj* diligent.
astudiaeth *f* (**·au**) study.
astudio *v* to study.
aswy *f* left-hand side.
asyn *m* (**·nod**) ass.
at *prep* towards.
atafaelu *v* to sequester.
atal *v* to restrain. • *m* stammer.
ataliad *m* (**·au**) stoppage.

atalnod *m* (**·au**) punctuation mark.
atalnodi *v* to punctuate.
atalwats *m/f* stopwatch.
atblygol *adj* reflexive.
ateb *v* to answer. • *m* (**·ion**) answer.
atebol *adj* responsible.
ategiad *m* support.
ategol *adj* corroborative.
ategu *v* to confirm.
ateli(ais) *from* **atal**.
atgas *adj* hateful.
atgasedd *m* hatred.
atgasrwydd *m* hatefulness.
atgno *m* remorse.
atgof *m* reminiscence.
atgoffa *v* to remind.
atgyfnerthu *v* to reinforce.
atgyfodi *v* to resurrect.
atgyfodiad *m* resurrection.
atgynhyrchu *v* to reproduce.
atgyrch *m* (**·ion**) reflex.
atgyweirio *v* to repair.
atgyweir·iwr *m* (**·wyr**) restorer.
atodi *v* to append.
atodiad *m* (**·au**) supplement.
atod·yn *m* (**·ion**) attachment.
atolwg *exclam* prithee!
atom·fa *f* (**·feydd**) nuclear power station.
atomig *adj* atomic.
atsain *f* (**atseiniau**) echo.
atseinio *v* to resound.
atyn·fa *f* (**·feydd**) attraction.
atyniad *m* (**·au**) attraction.
atyniadol *adj* attractive.
athletaidd *adj* athletic.
athletau *pl* athletics.
athrawes *f* (**·au**) teacher (female).
athrawiaeth *f* doctrine.
athrist *adj* sorrowful.
athr·o *m* (**·awon**) teacher.
athrod *m* (**·ion**) slander.
athrof·a *f* (**·âu**) college.
athroniaeth *f* philosophy.
athron·ydd *m* (**·wyr**) philosopher.
athronyddu *v* to philosophise.
athrylith *f* (**·oedd**) genius.
athrylithgar *adj* highly talented.
aur *m* gold.
awch *m* keenness.
awchus *adj* sharp, eager.
awdl *f* (**·au**) ode.
awdur *m* (**·on**) author.
awdurdod *m/f* (**·au**) authority.
awdurdodedig *adj* authorised.
awdurdodi *v* to authorise.
awdurdodol *adj* authoritative.
awdures *f* author (female).
awel *f* (**·on**) breeze.
awen *f* (**·au**) muse; rein.
awenyddol *adj* poetical.
awgrym *m* (**·iadau**) suggestion.
awgrymog *adj* suggestive.
awgrymu *v* to suggest.
awn *from* **mynd**.
awr *f* (**oriau**) hour.
awydd *m* desire.
awyddus *adj* eager.
awyr *f* air; sky.
awyren *f* (**·nau**) aeroplane.
awyren·dy *m* (**·dai**) hangar.
awyrgylch *m/f* atmosphere.
awyru *v* to ventilate.
ayb, ayyb *abb* etc.

B

baban *m* **(-od)** baby.
babandod *m* infancy.
babi *m* **(-s)** baby.
babïaidd *adj* childish.
babŵn *m* **(babwnod)** baboon.
bacas *f see* **bacsau.**
bacio, bagio *v* to back.
bacsau *pl* leg warmers; fetlocks.
bach *adj* small; dear (loved). • *m* **(-au)** hook.
bachgen *m* **(bechgyn)** boy.
bachgendod *m* boyhood.
bachgennaidd *adj* boyish.
bachgennyn *m* young boy.
bachog *adj* hooked.
bachu *v* to hook.
bach·wr *m* **(·wyr)** hooker (rugby).
bach·yn *m* **(·au)** hook.
bad *m* **(·au)** boat: **bad achub** lifeboat.
bae *m* **(·au)** bay.
baedd *m* **(·od)** boar.
baeddu *v* to soil.
bag *m* **(·iau)** bag.
bagl *f* **(·au)** crutch.
baglu *v* to trip.
bai *m* **(beiau)** fault. • *v from* **bod.**
baich *m* **(beichiau)** burden.
baidd *from* **beiddio.**
balaon *see* **bele.**
balch *adj* proud.
balchder *m* **(·au)** pride.
baldorddi *v* to babble.
bale, ballet *m* ballet.
baled *f* **(·i)** ballad.
baled·wr *m* **(·wyr)** ballad-monger.
balm *m* balm.
balŵn *m/f* **(balwnau)** balloon.
balwn·ydd *m* **(·wyr)** balloonist.
bambŵ *m* bamboo.
ban *m/f* **(·nau)** peak.
banadl *pl* broom (flowers).
banana *f* **(·s)** banana.
banc *m* **(·iau)** bank: **gŵyl banc** bank holiday.
bancio *v* to bank.
band *m* **(·iau)** band.
bando *m* (old Welsh game).
baner *f* **(·i)** flag.
banerog *adj* bannered.
baner·wr *m* **(·wyr)** standard-bearer.
banhadlen *f see* **banadl** *pl.*
banjô *m* banjo.
banllef *f* **(·au)** shout.
bannau *see* **ban.**
bannod *f* the definite article **(y)**.
bannog *adj* horned.
bar *m* **(·rau)** bar.
bâr *m* anger; greed.
bara *m* bread.
barbaraidd *adj* barbarous.
barbar·iad *m* **(·iaid)** barbarian.
barb·wr *m* **(·wyr)** barber.
barclod *m* **(·iau)** apron.
barcud *m* **(barcutiaid)** kite.
barcuta *v* to hang-glide.

bardd *m* (**beirdd**) poet.
barddol *adj* bardic.
barddoni *v* to compose poetry.
barddoniaeth *f* poetry.
barddonol *v* poetic.
barf *f* (**·au**) beard.
barfog *adj* bearded.
bargeinio *v* to bargain.
bargen *f* (**bargeinion**) bargain.
bargod *m* (**·ion**) eaves.
bargyfreith·iwr *m* (**·wyr**) barrister.
baril *m/f* barrel.
bario *v* to bar.
bariton *adj* baritone.
bariwns *m* barrier.
barlad, barlat *m* drake.
barlys *pl* barley.
barlysen *f see* **barlys** *pl.*
barlysyn *m see* **barlys** *pl.*
barn *f* (**·au**) judgement.
barnedigaeth *f* (**·au**) judgment.
barnol *adj* annoying.
barnu *v* to judge.
barn·wr *m* (**·wyr**) judge.
baromedr *m* barometer.
barrau *see* **bar**.
barrug *m* hoar frost.
barugo *v* to frost over.
barugog *adj* frosted.
barus *adj* greedy.
barwn *m* (**·iaid, baryniaid**) baron.
barwnes *f* (**·au**) baroness.
bas *adj* shallow; bass.
basâr *m* (**basarau, ·s**) bazaar.
basged *m/f* (**·i**) basket.
basged·aid *f* (**·eidiau**) basketful.
basgedu *v* to place in a basket.
basged·wr *m* (**·wyr**) basket-maker.
basn, basin *m* (**·au, basnys**) basin.
basnaid *m/f* (**basneidiau**) basinful.
baswn *m* (**baswnau**) bassoon.
bas·wr *m* (**·wyr**) bass.
bat *m* (**·iau**) bat.
batali·wn *m/f* (**·ynau**) battalion.
batiad *m* (**·au**) innings.
batio *v* to bat.
bat·iwr *m* (**·wyr**) batsman.
batr·i *m* (**·ïau**) battery.
bath[1], **bàth** *m* bath.
bath[2] *adj* minted.
bath·dy *m* (**·dai**) mint.
bathodyn *m* (**·nau**) badge.
bathu *v* to coin.
bath·wr *m* (**·wyr**) coiner.
baw *m* dirt.
bawd *m* (**bodiau**) thumb.
bawdd *from* **boddi**.
bawlyd *adj* dirty.
becsio, becso *v* to worry.
bechan *adj* (*f*) small.
bechgyn *see* **bachgen**.
bechingalw *m* thingummybob.
beddargraff *m* (**·iadau**) epitaph.
beiau *see* **bai**.
beichiau *see* **baich**.
beiddio *v* to dare.
beil·i *m* (**·ïau**) bailey; (**·ïaid**) bailiff.
beirdd *see* **bardd**.
beirn·iad *m* (**·iaid**) critic.
beirniadaeth *f* (**·au**) criticism.
beirniadol *adj* critical.
beirniadu *v* to criticise.
bele *m* (**balaon, beleod**) pine marten.
bendigedig *adj* blessed.
bendith *f* (**·ion**) blessing.

bendithio *v* to bless.
bendithiol *adj* beneficent.
benthyg *v* to lend. • *m* (**benthycion**) a loan.
benyw *adj* female. • *f* (**·od**) woman.
benywaidd *adj* feminine.
ber *adj* (*f*) short.
berdasen *f* (**berdys**) shrimp.
berdys *see* **berdasen; berdysyn.**
berdysyn *m* (**berdys**) shrimp.
berf *f* (**·au**) verb.
berf·a *f* (**·âu**) wheelbarrow.
berfâid *f* (**berfeidiau**) barrowful.
berfenw *m* (**·au**) infinitive (of verb).
bern(ais) *from* **barnu.**
berw *adj* boiled.
berwbwynt *m* boiling point.
berwedig *adj* boiling.
berwi *v* to boil.
berwr, berw *m* cress.
beryn *m* (**·nau**) bearing.
betgwn *m/f* night-dress.
betws *m* oratory.
betys *pl* beet.
beth *pn* what.
beu·dy *m* (**·dái**) cowshed.
beunos *adj* nightly.
beunyddiol *adv* daily.
bid *from* **bod.**
bidog *m/f* (**·au**) bayonet.
bing *m* (**·oedd**) alley.
bilidowcar *m* cormorant.
biliwn *m* (**biliynau**) billion.
bilwg *m* (**bilygau**) billhook.
bioleg *f* biology.
bioleg·ydd *m* (**·wyr**) biologist.
bisgïen *f* (**bisgedi**) biscuit.
biwrô *m/f* bureau.
biwrocrat *m* (**·iaid**) bureaucrat.
biwrocratiaeth *f* bureaucracy.
blacmêl *m* blackmail.
blaen *adj* front.
blaendal *m* (**·iadau**) deposit.
blaenddan·t *m* (**·nedd**) incisor.
blaenasgell·wr *m* (**·wyr**) wing forward.
blaengar *adj* progressive.
blaenllaw *adj* prominent.
blaenor *m* (**·iaid**) deacon.
blaenorol *adj* previous.
blaenoriaeth *m/f* (**·au**) priority.
blaen·wr *m* (**·wyr**) forward; leader.
blaguro *v* to sprout.
blaguryn *m* (**blagur**) shoot (bud).
blaidd *m* (**bleiddiaid**) wolf.
blas *m* (**·au**) taste.
blasu *v* to savour.
blasus *adj* tasty.
blawd *m* flour.
ble *adv* where.
bleidd·ast, bleiddi·ast *f* (**·eist**) she-wolf.
bleiddiaid *see* **blaidd.**
blêr *adj* untidy.
blewog *adj* hairy.
blewyn *m* (**blew**) hair.
blingo *v* to skin.
blin *adj* cross.
blinder *m* (**·au**) fatigue.
blinderog *adj* weary.
blinedig *adj* tiring.
blino *v* to tire.
blith draphlith *adj* topsy-turvy.
blodau *see* **blodyn.**
blodeugerdd *f* (**·i**) anthology.
blodeuo *v* to flower.

blodeuog *adj* florid.
blodfresychen *f* (**blodfresych**) cauliflower.
blodyn, blodeuyn *m* (**blodau**) flower.
bloedd *f* (**·iadau**) shout.
bloeddio *v* to shout.
bloesg *adj* husky.
blong *adj* (*f*) surly.
bloneg *m* fat, lard.
blwch *m* (**blychau**) box.
blwng *adj* surly.
blwydd *f* year old.
blwydd-dal *m* annuity.
blwyddlyfr *m* (**·au**) yearbook.
blwyddyn *f* (**blynedd, blynyddoedd**) year.
blych·aid *m* (**·eidiau**) boxful.
blychau *see* **blwch**.
blynedd *pl* years.
blynyddol *adj* annual.
blys *m* craving.
Bnr *abb* Mr.
Bns *abb* Mrs, Miss, Ms.
bo, byddo *from* **bod**.
bocsaid *m* (**bocseidi, bocseidiau**) boxful.
boch *f* (**·au**) cheek.
bochgoch *adj* red-cheeked.
bod *v* to be (*see* Appendix). • *m* (**·au**) being.
boda *m* (**·od**) buzzard.
bodan *f* girl.
bodiaid *f* pinch.
bodiau *see* **bawd**.
bodio *v* to thumb.
bodlon, boddlon *adj* content, willing.
bodloni *v* to satisfy.
bodlonrwydd *m* satisfaction.
bodo *f* auntie.
bodolaeth *f* existence.
bodoli *v* to exist.
bodd *m* (**·au**) consent.
boddfa *f* drenching.
boddhad *m* satisfaction.
boddhaol *adj* satisfactory.
boddhau *v* to satisfy.
boddi *v* to drown.
boddlon *see* **bodlon**.
boed *from* **bod**.
bogail *m/f* (**bogeiliau**) navel.
bol, bola *m* belly.
bolaheulo, bolheulo *v* to sunbathe.
bol·gi *m* (**·gwn**) glutton.
bolgodog *adj* marsupial.
bolgodogion *pl* marsupials.
bolheulo *see* **bolaheulo**.
boliaid *m* (**bolieidiau**) bellyful.
boliog *adj* pot-bellied.
bollt, bollten *f* (**byllt, bolltau**) bolt.
bolltio *v* to bolt.
bom *m/f* bomb.
bôm *from* **bod**.
bomio *v* to bomb.
bôn *m* (**bonion**) base.
boncath *m* (**·od**) buzzard.
bonclust *m* clout.
boncyff *m* (**·ion**) stump.
bondo *m* eaves.
boned, bonet *m/f* (**·au**) bonnet.
bonedd *m* gentry.
boneddigaidd *adj* polite.
boneddigeiddrwydd *m* courtesy.
boneddiges *f* (**·au**) lady.
boneddigion *see* **bonheddwr**.

bonesig *f* Miss; Lady.
bonet *see* **boned.**
bonheddig *adj* courteous.
bonheddwr *m* (**boneddigion**) gentleman.
bonllef *f* (**·au**) shout.
bônt *from* **bod.**
bonwr *m* Mister.
bonws *m* bonus.
bon·yn *m* (**·ion**) stub.
bopa *f* auntie.
bord *f* (**·ydd**) table.
bord·aid *f* (**·eidiau**) tableful.
bore *m* (**·au, ·uau**) morning. • *adj* early.
boreddydd *m* early morning.
boreol, boreuol *adj* morning.
bost *f* boast.
bostio *v* to boast.
botaneg *f* botany.
botaneg·ydd *m* (**·wyr**) botanist.
botasen, botysen *f* (**botas, botias, botys**) wellington boot.
botwm, botwn, bwtwm, bwtwn *m* (**botymau, botynau**) button.
botymog *adj* studded.
botymu *v* to button.
both *f* (**·au**) hub, boss.
bowlen *f* (**·ni**) bowl.
bowlen·naid *f* (**·eidiau**) bowlful.
bowlio *v* to bowl.
bowl·iwr *m* (**·wyr**) bowler.
braced *f* (**·i**) brackets.
bracsan, bracso *v* to wade.
bracty *see* **bragdy.**
brad *m* treachery.
brad·wr *m* (**·wyr**) traitor.
bradwrus *adj* treacherous.
bradychu *v* to betray.
braenar *m* fallow land.
braenaru *v* to fallow.
braf *adj* ample; fine.
brag *m* malt.
brag·dy, brac·ty *m* (**·dai, ·tai**) brewery.
bragu *v* to brew.
braich *f* (**breichiau**) arm.
braidd *adv* rather.
brain *see* **brân.**
braint *m/f* (**breiniau, breintiau**) privilege.
braith *adj* (*f*) speckled: **siaced fraith** coat of many colours.
brân *f* (**brain**) crow.
bras *adj* coarse; fat; general.
brasamcan *m* (**·ion**) approximation.
brasbwytho *v* to tack.
brasgamu *v* to stride.
braslun *m* (**·iau**) sketch.
braslunio *v* to sketch.
braster *m* (**·au**) fat.
brat *m* (**·iau**) apron.
bratiaith *f* poor language.
bratiog *adj* tattered.
brath, brathiad *m* bite.
brathu *v* to bite.
brau *adj* brittle.
braw *m* (**·iau**) terror.
brawd *m* (**brodyr**) brother; *f* (**brodiau**) judgement.
brawdgarol *adj* brotherly.
brawdgarwch *m* brotherly love.
brawdlys *m/f* (**·oedd**) assizes.
brawdol *adj* fraternal.
brawdoliaeth *f* brotherhood.

brawddeg *f* (**·au**) sentence.
brawddegu *v* to phrase; to enunciate.
brawychu *v* to terrify.
brawychus *adj* terrifying.
brêc *m* (**breciau**) brake.
brecwast *m* (**·au**) breakfast.
brech *f* (**·au**) pox. • *adj* (*f*) speckled.
brechdan *f* (**·au**) sandwich.
brechiad *m* (**·au**) vaccination.
brechu *v* to vaccinate.
bref *f* (**·iadau**) bleat.
brefu *v* to bleat.
bregedd *m/f* frailty.
bregliach *v* to jabber.
bregus *adj* frail.
breichiau *see* **braich.**
breichio *v* to dance arm in arm.
breichled *f* (**·au**) bracelet.
breindal *m* royalty fee.
breiniau, breintiau *see* **braint.**
breinio, breintio *v* to favour.
breiniog, breiniol *adj* privileged.
breinlen *f* charter.
breision *adj* (*pl*) large.
brenhines *f* (**breninesau**) queen.
brenhiniaeth *f* (**breniniaethau**) sovereignty.
brenhinoedd *see* **brenin.**
brenhinol *adj* regal.
brenigen *f* (**brennig**) limpet.
brenin *m* (**brenhinoedd**) king.
breninesau *see* **brenhines.**
breniniaethau *see* **brenhiniaeth.**
brennig *see* **brenigen.**
brest *f* chest.
bresus, bresys *pl* braces.
bresychen *f* (**bresych**) cabbage.
brethyn *m* (**·nau**) cloth.
breuder *m* frailty.
breuddwyd *m/f* (**·ion**) dreams.
breuddwydio *v* to dream.
breuddwydiol *adj* dreamy.
breuddwyd·iwr *m* (**·wyr**) dreamer.
breued, breuach, breuaf *from* **brau.**
bri *m* respect.
briallen *f* (**briallu**) primrose.
bribsyn *m* (**bribis, bribys**) fragment, bit.
bricio *v* to brick.
bric·iwr *m* (**·wyr**) bricklayer.
bricsen *f* (**briciau, brics**) brick.
bricyllen *f* (**bricyll**) apricot.
brifo *v* to hurt.
brig *m* (**·au**) top.
brigâd *f* (**brigadau**) brigade.
brigau *pl* twigs; tops.
briger *m/f* (**·au**) stamen.
brigo *v* to sprout.
brigyn *m* (**brigau, ·nau**) twig.
brith *adj* speckled; faint (*f* **braith**).
britho *v* to speckle.
brithwaith *m* mosaic.
brithyll *m* (**·od**) trout.
briw *m* (**·iau**) wound.
briwgig *m* mince.
briwio, briwo *v* to hurt.
briwsioni *v* to crumble.
briwsionyn *m* (**briwsion**) crumb.
bro *f* (**·ydd**) region.
broc *adj* grizzled. • *m* flotsam.
broch *m* (**·od**) badger.
brodiau *see* **brawd.**
brodio *v* to darn, to embroider.

brodor *m* (**-ion**) native.
brodorol *adj* indigenous.
brodwaith *m* embroidery.
brodyr *see* **brawd.**
broga *m* (**-od**) frog, toad.
brolian-t *hwn* (**-nau**) blurb.
brolio, brolian *v* to boast.
brol-iwr *m* (**brol-wyr**) braggart.
bron *f* (**-nau**) breast (body); (**-nydd**) breast of hill. • *adv* almost.
bronfraith *f* (**bronfreithiaid, bronfreithod**) thrush.
bront *adj* (*f*) dirty; nasty.
bronwen *f* weasel.
bru *m* womb.
brwd *adj* enthusiastic.
brwdfrydedd *m* enthusiasm.
brwdfrydig *adj* fervent.
brwmstan *m* brimstone.
brwnt *adj* dirty; nasty (*f* **bront**).
brws *m* (**-ys**) brush.
brwsio *v* to brush.
brwydr *f* (**-au**) battle.
brwydro *v* to fight.
brwynen *f* (**brwyn**) rush.
brwyn-iad *f* (**-iaid**) anchovy.
brwysg *adj* drunk.
brych *m* (**-au**) speck. • *adj* speckled.
brycheulyd *adj* bespotted.
brycheuyn *m* (**brychau**) speck.
brychni *m* freckles.
brychu *v* to fleck.
bryd *m* intent.
bryn *m* (**-iau**) hill.
bryncyn *m* hillock.
brynted *from* **brwnt.**
brynti, bryntni *m* filth.
brys *m* haste.
brysgennad *f* (**brysgenhadon**) courier.
brysgyll *m* mace.
brysio *v* to hurry.
brysiog *adj* hasty.
brysneges *f* (**-au**) telegram.
bu *from* **bod.**
buain *adj* (*pl*) swift.
bual *m* (**buail**) buffalo.
buan *adj* swift.
buander, buanedd *m* speed.
buarth *m* (**-au**) farmyard; school yard.
buchedd *f* (**-au**) conduct (of life).
buches *f* (**-au**) herd (cattle).
buchod *see* **buwch.**
budr *adj* filthy.
budredd, budreddi *m* filth.
budd *m* benefit.
budd-ai *f* (**-eiau**) churn.
budd-dâl *m* (**budd-daliadau**) benefit.
buddeiau *see* **buddai.**
buddian-t *m* (**-nau**) welfare.
buddiol *adj* beneficial.
buddsoddi *v* to invest.
buddugol *adj* victorious.
buddugoliaeth *f* (**-au**) victory.
buddugoliaethus *adj* triumphant.
buddug-wr *m* (**-wyr**) victor.
bugail *m* (**bugeiliaid**) shepherd.
bugeiles *f* shepherdess.
bugeilio *v* to shepherd.
bugunad *v* to roar.
bûm *from* **bod.**
bun *f* maiden.
burum *m* yeast.
busnes *m/f* (**-au**) business.

busnesa *v* to meddle.
busneslyd *adj* nosey.
bustach *m* (**bustych**) bullock.
bustachu *v* to bungle.
bustl *m* bile.
butred *from* **bydr**.
buwch *f* (**buchod**) cow.
buwch goch gota *f* ladybird.
bwa *m* (**bwâu**) bow.
bwaog *adj* arched.
bwbach *m* (**·od**) scarecrow.
bwced *m/f* (**·i**) bucket.
bwced·aid *m/f* (**·eidiau**) bucketful.
bwci *m* (**bwcïod**) bogy.
bwcl *m* (**byclau**) buckle.
bwch *m* (**bychod**) buck.
bwdram *m* flummery.
bwgan *m* (**·od**) bugbear.
bwi *m* (**bwïau**) buoy.
bwlb *m* (**bylbiau**) bulb.
bwlch *m* (**bylchau**) gap.
bwled *f* (**·i**) bullet.
bwli *m* (**bwlïod, bwlïaid**) bully.
bwlyn *m* (**·nau**) knob.
bwnglera *v* to bungle.
bwrdeistref *f* (**·i**) borough.
bwrdd *m* (**byrddau**) table, board.
bwriad *m* (**·au**) intention.
bwriadol *adj* intentional.
bwriadu *v* to intend.
bwr(iaf) *from* **bwrw**.
bwrlwm *m* (**byrlymau**) a bubbling.
bwrn *m* (**byrnau**) burden.
bwrw *v* to hit.
bws, bỳs *m* (**bysiau, bysys**) bus.
bwtsiasen *f* (**bwtsias, bwtias**) boot; wellington.
bwthyn *m* (**bythynnod**) cottage.
bwyall, bwyell *f* (**bwyeill**) axe.
bwyd *m* (**·ydd**) food.
bwydlen *f* (**·ni**) menu.
bwydo *v* to feed.
bwyeill *see* **bwyall**.
bwygilydd *adv* after another.
bwylltid *m* (**·au**) swivel.
bwystfil *m* (**·od**) beast.
bwyta *v* to eat.
bwytadwy *adj* edible.
bwy·ty *m* (**·tai**) restaurant.
byclau *see* **bwcl**.
bychain *adj* (*pl*) small.
bychan *adj* little.
bychander, bychandra *m* smallness.
bychanu *v* to belittle.
bychod *see* **bwch**.
byd *m* (**·oedd**) world.
byd-eang *adj* world-wide.
byd-enwog *adj* world-famous.
bydol *adj* worldly.
bydwraig *f* (**bydwragedd**) midwife.
bydysawd *m* universe.
bydd *from* **bod**.
byddar *adj* deaf.
byddarol *adj* deafening.
byddaru *v* to deafen.
byddin *f* (**·oedd**) army.
byddo *from* **bod**.
byg *m* (**·iau**) bug.
bygwth *v* to threaten.
bygythiad *m* (**·au**) threat.
bygythiol *adj* threatening.
byl *m/f* brim.
bylbiau *see* **bwlb**.
bylchau *see* **bwlch**.
bylchu *v* to breach.
byllt *see* **bollt**.

byngalo, bynglo *m* bungalow.
bynnag *prep* (what/where)soever.
bynnen, bynsen *f* (**byns**) bun.
byr *adj* short.
byrbryd *m* (**·au**) snack.
byrbwyll *adj* impulsive.
byrder, byrdra *m* brevity.
byrdwn *m* refrain.
byrdd·aid *m* (**·eidiau**) tableful.
byrddau *see* **bwrdd.**
byrfodd *m* (**·au**) abbreviation.
byrfyfr *adj* impromptu.
byrhau *v* to shorten.
byrhoedlog *adj* short-lived.
byrlymau *see* **bwrlwm.**
byrlymu *v* to bubble.
byrnau *see* **bwrn.**
byrred *from* **byr.**
byrstio *v* to burst.
bys *m* (**·edd**) finger.
bŷs *see* **bws.**
byseddu *v* to finger.
bysiau, bysys *see* **bws.**
byth *adv* ever.
bytheiad *m* (**bytheiaid**) hound.
bytheirio *v* to threaten.
bythgofiadwy *adj* memorable.
bythynnod *see* **bwthyn.**
bythol *adj* eternal.
bythwyrdd, bytholwyrdd *adj* evergreen.
bythynnod *see* **bwthyn.**
byw *v* to live. • *adj* alive.
bywgraffiad *m* (**·au**) biography.
bywgraffiadur *m* biographical dictionary.
bywhau *v* to enliven.
bywiocáu *v* to enliven.
bywiog *adj* lively.
bywiogrwydd *m* sprightliness.
bywoliaeth *f* (**·au**) livelihood.
bywyd *m* (**·au**) life.
bywyd·fa *f* (**·feydd**) vivarium.
bywyn *m* (**·nau**) core.

C

C *abb* **canrif.**
c *abb* **ceiniog.**
cabaetsen, cabeitsen, cabetsen *f* (**cabaets**) cabbage.
caban *m* (**·au**) cabin.
cabledd *m/f* blasphemy.
cableddus *adj* blasphemous.
cablu *v* to blaspheme.
caboledig *adj* polished.
caboli *v* to polish.
cacamwci *m* burdock.
cacen *f* (**·nau**) cake.
cacynen *f* (**cacwn**) wasps.
cacynyn *m* (**cacwn**) wasps.
cach·gi *m* (**·gwn**) sneak.
cachu *v* to defecate.
cad *f* (**·oedd**) battle.
cadach *m* (**·au**) cloth.
cad·air *f* (**·eiriau**) chair.
cadarn *adj* strong.

cadarnhad *m* confirmation.
cadarnhaol *adj* affirmative.
cadarnhau *v* to confirm.
cadeiriau *see* **cadair**.
cadeirio *v* to chair.
cadeiriol *adj* chaired: **eglwys g~** cathedral.
cadeirydd *m* (**·ion**) chairman.
cadernid *m* strength.
cadfridog *m* (**·ion**) general.
cadi ffan *m* sissy.
cadlas *f* (**cadlesydd**) enclosure.
cadnawes, cadnôes *f* vixen.
cadn·o *m* (**·awon, ·oid**) fox.
cadoediad *m* armistice.
cadw *v* to keep.
cadwedig *adj* saved.
cadw-mi-gei *m* money-box.
cadwraeth *f* conservation.
cadwyn *f* (**·au, ·i**) chain.
cadwyno *v* to chain.
caddug *m* mist.
cae *m* (**·au**) field.
caead *m* (**·au**) lid. • *adj* closed.
cae(af) *from* **cau**.
caeedig, caeëdig *adj* shut.
cael *v* to have (*see* Appendix).
caenen *f* (**·nau**) layer.
caentach *v* to wrangle.
caer *f* (**·au, ceyrydd**) fort.
caerog *adj* fortified.
caeth *adj* confined.
caethferch *f* slave.
caethglud *f* captivity.
caethgludo *v* to deport.
caethineb *m* addiction.
caethiwed *m* captivity.
caethiwo *v* to enslave.
caethwas *m* (**caethweision**) slave.
caethwasiaeth *f* slavery.
caf *from* **cael**.
cafell *f* chamber.
cafn *m* (**·au**) gutter.
caffael·iad *m* (**·iaid**) acquisition.
cafflo *v* to cheat.
caffo *from* **cael**.
cagl *m* (**·au**) clotted dirt.
cangell *f* (**canghellau, canghelloedd**) chancel.
cangen *f* (**canghennau**) branch.
canghellor *m* chancellor.
canghennog *adj* branching.
câi *from* **cael**.
caiac *m* (**·au**) kayak.
caib *f* (**ceibiau**) mattock.
caiff *from* **cael**.
caill *f* (**ceilliau**) testicle.
cain *adj* fine.
cainc *f* (**ceinciau**) branch.
cais *m* (**ceisiadau**) (an) attempt; (**ceisiau**) try (rugby).
cal, cala *f* (**caliau**) penis.
calan *m*: **Dydd Calan** New Year's Day.
calch *m* lime.
calchen *f* limestone.
calchfaen *m* (**calchfeini**) limestone.
calchu *v* to lime.
caled *adj* hard.
caledfwrdd *m* hardboard.
caledi *m* hardship.
caledu *v* to harden.
caledwch *m* hardness.
caledwedd *m* hardware.
calendr *m* (**·au**) calendar.

calennig *m/f* New Year gift.
caleted *from* **caled**.
calon *f* (**-nau**) heart.
calondid *m* encouragement.
calon-galed *adj* hard-hearted.
calonnog *adj* hearty.
calonogi *v* to encourage.
calonogol *adj* encouraging.
calori *m* (**caloriau**) calorie.
call *adj* sensible.
callestr *f* (**cellystr**) flint.
callineb *m* prudence.
callio *v* to get wiser.
cam *m* (**-au**) step. • *adj* crooked.
camamseru *v* to mistime.
camarfer *v* to abuse.
camargraff *m/f* false impression.
camarwain *v* to mislead.
camarweiniol *adj* misleading.
cambren *m* (**-ni**) coat-hanger.
camdreuliad *m* indigestion.
cam-drin *v* to ill-treat.
camdybio, camdybied *v* to misconceive.
camddeall *v* to misunderstand.
camddealltwriaeth *m* misunderstanding.
camddefnydd *m* misuse.
camddefnyddio *v* to misuse.
cam·fa *m* (**·feydd**) stile.
camfarnu *v* to misjudge.
camfihafio *v* to misbehave.
camgymer(af) *from* **camgymryd**.
camgymeriad *m* (**-au**) mistake.
camgymryd *v* to mistake.
camlas *f* (**camlesi**) canal.
camliwio *v* to misrepresent.
camocs, ciamocs *pl* pranks.
camochri *v* to be offside.
camp *f* (**-au**) feat.
camp·fa *f* (**·feydd**) gymnasium.
campreg *f* champion (woman).
campus *adj* splendid.
camp·waith *m* (**·weithiau**) masterpiece.
camp·wr *m* (**·wyr**) expert.
camre *m* footsteps.
camrifo *v* to miscount.
camsefyll *v* to be out of position.
camsyniad *m* (**-au**) error.
camsynied, camsynio, camsynnu *v* to mistake.
camsyniol *adj* mistaken.
camu *v* to pace.
camwedd *m* (**-au**) misdeed.
camwerthyd *f* camshaft.
camwri *m* wrong.
camymddwyn *v* to misbehave.
camymddygiad *m* misconduct.
can *m* flour; hundred.
cân *f* (**caneuon**) song.
canadwy *adj* singable.
can(ddo) *from* **gan**.
canawon *see* **cenau**.
cancr *m* cancer.
candryll *adj* shattered.
caneri *m* canary.
caneuon *see* **cân**.
canfasio *v* to canvass.
canfed *adj* hundredth.
canfod *v* to discern.
canfodydd *m* detector.
canfyddadwy *adj* perceptible.
canfyddiad *m* perception.
cangarŵ *m* (**cangarŵod, cangarwiaid**) kangaroo.

canhwyllarn, canhwyllbren (canwyllbrennau) *m* candlestick.
canhwyllau *see* **cannwyll.**
caniad *m* sounding.
caniadaeth *f* singing.
caniatâd *m* permission.
caniataol *adj* granted.
caniatáu *v* to permit.
canibaliaeth *f* cannibalism.
canlyn *v* to follow.
canlyniad *m* (**·au**) result.
canlynol *adj* following.
canlyn·wr *m* (**·wyr**) follower.
canllath *pl* hundred yards.
canllaw *m/f* (**·iau**) guideline.
canmlwyddian·t *m* (**·nau**) centenary.
canmol *v* to praise.
canmoladwy *adj* commendable.
canmoliaeth *f* praise.
canmoliaethus *adj* complimentary.
cannaid *adj* shining white.
cannoedd *see* **cant.**
cannu *v* to bleach.
cannwyll *f* (**canhwyllau**) candle.
cannydd *m* (**canyddion**) bleach.
canol *m* middle.
canolbarth *m* midlands.
canolbwynt *m* focus; centre.
canolbwyntio *v* to concentrate.
canoldir *m* inland region.
canolfan *f/m* (**·nau**) centre.
canoli *v* to centralise.
canolig *adj* middling.
canol oed middle age.
canol-oed middle-aged.
canoloesoedd *pl* Middle Ages.
canolog *adj* central.
canol·wr *m* (**·wyr**) centre; intermediary.
canradd *adj* centigrade.
canran *f* (**·nau**) percentage.
canrif *f* (**·oedd**) century.
cansen *hon* (**·nau, ·ni**) cane.
cant, can *m* (**cannoedd**) hundred; rim dome.
cânt *from* **cael.**
cantel *m* brim.
cantîn *m* canteen.
cantores *f* female singer.
cantorion *pl* singers.
cantref *m* (**·i**) hundred.
cantroed *m* (**·iaid**) centipede.
canu *v* to sing.
canŵ *m* (**canŵs**) canoe.
canwaith *adv* a hundred times.
can·wr *m* (**·wyr**) singer.
canwr·iad *m* (**·iaid**) centurion.
canwyllbrennau *see* **canhwyllbren.**
canyddion *see* **cannydd.**
canys *conj* because.
capan *m* (**·au**) cap.
capel *m* (**·i**) chapel.
capel·wr *m* (**·wyr**) chapel-goer.
caplan *m* (**·iaid**) chaplain.
capsiwl *m* (**·au**) capsule.
capten *m* (**capteiniaid**) captain.
car *m* (**ceir**) car.
câr *m* (**ceraint**) loved one.
carafán *f* (**carafannau**) caravan.
carbohydrad *m* (**·au**) carbohydrate.
carburedur *m* carburettor.
carbwl *adj* awkward.
carcio *v* to take care.
carcus *adj* careful.
carchar *m* (**·au**) jail.

carcharor *m* (**-ion**) prisoner.
carcharu *v* to imprison.
carden *f* (**cardiau**) cards.
cardfwrdd *m* cardboard.
cardod *f* charity.
cardota *v* to beg.
cardot·yn *m* (**-wyr**) beggar.
caredig *adj* kind.
caredigion *pl* friends.
caredigrwydd *m* kindness.
caregl *m* (**-au**) chalice.
caregog *adj* stony.
careiau *see* **carrai**.
carfan *f* (**-au**) faction.
cariad *m* love. • *m/f* lover.
cariadfab *m* sweetheart.
cariadferch *f* sweetheart.
cariadus *adj* affectionate.
caridým *m* (**-s**) down-and-out.
cario *v* to carry.
carlam *m* gallop.
carlamu *v* to gallop.
carlamus *adj* rash.
carlwm *m* (**carlymod**) stoat.
carn *m* (**-au**) hoof; hilt. • *f* tumulus.
cárnifal *m* carnival.
carnol *adj* hoofed.
carn-tro *m* brace (carpenter's).
carol·wr *m* (**-wyr**) carol singer.
carped *m* (**-i**) carpet.
carpedu *v* to carpet.
carpiau *see* **cerpyn**.
carpiog *adj* tattered.
carrai *f* (**careiau**) a lace.
carreg *f* (**cerrig**) stone.
cart *m* (**certi, ceirt**) cart.
cartio *v* to cart.
cartref *m* (**-i**) home.
cartrefol *adj* homely.
cartrefu *v* to make one's home.
cartrisen, cetrisen *f* (**certrys, cetris**) cartridge.
cartŵn *f* (**cartwnau**) cartoon.
cartwnydd *m* cartoonist.
carthen *f* (**-ni**) blanket.
carthffos *f* (**-ydd**) drain.
carthffosiaeth *f* sewage.
carthion *pl* excrement.
carthu *v* to muck out.
caru *v* to love.
carw *m* (**ceirw**) deer.
car·wr *m* (**-wyr**) lover.
carwriaeth *f* courtship.
cas *adj* nasty.
casáu *v* to hate.
casbeth *m* (**-au**) aversion.
caseg *f* (**cesig**) mare.
casét *m* (**casetiau**) cassette.
casgen *f* (**-ni**) cask.
casgliad *m* (**-au**) collection.
casglu *v* to collect.
casgl·wr *m* (**-wyr**) collector.
casineb *m* hatred.
cast *m* (**-iau**) prank.
castanwydden *f* (**castanwydd**) horse-chestnut tree; chestnut tree.
castell *m* (**cestyll**) castle.
castiog *adj* wily.
caswir *adj* unpalatable truth.
casyn *m* (**casiau**) casing.
catalydd *m* (**-ion**) catalyst.
categor·i *m* (**-ïau**) category.
caten *f* (**catiau**) bail.
catrawd *f* (**catrodau**) regiment.
catwad *m* chutney.

cath *f* (**·od**) cat.
catholig *adj* catholic.
cau *v* to close. • *adj* hollow.
caul *m* (**ceulion**) curd, rennet.
cawdel *m* hotchpotch.
cawell *m* (**cewyll**) basket.
cawg *m* (**·iau**) pitcher.
cawiau *see* **cewyn**.
cawio *v* to tie.
cawl *m* broth.
cawnen *f* (**cawn**) reed.
cawod *f* (**·au, ·ydd**) shower.
cawr *m* (**cewri**) giant.
cawres *f* (**·au**) giantess.
caws *m* cheese.
cawsu *v* to curdle.
CC *abb* BC.
ccc *abb* plc.
cêc *m* feed cake.
cecian *v* to stutter.
cecran, cecru *v* to quarrel.
cecren *f* shrew.
cecrus *adj* cantankerous.
cecryn *m* wrangler.
cedor *m/f* pubic hair.
cedowrach *m* burdock.
cedrwydden *f* (**cedrwydd**) cedar.
cedw(ais) *from* **cadw**.
cedyrn *from* **cadarn**.
cefais *from* **cael**.
cefn *m* (**·au**) back.
cefndedyn *m* sweetbread.
cefnder *m* (**cefndryd, cefnderoedd**) cousin (male).
cefndeudd·wr *m* (**·yrau**) watershed.
cefndir *m* (**·oedd**) background.
cefnen *f* (**·nau**) ridge.
cefnfor *m* (**·oedd**) ocean.
cefn·ffordd *m* (**·ffyrdd**) highway.
cefngefn *adv* back to back.
cefngrwm *adj* hunch-backed.
cefnog *adj* wealthy.
cefnogaeth *f* backing.
cefnogi *v* to support.
cefnogol *adj* supportive.
cefnog·wr *m* (**·wyr**) supporter.
cefnu *v* to withdraw.
cefn·wr *m* (**·wyr**) back, full-back.
ceffyl *m* (**·au**) horse.
ceg *f* (**·au**) mouth.
cega *v* to bicker.
ceg·aid *f* (**·eidiau**) mouthful.
cegiden *f* (**cegid**) hemlock.
cegin *f* (**·au**) kitchen.
cegog *adj* garrulous.
cegrwth *adj* gaping.
cengl *f* (**·au**) girth.
cei *m* (**·au**) quay. • *v from* **cael**.
ceian *f* carnation.
ceibiau *see* **caib**.
ceibio *v* to dig up.
ceidw *from* **cadw**.
ceidwad *m* (**ceidwaid**) keeper.
ceidwadol *adj* conservative.
ceidwad·wr *m* (**·wyr**) conservative.
ceiliagwydd *m* gander.
ceiliog *m* (**·od**) cock: **ceiliog y rhedyn** grasshopper.
ceilys *pl* skittles.
ceilliau *see* **caill**.
ceimion *from* **cam**.
ceinach *f* (**·od**) hare. • *adj from* **cain**.
ceinciau *see* **cainc**.
ceinciog *adj* branching; knotted.
ceinder *m* elegance.

ceiniog *f* (**·au**) penny.
ceinion *from* **cain**.
ceintach *v* to grumble.
ceintachlyd *adj* querulous.
ceir *see* **car**. • *v from* **cael**.
ceirchen *f* (**ceirch**) oats.
ceiriosen *f* (**ceirios**) cherry; cherry tree.
ceirt *see* **cart**.
ceirw *see* **carw**.
ceisiadau *see* **cais**.
ceisiau *see* **cais**.
ceisio *v* to seek.
cel *m* horse.
cêl *adj* hidden.
celain *f* (**celanedd**) corpse.
celc *m/f* hoard.
celf *f* art, craft.
celficyn *m* (**celfi**) (piece of) furniture.
celfydd *adj* skilful.
celfyddyd *m* (**·au**) art, craft.
celfyddydol *adj* artistic.
celu *v* to hide.
celwrn *m* (**celyrnau**) tub.
celwydd *m* (**·au**) lie.
celwydd·gi *m* (**·gwn**) liar.
celwyddog *adj* lying.
celyd *from* **caled**.
celynnen *f* (**celyn**) holly.
celyrnau *see* **celwrn**.
cell *f* (**·oedd**) cell.
celli *f* grove.
cellwair *m* (**cellweiriau**) banter. • *v* to banter.
cellweirus *adj* jocular.
cellystr *see* **callestr**.
cem(ais) *from* **camu**.
cemeg *f* chemistry.
cemegol *adj* chemical.
cemeg·ydd *m* (**·wyr**) chemist.
cemeg·yn *m* (**·au**, **·ion**) chemical.
cen *m* scale; lichen.
cenadaethau *see* **cenhadaeth**.
cenadwri *f* message.
cen(ais) *from* **canu**.
cenau *m* (**canawon**, **cenawon**) puppy.
cenawes *f* bitch.
cenedl *f* (**cenhedloedd**) nation.
cenedlaethau *see* **cenhedlaeth**.
cenedlaethol *adj* national.
cenedlaetholdeb *m* nationalism.
cenedlaetholi *v* to nationalise.
cenedlaethol·wr *m* (**·wyr**) nationalist.
cenedl-ddyn *m* gentile.
cenfaint *f* herd.
cenfigen *f* (**·nau**) envy.
cenfigennu *v* to envy.
cenfigennus *adj* jealous.
cenfydd *from* **canfod**.
cenhadaeth *f* (**cenadaethau**) mission.
cenhadau *see* **cennad**.
cenhadol *adj* missionary.
cenhadu *v* to conduct a mission.
cenhad·wr *m* (**·on**, **·wyr**) missionary.
cenhedlaeth *f* (**cenedlaethau**) generation.
cenhedloedd *see* **cenedl**.
cenhedlu *v* to beget.
cenhinen *f* (**cennin**) leek.
cen(ir) *from* **canu**.
cenllif *m/f* (**·oedd**) torrent.

cenllysg *pl* hailstones.
cennad *f* (**cenhadon, cenhadau**) messenger; message.
cennin *see* **cenhinen.**
cennog *adj* scaly.
cer *from* **mynd.**
ceraint *from* **câr.**
cerameg *m/f* ceramics.
cerbyd *m* (**·au**) coach.
cerdinen, cerddinen *f* (**cerdin, cerddin**) mountain ash.
cerdyn *m* (**cardiau**) card.
cerdd *f* (**·i**) poem; music.
cerdded *v* to walk.
cerddediad *m* walk.
cerddor *m* (**·ion**) musician.
cerddor·fa *f* (**·feydd**) orchestra.
cerddorfaol *adj* orchestral.
cerddoriaeth *f* music.
cerddorol *adj* musical.
cerdd·wr *m* (**·wyr**) walker.
cerfiedig *adj* carved.
cerfio *v* to carve.
cerflun *m* (**·iau**) statue.
cerflunio *v* to sculpt.
cerflunydd *m* (**cerflunwyr**) sculptor.
cerhyntau *see* **cerrynt.**
ceriach *f* equipment.
cerigyn *m* (**cerigos**) pebble.
ceriwb *m* (**·iaid**) cherub.
cern *f* (**·au**) cheekbone.
cernod *f* box on the ears.
cerpyn *m* (**carpiau**) rag.
cerrig *see* **carreg.**
cerrynt *m* (**ceryntau, cerhyntau**) current.
certrys *see* **cartrisen.**
cerwyn *f* (**·i**) cask.
cerydd *m* (**·on**) reprimand.
ceryddu *v* to reprimand.
ceryntau *see* **cerrynt.**
cesail *f* (**ceseiliau**) armpit.
cesair *pl* hail.
cesgl(ir) *from* **casglu.**
cesig *see* **caseg.**
cestyll *see* **castell.**
cetyn *m* (**catiau, ·nau**) pipe; piece.
cethin *adj* fierce, ugly.
ceubren *m* (**·nau**) hollow tree.
ceudod *m* cavity.
ceugrwm *adj* concave.
ceulan *f* (**·nau, ceulennydd**) hollow river bank.
ceulion *see* **caul.**
ceulo *v* to clot.
ceunant *m* (**ceunentydd**) ravine.
cewri *see* **cawr.**
cewyll *see* **cawell.**
cewyn *m* (**·nau, cawiau**) nappy.
ceyrydd *see* **caer.**
ci *m* (**cŵn**) dog.
ciaidd *adj* brutal.
cib *m* (**·au**) husk.
cibddall *adj* purblind.
cibwst *f* chilblain.
cibÅts *m* (**cibwtsau**) kibbutz.
cic·iwr *m* (**·wyr**) kicker.
cig *m* (**·oedd**) meat.
cigfran *f* (**cigfrain**) raven.
cignoeth *adj* raw.
cigydd *m* (**·ion**) butcher.
cigysol *adj* carnivorous.
cigysydd *m* (**·ion**) carnivore.
cil *m* (**·iau**) corner.
cilagor *v* to open partly.

cilagored *adj* ajar.
cilan *f* (**-nau**) cove.
cilcyn *m* chunk.
cildwrn, cil-dwrn *m* tip.
cilddant *m* (**cilddannedd**) molar.
ciledrych *v* to glance.
ciledrychiad *m* glance.
cilfach *f* (**-au**) creek.
cilgan·t *m* (**·nau, ·tau**) crescent.
cil-gnoi *v* to chew the cud.
cilio *v* to retreat.
cilwenu *v* to simper.
cilwg *m* (**cilygon**) scowl.
cim·wch *m* (**·ychiaid**) lobster.
ciniawa *v* to dine.
cinio *m/f* (**ciniawau**) dinner.
cip *m* glimpse.
cipio *v* to snatch.
cipol·wg *m* (**·ygon**) glimpse.
cis *m/f* (**·iau**) slap.
cist *f* (**·iau**) chest.
ciwcymber, cucumer *m* (**ciwcymerau, cucumerau**) cucumber.
ciwed *f* rabble.
ciwrad, ciwrat *m* curate.
ciwt *adj* smart.
clacwydd, clagwydd *m* gander.
claddedigaeth *m/f* burial.
cladd·fa *f* (**·feydd**) graveyard.
claddu *v* to bury.
claear *adj* lukewarm.
claer *adj* clear.
claerwyn *adj* pallid.
claf *adj* sick. • *m* (**cleifion**) patient.
clafr *m* mange.
clafychu *v* to fall ill.
clai *m* (**cleiau**) clay.
clais *m* (**cleisiau**) bruise.
clamp *m* whopper.
clap *m* (**·iau**) lump.
clap·gi *m* (**·gwn**) telltale.
clapian *v* to tell tales.
clapiog *adj* lumpy.
clarinét *m* (**clarinetau**) clarinet.
clas *m* (**·au**) Celtic monastery.
clasur *m* (**·on**) classic.
clasurol *adj* classical.
clatsian *v* to crackle.
clatsio *v* to slap.
clau *adj* cyflym.
clawdd *m* (**cloddiau**) hedge.
clawr *m* (**cloriau**) cover.
cleber, clebar *m/f* tittle-tattle.
clebran *v* to chatter.
clec *f* snap.
clecs *pl* gossip.
cledr, cledren *f* (**cledrau**) rail; palm of hand.
cledro *v* to wallop.
cledd, cleddyf *m* (**cleddyfau**) sword.
cleddyf·wr *m* (**·wyr**) swordsman.
clefyd *m* (**·au**) disease.
clegar *m* cluck, cackle.
cleiau *see* **clai**.
cleifion *see* **claf**.
cleiog *adj* clayey.
cleisio *v* to bruise.
cleisiau *see* **clais**.
clem *f* gumption.
clemio *v* to starve.
clên *adj* pleasant.
clensio *v* to clench.
clepian *v* to crackle.
clercio *v* to clerk.

cleren *f* (**clêr**) fly.
clerigol *adj* clerical.
cleuach *from* **clau**.
cliced, clicied *f* latch.
clindarddach *m* crackling.
clinigol *adj* clinical.
clir *adj* clear.
clirio *v* to clear.
clo *m* (**·eon, ·eau**) lock.
clocsen *f* (**clocsiau**) clogs.
clocs·iwr *m* (**·wyr**) clog-maker; clog-dancer.
clocwedd *adj* clockwise.
cloch *f* (**clychau**) bell.
clochdar *v* to cackle.
cloch·dy *m* (**·dai**) belfry.
clochydd *m* (**·ion**) sexton.
clod *m/f* (**·ydd**) praise.
clodfawr *adj* praiseworthy.
clodfori *v* to praise.
clodwiw *adj* commendable.
cloddiau *see* **clawdd**.
cloddio *v* to excavate.
cloëdig, cloiedig *adj* locked.
cloeon, cloeau *see* **clo**.
cloff *adj* lame.
cloffi *v* to lame.
cloffni *m* lameness.
clog *m/f* (**·au**) cloak; precipice.
clog·faen *m* (**·feini**) boulder.
clogwyn *m* (**·i**) cliff.
clogyn *m* (**·nau**) cloak.
clogyrnaidd *adj* rough.
cloi *v* to lock.
cloncian *v* to chatter.
clopa *f* (**clopâu**) head.
clorian *m/f* (**·nau**) scale (weighing).
cloriannu *v* to weigh.
cloriau *see* **clawr**.
clos *m* (**·ydd**) farmyard; trousers.
clòs *adj* close.
closio *v* to draw near.
cludadwy *adj* portable.
cludfelt *m* conveyor belt.
cludiad *m* postage, carriage.
cludiant *m* transport.
cludo *v* to carry, to transport.
clun *f* (**·iau**) hip.
clust *m/f* (**·iau**) ear; handle.
clusten *f* box on the ear.
clustfeinio *v* to eavesdrop.
clustl·ws, clustdl·ws *m* (**·ysau**) ear-ring.
clustnodi *v* to earmark.
clustog *m/f* (**·au**) cushion.
clwb *m* (**clybiau**) club.
clwc *adj* addled.
clwpa *m* bludgeon.
clwstwr *m* (**clystyrau**) cluster.
clwt, clwtyn *m* (**clytiau**) duster.
clwyd *f* (**·i**) gate; hurdle.
clwydo *v* to roost.
clwyf, clwy *m* (**clwyfau**) wound.
clwyfo *v* to wound.
clwyfus *adj* sick.
clybiau *see* **clwb**.
clychau *see* **cloch**.
clyd *adj* snug.
clydwch *m* warmth.
clyfrwch *m* cleverness.
clymau *see* **cwlwm**.
clymbl·aid *f* (**·eidiau**) coalition.
clymog *adj* knotted.
clymu *v* to tie.
clystyrau *see* **clwstwr**.
clytiau *see* **clwt, clwtyn**.

clytio *v* to patch.
clytiog *adj* patched.
clytwaith *m* patchwork.
clyw *m* hearing.
clywadwy *adj* audible.
clywed *v* to hear.
clyweled *adj* audiovisual.
clyweliad *m* audition.
cnaf *m* (**·on**) knave.
cnaif *m* (**cneifion**) fleece.
cnap *m* (**·iau**) chunk.
cnapan *m* old ball game.
cnau *see* **cneuen**.
cnawd *m* flesh.
cnawdol *adj* carnal.
cneifio *v* to shear.
cneifion *see* **cnaif**.
cneifi·wr *m* (**·wyr**) shearer.
cnepyn *m* (**·nau**) lump.
cneua *v* to collect nuts.
cneuen *f* (**cnau**) nut.
cnewyllyn *m* (**cnewyll**) kernel.
cnoad, cnoead *m* gnawing.
cnocell y coed *f* woodpecker.
cnocio *v* to knock.
cnoe(swn) *from* **cnoi**.
cnofil *m* (**·od**) rodent.
cnoi *v* to bite.
cnotiog *adj* gnarled.
cnu *m* (**·oedd**) fleece.
cnuchio *v* to copulate.
cnud *f* (**·oedd**) pack.
cnul *m* (**·iau**) knell.
cnwc *m* knoll.
cnwd *m* (**cnydau**) crop.
cnydio *v* to crop.
cob *m* (**·iau**) embankment.
coban *f* (**·au**) night-shirt.
coblyn *m* (**·nod**) goblin.
cocatŵ *m* cockatoo.
cocsen, cocosen *f* (**cocsenni**) cog; (**cocos**) cockles.
cocyn *m* (**·nau**) haycock.
coch *adj* red.
cochen *f* redhead.
cochi *v* to blush, to redden.
cochl *m/f* (**·au**) cloak.
cochyn *m* redhead.
cod *m* (**·au**) pod; code.
coden *f* (**·nau**) pouch.
codi *v* to lift.
codiad *m* (**·au**) rise, erection.
codwm *m* (**codymau**) fall.
coeden *f* (**coed**) tree.
coediog *adj* wooded.
coedlan *f* (**·nau**) glade.
coedwig *f* (**·oedd**) forest, wood.
coedwigaeth *f* forestry.
coedwig·wr *m* (**·wyr**) forester.
coedd *adj* public.
coeg *adj* false.
coegio, cogio *v* to pretend.
coeglyd *adj* sarcastic.
coegni *m* sarcasm.
coegyn *m* fop.
coel *f* (**·ion**).
coelbren *m* (**·nau**) lot, ballot.
coelcerth *f* (**·i**) bonfire.
coelio *v* to believe.
coes *f* (**·au**) leg. • *m* stem; handle.
coesog *adj* leggy.
coeten *f* (**coetiau, coets**) quoit.
coets *f* (**·ys**) coach.
coeth *adj* refined.
coethder *m* refinement.
coethi *v* to refine.

cof *m* (**·ion**) memory.
cofadail *f* cenotaph.
cofeb *f* (**·ion**) memorial.
cofgolofn *f* (**·au**) monument.
cofiadur *m* (**·on**) registrar.
cofiadwy *adj* memorable.
cofiannydd *m* (**cofianwyr**) biographer.
cofian·t *m* (**·nau**) biography.
cofio *v* to remember.
coflaid, cowlaid *f* armful.
cofleidio *v* to embrace.
cofnod *m* (**·ion**) record, minute.
cofnodi *v* to record.
cofrestr *f* (**·au**) register.
cofrestr·fa *f* (**·feydd**) registry.
cofrestru *v* to register.
cofrestrydd *m* (**·ion**) registrar.
coffa *m* remembrance.
coffâd *m* recollection.
coffadwriaeth *f* memorial.
coffáu *v* to commemorate.
coffor, coffr *m* (**coffrau**) coffer.
cog *f* (**·au**) cuckoo. • *m* cook.
còg *f* (**cogiau**) cog.
coginiaeth *f* cookery.
coginio *v* to cook.
cogio *v* to pretend.
cogor *v* to clatter.
cogor-droi *v* to spin.
cogydd *m* (**·ion**) cook.
cogyddes *f* (**·au**) cook.
congl *f* (**·au**) corner.
conglfaen *f* (**conglfeini**) cornerstone.
côl, cofl *f* lap, embrace.
coladu *v* to collate.
colbio *v* to thrash.
coleddu *v* to cherish.
coleg *m* (**·au**) college.
colegol *adj* collegiate.
colfach *m* (**·au**) hinge.
colfen *f* (**·ni, ·nnau**) branch.
colofn *f* (**·au**) column.
colomen *f* (**·nod**) dove; pigeon.
colomen·dy *m* (**·dai**) dovecot.
colsyn *m* (**cols**) cinder.
coluddyn *m* (**coluddion**) intestine.
colur *m* make-up.
coluro *v* to colour.
colyn *m* (**·nau**) sting; hinge.
coll *m* loss (of senses). • *adj* lost.
collddail *adj* deciduous.
colled *m/f* (**·ion**) loss.
colledig *adj* lost.
collen *f* (**cyll**) hazel.
collfarnu *v* to condemn.
colli *v* to lose.
collnod *m* apostrophe.
coll·wr *m* (**·wyr**) loser.
combein *m* combine harvester.
comed *f* (**·au**) comet.
comedi *f* (**comedïau**) comedy.
comedï·wr *m* (**·wyr**) comedian.
comin, cwmin *m* common.
comisi·wn *m* (**·ynau**) commission.
comisiynu *v* to commission.
comiwnydd *m* (**·ion**) communist.
comiwnyddiaeth *f* communism.
comiwnyddol *adj* communist.
compiwtereiddio *v* to computerise.
côn *m* (**conau**) cone.
conach, conan *v* to grumble.
concwer·wr *m* (**·wyr**) conqueror.
condemniad *m* condemnation.
condemnio *v* to condemn.

conen *f* grumbler.
confennau *pl* condiments.
confensiynol *adj* conventional.
congrinero *m* champion.
coniffer *m* (**-iaid**) conifer.
conigol *adj* conical.
cono *m* rascal.
consurio *v* to conjure.
consur·iwr *m* (**-wyr**) conjuror.
conwydden *f* (**conwydd**) coniferous trees.
conyn *m* grumbler.
cop, copyn *m* spider.
copa *m/f* (**copâu, copaon**) summit.
copi *m* (**copïau**) copy.
copïo *v* to copy.
copor, copr *m* copper.
cor *m* dwarf; spider.
côr *m* (**corau**) choir.
corachod *see* **corrach**.
corawl *adj* choral.
corben·fras *m* (**-freis**) haddock.
corcio, corco *v* to throb.
corcyn *m* (**cyrcs, corcau**) a cork.
cordeddu *v* to plait.
corden *f* (**-ni**) cord.
cordyn, cortyn *m* (**cordiau, cyrd, cyrt**) cord.
corddi *v* to churn.
cordd·wr *m* (**-wyr**) churner.
cored *f* (**-au**) weir.
corff *m* (**cyrff**) body.
corffil·yn *m* (**-od**) corpuscle.
corfflosgi *v* to cremate.
corfflu *m* (**-oedd**) corps.
corffolaeth *f* stature.
corfforaeth *f* (**-au**) corporation.
corffori *v* to embody.
corfforol *adj* bodily; physical.
cor·gi *m* (**-gwn**) corgi.
corgimwch *m* (**corgimychiaid**) prawn.
corlan *f* (**-nau**) fold.
corlannu *v* to pen (sheep).
corn *m* (**cyrn**) horn. • *adj* absolute.
cornant *m* (**cornentydd**) brook.
cornbilen *f* cornea.
cornchwig·len *f* (**-lod**) lapwing.
cornel *m/f* (**-i**) cornel.
cornelu *v* to corner.
cornicyll *m* (**-od**) lapwing.
cornio *v* to butt; to examine with stethoscope.
corniog *adj* horned.
cornwyd *m* (**-ydd**) boil.
coron *f* (**-au**) crown.
corongylch *m* (**-au**) halo.
coroni *v* to crown.
coroniad *m* coronation.
coronog *adj* crowned.
corrach, cor *m* (**corachod**) dwarf.
corryn, cor *m* (**corynnod**) spider.
cors *f* (**corsydd, cyrs**) bog.
corsen *f* (**-nau, cyrs**) reed.
corsog *adj* boggy.
corun *m* crown of head; tonsure.
corwgl *see* **cwrwgl**.
corygl·wr *m* (**-wyr**) coracle man.
corws *m* (**corysau**) chorus.
corwynt *m* (**-oedd**) hurricane.
corynnod *see* **corryn**.
corysau *see* **corws**.
cosb *f* (**-au**) punishment.
cosbedigaeth *f* punishment.
cosbi *v* to punish.
cos·fa *f* (**-feydd**) itch; thrashing.

cosi *v* to itch.
costio *v* to cost.
costrel *f* (**-au**) bottle.
costrelu *v* to bottle.
costus *adj* expensive.
cosyn *m* (**-nau**) a cheese.
cot *f* coat; a beating.
cota *adj* (*f*) short.
cotiar *f* (**cotieir**) coot.
cotwm *m* (**cotymau**) cotton.
cownt *m* reckoning.
crabysyn *m* (**crabas, crabys**) crab-apple.
crachach *pl* snobs.
crachboer *m* phlegm.
crachen *f* (**crach**) scab.
craen *m* (**-iau**) crane.
crafangu *v* to clutch.
crafanc *f* (**crafangau**) claw.
crafiad *m* (**-au**) scratch.
crafion *pl* scraps.
crafog *adj* cutting.
crafu *v* to scratch.
craff *adj* discerning.
craffter *m* discernment.
craffu *v* to look intently.
cragen *f* (**cregyn**) shell.
crai *adj* raw, crude.
craidd *m* (**creiddiau**) crux: **craidd disgyrchiant** centre of gravity.
craig *f* (**creigiau**) rock.
crair *m* (**creiriau**) relic.
craith *f* (**creithiau**) scar.
cramen *f* (**-nau**) crust.
cramennog *adj* encrusted.
cramenogion *pl* crustaceans.
cranc *m* (**-od**) crab; crank.
crancwerthyd *m* crankshaft.
crand *adj* grand.
crandrwydd *m* finery.
crap *m* inkling.
cras *adj* coarse; aired.
crasboeth *adj* scorching.
crasfa *f* a hiding.
crasiad *m* a baking.
craster *m* aridity.
crasu *v* to bake; to dry.
crau *m* (**creuau**) socket.
crawc *f* croak.
crawen *f* (**-nau**) crust.
crawn *m* pus.
crawni *v* to fester.
cread *m* creation.
creadigaeth *f* (**-au**) creation.
creadigol *adj* creative.
creadur *m* (**-iaid**) creature.
creadures *f* creature.
creawdwr, creawdur, creawdydd *m* (**creawdwyr**) creator.
crebachlyd *adj* wizened.
crebachu *v* to shrivel.
crebwyll *m* fancy.
crech *adj* (*f*) wrinkled.
crechwen *f* (**-au**) guffaw.
crechwenu *v* to guffaw.
cred *f* (**-au**) belief.
credadun *m* (**credinwyr**) believer.
credadwy *adj* credible.
crediniaeth *f* belief.
crediniol *adj* believing.
credu *v* to believe.
cred-wr *m* (**-wyr**) believer.
cref *adj* (*f*) strong.
crefu *v* to entreat.
crefydd *f* (**-au**) religion.
crefydda *v* to profess religion.

crefyddol *adj* religious.
crefft *f* (**·au**) craft.
crefft·waith *m* (**·weithiau**) craftsmanship.
crefft·wr *m* (**·wyr**) craftsman.
creg *adj (f)* hoarse.
cregyn *see* **cragen**.
crehyrod *see* **crëyr**.
creiddiau *see* **craidd**.
creifion *pl* peelings.
creigiau *see* **craig**.
creigiog *adj* rocky.
creiriau *see* **crair**.
creision *pl* crisps.
creithiau *see* **craith**.
creithio *v* to scar.
crempog *f* (**·au**) pancake.
crensian *v* to crunch.
creu *v* to create.
creuau *see* **crau**.
creulon *adj* cruel.
creulondeb, creulonder *m* cruelty.
crëwr *m* (**crewyr**) creator.
crëyr *m* (**crehyrod**) heron.
cri *m* (**·au**) cry. • *adj* unleavened.
criafolen *f* (**criafol**) rowan tree.
crib *m/f* (**·au**) comb.
cribddeilio *v* to extort.
cribin *m/f* (**·au, ·iau**) rake.
cribinio *v* to rake.
cribog *adj* crested.
criced *m* cricket.
criced·wr *m* (**·wyr**) cricketer.
crimog *f* (**·au**) shin.
crimp *adj* shrivelled.
crin *adj* brittle.
cringoch *adj* russet.
crino *v* to wither.
crintach, crintachlyd *adj* mean.
crio *v* to cry.
cripio *v* to creep.
crisial *m* (**·au**) crystal.
crisialu *v* to crystalise.
Cristion *m* (**·ogion, Cristnogion**) Christian.
criw *m* (**·iau**) crew.
crïwr *m* (**criwyr**) crier.
crocbren *m/f* (**·nau, ·ni**) gallows.
crocbris *m* (**·iau**) exorbitant price.
crocodil, crocodeil *m* (**crocodiliaid, crocodilod**) crocodile.
croch *adj* strident.
crochan *m* (**·au**) crock, cauldron.
crochen·dy *m* (**·dai**) pottery.
crochenwaith *m* pottery.
crochenydd *m* (**·ion**) potter.
croen *m* (**crwyn**) skin.
croendenau *adj* sensitive.
croendew *adj* thick-skinned.
croenddu *adj* black-skinned.
croes *f* (**·au**) cross.
croesair *m* (**croeseiriau**) crossword.
croesawgar *adj* hospitable.
croesawu *v* to welcome.
croesbren *m/f* (**·nau**) cross.
croes-ddweud *v* to contradict.
croesfan *f* (**·nau**) crossing.
croes·ffordd *f* (**·ffyrdd**) junction.
croesgad *f* (**·au**) crusade.
croesgad·wr *m* (**·wyr**) crusader.
croesgyfeirio *v* to cross-reference.
croeshoeliad *m* crucifixion.
croeshoelio *v* to crucify.
croesholi *v* to cross-examine.
croesi *v* to cross.

croeslin *f* (**·iau**) diagonal.
croeso *m* welcome.
croesymgroes *adj* criss-cross.
crofen, crawen *f* (**·nau, ·nau**) rind.
crog *f* (**·au**) cross. • *adj* suspended.
crogi *v* to hang.
crogian·t *m* (**·nau**) suspension.
croglith *f*: **Dydd Gwener y Groglith** Good Friday.
croglofft *f* (**·ydd**) attic.
cronglwyd *f* (**·ydd**) roof.
crom *adj* (*f*) round.
crombil *m/f* craw.
cromen *f* (**·nau**) dome.
cromfach *f* (**·au**) parenthesis.
cromlin *f* (**·iau**) curve; chord.
cron *adj* (*f*) round.
cronellau *see* **cronnell.**
cron·fa *f* (**·feydd**) reservoir; fund.
croniadur *m* (**·on**) accumulator.
croniclo *v* to chronicle.
cronnell *f* (**·au**) sphere.
cronni *v* to amass.
cronolegol *adj* chronological.
cropian, cropio *v* to crawl.
crosiet *m* (**·au**) crotchet.
crosio *v* to crochet.
crots *see* **crwt.**
croth *f* (**·au**) womb.
croyw *adj* pure.
croywder *m* clarity.
crud *m* cradle.
crug *m* (**·iau**) cairn.
crugyn *m* pile.
crwban *m* (**·od**) tortoise.
crwbi *m* (**crwbïod**) hump.
crwca *adj* crooked.
crwm *adj* curved.
crwn *adj* round.
crwner *m* (**·iaid**) coroner.
crwsâd *m/f* (**crwsadau**) crusade.
crwst *m* (**crystiau**) crust.
crwstyn, crystyn *m* (**crystiau**) crust.
crwt *m* (**crytiaid, crots, cryts**) lad.
crwth *m* (**crythau**) crwth, violin.
crwybr *m* (**·au**) honeycomb.
crwydr, crwydrad *m* wandering.
crwydro *v* to wander.
crwydrol *adj* wandering.
crwydryn *m* (**crwydriaid**) wanderer.
crwyn *see* **croen.**
crwys *f* (**·au**) cross.
crybwyll *v* to mention.
crych *adj* wrinkled. • *m* (**·au**) crease.
crychlyd *adj* wrinkled.
crychni *m* a wrinkling.
crychu *v* to wrinkle.
crychydd *m* heron.
cryd *m* (**·iau**) a shivering.
crydd *m* (**·ion**) cobbler.
cryf *adj* strong.
cryfder *m* strength.
cryfhau *v* to strengthen.
cryg, cryglyd *adj* hoarse.
crygni *m* hoarseness.
cryman *m* (**·au**) sickle.
crymanu *v* to swerve.
crymedd *m* curvature.
crymu *v* to stoop.
cryn *adj* quite.
cryndod *m* a shivering.
crynedig *adj* tremulous.
crynhoad *m* (**crynoadau**) collection.
crynhoi *v* to assemble.

crynion *from* **crwn**.
crynned *from* **crwn**.
cryno *adj* concise.
crynodeb *m/f* (**·au**) summary.
crynodedig *adj* concentrated.
crynodiad *m* (**·au**) concentration.
cryno-ddisg *m* (**·iau**) compact disc.
crynswth *m* entirety.
crynu *v* to shiver.
Cryn·wr *m* (**·wyr**) Quaker.
crys *m* (**·au**) shirt.
crys·bais *f* (**·beisiau**) jacket.
crystiau *see* **crwst**; **crwstyn**; **crystyn**.
cryts, crytiaid *see* **crwt**.
crythau *see* **crwth**.
crythor *m* (**·ion**) fiddler.
cu *adj* beloved.
cucumer *see* **ciwcymber**.
cuchiau *see* **cuwch**.
cuchio *v* to scowl.
cudyll *m* (**·od**) hawk.
cudyn *m* (**·nau**) ringlet.
cudd *adj* hidden.
cudd·fa *f* (**·fâu**, **·feydd**) hiding place.
cuddfan *f* (**·nau**) hiding place.
cuddiedig *adj* hidden.
cuddio *v* to hide.
cuddwedd *f* camouflage.
cufydd *m* cubit.
cul *adj* narrow.
culfor *m* (**·oedd**) channel.
culhau *v* to narrow.
culni *m* narrowness.
cun *adj* dear; beautiful.
cur *m* ache.
curad *m* (**·iaid**) curate.
cur·fa *f* (**·feydd**, **·fâu**) a beating.
curiad *m* (**·au**) a beat.
curlaw *m* driving rain.
curo *v* to strike.
curyll *m* (**·od**) hawk.
cusan *m/f* (**·au**) kiss.
cusanu *v* to kiss.
cut *m* (**·iau**) hut.
cuwch *m* (**cuchiau**) scowl.
cwafrio *v* to trill.
cwar *m* (**·rau**) quarry.
cwato *v* to hide.
cwb *m* (**cybiau**) kennel.
cwbl *adj* entire.
cwblhau *v* to complete.
cwcw *f* (**cwcŵod**) cuckoo.
cwcwll *m* (**cycyllau**) cowl.
cwch *m* (**cychod**) boat; hive.
cwd, cwdyn *m* (**cydau**) bag.
cweir *f* a hiding.
cwennod *see* **cywen**.
cweryl *m* (**·au**, **·on**) quarrel.
cweryla *v* to quarrel.
cwerylgar *adj* quarrelsome.
cwest *m* inquest.
cwestiwn *m* (**cwestiynau**) question.
cwfaint *m* convent.
cwfl *m* (**cyflau**) hood.
cwffio *v* to fight.
cwgen *f* (**·ni**, **·nod**) bread roll.
cwgn *m* (**cygnau**) knuckle.
cwil, cwilsyn *m* (**·s**, **·nau**) quill.
cwlff, cwlffyn *m* hunk.
cwlwm *m* (**clymau**) knot.
cwm *m* (**cymoedd**) glen.
cwmni *m* (**cwmnïau**) company.
cwmnïaeth *f* companionship.
cwmnï·wr *m* (**·wyr**) companion.

cwmpas *m*: **o gwmpas** about.
cwmpasog *adj* roundabout.
cwmpasu *v* to encompass.
cwmpawd *m* (**·au**) compass.
cwmpeini *m* company.
cwmwd *m* (**cymydau**) commote.
cwmwl *m* (**cymylau**) cloud.
cŵn *see* **ci**.
cwningen *f* (**cwningod**) rabbit.
cwnsela *v* to counsel.
cwnstabl *m* (**·iaid**) constable.
cwota *m* (**cwotâu**) quota.
cwpan *m/f* (**·au**) cup.
cwpanaid *m/f* (**cwpaneidiau**) cupful.
cwpl, cwpwl *m* (**cyplau**) couple.
cwpla, cwpláu *v* to finish.
cwpled *m* (**·i**) couplet.
cwpwrdd *m* (**cypyrddau**) cupboard.
cwr *m* (**cyrrau, cyrion**) corner.
cwrcath, cwrci *m* (**cwrcathod**) tomcat.
cwrcwd *m* (**cyrcydau**) squatting.
cwrdd *m* (**cyrddau**) meeting.
cwrel *m* coral.
cwricwlwm *m* (**cwricwla**) curriculum.
cwrlid *m* (**·au**) counterpane.
cwrs *m* (**cyrsiau**) course.
cwrt *m* (**cyrtiau**) court.
cwrtais *adj* courteous.
cwrteisi, cwrteisrwydd *m* courtesy.
cwrw *m* beer.
cwrwg, cwrwgl, corwgl *m* (**cyryglau**) coracle.
cwsg *m* (**cysgau**) sleep.
cwsmer *m* (**·iaid**) customer.
cwt *m* (**cytiau**) hut; tail.
cwta *adj* barely; curt.
cwter *f* (**·i**) gutter.
cwtogi *v* to shorten.
cwtsio, cwtsied *v* to crouch.
cwyd *from* **codi**.
cwymp *m* (**·au**) a fall.
cwympo *v* to fall.
cwyn *m/f* (**·ion**) complaint.
cwynfan *v* to complain.
cwynfanllyd *adj* grumbling.
cwyno *v* to complain.
cwyr *m* wax.
cwyrdeb *m* rennet.
cwys *f* (**·i, ·au**) furrow.
cybiau *see* **cwb**.
cybolfa *f* hotchpotch.
cyboli *v* to talk nonsense.
cybydd *m* (**·ion**) miser.
cybyddlyd *adj* mean.
cycyllau *see* **cwcwll**.
cycyllog *adj* hooded.
cychod *see* **cwch**.
cychwyn *v* to begin.
cychwynnol *adj* initial.
cyd *see* **cyhyd**.
cydadrodd *v* to recite together.
cydaid *m* (**cydeidiau**) bagful.
cydau *see* **cwd**.
cydbwysedd *m* equilibrium.
cydbwyso *v* to balance.
cyd-destun *m* (**·au**) context.
cyd-dynnu *v* to cooperate.
cyd-ddigwyddiad *m* (**·au**) coincidence.
cyd-ddyn *m* (**·ion**) fellow-man.
cydeidiau *see* **cydaid**.
cyd-fynd *v* to agree.
cyd-fyw *v* to live together.
cydganol *adj* concentric.

cydio *v* to hold.
cydlynu *v* to coordinate.
cydnabod *v* to acknowledge. • *m/f* (**cydnabyddion**) acquaintance.
cydnabyddedig *adj* acknowledged.
cydnabyddiaeth *f* recognition.
cydnaws *adj* congenial.
cydnerth *adj* strong.
cydol *m/f* whole.
cydosod *v* to assemble.
cydradd *adj* equal.
cydraddoldeb *m* equality.
cydran *f* (**-nau**) component.
cydryw *adj* homogeneous.
cydsynio *v* to agree.
cydweddu *v* to agree.
cydweithio *v* to cooperate.
cyd-weith·iwr *m* (**·wyr**) colleague.
cydweithrediad *m* cooperation.
cydweithredol *adj* cooperative.
cydweithredu *v* to cooperate.
cyd-weld *v* to agree.
cydwladol *adj* international.
cyd-wlad·wr *m* (**·wyr**) compatriot.
cydwybod *f* conscience.
cydwybodol *adj* conscientious.
cydymaith *m* (**cymdeithion**) companion.
cydymdeimlad *m* sympathy.
cydymdeimlo *v* to sympathise.
cydymffurfio *v* to conform.
cyddwysedd *m* condensation.
cyf. *abb* vol(ume); ltd; ref(erence).
cyfadran *f* (**·nau**) faculty (department).
cyfaddas *adj* suitable.
cyfaddawd *m* (**·au**) compromise.
cyfaddawdu *v* to compromise.
cyfaddef *v* to confess.
cyfagos *adj* adjoining.
cyfangu *v* to contract (draw in).
cyfaill *m* (**cyfeillion**) friend.
cyfaint *m* (**cyfeintiau**) volume.
cyfair *m* (**cyfeiriau**) acre.
cyfalaf *m* capital (money).
cyfalafiaeth *f* capitalism.
cyfamod *m* covenant.
cyfamodi *v* to covenant.
cyfamser *m* meantime.
cyfan *adj* complete.
cyfander *m* entirety.
cyfandir *m* (**·oedd**) continent.
cyfandirol *adj* continental.
cyfanheddu *v* to inhabit.
cyfannedd *m* (**cyfanheddau**) dwelling place.
cyfannu *v* to make whole.
cyfanrwydd *m* totality.
cyfansawdd *adj* composite.
cyfansoddi *v* to compose.
cyfansoddiad *m* (**·au**) constitution.
cyfansoddiadol *adj* constitutional.
cyfansodd·wr *m* (**·wyr**) composer.
cyfansodd·yn *m* (**·ion**) compound.
cyfanswm *m* (**cyfansymiau**) total.
cyfanwaith *m* (**cyfanweithiau**) entity.
cyfanwerthu *v* to sell wholesale.
cyfarch *v* to greet.
cyfarchiad *m* (**·au**) greeting.
cyfaredd *f* (**·au**) enchantment.
cyfareddol *adj* enchanting.
cyfareddu *v* to enchant.
cyfarfod *v* to meet. • *m* (**·ydd**) meeting, gathering.
cyfarfyddiad *m* (**·au**) meeting.

cyfarpar *m* apparatus.
cyfartal *adj* equal.
cyfartaledd *m* equality.
cyfarth *v* to bark.
cyfarthiad *m* (**·au**) a bark.
cyfarwydd *adj* familiar. • *m* (**·iaid**) story-teller.
cyfarwyddiad, cyfarwyddyd *m* (**cyfarwyddiadau**) direction.
cyfarwyddiadur *m* (**·on**) directory.
cyfarwyddo *v* to direct.
cyfarwydd·wr *m* (**·wyr**) director.
cyfateb *v* to correspond.
cyfatebiaeth *f* correspondence.
cyfatebol *adj* corresponding.
cyfath *adj* congruent.
cyfathrach *f* intercourse.
cyfathrachu *v* to have intercourse.
cyfathrebu *v* to communicate.
cyfddydd *m* daybreak.
cyfeb *adj* pregnant.
cyfebion *pl* pregnant animals.
cyfeddach *v* to carouse. • *f* carousal.
cyfeilian·t *m* (**·nau**) accompaniment.
cyfeilio *v* to accompany.
cyfeiliorn *m*: **ar gyfeiliorn** astray.
cyfeiliorni *v* to stray.
cyfeiliornus *adj* erroneous.
cyfeilydd *m* (**·ion**) accompanist.
cyfeillach *f* fellowship.
cyfeillachu *v* to associate.
cyfeilles *f* (**·au**) (female) friend.
cyfeillgar *adj* amicable.
cyfeillgarwch *m* friendship.
cyfeillion *see* **cyfaill**.
cyfeintiau *see* **cyfaint**.
cyfeiriad *m* (**·au**) direction; address.
cyfeiriadur *m* (**·on**) directory.
cyfeiriannu *v* to orienteer.
cyfeirio *v* to refer, to direct.
cyfenw *m* (**·au**) surname.
cyfer, cyfair *m* (**cyfeiriau**) acre: **ar gyfer** for.
cyferbyn *adj* opposite.
cyferbyniad *m* contrast.
cyferbyniol, cyferbynnol *adj* contrasting.
cyferbynnu *v* to contrast.
cyferfydd *from* **cyfarfod**.
cyfethol *v* to co-opt.
cyfiawn *adj* just.
cyfiawnder *m* justice.
cyfiawnhad *m* justification.
cyfiawnhau *v* to justify.
cyfieithiad *m* (**·au**) translation.
cyfieithu *v* to translate.
cyfieith·ydd *m* (**·wyr**) translator.
cyflafan *f* massacre.
cyflafareddu *v* to arbitrate.
cyflaith *m* toffee.
cyflanw(af) *from* **cyflenwi**.
cyflau *see* **cwfl**.
cyflawn *adj* entire.
cyflawnder *m* abundance.
cyflawni *v* to fulfil.
cyfle *m* (**·oedd**) opportunity.
cyfled *from* **llydan**.
cyflenwad *m* (**·au**) a supply.
cyflenwi *v* to supply.
cyflenwol *adj* complementary.
cyfleu *v* to convey.
cyfleus *adj* convenient.
cyfleustra, cyfleuster *m* (**cyfleusterau**) convenience.

cyflin *f* (**·iau**) parallel.
cyflog *m/f* (**·au**) wage.
cyflogaeth *f* employment.
cyflogedig *adj* employed.
cyflogi *v* to employ.
cyflogwr *m* employer.
cyflwr *m* (**cyflyrau**) condition.
cyflwyniad *m* (**·au**) presentation.
cyflwyno *v* to present.
cyflym *adj* quick.
cyflymder, cyflymdra *m* speed.
cyflymu *v* to accelerate.
cyflymydd *m* (**·ion**) accelerator.
cyflyrau *see* **cyflwr**.
cyflyru *v* to condition.
cyflythreniad *m* alliteration.
cyfnewid *v* to exchange.
cyfnewid·fa *f* (**·feydd**) clearing-house.
cyfnewidiol *adj* changeable.
cyfnither *f* (**·oedd**) (female) cousin.
cyfnod *m* (**·au**) period.
cyfnodol *adj* periodical.
cyfnodol·yn *m* (**·ion**) periodical.
cyfnos *m* dusk.
cyfochrog *adj* parallel.
cyfodi *v* to arise.
cyfoedion *pl* contemporaries.
cyfoes *adj* contemporary.
cyfoes·wr *m* (**·wyr**) contemporary.
cyfoeth *m* wealth.
cyfoethog *adj* rich.
cyfoethogi *v* to enrich.
cyfog *m* nausea.
cyfogi *v* to be sick.
cyfoglyd *adj* sickening.
cyforiog *adj* overflowing.
cyfosod *v* to set side by side.
cyfradd *m/f* (**·au**) rate.
cyfraith *f* (**cyfreithiau**) law.
cyfran *m/f* (**·nau**) portion.
cyfranddaliad *m* (**·au**) share.
cyfranddal·iwr, cyfranddeil·iad *m* (**·wyr, ·iaid**) shareholder.
cyfraniad *m* (**·au**) contribution.
cyfrannedd *f* (**cyfraneddau**) proportion.
cyfrannog *adj* participative.
cyfrannol *adj* contributory; proportional.
cyfrannu *v* to contribute.
cyfran·nwr *m* (**·wyr**) contributor.
cyfranogi *v* to partake.
cyfredol *adj* concurrent.
cyfreithiau *see* **cyfraith**.
cyfreithiol *adj* legal; judicial.
cyfreithiwr *m* (**cyfreithwyr**) lawyer, solicitor.
cyfreithlon *adj* lawful.
cyfreithloni *v* to legalise.
cyfres *f* (**·i**) series.
cyfrif *v* to count. • *m* (**·on**) account.
cyfrifiad *m* (**·au**) census.
cyfrifiadur *m* (**·on**) computer.
cyfrifiadureg *f* computer science.
cyfrifiannell *m* (**cyfrifianellau**) calculator.
cyfrifol *adj* responsible.
cyfrifoldeb *m* (**·au**) responsibility.
cyfrifydd *m* (**·ion**) accountant.
cyfrin *adj* mystic.
cyfrinach *f* (**·au**) secret.
cyfrinachol *adj* secret.
cyfrin·fa *f* (**·feydd**) lodge (trade union).
cyfrin-gyngor *m* privy council.

cyfriniaeth *f* mysticism.
cyfriniol *adj* mystical.
cyfrinydd *m* (**cyfrinwyr**) mystic.
cyfrodeddu *v* to plait.
cyfrol *f* (**-au**) volume.
cyfrwng *m* (**cyfryngau**) medium.
cyfrwy *m* (**-au**) saddle.
cyfrwyo *v* to saddle.
cyfrwys *adj* cunning.
cyfrwyster, cyfrwystra *m* craftiness.
cyfryngau *pl* media.
cyfryng-wr *m* (**-wyr**) mediator.
cyfryw *adj* such.
cyfuchlin *m* (**-au**) contour line.
cyfundeb *m* (**-au**) union.
cyfundrefn *f* (**-au**) system.
cyfundrefnu *v* to systemise.
cyfuniad *m* blend.
cyfuno *v* to combine.
cyfunrywiol *adj* homosexual.
cyfuwch *from* **uchel**.
cyf-weld *v* to interview.
cyfweliad *m* (**-au**) an interview.
cyfwerth *adj* equivalent.
cyfwng *m* (**cyfyngau**) interval.
cyfyd *from* **cyfodi; codi**.
cyfyng *adj* restricted.
cyfyngder *m* (**-au**) anguish.
cyfyngedig *adj* confined, limited.
cyfyng-gyngor *m* dilemma.
cyfyngu *v* to limit.
cyfyl *m* proximity.
cyfyrder *m* (**cyfyrdyr**) second cousin (male).
cyfyrdyres *m* (**-au**) second cousin (female).
cyfystyr *adj* synonymous.
cyfystyron *pl* synonyms.
cyff *m* (**-ion**) stock.
cyffaith *m* (**cyffeithiau**) preserve.
cyffeithio *v* to preserve.
cyffeithydd *m* (**-ion**) preservative.
cyffelyb *adj* like.
cyffelybiaeth *f* (**-au**) simile.
cyffelybu *v* to compare.
cyffes *f* (**-ion**) admission.
cyffesu *v* to confess.
cyffiniau *pl* borders.
cyffio *v* to stiffen.
cyffion *pl* stocks.
cyfflogiaid, cyfflogod *see* **cyffylog**.
cyffordd *f* (**cyffyrdd**) junction.
cyfforddus *adj* comfortable.
cyffredin *adj* common.
cyffredinedd *m* mediocrity.
cyffredinoli *v* to generalise.
cyffro *m* commotion.
cyffroi *v* to agitate.
cyffrous *adj* agitated.
cyffry *from* **cyffroi**.
cyffur *m* (**-iau**) drug.
cyffwrdd *v* to touch.
cyffylog *m/f* (**cyfflogod, cyfflogiaid**) woodcock.
cyffyrdd *see* **cyffordd**.
cyffyrddaf *from* **cyffwrdd**.
cyffyrddiad *m* (**-au**) touch.
cyffyrddus *adj* comfortable.
cynganeddion *see* **cynghanedd**.
cynganeddu *v* to write cynghanedd; to harmonise.
cyngerdd *m/f* (**cyngherddau**) concert.
cynghanedd *f* (**cynganeddion**) metrical verse form; harmony.

cynghorau *see* **cyngor**.
cynghori *v* to counsel.
cynghorion *see* **cyngor**.
cynghorwr, cynghorydd *m* (**cynghorwyr**) councillor.
cynghrair *m/f* (**cynghreiriau**) league.
cynghreiriad *m* (**cynghreiriaid**) ally.
cyngor *m* (**cynghorion**) counsel: (**cynghorau**) council.
cyngres *f* (**·au**) congress.
cyhoedd *m* the public.
cyhoeddi *v* to publish; to announce.
cyhoeddiad *m* (**·au**) publication; announcement.
cyhoeddus *adj* public.
cyhoeddusrwydd *m* publicity.
cyhoedd·wr *m* (**·wyr**) announcer.
cyhuddiad *m* (**·au**) accusation.
cyhuddo *v* to accuse.
cyhudd·wr *m* (**·wyr**) plaintiff.
cyhwfan *v* to flutter.
cyhyd, cyd *from* **hir**.
cyhydedd *m* equator.
cyhydnos *f* (**·au**) equinox.
cyhyr *m* (**·au**) muscle.
cyhyrog *adj* muscular.
cylch *m* (**·oedd**) circle.
cylchdaith *f* (**cylchdeithiau**) tour.
cylchdro *m* (**·eon**) rotation.
cylchdroi *v* to revolve.
cylched *f* (**·au**) circuit.
cylchedd *m* circumference.
cylch·fa *f* (**·faoedd, ·fâu**) zone.
cylchfan *m* (**·nau**) roundabout.
cylchgrawn *m* (**cylchgronau**) magazine.
cylchlythyr *m* (**·on**) circular.
cylchredeg *v* to circulate.
cylchrediad *m* circulation.
cylchynu *v* to surround.
cyll *see* **collen**.
cylla *m* stomach.
cyllell *f* (**cyllyll**) knife.
cyllid *m* income.
cyllideb *f* (**·au**) budget.
cyllidol *adj* financial.
cyllyll *see* **cyllell**.
cymaint *from* **mawr**.
cymal *m* (**·au**) joint; clause.
cymanfa *f* (**·oedd**) assembly.
cymanwlad *f* commonwealth.
cymar *m/f* (**cymheiriaid**) companion.
cymarebau *see* **cymhareb**.
cymariaethau *see* **cymhariaeth**.
cymathiad *m* assimilation.
cymathu *v* to assimilate.
cymdeithas *f* (**·au**) society.
cymdeithaseg *f* sociology.
cymdeithasol *adj* social.
cymdeithasu *v* to socialise.
cymdeithion *see* **cydymaith**.
cymdogaeth *f* (**·au**) neighbourhood.
cymdoges *f* (female) neighbour.
cymdogion *see* **cymydog**.
cymdogol *adj* neighbourly.
cymedrol *adj* moderate.
cymedroldeb *m* moderation.
cymedroli *v* to moderate.
cymell *v* to urge.
cymelliadau *see* **cymhelliad**.
cymen *adj* neat.
cymer *from* **cymryd**.

cymeradwy *adj* approved.
cymeradwyaeth *f* approval; applause.
cymeradwyo *v* to approve.
cymeriad *m* (**·au**) character.
cymesur *adj* symmetrical.
cymesuredd *m* symmetry.
cymhareb *f* (**cymarebau**) ratio.
cymhariaeth *f* (**cymariaethau**) comparison.
cymharol *adj* comparative.
cymharu *v* to compare.
cymheiriaid *see* **cymar**.
cymhell(af) *from* **cymell**.
cymhell·iad *m* (**·ion, cymelliadau**) incentive.
cymhenned *from* **cymen**.
cymhennu *v* to tidy.
cymhleth *adj* complicated. • *f* complex.
cymhlethdod *m* (**·au**) complexity.
cymhlethu *v* to complicate.
cymhorthdal *m* (**cymorthdaliadau**) subsidy.
cymhorthion *see* **cymorth**.
cymhwysed *from* **cymwys**.
cymhwysiad *m* adaptation.
cymhwyso *v* to adapt.
cymhwysol *adj* applied.
cymhwyster *m* (**cymwysterau**) suitability.
cymod *m* reconciliation.
cymodi *v* to reconcile.
cymodlon, cymodol *adj* conciliatory.
cymoedd *see* **cwm**.
cymoni *v* to tidy.
cymorth *m* (**cymhorthion**) aid.
cymorthdaliadau *see* **cymhorthdal**.
Cymraeg *f* Welsh (language).
Cymraes *f* (**Cymraësau**) Welshwoman.
cymrawd *m* (**cymrodyr**) fellow.
Cymreig *adj* Welsh.
Cymro *m* (**Cymry**) Welshman.
cymrodedd *m* arbitration.
cymrodeddu *v* to arbitrate.
cymrodoriaeth *f* fellowship.
cymrodyr *see* **cymrawd**.
Cymry *see* **Cymro**.
cymryd *v* to take.
cymudo *v* to commute.
cymud·wr *m* (**·wyr**) commuter.
cymun, cymundeb *m* communion.
cymuned *f* (**·au**) community.
cymunedol *adj* community.
cymwynas *f* (**·au**) favour.
cymwynasgar *adj* obliging.
cymwynasgarwch *m* benevolence.
cymwys *adj* suitable.
cymwysterau *see* **cymhwyster**.
cymydau *see* **cwmwd**.
cymydog *m* (**cymdogion**) neighbour.
cymylau *see* **cwmwl**.
cymylog *adj* cloudy.
cymylu *v* to cloud over.
cymynnu *v* to bequeath.
cymynrodd *f* (**·ion**) bequest.
cymynu *v* to hew.
cymyn·wr *m* (**·wyr**) woodcutter.
cymysg *adj* mixed.
cymysgedd *m/f* mixture.
cymysgfa *f* mixture.
cymysglyd *adj* muddled.
cymysgryw *adj* hybrid, mongrel.

cymysgu *v* to mix.
cymysgwch *m* mixture.
cyn *prep* before. • *adv* as, so.
cŷn *m* (**cynion**) chisel.
cynadledda *v* to attend conferences.
cynadleddau *see* **cynhadledd**.
cynaeafau *see* **cynhaeaf**.
cynaeafu *v* to harvest.
cynaniad *m* (**·au**) pronunciation.
cynanu *v* to pronounce.
cyndeidiau *pl* forefathers.
cynderfynol *adj* semi-final.
cyndyn *adj* stubborn.
cyndynrwydd *m* obstinacy.
cynddaredd *f* rage; rabies.
cynddeiriog *adj* rabid.
cynddeiriogi *v* to infuriate.
cynddelw *f* (**·au**) blueprint.
cynddrwg *from* **drwg**.
cyneddfau *see* **cynneddf**.
cynefin *adj* familiar. • *m* (**·oedd**) habitat.
cynefino *v* to become familiar with.
cyneu(af) *from* **cynnau**.
cynfrodorion *pl* aborigines.
cynfrodorol *adj* aboriginal.
cynfyd *m* antiquity.
cynffon *f* (**·nau**) tail.
cynffonna *v* to fawn.
cynffonnog *adj* tailed.
cynfon·nwr *m* (**·wyr**) sycophant.
cynhadledd *f* (**cynadleddau**) conference.
cynhaeaf *m* (**cynaeafau**) harvest.
cynhaliaeth *f* maintenance.
cynhal(iaf) *from* **cynnal**.
cynhal·iwr *m* (**·wyr**) supporter.
cynhanesyddol *adj* prehistoric.
cynhared *from* **cynnar**.
cynhebrwng *m* funeral.
cynheil·iad *m* (**·iaid**) supporter.
cynhel(iais) *from* **cynnal**.
cynhengar *adj* contentious.
cynhenid *adj* innate.
cynhenna, cynhennu *v* to quarrel.
cynhennau *see* **cynnen**.
cynhennus *adj* cantankerous.
cynhesed *from* **cynnes**.
cynhesrwydd *m* warmth.
cynhesu *v* to warm.
cynhorthwy *m* (**cynorthwyon**) aid.
cynhwys(af) *from* **cynnwys**.
cynhwysfawr *adj* comprehensive.
cynhwysiad *m* content.
cynhwysion *pl* contents.
cynhwysydd *m* (**cynwysyddion**) container.
cynhyrchiad *m* (**cynyrchiadau**) production.
cynhyrchiol *adj* productive.
cynhyrchion *see* **cynnyrch**.
cynhyrchu *v* to produce.
cynhyrch·ydd *m* (**·wyr, cynyrchyddion**) producer.
cynhyrfau *see* **cynnwrf**.
cynhyrfiad *m* (**cynyrfiadau**) a stirring.
cynhyrfu *v* to excite.
cynhyrfus *adj* stirring.
cynhyrf·wr *m* (**·wyr**) agitator.
cyni *m* hardship.
cynifer *adj* as many.
cyniferydd *m* quotient.

cynigiad *m* (**·au**) proposal.
cynig(iaf) *from* **cynnig.**
cynigion *see* **cynnig.**
cynigydd *m* (**cynigwyr**) proposer.
cynildeb, cynilder *m* thrift.
cyniled *from* **cynnil.**
cynilion *pl* savings.
cynilo *v* to save.
cyniwair, cyniweirio *v* to gather.
cynllun *m* (**·iau**) plan.
cynllunio *v* to plan, to design.
cynllunydd *m* (**cynllunwyr**) planner.
cynllwyn *m* (**·ion**) intrigue.
cynllwynio, cynllwyno *v* to conspire.
cynllwyn·iwr *m* (**·wyr**) conspirator.
cynnal *v* to support.
cynnar *adj* early.
cynnau *v* to light.
cynneddf *f* (**cyneddfau**) faculty.
cynnen *f* (**cynhennau**) contention.
cynnes *adj* warm.
cynnig *m* (**cynigion**) offer. • *v* to offer.
cynnil *adj* frugal.
cynnud *m* firewood.
cynnull *v* to gather together.
cynnwrf *m* (**cynhyrfau**) commotion.
cynnwys *m* (**cynhwysion**) content. • *v* to include.
cynnydd *m* increase.
cynnyrch *m* (**cynhyrchion**) produce.
cynoesol *adj* primeval.
cynorthwyo *v* to assist.
cynorthwyol *adj* assistant.
cynorthwyon *see* **cynhorthwy.**
cynorthwywr, cynorthwyydd *m* (**cynorthwywyr**) assistant.
cynradd *adj* primary.
cynrychioladol *adj* representative.
cynrychiolaeth *f* representation.
cynrychioli *v* to represent.
cynrychiolydd, cynrychiolwr *m* (**cynrychiolwyr**) representative.
cynrhonllyd *adj* maggot-ridden.
cynrhonyn *m* (**cynrhon**) maggot.
cynsail *f* (**cynseiliau**) precedent.
cynt *from* **cynnar; cyflym.** • *adv* formerly.
cyntaf *adj* first.
cyntaf-anedig *adj* first-born.
cynted *from* **cynnar.**
cyntedd *m* (**·au**) porch.
cyntefig *adj* primitive.
cyntun *m* nap.
cynullaf *from* **cynnull.**
cynulleidfa *f* (**·oedd**) audience.
cynulleidfaol *adj* congregational.
cynulliad *m* a gathering.
cynullydd *m* (**cynullwyr**) convenor.
cynwysedig *adj* inclusive.
cynwysyddion *see* **cynhwysydd.**
cynyddol *adj* increasing.
cynyddu *v* to increase.
cynyrchiadau *see* **cynhyrchiad.**
cynyrchyddion *see* **cynhyrchydd.**
cynyrfiadau *see* **cynhyrfiad.**
cynysgaeddu *v* to endow.
cyplad *m* copula.
cyplau *see* **cwpl, cwpwl.**
cyplysnod *m* (**·au**) hyphen.

cyplysu *v* to link.
cypreswydden *f* (**cypreswydd**) cypress tree.
cypyrddaid *m* (**cypyrddeidiau**) cupboardful.
cypyrddau *see* **cwpwrdd.**
cyraeddiadau *see* **cyrhaeddiad.**
cyrbibion *pl* smithereens.
cyrcs *see* **corcyn.**
cyrcydau *see* **cwrcwd.**
cyrcydu *v* to squat.
cyrch *m* (**·oedd**) attack.
cyrch·fa *f* (**·feydd**) rendezvous.
cyrchfan *m/f* (**·nau**) resort; rendezvous.
cyrchu *v* to attack.
cyrd *see* **cordyn.**
cyrddau *see* **cwrdd.**
cyrff *see* **corff.**
cyrhaedd(af) *from* **cyrraedd.**
cyrhaeddiad *m* (**cyraeddiadau**) reach.
cyrïau *see* **cyrri.**
cyrion *see* **cwr.**
cyrlen *f* (**cyrls**) a curl.
cyrliog *adj* curly.
cyrn *see* **corn.**
cyrraedd *v* to reach.
cyrrau *see* **cwr.**
cyrri *m* (**cyrïau**) curry.
cyrs *see* **corsen.**
cyrsiau *see* **cwrs.**
cyrt *see* **cordyn.**
cyrtiau *see* **cwrt.**
cyrydu *v* to erode.
cyryglau *see* **cwrwg.**
cysáct *adj* exact.
cysawd *m* (**cysodau**) system.
cysefin *adj* native.
cysegr *m* (**·au**) holy place.
cysegredig *adj* sacred.
cysegriad *m* consecration.
cysegru *v* to consecrate.
cyseinedd *m* alliteration.
cysetlyd *adj* finicky.
cysgadur *m* (**·iaid**) sleeper.
cysgau *see* **cwsg.**
cysglyd *adj* drowsy.
cysgod *m* (**·ion**) shadow.
cysgodi *v* to shelter.
cysgodol *adj* sheltered.
cysgu *v* to sleep.
cysg·wr *m* (**·wyr**) sleeper.
cysodau *see* **cysawd.**
cysodi *v* to set type.
cysodydd *m* compositor.
cyson *adj* regular.
cysondeb *m* consistency.
cysoni *v* to reconcile.
cystadleuaeth *f* (**cystadlaethau**) competition.
cystadleuol *adj* competitive.
cystadleu·wr, cystadleu·ydd *m* (**·wyr**) competitor.
cystadlu *v* to compete.
cystal *adj* as good as.
cystrawen *f* (**·nau**) syntax.
cystudd *m* (**·iau**) affliction.
cystuddio *v* to afflict.
cystwyo *v* to chastise.
cysur *m* (**·on**) consolation.
cysuro *v* to comfort.
cysurus *adj* comfortable.
cysur·wr *m* (**·wyr**) comforter.

cyswllt *m* (**cysylltau, cysylltiadau**) connection.
cysylltair *m* (**cysylltelriau**) conjunction.
cysylltiad *m* (**·au**) connection.
cysylltiedig *adj* connected.
cysylltiol *adj* connecting.
cysylltnod *m* (**·au**) hyphen.
cysylltu *v* to join.
cysylltydd *m* (**·ion**) contact.
cysyniad *m* (**·au**) concept.
cytbell *adj* equidistant.
cytbwys *adj* balanced.
cytbwysedd *m* balance.
cytew *m* batter.
cytgan *m/f* (**·au**) chorus.
cytgord *m* (**·iau**) concord.
cytiau *see* **cwt**.
cytir *m* common land.
cytsain *f* (**cytseiniaid**) consonant.
cytser *m* (**·au**) constellation.
cytûn *adj* in agreement.
cytundeb *m* (**·au**) agreement.
cytuno *v* to agree.
cythlwng *m* hunger.
cythraul *m* (**cythreuliaid**) fiend.
cythreulig *adj* diabolical.
cythru *v* to rush.
cythruddo *v* to annoy.
cythrwfl *m* commotion.
cythryblus *adj* turbulent.
cyw *m* (**·ion**) chick.
cywain *v* to garner.
cywair *m* (**cyweiriau**) key.
cywaith *m* (**cyweithiau**) project.
cywarchen *f* (**cywarch**) hemp.
cywasgiad *m* compression.
cywasgu *v* to compress.
cywasgydd *m* (**·ion**) compressor.
cywein(iaf) *from* **cywain**.
cyweiriau *see* **cywair**.
cyweirio *v* to repair; to tune.
cyweirnod *m* key signature.
cyweithiau *see* **cywaith**.
cywen *f* (**·nod, cwennod**) pullet.
cywilydd *m* shame.
cywilyddio *v* to shame.
cywilyddus *adj* shameful.
cywir *adj* correct.
cywirdeb *m* accuracy.
cywiriad *m* (**·au**) correction.
cywiro *v* to correct.
cywir·wr *m* (**·wyr**) corrector.
cywrain *adj* adroit.
cywreinrwydd *m* skill.
cywydd *m* (**·au**) Welsh strict-metre poem.
cywydd·wr *m* (**·wyr**) composer of a cywydd.

Ch

chwa *f* (**·on**) gust.
chw·aer *f* (**·iorydd**) sister.
chwaeth *f* (**·au, ·oedd**) taste.
chwaethach *adv* let alone.
chwaethus *adj* tasteful.
chwain *see* **chwannen**.
chwaith, ychwaith *adv* either, neither.
chwâl *adj* scattered.
chwal·fa *f* (**·feydd**) (a) scattering.
chwalu *v* to scatter.
chwannen *f* (**chwain**) flea.
chwannog *adj* inclined to.
chwant *m* (**·au**) appetite.
chwap *adj* at once.
chwarae *v* to play. • *m* (**·on**) game.
chwarae·wr *m* (**·wyr**) player.
chwardd *from* **chwerthin**.
chwarddiad *m* laugh.
chwarel *m/f* (**·i**) quarry.
chwarel·wr *m* (**·wyr**) quarryman.
chwarennau *see* **chwarren**.
chwareus *adj* playful.
chwar·ren *f* (**·ennau**) gland.
chwart *m* (**·(i)au**) quart.
chwarter *m* (**·i**) quarter.
chwe, chwech *num* six.
chweched *adj* sixth.
chwedl *f* (**·au**) tale.
chwedleua *v* to gossip.
chwedloniaeth *f* mythology.
chwedlonol *adj* legendary.
chwedyn *adv* after: **na chynt na chwedyn** neither before nor since.
Chwefror *m* February.
chwegr *f* (**·au**) mother-in-law.
chwegr·wn *m* (**·ynau, ·yniaid**) father-in-law.
chweinllyd *adj* flea-ridden.
chwel(ais) *from* **chwalu**.
chwennych *v* to covet.
chwerdd(ais) *from* **chwerthin**.
chwerf·an *f* (**·ain**) pulley.
chwerthin *v* to laugh.
chwerthiniad *m* (**·au**) a laugh.
chwerthinllyd *adj* laughable.
chwerw *adj* bitter.
chwerwder, chwerwdod, chwerwedd *m* bitterness.
chwerwi *v* to embitter.
chwery *from* **chwarae**.
chwîb *f* whistle.
chwiban *m/f* (**·au**) whistle.
chwibaniad *m* whistle.
chwibanogl *f* (**·au**) flute.
chwibanu *v* to whistle.
chwifio *v* to wave.
chwil *adj* reeling.
chwilboeth *adj* red-hot.
chwil·en *f* (**·od**) beetle.
chwiler *m* (**·od**) chrysalis, pupa.
chwilfriw *adj* shattered.
chwilfrydedd *m* curiosity.
chwilfrydig *adj* inquisitive.
chwilio *v* to search.

chwil·iwr *m* (**·wyr**) seeker.
chwilmanta, chwilmantan, chwilmentan *v* to rummage.
chwil·olau *m* (**·oleuadau**) searchlight.
chwilota *v* to rummage.
chwilot·wr *m* (**·wyr**) searcher.
chwim *adj* swift.
chwimder, chwimdra *m* nimbleness.
chwimwth *adj* nimble.
chwinciad *m* twinkling.
chwiorydd *from* **chwaer**.
chwip *f* (**·iau**) whip.
chwipio *v* to whip.
chwirligwgan, chwrligwgan, chwyrligwgan *m* whirligig.
chwistrell *f* (**·au, ·i**) syringe.
chwistrelliad *m* injection.
chwistrellu *v* to squirt; to inject.
chwit-chwat *adj* fickle.
chwith *adj* left.
chwithau *pron* you.
chwithdod *m* strangeness.
chwithig *adj* strange, awkward.
chwiw *f* (**·iau**) whim.
chwychwi *pron* you yourselves.
chwydu *v* to vomit.
chwydd, chwyddi *m* a swelling.
chwyddedig *adj* bloated.
chwyddhau *v* to magnify.
chwyddiant *m* inflation.
chwyddo *v* to swell.
chwyddwydr *m* (**·au**) magnifying glass.
chwyldro, chwyldroad *m* (**·(ad)au**) revolution.
chwyldroadol *adj* revolutionary.
chwyldroad·wr *m* (**·wyr**) revolutionary.
chwyldroi to revolve.
chwylolwyn *f* (**·ion**) fly-wheel.
chwyn *see* **chwynnyn**.
chŵyn *from* **cwyno**.
chwynleidd·iad *m* (**·iaid**) weed-killer.
chwynnu *v* to weed.
chwynnyn *m* (**chwyn**) weed.
chwyrlïo *v* to whirl.
chwyrlïydd *m* whisk.
chwyrn *adj* vigorous.
chwyrnellu *v* to whirl.
chwyrnu *v* to snore.
chwys *m* perspiration.
chwysfa *f* muck sweat.
chwysig·en *f* (**·od**) blister.
chwyslyd *adj* sweaty.
chwysu *v* to sweat.
chwyth *m* breath.
chwythbrennau *pl* woodwind (instruments).
chwythu *v* to blow.
chwyth·wr *m* (**·wyr**) blower.

D

da *adj* good. • *m* cattle.
dacw *adv* there.
da-da *pl* sweets.
dadansoddi *v* to analyse.
dadansoddiad *m* (**·au**) analysis.
dadansoddol *adj* analytical.
dadbacio *v* to unpack.
dadebru *v* to revive.
dadelfennu *v* to decompose.
dadeni *m* renaissance.
dadfeilio *v* to decay.
dadflino *v* to revive.
dadfygio *v* to debug.
dadhydradedd *m* dehydration.
dadl *f* (**·euon**) argument.
dadlaith *v* to thaw.
dadlau *v* to argue.
dadlennol *adj* revealing.
dadlennu *v* to disclose.
dadleuol *adj* controversial.
dadleuon *see* **dadl**.
dadleu·wr *m* (**·wyr**) debater.
dadlwytho *v* to unload.
dadlygru *v* to decontaminate.
dadmer *v* to thaw.
dadorchuddio *v* to unveil.
dadrithiad *m* disillusionment.
dadrithio *v* to disillusion.
dadwisgo *v* to undress.
dad-wneud, dadwneuthur *v* to undo.
dadwrdd *m* tumult.
dadwreiddio *v* to uproot.
daear *f* (**·oedd**) earth.
daeareg *f* geology.
daearegol *adj* geological.
daeareg·ydd *m* (**·wyr**) geologist.
daear·gi *m* (**·gwn**) terrier.
daeargryn *m/f* (**·fâu, ·feydd**) earthquake.
daearol *adj* earthly.
daearu *v* to earth.
daearyddiaeth *f* geography.
daearyddol *adj* geographical.
daeth *from* **dod**.
dafad *f* (**defaid**) sheep; (**·ennau**) wart.
dafadennog *adj* wart-covered.
dafn *m* (**·au, defni**) drop.
dagrau *see* **deigryn**.
dagreuol *adj* tearful.
dail *see* **deilen**.
daioni *m* goodness.
daionus *adj* beneficial.
dal, dala *v* to catch.
dalen *f* (**·nau**) sheet (of paper).
dal·fa *f* (**·feydd**) a catch.
dalgylch *m* (**·oedd**) catchment.
daliad *m* (**·au**) opinion.
dal·iwr *m* (**·wyr**) catcher.
dall *adj* blind.
dallineb *m* blindness.
dallu *v* to blind.
damcaniaeth *f* (**·au**) hypothesis.
damcaniaethol *adj* hypothetical.
damcaniaethu *v* to speculate.

dam·eg *f* (**·hegion**) parable.
damhegol *adj* allegorical.
damnedigaeth *f* damnation.
damnio *v* to curse.
damniol *adj* damning.
damsang *v* to trample.
dam·wain *f* (**·weiniau**) accident.
damweiniol *adj* accidental.
dan *prep* under.
danadl, dynad *see* **danhadlen**.
danas *m/f* fallow deer.
dandwn *v* to pamper.
danfon *v* to send.
dangos *v* to show.
danhadlen *f* (**danadl, dynad**) nettles.
danheddog *adj* serrated.
dannedd *see* **dant**.
dannod *v* to reproach.
dannoedd, dannodd *f* toothache.
danodd *adv* below.
dan·t *m* (**·nedd**) tooth.
dant·aith *m* (**·eithion**) delicacy.
danteithiol *adj* delicious.
darbodus *adj* prudent.
darbwyllo *v* to persuade.
darfod *v* to cease; to happen.
darfodedig *adj* transient.
darfodedigaeth *m/f* consumption.
darfudiad *m* convection.
darganfod *v* to discover.
darganfyddiad *m* (**·au**) discovery.
darganfydd·wr *m* (**·wyr**) discoverer.
dargludiad *m* conduction.
dargludo *v* to conduct.
dargludydd *m* (**·ion**) conductor.
dargopïo *v* to trace.
dargyfeiriad *m* (**·au**) diversion.
dargyfeirio *v* to divert; to diversify.
darlith *f* (**·iau, ·oedd**) lecture.
darlithio *v* to lecture.
darlith·ydd *m* (**·wyr**) lecturer.
darlun *m* (**·iau**) picture.
darluniadol *adj* illustrated.
darlunio *v* to illustrate.
darllediad *m* (**·au**) broadcast.
darlledu *v* to broadcast.
darlled·wr *m* (**·wyr**): **darlled·wraig** *f* broadcaster.
darllen *v* to read.
darllengar *adj* fond of reading.
darllenadwy *adj* legible; readable.
darllen·wr, darllenydd *m* (**·wyr, ·ion**) reader.
darn *m* (**·au**) part.
darnio *v* to break up.
darn-ladd *v* to thrash.
darogan *v* to predict.
darostwng *v* to subjugate.
darostyngedig *adj* subjugated.
darpar *adj* prospective.
darpariaeth *f* (**·au**) preparation.
darparu *v* to prepare.
darpar·wr *m* (**·wyr**) provider.
darseinydd *m* (**·ion**) loudspeaker.
daru *from* **darfod**.
darwden *f* ringworm.
datblygiad *m* (**·au**) development.
datblygu *v* to develop.
datblyg·ydd *m* (**·wyr**) developer.
datgan *v* to declare, to state.
datganiad *m* (**·au**) statement.
datganoli *v* to decentralise.
datgein·iad *m* (**·iaid**) narrator.
datgelu v to reveal.

datgloi *v* to unlock.
datglymu *v* to undo.
datod *v* to untie.
datrys *v* to solve.
datrysiad *m* (**-au**) solution.
datwm *m* (**data**) datum.
datysen *f* (**datys**) date.
dathliad *m* (**-au**) celebration.
dathlu *v* to celebrate.
dau *num* (**deuoedd**) two.
dauddyblyg *adj* twofold.
daufiniog *adj* double-edged.
dauwynebog *adj* hypocritical.
daw *from* **dod**.
dawn *m/f* (**doniau**) ability.
dawns *f* (**-iau, -feydd**) dance.
dawns·iwr *m* (**·wyr**) dancer.
dawnus *adj* gifted.
dawr as in **ni'm dawr**; **nis dawr** to be of interest.
de, deau *m* (the) South. • *adj* southern.
de *f* (the) right. • *adj* right.
deall *v* to understand. • *m* intellect.
dealladwy *adj* intelligible.
dealledig *adj* implicit.
dealltwriaeth *f* understanding.
deallus *adj* intelligent.
deallusion *pl* intelligentsia.
deallusrwydd *m* intelligence.
deau *see* **de**.
dechrau *v* to start. • *m* a start.
dechreuad *m* start.
dechreuol *adj* initial.
dechreu·wr *m* (**·wyr**) beginner.
dedfryd *f* (**-au**) verdict, sentence.
dedfrydu *v* to sentence.
dedwydd *adj* blissful.
dedwyddwch *m* bliss.
deddf *f* (**-au**) law; act.
deddfol *adj* legalistic.
deddfu *v* to legislate.
deddfwriaeth *f* legislation.
de-ddwyrain *adj* southeast.
deellir *from* **deall**.
defaid *see* **dafad**.
defni *see* **dafn**.
defnydd *m* (**-iau**) material.
defnyddio *v* to use.
defnyddiol *adj* useful.
defnyddioldeb *m* usefulness.
defnydd·iwr *m* (**·wyr**) user, consumer.
defnyn *m* (**-nau, dafnau**) drop.
defod *f* (**-au**) rite.
deffro *v* to wake.
deffroad *m* (**-au**) awakening.
deg, deng *num* (**-au**) ten.
degawd *m* (**-au**) decade.
degfed *adj* tenth.
degol *adj* decimal.
degol·yn *m* (**·ion**) a decimal.
deg·wm *m* (**·ymau**) tithe.
dengwaith *adv* ten times.
deheubarth *m* southern part.
deheuig *adj* adroit.
deheulaw *f* right hand.
deheuol *adj* southern.
deheurwydd *m* dexterity.
deheu·wr *m* (**·wyr**) Southerner.
dehongli *v* to interpret.
dehongliad *m* (**deongliadau**) interpretation.
deifio v to scorch.
deifiol *adj* withering.
deigryn *m* (**dagrau**) tear.

deil *from* **dal.**
deilen *f* (**dail**) leaf.
deilgoll *adj* deciduous.
deil·iad *m* (**·iaid**) tenant.
deilio *v* to sprout.
deiliog *adj* leafy.
deillio *v* to stem from.
deillion *pl* the blind.
deintio *v* to set one's teeth in.
deintydd *m* (**·ion**) dentist.
deintyddol *adj* dental.
deiseb *f* (**·au**) petition.
deisyf, deisyfu *v* to implore.
deisyfiad *m* (**·au**) entreaty.
del *adj* pretty.
dêl, del(o) *from* **dod.**
delfryd *m/f* (**·au**) ideal.
delfrydol *adj* ideal.
delfryd·wr *m* (**·wyr**) idealist.
deli *from* **dal.**
delio *v* to deal.
delw *f* (**·au**) statue, idol.
delwedd *f* (**·au**) image.
delweddu *v* to symbolise.
dellni *m* blindness.
dellten *f* (**dellt**) lath.
denfyn *from* **danfon.**
dengar *adj* attractive.
dengys *from* **dangos.**
deniadol *adj* attractive.
denu *v* to attract.
D. Enw *abb* A. N. Other.
deongliadau *see* **dehongliad.**
deon *m* (**·iaid**) dean.
deor, deori *v* to hatch.
deor·fa *f* (**·fâu, ·feydd**) hatchery.
de-orllewin *m* southwest.
deorydd *m* (**·ion**) incubator.
derbyn *v* to receive.
derbyniad *m* (**·au**) reception.
derbyniadwy *adj* admissible.
derbyniol *adj* acceptable.
derbynneb *f* (**derbynebau**) receipt.
derbynnydd *m* receiver.
dere *from* **dod.**
der(fydd) *from* **darfod.**
derw *adj* oaken. • *pl* oaks.
derwen *f* (**deri, derw**) oak tree.
derwreinyn *m/f* (**derwraint**) ringworm.
derwydd *m* (**·on**) druid.
deryn *see* **aderyn.**
destlus *adj* neat.
detrys *from* **datrys.**
detyd *from* **datod.**
dethau *adj* adroit.
dethol *adj* select. • *v* to select.
detholiad *m* (**·au**) selection.
deu(af) *from* **dod.**
deuaidd *adj* binary.
deuawd *m/f* (**·au**) duet.
deublyg *adj* twofold.
deuddeg, deuddeng *num* twelve.
deuddyn *m* couple.
deufin *adj* double-edged.
deufisol *adj* bi-monthly.
deugain *num* forty.
deunaw *num* eighteen.
deuoedd *see* **dau.**
deuol *adj* dual.
deuoliaeth *f* dualism.
deuparth *m* two-thirds.
deupen *m* two ends.
deurudd *m* the cheeks.
deusain *m* dipthong.
deuwch, dewch *from* **dod.**

dewin *m* (**-iaid**) wizard.
dewiniaeth *f* sorcery, wizardry.
dewinio *v* to divine.
dewis *v* to choose. • *m* (**-iadau**) choice.
dewis·iwr *m* (**·wyr**) selector.
dewisol *adj* select.
dewr *adj* brave.
dewrder *m* courage.
dewrion *pl* braves.
diacen *adj* unaccented.
diacon *m* (**·iaid**) deacon.
diachos *adj* needless.
diadell *f* (**·au, ·oedd**) flock.
diaddurn *adj* unadorned.
diafol *m* demon, devil.
diangen *adj* unnecessary.
diangfâu *see* **dihangfa**.
dianghenraid *adj* inessential.
di-ail *adj* incomparable.
diail *from* **dial**.
diainc *from* **dianc**.
dial *v* to avenge.
dialedd *m* vengeance.
dialgar *adj* vengeful.
di-alw-amdano *adj* uncalled-for.
dial·ydd *m* (**·wyr**) avenger.
diamau *adj* doubtless.
diamcan *adj* aimless.
diamheuol *adj* undeniable.
diamodol *adj* unconditional.
diamwys *adj* unambiguous.
diamynedd *adj* impatient.
dianaf *adj* uninjured.
dianc *v* to escape.
diarddel *v* to expel.
diarddeliad *m* expulsion.
diarfogi *v* to disarm.
diarffordd *adj* inaccessible.
diarhebion *see* **dihareb**.
diarhebol *adj* proverbial.
diaroglydd *m* (**·ion**) deodorant.
diarwybod *adj* unexpected.
diasbedain *v* to reverberate.
di-asgwrn-cefn *adj* invertebrate.
diatreg *adj* immediate.
diau *adj* certain.
diawl *m* (**·iaid**) devil.
diawledig *adj* diabolical.
diawlineb *m* devilment.
diawlio *v* to curse.
di-baid *adj* ceaseless.
di-ball *adj* unfailing.
diben *m* (**·ion**) purpose.
di-ben-draw *adj* interminable.
dibennu *v* to conclude.
diberfeddu *v* to disembowel.
dibetrus *adj* assured.
diboblogi *v* to depopulate.
dibriod *adj* unmarried.
dibris *adj* reckless.
dibrisio *v* to belittle.
dibrofiad *adj* inexperienced.
dibyn *m* precipice.
dibynadwy *adj* dependable.
dibynnol *adj* dependent.
dibynnu *v* to depend.
diced *from* **dig**.
dicllon *adj* wrathful.
dicter *m* wrath.
dichell *m* (**·ion**) guile.
dichellgar *adj* sly.
dichon *adv* perhaps.
di-chwaeth *adj* tasteless.
did *m* (**·au**) bit.
di-dâl *adj* unpaid.

didaro *adj* nonchalant.
di-daw *adj* ceaseless.
dideimlad *adj* numb.
diden *f* (**·nau**) teat.
diderfyn *adj* infinite.
didoli *v* to separate.
didolnod *m* diaeresis.
di-dor *adj* uninterrupted.
didoreth *adj* fickle.
didoriad *adj* unbroken.
didostur *adj* relentless.
didrafferth *adj* trouble-free.
di-drai *adj* unceasing.
didraidd *adj* opaque.
di-drais *adj* non-violent.
di-droi'n-ôl *adj* resolute.
didrugaredd *adj* merciless.
diduedd *adj* impartial.
didwyll *adj* sincere.
didwylledd *m* sincerity.
di-ddadl *adj* indisputable.
di-ddal *adj* fickle.
diddan *adj* amusing.
diddanu *v* to amuse.
diddanwch *m* entertainment.
diddan·wr *m* (**·wyr**) entertainer.
diddanydd *m* comforter.
di-ddawn *adj* untalented.
di-dderbyn-wyneb *adj* impartial.
diddig *adj* contended.
diddim *adj* useless.
diddordeb *m* (**·au**) interest.
diddori *v* to interest.
diddorol *adj* interesting.
diddos *adj* snug.
diddosrwydd *m* shelter.
diddrwg *adj* harmless.
di-ddweud *adj* taciturn.
diddyfnu *v* to wean.
diddymiad *m* dissolution.
diddymu *v* to abolish.
diedifar *adj* unrepentant.
dieflig *adj* diabolical.
diegwyddor *adj* unscrupulous.
dieisiau *adj* unnecessary.
dieithr *adj* strange.
dieithriad *adj* without exception.
dieithrio *v* to alienate.
dieithrwch *m* strangeness.
dieithr·yn *m* (**·laid**) stranger.
dienaid *adj* heartless.
dienw *adj* anonymous.
dienyddiad *m* (**·au**) execution.
dienyddio *v* to execute.
dienydd·iwr *m* (**·wyr**) executioner.
dieuog *adj* innocent.
difa *v* to destroy.
difai, di-fai *adj* faultless.
difancoll *f* oblivion.
difaol *adj* ravaging.
difater *adj* apathetic.
difaterwch *m* apathy.
difeddwl *adj* thoughtless.
difeddwl-drwg *adj* unsuspecting.
di-fefl *adj* flawless.
di-feind *adj* heedless.
difenwi *v* to defame.
diferol *adj* dripping.
diferu *v* to drip.
difer·yn *m* (**·ion, ·ynnau**) drop.
difesur *adj* immeasurable.
di-feth *adj* unerring.
Difiau *m* Thursday.
diflanedig *adj* fleeting.
diflaniad *m* (**·au**) disappearance.
diflannu *v* to disappear.

diflas *adj* dull.
di-flas *adj* tasteless.
diflastod *m* unpleasantness.
diflasu *v* to bore.
diflewyn-ar-dafod *adj* plain-speaking.
diflino *adj* indefatigable.
difodi *v* to annihilate.
difodiad, difodiant *m* extermination.
difrawder *m* apathy.
difreinio *v* to disenfranchise.
difrif *adj* serious.
difrifol *adj* grave.
difrifoldeb, difrifwch *m* earnestness.
difrifoli *v* to become serious.
difrïo *v* to disparage.
difrïol *adj* derogatory.
difrod *m* devastation.
difrodi *v* to devastate.
difrycheulyd *adj* immaculate.
di-fudd *adj* useless.
di-fwlch *adj* continuous.
difwyniant *m* defilement.
difwyno, dwyno *v* to soil.
di-fydr *adj* metreless.
difyfyr *adj* impromptu.
difyr *adj* entertaining.
difyrion *pl* amusements.
difyrru *v* to entertain.
difyrrwch *m* entertainment.
difywyd *adj* inanimate.
di-ffael *adj* without fail.
diffaith *adj* desolate.
diffeithwch *m* wilderness.
differyn *m* (**-nau**) differential.
diffiniad *m* (**-au**) definition.
diffinio *v* to define.
diffodd *v* to turn off.
diffodd-wr tân *m* (**-wyr**) fireman.
diffoddydd *m* (**-ion**) extinguisher.
di-ffrind *adj* friendless.
di-ffrwt *adj* listless.
diffrwyth *adj* barren.
diffuant *adj* sincere.
diffuantrwydd *m* sincerity.
di-ffurf *adj* amorphous.
diffwdan *adj* without a fuss.
diffydd *from* **diffodd**.
diffyg *m* (**-ion**) deficiency.
diffygio *v* to lose heart.
diffygiol *adj* defective.
diffyn-nydd *m* (**-yddion**) defendant.
dig *adj* irate. • *m* indignation.
digalon *adj* disheartened.
digalondid *m* dejection.
digalonni *v* to lose heart.
digamsyniol *adj* unmistakable.
digartref *adj* homeless.
digid *m* (**-au**) digit.
digidol *adj* digital.
digio *v* to anger.
di-glem *adj* inept.
di-glod *adj* unpraised.
digofaint *m* wrath.
digolledu *v* to compensate.
digon *m* enough. • *adj* sufficient.
digonedd *m* plenty.
digoni *v* to satisfy; to cook.
digonol *adj* adequate.
digornio *v* to dehorn.
di-gosb *adj* unpunished.
digrif *adj* funny.
digriflun *m* (**-iau**) caricature.
digrifwch *m* mirth.

digrif·wr *m* (**·wyr**) comedian.
digroeso *adj* unwelcoming.
digwydd *v* to happen.
digwyddiad *m* (**·au**) occurrence.
di-gŵyn *adj* uncomplaining.
digydwybod *adj* callous.
digyfaddawd *adj* uncompromising.
digyfeiliant *adj* unaccompanied.
digyfnewid *adj* unchanging.
digyffelyb *adj* peerless.
digyffro *adj* imperturbable.
digymar *adj* unequalled.
digymell *adj* spontaneous.
di-Gymraeg *adj* non-Welsh-speaking.
digymysg *adj* unalloyed.
digyswllt *adj* disjointed.
digywilydd *adj* impudent.
digywilydd-dra *m* effrontery.
di-had *adj* seedless.
dihafal *adj* incomparable.
dihang(af) *from* **dianc**.
dihangfa *f* (**diangfâu**) escape.
dihangol *adj* escaped.
di-haint *adj* sterile.
dihalog *adj* pure.
dihareb *f* (**diarhebion**) proverb.
dihatru *v* to strip.
diheng(ir) *from* **dianc**.
diheintio *v* to disinfect.
diheintydd *m* (**·ion**) disinfectant.
dihenydd *m* death.
di-hid, dihidio *adj* heedless.
dihidlo *v* to distil.
dihiryn *m* (**dihirod**) scoundrel.
dihoeni *v* to languish.
di-hun, dihun *adj* awake.
dihuno *v* to awake.
di-hwyl *adj* out of sorts.
dihyder *adj* lacking confidence.
dihysbydd *adj* inexhaustible.
dihysbyddu *v* to exhaust.
di-ildio *adj* unyielding.
dil *m* (**·iau**) honeycomb.
dilead *m* (**·au**) deletion.
diledryw *adj* thoroughbred.
di-les *adj* of no benefit.
dilestair *adj* unhindered.
dileu *v* to delete.
dilewyrch *adj* lacklustre.
di-liw *adj* drab.
di-log *adj* interest-free.
di-lol *adj* unaffected.
dilorni *v* to revile.
dilornus *adj* abusive.
di-lun *adj* shapeless.
di-lwgr *adj* incorruptible.
dilychwin *adj* spotless.
dilyffethair *adj* unfettered.
dilyn *v* to follow.
dilyniad *m* pusuit.
dilynian·t *m* (**·nau**) sequence.
dilynol *adj* following.
dilyn·wr *m* (**·wyr**) follower.
dilys *adj* valid.
dilysnod *f* (**·au**) hallmark.
dilysrwydd *m* validity.
dilysu *v* to guarantee.
dilyw *m* flood.
dillad *see* **dilledyn**.
dilladu *v* to clothe.
dilledyn *m* (**dillad**) garment.
dim *m* anything; nothing; nought.
dim·ai *f* (**·eiau**) halfpenny.
dimensi·wn *m* (**·ynau**) dimension.
di-nam *adj* immaculate.

dinas *m* (**·oedd**) city.
dinasol, dinesig *adj* municipal, civic.
dinasyddiaeth *f* citizenship.
dinesydd *m* (**dinasyddion**) citizen.
dinistr *m* destruction.
dinistrio *v* to destroy.
dinistriol *adj* destructive.
dinistriwr *m* destroyer.
diniwed *adj* innocent.
diniweidrwydd *m* innocence.
diniweited *from* **diniwed**.
di-nod, dinod *adj* obscure.
dinodedd *m* insignificance.
dinoethi *v* to expose.
diod *f* (**·ydd**) drink.
dioddef *v* to suffer.
dioddefaint *m* suffering.
dioddefgar *adj* long-suffering.
dioddef·wr *m* (**·wyr**) sufferer.
di-oed, dioed *adj* immediate.
diofal *adj* careless.
diofalwch *m* carelessness.
di-ofn, diofn *adj* unafraid.
diog *adj* lazy.
diogel *adj* safe.
diogelu *v* to secure.
diogelwch *m* security.
diogi *m* laziness. • *m* to laze.
dioglyd *adj* lazy.
diogyn *m* shirker.
diolch *v* to thank. • *m* (**·iadau**) gratitude.
diolchgar *adj* grateful.
diolchgarwch *m* thanksgiving.
diolwg *adj* plain.
diorffwys *adj* restless.
diorseddu *v* to dethrone.
di-os *adj* undoubted.
diosg *v* to strip.
diota *v* to tipple.
diplomydd *m* (**·ion**) diplomat.
dir *adj* necessary.
diraddio *v* to degrade.
diraddiol *adj* degrading.
di-raen, diraen *adj* lacklustre.
diragfarn *adj* impartial.
dirdynnol *adj* excruciating.
dirdynnu *v* to torture.
direidi *m* mischievousness.
direidus *adj* mischievous.
direol *adj* disorderly.
direswm *adj* without reason.
dirfawr *adj* immense.
dirgel *adj* secret.
dirgel·wch *m* (**·ion**) mystery.
dirgryniad *m* (**·au**) tremor.
dirgrynu *v* to vibrate.
diriaethol *adj* concrete.
diriaid *adj* wicked.
di-rif, dirifedi *adj* innumerable.
dirlawn *adj* saturated.
dirmyg *m* contempt.
dirmygedig *adj* despised.
dirmygu *v* to despise.
dirmygus, dirmygol *adj* contemptible.
dirnad *v* to understand.
dirnadaeth *f* understanding.
dirprwy *m* (**·on**) deputy.
dirprwyaeth *f* (**·au**) deputation.
dirprwyo *v* to deputise.
dirwasgiad *m* (**·au**) depression.
dirwest *m/f* temperance.
dirwgnach *adj* uncomplaining.
dirwy *f* (**·on**) fine.

dirwyn *v* to wind.
dirwyo *v* to fine.
di-rwystr *adj* unhindered.
di-rym, dirym *adj* powerless.
dirymu *v* to nullify.
diryw *adj* neuter.
dirywiad *m* deterioration.
dirywio *v* to deteriorate.
di-sail *adj* unfounded.
disbaddu *v* to castrate.
disberod *m*: **ar ddisberod** astray.
disbyddu *v* to exhaust, to empty.
diserch *adj* unendearing.
disglair *adj* bright.
disgled *m* a cup of.
disgleirdeb *m* brilliance.
disgleirio *v* to shine.
disgrifiad *m* (**-au**) description.
disgrifiadol *adj* descriptive.
disgrifio *v* to describe.
disgwyl *v* to expect.
disgwylgar *adj* expectant.
disgwyliedig *adj* anticipated.
disgybl *m* (**-ion**) pupil; disciple.
disgyblaeth *f* discipline.
disgybledig *adj* disciplined.
disgyblu *v* to discipline.
disgyn *v* to descend.
disgyniad *m* descent.
disgynnol *adj* descending.
disgynnydd *m* (**disgynyddion**) descendant.
disgyrchiant *m* gravity.
di-sigl *adj* steadfast.
disodli *v* to supplant.
di-sôn-amdan(o/i) *adj* insignificant.
dist *m* (**-iau**) rafter.
distadl *adj* insignificant.
di-staen *adj* unstained.
distaw *adj* quiet.
distaw(af) *from* **distewi**.
distawrwydd *m* silence.
distewi *v* to silence.
distryw *m* destruction.
distrywgar, distrywiol *adj* destructive.
distrywio *v* to destroy.
di-stŵr *adj* without fuss.
distyll *m* ebb.
distylliad *m* distillation.
distyllu *v* to distil.
di-sut *adj* inept.
diswta *adj* abrupt.
diswyddiad *m* (**-au**) dismissal.
diswyddo *v* to dismiss.
di-swyn *adj* unenchanting.
disychedu *v* to quench.
di-syfl *adj* steadfast.
disyfyd *adj* sudden.
di-sylw *adj* inattentive.
disylw *adj* unobserved.
disymwth *adj* abrupt.
disynnwyr *adj* senseless.
diurddas *adj* undignified.
diwaelod *adj* bottomless.
diwahân *adj* indiscriminate.
diwahardd, di-wardd *adj* unruly.
diwair *adj* uncorrupted.
di-waith *adj* unemployed.
diwallu *v* to satisfy.
diwarafun *adj* unstinting.
di-wardd *adj* unruly.
diwasgedd *m* (**-au**) depression (weather).
di-wast *adj* sparing.

diwedydd, diwetydd *m* eventide.
diwedd *m* end.
diweddar *adj* late.
diweddaru *v* to modernise.
diweddeb *f* (**-au**) cadence.
diweddglo *m* conclusion.
diweddu *v* to conclude.
diweirdeb *m* chastity.
diweithdra *m* unemployment.
diwel *v* to pour.
diwerth *adj* worthless.
diwethaf *adj* last.
di-wg *adj* without a frown.
diwinydd *m* (**-ion**) theologian.
diwinyddiaeth *f* theology.
diwinyddol *adj* theological.
di-wobr *adj* prizeless.
diwreiddio *v* to uproot.
diwrnod *m* (**-au**) day.
diwyd *adj* industrious.
diwydiannol *adj* industrial.
diwydian-nwr *m* (**-wyr**) industrialist.
diwydiant *m* (**diwydiannau**) industry.
diwydrwydd *m* diligence.
diwyg *m* format.
diwygiad *m* (**-au**) reform; revival.
diwygiedig *adj* revised.
diwygio *v* to revise.
diwyg-iwr *m* (**-wyr**) reformer.
diwylliadol *adj* cultural.
diwylliannol *adj* cultural.
diwyllian-t *m* (**-nau**) culture.
diwylliedig *adj* cultured.
diwyllio *v* to cultivate.
diwyro *adj* undeviating.
diymadferth *adj* helpless.
diymdrech *adj* effortless.
diymdroi *adj* without delay.
diymffrost *adj* unassuming.
diymgeledd *adj* uncared-for.
diymhongar *adj* unpretentious.
diymwad, diymwâd *adj* indubitable.
diymwybod *adj* unaware.
diysgog *adj* immovable.
diystyr *adj* meaningless.
diystyriol *adj* inconsiderate.
diystyrllyd *adj* disdainful.
diystyru *v* to disregard.
do *adv* yes.
dobio *v* to hit.
doctora *v* to doctor.
dod, dyfod *v* to come (*see* Appendix).
dodi *v* to put.
dodrefnu *v* to furnish.
dodrefnyn *m* (**dodrefn**) (a piece of) furniture.
dodwy *v* to lay eggs.
doe, ddoe *adv* yesterday.
doeth *adj* wise.
doethineb *m/f* wisdom.
doethinebu *v* to pontificate.
doethion *pl* wise-men.
doethur *m* (**-iaid**) doctor (academic).
dof *adj* tame.
dofednod *pl* poultry.
dofi *v* to tame.
dofn *adj* (*f*) deep.
dogfen *f* (**-nau**) document.
dogfennol *adj* documentary.
dogn *m* (**-au**) ration.
dogni *v* to apportion.
dôl *f* (**dolau, dolydd**) meadow. • *m* dole.

dolef *f* (**·au**) bleat.
dolefain *v* to cry out.
dolefus *adj* doleful.
dolen *f* (**·nau, ·ni**) link; handle.
dolennog *adj* winding.
dolennu *v* to coil.
dolur *m* (**·iau**) ailment.
dolurio *v* to ache.
dolurus *adj* painful.
doniau *see* **dawn.**
donio *v* to endow.
doniol *adj* humorous.
doniolwch *m* humour.
dôr *f* (**dorau**) door.
dos *from* **mynd.**
dosbarth *m* (**·iadau**) class.
dosbarthu *v* to distribute.
dosbarth·wr *m* (**·wyr**) distributor.
dosraniad *m* (**·au**) analysis.
dosrannu *v* to distribute.
drachefn *adv* again.
drachtio *v* to quaff.
draenen, draen *f* (**drain**) thorn.
draenog *m* (**·od**) hedgehog.
draenog·iad, draenogyn *m* (**·iaid**) perch.
draig *f* (**dreigiau**) dragon.
drain *see* **draenen.**
drama *f* (**dramâu**) drama.
dramateiddio *v* to dramatise.
dramod·ydd *f* (**·wyr**) dramatist.
drâr *m* (**dreiriau**) drawer.
draw *adv* yonder.
dreng *adj* surly.
dreigiau *see* **draig.**
dreiniog *adj* prickly.
dreiriau *see* **drâr.**
dresel, dreser *f* dresser.
drewdod *m* stench.
drewi *v* to stink.
drewllyd *adj* stinking.
dringo *v* to climb.
dring·wr *m* (**·wyr**) climber.
dros *see* **tros.**
drud *adj* expensive.
drudfawr *adj* costly.
drudw, drudwy *m* (**·od**) starling.
drudwen *f* starling.
drwg *m* (**drygau**) harm. • *adj* bad.
drwgdeimlad *m* (**·au**) ill-feeling.
drwgdybiaeth *f* (**·au**) suspicion.
drwgdybio, drwgdybied *v* to suspect.
drwgdybus *adj* suspicious.
drwgweithred·wr *m* (**·wyr**) offender.
drwm *m* (**drymiau**) drum.
drws *m* (**drysau**) door.
drwy *see* **trwy.**
drycin *f* (**·oedd**) stormy weather.
drych *m* (**·au**) mirror.
drychiolaeth *f* (**·au**) spectre.
drygau *see* **drwg.**
drygioni *m* wickedness.
drygionus *adj* mischievous.
drygu *v* to harm.
dryll *m* (**·iau**) fragment. • *m/f* gun.
drylliedig *adj* shattered.
dryllio *v* to shatter.
drylliog *adj* shattered.
drymiau *see* **drwm.**
drysau *see* **drws.**
drysf·a *f* (**·eydd**) maze.
drysïen *f* (**drysi**) briar.
dryslyd *adj* confused.
drysni *m* tangle.
drysu *v* to bewilder.

dryswch *m* bewilderment.
dryw *m/f* (**-od**) wren.
D.S. *abb* N.B.
du *adj* black.
ducpwyd *from* **dwyn**.
dudew *adj* pitch black.
dueg *f* spleen.
dug *from* **dwyn**. • *m* duke.
dugiaeth *f* (**-au**) duchy.
du-las, dulas *adj* black and blue.
dull *m* (**-iau**) manner.
duo *v* to blacken.
dur *m* steel.
duryn *m* (**-nau**) trunk (elephant).
duw *m* (**-iau**) god.
dŵwch *m* blackness.
duwies *f* (**-au**) goddess.
duwiol *adj* pious.
duwioldeb *m* piety.
dwbl, dwbwl *m* (**dyblau**) double.
dweud, dywedyd *v* to say.
dwfn *adj* deep.
dwfr *see* **dŵr**.
dwg *from* **dwyn**.
dwl *adj* foolish.
dwlu *v* to dote.
dwndwr *m* clamour.
dŵr, dwfr *m* (**dyfroedd**) water.
dwrdio *v* to scold.
dwrglos *adj* watertight.
dwrn *m* (**dyrnau**) fist.
dwsin *m* (**-au, dwsenni**) dozen.
dwsmel *m* dulcimer.
dwthwn *m* (particular) time.
dwy *num* (*f*) two.
dwyfol *adj* divine.
dwyfoldeb *m* divinity.
dwyfoli *v* to deify.
dwyfron *f* breast.
dwyfron-neg *f* (**-egau**) breastplate.
dwyffordd *adj* two-way.
dwyieitheg *f* (study of) bilingualism.
dwyieithog *adj* bilingual.
dwyieithrwydd *m* bilingualism.
dwylo, dwylaw *see* **llaw**.
dwyn *v* to steal.
dwyrain *m* east.
dwyreiniol *adj* eastern.
dwys *adj* serious.
dwysáu *v* to intensify.
dwysbigo *v* to prick.
dwysedd *m* density.
dwyster, dwystra *m* seriousness.
dwythell *f* (**-au**) duct.
dwywaith *adv* twice.
dy *pron* your; you.
dybiwn i *from* **tybio**.
dyblau *see* **dwbl**.
dyblu *v* to double.
dyblyg *adj* folded.
dyblygu *v* to duplicate.
dybryd *adj* dire.
dycned *from* **dygn**.
dychan *f* satire.
dychanol *adj* satirical.
dychanu *v* to satirise.
dychlamu *v* to leap.
dychmygion *see* **dychymyg**.
dychmygol *adj* imaginary.
dychmygu *v* to imagine.
dychmygus *adj* imaginative.
dychryn *m* (**-iadau**) fright. • *v* to frighten.
dychrynllyd *adj* frightful.
dychweliad *m* (**-au**) return.

dychwelyd, dychwel *v* to return.
dychymyg *m* (**dychmygion**) imagination.
dyd *from* **dodi**.
dydd *m* (**·iau**) day.
dyddiad *m* (**·au**) date.
dyddiadur *m* (**·on**) diary.
dyddiedig *adj* dated.
dyddio *v* to date, to dawn.
dyddiol *adj* daily.
dyddodi *v* to deposit.
dyf·ais *f* (**·eisiadau**) device.
dyfal *adj* diligent.
dyfalbarhad *m* perseverance.
dyfalbarhau *v* to persevere.
dyfaliad *m* (**·au**) supposition.
dyfalu *v* to conjecture.
dyfarniad *m* (**·au**) verdict.
dyfarnu *v* to pronounce; to referee.
dyfarn·wr *m* (**·wyr**) referee.
dyfeisgar *adj* resourceful.
dyfeisgarwch *m* inventiveness.
dyfeisiadau, dyfeisiau *see* **dyfais.**
dyfeisio *v* to invent.
dyfeis·iwr *m* (**·wyr**) inventor.
dyfnder *m* (**·oedd, ·au**) depth.
dyfned *from* **dwfn.**
dyfnhau *v* to deepen.
dyfnion *from* **dwfn.**
dyfod *see* **dod, dyfod.**
dyfodiad *m* arrival.
dyfodol *m* future.
dyfradwy *adj* watered.
dyfr·ast *f* (**·eist**) otter (female).
dyfr·farch *m* (**·feirch**) hippopotamus.
dyfr·gi, dwrgi *m* (**·gwn**) otter.
dyfrhau, dyfrio *v* to water.
dyfrliw, dyfrlliw *m* (**·iau**) watercolour.
dyfrllyd *adj* watery.
dyfyniad *m* (**·au**) quotation.
dyfyn·nod *m* (**·odau**) quotation mark.
dyfynnu *v* to quote.
dyffryn *m* (**·noedd**) vale.
dyg(af) *from* **dwyn.**
dygn *adj* diligent.
dygnu *v* to persevere.
dygnwch *m* perseverance.
dygwyl *m* holy day.
dygyfor *m* a surging.
dygymod *v* to come to terms with.
dyhead *m* (**·au**) aspiration.
dyheu *v* to yearn.
dyladwy *adj* fitting.
dyl(ai) *from* **dylu***.
dylanwad *m* (**·au**) influence.
dylanwadol *adj* influential.
dylanwadu *v* to influence.
dyled *f* (**·ion**) debt.
dyledus *adj* due.
dyled·wr *m* (**·wyr**) debtor.
dyletswydd *m* (**·au**) duty.
dylifiad *m* (**·au**) flood.
dylifo *v* to flow.
dylu *v* ought (hypothetical form that is the base of other common forms).
dyluniad *m* (**·au**) design.
dylunio *v* to design.
dylyfu gên *v* to yawn.
dyma *adv* here is.
dymchwel, dymchwelyd *v* to overturn.
dymuniad *m* (**·au**) desire.

dymuno *v* to desire.
dymunol *adj* pleasant.
dyn *m* (**-ion**) man.
dyna *adv* that is.
dyndod *m* manhood.
dyneiddiaeth *f* humanism.
dynes *f* woman.
dynesiad *m* approach.
dynesu *v* to draw near.
dyn·farch *m* (**-feirch**) centaur.
dyngarol *adj* philanthropic.
dyngarwch *m* philanthropy.
dyn-laddiad *m* manslaughter.
dynn *from* **tyn**.
dynodi *v* to indicate.
dynol *adj* mortal.
dynoliaeth *f* humanity.
dynolryw, dynol-ryw *f* mankind.
dynwared *v* to imitate.
dynwarediad *m* (**-au**) impersonation.
dynwared·wr *m* (**-wyr**) impersonator.
dyodiad *m* precipitation.
dyraniad *m* (**-au**) allocation.
dyrannu *v* to allocate.
dyrchafael *m* ascension.
dyrchafiad *m* promotion.
dyrchafu *v* to lift up.
dyri *f* (**dyrïau**) ballad.
dyrn·aid *m* (**-eidiau**) handful.
dyrnau *see* **dwrn**.
dyrnfedd *m/f* (**-i**) hand.
dyrnod *m/f* punch.
dyrnu *v* to thresh.
dyrn·wr *m* (**-wyr**) thresher.
dyr(o) *from* **rhoi**.
dyrys *adj*. entangled.
dysg *m/f* learning.
dysgedig *adj* learned.
dysgeidiaeth *f* doctrine.
dysgl *f* (**-au**) platter.
dysgl·aid *f* (**-eidiau**) plateful; cup (of).
dysgu *v* to learn; to teach.
dysg·wr *m* (**-wyr**) learner.
dyw(aid) *from* **dweud**.
dywediad *m* (**-au**) saying.
dywedwst *adj* taciturn.
dyweddi *m/f* fiancé; fiancée.
dywedd·ïad *m* (**-iadau**) engagement.
dyweddïo *v* to become engaged.

E

eang *adj* broad.
eangderau *see* **ehangder**.
eangfrydedd *m* magnanimity.
eangfrydig *adj* magnanimous.
ebargofiant *m* oblivion.
ebe, eb, ebr *v* said.
ebill *m/f* (**-ion**) auger.
ebol *m* (**-ion**) colt.
eboles *f* filly.
Ebrill *m* April.
ebrwydd *adj* quick.
ebychiad *m* (**-au**) exclamation.
ebychnod *m* (**-au**) exclamation mark (!).

ebychu *v* to exclaim.
ebyrth *see* **aberth**.
eciwmenaidd *adj* ecumenical.
ecoleg *f* ecology.
economaidd *adj* economical.
economeg *f* economics.
economeg·ydd *m* (**·wyr**) economist.
econom·i *m* (**·ïau**) economy.
echdoe *adv* day before yesterday.
echdoriad *m* (**·au**) eruption.
echdorri *v* to erupt.
echdynnu *v* to extract.
echel *f* (**·au, ·ydd**) axle.
echelin *f* (**·au**) axis.
echnos *f* night before last.
echreiddig *adj* eccentric.
echrydus *adj* fearful.
eda·u *f* (**·fedd**) yarn.
edefyn *m* (**·nau**) thread.
edfryd *from* **adfer**.
edifar *adj* repentant.
edifarhau *v* to repent.
edifeiriol *adj* repentant.
edifeirwch *m* repentance.
edliw *v* to reproach.
edmygedd *m* admiration.
edmygu *v* to admire.
edmyg·ydd *m* (**·wyr**) admirer.
edrych *v* to look.
edrychiad *m* (**·au**) a look.
edryd *v* to move.
edrydd *from* **adrodd**.
edwi, edwino *v* to fade.
edwyn *from* **adnabod**.
eddyf *from* **addef**.
e.e. *abb* e.g..
ef *pron* he, him, it.
efallai *adv* perhaps.
efe, efô *pron* he; him; it.
efengyl *f* (**·au**) gospel.
efengylaidd *adj* evangelical.
efengyl·wr *m* (**·wyr**) evangelist.
efelychiad *m* (**·au**) imitation.
efelychu *v* to imitate.
efrau *see* **efryn**.
efrydiau *pl* studies.
efryd·ydd *m* (**·wyr**) student.
efrydd *m* a cripple.
efr·yn *m* (**·au**) tare(s).
efydd *m* brass.
eff·aith *f* (**·eithiau**) effect.
effeithio *v* to effect.
effeithiol *adj* effective.
effeithiolrwydd *m* effectiveness.
effeithlon *adj* efficient.
effeithlonrwydd *m* efficiency.
effro *adj* vigilant.
eger *m* (**·au**) eagre, bore.
egino *v* to germinate.
eginyn *m* (**egin**) bud.
eglur *adj* clear.
eglurder *m* clarity.
eglurhad *m* explanation.
eglwys *f* (**·i**) church.
Eglwys Loegr *f* Church of England.
Eglwys Rufain *f* Roman Catholic Church.
eglwysig *adj* ecclesiastical.
eglwys·wr *m* (**·wyr**) church-goer.
eglwys·wraig, eglwys·wreg *f* (**·wragedd**) churchwoman.
egni *m* (**egnïon**) energy.
egnïol *adj* energetic.
egr *adj* impudent; rough; tart.
egroesen *f* (**egroes**) rose-hip.

egwan *adj* puny.
egwyd *f* (**·ydd**) pastern.
egwyddor *f* (**·ion**) principle.
egwyddorol *adj* principled.
egwyl *f* (**·iau**) intermission.
egyr *from* **agor**.
enghraifft *f* (**enghreifftiau**) example.
englyn *m* (**·ion**) Welsh verse form.
engyl *see* **angel**.
ehangder *m* (**eangderau**) expanse.
ehanged *from* **eang**.
ehangu *v* to expand.
ehedeg *v* to fly.
ehediad *m* (**ehediaid**) bird; (**·au**) flight.
ehedog *adj* flying.
ehedydd *m* (**·ion**) lark.
ehofndra *m* presumption.
ei *pron* his; her; its. • *from* **mynd**.
eich *pron* your; you.
eidion *m* (**·nau**) bullock.
eidionyn *m* (**·nau**) beefburger.
eiddew *m* ivy.
eiddgar *adj* zealous.
eiddi *from* **eiddo**.
eiddigedd *m* jealousy.
eiddigeddu *v* to be jealous.
eiddigeddus *adj* envious.
eiddil *adj* frail.
eiddilwch *m* frailty.
eiddo *m* property.
eidduniad *m* wish.
eigion *m* the deep.
eigioneg *f/m* oceanography.
eingion, einion *f* (**·au**) anvil.
Eingl-Gymreig *adj* Anglo-Welsh.
eil *f* (**·ion**) shed.
eilch *see* **alch**.
eilchwyl *adj* again.
eildwym *adj* reheated.
eiledol *adj* alternating.
eilfed *adj* second.
eiliad *m/f* (**·au**) second.
eiliadur *m* (**·on**) alternator.
eilio *v* to second.
eilradd *adj* secondary.
eilrif *m* (**·au**) even number.
eilun *m* (**·od**) idol.
eilunaddoliad *m* idolatry.
eilwaith *adv* again.
eilydd *m* (**·ion**) seconder; substitute.
eillio *v* to shave.
ein *pron* our.
einioes *f* life.
einion *see* **eingion**.
eir *from* **mynd**.
eira *m* snow.
eirch *from* **arch**; **erchi**.
eirinen *f* (**eirin**) plum, berry.
eiriol *v* to beseech.
eiriolaeth *f* intercession.
eiriol·wr *m* (**·wyr**) mediator.
eirlaw *m* sleet.
eirlithriad *m* (**·au**) avalanche.
eirlys *m* (**·iau**) snowdrop.
eirth *see* **arth**.
eisiau *m* a want.
eisinyn *m* (**eisin**) husk(s).
eisoes *adv* already.
eistedd *v* to sit.
eisteddfod *f* (**·au**) eisteddfod.
eisteddfodol *adj* eisteddfodic.
eisteddfod·wr *m* (**·wyr**) eisteddfod-goer.
eisteddiad *m* (**·au**) sitting.

eisteddle *m/f* (**·oedd**) stand.
eithaf *adj* quite.
eithafbwynt *m* (**·iau**) extremity.
eithafoedd, eithafion *pl* extremities.
eithafol *adj* extreme.
eithaf·wr *m* (**·wyr**) extremist.
eithinen *f* (**eithin**) gorse.
eithr *conj* save that.
eithriad *f* (**·au**) exception.
eithriadol *adj* exceptional.
eithrio *v* to opt out: **ac eithrio** except.
êl *from* **mynd**.
elain *f* (**elanedd**) doe.
eleni *adv* this year.
elfen *f* (**·nau**) element.
elfennol *adj* elementary.
eli *m* (**elïau**) ointment.
eliffant *m* (**·od**) elephant.
eliffantaidd *adj* elephantine.
elin *f* (**·au, ·oedd**) elbow.
elor *f* (**·au**) bier.
elusen *f* (**·nau**) charity.
elusengar *adj* benevolent.
elusennol *adj* charitable.
elw *m* (**·au**) profit.
elwa *v* to profit.
elwach *adj* better off.
elwl·en *f* (**·od**) kidney.
elyrch *see* **alarch**.
elltydd *see* **allt**.
ellyll *m* (**·on**) fiend.
ellyn *m* (**·nau, ·nod**) razor.
emosi·wn *m* (**·ynau**) emotion.
emosiynol *adj* emotional.
emrallt *m* emerald.
emyn *m* (**·au**) hymn.
emyn-dôn *f* hymn tune.
emyn·ydd *m* (**·wyr**) hymn-writer.
en·aid *m* (**·eidiau**) soul.
enbyd *adj* grievous.
enbydrwydd *m* peril.
encil *m* (**·ion**) retreat.
encilio *v* to retreat.
eneidiau *see* **enaid**.
eneiniad *m* inspiration.
eneiniau, eneintiau *see* **ennaint**.
eneinio *v* to anoint.
enfawr *adj* colossal.
enfyn *from* **anfon**.
enfys *f* (**·au**) rainbow.
enill(af) *from* **ennill**.
enill·wr, enillydd *m* (**·wyr**) winner.
enllib *m* (**·ion**) libel, slander.
enllibus *adj* slanderous.
enllyn *m* relish.
ennaint *m* (**eneiniau, eneintiau**) ointment.
ennill *v* to win.
ennyd *m/f* a while.
ennyn *v* to kindle.
ensyniad *m* (**·au**) insinuation.
ensynio *v* to insinuate.
entrych *m* (**·ion**) zenith.
enw *m* (**·au**) name.
enwad *m* (**·au**) denomination.
enwadol *adj* sectarian.
enwadur *m* denominator.
enwaedu *v* to circumcise.
enwebu *v* to nominate.
enwedig *adj*: **yn enwedig** particularly.
enwi *v* to name.
enwog *adj* famous.
enwogion *pl* celebrities.

enwogrwydd *m* fame.
enwol *adj* nominative.
enwyn *m*: **llaeth enwyn** buttermilk.
enynn(af) *from* **ennyn.**
eofn, eon *adj* bold.
eog *m* (**-iaid**) salmon.
eos *f* (**-iaid**) nightingale.
epa *m* (**-od**) ape.
epil *m* offspring.
epilio *v* to breed.
epistol *m* (**-au**) epistle.
eples *m* leaven.
eplesu *v* to ferment.
er *prep* in order; since.
eraill *see* **arall.**
erbyn *prep* against.
erch *adj* frightful.
erchi *v* to plead.
erchwyn *m/f* (**-nau**) edge (of bed).
erchyll *adj* hideous.
erchyll·tra *m* (**-terau**) atrocity.
erdd(ais) *from* **aredig.**
erfinen *f* (**erfin**) swede, turnip.
erfyn *m* (**arfau**) tool. • *v* to entreat.
erfyniad *m* (**-au**) entreaty.
erglyw *v* hark.
ergyd *m/f* (**-ion**) a blow.
ergydio *v* to strike.
erioed *adv* ever; never.
erledigaeth *f* (**-au**) persecution.
erlid *v* to persecute.
erlyn *v* to pursue.
erlyniad *m* (**-au**) prosecution.
erlyn·ydd *m* (**-wyr**) prosecutor.
ernes *f* (**-au**) deposit.
erof *from* **er.**
ers *prep* since.
erstalwm *adv* long time ago.
erthygl *m/f* (**-au**) article.
erthyliad *m* (**-au**) abortion.
erthylu *v* to abort.
erw *f* (**-au**) acre.
erwydd *m* (**-i**) stave (music).
ery *from* **aros.**
erydr *see* **aradr.**
erydu *v* to erode.
eryr *m* (**-od**) eagle; shingles (of skin).
erys *from* **aros.**
esblygiad *m* (**-au**) evolution.
esblygu *v* to evolve.
esboniad *m* (**-au**) explanation; commentary.
esboniadol *adj* explanatory.
esbonio *v* to explain.
esg·air *f* (**-eiriau**) ridge.
esgeulus *adj* slipshod.
esgeuluso *v* to neglect.
esgeulustod *m* negligence.
esgid *f* (**-iau**) shoe.
esgob *m* (**-ion**) bishop.
esgobaeth *f* (**-au**) diocese.
esgor *v* to give birth to.
esgud *adj* quick.
esgus *m* (**-odion, -ion**) an excuse.
esgusodi *v* to excuse.
esgyll *see* **asgell.**
esgymuno *v* to excommunicate.
esgyn *v* to ascend.
esgynfaen *m* mounting-block.
esgyniad *m* ascension.
esgyrn *see* **asgwrn.**
esgyrnog *adj* bony.
esmwyth *adj* smooth.
esmwythâu *v* to smooth.
esmwythder *m* ease.
estraddodi *v* to extradite.

estron *adj* foreign. • *m* (**·iaid**) foreigner.
estrys *m/f* (**·iaid**) ostrich.
estyllen *f* (**estyll**) plank.
estyn *v* to extend.
estyniad *m* (**·au**) extension.
eteil *from* **atal**.
etifedd *m* (**·ion**) heir.
etifeddeg *f* heredity.
etifeddes *f* (**·au**) heiress.
etifeddiaeth *f* inheritance.
etifeddu *v* to inherit.
eto *conj*, *adv* yet.
etyb *from* **ateb**.
etyl *from* **atal**.
ethol *v* to elect.
etholaeth *f* (**·au**) constituency.
etholedig *adj* elect.
etholiad *m* (**·au**) election.
etholwr *m* (**·wyr**) constituent.
eu *pron* their, them.
euog *adj* guilty.
euogrwydd *m* guilt.
euraid, euraidd *adj* golden.
euro *v* to guild.
eurych *m* (**·iaid**) goldsmith.
euthum *from* **mynd**.
ewig *f* (**·od**) hind.
ewin *m/f* (**·edd**) nail.
ewinog *adj* clawed.
ewinor *f* whitlow.
ewinrhew *m* frost-bite.
ewyllys *f* (**·iau**) will.
ewyllysgar *adj* desirous.
ewyllysio *v* to bequeath.
ewyn *m* foam.
ewynnog *adj* foaming.
ewynnu *v* to foam.
ewythr, ewyrth *m* (**ewythredd, ewythrod**) uncle.

F

fagddu *f* hell.
fandal *m* (**·iaid**) vandal.
fandaleiddio *v* to vandalise.
fandaliaeth *f* vandalism.
farnais *m* varnish.
farneisio *v* to varnish.
fawr *adv* not much.
fe *pron* he, him.
fei *m*: **dod i'r fei** to come to light.
fel *prep* like.
felly *adv* therefore.
fersiwn *m* (**fersiynau**) version.
festr·i *f* (**·ïoedd, ·ïau**) vestry.
fi, i *pron* me, I.
ficer *m* (**·iaid**) vicar.
ficer·dy *m* (**·dai**) vicarage.
fiol·a *m* (**·âu**) viola.
firws *m* (**firysau**) virus.
y Fns *abb* Mrs; Miss; MS.
foltedd *m* voltage.
fwltur *m* (**·iaid**) vulture.
fy *pron* my; me.
fyny *adv* up.

Ff

ffa *see* **ffeuen**.
ffacbysen *f* (**ffacbys**) lentil(s).
ffaeledig *adj* feeble.
ffaelu *v* to fail.
ffãen *see* **ffeuen**.
ffafrio *v* to favour.
ffafriol *adj* favourable.
ffagl *f* (**·au**) torch.
ffagotsen *f* (**ffagots**) faggot.
ffair *f* (**ffeiriau**) fair.
ffaith *f* (**ffeithiau**) fact.
ffald *f* (**·au**) fold.
ffals *adj* false.
ffalsio *v* to flatter.
ffans·i *f* (**·ïau**) fancy.
ffansïo *v* to fancy.
ffantas·i *f* (**·ïau**) fantasy.
ffárwel *m/f* a farewell.
ffarwél *interj* Farewell!
ffas *f* (coal) face.
ffas·iwn *f* (**·iynau**) fashion.
ffasiynol *adj* fashionable.
ffatr·i *f* (**·ïoedd**) factory.
ffau *f* (**ffeuau**) lair.
ffawd *f* fate.
ffawt *m* (**·iau**) fault.
ffawydden *f* (**ffawydd**) beech.
FfCM *abb* Highest Common Factor (hcf).
ffedog *f* (**·au**) apron.
ffefryn *m* (**·nau, ·nod**) favourite.
ffeil *f* (**·iau**) file.
ffeilio *v* to file.
ffein *adj* kind; delicious.
ffeind *adj* kind.
ffeiriau *see* **ffair**.
ffeirio *v* to exchange.
ffeithiau *see* **ffaith**.
ffeithiol *adj* factual.
ffel *adj* sagacious, dear.
ffelwm *m* whitlow.
ffeministiaeth *f* feminism.
ffenestr *f* (**·i**) window.
ffensio *v* to fence.
ffêr *f* (**fferau**) ankle.
fferen *f* (**fferins**) sweet(s).
fferf *adj* (*f*) firm.
fferi *f* (**fferïau**) ferry.
fferins *pl* sweets.
fferm, ffarm *f* (**·ydd**) farm.
fferm·dy *m* (**·dai**) farmhouse.
ffermio, ffarmio *v* to farm.
fferm·wr, ffarmwr *m* (**·wyr**) farmer.
fferru *v* to numb.
fferyll·fa *f* (**·feydd**) pharmacy.
fferyll·ydd *m* (**·wyr**) pharmacist.
ffesant *m/f* (**·od**) pheasant.
ffetan *f* (**·au**) sack.
ffeuau *see* **ffau**.
ffeuen, ffãen *f* (**ffa**) bean.
ffi *f* (**·oedd**) fee.
ffiaidd *adj* despicable.
ffieidd-dra *m* abomination.
ffieiddio *v* to abhor.
ffigur *f* (**·au**) figure.
ffigurol *adj* figurative.

ffigysbren *m* (**·nau**) fig tree.
ffigysen *f* (**ffigys**) fig(s).
ffilmio *v* to film.
ffiloreg *f* rigmarole.
ffin *f* (**·iau**) boundary.
ffinio *v* to border on.
ffiol *f* (**·au**) cup.
ffiseg *f* physics.
ffiseg·ydd *m* (**·wyr**) physicist.
ffisig *m* medicine.
ffisioleg *m* physiology.
ffitiach *adj* more fitting.
ffitio *v* to fit.
ffitrwydd *m* fitness.
ffiwdaliaeth *f* feudalism.
ffiwsio *v* to fuse.
fflach *f* (**·iau**) flash.
fflachio *v* to flash.
fflangell *f* (**·au**) scourge.
fflangellu *v* to scourge.
fflam *f* (**·au**) flame.
fflamgoch *adj* flame coloured.
fflamio *v* to blaze.
fflat *adj* flat. • *m* (**·iau**) flat.
ffloch *m* (**·au**) floe.
fflodiar·t *f* (**·dau**) floodgate.
fflŵr *m* flour.
ffo *m* flight.
ffoadur *m* (**·iaid**) fugitive.
ffoc·ws *m* (**·ysau**) focus.
ffodus *adj* fortunate.
ffoëdig *adj* fleeing.
ffōedigaeth *f* flight.
ffōedigion, ffoaduriaid *pl* refugees.
ffoi *v* to flee.
ffôl *adj* foolish.
ffoli *v* to be infatuated.
ffolineb *m* (**·au**) folly.
ffon *f* (**ffyn**) stick.
ffôn *m* (**ffonau**) telephone.
ffonio *v* to phone.
ffonnod *f* (**ffonodiau**) a whack.
fforc *f* (**ffyrc**) ffork.
fforch *f* (**·au, ffyrch**) fork.
fforchi *v* to fork.
fforchog *adj* forked.
ffordd *f* (**ffyrdd**) way.
fforddio *v* to afford.
fforddol·yn *m* (**·ion**) wayfarer.
fforest *f* (**·ydd**) forest.
fforffedu *v* to forfeit.
ffor·iwr *m* (**·wyr**) explorer.
ffformwl·a *f* (**·âu**) formula.
ffort·iwn *f* (**·iynau**) fortune.
ffos *f* (**·ydd**) trench.
ffosileiddio *v* to fossilise.
ffotograffiaeth *f* photography.
ffotograff·ydd *m* (**·wyr**) photographer.
ffowlyn *m* (**ffowls**) poultry.
ffowndr·i *f* (**·ïau**) foundry.
ffracs·iwn *m* (**·iynau**) fraction.
ffradach *m* shambles.
ffrae *f* (**·au, ·on**) quarrel.
ffraeo *v* to squabble.
ffraeth *adj* witty.
ffraethineb *m* (**·au**) wit.
ffrâm *f* (**fframiau**) frame.
fframio *v* to frame.
ffram·waith *m* (**·weithiau**) framework.
fframyn *m* (**fframiau**) frame.
ffres *adj* fresh.
ffresni *m* freshness.
ffreutur *m/f* refectory.
ffrewyll *f* scourge.

ffridd *f* (**-oedd**) mountain pasture.
ffrimpan *f* (**-au**) frying-pan.
ffrind *m* (**-iau**) friend.
ffrio *v* to fry.
ffris *f* (**-iau**) frieze.
ffrit *adj* worthless.
ffrith *f* (**-oedd**) mountain pasture.
ffrithiant *m* friction.
ffroen *f* (**-au**) nostril.
ffroeni *v* to sniff.
ffroenuchel *adj* haughty.
ffroesen, ffroisen *f* (**ffroes, ffrois**) pancake.
ffrog *f* (**-iau**) frock.
ffromi *v* to bluster.
ffrwcslyd *adj* confused.
ffrwd *f* (**ffrydiau**) stream.
ffrwgwd *m* (**ffrygydau**) brawl; fray.
ffrwst *m* bustle.
ffrwt *m* energy.
ffrwtian *v* to splutter.
ffrwydrad *m* (**-au**) explosion.
ffrwydro *v* to explode.
ffrwydrol *adj* explosive.
ffrwydr·yn *m* (**-on**) explosive.
ffrwyn *f* (**-au**) bridle.
ffrwyth *m* (**-au**) fruit.
ffrwythlon *adj* fertile.
ffrwythlondeb *m* fertility.
ffrwythloni *v* to fertilise.
ffrydiau *see* **ffrwd**.
ffrydio *v* to flow.
ffrygydau *see* **ffrwgwd**.
ffuantus *adj* insincere.
ffug *adj* false.
ffugbasio *v* to sell a dummy.
ffugenw *m* (**-au**) pseudonym.
ffugio *v* to pretend.
ffuglen *f* fiction.
ffunen *f* (**-nau, -ni**) handkerchief.
ffunud *m*: **yr un ffunud** the spitting image.
ffured *f* (**-au**) ferret.
ffureta *v* to ferret.
ffurf *f* (**-iau**) form.
ffurfafen *f* (**-nau**) firmament.
ffurfio *v* to form.
ffurfiol *adj* formal.
ffurflen *f* (**-ni**) form.
ffust *f* (**-iau**) flail.
ffusto *v* to beat.
ffwdan *f* bother.
ffwdanu *v* to bother.
ffwdanus *adj* fussy.
ffwng *m* (**ffyngau, ffyngoedd**) fungus.
ffŵl *m* (**ffyliaid**) fool.
ffwlbart *m* (**-iaid**) polecat.
ffwlbri *m* folly.
ffwlc·rwm *m* (**-rymau**) fulcrum.
ffwndro *v* to bewilder.
ffwndrus *adj* bewildered.
ffwr *m* (**ffyrrau**) fur.
ffwr-bwt *adj* abrupt.
ffwrdd *adv* away.
ffwrdd-â-hi *adj* easy-going.
ffwrn *f* (**ffyrnau**) oven.
ffwrn·ais *f* (**-eisi, -eisiau**) furnace.
ffwrwm *f* (**ffwrymau**) bench.
ffwythian·t *m* (**-nau**) function (mathematical).
ffy *from* **ffoi**.
ffydd *f* faith.
ffyddiog *adj* confident.
ffyddlon *adj* faithful.
ffyddlondeb *m* fidelity.

ffyddloniaid *pl* the faithful.
ffyngau, ffyngoedd *see* **ffwng.**
ffyliaid *see* **ffŵl.**
ffyn *see* **ffon.**
ffynhonnau *see* **ffynnon.**
ffynhonnell *f* (**ffynonellau**) fount.
ffyniannus *adj* prosperous.
ffyniant *m* prosperity.
ffynidwydden *f* (**ffynidwydd**) fir tree.
ffyn·non *f* (**·honnau**) well.
ffynnu *v* to thrive.
ffynonellau *see* **ffynhonnell.**
ffyrc *see* **fforc.**
ffyrch *see* **fforch.**
ffyrdd *see* **ffordd.**
ffyrf *adj* firm; solid.
ffyrling *f* farthing.
ffyrn·aid *f* (**·eidiau**) batch.
ffyrnig *adj* fierce.
ffyrnigo *v* to enrage.
ffyrnigrwydd *m* ferocity.
ffyrrau *see* **ffwr.**

G

gadael *v* to leave.
gaeaf *m* (**·au**) winter.
gaeafgwsg *m* hibernation.
gaeafgysgu *v* to hibernate.
gaeafol *adj* wintry.
gaeafu *v* to winter.
gafael *v* to grip. • *f* grasp.
gafaelgar *adj* gripping.
gafr *f* (**geifr**) goat.
gafrewig *f* (**·od**) antelope.
gaing *f* (**geingiau**) chisel.
gair *m* (**geiriau**) word.
galaeth *m/f* (**·au**) galaxy.
galanas *f* massacre.
galar *m* grief.
galarnad *f* (**·au**) lament.
galarnadu *v* to lament.
galaru *v* to grieve.
galar·wr *m* (**·wyr**) mourner.
galfaneiddio *v* to galvanise.
galw *v* to call. • *m* a call.
galwad *f* (**·au**) a call.
galwedigaeth *f* (**·au**) vocation.
galwyn *m* (**·au, ·i**) gallon.
gallt, allt *f* (**gelltydd, elltydd**) slope (wooded).
gallu *v* to be able. • *m* (**·oedd**) ability.
galluog *adj* gifted.
galluogi *v* to enable.
gan *prep* with, by.
ganed, ganwyd *from* **geni.**
gar *m/f* (**·rau**) thigh; shank.
garan *m/f* (**·od**) heron.
gardas *m/f* garter.
gardd *f* (**gerddi**) garden.
garddio *v* to garden.
garddwest *f* fête.
gardd·wr *m* (**·wyr**) gardener.
garddwriaeth *f* horticulture.
garddwrn *see* **arddwrn.**
garllegen *f* (**garlleg**) garlic.
garrau *see* **gar.**

garsiwn *m* (**garsiynau**) garrison.
gartref *adv* at home.
garw *adj* rough.
gast *f* (**geist**) bitch.
gau *adj* false.
gedy *from* **gadael.**
gef·ail *f* (**·eiliau**) a forge.
gefeilliaid *see* **gefell.**
gefeillio *v* to twin.
gefeilltref *f* (**·i**) twin town.
gefel *f* (**gefeiliau**) tongs.
gefelen *f* (**gefeiliau**) pliers.
gefell *m/f* (**gefeilliaid**) twin.
gefyn *m* (**·nau**) fetter.
geifr *see* **gafr.**
geingiau *see* **gaing.**
geilw *from* **galw.**
geirfa *f* vocabulary.
geiriad *m* wording.
geiriadur *m* (**·on**) dictionary.
geiriadurol *adj* lexicographical.
geiriadur·wr *m* (**·wyr**) lexicographer.
geiriau *see* **gair.**
geirio *v* to phrase.
geiriol *adj* verbal.
geirw, geirwon *adj* (*pl*) rough.
geirwir *adj* truthful.
geirwiredd *m* truthfulness.
geiryn *m* (**·nau**) particle.
geist *see* **gast.**
gelen, gel·e *f* (**·od**) leech.
gelw(ir) *from* **galw.**
gelyn *m* (**·ion**) enemy.
gelyniaeth *f* animosity.
gell(ir) *from* **gallu.**
gelltydd *see* **gallt.**
gellygen *f* (**gellyg**) pear.
gem *m/f* (**·au**) gem.
gêm *f* (**gêmau**) game.
gemydd *m* jeweller.
gên *f* (**genau**) jaw.
genau *m* (**geneuau**) mouth.
genau-goeg *m* (**genau-goegion**) lizard.
genedigaeth *f* (**·au**) birth.
genedigol *adj* native.
generadur *m* (**·on**) generator.
geneteg *f* genetics.
geneth *f* (**·od**) lass.
geneuau *see* **genau.**
genfa *f* (**genfâu**) bit.
genglo *m* lockjaw.
geni *v* to give birth.
gennod *pl* girls.
genn(yf) *from* **gan.**
gen·wair *f* (**·weiriau**) fishing-rod.
genweir·iwr *m* (**·wyr**) angler.
genyn *m* (**·nau**) gene.
geometreg *f* geometry.
ger *prep* by.
gêr *m/f* (**gerau, gêrs**) gear.
gerbron *prep* before.
gerddi *see* **gardd.**
gerfydd *prep* by.
geri marwol *m* cholera.
geriach *pl* odds and ends.
gerllaw *prep* beside.
gerwin *adj* severe.
gerwindeb, gerwinder *m* roughness.
gesyd *from* **gosod.**
gewyn, giewyn *m* (**·nau, gïau**) sinew.
gewynnog *adj* sinewy.
gïach *m* (**giâchod**) snipe.

giamocs, gamocs *pl* pranks.
gïau *see* **gewyn.**
gilydd *pron*: **ei gilydd** each other.
glafoerio *v* to slobber.
glafoerion *pl* drivel.
glain *m* (**gleiniau**) bead.
glan *f* (**·nau, glennydd**) bank.
glân *adj* clean.
glandeg *adj* fair.
glanedydd *m* (**·ion**) detergent.
glanf·a *f* (**·eydd**) landing-place.
glanhad, glanheuad *m* a cleaning.
glanhau *v* to clean.
glanio *v* to land.
glannau *see* **glan.**
glanweithdra *m* cleanliness.
glas *adj* blue.
glasenw *m* (**·au**) nickname.
glasfyfyr·iwr *m* (**·wyr**) fresher.
glasgroen *m* epidermis.
glaslanc *m* (**·iau**) lad.
glasog *f* (**·au**) gizzard.
glastwr *m* milk and water.
glastwraidd *adj* insipid.
glastwreiddio *v* to dilute.
glasu *v* to turn blue/green.
glaswelltyn *m* (**glaswellt**) blade of grass.
glaswenu *v* to smirk.
glaw *m* (**·ogydd**) rain.
gleiniau *see* **glain.**
gleisi·ad *m* (**·aid**) grilse.
gleision *adj* (*pl*) blue.
glendid *m* cleanliness; comeliness.
glenn(ir) *from* **glanio.**
glennydd *see* **glan.**
glesni *m* blueness.
glew *adj* valiant.
glin *m* (**·iau**) knee.
glo *m* coal.
gloddesta *v* to carouse.
gloes, loes *f* wound.
glof·a *f* (**·eydd**) colliery.
glöwr *m* (**glowyr**) collier.
glöyn byw *m* (**gloÿnnod**) butterfly.
gloyw *adj* bright.
gloywder *m* brightness.
gloywi *v* to burnish.
glud *m* (**·ion**) glue.
gludio, gludo *v* to stick.
gludiog *adj* sticky.
gludlun *m* (**·iau**) collage.
glwth *m* glutton.
glwys *adj* fair.
glyn *m* (**·noedd**) glen.
glŷn *from* **glynu.**
glynu *v* to stick.
go *adv* rather.
gob·aith *m* (**·eithion**) hope.
gobeithio *v* to hope.
gobeithiol *adj* hopeful.
goben·nydd *m* (**·yddiau, ·yddion**) pillow.
goblygiad *m* (**·au**) implication.
gochel *v* to avoid.
gochelgar *adj* cautious.
godidog *adj* wonderful.
godidowgrwydd *m* splendour.
godineb *m* adultery.
godinebu *v* to commit adultery.
godinebus *adj* adulterous.
godre *m* (**·on, ·uon**) edge.
godro *v* to milk.
godd·aith *f* (**·eithiau**) bonfire.
goddef *v* to endure.

goddefgar *adj* tolerant.
goddefgarwch *m* tolerance.
goddefol *adj* passive.
goddiweddyd *v* to overtake.
goddrych *m* (**·au**) subject.
goddrychol *adj* subjective.
gof *m* (**·aint**) blacksmith.
gofal *m* (**·on**) care.
gofalu *v* to take care.
gofalus *adj* careful.
gofal·wr *m* (**·wyr**) caretaker.
goferu *v* to stream.
goferwi *v* to simmer.
gofid *m* (**·iau**) grief.
gofidio *v* to worry.
gofidus *adj* sorrowful.
gofod *m* (**·au**) space.
gofod·wr *m* (**·wyr**) astronaut.
gofwy *m* tribulation.
gofyn *m* (**·ion**) a request. • *v* to ask.
gofynnod *m* (**gofynodau**) question mark (?).
gofynnol *adj* necessary.
goganu *v* to lampoon.
goglais, gogleisio *v* to tickle.
gogledd *m* north.
gogledd-ddwyrain *m* northeast.
gogleddol *adj* northerly.
gogledd-orllewin *m* northwest.
gogleisiol *adj* titillating.
gogoneddu *v* to glorify.
gogoneddus *adj* glorious.
gogonian·t *m* (**·nau**) splendour.
gogr, gogor *m* (**·au**) sieve.
gogrwn *v* to sift.
gogwydd *m* (**·ion**) tendency.
gogwyddo *v* to veer.
gogyfer *prep* for.
gogynderfynol *adj* quarter-final.
gohebiaeth *f* correspondence.
gohebu *v* to correspond.
goheb·ydd *m* (**·wyr, ·yddion**) correspondent.
gohiriad *m* (**·au**) postponement.
gohirio *v* to postpone.
gol. *abb* ed.
gôl *f* (**goliau, gôls**) goal.
gol·au *m* (**·euadau**) a light. • *adj* fair.
golch *m* (**·ion**) the wash.
golchi *v* to wash.
golchwra·ig *f* (**·gedd**) washerwoman.
goleddf *m* incline.
goleddfu *v* to slant.
goleuadau *see* **golau.**
goleu·dy *m* (**·dai**) lighthouse.
goleuedig *adj* enlightened.
goleuni *m* light.
goleuo *v* to lighten.
gôl-geid·wad *m* (**·waid**) goalkeeper.
golosg *m* coke.
golud *m* (**·oedd**) wealth.
goludog *adj* wealthy.
gol·wg *m* (**·ygon**) sight. • *f* appearance.
golwyth *m* (**·ion**) chop.
golyg·fa *f* (**·feydd**) scene.
golygon *see* **golwg.**
golygu *v* to intend; to edit.
golygus *adj* handsome.
golygydd *m* (**·ion**) editor.
golygyddol *adj* editorial.
gollwng *v* to release.
gollyngdod *m* relief.

gomedd to refuse.
gonest *adj* honest.
gonestrwydd *m* honesty.
gorau *adj* (**goreuon**) best.
gorawyddus *adj* over-eager.
gorberffaith *adj* pluperfect.
gorchest *f* (**·ion**) feat.
gorchestol *adj* outstanding.
gorchfygiad *m* (**·au**) defeat.
gorchfygu *v* to overcome.
gorchfyg·wr *m* (**·wyr**) conqueror.
gorchmynion *see* **gorchymyn**.
gorchmynn(af) *from* **gorchymyn**.
gorchmynnol *adj* imperative.
gorchymyn *m* (**gorchmynion**) command. • *v* to command.
gordd *f* (**gyrdd**) sledge-hammer.
gorddefnyddio *v* to over-use.
gordderch *f* (**·adon**) concubine.
gorddibynnu *v* to be overdependent.
gor-ddweud *v* to exaggerate.
goresgyn *v* to vanquish.
goresgyniad *m* (**·au**) conquest.
goresgyn·nwr *m* (**·wyr**) conqueror.
goreuon *adj* (*pl*) best.
goreuro *v* to gild.
gorfod *v* to have to. • *m* obligation.
gorfodaeth *f* (**·au**) compulsion.
gorfodi *v* to compel.
gorfodol *adj* compulsory.
gorfoledd *m* jubilation.
gorfoleddu *v* to rejoice.
gorfoleddus *adj* jubilant.
gorfwyta *v* to overeat.
gorffen *v* to finish.
gorffenedig *adj* completed.
Gorffennaf *m* July.
gorffennol *m* the past.
gorffwyll *adj* delirious.
gorffwys, gorffwyso *v* to rest.
gorgymhleth *adj* over-complicated.
gorgyffwrdd *v* to overlap.
gorhendad *m* (**·au**) great-grandfather.
gorhenfam *m* (**·au**) great-grandmother.
gorhoffedd *m* metrical verse.
gori *v* to hatch.
gorifyny *m* ascent.
goriwaered *m* descent.
gorlawn *adj* overflowing.
gorlenwi *v* to overfill.
gorlifo *v* to overflow.
gorliwio *v* to exaggerate.
gorlwytho *v* to overburden.
gorllewin *m* west.
gorllewinol *adj* western.
gorllyd *adj* festering.
gormes *m* oppression.
gormesol *adj* oppressive.
gormesu *v* to oppress.
gormes·wr *m* (**·wyr**) oppressor.
gormod *m* (**·ion**) too much.
gormodedd *m* excess.
gormodiaith *f* hyperbole.
gormodol *adj* excessive.
gornest, ornest *f* (**·au**) contest.
goroesi *v* to survive.
goroes·wr *m* (**·wyr**) survivor.
goror *m/f* (**·au**) frontier.
gorsaf *f* (**·oedd**) station.
gorsaf-feistr *m* (**·i**) station-master.
gorsedd, gorsedd·fainc *f* (**·au, ·feinciau**) throne.

gorseddu *v* to enthrone.
gorthrech *m* oppression.
gorthr·wm *m* (**·ymau**) oppression.
gorthrymder *m* (**·au**) tribulation.
gorthrymedig *adj* oppressed.
gorthrymu *v* to oppress.
gorthrym·wr *m* (**·wyr**) oppressor.
goruchaf *adj* supreme.
goruchafiaeth *f* (**·au**) supremacy.
goruchel *adj* eminent.
goruchwyliaeth *f* supervision.
goruchwylio *v* to oversee.
goruchwyl·iwr *m* (**·wyr**) supervisor.
goruwch *prep* above.
goruwchnaturiol *adj* supernatural.
gorwedd *v* to lie.
gorweddian *v* to sprawl.
gorweiddiog *adj* bedridden.
gorweithio *v* to overwork.
gorwel *m* (**·ion**) horizon.
gorwneud *v* to overdo.
gorwyr *m* (**·ion**) great-grandson.
gorwyres *f* (**·au**) great-granddaughter.
gorymd·aith *f* (**·eithiau**) procession.
gorymdeithio *v* to march.
gorynys *f* (**·oedd**) peninsula.
goryrru *v* to speed.
gosber *m* vesper.
gosgeiddig *adj* graceful.
gosgordd *f* (**·ion**) retinue.
goslef *f* (**·au**) tone.
gosod *v* to set; to put. • *adj* false.
gosodiad *m* (**·au**) a setting.
gosteg *m* silence.
gostegion *pl* banns.
gostegu *v* to silence.
gostwng *v* to lower.
gostyngedig *adj* humble.
gostyngeiddrwydd *m* humility.
gostyngiad *m* (**·au**) reduction.
gostyngol *adj* reduced.
gradell *f* (**gredyll**) griddle.
gradd *f* (**·au**) grade, degree.
graddedig *adj* graded.
graddedigion *pl* graduates.
gradd·fa *f* (**·feydd**) scale.
graddian·t *m* (**·nau**) gradient.
graddio *v* to graduate; to grade.
graddol *adj* gradual.
graean *pl* shingle.
graen *m* lustre.
graenus *adj* polished.
gramadeg *m* (**·au**) grammar.
gramadegol *adj* grammatical.
gras *m* (**·usau**) grace.
grasion, grasol *adj* gracious.
graslonrwydd *m* graciousness.
grât *m/f* (**gratiau**) grate.
grawn *see* **gronyn**.
grawnfwyd *m* (**·ydd**) cereal.
grawnffrwyth *m* (**·au**) grapefruit.
grawnwinen *f* (**grawnwin**) grape(s).
Grawys *m* Lent.
gre *f* (**·oedd**) flock.
gredyll *see* **gradell**.
greddf *f* (**·au**) instinct.
greddfol *adj* instinctive.
gresyn *m* a shame.
gresynu *v* to deplore.
gresynus *adj* wretched.
gridyll *m/f* (**·au**) griddle.
griddfan *m* (**·nau**) a groan. • *v* to groan.
grifft *m* frog-spawn.

gris *m/f* (**·iau**) step, stair.
grisial *m* (**·au**) crystal.
grisialaidd *adj* crystalline.
gro *pl* pebbles.
gronell *f* (**·au**) roe.
gronyn *m* (**·nau, grawn**) grain.
groser *m* (**groseriaid**) grocer.
grudd *f* (**·iau**) cheek.
grug *m* heather.
grug·iar *f* (**·ieir**) grouse.
grwgnach *v* to grumble.
grwgnachlyd *adj* prone to moan.
grwn *m* (**grynnau**) ploughed section.
grwndi *m* a purring.
grŵp *m* (**grwpiau**) group.
grym *m* (**·oedd**) force.
grymus *adj* poweful.
grymuso *v* to fortify.
grynnau *see* **grwn**.
gw. *abb* see.
gwacáu *v* to empty.
gwaced *from* **gwag**.
gwacsaw *adj* trivial.
gwacter *m* (**·au**) void.
gwachul *adj* feeble.
gwadadwy *adj* deniable.
gwadiad *m* denial.
gwadn *m/f* (**·au**) sole.
gwadnu *v* to sole; to hoof it.
gwadu *v* to deny.
gwad·wr *m* (**·wyr**) denier.
gwadd[1] *adj* guest.
gwadd[2], **gwadden**, **gwahadd·en** *f* (**·od**) mole.
gwaddod *m* (**·ion**) sediment.
gwaddol *m* endowment.
gwaddoli *v* to endow.
gwae *m* (**·au**) woe.
gwaed *m* blood.
gwaed-gynnes *adj* warm-blooded.
gwaedlif *m* haemorrhage.
gwaedlyd *adj* bloody.
gwaedoer *adj* cold-blooded.
gwaedu *v* to bleed.
gwaedd *f* (**·au**) shout.
gwaedd(af) *from* **gweiddi**.
gwaeg *f* (**·au**) buckle.
gwael *adj* poor.
gwaeledd *m* illness.
gwaelod *m* (**·ion**) bottom.
gwaelu *v* to sicken.
gwäell *f* (**gweill, gwëyll**) knitting needle.
gwaered *m* downward slope.
gwaeth *adj* worse.
gwaethwaeth *adj* from bad to worse.
gwaethygu *v* to deteriorate.
gwag *adj* empty.
gwagedd *m* frivolity.
gwagio, gwagu *v* to empty.
gwaglaw *adj* empty-handed.
gwagle *m* (**·oedd**) void.
gwagnod *m* (**·au**) zero.
gwag-siarad *m* tittle-tattle.
gwahadden *see* **gwadd**.
gwahân *m* apart.
gwahanf·a ddŵr *f* (**·eydd dŵr**) watershed.
gwahangleifion *pl* lepers.
gwahanglwyf *m* leprosy.
gwahanglwyfus *adj* leprous. • *m* leper.
gwahaniaeth *m* (**·au**) difference.
gwahaniaethu *v* to distinguish.

gwahanol *adj* different.
gwahanu *v* to separate.
gwahardd *v* to forbid.
gwaharddedig *adj* prohibited.
gwaharddiad *m* (**·au**) prohibition.
gwahodd *v* to invite.
gwahoddedigion *pl* guests.
gwahoddiad *m* (**·au**) invitation.
gwain *f* (**gweiniau**) sheath.
gwair *m* (**gweiriau, gweirydd**) hay.
gwaith *m* (**gweithiau**) work. • *f* occasion.
gwâl *f* (**gwalau**) lair.
gwala *f* plenty.
gwalch *m* (**gweilch**) hawk.
gwall *m* (**·au**) mistake.
gwallgof *adj* insane.
gwallgof·dy *m* (**·dai**) lunatic asylum.
gwallgofddyn *m* (**·ion**) lunatic.
gwallgofrwydd *m* insanity.
gwallt *m* (**gwalltiau**) hair (of head).
gwalltog *adj* hairy.
gwallus *adj* incorrect.
gwamal *adj* fickle.
gwamalrwydd *m* frivolity.
gwamalu *v* to waver.
gwan *adj* weak.
gwanaf *f* (**·au, gwaneifiau**) swath.
gwanc *m* lust.
gwancus *adj* greedy.
gwanedig *adj* diluted.
gwanedu *v* to dilute.
gwaneg *f* (**·au, gwenyg**) a billow.
gwaneifiau *see* **gwanaf.**
gwangalon *adj* timid.
gwangalonni *v* to despair.
gwanhau *v* to weaken.
gwanllyd, gwannaidd *adj* feeble.
gwanned *from* **gwan.**
gwant *m* caesura.
gwantan *adj* feeble; fickle.
gwanu *v* to stab.
gwanwyn *m* spring.
gwanwynol *adj* vernal.
gwanychu *v* to weaken.
gwar *m/f* (**·rau**) nape.
gwâr *adj* civilised.
gwaradwydd *m* shame.
gwaradwyddo *v* to shame.
gwaradwyddus *adj* shameful.
gwarafun *v* to forbid.
gwaraidd *adj* civilised.
gwarant *f* (**·au**) warrant.
gwarantu *v* to justify.
gwarchae *m* (**·au**) siege. • *v* to besiege.
gwarcheid·wad *m* (**·waid**) keeper.
gwarchod *v* to look after.
gwarchodaeth *f* custody.
gwarchod·fa *f* (**·feydd**) reservation.
gwarchodliw *m* camouflage.
gwarchodlu *m* (**·oedd**) guards.
gwarchod·wr *m* (**·wyr**) guardian.
gware *m/f* game.
gwared, gwaredu *v* to rid.
gwaredigaeth *f* deliverance.
gwared·wr *m* (**·wyr**) saviour.
gwareiddiad *m* (**·au**) civilisation.
gwareiddiedig *adj* civilised.
gwareiddio *v* to civilise.
gwargaled *adj* stubborn.
gwarged *m* (**·ion**) surplus.
gwargrwm *adj* stooping.
gwargrymu *v* to stoop.
gwarian·t *m* (**·nau**) expenditure.

gwarineb *m* civility.
gwario *v* to spend.
gwarrau *see* **gwar**.
gwarth *m* shame.
gwarthaf *m*: **ar warthaf** upon.
gwarthafl *see* **gwarthol**.
gwartheg *pl* cattle.
gwarthol *f* (**·ion**) stirrup.
gwarthus *adj* disgraceful.
gwas *m* (**gweision**) servant.
gwasaidd *adj* servile.
gwasanaeth *m* (**·au**) service.
gwasanaethu *v* to serve.
gwaseidd-dra *m* servility.
gwasg *f* (**gweisg**) a press. • *m/f* waist.
gwasgar *m*: **ar wasgar** scattered.
gwasgaredig *adj* scattered.
gwasgarog *adj* dispersed.
gwasgaru *v* to scatter.
gwasgedd *m* (**·au**) pressure.
gwasg·fa *f* (**·feydd**) pang.
gwasgiad *m* (**·au**) a squeeze.
gwasgod *f* (**·au**) waistcoat.
gwasgu *v* to squeeze.
gwasod *adj* in heat.
gwastad *adj* level; always.
gwastad, gwastadedd *m* (**·au**) plain, level.
gwastadol *adj* perpetual.
gwastadrwydd *m* evenness.
gwastatáu, gwastatu *v* to level.
gwastatir *m* (**·oedd**) plain.
gwastraff *m* waste.
gwastrafflyd *adj* wasteful.
gwastraffu *v* to waste.
gwastraffus *adj* extravagant.
gwastr·awd *m* (**·odion**) groom.
gwatwar *m* mockery. • *v* to mock.
gwatwarus *adj* mocking.
gwatwar·wr *m* (**·wyr**) mocker.
gwau *m* knitting.
gwau, gweu *v* to weave.
gwaun *f* (**gweunydd**) moorland.
gwawch *f* yell.
gwawd *m* scorn.
gwawdio *v* to ridicule.
gwawdlyd *adj* scornful.
gwawl *m* radiance.
gwawn *m* gossamer.
gwawr *f* dawn.
gwawrio *v* to dawn.
gwayw *m* (**gwewyr**) pang.
gwayw·ffon *f* (**·ffyn**) spear.
gwdihŵ *f* owl.
gwddf, gwddwg *m* (**gyddfau, gyddygau**) neck.
gwe *f* (**·oedd**) web.
gwead *m* (**·au**) texture.
gwe(af) *from* **gwau**.
gwed(ir) *from* **gwadu**.
gwedd *f* (**·au**) appearance. • *f* (**·oedd**) yoke.
gweddaidd *adj* suitable.
gwedd·er *m* (**·rod**) wether.
gwedd·i *f* (**·ïau**) prayer.
gweddill *m* (**·ion**) remnant.
gweddïo *v* to pray.
gweddol *adj* fairly.
gweddu *v* to suit.
gweddus *adj* seemly.
gweddustra *m* propriety.
gweddw *f* (**·on**) widow.
gweddwdod *m* widowhood.
gwefl *f* (**·au**) lip.
gwefr *m* (**·au**) thrill.

gwefreiddio *v* to electrify.
gwefreiddiol *adj* electrifying.
gwefus *f* **(·au)** lip.
gwegian *v* to totter.
gwegil *m/f* nape.
gweheirdd *from* **gwahardd**.
gwehelyth *m/f* lineage.
gwehilion *pl* dregs.
gwehydd, gwŷdd (gwehyddion) weaver.
gweiddi *v* to shout.
gweigion *adj (pl)* empty.
gweilch *see* **gwalch**.
gweilgi *f* the deep.
gweill *see* **gwäell**.
gweini *v* to serve.
gweiniau *see* **gwain**.
gweinidog *m* **(·ion)** minister.
gweinidogaeth *f* ministry.
gweinidogaethu *v* to officiate.
gweinion *adj (pl)* weak.
gweinydd *m* **(·ion)** waiter.
gweinyddes *f* **(·au)** waitress.
gweinyddiaeth *f* **(·au)** administration.
gweinyddol *adj* administrative.
gweinyddu *v* to administer.
gweinydd·wr *m* **(·wyr)** administrator.
gweinyddwraig *f* administratrix.
gwëir *from* **gwau**.
gweirglodd *f* **(·iau)** meadow.
gweiriau, gweirydd *see* **gwair**.
gweiryn *m* **(gwair)** blade of grass.
gweisg *see* **gwasg**.
gweision *see* **gwas**.
gweith·dy *m* **(·dai)** workshop.
gweithfeydd *pl* industrial works.
gweithgar *adj* diligent.
gweithgaredd, gweithgarwch *m* **(·au)** activity.
gweithgor *m* **(·au)** working party.
gweithgynhyrchu *v* to manufacture.
gweithiau *see* **gwaith**.
gweithio *v* to work.
gweith·iwr *m* **(·wyr)** worker.
gweithred *f* **(·oedd)** action.
gweithredoedd *pl* deeds.
gweithredol *adj* executive.
gweithredu *v* to act.
gweithred·wr *m* **(·wyr)** operator.
gwêl *from* **gweld**.
gweladwy *adj* visible.
gwelâu *see* **gwely**.
gweld, gweled *v* to see.
gweledig *adj* visible.
gweledigaeth *f* **(·au)** vision.
gweledol *adj* visual.
gwelw *adj* pale.
gwelwder, gwelwedd *m* pallor.
gwelwi *v* to pale.
gwel·y *m* **(·yau, ·âu, gwlâu)** bed.
gwell *adj* better.
gwella *v* to get better.
gwell·aif, gwell·au *m* **(·eifiau)** shears.
gwellhad *m* recovery.
gwellian·t *m* **(·nau)** improvement.
gwelltglas *pl* grass.
gwelltog *adj* grassy.
gwelltyn *m* **(gwellt)** straw.
gwellwell *adj* better and better.
gwemp *adj (f)* fair.
gwen *adj (f)* white.
gwên *f* **(gwenau)** smile.

gwenc·i *f* (·ïod) weasel.
gwendid *m* (**·au**) weakness.
Gwener *f* Friday; Venus.
gwenerol *adj* venereal.
gwenfflam *adj* blazing.
gweniaith *f* flattery.
gwenieithio *v* to blandish.
gwenieith·iwr *m* (**·wyr**) flatterer.
gwenieithus *adj* flattering.
gwenithen *f* (**gwenith**) wheat.
gwenithfaen *m/f* granite.
gwennaf *from* **gwen**.
gwen·nol *f* (**·oliaid**) swallow.
gwenu *v* to smile.
genwyn *m* poison.
genwynig *adj* poisonous.
gwenwynllyd *adj* venemous.
genwyno *v* to poison.
gwenyg *see* **gwaneg**.
gwenynen *f* (**gwenyn**) bee.
gweog *adj* webbed.
gwep *f* jib.
gwêr *m* tallow.
gwerdd *adj* (*f*) green.
gwerddon *f* (**·au**) oasis.
gweren *f* suet.
gwerin *f* folk.
gweriniaeth *f* (**·au**) republic.
gwerinol *adj* common.
gwerin·wr *m* (**·wyr**) countryman.
gwern *f* (**·i, ·ydd**) alder.
gwernen *f* (**·ni, ·nau**) alder.
gwers *f* (**·i**) lesson.
gwerslyfr *m* (**·au**) textbook.
gwersyll *m* (**·oedd**) camp.
gwersylla, gwersyllu *v* to camp.
gwerth *m* (**·oedd**) value.
gwerthfawr *adj* precious.
gwerthfawrogi *v* to appreciate.
gwerthfawrogiad *m* appreciation.
gwerthfawrogol *adj* appreciative.
gwerthian·t *m* (**·nau**) sale.
gwerthu *v* to sell.
gwerth·wr *m* (**·wyr**) seller.
gwerthyd *f* (**·au, ·oedd**) axle.
gweryd *m* earth; grave.
gweryrad *m* whinny.
gweryru *v* to neigh.
gwest·ai *m* (**·eion**) guest.
gwest·y *m* (**·ai, ·yau**) guest-house.
gweu *v* to weave, to knit.
gweunydd *see* **gwaun**.
gwëwyd *from* **gwau**.
gwewyr *see* **gwayw**.
gwëydd *see* **gwehydd, gwëydd**.
gwëyll *see* **gwäell**.
gwg *m* frown.
gwgu *v* to frown.
gwialen *f* (**gwiail**) cane.
gwib *f* rush.
gwib·daith *f* (**·deithiau**) outing.
gwiber *f* (**·od**) viper.
gwich *f* (**·iau**) squeal.
gwich·iad *m* (**·iaid**) winkle.
gwichian *v* to squeal.
gwichlyd *adj* squeaky.
gwiddon *f* witch.
gwifr, gwifr·en *f* (**·au**) wire.
gwig *f* woodland.
gwingo *v* to writhe.
gwin *m* (**·oedd**) wine.
gwinau *adj* auburn.
gwinllan *f* (**·nau, ·noedd**) vineyard.
gwinwydden *f* (**gwinwydd**) vine.
gwir *adj* true.
gwireb *f* maxim.

gwireddu *v* to make true.
gwirfodd *m* voluntary consent.
gwirfoddol *adj* voluntary.
gwirfoddoli *v* to volunteer.
gwirfoddol·wr *m* (**·wyr**) volunteer.
gwirgroen *m* dermis.
gwiriad *m* a check.
gwirio *v* to verify.
gwirion *adj* silly.
gwiriondeb *m* silliness.
gwirionedd *m* truth.
gwirioneddol *adj* true.
gwirioni *v* to dote.
gwirod *m* (**·ydd**) liquor.
gwisg *f* (**·oedd**) clothing.
gwisgi *adj* nimble.
gwisgo *v* to wear.
gwiw *adj* worthy.
gwiwer *f* (**·od**) squirrel.
gwlad *f* (**gwledydd**) country.
gwladaidd *adj* rustic.
gwladf·a *f* (**·eydd**) colony.
gwladgarol *adj* patriotic.
gwladgarwch *m* patriotism.
gwladgar·wr *m* (**·wyr**) patriot.
gwladol *adj* state.
gwladoli *v* to nationalise.
gwladwein·ydd *m* (**·wyr**) statesman.
gwlad·wr *m* (**·wyr**) countryman.
gwladwriaeth *f* (**·au**) state.
gwladychu *v* to colonise.
gwlân *m* (**gwlanoedd**) wool.
gwlanen *f* (**·ni**) flannel.
gwlanog *adj* woolly.
gwlatgar *adj* patriotic.
gwlâu *see* **gwely**.
gwleb *adj* (*f*) wet.
gwledig *adj* rural.
gwledydd *see* **gwlad**.
gwledd *f* (**·oedd**) feast.
gwledda *v* to feast.
gwleidydd *m* (**·ion**) politician.
gwleidyddiaeth *f* politics.
gwleidyddol *adj* political.
gwleidydd·wr *m* (**·wyr**) politician.
gwlith *m* dew.
gwlith·en *f* (**·od, gwlithenni**) slug.
gwlithyn *m* dewdrop.
gwlyb *adj* wet.
gwlybaniaeth *m* moisture.
gwlybwr *m* fluid.
gwlych *m* liquid; gravy.
gwlychu *v* to wet.
gwlydd *pl* stalks.
gwm *m* gum.
gwn *m* (**gynnau**) gun. • *from* **gwybod**.
gŵn *m* (**gynau**) gown.
gwndwn *m* ley.
gwnêl, gwnelo *from* **gwneud**.
gwneud, gwneuthur *v* to do (*see* Appendix).
gwneuthuriad *m* composition.
gwneuthur·wr *m* (**·wyr**) maker.
gwniadur *m* (**·on**) thimble.
gwniadwaith *m* needlework.
gwniad·wraig, gwniad·wreg *f* (**·wragedd**) seamstress.
gwnïo *v* to sew.
gwobr *f* (**·au, ·wyon**) prize.
gwobrwyo *v* to reward.
gŵr *m* (**gwŷr**) man; husband.
gwrach *f* (**·od, ·ïod**) witch.
gwragedd *see* **gwraig**.
gwraidd, gwreiddyn *m* (**gwreiddiau**) root.

gwraig *f* (**gwragedd**) woman; wife.
gwrandaw(af) *from* **gwrando.**
gwrandawiad *m* (**·au**) hearing.
gwranda·wr *m* (**·wyr**) listener.
gwrando *v* to listen.
gwrant(af) *from* **gwarantu.**
gwrcath, gwrc·i, gwrcyn *m* (**·od, ·ïod, ·od**) tom-cat.
gwregys *m* (**·au**) seat-belt.
gwregysu *v* to girdle.
gwrêng *m* common people.
gwreichionen *f* (**gwreichion**) spark.
gwreichioni *v* to sparkle.
gwreichionyn *m* (**gwreichion**) spark.
gwreiddiau *see* **gwraidd, gwreiddyn.**
gwreiddio *v* to take root.
gwreiddiol *adj* original.
gwreiddioldeb *m* originality.
gwreiddyn *see* **gwraidd.**
gwrendy *from* **gwrando.**
gwresog *adj* hot.
gwresogi *v* to heat.
gwresogydd *m* (**·ion**) heater.
gwrhyd, gwryd *m* fathom.
gwrhydri *m* valour.
gwrid *m* blush.
gwrido *v* to blush.
gwridog *adj* rosy-cheeked.
gwritgoch *adj* ruddy.
gwrogaeth *f* homage.
gwrol *adj* brave.
gwroldeb *m* valour.
gwron *m* (**·iaid**) brave man.
gwrt·aith *m* (**·eithiau**) fertiliser.
gwrthban *m* (**·nau**) blanket.
gwrteithio *v* to manure.
gwrthban *m* (**·nau**) blanket.
gwrthbl·aid *f* (**·eidiau**) the opposition.
gwrthbrofi *v* to disprove.
gwrthbwynt *m* counterpoint.
gwrthdaro *v* to clash.
gwrthdrawiad *m* (**·au**) collision.
gwrthdystiad *m* (**·au**) protest.
gwrthdystio *v* to protest.
gwrth-ddweud *v* to contradict.
gwrthddywediad *m* (**·au**) contradiction.
gwrthfiotig *m* antibiotic.
gwrthgilio *v* to backslide.
gwrthgil·iwr *m* (**·wyr**) backslider.
gwrthgl·awdd *m* (**·oddiau**) rampart.
gwrthglocwedd *adj* anticlockwise.
gwrthgyferbyniad *m* (**·au**) contrast.
gwrthgyferbyniol *adj* opposite.
gwrthgyferbynnu *v* to contrast.
gwrthian·t *m* (**·nau**) resistance.
gwrthnysig *adj* perverse.
gwrthod *v* to refuse.
gwrthodedig *adj* rejected.
gwrthodiad *m* (**·au**) refusal.
gwrthrewydd *m* antifreeze.
gwrthrych *m* (**·au**) object.
gwrthrychol *adj* objective.
gwrthryfel *m* (**·oedd**) rebellion.
gwrthryfela *v* to rebel.
gwrthryfelgar *adj* rebellious.
gwrthryfel·wr *m* (**·wyr**) a rebel.
gwrthsafiad *m* stance against.
gwrthsefyll *v* to withstand.
gwrthsoddi *v* to countersink.
gwrthun *adj* repugnant.
gwrthuni *m* repugnance.
gwrthwenwyn *m* antidote.

gwrthwyneb *m* contrary.
gwrthwynebiad *m* (**·au**) objection.
gwrthwynebu *v* to oppose.
gwrthwynebus *adj* antagonistic.
gwrthwyneb·wr *m* (**·wyr**) opponent.
gwrthyd *from* **gwrthod**.
gwrych *m* (**·oedd**) hedge.
gwrychyn *m* (**gwrych**) hackle.
gwryd *m* fathom.
gwrym *m* (**·iau**) welt.
gwrysgen *f* (**gwrysg**) haulm.
gwrysgyn *m* (**gwrysg**) haulm.
gwryw *adj* male.
gwrywaidd *adj* masculine.
gwrywgydiaeth *f* homosexuality.
gwrywgyd·iwr *m* (**·wyr**) homosexual.
gwsber·en *f* (**·ins**, **gwsberis**) gooseberry.
gwth, gwthiad *m* (**·iau**, **·au**) shove.
gwthio *v* to push.
gwyach *f* (**·od**) grebe.
gwybedyn *m* (**gwybed**) midges.
gwybod *v* to know.
gwybodaeth *f* knowledge; information.
gwybodus *adj* learned.
gwybyddus *adj* known.
gwych *adj* excellent.
gwychder *m* splendour.
gwydn *adj* tough.
gwydnwch, gwytnwch *m* toughness.
gwydr *m* (**·au**) glass.
gwydr·aid *m* (**·eidiau**) glassful.
gwydro *v* to glaze.
gwydryn *m* (**·nau**) tumbler.
gŵydd *m* presence.
gŵydd *f* (**gwyddau**) goose.
gwŷdd *m* (**gwyddion**) loom; plough.
gwŷdd *pl* trees.
gwydd(ai) *from* **gwybod**.
gwyddbwyll *f* chess.
Gwyddel *m* (**·od**) Irishman.
Gwyddeleg *f* Irish.
gwyddfid *m* honeysuckle.
gwyddoniadur *m* (**·on**) encyclopedia.
gwyddoniaeth *f* science.
gwyddonol *adj* scientific.
gwyddon·ydd *m* (**·wyr**) scientist.
gwyddor *f* (**·au**) rudiment(s); science: **yr wyddor** the alphabet.
gwyfyn *m* (**·od**) moth.
gŵyl *f* (**gwyliau**) holiday; festival.
gŵyl Dewi, gŵyl Ddewi St David's Day.
gwylaidd *adj* unassuming.
gwylan *f* (**·od**) seagull.
gwyleidd-dra *m* modesty.
gwyl·fa *f* (**·âu**) lookout.
gwyliadwriaeth *f* alertness.
gwyliadwrus *adj* cautious.
gwyliedydd *m* watchman.
gwylio *v* to watch.
gwyl·iwr *m* (**·wyr**) watcher.
gwylmabsant *f* wake.
gwylnos *f* (**·au**) vigil.
gwylog *f* (**·od**) guillemot.
gwyll *m* gloom.
gwyll·iad *m* (**·iaid**) bandit.
gwyllt *adj* wild.
gwylltineb *m* wildness.
gwylltio, gwylltu *v* to become angry.
gwymon *m* seaweed.

gwymp *adj* fine.
gwyn *adj* white.
gwŷn *m* (**gwyniau**) ache; rage.
gwynder *m* whiteness.
gwynegon *pl* rheumatism.
gwynegu *v* to throb.
gwynfa *f* paradise.
gwynfyd *m* (**·au**) bliss.
gwynfydedig *adj* blessed.
gwyngalch *m* whitewash.
gwyngalchu *v* to whitewash.
gwyn·iad *m* (**·iaid**) fish unique to Bala Lake.
gwynias *adj* white-hot.
gwynio *v* to ache.
gwynned *from* **gwyn**.
gwynnin *m* sap-wood.
gwynnu *v* to whiten.
gwynnwy *m* albumen.
gwynt *m* (**·oedd**) wind.
gwyntio, gwynto *v* to smell.
gwyntog *adj* windy.
gwyntyll *f* (**·au**) fan.
gwypo *from* **gwybod**.
gŵyr[1] *from* **gwybod**.
gŵyr[2] *adj* aslant.
gŵyr[3] *mutated form of* **cwyr**.
gwŷr *see* **gŵr**.
gwyr·an *m/f* (**·ain**) barnacle.
gwyrdroad *m* (**·au**) perversion.
gwyrdroëdig *adj* perverted.
gwyrdroi *v* to distort.
gwyrdd *adj* green.
gwyrddlas *adj* sea-green.
gwyrddlesni *m* verdure.
gwyrgam *adj* crooked.
gwyriad *m* (**·au**) deviation.
gwyro *v* to bend.
gwyrth *f* (**·iau**) miracle.
gwyrthiol *adj* miraculous.
gwyryf, gwyry (**·(f)on**) virgin.
gwyryfol *adj* virgin.
gwŷs *f* (**gwysion**) summons.
gwysio *v* to summon.
gwystl *m* (**·on**) hostage.
gwystlo *v* to pledge.
gwytned *from* **gwydn**.
gwytnwch *see* **gwydnwch**.
gwythïen *f* (**gwythiennau**) vein.
gwyw *adj* withered.
gwywo *v* to wither.
gyda, gydag *prefix* with.
gyddfau, gyddygau *see* **gwddf, gwddwg**.
gyddfol *adj* guttural; jugular.
gylch *from* **golchi**.
gylfin *m* (**·au**) beak.
gylfinir *m* (**·od**) curlew.
gynau *see* **gŵn**.
gynnau *see* **gwn**.
gynnau *adv* just now.
gynt *adv* formerly.
gyr *m* (**·roedd**) flock.
gyrdd *see* **gordd**.
gyrfa *f* (**·oedd**) career.
gyrru *v* to drive.
gyrrwr *m* (**gyrwyr**) driver.
gyrwynt *m* (**·oedd**) hurricane.

H

ha *abb* hectar (ha).
hacio *v* to hack.
haclif *f* (**-iau**) hacksaw.
hacred *from* **hagr**.
had *m* seed.
haden *f* (**hadau**) a seed.
hadu *v* to go to seed.
had·yn *m* (**-au**) seed.
haearn *m* (**heyrn**) iron.
haearnaidd *adj* iron-like.
haeddiannau *see* **haeddiant**.
haeddiannol *adj* deserving.
haeddian·t *m* (**-nau**) merit.
haeddu *v* to deserve.
hael *adj* generous.
haelfrydedd *m* generosity.
haelfrydig *adj* liberal.
haelioni *m* generosity.
haelionus *adj* generous.
haen, haenen *f* (**-au, -nau**) layer.
haeriad *m* (**-au**) allegation.
haerllug *adj* arrogant.
haerllugrwydd *m* cheek.
haeru *v* to allege.
haf *m* (**-au**) *m* summer.
hafaidd *adj* summery.
hafal *adj* equal.
hafaliad *m* (**-au**) equation.
hafalnod *m* (**-au**) equal sign.
hafan *f* haven.
haflug *m/f* plenty.
hafn *m/f* (**-au**) pass.
hafod *f* (**-au, -ydd**) upland farm.
hafflau *m* clutches.
hagr *adj* ugly.
hagru *v* to disfigure.
hagrwch *m* ugliness.
haid *f* (**heidiau**) swarm.
haidd *see* **heidden**.
haig *f* (**heigiau**) shoal.
haint *m/f* (**heintiau**) disease.
halen *m* salt.
halio *v* to hall.
halogedig *adj* defiled.
halogi *v* to defile.
halwyn *m* (**-au**) salt.
hallt *adj* salty.
halltu *v* to salt.
hamb·wrdd *m* (**-yrddau**) tray.
hamdden *m/f* leisure.
hamddena *v* to laze.
hamddenol *adj* leisurely.
hances *f* (**-i**) handkerchief.
haneri *pl* half-backs (rugby).
haneru *v* to halve.
hanes *m* (**-ion**) tale; history.
hanes·ydd *m* (**-wyr**) historian.
hanfod *m* (**-ion**) essence.
hanfodol *adj* essential.
haniaeth *f* (**-au**) abstraction.
haniaethol *adj* abstract.
hanner *m* (**haneri**) half.
hanner tôn *m* (**~ tonau**) semitone.
hanu *v* to derive from.
hap *f* (**-iau**) chance.
hapchwarae *m* (**-on**) gambling.

hapnod *m* (**·au**) an accidental.
hapus *adj* happy.
hapusrwydd *m* happiness.
hardd *adj* handsome.
harddu *v* to beautify.
harddwch *m* beauty.
harmon·i *m* (**·ïau**) harmony.
harn·ais *m* (**·eisiau**) harness.
harneisio *v* to harness.
hastus *adj* rushed.
hatling *f* mite (*widow's mite*).
hau *v* to sow.
haul *m* (**heuliau**) sun.
hawdd *adj* easy.
hawddfyd *m* prosperity.
hawddgar *adj* amiable.
hawddgarwch *m* amiability.
hawl *f* (**·iau**) right.
hawl *from* **holi**.
hawl·fraint *f* (**·freintiau**) copyright.
hawlio *v* to claim.
haws *adj* easier.
heb *prep* without.
heblaw *prep* besides.
hebog *m* (**·au, ·iaid**) hawk.
Hebread *m* (**Hebreaid**) Hebrew.
hebrwng *v* to accompany.
hebryngydd *m* guide.
hed *from* **ehedeg**.
hedegog *adj* flying.
hedfan *v* to fly.
hedyn *m* (**hadau**) seed.
heddgeid·wad *m* (**·waid**) policeman.
heddiw *adv* today.
heddlu *m* police force.
hedd·was *m* (**·weision**) policeman.
heddwch, hedd *m* peace.
heddychiaeth *f* pacifism.
heddychlon, heddychol *adj* peaceful.
heddych·wr *m* (**·wyr**) pacifist.
hefelydd *m* peer.
hefyd *adv* also.
heff·er *f* (**·rod**) heifer.
heglog *adj* leggy.
heglu *v* to leg it.
heibio *adv* past.
heicio *v* to hike.
heidiau *see* **haid**.
heidio *v* to swarm.
heidden *f* (**haidd**) (grain of) barley.
heigiau *see* **haig**.
heilltion *adj* (*pl*) salty.
heini *adj* active.
heintiau *see* **haint**.
heintio *v* to infect.
heintus *adj* infectious.
heirdd *adj* (*pl*) beautiful.
hel *v* to send.
hela *v* to hunt.
helaeth *adj* extensive.
helaethrwydd *m* extent.
helaethu *v* to enlarge.
helbul *m* (**·on**) trouble.
helbulus *adj* troublesome.
helcyd *v* to lug.
helf·a *f* (**·eydd, ·âu**) (a) hunt.
hel·gi *m* (**·gwn**) hound.
heli *m* sea.
hel·iwr *m* (**·wyr**) hunter.
helm *f* (**·au**) helmet; (**·ydd**) rick.
helogan *f* celery.
helpu *v* to help.
helygen *f* (**helyg**) willow.
helynt *f* (**·ion**) trouble.

hell *adj* (*f*) ugly.
hemio *v* to hem; to belt.
hen *adj* old.
henadur *m* (**-iaid**) alderman.
henaduriaeth *f* presbytery.
henaidd *adj* old-fashioned.
henaint *m* old age.
hen dad-cu, hen-daid *m* great-grandfather.
hendref *f* (**-i**) lowland farm.
heneb·yn *m* (**-ion**) ancient monument.
heneiddio *v* to grow old.
hen fam-gu, hen-nain *f* great-grandmother.
henffasiwn *adj* old-fashioned.
henffych *exclam* greetings!
hen-nain *f* (**hen-neiniau**) great-grandmother.
heno *adv* tonight.
henoed *m* elderly people.
henur·iad *m* (**-iaid**) an elder.
heol, hewl *f* (**heolydd**) road.
hepgor *v* to forgo.
hepian *v* to doze.
her *f* (**-iau**) challenge.
herc *f* (**-iau**) hop.
hercian *v* to hobble.
herciog *adj* limping.
herfeiddiol *adj* defiant.
hergwd *m* push.
herio *v* to challenge.
herodraeth *f* heraldry.
herw *m*: **ar herw** outlawed.
herwgipio *v* to hijack, to kidnap.
herwgip·iwr *m* (**-wyr**) kidnapper.
herwhela *v* to poach.
her·wr *m* (**-wyr**) outlaw.
hesb *adj* (*f*) barren.
hesbin, hesben *f* (**-od**) (yearling) ewe.
hesgen *f* (**hesg**) sedge.
het *f* (**-iau**) hat.
hetar *m* (**-s**) iron.
heth *f* cold spell.
heuaf *from* **hau**.
heuldro *m* (**-eon**) solstice.
heuliau *see* **haul**.
heulog *adj* sunny.
heulwen *f* sunshine.
heu·wr *m* (**-wyr**) sower.
heyrn *see* **haearn**.
hi *pron* she; her.
hidio *v* to mind.
hidl *f* (**-au**) sieve. • *adj* streaming.
hidlen *f* (**-ni**) filter.
hidlo *v* to filter.
hil *f* (**-ion, -oedd**) race.
hiliogaeth *f* descendants.
hiliol *adj* racist.
hilyddiaeth *f* racism.
hin *f* weather.
hiniog *see* **rhiniog**.
hinon *f* fair weather.
hins·awdd *m/f* (**-oddau**) climate.
hir *adj* long.
hiraeth *m* nostalgia.
hiraethu *v* to long for.
hiraethus *adj* homesick.
hirbell *adj* afar.
hirben *adj* shrewd.
hirgrwn *adj* oval.
hirgron *adj* (*f*) oval.
hirhoedledd *m* longevity.
hirhoedlog *adj* long-lived.
hirlwm *m* lean period.

hirwyntog *adj* long-winded.
hirymarhous *adj* long-suffering.
hithau *pron* she too; her too.
hoced *m/f* chicanery.
hoe *f* rest.
hoedl *f* lifetime.
hoel, hoel·en *f* (**·ion**) nail.
hoelbren *m* (**·nau**) dowel.
hoelio *v* to nail.
hoen *m/f* zest.
hoenus *adj* vivacious.
hof *f* (**·iau**) hoe.
hofio *v* to hoe.
hofran *v* to hover.
hofranfad *m* (**·au**) hovercraft.
hofrenydd *m* (**·ion**) helicopter.
hoff *adj* favourite.
hoffi *v* to like.
hoffter *m* (**·au**) fondness.
hoffus *adj* likeable.
hogen, hogan *f* (**·nod, gennod**) lass.
hogi *v* to sharpen.
hogwr *m* sharpener.
hog·yn *m* (**·iau**) lad.
hongiad *m* (**·au**) suspension.
hongian *v* to hang.
holgar *adj* inquisitive.
holi *v* to question.
holiadur *m* (**·on**) questionnaire.
hol·wr *m* (**·wyr**) question-master.
holwyddoreg *f* catechism.
holl *adj* all.
hollalluog *adj* omnipotent.
hollfyd *m* universe.
holliach *adj* sound.
hollol *adj* entire.
hollt *m/f* (**·au**) cleft.
hollti *v* to split.
hollwybodol *adj* omniscient.
hollysydd *m* omnivore.
hon *pron* this (*f*).
honcian *v* to limp.
honedig *adj* alleged.
honiad *m* (**·au**) claim.
honni *v* to allege.
honno *pron* that (*f*).
hopran *f* mill-hopper.
hosan *f* (**·au, sanau**) sock.
hosanną *exclam* hosanna.
hoyw *adj* gay.
hual *m* (**·au**) fetter.
huawdl *adj* eloquent.
hud *m* magic.
hudlath *f* (**·au**) magic wand.
hudo *v* to enchant.
hudol, hudolus *adj* beguiling.
hudoliaeth *f* enchantment.
huddygl *m* soot.
hufen *m* cream.
hufen·fa *f* (**·feydd**) creamery.
hugan *f* (**·au**) cloak; gannet.
huling *f* a covering.
hulio *v* to cover.
hun *f* slumber.
hun, hunan *pron* self.
hunan-barch *m* self-respect.
hunanbwysig *adj* bumptious.
hunandosturiol *adj* self-pitying.
hunandybus *adj* self-important.
hunanddisgyblaeth *f* self-discipline.
hunanfeddiannol *adj* self-possessed.
hunangofian·t *m* (**·nau**) autobiography.

hunangyfiawn *adj* self-righteous.
hunangynhaliol *adj* self-sufficient.
hunanhyder *m* self-confidence.
hunaniaeth *f* identity.
hunanladdiad *m* suicide.
hunanlywodraeth *f* autonomy.
hunanol *adj* selfish.
hunanoldeb *m* selfishness.
hunanymwadiad *m* self-denial.
hunanymwybodol *adj* self-conscious.
hunllef *f* (**-au**) nightmare.
huno *v* to sleep.
huodledd *m* eloquence.
huotled *from* **huawdl**.
hur *m* hire.
hur-bwrcas *m* hire-purchase.
hurio *v* to hire.
hurt *adj* stupid.
hurtio, hurto *v* to stupify.
hurtrwydd *m* stupidity.
hurtyn *m* (**-nod**) idiot.
hwb, hwp *m* a shove.
hwch *f* (**hychod**) sow.
hwiangerdd *f* (**-i**) nursery rhyme.
hwliganiaeth *f* hooliganism.
hwn *pron* this (*m*).
hwnnw *pron* that (*m*).
hwnt *adv* yonder.
hwp *see* **hwb, hwp**.
hwrdd *m* (**hyrddod**) ram.
hwre *exclam* take this.
hws·mon *m* (**-myn**) husbandman.
hwy, nhw *pron* them.
hwy *from* **hir**.
hwy·ad, hwy·aden *f* (**-aid**) duck.
hwyhau *v* to lengthen.
hwyl *f* (**-iau**) sail; mood.
hwylbren *m* (**-nau, -ni**) mast.
hwylio *v* to sail.
hwyliog *adj* humorous.
hwylus *adj* convenient.
hwyluso *v* to facilitate.
hwylustod *m* convenience.
hwynt-hwy *pron* they themselves.
hwyr *adj* late.
hwyrach *adv* perhaps; later.
hwyrddyfod·iad *m* (**-iaid**) latecomer.
hwyrfrydig *adj* reluctant.
hwyrhau *v* to become late.
hwyrol *adj* evening.
hwythau *pron* they too.
h.y. *abb* i.e.
hy, hyf *adj* bold.
hybarch *adj* very reverend.
hyblyg *adj* flexible.
hyblygrwydd *m* flexibility.
hybu *v* to promote.
hychod *see* **hwch**.
hyd *m* length. • *prep* until.
hydawdd *adj* soluble.
hyder *m* confidence.
hyderu *v* to rely.
hyderus *adj* confident.
hydraidd *adj* pervious.
hydred *m* (**-au**) longitude.
hydredol *adj* longitudinal.
Hydref *m* October.
hydref *m* autumn.
hydrefol *adj* autumnal.
hydrin *adj* tractable.
hydwyth *adj* resilient.
hydwythedd *m* elasticity.
hydyn *adj* docile.
hydd *m* (**-od**) stag.
hyddysg *adj* learned.

hyf *see* **hy**.
hyfder, hyfdra *m* audacity.
hyfedr *adj* expert.
hyfryd *adj* lovely.
hyfrydu *v* to delight.
hyfrydwch *m* delight.
hyfwyn *adj* genial.
hyfforddai *m* trainee.
hyfforddi *v* to train.
hyfforddiant *m* training.
hyfford·wr *m* (**·wyr**) trainer.
hyfford·wraig *f* (**·wragedd**) instructress.
hygar *adj* amiable.
hyglyw *adj* audible.
hygoelus *adj* gullible.
hygrededd *m* credibility.
hygyrch *adj* accessible.
hygyrchedd *m* accessibility.
hyhi *pron* she herself.
hylaw *adj* handy.
hylendid *m* hygiene.
hylif *m* (**·au**) liquid.
hylifo *v* to liquify.
hylifydd *m* (**·ion**) liquidiser.
hylosg *adj* combustible.
hylosgiad *m* combustion.
hyll *adj* ugly.
hyllt *from* **hollti**.
hylltra, hylltod *m* ghastliness, ugliness.
hyn *pron* these.
hŷn *adj* older.
hynafg·wr *m* (**·wyr**) old man.
hynaf·iad *m* (**·iaid**) ancestor.
hynafiaeth *f* (**·au**) antiquity.
hynafiaethol *adj* antiquarian.
hynafiaeth·ydd *m* (**·wyr**) antiquary.
hynafol *adj* ancient.
hynaws *adj* genial.
hynawsedd *m* geniality.
hyned *from* **hen**.
hynny *pron* those; that.
hynod *adj* remarkable.
hynodrwydd *m* peculiarity.
hynt *f* course.
hyrddio *v* to hurl.
hyrddod *see* **hwrdd**.
hyrwyddo *v* to further.
hysb *adj* barren.
hysbyddu *v* to drain.
hysbys *adj* evident.
hysbyseb *f* advertisment.
hysbysebu *adj* to advertise.
hysbys·fwrdd *m* (**·fyrddau**) notice-board.
hysbysiad *m* (**·au**) announcement.
hysbysion *pl* notices.
hysbysrwydd *m* information.
hysbysu *v* to inform.
hysian, hysio *v* to incite.
hytrach *adv*: **yn hytrach** rather.
hywedd *adj* trained.
hyweddu *v* to train.

I

i *prep* to. • *pron* me; my.
iâ *m* ice.
iach *adj* healthy.
iachâd *m* cure.
iacháu *v* to make better.
iachawdwr *m* saviour.
iachawdwriaeth *f* salvation.
iachus *adj* bracing.
iad *f* (**-au**) cranium.
iâen *f* (**iaënnau**) sheet of ice.
iaith *f* (**ieithoedd**) language.
iâr *f* (**ieir**) hen.
iard *f* (**-iau, ierdydd**) yard.
iarll *m* (**ieirll**) earl.
iarlles *f* countess.
ias *f* (**-au**) shiver.
iasoer *adj* chilling.
iasol *adj* eerie.
iau *f* (**ieuau, ieuoedd**) yoke. • *m* liver.
iau *adj* younger.
Iau *m* Thursday; Jupiter.
iawn *adv* very. • *adj* right.
iawndal *m* compensation.
iawnderau *pl* rights.
iddi, iddo, iddynt *from* **i**.
ie *adv* yes.
iechyd *m* health.
ieir *see* **iâr**.
ieirll *see* **iarll**.
ieitheg *f* philology.
ieithoedd *see* **iaith**.
ieithwedd *f* style.
ieithydd *m* (**-ion**) linguist.
ieithyddiaeth *f* philology.
ieithyddol *adj* linguistic.
ierdydd *see* **iard**.
iet *f* (**-iau**) gate.
ieuanc, ifanc *adj* young.
ieuau *see* **iau**.
ieuenctid *m* youth.
ieuo *v* to yoke.
ieuoedd *see* **iau**.
ifanc *adj* young.
ig *m* (**-ion**) hiccup.
igam-ogam *adj* zigzag.
igian *v* to hiccup.
iglw *m* (**iglŵau, iglws**) igloo.
ing *m* (**-oedd**) anguish.
ingol *adj* agonising.
ildio *v* to yield.
ill *pron* they.
imperialaeth *f* imperialism.
imperialaidd *adj* imperial.
impio *v* to graft; to sprout.
imp·yn *m* (**-iau**) sprout; graft.
imwneiddio *v* to immunise.
Ind·iad *m* (**-iaid**) Indian.
indrawn *m* maize.
innau *see* **minnau**.
inswleiddio *v* to insulate.
iòd *see* **iot, iòd**.
iolyn *m* nincompoop.
Iôn, Iôr *m* (the) Lord.
ïon *m* (**ïonau**) ion.
Ionawr *m* January.

iorwg *m* ivy.
iot, iòd *m* jot; iota.
ir, iraidd *adj* succulent.
iraid *m* (**ireidiau**) lubricant.
iro *v* to oil.
is *adj* lower.
isadran *f* (**·nau**) subsection.
isaf *adj* lowest.
isaf·swm *m* (**·symiau**) minimum.
is-bwyllgor *m* (**·au**) subcommittee.
isel *adj* low.
iselder *m* (**·au**) depression.
iseldir *m* (**·oedd**) lowland.
iselhau *v* to lower.
iselradd *adj* inferior.
isetholiad *m* (**·au**) by-election.
is-gadeirydd *m* vice-chairman.
is-ganghellor *m* vice-chancellor.
is-gapt·en *m* (**·einiaid**) lieutenant.
isgell *m* stock.
is-iarll *m* (**is-ieirll**) viscount.
is·lais *m* (**·leisiau**) undertone.
islaw *prep* below.
isobar *m* (**·rau**) isobar.
isod *adv* below.
isradd *m* (**·au**) (mathematical) root.
israddol *adj* subordinate.
israddoldeb *m* inferiority.
israniad *m* (**·au**) subdivision.
isrannu *v* to subdivide.
isymwybod *m* subconscious.
ith·faen *m* (**·feini**) granite.
iwrch *m* (**iyrchod**) roebuck.
iyrches *f* roe-deer.

J

J *abb* joule (J).
jac codi baw *m* JCB.
jac-y-do *m* jackdaw.
jadan, jaden *f* harridan.
jamio *v* to jam.
jariaid *f* (**jareidiau**) jarful.
jazz *m* jazz.
jêl *f* jail.
jest *adv* almost.
jib *m* (**·s**) grimace.
jibidêrs *pl* smithereens.
ji-binc *m* (**jibincod**) chaffinch.
jîns *m* jeans.
jiráff *m* (**jiraffod**) giraffe.
jiwbilî *m/f* (**jiwbilîau**) jubilee.
jòb *f* (**jobsys**) job.
jôc *f* (**jôcs**) joke.
jocan *v* to joke.
jocôs *adj* contented.
joch *m* (**·iau**) swig.
jolihoetio, jolihoitio *v* to gallivant.
jŵg *m/f* (**jygiau**) jug.
jygaid *m* jugful.

L

labelu *v* to label.
labor·dy *m* (**·dai**) laboratory.
lafant *m* lavender.
lagŵn *m* (**lagwnau**) lagoon.
lambastio *v* to lambaste.
lamineiddio *v* to laminate.
lan *adv* up.
lander *m* (**·i, ·au**) gutter.
lansio *v* to launch.
lapio *v* to wrap.
larts *adj* conceited.
lar·wm *m* (**·ymau**) alarm.
las *m* (**lasys**) lace.
law yn llaw *adj* hand-in-hand.
lawnt *f* (**·iau**) lawn.
lawr *adv* down. • *m* **bara lawr** laver bread.
lecsiwn *f* (**lecsiynau**) election.
ledio *v* to lead.
ledled *adv* throughout.
lefain *m* leaven.
lefeinio *v* to leaven.
lefr·en *f* (**·od**) leveret.
leinio *v* to line; to thrash.
lelog *m/f* lilac.
lembo *m* numbskull.
lemonêd, lemwnêd *m* lemonade.
les *f* (**·oedd**) lease; (**·au**) lace.
letysen *f* (**letys**) lettuce.
libart *m* mountain pasture.
lifr·ai *m/f* (**·eiau**) livery.
ling-di-long, linc-di-lonc *adv* leisurely.
lili *f* (**liliau**) lily.
lindysen *f* (**lindys**) caterpillar.
lindysyn *m* (**lindys**) caterpillar.
lintel *f* (**·ydd**) window-sill.
liw dydd, liw nos *adv* by (day, night).
lobi *m/f* (**lobïau**) lobby.
locust *m* (**·iaid**) locust.
lodes *f* (**·i, ·au**) girl.
loetran *v* to loiter.
lòg *m* (**logiau**) log.
lol *f* nonsense.
lolf·a *f* (**·eydd**) lounge.
lolian *v* to joke; to lounge.
lôn *f* (**lonydd**) lane.
loncian *v* to jog.
lonc·iwr *m* (**·wyr**) jogger.
lordio *v* to domineer.
lorri *f* (**lorïau**) lorry.
losin *m/pl* sweets.
lwcus *adj* lucky.
lwfans *m* (**·au**) allowance.
lwmp(yn) *m* (**lympiau**) lump.

Ll

llabed *f* (**·au**) flap; lapel.
llab·wst *m* (**·ystau**) lout.
llabyddio *v* to stone.
llac *adj* slack.
llaca *m* muck.
llacio *v* to slacken.
llacrwydd *m* laxity.
llach, lach *f* (**·iau**) lash.
llachar *adj* glittering.
lladmerydd *m* (**·ion**) interpreter.
lladrad *m* (**·au**) theft.
lladradaidd *adj* surreptitious.
lladrata *v* to steal.
lladron *see* **lleidr**.
lladd *v* to kill.
lladd-dy *m* (**lladd-dai**) abattoir.
lladdfa *f* massacre.
llaes *adj* flowing.
llaesu *v* to slacken.
llaeth *m* milk.
llaeth·dy *m* (**·dai**) dairy.
llaethog *adj* milky.
llafar *adj* vocal.
llafarganu *v* to chant.
llafar·iad *f* (**·iaid**) vowel.
llafn *m* (**·au**) blade.
llafur *m* labour; toil.
llafurio *v* to toil.
llafurus *adj* laborious.
llafur·wr *m* (**·wyr**) labourer.
llai *adj* smaller.
llaid *m* mud.
llain *f* (**lleiniau**) strip (of land).
llais *m* (**lleisiau**) voice.
llaith *adj* damp.
llall *pron* (**lleill**) other.
llam *m* (**·au**) leap.
llamhidydd *m* (**llamidyddion**) porpoise.
llamsachus *adj* prancing.
llamu *v* to leap.
llan *f* (**·nau**) (parish) church.
llanastr *m* disorder.
llanc *m* (**·iau**) lad.
llances *f* (**·i, ·au**) lass.
llannerch *f* (**llennyrch**) glade.
llanw *v* to fill. • *m* (**·au**) tide.
llariaidd *adj* benign.
llarieidd-dra *m* meekness.
llarieiddio *v* to soothe.
llarpiau *pl* tatters.
llarpio *v* to tear to shreds.
llarpiog *adj* tattered.
llarwydden *f* (**llarwydd**) larch.
llatai *m* (**llateion**) negesydd cariad.
llath, llathen *f* (**·au, ·ni**) yard.
llathaid *f* (**llatheidi, llatheidiau**) yard's length.
llathraid, llathraidd *adj* glossy.
llau *see* **lleuen**.
llaw *m* (**dwylo, dwylaw**) hand.
llawcio, llowcio *v* to gulp.
llawchwith *adj* left-handed.
llawdriniaeth *f* (**·au**) operation.
llawdrwm *adj* hypercritical.
llawdde *adj* right-handed.

llawen *adj* happy.
llawenhau *v* to rejoice.
llawenychu *v* to rejoice.
llawenydd *m* happiness.
llawer *adv* much.
llawes *f* (**llewys**) sleeve.
llawfeddyg *m* (**·on**) surgeon.
llawfeddygaeth *f* surgery.
llaw-fer *f* shorthand.
llawfor·wyn *f* (**·ynion**) maidservant.
llawlyfr *m* (**·au**) handbook.
llawn *adj* full. • *adv* quite.
llawnder, llawndra *m* fullness.
llawr *m* (**lloriau**) floor.
llawryf *m* (**·au, ·oedd**) laurel.
llawysgrif *f* (**·au**) manuscript.
llawysgrifen *f* handwriting.
LICLl *abb* Lowest Common Multiple (LCM).
lle *m* (**·oedd, ·fydd**) place.
llecyn *m* (**·nau**) spot.
llech, llechen *f* (**llechi**) slate.
llech·faen *m/f* (**·feini**) slate.
llechres *f* (**·i**) list.
llechu *v* to lurk.
llechwedd *m* (**·au**) hillside.
llechwraidd *adj* furtive.
lled *m* width. • *adv* fairly.
lledaenu *v* to spread.
lled-ddargludydd *m* (**·ion**) semiconductor.
lled·en *f* (**·od**) plaice.
llediaith *f* twang.
lednais *adj* courteous.
lleidneisrwydd *m* modesty.
lled-orwedd *v* to recline.
lledr *m* leather.
lledred *m* (**·au**) latitude.
lledrith *m* magic.
lledrithiol *adj* illusory.
lledu *v* to widen.
lleddf *adj* mournful; minor (music).
lleddfu *v* to soothe.
lledd(ir) *from* **lladd.**
llef *f* (**·au**) cry.
llefain *v* to cry.
llefair *from* **llefaru.**
llefaru *v* to speak.
llefarydd *m* spokesperson.
llefelyn, llyfelyn *m* (**·od**) sty.
lleferydd *m/f* speech.
llefn *adj* (*f*) smooth.
llefrith *m* milk.
llefydd *see* **lle.**
llegach *adj* feeble.
lleng *f* (**·oedd**) legion.
llengfil·wr *m* (**·wyr**) legionnaire.
lleiaf *adj* smallest.
lleiafrif *m* (**·oedd**) minority.
lleiafrifol *adj* minority.
lleiaf·swm *m* (**·symiau**) minimum.
lleian *f* (**·od**) nun.
lleian·dy *m* (**·dai**) nunnery.
lleidiog *adj* muddy.
lleidr *m* (**lladron**) thief.
lleidd·iad *m* (**·iaid**) killer.
lleihad *m* decrease.
lleihau *v* to lessen.
lleill *see* **llall.**
lleiniau *see* **llain.**
lleinw *from* **llanw.**
lleisiau *see* **llais.**
lleisio *v* to voice.
lleisiol *adj* vocal.
lleisiwr *m* vocalist.
lleithder *m* moisture.

llem *adj* (*f*) acute.
llem(ir) *from* **llamu.**
llen *f* (**·ni**) curtain.
llên *f* literature.
llencyn *m* stripling.
llencyndod *m* adolescence.
llengar *adj* literary.
llengig *m/f* diaphragm.
llên-ladrad *m* (**·au**) plagiarism.
llenni *see* **llen.**
llennyrch *see* **llannerch.**
llenor *m* (**·ion**) author.
llenw(ir) *from* **llanw.**
llenydda *v* to practise literature.
llenyddiaeth *f* (**·au**) literature.
llenyddol *adj* literary.
lleol *adj* local.
lleoli *v* to locate.
lleoliad *m* (**·au**) location.
llercian *v* to lurk.
lles *m* benefit.
llesâd *m* benefit.
llesáu *v* to be of benefit.
llesg *adj* weak.
llesgáu *v* to weaken.
llesgedd *m* weakness.
llesm·air *m* (**·eiriau**) swoon.
llesmeirio *v* to swoon.
llesmeiriol *adj* enchanting.
llesol *adj* beneficial.
llest·air *m* (**·eiriau**) obstruction.
llesteirio *v* to impede.
llestr *m* (**·i**) dish; vessel.
lletach *from* **llydan.**
lle tân *m* (**llefydd tân**) fireplace.
lletchwith *adj* awkward.
lletchwithdod *m* awkwardness.
lletem *f* (**·au**) wedge.
lletraws *adj* diagonal.
lletwad *f* (**·au**) ladle.
llety *m* (**·au**) lodging house.
lletya *v* to lodge.
lletygarwch *m* hospitality.
llethol *adj* overpowering.
llethr *m/f* (**·au**) slope.
llethrog *adj* sloping.
llethu *v* to overwhelm.
lleuad *f* (**·au**) moon.
lleuen *f* (**llau**) louse.
lleufer *m* light.
lleuog *adj* lousy.
lleurith *m* (**·iau**) mirage.
llew *m* (**·od**) lion.
llewes *f* lioness.
llewpart *m* (**·iaid**) leopard.
llewych *m* light.
llewyg *m* (**·on**) swoon.
llewygu *v* to faint.
llewyrch *m* brightness.
llewyrchu *v* to shine.
llewyrchus *adj* flourishing.
llewys *see* **llawes.**
lleyg *adj* lay.
lleygwr *m* (**·wyr**) layman.
LlGC *abb* Llyfrgell Genedlaethol Cymru.
lli·ain *m* (**·einiau**) towel; linen.
lliaws *m* multitude.
llid *m* wrath.
llidiar·t *m/f* (**·dau**) gate.
llidiog, llidus *adj* inflamed.
llidiowgrwydd *m* wrath.
llieiniau *see* **lliain.**
llif, lli *m* (**·(f)ogydd**) current.
llif *f* (**·iau**) saw.
llifanu *v* to whet.

llifddor *f* (**·au**) floodgate.
llifeiriant *m* spate.
llifeirio *v* to flow.
llifio *v* to saw.
llifion *see* **llifyn.**
llifo *v* to gush; to dye; to whet.
llifogydd *see* **llif.**
llifol·au *m* (**·euadau**) floodlight.
llifoleuo *v* to floodlight.
llifyddol *adj* fluid.
llifyn *m* (**·nau, llifion**) dye.
llilin *adj* streamlined.
llin *m* flax.
llinach *f* lineage.
llindagu *v* to strangle.
llinell *f* (**·au**) line.
lliniarol *adj* soothing.
lliniaru *v* to alleviate.
llinos *f* (**·od**) linnet.
llinyn *m* (**·nau**) string.
llinynnol *adj* stringed.
llipa *adj* limp.
llipryn *m* (**·nod**) weakling.
llith *f* (**·au, ·oedd**) lesson. • *m* (**·iau**) mash.
llithio *v* to entice.
llithren *f* slide.
llithriad *m* (**·au**) slip.
llithrig *adj* slippery.
llithrigrwydd *m* slipperiness.
llithro *v* to slip.
lliw *m* colour.
lliwgar *adj* colourful.
lliwio *v* to colour.
lliwur *m* (**·au**) dye.
llo *m/f* (**·i, ·eau**) calf.
lloc *m* (**·iau**) enclosure.
llocio *v* to pen.
lloches *f* (**·au**) refuge.
llochesu *v* to shelter.
llodig *adj* in heat (of sow).
llodrau *pl* trousers.
lloer *f* (**·au**) moon.
lloeren *f* (**·ni, ·nau**) satellite.
lloergan *m* moonlight.
lloerig *adj* mad.
llofnod *m* (**·ion, ·au**) signature.
llofnodi *v* to sign.
llofr *adj* (*f*) cowardly.
llofrudd *m* (**·ion**) murderer.
llofruddiaeth *f* (**·au**) murder.
llofruddio *v* to murder.
lloffa *v* to glean.
lloffion *pl* gleanings.
llofft *f* (**·ydd**) upstairs.
lloff·wr *m* (**·wyr**) gleaner.
llog *m* (**·au**) interest.
llogell *f* (**·au**) pocket.
llogi *v* to hire.
llog·wr *m* (**·wyr**) hirer.
llong *f* (**·au**) ship.
llongddrylliad *m* (**·au**) shipwreck.
llong·wr *m* (**·wyr**) sailor.
lloi *see* **llo.**
llom *adj* (*f*) bare.
llon *adj* happy.
llond *m* full.
llonder *m* gaiety.
llongyfarch *v* to congratulate.
llongyfarchiad *m* (**·au, llongyfarchion**) congratulation.
llonned *from* **llon.**
llonni *v* to cheer.
llonnod *m* (**llonodau**) sharp (music).
llonydd *adj* still. • *m* quiet.
llonyddu *v* to still.

llonyddwch *m* stillness.
lloriau *see* **llawr**.
llorio *v* to floor.
llorp *f* (**·iau**) shaft.
llorwedd *adj* horizontal.
llosg *adj* burning.
llosgach *m* incest.
llosgadwy *adj* combustible.
llosgfynydd *m* (**·oedd**) volcano.
llosgi *v* to burn.
llosgiad *m* (**·au**) burn.
llosg·wrn *m* (**·yrnau**) tail.
llosgydd *m* (**·ion**) incinerator.
llostlydan *m* (**·od**) beaver.
llsgr. *abb* manuscript (ms).
llu *m* (**·oedd**) throng.
llucheden *f* (**lluched**) thunderbolt.
lluchio *v* to throw.
lluch·iwr *m* (**·wyr**) thrower.
lludw, lludu *m* ash.
lludded *m* fatigue.
lluddedig *adj* fatigue.
lluest *m* tent.
llugoer *adj* tepid.
lluman *m* (**·au**) banner.
llumanu *v* to flag.
lluman·wr *m* (**·wyr**) linesman.
llun *m* (**·iau**) picture.
Llun *m* Monday.
llungop·i *m* (**·ïau**) photocopy.
lluniad *m* (**·au**) drawing.
lluniadu *v* to draw.
lluniaeth *m* sustenance.
lluniaidd *adj* graceful.
llunio *v* to fashion.
llun·iwr *m* (**·wyr**) maker.
lluo *see* **llyo, lluo**.
lluosflwydd *adj* perennial.
lluosi *v* to multiply.
lluosiad *m* (**·au**) multiplication.
lluosill *adj* polysyllabic.
lluosog *adj* numerous; plural.
lluosogi *v* to multiply.
lluosrif *m* (**·au**) multiple.
lluo·swm *m* (**·symiau**) product (mathematics).
llurgunio *v* to distort.
llurig *f* (**·au**) cuirass.
llurs *f* (**·od**) razorbill.
llusen *f* (**llus, llusi**) whinberry.
llusern *m* (**·au**) lamp.
llusg *adj* drawn.
llusgo *v* to drag.
llutrod *m* mire.
lluwch *m* (**·feydd**) snowdrift.
lluwchio *v* to drift.
llw *m* (**·on**) oath.
llwch *m* dust.
llwdn *m* (**llydnod**) young animal.
llwfr *adj* cowardly.
llwfrgi, llyfrgi *m* coward.
llwfrdra *m* cowardice.
llwglyd *adj* famished.
llwgr *adj* corrupt.
llwgrwobrwyo *v* to bribe.
llwgu *v* to starve.
llwm *adj* bare.
llwnc *m* gullet.
llwncdestun *m* a toast.
llwrw *adv*: **llwrw ei ben** headlong.
llwy *f* (**·au**) spoon.
llwy·aid *f* (**·eidiau**) spoonful.
llwybr *m* (**·au**) path.
llwybreiddio *v* to make one's way.
llwyd *adj* grey.
llwydaidd *adj* drab.

llwydni, llwydi *m* mildew.
llwydo *v* to turn mouldy.
llwydrew *m* hoar frost.
llwydrewi *v* to frost up.
llwyddiannus *adj* successful.
llwyddian·t, llwydd *m* (**·nau**) success.
llwyddo *v* to succeed.
llwyfan *m/f* (**·nau**) stage.
llwyfandir *m* (**·oedd**) plateau.
llwyfannu *v* to stage.
llwyfen *f* (**llwyf**) elm.
llwyn *m* (**·i**) grove. • *f* (**·au**) loin.
llwynog *m* (**·od**) fox.
llwynoges *f* vixen.
llwyr *adj* complete.
llwyrymwrthod·wr *m* (**·wyr**) teetotaller.
llwyted *from* **llwyd**.
llwyth *m* (**·i**) load; (**·au**) tribe.
llwytho *v* to load.
llwythog *adj* laden.
llycrach *from* **llwgr**.
llychlyd *adj* dusty.
Llychlyn·nwr *m* (**·wyr**) Viking.
llychwino *v* to tarnish.
llydain *adj* (*pl*) wide.
llydan *adj* wide.
llydnu *v* to foal.
llyfn *adj* smooth.
llyfnder, llyfndra *m* smoothness.
llyfnhau *v* to smooth.
llyfnu *v* to harrow.
llyfr *m* (**·au**) book.
llyfrach *from* **llwfr**.
llyfrbryf *m* (**·ed**) bookworm.
llyfrgell *f* (**·oedd**) library.
llyfrgell·ydd *m* (**·wyr**) librarian.
llyfrgi *see* **llwfrgi**.
llyfrith·en *f* (**·od**) sty.
llyfrwerth·wr *m* (**·wyr**) bookseller.
llyfryddiaeth *f* (**·au**) bibliography.
llyfryn *m* (**·nau**) booklet.
llyfu, llyo *v* to lick.
llyffant *m* (**·od**) toad; frog.
llyffeth·air *f* (**·eiriau**) fetter.
llyffetheirio *v* to shackle.
llyg *m* shrew.
llygad *m* (**llygaid**) eye.
llygad-dynnu *v* to attract.
llygad-dyst *m* (**·ion**) eyewitness.
llygad maharen *m* (**llygaid meheryn**) limpet.
llygad y dydd *m* (**llygaid y dydd**) daisy.
llygadu *v* to eye.
llygaeron *pl* cranberries.
llygaid *see* **llygad**.
llygatgam *adj* squint-eyed.
llygatgraff *adj* sharp-eyed.
llygedyn *m* gleam.
llygoden *f* (**llygod**) mouse.
llygoden fawr *f* (**llygod mawr**) rat.
llygoden gota *f* (**llygod cwta**) guinea-pig.
llygotwr *m* mouser.
llygredig *adj* corrupt.
llygredigaeth *f* corruption.
llygredd *m* depravity.
llygru *v* to contaminate.
llynges *f* (**·au**) navy.
llyngesydd *m* admiral.
llyngyren *f* (**llyngyr**) tapeworm.
llym *adj* sharp.
llym·aid *m* (**·eidiau**) sip.
llym·arch *m* (**·eirch**) oyster.

llymder *m* sharpness.
llymed *from* **llwm** *and* **llym**.
llymeitian *v* to tipple.
llymion *from* **llwm** *and* **llym**.
llymru *n* flummery.
llyn *m* (**·noedd**) lake.
llyncu *v* to swallow.
llynedd *adv* last year.
llyo *v* to lick.
llys *m* (**·oedd**) court.
llys·chwaer *f* (**·chwiorydd**) stepsister.
llysenw *m* (**·au**) nickname.
llys·fab *m* (**·feibion**) stepson.
llysfam *f* (**·au**) stepmother.
llysferch *f* (**·ed**) stepdaughter.
llys·frawd *m* (**·frodyr**) stepbrother.
llysg *from* **llosgi**.
llysgen·hadaeth *f* (**·adaethau**) embassy.
llysgen·nad *m* (**·hadon**) ambassador.
llysieueg *f* botany.
llysieu·wr, **llysieuydd** *m* (**·wyr**) herbalist; vegetarian.
llysieuyn *m* (**llysiau**) plant.
llysleuen *f* (**llyslau**) aphid.
llysnafedd *m* mucus.
llystad *m* (**·au**) stepfather.
llystyfiant *m* vegetation.
llysysydd *m* (**·ion**) herbivore.
llysywen *f* (**llyswennod, llysywod**) eel.
llythrennau *see* **llythyren**.
llythrennedd *m* literacy.
llythrennog *adj* literate.
llythrennol *adj* literal.
llythrennu *v* to inscribe.
llythyr *m* (**·au, ·on**) letter.
llythyr·dy *m* (**·dai**) post office.
llythyren *f* (**llythrennau**) letter.
llythyru *v* to correspond.
llythyr·wr *m* (**·wyr**) letter writer.
llyw *m* (**·iau**) rudder.
llywaeth *adj* tame.
llyweth *f* (**·au**) ringlet.
llywio *v* to steer.
llywionen, llywanen *f* sheet.
llyw·iwr *m* (**·yr**) helmsman.
llywodraeth *f* (**·au**) government.
llywodraethol *adj* governing.
llywodraethu *v* to govern.
llywodraeth·wr *m* (**·wyr**) governor.
llywydd *m* (**·ion**) president.
llywyddiaeth *f* presidency.
llywyddu *v* to preside.

M

m *abb* metre.
mab *m* (**meibion**) son.
maban *m* baby.
maboed *m* childhood.
mabolgampau *pl* athletics.
mabsant *m* patron saint.
mabwysiad *m* adoption.
mabwysiadu *v* to adopt.
macrell *m/f* (**mecryll**) mackerel.
macsu *v* to brew.
macwy *m* (**·aid**) page (boy).
mach *m* (**meichiau**) surety.

machlud *v* to set. • *m* sunset.
mad *adj* seemly.
madarch *pl* mushrooms.
madfall *f* (**-od**) lizard.
madroni *v* to become giddy.
madru *v* to putrefy.
madruddyn *m* cartilage.
maddau *v* to forgive.
maddeuant *m* forgiveness.
maddeugar *adj* forgiving.
maddeuol *adj* pardoning.
mae (*from* **bod**) is, are.
maeddu *v* to conquer.
maen *m* (**main, meini**) stone.
maenor, maenol *f* (**-au**) manor.
maenor·dy *m* (**-dai**) manor-house.
maentumio *v* to maintain.
maer *m* (**meiri**) mayor.
maeres *f* mayoress.
maes *m* (**meysydd**) field.
maestir *m* (**-oedd**) plain.
maestref *f* (**-i**) suburb.
maesu *v* to field.
maes·wr *m* (**-wyr**) fielder.
maeth *m* nourishment.
maethlon *adj* nourishing.
mafonen *f* (**mafon**) raspberry.
magïen *f* (**magïod**) glow-worm.
magl *f* (**-au**) snare.
maglu *v* to snare.
magnel *f* (**-au**) cannon.
magnetedd *m* magnetism.
magneteiddio *v* to magnetise.
magu *v* to breed.
magwraeth *f* upbringing.
magwyr *f* (**-ydd**) wall.
maharen *m* (**meheryn**) ram.
mai *conj* that.
Mai *m* May.
maidd *m* whey. • *v from* **meiddio**.
main *adj* thin. • *pl see* **maen**.
mainc *f* (**meinciau**) bench.
maint *m* (**meintiau**) size.
maintioli *m* stature.
maip *see* **meipen**.
maith *adj* long.
mâl *adj* ground.
malais *m* malice.
maldod *m* pampering.
maldodi *v* to pamper.
maleisus *adj* malicious.
maleithiau *pl* chilblains.
malio *v* to heed.
malu *v* to grind.
malurio *v* to pulverise.
malwen, malwoden *f* (**malwod**) snail.
malwr *m* grinder.
mall *adj* blasted.
malltod *m* blight.
mam *f* (**-au**) mother.
mamaeth *f* nurse.
mamfaeth *f* foster-mother.
mam-gu *f* grandmother.
mamiaith *f* mother-tongue.
mamog *f* (**-iaid**) pregnant sheep.
mamolaeth *f* maternity.
mamol·yn *m* (**-ion**) mammal.
man *m* (**-nau**) place. • *f* **yn y fan** immediately.
mân *adj* small.
manblu *pl* down.
man·dwll *m* (**-dyllau**) pore.
mandyllog *adj* porous.
maneg *f* (**menig**) glove.
mangre *f* (**-oedd**) place.

manion *adj* (*pl*) trivia.
mannau *see* **man.**
mant·ais *f* (**·eision**) advantage.
manteisio *v* to take advantage.
manteisiol *adj* advantageous.
mantell *f* (**mentyll**) mantle.
mantol *f* (**·ion**) balance.
mantolen *f* (**·ni**) balance-sheet.
mân-werthu *v* to retail.
mân-werth·wr *m* (**·wyr**) retailer.
manwl *adj* detailed.
manwl-gywir *adj* precise.
manylrwydd, manyldeb, manylder, manyldra *m* the detail.
manylu *v* to detail.
manyl·yn *m* (**·ion**) a detail.
mapio *v* to map.
map·iwr *m* (**·wyr**) cartographer.
marblen *f* (**marblis, marblys**) marble.
marcio *v* to mark.
march *m* (**meirch**) stallion.
marchnad *f* (**·oedd**) market.
marchnata *v* to market.
marchnat·wr *m* (**·wyr**) merchant.
marchnerth *m* horsepower.
marchog *m* (**·ion**) knight.
marchogaeth *v* to ride.
marchwellt *m* coarse grass.
marian *m* strand.
marlat, marlad *m* drake.
marmor *m* marble.
marsiandïaeth *f* merchandise.
marsiand·ïwr *m* (**·ïwyr**) merchant.
marswpial *m* (**·od**) marsupial.
marw *v* to die. • *adj* dead.
marwaidd *adj* lifeless.
marwdon *f* dandruff.
marweidd-dra *m* sluggishness.
marwnad *f* (**·au**) elegy.
marwol *adj* lethal.
marwolaeth *f* (**·au**) death.
marworyn *m* (**marwor**) ember.
marwydos *pl* embers.
màs *m* (**masau**) mass (physics).
ma's, maes *adv* out.
masarnen *f* (**masarn**) maple.
masgl *m* (**·au**) pod.
masi·wn *m* (**·yniaid**) mason.
masnach *f* (**·au**) trade.
masnachol *adj* commercial.
masnachu *v* to trade.
masnach·wr *m* (**·wyr**) merchant.
maswedd *m* wantonness.
masweddol, masweddus *adj* ribald.
mas·wr *m* (**·wyr**) outside half.
mater *m* (**·ion**) matter.
materol *adj* materialistic.
matr·as *m/f* (**·esi**) mattress.
mats·en *f* (**·ys**) match.
math *f* (**·au**) sort.
mathemateg *f* mathematics.
mathemategol *adj* mathematical.
mathemategwr, mathemategydd *m* mathematician.
mawl *m* worship. • *v from* **moli.**
mawnen *f* (**mawn**) peat.
mawnog *f* (**·ydd**) peat bog.
mawr *adj* big.
mawredd *m* grandeur.
mawreddog *adj* pompous.
mawrfrydig *adj* magnanimous.
mawrhau *v* to enlarge.
mawrhydi *m* majesty.
Mawrth *m* Tuesday; March; Mars.
mawrygu *v* to glorify.

MC *abb* Methodist(iaid) Calfinaidd.
mebyd, maboed *m* childhood.
mecaneg *f* mechanics.
mecan·waith *m* (**·weithiau**) mechanism.
mecanyddol *adj* mechanical.
mecryll *see* **macrell.**
mechnïaeth *f* bail.
medel *f* (**·au**) reaping.
medel·wr *m* (**·wyr**) reaper.
medi *v* to reap.
Medi *m* September.
medr *m* (**·au**) skill.
medru *v* to be able.
medrus *adj* skilful.
medrusrwydd *m* skill.
medrydd *m* (**·ion**) gauge.
medd *m* mead.
medd, meddai *v* says, said.
meddal *adj* soft.
meddalnod *m* (**·au**) flat (music).
meddalu *v* to soften.
meddalwch *m* softness.
meddalwedd *m* software.
medd-dod, meddwdod *m* intoxication.
meddiannau *see* **meddiant.**
meddiannol *adj* possessive.
meddiannu *v* to take possession of.
meddian·t *m* (**·nau**) possession.
meddu *v* to possess.
meddw *adj* drunk.
meddwdod *m* drunkenness.
meddwi *v* to get drunk.
medd·wl *m* (**·yliau**) the mind. • *v* to think.
meddwol *adj* intoxicating.
meddw·yn *m* (**·on**) drunkard.
meddyg *m* (**·on**) doctor.
meddygaeth *f* medicine.
meddyg·fa *f* (**·feydd**) surgery.
meddyginiaeth *f* (**·au**) medication.
meddygol *adj* medical.
meddylgar *adj* thoughtful.
meddyl(iaf) *from* **meddwl.**
meddyliau *see* **meddwl.**
meddyliol *adj* mental.
meddyl·iwr *m* (**·wyr**) thinker.
mefusen *f* (**mefus**) strawberry.
meg(ir) *from* **magu.**
megin *f* (**·au**) bellows.
megis *conj* like.
Mehefin *m* June.
meheryn *see* **maharen.**
meibion *see* **mab.**
meicrobioleg *m/f* microbiology.
meicro-brosesydd *m* microprocessor.
meicro-sglod·yn *m* (**·ion**) microchip.
meich·iad *m* (**·iaid**) swine-herd.
meichiau *m* surety.
meidrol *adj* finite.
meiddio *v* to dare.
meilart *m* drake.
meillionen *f* (**meillion**) clover.
meimio *v* to mime.
meinciau *see* **mainc.**
meincnod *m* (**·au**) benchmark.
meinder *m* slenderness.
meindio *v* to mind.
meined *from* **main.**
meingefn *m* small of the back; spine (of book).
meini *see* **maen.**
meinion *adj* (*pl*) slender.
meinir *f* maiden.

meintiau *see* **maint**.
meinwe *m* (**·oedd**) tissue.
meinwen *f* maiden.
meipen *f* (**maip**) swede.
meirch *see* **march**.
meiri *see* **maer**.
meirioli *v* to thaw.
meirw, meirwon *pl* the dead.
meistr *m* (**·i, ·iaid**) master.
meistres *f* (**·i**) mistress.
meistrolaeth *f* mastery.
meistrolgar *adj* masterly.
meistroli *v* to master.
meitin *m* some time.
meitrog *adj* mitred.
meithed *from* **maith**.
meithrin *v* to nourish.
meithrin·fa *f* (**·feydd**) nursery.
mêl *m* honey.
mela *v* to gather honey.
melan *f* depression.
melen *adj* (*f*) yellow.
melfaréd *m* corduroy.
melfed *m* velvet.
melfedaidd *adj* velvety.
melin *f* (**·au**) mill.
melinydd *m* miller.
mel(ir) *from* **malu**.
melodaidd *adj* melodious.
melod·i *f* (**·ïau**) melody.
melyn *adj* yellow.
melynaidd *adj* yellowish.
melynder, melyndra *m* yellowness.
melyngoch *adj* orange.
melynu *v* to yellow.
melys *adj* sweet.
melysion *pl* sweets.
melyster, melystra *m* sweetness.
melysu *v* to sweeten.
mellten *f* (**mellt**) lightning.
melltennu, melltio *v* to flash.
melltigedig *adj* accursed.
melltith *f* (**·ion**) curse.
melltithio *v* to curse.
memr·wn *m* (**·ynau**) parchment.
men *f* (**·ni**) wagon.
mên *adj* mean.
mendio *v* to mend.
menig *see* **maneg**.
menni *see* **men**.
menter, mentr *f* venture.
mentro *v* to venture.
mentrus *adj* adventurous.
mentr·wr *m* (**·wyr**) entrepreneur.
mentyll *see* **mantell**.
menu, mennu *v* to affect.
menyn, ymenyn *m* butter.
menyw *f* (**·od**) woman.
mêr *m* marrow.
merch *f* (**·ed**) girl; daughter.
Mercher *m* Wenesday; Mercury.
mercheta *v* to womanise.
merchetaidd *adj* effeminate.
merchyg *from* **marchogaeth**.
merdd·wr *m* (**·yfroedd**) stagnant water.
merfaidd *adj* insipid.
merl·en *f* (**·od**) pony (female).
merlota *v* to pony-trek.
merl·yn *m* (**·od**) pony.
merllyd *adj* insipid.
merllys·en *m* (**merllys, ·iau**) asparagus.
merthyr *m* (**·on**) martyr.
merthyrdod *m* martyrdom.
merthyru *v* to martyr.

merwino *v* to benumb.
mesen *f* (**mes**) acorn.
mesmereiddio *v* to mesmerise.
mesul *prep* by.
mesur, mesuro *v* to measure.
mesur *m* (**·au**) measurement.
mesuradwy *adj* measurable.
mesuriad *m* (**·au**) measurement.
mesurydd *m* (**·ion**) meter.
metabolaeth *f* metabolism.
metel *m* (**·au**) metal.
metelaidd *adj* metallic.
meteleg *m/f* metallurgy.
meteoroleg *f* meteorology.
meteoroleg·ydd *m* (**·wyr**) meteorologist.
methdaliad *m* bankruptcy.
methdal·wr *m* (**·wyr**) bankrupt.
methedig *adj* disabled.
methian·t *m* (**·nau**) failure.
methodoleg *f* methodology.
methu *v* to fail.
meudwy *m* (**·aid, ·od**) hermit.
meudwyaidd *adj* retiring.
mewian, mewial *v* to mew.
mewn *prep* in.
mewnblyg *adj* introverted.
mewn·bwn *m* (**·bynnau**) input.
mewndirol *adj* inland.
mewnforio *v* to import.
mewnforion *pl* imports.
mewnfudo *v* to immigrate.
mewnfud·wr *m* (**·wyr**) immigrant.
mewnlifiad *m* influx.
mewnol *adj* internal.
mewn·wr *m* (**·wyr**) scrum half.
meysydd *see* **maes**.
mi *pron* I, me.
miaren *f* (**mieri**) bramble.
microbrosesydd *m* (**·ion**) microprocessor.
microdon *f* (**·nau**) microwave.
microgyfrifiadur *m* (**·on**) microcomputer.
mieri *see* **miaren**.
mig *f*: **chwarae mig** to play hide and seek.
mignen *f* (**·ni**) marsh.
mig·wrn *m* (**·yrnau**) ankle; knuckle.
mil *m* (**·od**) animal.
mil *f* (**·oedd**) thousand.
milain, mileinig *adj* vicious.
milfed *adj* thousandth.
milfeddyg *m* (**·on**) vet.
milfeddygol *adj* veterinary.
milflwyddiant *m* millennium.
mil·gi *m* (**·gwn**) greyhound.
mili·ast *f* (**·eist**) female greyhound.
mili·wn *f* (**·ynau**) million.
miliwnydd, miliynydd *m* (**miliynyddion**) millionaire.
mil·wr *m* (**·wyr**) soldier.
milwriaethus *adj* militant.
milwrio *v* to militate.
milwrol *adj* military.
mill *see* **millyn**.
milltir *f* (**·oedd**) mile.
millyn *m* (**mill**) violet.
min *m* (**·ion**) edge.
miniog *adj* sharp.
minlliw *m* lipstick.
minnau, innau *pron, conj* I for my part.
min·tai *f* (**·teioedd**) troop.
mintys *m* mint.
min·ws *m* (**·ysau**) minus.

mirain *adj* fair.
mireinder *m* beauty.
miri *m* merriment.
mis *m* (**·oedd**) month.
misglen *f* (**misgl**) mussel.
misglwyf *m* menses.
misol *adj* monthly.
misol·yn *m* (**·ion**) (monthly) magazine.
mitsio *v* to play truant.
miw *m*: **siw na miw** no sound.
mo *abb* no.
mochaidd *adj* filthy.
mochyn *m* (**moch**) pig.
mochynnaidd *adj* filthy.
moderneiddio *v* to modernise.
modfedd *f* (**·i**) inch.
modrwy *f* (**·au**) ring.
modrwyog *adj* curly.
modryb *f* (**·edd**) aunt.
modur *m* (**·on**) automobile.
modur·dy *m* (**·dai**) garage.
moduro *v* to motor.
modur·wr *m* (**·wyr**) motorist.
modd *m* (**·ion**) means.
modd *m* (**·au**) mode.
moddion *m* medicine.
moel *adj* bald.
moeli *v* to become bald.
moelni *m* baldness.
moelyd *v* to topple.
moes *v* give!
moesau *pl* morals.
moesgar *adj* courteous.
moesgarwch *m* politeness.
moesol *adj* moral.
moesoldeb *m* morality.
moeswers *f* (**·i**) moral.
moesymgrymu *v* to bow.
moethus *adj* sumptuous.
moethusrwydd *m* luxury.
mogfa *f* asthma.
mogi, mygu *v* to smother.
mohoni, moni *from* **mo.**
molawd *m/f* eulogy.
moli *v* to praise.
moliannu *v* to praise.
molian·t *m* (**·nau**) praise.
moll *adj* (*f*) sultry.
mollt *m* (**myllt**) wether (sheep).
moment·wm *m* (**·a**) momentum.
monarchiaeth *f* monarchy.
monopoli *m* (**monopolïau**) monopoly.
mon·sŵn *m* (**·synau**) monsoon.
mor *adv* as; so.
môr *m* (**moroedd**) sea.
mor·daith *f* (**·deithiau**) voyage.
mordwyo *v* to navigate.
morddwyd *f* (**·ydd**) thigh.
moresg *pl* sedge.
mor·fa *m* (**·feydd**) fen.
môr-farch *m* (**môr-feirch**) walrus.
morfil *m* (**·od**) whale.
môr-for·wyn *f* (**·ynion**) mermaid.
mor·fran *f* (**·frain**) cormorant.
morffoleg *m/f* morphology.
morg·ais *m* (**·eisi, ·eisiau**) mortgage.
morgeisio *v* to mortgage.
mor·glawdd *m* (**·gloddiau**) embankment.
morgrugyn *m* (**morgrug**) ant.
môr-hwch *f* (**môr-hychod**) dolphin.
morio *v* to sail.
môr-leidr *m* (**môr-ladron**) pirate.
morlo *m* (**·i**) seal.

morlyn *m* (**môr-lynnoedd**) lagoon.
morol *adj* maritime.
moronen *f* (**moron**) carrot.
morthwyl, mwrthwl *m* (**-ion, myrthylau**) hammer.
morthwylio *v* to hammer.
mor·wr *m* (**·wyr**) sailor.
morwriaeth *f* seamanship.
morwydden *f* (**morwydd**) mulberry.
morwyn *f* (**morynion**) maid.
morwyndod *m* virginity.
morwynol *adj* maiden.
moryd *f* (**·au**) estuary.
muchudd *m* jet.
mud, mudan *adj* silent.
mudandod *m* silence.
mudferwi *v* to simmer.
mudiad *m* (**·au**) movement.
mudian·t *m* (**·nau**) motion.
mudlosgi *v* to smoulder.
mudo *v* to migrate.
mudol *adj* migratory.
mul *m* (**·od**) mule.
mul·fran *f* (**·frain**) cormorant.
munud *m/f* minute.
mur *m* (**iau**) wall.
murddun *m* (**·nod**) ruin.
murlun *m* (**·iau**) mural.
murmur *m* (**·on**) murmur.
mursendod *m* affectation.
mursennaidd *adj* prudish.
musgrell *adj* feeble.
MW *abb* Merched y Wawr.
mwclis *pl* beads.
mwdlyd *adj* muddy.
mwdwl *m* (**mydylau**) haycock.
mẁg *m* (**mygiau**) mug.
mwg *m* smoke.
mwgwd *m* (**mygydau**) mask.
mwng *m* (**myngau**) mane.
mwlsyn *m* nincompoop.
mwll *adj* muggy.
mwm·i *m/f* (**·ïau**) mummy.
mwmian, mwmial *v* to mutter.
mwnci *m* (**mwncïod**) monkey.
mwnt *m* motte, mound.
mwnwgl *m* (**mynyglau**) neck.
mwrllwch *m* smog.
mwrn *adj* sultry.
mwrthwl *m* (**myrthylau**) hammer.
mwsogl, mwswgl *m* moss.
mwstás(h) *m* moustache.
mwstro *v* to hurry.
mwy *adj* more.
mwyach *adv* any more.
mwyaduron *see* **mwyhadur**.
mwyafrif *m* (**·au, ·oedd**) majority.
mwyalchen *f* (**mwyeilch**) blackbird.
mwyara *v* to gather blackberries.
mwyaren *f* (**mwyar**) blackberry.
mwydion *pl* pulp; pith.
mwydo *v* to soak.
mwydro *v* to confuse.
mwydyn *m* (**mwydod**) worm.
mwyeilch *see* **mwyalchen**.
mwyfwy *adv* increasingly.
mwyhadur *m* (**mwyaduron**) amplifier.
mwyhau *v* to enlarge.
mwyn *adj* fine.
mwyn *m* (**·au**) mineral.
mwynder *m* gentleness.
mwyneidd-dra *m* gentleness.
mwyn·glawdd *m* (**·gloddiau**) mine.
mwyngloddio *v* to mine.
mwynhad *m* pleasure.

mwynhau *v* to enjoy.
mwynian·t *m* (**·nau**) pleasure.
mwyn·wr *m* (**·wyr**) miner.
mwys *adj* ambiguous.
mwyth *adj* delicate.
mwythau *pl* caresses.
mwytho *v* to fondle.
m.y.a. *abb* milltir yr awr (mph).
mydr *m* (**·au**) metre.
mydryddiaeth *f* versification.
mydryddol *adj* metrical.
mydylau *see* **mwdwl**.
myfi *pron* me myself.
myfiol *adj* egoistic.
myfyrdod *m* (**·au**) meditation.
myfyrgar *adj* meditative.
myfyrio *v* to meditate.
myfyr·iwr *m* (**·wyr**) student.
myfyr·wraig *f* (**·wragedd**) (female) student.
mygdarth *m* fumes.
mygedol *adj* honorary.
mygiau *see* **m²g**.
myglyd *adj* smoky.
myglys *m* tobacco.
mygu *v* to smoke; to suffocate.
mygydau *see* **mwgwd**.
mygydu *v* to blindfold.
myngau *see* **mwng**.
mylled *from* **mwll**.
myllni *m* mugginess.
myllt *see* **mollt**.
MYM *abb* Mudiad Ysgolion Meithrin.
mympwy *m* (**·on**) whim.
mympwyol *adj* whimsical.
mymryn *m* (**·nau**) bit.
myn *m* (**·nod**) kid (goat).
myn *prep* by.
mynach *m* (**·od, mynaich**) monk.
mynachlog *f* (**·ydd**) monastery.
mynawyd *m* (**·au**) awl.
mync·i *m* (**·ïau**) hames.
mynd, myned *v* to go (*see* Appendix).
myned·fa *f* (**·feydd**) entrance.
mynediad *m* (**·au**) admission.
myneg·ai *m* (**·eion**) index.
myneg·bost *m* (**·byst**) signpost.
mynegeio *v* to index.
mynegi *v* to tell.
mynegian·t *m* (**·nau**) expression.
mynegol *adj* indicative.
mynnod *see* **myn**.
mynnu *v* to insist.
mynor *m* (**·ion**) marble.
mynwent *f* (**·ydd**) cemetery.
mynwes *f* (**·au**) bosom.
mynwesol *adj* dear.
mynych *adj* frequent.
mynychu *v* to frequent.
mynydd *m* (**·oedd**) mountain.
mynydd iâ *m* iceberg.
mynydda *v* mountaineer.
mynydd-dir *m* hill country.
mynyddig *adj* mountainous.
mynydd·wr *m* (**·wyr**) mountaineer.
mynyglau *see* **mwnwgl**.
myrdd, myrdd·iwn *m* (**·iynau**) myriad.
myrr *m* myrrh.
myrtwydden *f* (**myrtwydd**) myrtle.
myrthylau *see* **morthwyl, mwrthwl**.
mysg *m*: **ym mysg** midst.
myswynog *f* (**·ydd**) barren cow.
mytholeg *f* mythology.
mytholegol *adj* mythological.

N

N *abb* newton.
na *conj* nor. • *adv* no.
nacâd *m* refusal.
nacaol *adj* negative.
nacáu *v* to refuse.
nad *adv* not.
nâd *f* (**nadau**) cry.
nâd-fi'n-angof *m* forget-me-not.
Nadolig *m* (**·au**) Christmas.
Nadoligaidd *adj* Christmassy.
nadredd, nadroedd *see* **neidr**.
nadu *v* to bray; to prevent.
naddion *pl* chips.
naddo *adv* no.
naddu *v* to carve.
nag *conj* than.
nage *adv* not so.
nai *m* (**neiaint**) nephew.
naid *f* (**neidiau**) leap.
naid *from* **neidio**.
naill *pron* the one; either.
nain *f* (**neiniau**) grandmother.
nam *m* (**·au**) blemish.
namyn *prep* except.
nant *f* (**nentydd**) stream.
Natsi *m* (**Natsïaid**) Nazi.
natur *f* nature; temper.
naturiaeth·wr *m* (**·wyr**) naturalist.
naturiol *adj* natural.
naturioldeb *m* naturalness.
naw *num* nine.
nawdd *m* patronage.
nawddogi *v* to patronise.
nawddoglyd, nawddogol *adj* patronising.
nawdd·sant *m* (**·seintiau**) patron saint.
nawf *from* **nofio**.
nawfed *adj* ninth.
nawn *m* noon.
nawr *adv* now.
naws *f* (**·au**) disposition.
neb *m* anyone; no one.
nedden *f* (**nedd**) nit.
nef, nefoedd *f* heaven.
nefol, nefolaidd *adj* heavenly.
neges *f* (**·au, ·euon**) message; errand.
negeseua *v* to run errands.
neges·ydd *m* (**·wyr**) messenger.
negodi *v* to negotiate.
negydd *m* (**·ion**) negative.
negyddol *adj* negative.
negyddu *v* to negate.
neiaint *see* **nai**.
neidiau *see* **naid**.
neidio *v* to leap.
neid·iwr *m* (**·wyr**) leaper.
neidr *f* (**nadredd, nadroedd**) snake.
Neifion *m* Neptune.
neilltu *m* one side.
neilltuo *v* to separate.
neilltuol *adj* special.
neiniau *see* **nain**.
neisied *f* (**·i**) handkerchief.

neithdar *m* nectar.
neithior *f* (**·au**) wedding breakfast.
neithiwr *adv* last night.
nemor *adv* hardly.
nen *f* (**·nau, ·noedd**) heavens.
nen·fwd *f* (**·fydau**) ceiling.
nentydd *see* **nant.**
nepell *adv* far: **nid nepell** near.
nerfol *adj* nervous.
nerfus *adj* nervous.
nerfusrwydd *m* nervousness.
nerth *m* (**·oedd**) strength.
nerthol *adj* mighty.
nes *adj* nearer.
nes *adv* until.
nesaf *adj* next.
nesáu, nesu *v* to draw near.
nesnes *adv* ever nearer.
nesu *v* to draw near.
neu *conj* or.
neuadd *f* (**·au**) hall.
newid *m* (**·iadau**) change. • *v* to change.
newidiol *adj* changeable.
newidyn *m* variable.
newydd *m* (**·ion**) news. • *adj* new.
newydd-anedig *adj* new-born.
newyddbeth *m* (a) novelty.
newydd-deb *m* novelty.
newydd-ddyfod·iad *m* (**·iaid**) newcomer.
newyddiaduraeth, newyddiaduriaeth *f* journalism.
newyddiadur·wr *m* (**·wyr**) journalist.
newyddian *m* (**·od**) novice.
newyddion *see* **newydd.**
newyn *m* famine.
newynog *adj* hungry.
newynu *v* to starve.
nhw *pron* they, them.
ni *pron* we, us.
ni, nid *negative conj* not.
nico *m* goldfinch.
nifer *m/f* (**·oedd**) number.
niferus *adj* numerous.
nif·wl *m* (**·ylau**) nebula.
ninnau *pron conj* we for our part.
nion·yn *m* (**·od**) onion.
nis *adv* not.
nith *f* (**·oedd**) niece.
nithio *v* to winnow.
niwcl·ews *m* (**·ysau**) nucleus.
niwed *m* (**niweidiau**) harm.
niweidio *v* to harm.
niweidiol *adj* harmful.
niwl *m* (**·oedd**) fog.
niwlog *adj* foggy.
niwtraleiddio *v* to neutralise.
niwtraliaeth *f* neutrality.
nobl *adj* fine.
nob·yn *m* (**·iau**) knob.
nod *m/f* (**·au**) objective.
nodedig *adj* notable.
nodi *v* to note.
nodiadau *see* **nodyn.**
nodiadur *m* (**·on**) notebook.
nodiant *m* notation.
nodwedd *f* (**·ion**) feature.
nodweddiadol *adj* characteristic.
nodweddu *v* to typify.
nodwydd *f* (**·au**) needle.
nod·yn *m* (**·au, ·iadau**) note.
nodd *m* juice.
nodded *m* protection.
nodd·fa *f* (**·feydd**) refuge.

noddi *v* to patronise.
nodd·wr *m* (**·wyr**) patron.
noe *f* (**·au**) dish.
noeth *adj* bare.
noethi *v* to bare.
noeth lymun, noethlymun *adj* nude.
noethni *m* nakedness.
nofel·ydd *m* (**·wyr**) novelist.
nofio *v* to swim, to float.
nof·iwr *m* (**·wyr**) swimmer.
nogio *v* to jib.
nôl *v* to fetch.
nomad *m* (**·iaid**) nomad.
nos *f* (**·au**) night.
nosi *v* to get dark.
nosol *adj* nocturnal.
nos·on, nos·waith *f* (**·weithiau**) evening; night.
noswyl *f* eve of festival.
noswylio *v* to take an evening break.
nudd, nudden *f* mist.
nwy *m* (**·on**) gas.
nwyd *m* (**·au**) passion.
nwydus *adj* passionate.
nwyddau *pl* goods.
nwyf *m* vivacity.
nwyfiant *m* vigour.
nwyfus *adj* vivacious.
nychdod *m* feebleness.
nychlyd *adj* sickly.
nychu *v* to languish.
nyddu *v* to spin.
nydd·wr *m* (**·wyr**) spinner.
nyni *pron* us.
nyrs *m/f* (**·ys**) nurse.
nyrsio *v* to nurse.
nyt·en *f* (**·iau**) nut.
nyth *m/f* (**·od**) nest.
nyth·aid *m* (**·eidiau**) nestful.
nythu *v* to nest.

O

o *prep* from.
oblegid *conj* on account of.
obry *adv* below.
OC *abb* Oed Crist (AD).
ocs·iwn *f* (**·iynau**) auction.
ocsygen *m* oxygen.
ochain, ochneidio *v* to sigh.
ochen·aid *f* (**·eidiau**) groan.
ochr *f* (**·au**) side.
ochrgamu *v* to side-step.
ochri *v* to side.
ôd *m* snow.
o dan *prep* below.
odiaeth *adj* exquisite.
odid *adv* hardly.
odl *f* (**·au**) rhyme.
odli *v* to rhyme.
odrif *m* (**·au**) odd number.
odrwydd *m* eccentricity.
odyn *f* (**·au**) kiln.
oddeutu *adv* approximately.
oddi *prep* from.
oddieithr, oddigerth *prep* unless.
oed, oedran *m* (**·nau**) age; (**oedau**) tryst.
oedfa *f* (**·on**) service.

oedi *v* to postpone.
oediad *m* (**·au**) delay.
oedol·yn *m* (**·ion**) adult.
oedran *m* age.
oedrannus *adj* elderly.
oedd *from* **bod**.
oelio *v* to oil.
oen *m* (**ŵyn**) lamb.
oena *v* to lamb.
oenig *f* ewe lamb.
oer *adj* cold.
oeraidd *adj* chilly.
oerfel, oerni *m* cold.
oergell *f* (**·oedd**) refrigerator.
oeri *v* to get cold.
oernadu *v* to howl.
oerni *m* (the) cold.
oes *f* (**·au, ·oedd**) age.
oes *from* **bod**.
oesol *adj* perpetual.
ofari *m* (**ofarïau**) ovary.
ofer *adj* worthless.
ofera *v* to squander.
oferedd *m* dissipation.
ofergoel *f* (**·ion**) (a) superstition.
ofergoeledd *m* superstition.
ofergoeliaeth *f* superstition.
ofergoelus *adj* superstitious.
ofn *m* (**·au**) fear.
ofnadwy *adj* awful.
ofni *v* to fear.
ofnus *adj* fearful.
ofnusrwydd *m* timidity.
ofydd *m* (**·ion**) ovate.
offeir·iad *m* (**·iaid**) priest.
offeiriadaeth *f* priesthood.
offeiriades *f* priestess.
offeiriadol *adj* priestly.
offer *pl* implements.
offeren *f* (**·nau**) mass.
offeryn *m* (**offer, ·nau**) instrument.
offerynnol *adj* instrumental.
offeryn·nwr *m* (**·wyr**) instrumentalist.
offr·wm *m* (**·ymau**) offering.
offrymu *v* to sacrifice.
offthalmolegydd *m* ophthalmologist.
og, oged *f* (**·au**) harrow.
ogedu *v* to harrow.
ogof *f* (**·âu, ·eydd**) cave.
ogof·wr *m* (**·wyr**) pot-holer.
ogylch *prep* about.
ongl *f* (**·au**) angle.
onglog *adj* angular.
onglydd *m* (**·ion**) protractor.
oherwydd *conj* because.
ohonof *from* **o**.
ôl *m* (**olion**) impression. • *adj* behind.
olaf *adj* last.
olddod·iad, ôl-ddod·iad *m* (**·iaid**) suffix.
olew *m* oil.
ôl-ddyddio *v* to post-date.
ôl-ddyled *f* (**ôl-ddyledion**) arrears.
olewydden *f* (**olewydd**) olive tree.
olion *see* **ôl**[1].
ôl-nodyn *m* postscript.
olrhain *v* to trace.
ol·wr *m* (**·wyr**) back (rugby).
olwyn *f* (**·ion**) wheel.
olwyno *v* to wheel.
olwynog *adj* wheeled.
Olympaidd *adj* Olympic.
olyniaeth *f* succession.

olynol *adj* consecutive.
olyn·ydd *m* (**·wyr**) successor.
oll *adv* all.
ON *abb* ôl-nodyn (PS).
ond *conj* but.
oni, onid *adv* unless.
onis *conj* if it is not.
onnen *f* (**ynn, onn**) ash tree.
OON *abb* ôl-ôl-nodiad (PPS).
opera *f* (**operâu**) opera.
opteg *f* optics.
opteg·wr, opteg·ydd *m* (**·wyr**) optician.
optimistiaeth *f* optimism.
ordeinio *v* to ordain.
ordinhad *f* (**·au**) sacrament.
oren *m* (**orenau**) orange.
organaidd *adj* organic.
organeb *f* organism.
organydd *m* (**·ion**) organist.
orgraff *f* orthography.
oriau *see* **awr**.
oriawr *f* watch.
oriel *f* (**·au**) gallery.
orig *f* a little while.
oriog *adj* fickle.
os *conj* if.
osgo *m* stance.
osgoi *v* to avoid.
osôn *m* ozone.
ots, ods *m* care.
owmal *m* enamel.

P

pa *adj* what, which.
pab *m* (**·au**) pope.
pabaidd *adj* papal.
pabell *f* (**pebyll**) tent.
pab·i *m* (**·ïau, ·s**) poppy.
pabwyr *m* wick.
pabwyren *f*, **pabwyryn** *m* (**pabwyr**) rush(es).
Pabydd *m* (**·ion**) (a) Roman Catholic.
Pabyddiaeth *f* Roman Catholicism.
pabyddol *adj* Catholic.
pacio *v* to pack.
padell *f* (**·au, ·i, pedyll**) pan.
padell·aid *f* (**·eidiau**) panful.
pader *m* (**·au**) prayers.
padlen *f* (**·nau**) paddle.
pae *m* pay.
paent *m* paint.
paentiad *m* (**·au**) painting.
paentio, peintio *v* to paint.
pafiliwn *m* (**pafiliynau**) pavilion.
pafin *m* pavement.
paffio *v* to box.
paff·iwr *m* (**·wyr**) boxer.
pagan *m* (**·iaid**) pagan.
paganaidd *adj* pagan.
pang·fa *f* (**·feydd**) fit.
paham, pam *adv* why.
paid *from* **peidio**.
paill *m* pollen.
pair *m* (**peiriau**) cauldron. • *v from* **peri**.
pais *f* (**peisiau**) petticoat.

paith *m* (**peithiau**) prairie.
pâl *f* (**palau**) spade.
pâl *m* (**palod**) puffin.
paladr *m* (**pelydr**) ray.
palalwyfen *f* (**palalwyf**) linden (tree).
palf *f* (**·au**) palm.
palfalu *v* to grope.
palis *m* (**·au**) partition.
palmant *m* (**·au, palmentydd**) pavement.
palmantu *v* to pave.
palmwydden *f* (**palmwydd**) palm.
palu *v* to dig.
pall *m* lack.
pallu *v* to fail.
pam *adv* why.
pâm *m* (**pamau**) bed (of earth).
pamffled·yn *m* (**·au**) pamphlet.
pan *conj* when.
pan *adj* fulling.
panasen *f* (**pannas**) parsnip.
pancosen *f* (**pancos**) pancake.
pan·dy *m* (**·dai**) fulling mill.
pannas *see* **panasen**.
pannu *v* to full cloth.
pannwl *m* (**panylau**) dimple.
pan·nwr *m* (**·wyr**) fuller.
pant *m* (**·iau**) hollow.
pantio *v* to dent.
pantiog *adj* dented.
panylau *see* **pannwl**.
papur *m* (**·au**) paper.
papurfrwyn *pl* papyrus.
papuro *v* to paper.
pâr *m* (**parau, peiri**) pair.
pâr *from* **peri**.
para, parhau *v* to last.
parabl *m* (**·au**) speech.
parablu *v* to prattle.
paradwys *f* paradise.
paraf *from* **peri**.
paratoi *v* to prepare.
parcio *v* to park.
parch *m* respect.
parchedig *adj* revered.
Parchg *abb* parchedig (Revd).
parchu *v* to respect.
parchus *adj* respectable.
parchusrwydd *m* respectability.
pard·wn *m* (**·ynau**) pardon.
parddu *m* soot.
pardduo *v* to malign.
par·ed *m* (**·wydydd**) wall.
parhad *m* continuation.
parhaol *adj* perpetual.
parhau *v* to continue.
parhaus *adj* continuing.
parl·wr *m* (**·yrau**) parlour.
parlys *m* paralysis.
parlysu *v* to paralyse.
parod *adj* ready.
parod·i *m* (**·ïau**) parody.
parodrwydd *m* readiness.
parôl *m* parole.
parot *m* (**·iaid**) parrot.
paroted *from* **parod**.
part·i *m* (**·ïon**) party.
partneriaeth *f* (**·au**) partnership.
parth *m* (**·au**) region.
parthed *prep* concerning.
parwydydd *see* **pared**.
pàs *f* (**pasiau**) pass; (a) lift.
pas *m* whooping cough.
Pasg *m* Easter.
pasgaf *from* **pesgi**.

pasgedig *adj* fatted.
pasian·t *m* (**·nau, ·tau**) pageant.
pasio *v* to pass.
past *m* (**·au**) paste.
past·ai *f* (**·eiod**) pie.
pastio *v* to paste.
past·wn *m* (**·ynau**) cudgel.
patriarchaidd *adj* patriarchal.
pat·rwm, pat·rwn *m* (**·rymau, ·rynau**) pattern.
patrymog *adj* patterned.
pathew *m* (**·od**) dormouse.
patholeg *f* pathology.
pau *f* (**peuau**) country.
paun *m* (**peunod**) peacock.
pawen *f* (**·nau**) paw.
pawr *from* **pori**.
pe *conj* if.
pebyll *see* **pabell**.
pecyn *m* (**·nau**) package.
pechadur *m* (**·iaid**) sinner.
pechadures *f* sinner (female).
pechadurus *adj* sinful.
pechod *m* (**·au**) sin.
pechu *v* to sin.
pedair *num* (*f*) four.
pedlera *v* to peddle.
pedol *f* (**·au**) horseshoe.
pedoli *v* to shoe.
ped·rain *f* (**·reiniau**) hindquarters.
pedrongl *f* (**·au**) quadrangle.
pedwar *num* four.
pedwaredd *adj* (*f*) fourth.
pedwerydd *adj* fourth.
pedyll *see* **padell**.
pefrio *v* to sparkle.
pegio *v* to peg.
peg·wn *m* (**·ynau**) pole.
pegynol *adj* axial.
peidio *v* to cease.
peilot *m* (**·iaid**) pilot.
peillio *v* to pollinate.
peintiad *m* (**·au**) painting.
peintio to paint.
peint·iwr *m* (**·wyr**) painter.
peip·en *f* (**·iau**) pipe.
peiran *m* (**·nau**) corrie.
peirch *from* **parchu**.
peiri *see* **pâr**.
peirianneg *m* engineering.
peiriannau *see* **peiriant**.
peiriannol *adj* mechanical.
peirian·nydd *m* (**·wyr, ·yddion**) engineer.
peirian·t *m* (**·nau**) machine.
peirianwaith *m* machinery.
peirianyddol *adj* mechanical.
peiriau *see* **pair**.
peisiau *see* **pais**.
peiswyn *m* chaff.
peithiau *see* **paith**.
pêl *f* (**peli**) ball.
pelawd *f* (**·au**) over (cricket).
pêl-droed *f* football.
pêl-droed·iwr *m* (**·wyr**) footballer.
pelen *f* (**·ni**) ball.
pêl-fas *f* baseball.
pêl-fasged *f* basketball.
pelferyn *f* (**·nau**) ball-bearing.
pêl-rwyd *f* netball.
pelten *f* (a) blow.
pelydr *see* **paladr**.
pelydru *v* to radiate.
pelydr·yn *m* (**·au**) ray.
pell *adj* far.
pellen *f* (**·ni**) ball (of wool).

pellennig *adj* remote.
pellgyrhaeddol *adj* far-reaching.
pellhau *v* to move away.
pellter *m* (**·au**) distance.
pen *m* (**·nau**) head.
penaethiaid *see* **pennaeth**.
penagored *adj* undecided.
penarglwyddiaeth *f* sovereignty.
penawdau *see* **pennawd**.
penbaladr *adv* universal.
penbleth *f* quandry.
pen blwydd *m* (**pennau blwydd**) birthday.
penboeth *adj* hot-headed.
penboeth·yn *m* (**·iaid**) fanatic.
pen·bwl *m* (**·byliaid**) tadpole.
pencadlys *m* (**·oedd**) headquarters.
pencamp·wr *m* (**·wyr**) champion.
pencampwriaeth *f* (**·au**) championship.
pen·cerdd *m* (**·ceirddiaid**) head musician.
pen·ci *m* (**·cwn**) dogfish.
penchwiban *adj* frivolous.
pendant *adj* positive.
pendantrwydd *m* decisiveness.
pendefig *m* (**·ion**) lord.
pendefigaeth *f* aristocracy.
pendefigaidd *adj* aristocratic.
penderfyniad *m* (**·au**) decision.
penderfynol *adj* resolute.
penderfynu *v* to decide.
pendifaddau *adv* verily.
pendil *m* (**·iau**) pendulum.
pendramwnwgl *adj* headlong.
pendraphen *adj* helter-skelter.
pendro *f* giddiness.
pendroni *v* to brood.
pendwmpian *v* to drowse.
penddaredd *m* giddiness.
penddelw *f* (**·au**) bust.
pendduyn *m* (**·nod**) boil; blackhead.
penelin *m/f* (**·oedd**) elbow.
pengaled *adj* stubborn.
pen-glin *m* (**pennau gliniau**) knee.
penglog *f* (**·au**) skull.
Pengryn·iad *m* (**·iaid**) Roundhead.
penhwy·ad *m* (**·aid**) pike.
peniad *m* (**·au**) header.
penigamp *adj* first-rate.
penillion *see* **pennill**.
penio *v* to head.
peniog *adj* brainy.
penisel *adj* downcast.
pen-lin *hon* (**penliniau**) knee.
penlinio *v* to kneel.
penllâd *m* supreme good.
penllanw *m* high water.
penllinyn *m* end.
pen·naeth *m* (**·aethiaid**) chief.
pennaf *adj* chief.
pennau *see* **pen**.
pen·nawd *m* (**·awdau**) heading.
pen·nill *m* (**·illion**) verse.
pen·nod *f* (**·odau**) chapter.
pennoeth *adj* bare-headed.
pen·nog *m* (**·waig**) herring.
pennu *v* to determine.
penodi *v* to appoint.
penodau *see* **pennod**.
pen-ôl *m* (**penolau**) backside.
penrhydd *adj* uncurbed.
penrhydd *adj* unbridled.
penrhyddid *m* licentiousness.
penrhyn *m* (**·nau**) promontory.

pen·saer *m* (**·seiri**) architect.
pensaernïaeth *f* architecture.
pensel *f* (**·i**) pencil.
pensi·wn *m* (**·ynau**) pension.
penstiff *adj* stubborn.
pensyfrdan *adj* stunned.
pensyth *adj* perpendicular.
pentan *m* inglenook.
penteulu *m* householder.
pentewyn *m* (**·ion**) firebrand.
pentir *m* (**·oedd**) headland.
pentref *m* (**·i**) village.
pentref·wr *m* (**·wyr**) villager.
pent·wr *m* (**·yrrau**) pile.
penty *m* cottage, shed.
pentyrru *v* to heap.
penwaig *see* **pennog.**
penwan *adj* silly.
penwythnos *m/f* (**·au**) weekend.
penyd *m* (**·iau**) penance.
penysgafn *adj* dizzy.
penysgafnder *m* giddiness.
pêr[1], **peraidd** *adj* sweet.
pêr[2] *see* **peren.**
peraidd *adj* pure.
perarogl *m* (**·au**) perfume.
peraroglus *adj* perfumed.
percoladur *m* (**·on**) percolator.
perch(ais) *from* **parchu.**
perchen·nog *m* (**·ogion**) owner.
perchenogaeth *f* ownership.
perchenogi *v* to possess.
perchyll *see* **porchell.**
perdysen *f* (**perdys**) shrimp.
pereidd-dra *m* sweetness.
pereiddied *from* **peraidd.**
pereiddio *v* to sweeten.
peren *f* (**pêr**) pear.
pererin *m* (**·ion**) pilgrim.
pererindod *m/f* (**·au**) pilgrimage.
perfedd *m* (**·ion**) intestine.
perffaith *adj* perfect.
perffeithio *v* to perfect.
perffeithrwydd *m* perfection.
perffeithydd *m* perfectionist, perfecter.
perfformiad *m* (**·au**) performance.
perfformio *v* to perform.
peri *v* to cause.
perlewyg *m* (**·on**) trance.
perlysiau *pl* herbs; spices.
perllan *f* (**·nau**) orchard.
persain *adj* melodious.
persain *adj* melodious.
persawr *m* fragrance.
persawrus *adj* fragrant.
perseiniol *adj* melodious.
persli *m* parsley.
person *m* (**·au**) person; (**·iaid**) parson.
personol *adj* personal.
personoliaeth *f* (**·au**) personality.
perswâd *m* persuasion.
perswadio *v* to persuade.
pert *adj* pretty.
perth *f* (**·i**) hedge.
perthnasau *see* **perthynas.**
perthnasol *adj* relevant.
perthyn *v* to be related; to belong.
perthynas *m/f* (**perthnasau**) relative.
perthynol *adj* relative.
perwyl *m* purpose.
pery *from* **para, parhau.**
perygl *m* (**·on**) danger.
peryglu *v* to endanger.
peryglus *adj* dangerous.
pesgi *v* to get fat; to fatten.

pesimist *m* (**·iaid**) pessimist.
pesimistaidd *adj* pessimistic.
pesimistiaeth *f* pessimism.
peswch, pesychu *v* to cough.
peswch, pesychiad *m* (**·au**) (a) cough.
petawn i *v* were I, etc.
petrisen *f* (**petris**) partridge.
petrus *adj* hesitant.
petruso *v* to hesitate.
petruster *m* hesitation.
petryal *m* (**·au**) oblong.
peth *m* (**·au**) thing.
petheuach *pl* odds and ends.
peuau *see* **pau.**
peunes *f* peahen.
peunod *see* **paun.**
pianydd *m* (**·ion**) pianist.
piau *v* to possess.
pib *f* (**·au**) pipe; diarrhoea.
pibell *f* (**·au, ·i**) pipe.
pibell·aid *f* (**·eidiau**) pipeful.
piben *f* (**·ni**) pipe.
pibo *v* to pipe; to squirt.
pibonwy *pl* icicles.
pibydd *m* (**·ion**) piper.
picas *m/f* pickaxe.
picedu *v* to picket.
picell *f* (**·au**) spear.
picellu *v* to spear.
piced·wr *m* (**·wyr**) (a) picketer.
pic·fforch *f* (**·ffyrch**) pitchfork.
picio *v* to pop (out).
piclo *v* to pickle.
picti·wr *m* (**·yrau**) picture.
pictiwrs *pl* cinema.
pic·warch *f* (**·weirch**) pitchfork.
picwnen *f* (**picwn**) wasp.
pidyn *m* penis.
piffian *v* to giggle.
pig *f* (**·au**) beak.
pigfain *adj* pointed.
pigiad, pigad *m* (**·au**) a prick.
pigion *pl* selections.
pigm·i *m* (**·ïaid**) pygmy.
pigo *v* to pick.
pigog *adj* prickly.
pigoglys *m* spinach.
pig·yn *m* (**·au**) prick.
pil *m* peel.
pilen *f* (**·nau**) membrane.
piler *m* (**·i**) pillar.
pilio, pilo *v* to peel.
pilipala *m* butterfly.
pilsen *f* (**pils**) pill.
pilyn *m* (**·nau**) garment.
pìn *m* (**pinnau**) pin.
pin *see* **pinwydden.**
pinafal *m* (**·au**) pineapple.
pinc *m* (**·od**) chaffinch.
pincas *m* pincushion.
piner *m* pinafore.
pinio *v* to pin.
pin·iwn *m* (**·iynau**) opinion.
pinnau *see* **pìn.**
pinsiad *m* (a) pinch.
pinsio *v* to pinch.
pins·iwrn, pins·iwn *m* (**·iyrnau, ·iynau**) pincers.
pinwydden *f* (**pinwydd, coed pin**) pine tree.
pioden *f* (**piod**) magpie.
piser *m* (**·i**) pitcher.
pisgwydden *f* (**pisgwydd**) lime tree.
pistyll *m* (**·oedd**) well.
pistyllio *v* to spout.

pisyn *m* (**-nau, pisys**) piece.
pitïo *v* to pity.
pitw *adj* paltry.
piw *m* (**-au**) udder.
piwis *adj* peevish.
Piwritan *m* (**-iaid**) Puritan.
piwritanaidd *adj* puritanical.
pla *m* (**plâu**) plague.
pladur *f* (**-iau**) scythe.
plaen *adj* plain.
plaen, plân *m* (**-au, plaeniau**) plane (carpenter).
plagio *v* to pester.
plaid *f* (**pleidiau**) party.
plân *m* (**planau**) plane (geometry); (**plaenau**) plane (carpentry).
planced *f* (**-i**) blanket.
planed *f* (**-au**) planet.
planhigfa *f* (**planigfeydd**) plantation.
planhig·yn *m* (**-ion**) plant.
plannu *v* to plant.
plant *see* **plentyn**.
planta *v* to beget children.
plantos *pl* little children.
planwydden *f* (**planwydd**) plane trees.
plas *m* (**-au**) mansion.
plastig *m* (**-ion**) (a) plastic.
plastro *v* to plaster.
plasty *m* (**plastai**) mansion.
plât *m* (**platiau**) plate.
plat·aid *m* (**-eidi, -eidiau**) plateful.
ple *m* plea.
pledio *v* to plead.
pledren *f* (**-ni, -nau**) bladder.
pleidiau *see* **plaid**.
pleidiol *adj* partial.
pleid·lais *f* (**-leisiau**) vote.
pleidleisio *v* to vote.
plencyn *m* (**planciau**) plank.
plenn(ais) *from* **plannu**.
plentyn *m* (**plant**) child.
plentyndod *m* childhood.
plentynnaidd *adj* infantile.
pleser *m* (**-au**) pleasure.
pleserus *adj* pleasant.
plesio *v* to please.
plet, pleten *f* (**pletau**) crease.
pletio *v* to pleat.
pleth *f* (**-au**) plait.
plethu *v* to plait.
plicio *v* to pluck.
plisgyn *m* (**plisg**) pod.
plisman, plismon *m* (**plismyn**) policeman.
plismona *v* to police.
plismones *f* policewoman.
plith *m* midst.
ploc·yn *m* (**-iau**) block.
ploryn *m* (**-nod, plorod**) acne.
pluen *f* (**plu**) feather.
pluo, plufio *v* to pluck.
pluog *adj* feathered.
plwc *m* (**plyciau**) pluck.
plwg *m* (**plygiau**) plug.
plwm *m* lead.
plws *m* (**plysau**) plus.
Plwton *f* Pluto.
plwyf *m* (**-i**) parish.
plwyfol *adj* parochial.
plwyfolion *pl* parishioners.
plyciau *see* **plwc**.
plycio *v* to jerk.
plyg *m* (**-ion**) fold.
plyg·ain *m/f* (**-einiau**) dawn; matins.

plygeiniol *adj* early (morning).
plygell *m* (**·au**) folder.
plygiad, plygiant *m* (**·au**) crease.
plygiau *see* **plwg**.
plygu *v* to bend.
plymio *v* to plumb.
plysau *see* **plws**.
pob *adj* each; baked.
pobi *v* to bake.
pobiad *m* (**·au**) (a) baking.
pobl *f* (**·oedd**) people.
poblog *adj* populous.
poblogaeth *f* population.
poblogaidd *adj* popular.
poblogeiddio *v* to poularise.
poblogi *v* to populate.
poblogrwydd *m* popularity.
pobydd *m* (**·ion**) baker.
poced *m/f* (**·i**) pocket.
poced·aid *f* (**·eidiau**) pocketful.
pocedu *v* to pocket.
pocer, procer *m* (**·i**) poker.
poen *m/f* (**·au**) pain.
poendod *m* pest.
poeni *v* to hurt; to worry.
poenus *adj* painful.
poenydio *v* to torment.
poenyd·iwr *m* (**·wyr**) tormentor.
poenyn *m* tease.
poer *m* saliva.
poeri *v* to spit.
poeth *adj* hot.
poethder *m* heat.
poethi *v* to heat.
polareiddio *v* to polarise.
polyn *m* (**polion**) pole.
pomgranad *m* (**·au**) pomegranate.
pompren *f* footbridge.
ponc *f* (**·au, ·iau**) hillock.
ponsio *v* to bungle.
pont *f* (**·ydd**) bridge.
pontio *v* to bridge.
popeth *m* everything.
poplysen *f* (**poplys**) poplar.
poptu *m* all sides.
pop·ty *m* (**·tai**) oven.
porchell *m* (**perchyll**) porker.
porf·a *f* (**·eydd**) grass.
porffor *adj* purple.
pori *v* to graze.
pornograffiaeth *f* pornography.
portread *m* (**·au**) portrait.
portreadu *v* to portray.
porth *m* (**pyrth**) door. • *f* (**pyrth**) harbour.
porthi *v* to feed.
porthiannus *adj* well-fed.
porthiant *m* food.
porthladd *m* (**·oedd**) harbour.
porthmon *m* (**porthmyn**) drover.
porthor *m* (**·ion**) porter.
pos *m* (**·au**) puzzle.
posibil·rwydd *m* (**·iadau**) possibilities.
poster *m* (**·i**) poster.
postio *v* to post.
post·man, post·mon *m* (**·myn**) postman.
postyn, post *m* (**pyst**) post.
potel *f* (**·i**) bottle.
potel·aid *f* (**·eidi, ·eidiau**) bottleful.
potelu *v* to bottle.
potes *m* broth.
potio *v* to pot; to booze.
potsio *v* to poach.
pothell *f* (**·au, ·i**) blister.

powdr, powdwr *m* (**-au**) powder.
powld *adj* cheeky.
powlen *f* (**-ni**) bowl.
powlennaid *f* bowlful.
powlio *v* to bowl.
praff *adj* stout.
praffter *m* girth.
praidd *m* (**preiddiau**) flock.
prancio *v* to caper.
prawf, praw *m* (**profion**) proof.
prawf *from* **profi.**
preblan *v* to chatter.
pregeth *f* (**-au**) sermon.
pregethu *v* to preach.
pregeth·wr *m* (**-wyr**) preacher.
preiddiau *see* **praidd.**
preifat *adj* private.
preifateiddio *v* to privatise.
preifatrwydd *m* privacy.
preiffion *see* **praff.**
preimin *m* ploughing match.
pren *m* (**-nau**) wood.
prennaidd *adj* wooden.
prentis *m* (**-iaid**) apprentice.
prentisiaeth *f* apprenticeship.
prentisio *v* to apprentice.
prepian *v* to babble.
pres *m* brass; money.
preseb *m* (**-au**) crib.
presennol *adj* present.
presenoldeb *m* presence.
preswyl *adj* residential.
preswyl·fa *f* (**-feydd**) dwelling.
preswylio *v* to dwell.
preswyl·ydd *m* (**-wyr**) dweller.
pric *m* (**-iau**) stick.
prid *adj* expensive.
pridwerth *m* ransom.
pridd *m* (**-oedd**) soil.
priddio, priddo *v* to earth up.
prif *adj* chief.
prif·ardd *m* (**-eirdd**) chief poet.
prifathrawes *f* (**-au**) headmistress.
prifathr·o *m* (**-awon**) headmaster.
prifddinas *f* (**-oedd**) capital city.
prifiant *m* growth.
prifio *v* to grow.
priflyth·yren *f* (**-rennau**) capital letter.
prifol *adj* cardinal.
prifysgol *f* (**-ion**) university.
priff·ordd *f* (**-yrdd**) highway.
prin *adj* scarce.
prinder *m* scarcity.
prinhau *v* to become scarce.
prinned *from* **prin.**
printiedig *adj* printed.
printio *v* to print.
priod *adj* married; appropriate.
priod *m/f* spouse.
priodas *f* (**-au**) marriage.
priodasol *adj* marital.
priod-ddull *m* (**-iau**) idiom.
priodfab, priodasfab *m* bridegroom.
priodferch, priodasferch *f* bride.
priodi *v* to marry.
priodol *adj* proper.
priodoldeb *m* (**-au**) propriety.
priodoledd *f* (**-au**) attribute.
priodoli *v* to attribute.
prior *m* (**-iaid**) prior.
prior·dy *m* (**-dai**) priory.
pris *m* (**-iau**) price.
prisiad, prisian·t *m* (**-au, -nau**) valuation.

prisio *v* to value.
pris·iwr *m* (**·wyr**) valuer.
proc *m* (**·iau**) (a) poke.
procio *v* to poke.
proest *m* (**·au**) half-rhyme.
profedigaeth *f* (**·au**) tribulation.
profi *v* to test; to prove.
profiad *m* (**·au**) experience.
profiadol *adj* experienced.
profiannaeth *f* probation.
profion *see* **prawf**.
proflen *f* (**·ni**) (copy) proof.
proffes *f* (**·au**) (a) profession.
proffes·iwn *m* (**·iynau**) profession.
proffesiynol *adj* professional.
proffesu *v* to profess.
proffidiol *adj* profitable.
proffwyd *m* (**·i**) prophet.
proffwydo *v* to prophesy.
proffwydol *adj* prophetic.
proffwydoliaeth *f* (**·au**) prophecy.
prosesydd geiriau *m* (**·ion geiriau**) word processor.
Protestannaidd *adj* Protestant.
prudd *adj* serious.
pruddglwyfus *adj* melancholic.
pryd[1] *m* (**·iau**) time; (**·au**) meal.
pryd[2] *adj* when.
pryder *m* (**·on**) worry.
pryderu *v* to fret.
pryderus *adj* anxious.
prydferth *adj* beautiful.
prydferthu *v* to adorn.
prydferthwch *m* beauty.
prydles *f* (**·au**, **·i**) lease.
prydlon *adj* punctual.
prydlondeb *m* punctuality.
prydydd *m* (**·ion**) bard.
prydyddiaeth *f* poetry.
pryddest *f* (**·au**) bardic poem.
pryf, pry *m* (**·ed**) fly.
pryfetach *pl* vermin; flies.
pryfocio *v* to provoke.
pryfoclyd *adj* provocative.
pryfysydd *m* (**·ion**) insectivore.
prŷn *v from* **prynu**. • *adj* bought.
prynedigaeth *f/m* redemption.
prynhawn *m* (**·iau**) afternoon.
prynhawnol *adj* afternoon.
prynu *v* to buy.
pryn·wr *m* (**·wyr**) buyer.
prysglwyn *m* (**·i**) copse.
prysgwydden *f* (**prysgwydd**) shrub.
prysur *adj* busy.
prysurdeb *m* busyness.
prysuro *v* to hasten.
pulpud *m* (**·au**) pulpit.
pumawd *m* (**·au**) quintet.
pumed *adj* fifth.
pump, pum *num* five.
pun·t *f* (**·noedd**, **·nau**) pound.
pur *adj* pure. • *adv* quite.
purdan *m* purgatory.
purdeb *m* purity.
pur·fa *f* (**·feydd**) refinery.
purion *adj* right.
puro *v* to purify.
purydd *m* (**·ion**) purist.
put·ain *f* (**·einiaid**) prostitute.
puteindra *m* prostitution.
pwca, pwc·i *m* (**·od**, **·iod**) imp.
pwdin *m* (**·au**) pudding.
pwdlyd *adj* sulky.
pwdr *adj* rotten.
pwdryn *m* waster.
pwdu *v* to sulk.

pŵer *m* (**pwerau**) power.
pwer·dy *m* (**·dai**) powerhouse.
pwerus *adj* powerful.
pwff *m* (**pyffiau**) puff.
pwffian, pwffio *v* to puff.
pwl *m* (**pyliau**) (a) fit.
pŵl *adj* matt.
pwll *m* (**pyllau**) pool.
pwmp *m* (**pympiau**) pump.
pwmpen *f* (**·ni**) marrow.
pwn *m* (**pynnau**) pack.
pwnc *m* (**pynciau**) subject.
pwniad, pwnad *m* (**·au**) nudge.
pwnio *v* to nudge.
pwrcas *m* (**·au**) (a) purchase.
pwrcasu *v* to purchase.
pwrpas *m* (**·au**) purpose.
pwrpasol *adj* purposeful.
pwrs *m* (**pyrsau**) purse.
pwt *m* (**pytiau**) bit.
pwti *m* putty.
pwy *pron* who.
pwyll *m* caution.
pwyllgor *m* (**·au**) committee.
pwyllgor·wr *m* (**·wyr**) committee-man.
pwyllo *v* to pause.
pwyllog *adj* prudent.
pwynt *m* (**·iau**) point.
pwyntio *v* to point.
pwyo *v* to batter.
pwys *m* (**·i**) pound; (**·au**) weight.
pwysau *m* weight.
pwysedd *m* (blood) pressure.
pwys·i *m* (**·ïau**) posy.
pwysig *adj* important.
pwysigrwydd *m* importance.
pwys·lais *m* (**·leisiau**) emphasis.
pwysleisio *v* to emphasise.
pwyso *v* to weigh.
pwys·wr *m* (**·wyr**) weigher.
pwysyn *m* (**·nau**) (a) weight.
pwyth *m* (**·au**) stitch.
pwytho *v* to stitch.
pybyr *adj* staunch.
pydew *m* well, pit.
pydredd *m* decay.
pydru *v* to rot.
pyffiau *see* **pwff**.
pyg *m* pitch.
pygddu *adj* pitch black.
pyliau *see* **pwl**.
pylni *m* dullness.
pylu *v* to blunt.
pyllau *see* **pwll**.
pympiau *see* **pwmp**.
pymtheg, pymtheng *num* fifteen.
pymthegfed *adj* fifteenth.
pymthengwaith *adv* fifteen times.
pynciau *see* **pwnc**.
pyncio *v* to sing.
pynfarch *m* pack-horse; mill-race.
pynnau *see* **pwn**.
pyrsau *see* **pwrs**.
pyrth *see* **porth**.
pyrwydden *f* (**pyrwydd**) spruce.
pysen *f* (**pys**) pea.
pysgodyn *m* (**pysgod**) fish.
pysgota *v* to fish.
pysgot·wr *m* (**·wyr**) fisherman.
pyst *see* **postyn**.
pystylad *v* to stamp.
pytat·en *f* (**·ws**) potato.
pytiau *see* **pwt**.
pythefnos *m/f* (**·au**) fortnight.
pythefnosol *adj* fortnightly.

Ph

Pharise·ad *m* (**·aid**) Pharisee.
Philist·iad *m* (**·iaid**) Philistine.
Philistiaeth *f* Philistinism.

R

rab(b)i *m* (**·niaid**) rabbi.
rabinaidd *adj* rabbinical.
raced *m/f* (**·i**) racket.
radicalaidd *adj* radical.
ras *f* (**·ys**) race.
ras·al *f* (**·elydd**) razor.
rasio *v* to race.
realydd *m* realist.
recordiad *m* (**·au**) recording.
recordydd *m* (**·ion**) recorder.
reit *adv* quite.
ridens *f* fringe.
roboteg *f* robotics.
rŵan *adv* now.
rwbel *m* rubble.
rwden *f* (**rwdins**) swede.
rwdlan, rwdlian *v* to natter on.
Rwsiad *m* (**Rwsiaid**) Russian.
rwyf *from* **bod**.
rys·áit *f* (**·eitiau**) recipe.

Rh

rhaca *f* (**·nau**) rake.
rhacanu *v* to rake.
rhacsyn, rhecsyn *m* (**rhacs**) rags.
rhad *adj* cheap. • *m* (**·au**) blessing.
rhadlon *adj* gracious.
rhadlonrwydd *m* graciousness.
rhaeadr *f* (**·au, rhěydr**) waterfall.
rhaff *f* (**·au**) rope.
rhaffu, rhaffo *v* to string together.
rhag *prep* lest.
rhag·air *m* (**·eiriau**) foreword.
rhagarweiniad *m* introduction.
rhagarweiniol *adj* introductory.
rhagbaratoawl *adj* preparatory.
rhag·brawf *m* (**·brofion**) prelim.
rhagdybio, rhagdybied *v* to assume.
rhagddod·iad *m* (**·iaid**) prefix.
rhag-ddweud *v* to foretell.
rhageiriau *see* **rhagair**.
rhagenw *m* (**·au**) pronoun.
rhagflaenu *v* to precede.
rhagflaen·ydd *m* (**·wyr**) predecessor.
rhagflas *m* foretaste.
rhagfur *m* (**·iau**) rampart.
rhagfynegi *v* to foretell.

Rhagfyr *m* December.
rhaglaw *m* (**-laid, rhaglofiaid**) governor.
rhaglen *f* (**-ni**) programme.
rhaglennu *v* to program.
rhaglofiaid *see* **rhaglaw.**
rhagluniaeth *f* providence.
rhagluniaethol *adj* providencial.
rhagofalon *pl* precautions.
rhag-olwg *m* (**-olygon**) prospect.
rhagor *m* more.
rhagor-fraint *f* (**-freintiau**) privilege.
rhagori *v* to excel.
rhagoriaeth *f* (**-au**) superiority.
rhagorol *adj* excellent.
rhagredegydd *m* forerunner.
rhagrith *m* (**-ion**) hypocrisy.
rhagrithio *v* to be hypocritical.
rhagrithiol *adj* hypocritical.
rhagrith-iwr *m* (**-wyr**) hypocrite.
rhagrybuddio *v* to forewarn.
rhag-weld, rhagweled *v* to foresee.
rhagymadrodd *m* (**-ion**) introduction.
rhai *adj* some.
rhaib *f* spell.
rhaid *m* (**rheidiau**) necessity.
rhaidd *f* (**rheiddiau**) antler.
rhain *pron* these.
rhamant *f* romance.
rhamantus *adj* romantic.
Rhamantiaeth *f* Romanticism.
rhan *f* (**-nau**) part.
rhanadwy *adj* divisible.
rhanbarth *m* (**-au**) region.
rhanbarthol *adj* regional.
rhanedig *adj* divided.
rhaniad *m* (**-au**) division.
rhannol *adj* in part.
rhannu *v* to share.
rhated *from* **rhad.**
rhathell *f* (**-au**) rasp.
rhaw *f* (**-iau, rhofiau**) shovel.
rhawd *f* course, career.
rhawg *adv* after a time.
rhawn *m* horsehair.
rhech *f* fart.
rhechain, rhechian *v* to fart.
rhedeg *v* to run.
rhedegog *adj* running.
rhediad *m* (**-au**) run, flow.
rhed-wr *m* (**-wyr**) runner.
rhedynen *f* (**rhedyn**) fern.
rhefr *m* anus.
rheffyn *m* (**-nau**) halter.
rheg *f* (**-feydd**) swear word.
rhegen yr ŷd *f* corncrake.
rhegi *v* to swear.
rheng *f* (**-oedd**) row.
rheibio *v* to bewitch; to ravage.
rheibus *adj* rapacious.
rheidiau *see* **rhaid.**
rheidrwydd *m* compulsion.
rheiddiadur *m* (**-on**) radiator.
rheiddiau *see* **rhaidd.**
rheil-en *f* (**-iau**) rail.
rheil-ffordd *f* (**-ffyrdd**) railway.
rheini *pron* those.
rheitied *from* **rhaid.**
rheithfarn *f* (**-au**) verdict.
rheithgor *m* jury.
rheithor *m* (**-ion, -iaid**) rector.
rhelyw *m* remainder.
rhemp *f* excess.
rhenn(ais) *from* **rhannu.**

rhent *m* (·i) rent.
rhentu *v* to rent.
rheol *f* (·**au**) rule.
rheolaeth *f* control.
rheolaidd *adj* regular.
rheoleiddio *v* to regulate.
rheoli *v* to rule.
rheol·wr *m* (·**wyr**) ruler.
rhes *f* (·**i**, ·**au**) row.
rhesel, rhestl *f* (·**i**, ·**au**) rack.
rhes·en *f* (·i) parting.
rhesinen *f* (**rhesin**) raisin.
rhestr *f* (·**i**, ·**au**) (a) list.
rhestru *v* to list.
rhes·wm *m* (·**ymau**) reason.
rhesymeg *f* logic.
rhesymegol *adj* logical.
rhesymol *adj* reasonable.
rhesymu *v* to reason.
rhethreg *f* rhetoric.
rhew *m* frost.
rhewbwynt *m* (·**iau**) freezing-point.
rhewgell *f* (·**oedd**) freezer.
rhewi *v* to freeze.
rhewlif *m* (·**au**) glacier.
rhewllyd *adj* icy.
rhewynt *m* (·**oedd**) ice-cold wind.
rhēydr *see* **rhaeadr.**
rhi *m* king.
rhia·in *f* (·**nedd**) maiden.
rhialtwch *m* jollification.
rhiant *m* (**rhiaint, rhieni**) parent.
rhibidirês *f* string (of).
rhibin *m* streak.
rhic *m* (·**iau**) notch.
rhidens *pl* fringe.
rhidyll *m* (·**au**) sieve.
rhidyllu *v* to sieve.
rhieni *pl* parents.
rhif *m* (·**au**) number.
rhifo *v* to number; to count.
rhifol *m* (·**ion**) numeral.
rhifyddeg *f* arithmetic.
rhifyn *m* (·**nau**) issue.
rhigol *f* (·**au**, ·**ydd**) groove.
rhig·wm *m* (·**ymau**) rhyme.
rhigym·wr *m* (·**wyr**) rhymester.
rhingyll *m* (·**iaid**) sergeant.
rhimyn *m* (·**nau**) rim.
rhin *f* (·**iau**) virtue.
rhincian *v* to gnash.
rhiniog *m* (·**au**) threshold.
rhinwedd *m/f* (·**au**) virtue.
rhinweddol *adj* virtuous.
rhisgl *m* bark.
rhith *m* (·**iau**) guise.
rhithio *v* to appear.
rhithyn *m* particle.
rhiw *f* (·**iau**) hill.
rhocen, rhoces *f* (·**i**) lass.
rhochian *v* to grunt.
rhod *f* (·**au**) wheel.
rhoden *f* (·**ni**) rod.
rhod·fa *f* (·**feydd**) promenade.
rhodio *v* to walk.
rhodres *m* ostentation.
rhodresgar *adj* ostentatious.
rhodd *f* (·**ion**) gift.
rhoddi *v* to give.
rhodd·wr *m* (·**wyr**) donor.
rhof·iad *f* (·**ieidiau**) shovelful.
rhofiau *see* **rhaw.**
rhoi, rhoddi *v* to give.
rholbren *m* (·**ni**) rolling pin.
rholio *v* to roll.
rholyn *m* (**rholiau**) roll.

rhonc *adj* rank.
rhos *f* (**·ydd**) moor.
rhostio *v* to roast.
rhosyn *m* (**·nau, rhosod**) rose.
rhu, rhuad *m* (**·au**) (a) roar.
rhudd *adj* ruddy.
rhuddem *f* ruby.
rhuddin *m* heart of timber.
rhuddo *v* to scorch.
rhuddygl *m* radish.
rhugl *adj* fluent.
rhuo *v* to roar.
rhusio *v* to take fright.
rhuthr *m* (**·au, ·adau**) rush; attack.
rhûwr *m* roarer.
rhwbio, rhwto *v* to rub.
rhwd *m* rust.
rhwng *prep* between.
rhwth *adj* gaping.
rhwyd *f* (**·au, ·i**) net.
rhwyden *f* (**·ni**) retina.
rhwydo *v* to net.
rhwyd·waith *m* (**·weithiau**) network.
rhwydd *adj* easy.
rhwyddineb *m* ease.
rhwyf *f* (**·au**) oar.
rhwyfo *v* to row.
rhwyfus *adj* restless.
rhwyf·wr *m* (**·wyr**) oarsman.
rhwyg *f* (**·iadau**) tear.
rhwygo *v* to tear.
rhwyll *f* (**·au**) lattice.
rhwyllog *adj* perforated.
rhwyllwaith *m* fretwork.
rhwym *m* (**·au**) tie. • *adj* constipated.
rhwymedig *adj* bound.
rhwymedigaeth *f* (**·au**) bond.
rhwymedd *m* constipation.
rhwymo *v* to bind.
rhwym·wr *m* (**·wyr**) binder.
rhwymyn *m* (**·nau**) bandage.
rhwysg *m* pomp.
rhwystr *m* (**·au**) obstruction.
rhwystro *v* to hinder.
rhy[1] *adv* too.
rhy[2] *from* **rhoi.**
rhybed *m* (**·ion**) rivet.
rhybudd *m* (**·ion**) warning.
rhybuddio *v* to warn.
rhych *m/f* (**·au**) furrow.
rhychiog, rhychog *adj* corrugated, furrowed.
rhychwant *m* (**·au**) span.
rhychwantu *v* to span.
rhyd *f* (**·au**) ford.
rhydlyd *adj* rusty.
rhydu, rhwdu *v* to rust.
rhydwel·i *f* (**·ïau**) artery.
rhydd *adj* loose.
rhydd *from* **rhoddi.**
rhydd·fraint *f* (**·freiniau**) emancipation.
Rhyddfrydiaeth *f* Liberalism.
rhyddfrydig *adj* liberal.
Rhyddfrydol *adj* Liberal.
Rhyddfryd·wr *m* (**·wyr**) (a) Liberal.
rhyddhad *m* liberation, relief.
rhyddhau *v* to release.
rhyddiaith *f* prose.
rhyddid *m* freedom.
rhyddieithol *adj* prosaic.
rhyfedd *adj* strange.
rhyfeddod *m* (**·au**) marvel.
rhyfeddol *adj* marvellous.
rhyfeddu *v* to amaze.
rhyfel *m/f* (**·oedd**) war.

rhyfela *v* to wage war.
rhyfelgar *adj* bellicose.
rhyfel·wr *m* (**·wyr**) warrior.
rhyferthwy *m* tempest.
rhyfon *pl* currants.
rhyfyg *m* presumption.
rhyfygu *v* to presume.
rhyfygus *adj* presumptuous.
rhyg *m* rye.
rhygnu *v* to grate.
rhygyngu *v* to canter.
rhyng(ddi) *see* **rhwng.**
rhyngu bodd *v* to satisfy.
rhyngwladol *adj* international.
rhynllyd *adj* shivering.
rhynnu *v* to freeze.
rhysedd *m* abundance.
rhython *pl* cockles.
rhythu *v* to stare.
rhyw *adj* some. • *f* (**·iau**) sex.
rhywbeth *m* something.
rhywbryd *adv* sometime.
rhywfaint *m* some amount.
rhywfodd, rhywsut *adv* somehow.
rhywiog *adj* proper.
rhywiol *adj* sexual.
rhywle *adv* somewhere.
rhywogaeth *f* (**·au**) species.
rhywsut *adv* somehow.
rhyw·un *m* (**·rai**) someone.

S

Sab(b)ath, Saboth *m* (**Sabathau, Sabothau**) Sabbath.
sach *f* (**·au**) sack.
sach·aid *f* (**·eidiau**) sackful.
sachlïain *m* sackcloth.
sad *adj* stable.
sadio *v* to steady.
sadrwydd *m* steadiness.
Sadwrn *m* (**Sadyrnau**) Saturday.
Sadwrn *f* Saturn.
saer *m* (**seiri**) carpenter.
saernïaeth *f* workmanship.
saernïo *v* to construct.
Saesneg *f* English.
Saeson *see* **Sais.**
saeth *f* (**·au**) arrow.
saethu *v* to shoot.
saethydd *m* (**·ion**) archer.
saethyddiaeth *f* archery.
saf *from* **sefyll.**
safadwy *adj* steadfast.
safann·a *m* (**·au**) savannah.
safbwynt *m* (**·iau**) standpoint.
safiad *m* (a) stand.
safle *m/f* (**·oedd**) site.
safn *f* (**·au**) mouth.
safnrhwth *adj* gaping.
safon *f* (**·au**) standard.
safoni *v* to standardise.
safonol *adj* standard.
saff *adj* safe.
saffrwm, saffrwn *m* crocus.
sang *f* (**·au**) chock-a-block.
sangu, sengi *v* to tread.
saib, seibian·t *m* (**seibiau, ·nau**) pause.
saif from **sefyll.**
saig *f* (**seigiau**) dish.

sail *f* (**seiliau**) foundation.
saim *m* (**seimiau**) grease.
sain *f* (**seiniau**) sound.
saint *see* **sant**.
Sais *m* (**Saeson**) Englishman.
saith *num* seven.
sâl *adj* ill.
salm *f* (**·au**) psalm.
salm-dôn *f* (**salmdonau**) chant.
salmydd *m* psalmist.
salw *adj* ugly.
salwch *m* illness.
Sallwyr *m* Psalter.
samona *v* to fish for salmon.
sanau *see* **hosan**.
sanctaidd, santaidd *adj* sacred.
sancteiddio *v* to sanctify.
sancteiddrwydd *m* holiness.
sant *m* (**saint, seintiau**) saint.
santes *f* female saint.
sarff *f* (**seirff**) serpent.
sarhad *m* insult.
sarhau *v* to insult.
sarhaus *adj* insulting.
sarn *f* (**·au**) causeway.
sarnu *v* to spill.
sarrug *adj* surly.
sas·iwn *m/f* (**·iynau**) Methodist Association.
sathredig *adj* debased.
sathru *v* to trample.
sawdl *m/f* (**sodlau**) heel.
sawl *pron* whoso.
sawr *m* savour.
sawru *v* to smell.
sawrus *adj* savoury.
saws *m* sauce.
sbâr *adj* spare.
sbardun, ysbardun *m* (**·au**) accelerator.
sbario *v* to spare.
sbectol *f* spectacles.
sbectrwm *m* (**sbectra**) spectrum.
sbeislyd *adj* spicy.
sbeitio *v* to spite.
sbeitlyd *adj* spiteful.
sbio *v* to look.
sbel *f* period.
sbon *adj*: **newydd sbon** brand-new.
sbonc *f* leap.
sboncen *f* squash.
sboncio *v* to bounce.
sbri *m* fun.
sbrigyn *m* (**·nau**) sprig.
sbwng, ysbwng *m* (**sbyngau**) sponge.
sbŵl *m* (**sbwliau**) spool.
sbwriel *m* rubbish.
sbwylio *v* to spoil.
sbyngau *see* **sbwng**.
sebon *m* (**·au**) soap.
seboni *v* to flatter.
sebon·wr *m* (**·wyr**) flatterer.
secretu *v* to secrete.
sebra *m* (**·od**) zebra.
sech *adj* (*f*) dry.
sedd *f* (**·au**) seat.
sef *conj* namely.
sefydledig *adj* established.
sefydliad *m* (**·au**) institution.
sefydlog *adj* settled.
sefydlogrwydd *m* stability.
sefydlu *v* to establish.
sefyll *v* to stand.
sefyllfa *f* (**·oedd**) situation.
sefyllian *v* to stand about.
segur *adj* unemployed.

segurdod *m* idleness.
sengi *see* **sangu.**
sengl *adj* single.
seia·t *f* (**·dau**) religious meeting.
seibian·t *m* (**·nau**) leisure.
seiciatreg *m/f* psychiatry.
seiciatrydd *m* psychiatrist.
seicoleg *m/f* psychology.
seicolegol *adj* psychological.
seicolegydd *m* psychologist.
seigiau *see* **saig.**
seiliau *see* **sail.**
seilio *v* to base.
seimiau *see* **saim.**
seimlyd, seimllyd *adj* greasy.
seindorf *f* band.
seingl·awr *m* (**·oriau**) keyboard.
seiniau *see* **sain.**
seinio *v* to sound.
seintiau *see* **sant.**
seintwar *f* sanctuary.
seirff *see* **sarff.**
seiri *see* **saer.**
Seisnig *adj* English.
Seisnigeiddio *v* to Anglicise.
seithfed *adj* seventh.
seithug *adj* wasted.
seithwaith *adv* seven times.
sêl *f* zeal; seal; sale.
seld *f* (**·au**) dresser.
selio *v* to seal.
selog *adj* zealous.
selsigen *f* (**selsig**) sausage.
seml *adj* (*f*) simple.
sen *f* (**·nau**) reproof.
senedd *f* (**·au**) parliament.
seneddol *adj* parliamentary.
sensitifrwydd *m* sensitivity.
sensoriaeth *f* censorship.
sentimentaliaeth *f* sentimentality.
sêr *see* **seren.**
sercol *m* charcoal.
serch *m* love. • *conj* although.
serchog, serchus *adj* affectionate.
sêr-ddewin *m* (**·iaid**) astrologer.
sêr-ddewiniaeth *f* astrology.
seremoni *f* (**seremonïau**) ceremony.
seremonïol *adj* ceremonial.
seren *f* (**sêr**) star.
serenâd *m* serenade.
serennog, serog *adj* starry.
serennu *v* to twinkle.
serth *adj* steep.
seryddiaeth *f* astronomy.
serydd·wr *m* (**·wyr**) astronomer.
sesbin *m* shoehorn.
sêt *f* (**seti**) seat.
setin *m* (**·oedd**) hedge.
seth *adj* (*f*) straight.
sewin, siwin *m* sea-trout.
sffêr *f* (**sfferau**).
sfferaidd *adj* spherical.
sgadenyn *m* (**sgadan**) herring.
sgaprwth *adj* uncouth.
sgarmesydd *m* (**·ion**) fighter (plane).
sgeintio *v* to sprinkle.
sgerb·wd *m* (**·ydau**) skeleton.
sgert *f* (**·iau**) skirt.
sgìl *m* (**sgiliau**) skill.
sgil *m* (on the) back (of).
sgio *v* to ski.
sgiw *f* (**·ion**) settle.
sgiw *adj*: **ar sgiw** askew.
sglefren *f* slide.
sglefrio *v* to skate.
sglefrholio *v* to roller-skate.

sglein *m* shine.
sgleinio *v* to shine.
sglod·yn *m* (**·ion**) chip.
sgolor *m* (**·ion**) (able) schoolchild.
sgrech *f* (**·iadau**) scream.
sgrechain, sgrechian *v* to shriek.
sgrwb *m* stiffness.
sgrwbio *v* to scrub.
sguthan *f* (**·od**) wood pigeon.
sgwâr *m/f* (**sgwariau**) square.
sgwaryn *m* (**·nau**) square.
sgwd *m* (**sgydau**) cascade.
sgwïer *m* (**sgwierlaid**) squire.
sgwlyn *m* headmaster.
sgwrio *v* to scour.
sgwrs *f* (**sgyrsiau**) conversation.
sgwrsio *v* to talk.
sgydau *see* **sgwd**.
sgyrsiau *see* **sgwrs**.
si, su *m* (**sïon, suon**) buzz; whisper.
siaced *f* (**·i**) jacket.
siachmat *m* checkmate.
siafio *v* to shave.
sialc *m* (**·au**) chalk.
siambr *f* chamber.
siampŵ *m* (**·au**) shampoo.
sianel *f* (**·i**) channel.
siâp *m* (**siapau, siapiau**) shape.
siapo, siapio *v* to take shape.
siapus *adj* shapely.
siâr *f* (**siariau**) share.
siarad *v* to speak.
siaradus *adj* garrulous.
siarad·wr *m* (**·wyr**) speaker.
siario *v* to share.
siarp *adj* sharp.
siarsio *v* to warn.
siasbi *m* shoehorn.
siawns *f* chance.
sibrwd *v* to whisper.
sibr·wd *m* (**·ydion**) whisper.
sicr *adj* sure.
sicrhau *v* to ensure.
sicrwydd *m* assurance.
sidan *m* (**·au**) silk.
sidanaidd *adj* silky.
sideru *v* to make lace.
sidydd *m* zodiac.
siersi *m/f* sweater.
sieryd *from* **siarad**.
siesbin *m* shoehorn.
siew *f* (**·iau**) show.
siffrwd *v* to rustle.
sigâr *f* (**sigarau**) cigar.
sigarét *f* (**sigaretau**) cigarette.
siglad *m* (**·au**) (a) shaking.
sigledig *adj* shaky.
siglen *f* (**·ni, ·nydd**) swamp; swing.
sigl-i-gwt *m* wagtail.
siglo *v* to shake.
sil *m* spawn.
silff *f* (**·oedd**) shelf.
silidón *m* minnow.
silwair *m* silage.
sill, sillaf *f* (**·au**) syllable.
sillafiad *m* spelling.
sillafu *v* to spell.
simdde, simnai *f* (**simneiau**) chimney.
simsan *adj* unsteady.
simsanu *v* to totter.
sinach *f* skinflint.
sin·ws *m* (**·ysau**) sinus.
sïo *v* to hum.
sioe *f* (**·au**) show.
siôl *f* (**siolau**) shawl.

siom *m/f* disappointment.
siomedig *adj* disappointed.
siomedigaeth *f* (**·au**) disappointment.
siomi *v* to disappoint.
Siôn Corn *m* Santa Claus.
sionc *adj* nimble.
sioncrwydd *m* alacrity.
sioncyn y gwair *m* grasshopper.
siop *f* (**·au**) shop.
siopa *v* to shop.
siop·wr *m* (**·wyr**) shopkeeper.
sipian, sipio *v* to sip; to zip.
siprys *m* mixed corn.
sipsi *m* (**·wn**) gypsy.
sir *f* (**·oedd**) county.
siriol *adj* pleasant.
sirioldeb *m* serenity.
sirioli *v* to cheer up.
sirydd, siryf *m* (**·ion**) (high) sheriff.
sisial *v* to whisper.
sis·wrn *m* (**·yrnau**) scissors.
siwgr *m* sugar.
siwmper *f* (**·i**) jumper.
siwr, siŵr *adj* sure.
siwrn·ai *f* (**·eiau, ·eion**) journey.
slafaidd *adj* slavish.
slefren fôr *f* jellyfish.
slei *adj* sly.
sleifio *v* to slink.
sleis·en *f* (**·ys**) slice.
slic *adj* slippery.
slotian *v* to tipple.
smala *adj* droll.
smaldod *m* banter.
smalio *v* to joke, to pretend.
smonach *f* mess.
smot·yn *m* (**·iau**) spot.
smwddio *v* to iron.
smwt *adj* snub.
smygu *v* to smoke.
sniffian, snwffian *v* to sniff.
snisin *m* snuff.
snobyddiaeth *f* snobbishness.
snobyddlyd *adj* snobbish.
sobr *adj* serious.
sobri *v* to sober.
sobrwydd *m* sobriety.
sodlau *see* **sawdl.**
sodr, sawdur *m* (**sodrau**) solder.
sodro *v* to solder.
sodd·grwth *m* (**·grythau**) cello.
soeglyd *adj* soggy.
sofl·iar *f* (**·ieir**) quail.
soflyn *m* (**sofl**) stubble.
sofraniaeth *f* (**·au**) sovereignty.
solet *adj* solid.
solffaeo *v* to sing sol-fa.
sôn *v* to mention.
soniarus *adj* sonorous.
sorod *pl* dross.
sorri *v* to sulk.
sorth *adj* (*f*) sullen.
sosb·an *f* (**·annau, ·enni**) saucepan.
sosej *f* (**·ys**) sausage.
soser *f* (**·i**) saucer.
sosialaeth *f* socialism.
sosial·ydd *m* (**·wyr**) socialist.
sothach *m* rubbish.
sownd *adj* fast.
St *abb* sant (St).
staen *m* (**·iau**) stain.
staenio *v* to stain.
stâl *f* (**stalau**) stall.
stampio *v* to stamp.
statudol *adj* statutory.

stên *f* (**stenau**) pitcher.
sterylledig *adj* sterilised.
steryllu *v* to sterilise.
sticil, sticill *f* stile.
stilio *v* to question.
stôl *f* (**stolion**) stool; chair.
stomp *f* bungle.
stond *adj* stock (still).
stondin *m/f* (**·au**) stall.
stor·dy *m* (**·dai**) storehouse.
stor·i *f* (**·ïau, ·iâu, straeon**) story.
stor·ïwr *m* (**·ïwyr**) story-teller.
stormus *adj* stormy.
straegar *adj* gossipy.
straeon *see* **stori**.
stranc *f* (**·iau**) prank.
strancio *v* to struggle.
strap·en *f* (**·iau**) strap.
strategaeth *f* strategy.
strategol *adj* strategic.
streic *f* (**·iau**) strike.
stribed *m* (**·i**) strip.
strim-stram-strellach *adv* helter-skelter.
strôc *f* (**strociau**) seizure.
strwythur *m* structure.
stryd *f* (**·oedd**) street.
stumog *f* (**·au**) stomach.
stwc *m* (**stycau**) oil.
stwffio *v* to stuff.
stwffwl *m* (**styffylau**) staple.
stwnsh *m* mash.
stwnsio, stwmpo *v* to mash.
stŵr *m* rumpus.
stwrllyd *adj* rowdy.
styd·en *f* (**·iau**) stud.
su *m* hum.
sudd *m* (**·ion**) juice.
suddlon *adj* succulent.
suddo *v* to sink.
sugnedd *m* (**·au**) quagmire.
sugno *v* to suck.
Sul *m* (**·iau**) Sunday.
Sulgwyn *m* Whitsun.
suo *v* to hum.
sur *adj* sour.
surbwch *adj* surly.
surdoes *m* leaven.
surni *m* sourness.
suro *v* to sour.
sut *pron* how; what sort.
sw *m* (**sŵau**) zoo.
swaden *f* clout.
swatio *v* to squat.
swci *adj* tame.
swclen *f* filly.
swclyn *m* colt.
swcro *v* to succour.
swch *f* (**sychau**) ploughshare.
sweden *f* (**swêds**) swede.
swil *adj* shy.
swildod *m* shyness.
switsio *v* to switch.
swllt *m* (**sylltau**) shilling.
swm *m* (**symiau**) sum.
swmbwl *m* (**symbylau**) goad.
swmp *m* bulk.
swmpus *adj* bulky.
sŵn *m* (**synau**) noise.
swnian *v* to grumble.
swnio *v* to sound.
swnllyd *adj* noisy.
swnt *m* (**·iau**) strait.
sŵoleg *f* zoology.
sŵoleg·wr, sŵoleg·ydd *m* (**·wyr**) zoologist.

swp *m* (**sypiau**) pile.
swper *m/f* (**·au**) supper.
swpera *v* to eat supper.
swrealaeth *f* surrealism.
swrn *f* (**syrnau**) ankle.
swrth *adj* sullen.
sws *m* (**·ys**) kiss.
swta *adj* abrupt.
swydd *f* (**·i**) job.
swydd·fa *f* (**·feydd**) office.
swyddog *m* (**·ion**) officer.
swyddogaeth *f* (**·au**) function.
swyddogol *adj* official.
swyn *m* (**·ion**) charm.
swyngyfaredd *f* (**·ion**) enchantment.
swyno *v* to enchant.
swynol *adj* enchanting.
swyn·wr *m* (**·wyr**) enchanter.
sy, sydd *v* are.
syber *adj* gracious.
sycamorwydden *f* (**sycamorwydd**) sycamore.
sych *adj* dry.
sychau *see* **swch**.
sychder *m* dryness, drought.
syched *m* thirst.
sychedig *adj* thirsty.
sychedu *v* to thirst.
sychlyd *adj* dry.
sychu *v* to dry.
sychydd *m* dryer.
sydyn *adj* sudden.
sydynrwydd *m* suddenness.
sydd *v* is, are.
syfïen *f* (**syfi**) strawberry.
syflyd *v* to flinch.
syfrdan *adj* stunned.
syfrdandod *m* stupor.
syfrdanol *adj* stunning.
syfrdanu to shock.
syl·faen *m/f* (**·feini**) foundation.
sylfaenol *adj* fundamental.
sylfaenu *v* to found.
sylfaen·wr, sylfaen·ydd *m* (**·wyr**) founder.
sylw *m* (**·adau**) observation.
sylwadaeth *f* observation.
sylwebaeth *f* commentary.
sylwebydd *m* (**·ion**) commentator.
sylwedydd *m* (**·ion**) observer.
sylwedd *m* substance.
sylweddol *adj* substantial.
sylweddoli *v* to realise.
sylwgar *adj* observant.
sylwi *v* to notice.
sylltau *see* **swllt**.
syllu *v* to gaze.
symbolaidd *adj* symbolic.
symbylau *see* **swmbwl**.
symbyliad *m* incentive.
symbylu *v* to encourage.
syml *adj* simple.
symleiddio *v* to simplify.
symlrwydd *m* simplicity.
symol *adj* fair.
symud *v* to move.
symudiad *m* (**·au**) movement.
symudol *adj* mobile.
syn *adj* amazed.
synau *see* **sŵn**.
syndod *m* wonder.
synfyfyrio *v* to muse.
synhwyrau *see* **synnwyr**.
synhwyro *v* to sense.
synhwyrol *adj* sensible.
syniad *m* (**·au**) idea.

synied, synio *v* to imagine.
synned *from* **syn.**
synnu *v* to be surprised.
syn·nwyr *m* (**·hwyrau**) sense.
sypiau *see* **swp.**
sypyn *m* (**·nau**) heap.
syr *m* sir.
syrcas *f* circus.
syrffed *m* surfeit.
syrffedu *v* to be fed up.
syrr *from* **sorri.**
syrthiedig *adj* fallen.
syrthio *v* to fall.
syrthni *m* lethargy.
syth *adj* straight.
sythu *v* to benumb.
sythwelediad *m* insight.

T

t. *abb* tudalen p.
tablen *f* beer.
tab·wrdd *m* (**·yrddau**) tabor.
tacio *v* to tack.
taclau *pl* kit.
taclo *v* to tackle.
taclus *adj* tidy.
tacluso *v* to trim.
taclusrwydd *m* neatness.
tacteg *f* (**·au**) tactics.
Tachwedd *m* November.
tad *m* (**·au**) father.
tad-cu *m* grandfather.
tadmaeth *m* (**tadau maeth**) foster-father.
tadogaeth *f* derivation.
tadogi *v* to ascribe.
tadol *adj* fatherlike.
tad-yng-nghyfraith *m* father-in-law.
taenelliad *m* sprinkling.
taenellu *v* to sprinkle.
taenu *v* to spread.
taeog *m* (**·ion**) serf.
taeogaidd *adj* churlish.
taer *adj* earnest.
taeru *v* to insist.
tafarn *f* (**·au**) pub.
tafarn·dy *m* (**·dai**) public house.
tafarn·wr *m* (**·wyr**) publican.
tafell *f* (**·au, ·i**) slice.
taflegr·yn *m* (**·au**) missile.
tafleis·ydd *m* (**·wyr**) ventriloquist.
taflen *f* (**·ni**) leaflet.
taflennu *v* to tabulate.
tafliad *m* (**·au**) a throw.
taflod *f* (**·ydd**) loft.
taflu *v* to throw.
tafluniad *m* (**·au**) projection.
taflunydd *m* (**·ion**) projector.
tafod *m* (**·au**) tongue.
tafodi *v* to scold.
tafod·iaith *f* (**·ieithoedd**) dialect.
tafodieithol *adj* colloquial.
tafod-leferydd *m* speech.
tafol *f* scales.
tafolen *f* (**tafol**) dock (plant).
tafoli *v* to weigh up.
tagell *f* (**·au**) chin; gill.
tag·fa *f* (**·feydd**) blockage.

tagu *v* to choke.
tagydd *m* (a) choke.
tangnefedd *m/f* peace.
tangnefeddus *adj* peaceful.
tangnefeddwyr *pl* peacemakers.
tai *see* **tŷ**.
taid *m* (**teidiau**) grandfather.
tair *num* (*f*) three.
taith *f* (**teithiau**) journey.
tal *adj* tall.
tâl, taliad *m* (**taliadau**) fee.
taladwy *adj* payable.
tal·aith *f* (**·eithiau**) state.
talar *f* (**·au**) headland (ploughing).
talcen *m* (**·ni, ·nau**) forehead.
talch *m* (**teilchion**) smithereen.
talchu *v* to shatter.
taldra *m* height.
taleb *f* (**·au**) voucher.
taleithiol *adj* provincial.
talentog *adj* talented.
talfyriad *m* (**·au**) abridgement.
talfyrru *v* to abbreviate.
talgrynnu *v* to round off.
taliad *m* (**·au**) payment.
talïaidd *adj* noble.
talm, talwm *m* (**·au**) period.
talog *adj* lively.
talp *m* (**·au**) chunk.
talpiog *adj* lumpy.
talu *v* to pay.
tal·wrn *m* (**·yrnau**) cockpit.
tam·aid *m* (**·eidiau**) bit.
tameidiog *adj* bitty.
tamprwydd *m* dampness.
tan *prep* under. • *conj* until.
tân *m* (**tanau**) fire.
tanbaid *adj* fiery.
tanbeidio *v* to glow.
tanbeidiol *adj* glowing.
tanchwa *f* (**·oedd**) explosion.
tanddaearol *adj* underground.
taner·dy *m* (**·dai**) tannery.
tanfor *adj* submarine.
tangloddio *v* to undermine.
taniad *m* ignition.
tanio *v* to ignite.
tan·iwr *m* (**·wyr**) firer.
tanlinellu *v* to underline.
tanllwyth *m* (**·i**) blazing fire.
tanllyd *adj* fiery.
tannau *see* **tant**.
tannu *v* to spread.
tanodd *adv* beneath.
tan·t *m* (**·nau**) string.
tanwydd *m* (**·au**) fuel.
tanysgrifiad *m* (**·au**) subscription.
tanysgrifio *v* to subscribe.
tanysgrif·iwr *m* (**·wyr**) subscriber.
tâp *m* (**tapiau**) tape.
taradr *m* (**terydr**) auger.
taran *f* (**·au**) thunder.
taranfollt *f* thunderbolt.
taranu *v* to thunder.
tarddiad *m* (**·au**) source.
tarddian·t *m* (**·nau**) eruption.
tarddle *m* (**·oedd**) source.
tarddu *v* to derive from.
tarfu *v* to interrupt.
targed *m* (**·au**) target.
tarian *f* (**·au**) shield.
taro *v* to hit.
tarten *f* (**·nau, ·ni**) tart.
tarth *m* (**·au**) vapour.
tarw *m* (**teirw**) bull.
tarwden *f* ringworm.

tas *f* (**teisi**) haystack.
tasg *f* (**-au**) task.
tasgu *v* to splash.
taten *f* (**tatws, tato, tatw**) potato.
tau *from* **tewi**.
taw[1] *m* silence.
taw[2] *conj* that.
TAW *abb* Treth ar Werth (VAT).
taw(af) *from* **tewi**.
tawch *m* vapour.
tawdd *adj* molten. • *v from* **toddi**.
tawedog *adj* taciturn.
tawel *adj* quiet.
tawelu *v* to calm.
tawelwch *m* stillness.
tawnod *m* (**-au**) rest.
te *m* tea.
tebot *m* (**-au**) teapot.
tebyg *adj* similar.
tebygol *adj* likely.
tebygolrwydd *m* likelihood.
tebygrwydd *m* similarity.
tebygu *v* to liken.
tecáu *v* to get finer.
teced *from* **teg**.
teclyn *m* (**taclau**) tool.
techneg *f* (**-au**) technique.
technegol *adj* technical.
techneg·ydd *m* (**-wyr**) technician.
tefl(ais) *from* **taflu**.
teg *adj* fair.
tegan *m* (**-au**) toy.
tegeirian *m* orchid.
tegell *m* (**-au, -i**) kettle.
tegwch *m* beauty.
teidiau *see* **taid**.
teifl *from* **taflu**.
teigr *m* (**-od**) tiger.
teilchion *see* **talch**.
teil·iwr *m* (**-wriaid**) tailor.
teilsen *f* (**teils**) tile.
teilwng *adj* worthy.
teilwra *v* to tailor.
teilyngdod *m* merit.
teilyngu *v* to merit.
teimlad *m* (**-au**) feeling.
teimladol *adj* sentimental.
teimladwy *adj* impassioned.
teimlo *v* to feel.
teimlydd *m* (**-ion**) antenna.
teios *pl* cottages.
teipiadur *m* (**-on**) typewriter.
teipio *v* to type.
teipydd *m* (**-ion**) typist.
teipyddes *f* (**-au**) typist.
teipysgrif *f* (**-au**) typescript.
teirf *from* **tarfu**.
teirw *see* **tarw**.
teisen *f* (**-nau**) cake.
teisi *see* **tas**.
teithi *pl* characteristics.
teithiau *see* **taith**.
teithio *v* to travel.
teithiol *adj* travelling.
teith·iwr *m* (**-wyr**) traveller.
tel(ais) *from* **talu**.
telathrebiaeth *f* telecommunication.
telathrebu *v* to print.
telediad *m* telecast.
teledu *m* television.
teleffon, teliffon *m* (**-au**) telephone.
telerau *pl* terms.
telor *m* (**-iaid**) warbler.
telori *v* to warble.
telpyn *m* (**talpau**) lump.

telyn *f* (**·au**) harp.
telyneg *f* (**·ion**) lyric.
telynegol *adj* lyrical.
telynor *m* (**·ion**) harpist.
telynores *f* (**·au**) harpist.
teml *f* (**·au**) temple.
tempro *v* to temper.
temp·o *m* (**·i**) tempo.
temtas·iwn *m/f* (**·iynau**) temptation.
temtio *v* to tempt.
ten *adj* (*f*) tight.
tenant *m* (**·iaid**) tenant.
tenantiaeth *f* tenancy.
tenau *adj* thin.
tendio *v* to tend.
teneued *from* **tenau**.
teneuo *v* to thin.
tenewyn *m* (**·nau**) flank.
tennis *m* tennis.
ten·nyn *m* (**·ynnau**) tether.
têr *adj* clear.
teras *m* (**·au**) terrace.
terf(ais) *from* **tarfu**.
terfyn *m* (**·au**) boundary.
terfynell *f* (**·au**) terminal.
terfynol *adj* final.
terfyniad *m* (**·au**) ending.
terfynu *v* to terminate.
terfysg *m* (**·oedd**) tumult.
terfysgaeth *f* terrorism.
terfysglyd *adj* riotous.
terfysgu *v* to terrorise.
terfysg·wr *m* (**·wyr**) rioter.
terminoleg *f* terminology.
tery *from* **taro**.
terydr *see* **taradr**.
tes *m* heat.
tesog *adj* hot.
testun *m* (**·au**) subject.
teth *f* (**·au**) teat.
teulu *m* (**·oedd**) family.
teuluol *adj* domestic.
tew *adj* fat.
tew·dra, ·dwr, ·der *m* thickness.
tewhau *v* to fatten.
tewi *v* to become silent.
tewychu *v* to fatten.
teyrn *m* monarch.
teyrnas *f* (**·oedd**) kingdom.
teyrnasiad *m* (**·au**) (a) reign.
teyrnasu *v* to reign.
teyrnfrad·wr *m* (**·wyr**) traitor.
teyrnfradwriaeth *f* high treason.
teyrngar *adj* loyal.
teyrngarwch *m* loyalty.
teyrnged *f* (**·au**) tribute.
teyrn·wialen *f* (**·wiail**) sceptre.
TGAU *abb* Tystysgrif Gyffredinol Addysg Uwchradd (GCSE).
ti *pron* you.
ticed *m* (**·i**) ticket.
tician *v* to tick.
tid *f* (**·au**) chain.
tila *adj* feeble.
tîm *m* (**timau, timoedd**) team.
tin *f* (**·au**) bum.
tinc *m* (a) hint.
tincial *v* to tinkle.
tindroi *v* to dawdle.
tipian *v* to tick.
tip·yn *m* (**·iau**) (a) little.
tir *m* (**·oedd**) land.
tirf *adj* verdant.
tirfeddian·nwr *m* (**·wyr**) landowner.
tirfesur·ydd *m* (**·wyr**) surveyor.
tirio *v* to ground.

tiriogaeth *f* (**·au**) territory.
tiriogaethol *adj* territorial.
tirion *adj* gentle.
tiriondeb *m* kindness.
tirlun *m* (**·iau**) landscape.
tirwedd *f* (**·au**) (geographical) relief.
tisian *v* to sneeze.
titw *m* (**titŵod**) tit.
tithau *pron* you (too).
tiwnio *v* to tune.
tlawd *adj* poor.
tlos *adj* (*f*) pretty.
tloted *from* **tlawd**.
tlo·ty *m* (**·tai**) poorhouse.
tlotyn *m* (**tlodion**) pauper.
tlws *m* (**tlysau**) jewel.
tlws *adj* pretty.
tlysni *m* prettiness.
t/o *abb* tan ofal (c/o).
to *m* (**·au**) roof.
to *m* generation.
toc *adv* soon.
tocio *v* to clip.
tocyn *m* (**·nau**) ticket; slice of bread.
tocyn·nwr *m* (**·wyr**) ticket collector.
toddadwy *adj* soluble.
toddedig *adj* molten.
toddi *v* to melt.
toddian·t *m* (**·nau**) solution.
toddion *pl* dripping.
toddydd *m* (**·ion**) solvent.
todd·yn *m* (**·ion**) solute.
toes *m* dough.
toesen *f* (**·ni**) doughnut.
toi *v* to roof.
toili *m* ghostly funeral.
tolach *v* to fondle.
tolc *m* (**·iau**) dent.
tolciog *adj* dented.
tolch, tolchen *f* (**·au, ·ni**) clot.
tolchennu *v* to coagulate.
tolio *v* to stint.
toll *f* (**·au**) toll.
toll·borth *m* (**·byrth**) tollgate.
tollty *m* (**tolltai**) custom-house.
tom *f* manure.
tomen *f* (**·ni, ·nydd**) dunghill.
ton *f* (**·nau**) wave.
tôn *f* (**tonau**) tune.
tôn *m* (**tonau**) tone.
tonc *f* (a) tinkle.
tonfedd *f* (**·i**) wavelength.
tonnau *see* **ton**.
tonnen *f* bog.
tonni *v* to billow.
tonnog *adj* wavy.
tonyddiaeth *f* intonation.
tor *f* (**·rau**) litter.
torcalonnus *adj* heart-breaking.
torcyfraith *m* breach of law.
torch *m/f* (**·au**) torque.
torchi *v* to coil.
torchog *adj* coiled.
toreithiog *adj* fertile.
toreth *f* abundance.
torf *f* (**·eydd**) crowd.
torgoch *m* roach.
torheulo *v* to bask.
toriad *m* (**·au**) break.
torlan *f* (**·nau**) (hollow) river bank.
torllengig *m* rupture.
torllwyth, torraid *f* litter.
torrau *see* **tor**.
torri *v* to break.

tor·rwr *m* (**·wyr**) cutter.
torsythu *v* to swagger.
torth *f* (**·au**) loaf.
torthen *f* (**·ni**) clot.
tost *adj* ill.
tostedd, tostrwydd *m* illness.
tostio *v* to toast.
tosturi *m* compassion.
tosturio *v* to pity.
tosturiol *adj* compassionate.
tosyn *m* (**tosau**) pimple.
tô·wr *m* (**·wyr**) roofer.
tra *adj* very.
tra *conj* while.
tra-arglwyddiaeth *f* (**·au**) tyranny.
tra-arglwyddiaethu *v* to lord it.
trabŵd *adj* soaking.
tracwisg *f* (**·oedd**) tracksuit.
trachefn *adv* again.
trachwant *m* (**·au**) greed.
trachwantus *adj* avaricious.
trachywir *adj* precise.
tradwy *adv* three days hence.
traddodi *v* to deliver (a speech).
traddodiad *m* (**·au**) tradition.
traddodiadol *adj* traditional.
traddod·wr *m* (**·wyr**) deliverer.
traean *m* one third.
traed *see* **troed**.
traeth *m* (**·au**) beach.
traeth·awd *m* (**·odau**) composition.
traethell *f* (**·au**) shore.
traethiad *m* (**·au**) narrative; predicate.
traethu *v* to relate.
traflyncu *v* to devour.
trafnidiaeth *f* traffic.
trafod *v* to discuss.
trafodaeth *f* (**·au**) discussion.
trafodion *pl* transactions.
trafferth *m/f* (**·ion**) trouble.
trafferthu *v* to take trouble.
trafferthus *adj* troublesome.
tra·ffordd *f* (**·ffyrdd**) motorway.
tragwyddol, tragywydd *adj* eternal.
tragwyddoldeb *m* eternity.
traha, trahauster *m* arrogance.
trahaus *adj* haughty.
trai *m* ebb.
traidd *from* **treiddio**.
trais *m* violence, rape.
trallod *m* (**·ion**) tribulation.
trallodus *adj* troubled.
trallwysiad *m* (**·au**) transfusion.
trallwyso *v* to transfuse.
tramgwydd *m* (**·au**) hindrance.
tramgwyddo *v* to offend.
tramor *adj* foreign.
tramor·wr *m* (**·wyr**) foreigner.
tramwyo *v* to pass.
tranc *m* death.
trannoeth *adv* the next day.
trapes·iwm *m* (**·iymau**) trapezium.
traphont *f* (**·ydd**) viaduct.
tras *f* lineage.
traserch *m* infatuation.
trasied·i *m* (**·ïau**) tragedy.
traul *f* (**treuliau**) expense; wear.
traw *m* pitch (in music).
traw(af) *from* **taro**.
trawiad *m* (**·au**) blow.
trawiadol *adj* striking.
traws *adj* cross.
trawsacennu *v* to syncopate.
trawsblannu *v* to transplant.

trawsdoriad *m* (**·au**) cross-section.
trawsffurfiad *m* (**·au**) transformation.
trawsgludo *v* to transport.
trawsgyweirio *v* to modulate, to transpose.
trawst *m* (**·iau**) beam.
treblu *v* to treble.
trech *adj* superior.
trechu *v* to defeat.
trech·wr *m* (**·wyr**) victor.
tref, tre *f* (**·i, ·ydd**) town.
trefedigaeth *f* (**·au**) colony.
treflan *f* (**·nau**) small town.
trefn *f* order.
trefniad, trefniant *m* (**trefniadau**) arrangement.
trefnlen *f* (**·ni**) schedule.
trefnu *v* to arrange.
trefnus *adj* orderly.
trefnusrwydd *m* orderliness.
trefnydd *m* (**·ion**) organiser.
trefol *adj* urban.
treftadaeth *f* inheritance.
trengi *v* to die.
treial *m* (**·on**) trial.
treiddgar *adj* penetrating.
treiddgarwch *m* acumen.
treiddio *v* to penetrate.
treiglad *m* (**·au**) mutation.
treigliad *m* (**·au**) (the) passing.
treiglo *v* to mutate; to roll.
treillio *v* to trawl.
treio *v* to ebb.
treis·iad *f* (**·iedi**) heifer.
treisio *v* to rape.
treisiol *adj* violent.
treis·iwr *m* (**·wyr**) rapist.
trem *f* (a) glance.
tremio *v* to gaze.
trên *m/f* (**trenau**) train.
trennydd *adv* the day after next.
tresbasu *v* to trespass.
tresglen *f* missel-thrush.
tresi *pl* traces (straps).
treth *f* (**·i**) tax.
trethadwy *adj* taxable.
trethdal·wr *m* (**·wyr**) ratepayer.
trethu *v* to tax.
treuliad *m* digestion.
treuliau *pl* expenses.
treulio *v* to wear.
trew(ir) *from* **taro**.
tri *num* three.
triagl, triog *m* treacle.
triawd *m* (**·au**) trio.
tribiwnlys *m* (**·oedd**) tribunal.
tridiau *pl* three days.
trigain *num* sixty.
trig·fa, trigfan *f* (**·feydd, ·nau**) dwelling.
trigo *v* to dwell; to die (of animals).
trigolion *pl* inhabitants.
trilliw *adj* tortoiseshell.
trin *f* battle. • *v* to treat.
trindod *f* trinity.
tringar *adj* tender.
triniaeth *f* (**·au**) treatment.
trioedd *pl* triads.
triongl *m* (**·au**) triangle.
trionglog *adj* triangular.
tripled *m* (**·i**) triplet.
trist *adj* sad.
tristáu *v* to sadden.
tristwch *m* sadness.
triw *adj* loyal.

tro *m* (**·eon**) turn.
troad *m* (**·au**) bend, turning.
tro·bwll *m* (**·byllau**) whirlpool.
trobwynt *m* (**·iau**) turning-point.
troch·fa *f* (**·feydd**) (a) soaking.
trochi *v* to dip.
trochiad *m* (**·au**) immersion.
trochion *pl* suds.
troch·iwr, troch·wr *m* (**·wyr**) dipper.
troed *m/f* (**traed**) foot.
troedfedd *f* (**·i**) foot (12 inches).
troëdig *adj* turned; perverse.
tröedigaeth *f* (**·au**) conversion.
troedio *v* to tread.
troedlath *f* (**·au**) treadle.
troednod·yn *m* (**·iadau**) footnote.
troednoeth *adj* barefooted.
troell *f* (**·au**) spinning-wheel.
troelli *v* to spin.
troellog *adj* twisting.
troes *from* **troi**.
trof·a *f* (**·âu, ·eydd**) bend.
trofan *m* (**·nau**) tropic.
trofannol *adj* tropical.
trofeydd *see* **tro**.
trof·wrdd *m* (**·yrddau**) turntable.
trog·en *f* (**·od**) tick.
trogylch *m* (**·au**) orbit.
troi *v* to turn.
trol *f* (**·iau**) cart.
trom *adj* (*f*) heavy.
trôns *m* (**tronsiau**) pants.
tros, dros *prep* over.
trosedd *m/f* (**·au**) offence.
troseddu *v* to commit an offence.
trosedd·wr *m* (**·wyr**) offender.
trosg·ais *m* (**·eisiau**) converted try.
trosgl *adj* (*f*) clumsy.
trosglwyddo *v* to transfer.
trosglwyddydd *m* (**·ion**) transmitter.
trosgynnol *adj* transcendental.
trosi *v* to translate; to convert.
trosiad *m* (**·au**) translation.
trosodd, drosodd *adv* over.
trosol *m* (**·ion**) lever.
trotian *v* to trot.
trothwy *m* (**·au**) threshold.
tru·an *m* (**·einiaid**) wretch.
trueni *m* pity.
truenus *adj* wretched.
trugaredd *m/f* (**·au**) mercy.
trugarhau *v* to have mercy.
trugarog *adj* merciful.
trugarowgrwydd *m* mercifulness.
trull·iad *m* (**·iaid**) butler.
trum *m* (**·iau**) ridge.
truth *m* rigmarole.
trwbad·ŵr *m* (**·wriaid**) troubadour.
trwch *m* (**trychion**) thickness.
trwchus *adj* thick.
trwm *adj* heavy.
trwnc *m* (**tryncIau**) trunk.
trwodd *adv* through.
trw(of) *from* **trwy**.
trwser *m* (**·i**) trousers.
trwsgl *adj* clumsy.
trwsiadus *adj* dapper.
trwsio *v* to mend.
trws·iwr *m* (**·wyr**) repairer.
trwst *m* (**trystau**) uproar.
trwstan *adj* awkward.
trwy, drwy *prep* through.
trwyadl *adj* thorough.
trwydded *f* (**·au**) licence.

trwyddedig *adj* licensed.
trwyddedu *v* to license.
trwyn *m* (**-au**) nose.
trwynol *adj* nasal.
trwynsur *adj* morose.
trwytho *v* to steep.
try *from* **troi**.
trybedd *f* (**-au**) tripod.
trybeilig *adj* awful.
trybestod *m* commotion.
trybini *m* misfortune.
tryblith *m* muddle.
trychfil, trychfil-yn *m* (**-od**) insect.
trychiad *m* (**-au**) section.
trychineb *m/f* disaster.
trychinebus *adj* disastrous.
trychion *see* **trwch**.
trychu *v* to amputate.
trydan *m* electricity.
trydaneg *f* electrical engineering.
trydanol *adj* electric.
trydanu *v* to electrify.
trydar *v* to chirp.
trydedd *adj* (*f*) third.
trydydd *adj* third.
tryfer *f* (**-i**) trident.
tryloyw *adj* transparent.
tryloywder *m* (**-au**) transparency.
trylwyr *adj* thorough.
trylwyredd *m* thoroughness.
trymaidd, trymllyd *adj* oppressive.
trymder *m* heaviness.
trymhau *v* to grow heavier.
trynewid *v* to permutate.
trysor *m* (**-au**) treasure.
trysor-fa *f* (**-feydd**) treasury.
trysori *v* to treasure.
trysorlys *m* treasury.
trysorydd *m* (**-ion**) treasurer.
trystau *see* **trwst**.
trystiog *adj* rowdy.
trythyllwch *m* lasciviousness.
trywanu *v* to pierce.
trywser, trywsus *m* (**-au**) trousers.
trywydd *m* track.
tsieini *m* china.
tsimpansî *m* chimpanzee.
tu *m* side.
tua, tuag *prep* about, towards.
tud *m* land; people.
tudalen *m/f* (**-nau**) page.
tuedd *f* (**-iadau**) tendency.
tueddfryd *m* inclination.
tueddiad *m* (**-au**) tendency.
tueddol *adj* inclined.
tueddu *v* to be inclined to.
tulath *f* (**-au**) beam.
tun-nell *f* (**-elli**) ton.
turio *v* to burrow.
turn *m* lathe.
turnio *v* to turn (wood).
turn-iwr *m* (**-wyr**) turner.
turtur *f* (**-od**) turtle-dove.
tus-w *m* (**-ŵau**) posy.
tuth *m* (**-iau**) trot.
tuthio, tuthian *v* to trot.
twb, twba, twbyn *m* (**tybau, tybiau**) tub.
twca *m* (carving) knife.
twff-yn *m* (**-iau**) tuft.
twng *from* **tyngu**.
twlc *m* (**tylcau, tylciau**) pigsty.
twll *m* (**tyllau**) hole.
twll *adj* broken.
twmffat *m* (**-au**) funnel.
twmpath *m* (**-au**) mound; folk dance.

twmplen *f* (**·ni**) dumpling.
twndis *m* (**·au**) funnel.
twn·nel *m* (**·elau, ·eli**) tunnel.
twp *adj* daft.
twpdra *m* stupidity.
twpsen *f* silly (woman).
twpsyn *m* silly (man).
twr *m* (**tyrrau**) heap.
tŵr *m* (**tyrau**) tower.
twrc·i *m* (**·ïod**) turkey.
twrch *m* (**tyrchod**) boar.
twrf *m* (**tyrfau**) noise; thunder.
twrio *v* to burrow.
twristiaeth *f* tourism.
twrn·ai *m* (**·eiod**) lawyer.
twrnameint *m* (**·iau**) tournament.
twrw, twrf *m* (**tyrfau**) thunder.
twsian *v* to sneeze.
twt *adj* neat.
twtio *v* to tidy.
twyll *m* deceit.
twyllo *v* to deceive.
twyllodrus *adj* deceitful.
twyll·wr *m* (**·wyr**) cheat.
twym *adj* warm.
twymder, twymdra *m* warmness.
twymgalon *adj* warm-hearted.
twymo *v* to warm.
twymyn *f* (**·au**) fever.
twyn *m* (**·i**) dune.
tŷ *m* (**tai**) house.
tyb *m/f* (**·iau**) opinion.
tybed *adv* I wonder.
tybiaeth *f* (**·au**) supposition.
tybied, tybio *v* to suppose.
tybiedig *adj* supposed.
tycio *v* to avail.
tydi *pron* thou.
tydy isn't (it).
tyddyn *m* (**·nod, ·nau**) smallholding.
tyddyn·nwr *m* (**·wyr**) small-holder.
tyfadwy *adj* growing.
tyfiant *m* growth.
tyfu *v* to grow.
tyf·wr *m* (**·wyr**) grower.
tyng·ed *f* (**·hedau**) fate.
tyngedfennol *adj* fateful.
tynghedu *v* to destine.
tyngu *v* to swear.
tylciau *see* **twlc**.
tyle *m* ascent.
tylino *v* to knead; to massage.
tyllau *see* **twll**.
tyllog *adj* perforated.
tyllu *v* to excavate.
tylluan *f* (**·od**) owl.
tym·er *f* (**·herau**) temper.
tym·estl *f* (**·hestloedd**) tempest.
tym·heredd *m* (**·ereddau**) temperature.
tymheru *v* to temper.
tymherus *adj* temperate.
tymhestloedd *see* **tymestl**.
tymhestlog *adj* stormy.
tymhorol *adj* seasonal.
tym·or *m* (**·horau**) season.
tymp *m* appointed time.
tyn *adj* tight.
tynder, tyndra *m* tension.
tyndro *m* (**·eon**) wrench.
tyner *adj* tender.
tyneru *v* to soften.
tynerwch *m* tenderness.
tynf·a *f* (**·eydd**) (a) draw.
tynfad *m* (**·au**) tug.

tynhau *v* to tighten.
tynned *from* **tyn.**
tynnu *v* to pull; to draw.
tyr *from* **torri.**
tyrau *see* **tŵr.**
tyrchod *see* **twrch.**
tyrchu *v* to burrow.
tyrd, tyred *from* **dod.**
tyrfa *f* (**·oedd**) crowd.
tyrfau *see* **twrw, twrf.**
tyrfedd *m* turbulence.
tyrnsgriw *m* (**·iau**) screwdriver.
tyrrau *see* **twr.**
tyrru *v* to cluster.
tyst *m/f* (**·ion**) witness.
tysteb *f* (**·au**) testimonial.
tystio, tystiolaethu *v* to testify.
tystiolaeth *f* (**·au**) evidence.
tystlythyr *m* (**·au**) reference.
tystysgrif *f* (**·au**).
tywallt *v* to pour.
tywalltiad *m* (**·au**) outpouring.
tywarchen *f* (**tywyrch**) clod (of turf).
tywel *m* (**·ion**) towel.
tywell *adj* (*f*) dark.
tywod *m* sand.
tywodfaen *m* sandstone.
tywodlyd *adj* sandy.
tywydd *m* weather.
tywyll *adj* dark.
tywyllu *v* to darken.
tywyllwch *m* dark.
tywyn *m* (**·nau**) sand dune.
tywynnu *v* to shine.
tywyrch *see* **tywarchen.**
tywys *v* to lead.
tywysen *f* (**·nau**) ear of corn.
tywysog *m* (**·ion**) prince.
tywysogaeth *f* (**·au**) principality.
tywysogaidd *adj* princely.
tywysoges *f* (**·au**) princes.
tywys·ydd, tywys·wr *m* (**·wyr**) leader, usher.

Th

theatr *f* (**·au**) theatre.
theatraidd *adj* theatrical.
thema *f* (**themâu**) theme.
theori *f* (**theorïau**) theory.
therap·i *m* (**·ïau**) therapy.
thermomedr *m* (**·au**) thermometer.
thus *m* frankincense.

U

ubain *v* to wail.
UCAC *abb* Undeb Cenedlaethol Athrawon Cymru.
uchaf *adj* highest.
uchafbwynt *m* (**·iau**) pinnacle.
uchafiaeth *f* supremacy.
uchafion *pl* heights.
uchaf·swm *m* (**·symiau**) maximum.
uchder *m* height.
uchel *adj* high.
uchel-ael *adj* highbrow.
uchelder *m* (**·au**) height.
ucheldir *m* (**·oedd**) highland.
uchel·gais *m/f* (**·geisiau**) ambition.
uchelgeisiol *adj* ambitious.
uchelseinydd *m* (**·ion**) loudspeaker.
uchel·wr *m* (**·wyr**) nobleman.
uchelwydd *m* mistletoe.
uchgapt·en *m* (**·einiaid**) major.
uchod *adv* above.
UDA *abb* Unol Daleithiau America (USA).
udfil *m* (**·od**) hyena.
udo *v* to howl.
UFA *abb* unrhyw fater arall (AOB).
ufudd *adj* obedient.
ufudd-dod *m* obedience.
ufuddhau *v* to obey.
uffern *f* hell.
uffernol *adj* infernal.
ugain *num* (**ugeiniau**) twenty.
ugeinfed *adj* twentieth.
UH *abb* Ustus Heddwch (JP).
un *num* one. • *adj* same. • *m/f* one.
unawd *m* (**·au**) solo.
unawd·ydd *m* (**·wyr**) soloist.
unben *m* (**·iaid**) dictator.
unbenaethol *adj* despotic.
unbennaeth *m* dictatorship.
undeb *m* (**·au**) unity; union.
undebol *adj* united.
undeb·wr *m* (**·wyr**) unionist.
undod *m* (**·au**) unity.
Undod·wr *m* (**·wyr**) Unitarian.
undonedd *m* monotony.
undonog *adj* monotonous.
uned *f* (**·au**) unit.
unedig *adj* united.
unfan *m* same place.
unfarn *adj* unanimous.
unfath *adj* identical.
unfed *adj* first.
unfryd, unfrydol *adj* unanimous.
unfrydedd *m* unanimity.
un-ffordd *adj* one-way.
unffurf *adj* uniform.
unffurfiaeth *f* uniformity.
uniad *m* (**·au**) (a) joining.
uniaethu *v* to identify (with).
uniaith *adj* monoglot.
unig *adj* only; lonely.
unigedd *m* (**·au**) solitude.
unigol *adj* singular.
unigol·yn *m* (**·ion**) individual.
unigrwydd *m* loneliness.
unigryw *adj* unique.

union *adj* straight; exact.
uniondeb, unionder *m* rectitude.
uniongred *adj* orthodox.
uniongyrchol *adj* direct.
unioni *v* to straighten; to rectify.
unionsyth *adj* upright.
unlliw *adj* monochrome.
unllygeidiog *adj* blinkered.
unman *m* anywhere.
unnos *adv* (in) one night.
uno *v* to amalgamate.
unochrog *adj* biased.
unodl *adj* of the same rhyme.
unol *adj* united.
unoliaeth *f* (**·au**) unity.
unplyg *adj* upright.
unplygrwydd *m* single-mindedness.
unrhyw *adj* any.
unsain *adj* unison.
unsill *adj* monosyllabic.
unswydd *adj* (with the) sole intention.
unwaith *adv* once.
urdd *f* (**·au**) order.
urddas *m* dignity.
urddasol *adj* dignified.
urddo *v* to ordain.
us *pl* chaff.
ust *exclam* hush!
ustus *m* (**·iaid**) magistrate.
utg-orn *m* (**·yrn**) trumpet.
uwch *adj* higher.
uwch- *prefix* senior.
uwchben *adv* overhead.
uwchbridd *m* topsoil.
uwchfarchnad *f* (**·oedd**) supermarket.
uwchlaw *prep* above.
uwchradd *adj* secondary (school).
uwch-ringyll *m* sergeant-major.
uwchseinaidd *adj* supersonic.
uwchsonig *adj* ultrasonic.
uwd *m* porridge.

W

wado, whado *v* to wallop.
wagen *f* (**·i**) wagon.
wal *f* (**·iau**) wall.
waldio *v* to wallop.
wats *f* (**·ys**) watch.
wedi *prep* after.
wedyn *adv* after.
weindio *v* to wind.
weiren *f* wire.
weirio *v* to wire.
weithian *adv* now.
weithiau *adv* sometimes.
wermod *f* wormwood.
wfftio, wfftian *v* to pooh-pooh.
whilber *m/f* wheelbarrow.
whilberaid *m* barrowload.
wiced *f* (·i) wicket.
wiced·wr *m* (**·wyr**) wicket-keeper.
widw *f* widow.
wmbredd *m* abundance.
woblyn *m* lather.
Wranws *f* Uranus.

wrlyn *m* lump.
wrth *prep* by.
wy *m* (**·au**) egg.
wybren *f* (**·nau**) sky.
yr wyddor *see* **gwyddor**.
wyf *from* **bod** I am.
wylo *v* to weep.
wylofain *v* to lament.
ŵyn *see* **oen**.
wyna *v* to lamb.
wyneb *m* (**·au**) face.
wyneb-ddalen *f* title page.
wynebgaled *adj* barefaced.
wynebu *v* to face.
wynepryd *m* countenance.
wynion·yn, wynwynyn *m* (**·od, wynwyn**) onion.
ŵyr *m* (**wyrion**) grandchild.
wyres *f* (**·au**) granddaughter.
wysg *m* track.
wystrysen *f* (**wystrys**) oyster.
wyth *num* eight.
wythawd *m* (**·au**) octet.
wythfed *m* (**·au**) octave.
wythfed *adj* eighth.
wythnos *f* (**·au**) week.
wythnosol *adj* weekly.
wythnosol·yn *m* (**·ion**) weekly.
wyth·wr *m* (**·wyr**) number eight (rugby).

YZ

y, yr, 'r *art* the.
ych *m* (**·en**) ox.
ychwaith *adv* either, neither.
ychwaneg *m* more.
ychwanegiad *m* (**·au**) addition.
ychwanegol *adj* additional.
ychwanegu *v* to add.
ychydig *adj* few.
ŷd *m* (**ydau**) corn.
yd·fran *f* (**·frain**) rook.
ydlan *f* (**·nau**) rickyard.
yd(w), yd(wyf) *from* **bod**.
yfed *v* to drink.
yfory *adv* tomorrow.
yf·wr *m* (**·wyr**) drinker.
yfflon *pl* smithereens.
yng *see* **yn**.
yngan, ynganu *v* to utter.
ynganiad *m* pronunciation.
ynghau *adv* shut.
ynghlwm *adv* tied up.
ynghudd *adv* hidden.
ynghwsg *adv* asleep.
ynghyd *adv* together.
ynghylch *prep* concerning.
ynghynn *adv* alight.
ynglŷn â *adv* concerning.
YH *abb* Ynad Heddwch (JP).
ym *from* **yn**.
yma *adv* here.
ymadael *v* to leave.
ymadawedig *adj* deceased.
ymadawiad *m* (**·au**) departure.
ymadawol *adj* valedictory.
ymadrodd *m* (**·ion**) phrase.
ymaelodi *v* to join.

ymafael, ymaflyd *v* to seize.
ymagor *v* to yawn.
ymagweddiad *m* (**-au**) attitude.
ymaith *adv* away.
ymarfer *v* to practise.
ymarferiad *m* (**-au**) exercise.
ymarferol *adj* practical.
ymarhous *adj* long-suffering.
ymarweddiad *m* conduct.
ymatal *v* to refrain.
ymateb *v* to respond.
ymbalfalu *v* to grope.
ymbarél *m* umbrella.
ymbelydredd *m* radiation.
ymbelydrol *adj* radioactive.
ymbil, ymbilio *v* to plead.
ymbincio *v* to titivate oneself.
ymborth *m* sustenance.
ymchwil *f* research.
ymchwiliad *m* (**-au**) investigation.
ymchwilio *v* to investigate.
ymchwil·ydd *m* (**-wyr**) researcher.
ymdeimlad *m* sense.
ymdeithio *v* to journey.
ymdoddi *v* to melt.
ymdopi *v* to cope.
ymdrech *f* (**-ion**) effort.
ymdrechu *v* to strive.
ymdrin *v* to deal (with).
ymdriniaeth *f* (**-au**) treatment.
ymdrochi *v* to bathe.
ymdroch·wr *m* (**-wyr**) bather.
ymdroi *v* to linger.
ymdrybaeddu *v* to wallow.
ymddangos *v* to appear.
ymddangosiad *m* (**-au**) appearance.
ymddangosiadol *adj* seeming.
ymddarostwng *v* to submit.
ymddarostyngiad *m* submission.
ymddatod *v* to become undone.
ymddeol *v* to retire.
ymddeoliad *m* (**-au**) retirement.
ymddiddan *v* to converse.
ymddihatru *v* to undress.
ymddiheuriad *m* (**-au**) apology.
ymddiheuro *v* to apologise.
ymddiried *v* to trust.
ymddiriedolaeth *f* (a) trust.
ymddiriedol·wr *m* (**-wyr**) trustee.
ymddiswyddiad *m* (**-au**) resignation.
ymddiswyddo *v* to resign.
ymddwyn *v* to behave.
ymddygiad *m* (**-au**) behaviour.
ymefl(ir) *from* **ymafael, ymaflyd**.
ymen·nydd *m* (**-yddiau**) brain.
ymenyn, menyn *m* butter.
ymerawd·wr *m* (**-wyr**) emperor.
ymerodraeth *f* (**-au**) empire.
ymerodres *f* empress.
ymestyn *v* to stretch.
ymesyd *from* **ymosod**.
ymetyb *from* **ymateb**.
ymfalchïo *v* to take pride.
ymfudo *v* to emigrate.
ymfud·wr *m* (**-wyr**) emigrant.
ymfflamychol *adj* inflamatory.
ymffrost *m* boast.
ymffrostgar *adj* boastful.
ymffrostio *v* to boast.
ymgadw *v* to keep oneself (from).
ymgais *m/f* effort.
ymgeis·ydd *m* (**-wyr**) applicant.
ymgeledd *m* succour.
ymgeleddu *v* to cherish.
ymgiprys *v* to vie.

ymglywed *v* to be inclined (to).
ymgnawdoliad *v* incarnation.
ymgodymu *v* to wrestle.
ymgolli *v* to lose oneself.
ymgom *m/f* (**·ion**) conversation.
ymgomio *v* to converse.
ymgorffori *v* to embody.
ymgreinio *v* to grovel.
ymgroesi *v* to cross oneself.
ymgrymu *v* to bow.
ymgynghori *v* to consult.
ymgynghorol *adj* consultative.
ymgynghor·ydd *m* (**·wyr**) adviser.
ymgymryd *v* to undertake.
ymgynnull *v* to assemble.
ymgyrch *m/f* campaign.
ymgyrraedd *v* to stretch.
ymgysegru *v* to consecrate oneself.
ymhél *v* to meddle.
ymhelaethu *v* to expand upon.
ymhell *adv* afar.
ymhellach *adv* further.
ymherodr *m* (**ymerodron**) emperor.
ymhlith *prep* among.
ymhlyg *adj* implicit.
ymholiad *m* (**·au**) enquiry.
ymhonni *v* to pretend.
ymhŵedd *v* to implore.
ymladd *v* to fight.
ymlâdd *v* to grow tired.
ymladd·wr *m* (**·wyr**) fighter.
ymlaen *adv* onward.
ymlafnio *v* to strive.
ymlawenhau *v* to rejoice.
ymledu *v* to expand.
ymlid *v* to pursue.
ymlonyddu *v* to grow calm.
ymlusg·iad *m* (**·iaid**) reptile.
ymlusgo *v* to crawl.
ymlwybro *v* to make one's way.
ymlyniad *m* attachment.
ymlynu *v* to adhere.
Ymneilltuaeth *f* Nonconformity.
ymneilltuo *v* to withdraw.
ymochel *v* to shelter.
ymofyn *v* to seek.
ymolchi *v* to wash oneself.
ymollwng *v* to let oneself go.
ymorol *v* to seek.
ymosod *v* to attack.
ymosodiad *m* (**·au**) (an) attack.
ymosod·wr *m* (**·wyr**) assailant.
ymostwng *v* to submit.
ymostyngiad *m* submission.
ympryd *m* (**·iau**) (a) fast.
ymprydio *v* to fast.
ymrafael *m* (**·ion**) strife.
ymraniad *m* schism.
ymrannu *v* to separate.
ymresymu *v* to reason.
ymrithio *v* to appear.
ymroddiad *m* devotion.
ymroi *v* to devote.
ymron *adv* nearly.
ymrwymiad *m* (**·iau**) commitment.
ymrwymo *v* to bind oneself.
ymryson *v* to contest.
ymson *v* soliloquy.
ymuno *v* to join.
ymwadu *v* to renounce.
ymwared *m* relief.
ymweld *v* to visit.
ymweliad *m* (**·au**) (a) visit.
ymwel·ydd *m/f* (**·wyr**).
ymwneud *v* to concern.

ymwrthod *v* to abstain.
ymwthgar *adj* pushy.
ymwthiol *adj* obtrusive.
ymwybodol *adj* conscious.
ymwybyddiaeth *f* consciousness.
ymyl *m/f* (**·on**) edge.
ymylol *adj* marginal.
ymylu *v* to border.
ymyrraeth *f* interference.
ymyrryd *v* to intervene.
ymysg *prep* amid.
ymysgaroedd *pl* bowels.
yn, yng, ym *prep* in.
yna *adv* there, then.
ynad *m* (**·on**) magistrate.
ynfyd *adj* idiotic.
ynfydrwydd *m* folly.
ynfy·tyn *m* (**·dion**) simpleton.
ynn *see* **onnen.**
ynni *m* energy.
yno *adv* there.
yn(of) *from* **yn.**
yntau *pron* he too.
ynteu *conj* or.
Ynyd *m* Shrove (Tuesday).
ynys *f* (**·oedd**) island.
ynysfor *m* (**·oedd**) archipelago.
ynysol *adj* insular.
ynysu *v* to isolate.
ynys·wr *m* (**·wyr**) islander.
ynysydd *m* (**·ion**) insulator.
yr *see* **y.**
yrŵan, rŵan *adv* now.
yrhawg *adv* for a long time to come.
ys *conj* as.
ysbaddu *v* to castrate.
ysb·aid *m/f* (**·eidiau**) respite.
ysb·ail *f* (**·eiliau**) booty.
ysbardun *m* (**·au**) spur.
ysbarduno *v* to spur.
ysbeidiol *adj* intermittent.
ysbeilio *v* to plunder.
ysbeil·iwr *m* (**·wyr**) robber.
ysbienddrych *m* (**·au**) telescope.
ysbïo *v* to spy.
ysbï·wr *m* (**·wyr**) spy.
ysblander *m* splendour.
ysblennydd *adj* resplendent.
ysbryd *m* (**·ion**) spirit.
ysbrydol *adj* spiritual.
ysbrydoli *v* to inspire.
ysbrydiaeth *f* inspiration.
ysbrydoliaeth *f* inspiration.
ysby·ty *m* (**·tai**) hospital.
ys·fa *f* (**·feydd**) craving.
ysgafala *adj* careless.
ysgafn *adj* light.
ysgafnder *m* lightness.
ysgafnhau, ysgafnu *v* to lighten.
ysgaldanu *v* to scald.
ysgallen *f* (**ysgall**) thistle.
ysgariad *m* (**·au**) divorce.
ysgarlad *adj* scarlet.
ysgarthion *pl* excreta.
ysgarthu *v* to excrete.
ysgatfydd *adv* peradventure.
ysgawen *f* (**ysgaw**) elder.
ysgeler *adj* villainous.
ysgellyn *m* (**ysgall**) thistle.
ysgerbwd *m* (**sgerbydau**) skeleton.
ysgewyll *pl* sprouts.
ysgithr *m* (**·au, ·edd**) tusk.
ysgithrog *adj* craggy, tusked.
ysglyfaeth *f* (**·au**) prey.

ysglyfaethus *adj* predatory.
ysgogi *v* to impel.
ysgogiad *m* (**·au**) impulse.
ysgol *f* (**·ion**) school; ladder.
ysgol·dy *m* (**·dai**) schoolroom.
ysgolfeistr *m* (**·i**) schoolmaster.
ysgol·haig *m* (**·heigion**) intellectual.
ysgolheictod *m* scholarship.
ysgolheigaidd *adj* intellectual.
ysgoloriaeth *f* (**·au**) scholarship.
ysgrafell *f* (**·od**) scraper.
ysgraffinio *v* to scrape.
ysgrepan, sgrepan *f* (**·au**) satchel.
ysgrif *f* (**·au**) essay.
ysgrifen *f* handwriting.
ysgrifenedig *adj* written.
ysgrifennu *v* to write.
ysgrifen·nwr *m* (**·wyr**) writer.
ysgrifen·nydd *m* (**·yddion**) secretary.
ysgrifenyddes *f* (**·au**) secretary.
ysgr·în *f* (**·iniau**) screen.
ysgryd *m* shiver.
ysgrythur *f* (**·au**) scripture.
ysgrythurol *adj* scriptural.
ysgub *f* (**·au**) sheaf.
ysgubell *f* (**·au**) broom.
ysgubo *v* to sweep.
ysgubol *adj* sweeping.
ysgubor *f* (**·iau**) barn.
ysgutor *m* (**·ion**) executor.
ysguthan *f* (**·od**) wood-pigeon.
ysgwâr *m/f* (**sgwariau**) square.
ysgwyd *v* to shake.
ysgwydd *f* (**·au**) shoulder.
ysgwyddo *v* to shoulder.
ysgydwad, ysgytwad *m* (**·au**) (a) shaking.
ysgyf·ant *m* (**·aint**) lungs.
ysgyfarnog *f* (**·od**) hare.
ysmygu *v* to smoke.
ysol *adj* consuming.
ystad *f* (**·au**) estate.
ystadegau *pl* statistics.
ystadegol *adj* statistical.
ystadegydd *m* statistician.
ystafell *f* (**·oedd**) room.
ystanc *m* (**·iau**) stake.
ystlum, slumyn *m* (**·od**) bat.
ystlys *m/f* (**·au**) flank.
ystod *f* (**·au**) course; swath.
ystofi *v* to weave, to plan.
ystor·i, stor·i *f* (**·ïau**) story.
ystorm *f* (**·ydd**) storm.
ystrad *m* (**·au**) vale.
ystrydeb *f* (**·au**) cliché.
ystrydebol *adj* hackneyed.
ystryw *f* (**·iau**) ruse.
ystrywgar *adj* crafty.
ystum *m/f* (**·iau**) pose; curve.
ystumio *v* to contort.
Ystwyll *m* Epiphany.
ystwyrian *v* to stir oneself.
ystwyth *adj* flexible.
ystwythder *m* flexibility.
ystwytho *v* to make flexible.
ystyfnig *adj* stubborn.
ystyfnigo *v* to become more obstinate.
ystyfnigrwydd *m* obstinacy.
ystyll·en, styll·en *f* (**·od**) plank.
ystyr *m/f* (**·on**) meaning.
ystyriaeth *f* (**·au**) consideration.

ystyried *v* to consider.
ystyriol *adj* considerate.
ysu *v* to consume; to crave.
Ysw. *abb* Yswain (Esq.).
ysw·ain *m* (**·einiaid**) squire.
yswiriant *m* insurance.
yswirio *v* to insure.
ysywaeth *adv* more's the pity.
yw *from* **bod**.
ywen *f* (**yw**) yew.
zinc *m* zinc.

English-Welsh Dictionary

A

abacus *n* abacws *m.*
abandon *v* gadael, rhoi'r gorau i.
abash *v* cywilyddio.
abate *v* gostegu.
abbatoir *n* lladd-dy *m.*
abbey *n* abaty *m.*
abbreviate *v* talfyrru.
abbreviation *n* byrfodd *m.*
abdicate *v* ymddiswyddo.
abdomen *n* bol, bola *m.*
abduct *v* cipio.
abet *v* cefnogi.
abeyance *n* oediad *m.*
abhor *v* ffieiddio.
abhorrent *adj* atgas.
abide *v* trigo; goddef.
abiding *adj* arhosol.
ability *n* dawn *m/f.*
abject *adj* distadl.
ablaze *adv* yn wenfflam.
able *adj* atebol, galluog.
abnegation *n* ymwadiad *m.*
abnormal *adj* anghyffredin.
aboard *adv* ar fwrdd.
abode *n* annedd *m/f.*
abolish *v* diddymu.
abolition *n* diddymiad *m.*
abominable *adj* ffiaidd.
abomination *n* ffieidd-dra *m.*
aboriginal *adj* cynfrodorol.
aborigines *n* cynfrodorion *pl.*
abort *v* erthylu.
abortion *n* erthyliad *m.*
abortive *adj* seithug.
abound *v* heigio.
about *prep* am, tua. • *adv* o gwmpas.
above *prep* uwch, uwchlaw. • *adv* fry.
abrasion *n* ysgraffiniad *m.*
abrasive *adj* crafog.
abridge *v* talfyrru.
abroad *adv* dramor.
abrupt *adj* disymwth.
abscess *n* cornwyd *m.*
absence *n* absenoldeb *m.*
absent *adj* absennol.
absenteeism *n* absenolaeth *f.*
absent-minded *adj* anghofus.
absolute *adj* hollol.
absolve *v* rhyddhau.
absorb *v* amsugno, llyncu.
absorption *n* amsugniad *m.*
abstain *v* ymatal.
abstinence *n* dirwest *m/f.*
abstinent *adj* cymedrol.
abstract *adj* haniaethol.
abstraction *n* haniaeth *m/f.*
abstruse *adj* astrus.
absurd *adj* hurt, abswrd.

absurdity *n* hurtrwydd *m*.
abundance *n* digonedd *m*; toreth *f*.
abundant *adj* toreithiog.
abuse *v* camdrin; difenwi.
abyss *n* agendor, gagendor *m/f*.
academic *adj* academaidd.
academy *n* academi *f*.
accede *v* cydsynio.
accelerate *v* cyflymu.
accelerator *n* cyflymydd, sbardun *m*.
accent *n* acen *f*. • *v* acennu.
accept *v* derbyn.
acceptable *adj* derbyniol.
acceptance *n* derbyniad *m*.
access *n* mynediad *m*.
accessible *adj* hygyrch.
accident *n* damwain *f*.
accidental *adj* damweiniol.
acclaim *v* cymeradwyo.
accommodate *v* lletya.
accommodation *n* llety *m*.
accompaniment *n* cyfeiliant *m*.
accompany *v* cyfeilio; hebrwng.
accomplish *v* cyflawni.
accomplishment *n* camp *f*.
accord *n* cytundeb *m*.
accordance *n*: **in ~ with** yn unol â.
according to *adv* yn ôl.
accost *v* cyfarch.
account *n* cyfrif *m*.
accountability *n* atebolrwydd *m*.
accountancy *n* cyfrifyddiaeth *f*.
accountant *n* cyfrifydd *m*.
accumulate *v* crynhoi.
accumulation *n* crynhoad *m*.
accuracy *n* cywirdeb *m*.
accurate *adj* cywir.
accursed *adj* melltigedig.
accusation *n* cyhuddiad *m*.
accuse *v* cyhuddo.
accused *n* cyhuddedig *m*.
accustom *v* arfer.
accustomed *adj* cynefin.
ace *n* as *f*.
ache *n* cur *m/f*. • *v* gwynegu.
achieve *v* cyflawni.
achievement *n* gorchest *f*.
acid *adj* sur. • *n* asid *m*.
acknowledge *v* cydnabod.
acknowledgment *n* cydnabyddiaeth *f*.
acne *n* plorod *pl*.
acoustics *n* acwsteg *f*.
acquaint *v* hysbysu.
acquaintance *n* cydnabod *m/f*.
acquiesce *v* cydsynio.
acquiescent *adj* cydsyniol.
acquire *v* cael, ennill.
acquisition *n* caffaeliad *m*.
acquit *v* gollwng yn rhydd.
acrimonious *adj* chwerw.
across *adv* ar draws.
act *v* actio; gweithredu. • *n* act *f*.
action *n* gweithred *f*.
activate *v* cychwyn; actifadu.
active *adj* heini; gweithredol.
activity *n* gweithgarwch *m*.
actor *n* actor *m*.
actress *n* actores *f*.
actual *adj* gwir.
acute *adj* llym.
ad lib *adv* yn fyrfyfyr.
ad nauseam *adv* hyd syrffed.
adage *n* dywediad *m*.
adamant *adj* diysgog.

adapt *v* addasu.
adaptable *adj* cymwysadwy; hyblyg.
adaptation *n* cyfaddasiad *m.*
add *v* adio.
addicted *adj* yn gaeth i.
addiction *n* gorddibyniaeth *f.*
addition *n* ychwanegiad *m.*
additional *adj* ychwanegol.
address *v* annerch; cyfeirio (a letter).
adept *adj* deheuig.
adequate *adj* digonol.
adhere *v* glynu wrth.
adhesion *n* ymlyniad *m.*
adhesive *adj* adlynol.
adjacent *adj* cyfagos.
adjective *n* ansoddair *m.*
adjourn *v* gohirio.
adjournment *n* gohiriad *m.*
adjudicate *v* beirniadu.
adjudicator *n* beirniad *m.*
adjust *v* addasu, cymhwyso.
adjustable *adj* modd i'w (h)addasu.
adjustment *n* addasiad *m.*
administer *v* gweinyddu.
administration *n* gweinyddiaeth *f.*
administrative *adj* gweinyddol.
admirable *adj* campus.
admiral *n* llyngesydd *m.*
admiration *n* edmygedd *m.*
admire *v* edmygu.
admirer *n* edmygydd *m.*
admission *n* cyfaddefiad *m*; mynediad *m.*
admit *v* cyfaddef.
admonish *v* ceryddu.
admonition *n* cerydd *m.*
adolescence *n* llencyndod *m.*
adopt *v* mabwysiadu.
adoption *n* mabwysiad *m.*
adoptive *adj* mabwysiol.
adorable *adj* swynol.
adore *v* dwlu, dylu.
adorn *v* addurno.
adrift *adv* yn rhydd.
adroit *adj* deheuig.
adulation *n* gweniaith *f.*
adult *n* oedolyn. • *adj* mewn oed.
adulterate *v* llygru.
adultery *n* godineb *m.*
advance *v* symud ymlaen.
advantage *n* mantais *f.*
advantageous *adj* manteisiol.
adventure *n* antur *f.*
adventurous *adj* anturus.
adversary *n* gwrthwynebydd *m.*
adverse *adj* croes.
adversity *n* adfyd *m.*
advertise *v* hysbysebu.
advertisement *n* hysbyseb *f.*
advice *n* cyngor *m.*
advise *v* cynghori.
advisory *adj* ymgynghorol.
advocacy *n* eiriolaeth *f.*
advocate *v* pleidio.
aerial *n* erial *m/f.*
aerobic *adj* aerobig.
aeroplane *n* awyren *f.*
aerosol *n* chwistrell *f.*
aesthetic *adj* esthetig.
affability *n* hynawsedd *m.*
affable *adj* hynaws.
affair *n* mater; achos *m.*
affect *v* effeithio.

affected *adj* mursennaidd.
affection *n* hoffter *m.*
affectionate *adj* serchog.
affiliate *v* derbyn yn aelod.
affinity *n* cydnawsedd *m.*
affirm *v* cadarnhau; haeru.
affirmative *adj* cadarnhaol.
afflict *v* cystuddio, blino.
affliction *n* cystudd *m.*
affluent *adj* goludog.
afford *v* fforddio.
affront *n* sarhad *m.* • *v* sarhau.
afoot *adv* ar droed.
afraid *adj* ofnus.
after *prep* ar ôl. • *adv* wedyn.
afterbirth *n* brych, garw *m.*
aftermath *n* adladd; sgil *m.*
afternoon *n* prynhawn *m.*
afterward(s) *adv* wedyn.
again *adv* eto, drachefn.
against *prep* yn erbyn.
age *n* oedran; oes *m.* • *v* heneiddio.
agency *n* asiantaeth *f.*
agenda *n* agenda *f.*
agent *n* asiant *m.*
aggravate *v* gwneud yn waeth, gwaethygu.
aggression *n* gormes *m.*
aggressive *adj* ymosodol.
aggressor *n* ymosodwr *m.*
agile *adj* gwisgi; sionc.
agility *n* sioncrwydd *m.*
agitate *v* cyffroi.
agitation *n* cynnwrf *m.*
ago *adv* yn ôl.
agony *n* gwewyr, ing *m.*
agree *v* cytuno.
agreeable *adj* dymunol.
agreed *adj* cytûn.
agreement *n* cytundeb *m.*
agricultural *adj* amaethyddol.
agriculture *n* amaethyddiaeth *f.*
ahead *adv* o flaen.
aid *v* cynorthwyo. • *n* cymorth *m.*
AIDS *n* AIDS.
ailment *n* anhwyldeb *m.*
aim *v* anelu. • *n* amcan *m.*
air *n* awyr *f.*
air-conditioned *adj* wedi'i (h)aerdymheru.
air-conditioning *vn* aerdymheru.
aircraft *n* awyren *f.*
airline *n* cwmni hedfan *m.*
airport *n* maes awyr *m.*
airsick *adj* sâl awyr.
airtight *adj* aer-dynn.
aisle *n* eil *f.*
ajar *adj* cilagored.
akin *adj* yn perthyn; yn debyg.
alarm *n* larwm *m/f.* • *v* dychryn.
alarm bell *n* cloch larwm *f.*
alarmist *n* codwr bwganod *m.*
albeit *conj* er, er hynny.
album *n* albwm *m.*
alcohol *n* alcohol *m.*
alcoholic *adj* meddwol.
ale *n* cwrw *m.*
alert *adj* gwyliadwrus.
alertness *n* gwyliadwriaeth *f.*
alien *adj* estron.
alienate *v* dieithrio.
alight *v* disgyn.
alike *adj* tebyg.
alive *adj* byw.
alkali *n* alcali *m.*
all *adj* holl; oll, i gyd.

allege *v* haeru.
allegiance *n* teyrngarwch *m.*
allergy *n* alergedd *m.*
alleviate *v* lliniaru.
alley *n* ale *f.*
alliance *n* cynghrair *m/f.*
allocate *v* dosrannu.
allocation *n* dyraniad *m.*
allot *v* pennu.
allow *v* caniatáu.
allowance *n* lwfans *m.*
allude *v* crybwyll.
allure *n* hudoliaeth *f.*
allusion *n* cyfeiriad *m.*
allusive *adj* awgrymog.
ally *n* cynghreiriad *m.* • *v* cynghreirio.
almond *n* almon *m/f.*
almost *adv* bron.
aloft *adv* fry.
alone *adj* unig.
along *adv* ymlaen, hyd.
aloud *adv* yn uchel.
alphabet *n* (yr) wyddor *f.*
alphabetical *adj* yn nhrefn yr wyddor.
already *adv* yn barod, eisoes.
also *adv* hefyd.
altar *n* allor *f.*
alter *v* newid.
alteration *n* newid *m.*
alternate *adj* bob yn ail.
alternating *adj* eiledol.
alternative *n* dewis arall *m.* • *adj* amgen.
although *conj* er.
altitude *n* uchder *m.*
always *adv* yn wastad.
a.m. *adv* y bore.
amalgamate *v* uno.
amalgamation *n* cyfuniad *m.*
amass *v* cronni.
amateur *n* amatur *m/f.*
amaze *v* synnu.
amazement *n* syndod *m.*
amazing *adj* rhyfeddol.
ambassador *n* llysgennad *m.*
ambidextrous *adj* deheuig â dwy law.
ambiguity *n* amwysedd *m.*
ambiguous *adj* amwys.
ambition *n* uchelgais *m/f.*
ambitious *adj* uchelgeisiol.
ambulance *n* ambiwlans *m.*
ambush *n* rhagod *m.*
ameliorate *v* lleddfu.
amelioration *n* gwelliant *m.*
amenable *adj* hydrin.
amend *v* diwygio.
amendment *n* gwelliant *m.*
amenities *n* mwynderau *pl.*
America *n* yr Amerig *f.*
American *adj* Americanaidd.
amiability *n* hawddgarwch *m.*
amiable *adj* hawddgar.
amicable *adj* cyfeillgar.
amid(st) *prep* ymhlith.
ammunition *n* bwledi *pl.*
amnesia *n* anghofrwydd *m.*
amnesty *n* amnest *m.*
among(st) *prep* ymysg.
amorous *adj* carwriaethol.
amount *n* swm *m.*
amphibian *n* amffibiad *m.*
ample *adj* digonol.
amplify *v* mwyhau; ehangu.

amplitude *n* amlder *m*.
amputate *v* trychu.
amputation *n* trychiad *m*.
amuse *v* difyrru.
amusement *n* difyrrwch *m*.
amusing *adj* digrif.
anachronism *n* camamseriad *m*.
anaemia *n* diffyg gwaed *m*.
anaesthetic *n* anesthetig *m*.
analogy *n* cyfatebiaeth *f*.
analyse *v* dadansoddi.
analysis *n* dadansoddiad *m*.
analytical *adj* dadansoddol.
anarchic *adj* anarchaidd.
anarchy *n* anarchiaeth *f*.
anatomical *adj* anatomegol.
anatomy *n* anatomeg *f*.
ancestor *n* hynafiad *m/f*.
anchor *n* angor *m*.
ancient *adj* hynafol.
and *conj* a, ac.
anecdote *n* hanesyn *m*.
angel *n* angel *m*, angyles *f*.
anger *n* dicter *m*.
angle *n* ongl *f*.
angler *n* genweiriwr; pysgotwr *m*.
Anglicise *v* Seisnigeiddio.
Anglo-Welsh *adj* Eingl-Gymreig.
angry *adj* dig.
anguish *n* ing *m*.
angular *adj* onglog.
animal *n* anifail *m*.
animate *v* bywhau. • *adj* byw.
animation *n* animeiddiad *m*.
animosity *n* atgasedd *m*.
ankle *n* migwrn *m*, ffêr *f*.
annex *v* atodi. • *n* atodiad *m*.
annihilate *v* difodi.
annihilation *n* difodiad *m*.
anniversary *n* pen blwydd *m*.
annotate *v* gwneud nodiadau.
annotation *n* nodiadau *pl*.
announce *v* cyhoeddi, datgan.
announcement *n* cyhoeddiad *m*.
annoy *v* cythruddo.
annoyance *n* dicter *m*.
annoyed *adj* penwan.
annual *adj* blynyddol.
annul *v* diddymu.
anomaly *n* anghysonder *m*.
anonymity *n* anhysbysrwydd *m*.
anonymous *adj* dienw.
another *adj* arall.
answer *v* ateb. • *n* ateb *m*.
ant *n* morgrugyn *m*.
antagonise *v* digio.
antagonism *n* gelyniaeth *f*.
Antarctic *adj/n* Antarctig *f*.
antenna *n* teimlydd *m*.
anterior *adj* blaenorol.
anthem *n* anthem *f*.
anthology *n* blodeugerdd *f*.
anthracite *n* glo caled, glo carreg *m*.
anthropology *n* anthropoleg *f*.
antibiotic *n* gwrthfiotig *m*.
anticipate *v* achub y blaen, disgwyl.
antics *n* stranciau *pl*.
antidote *n* gwrthwenwyn *m*.
antipathy *n* gelyniaeth *f*.
antiquarian *n* hynafiaethydd *m*.
antiques *n* hynafion *pl*.
antiquity *n* cynfyd *m*.
antithesis *n* gwrthgyferbyniad *m*.
antler *n* rhaidd *f*.

anvil *n* einion *f*.
anxiety *n* pryder *m*.
anxious *adj* pryderus.
any *adj* unrhyw; dim.
apart *adv* ar wahân.
apartment *n* fflat *f*.
apathetic *adj* di-hid.
apathy *n* difrawder *m*.
aperture *n* twll *m*.
apex *n* apig *f*; copa *m/f*.
apologise *v* ymddiheuro.
apology *n* ymddiheuriad *m*.
apostle *n* apostol *m*.
appal *v* brawychu.
apparatus *n* offer *pl*, cyfarpar *m*.
apparent *adj* amlwg.
apparition *n* drychiolaeth *f*.
appeal *v* apelio. • *n* apêl *f*.
appear *v* ymddangos.
appearance *n* ymddangosiad *m*; golwg *f*.
append *v* atodi.
appendix *n* atodiad; coluddyn crog *m*.
appetising *adj* blasus.
appetite *n* archwaeth *m*.
applaud *v* cymeradwyo.
applause *n* cymeradwyaeth *f*.
apple *n* afal *m*.
apple tree *n* coeden afalau *f*.
appliance *n* teclyn *m*; dyfais *f*.
applicable *adj* perthnasol.
applicant *n* ymgeisydd *m*.
apply *v* cynnig; cymhwyso; ymroi.
appoint *v* penodi.
appointment *n* penodiad; oed *m*.
apportion *v* rhannu.
apposite *adj* addas.
appraisal *n* gwerthusiad *m*.
appraise *v* pwyso a mesur gwerth.
appreciate *v* gwerthfawrogi.
appreciation *n* gwerthfawrogiad *m*.
appreciative *adj* gwerthfawrogol.
apprehend *v* dal.
apprehension *n* ofn *m*.
apprentice *n* prentis *m*.
approach *v* dynesu, nesáu.
appropriate *adj* addas, priodol.
approval *n* cymeradwyaeth *f*.
approve *v* cymeradwyo.
approximately *adv* fwy neu lai.
approximation *n* brasamcan *m*.
April *n* Ebrill *m*.
apron *n* brat *m*; ffedog *f*.
apt *adj* priodol.
aqualung *n* tanc anadlu *m*.
aquarium *n* acwariwm *m*.
aquatic *adj* dyfrol.
arable *adj* âr.
arbiter *n* beirniad *m*.
arbitrary *adj* mympwyol.
arbitrate *v* cyflafareddu.
arbitration *n* cyflafareddiad *m*.
arcade *n* arcêd *f*.
arch *n* bwa *m*; pont *f*.
archaeological *adj* archaeolegol.
archaeology *n* archaeoleg *f*.
archaic *adj* hynafol.
archbishop *n* archesgob *m*.
archdruid *n* archdderwydd *m*.
architect *n* pensaer *m*.
architecture *n* pensaernïaeth *f*.
archives *n* archifau *pl*.
Arctic *n* Yr Arctig *m*.
ardent *adj* selog.
ardour *n* angerdd *m*.

area *n* arwynebedd *m*; ardal *f*.
argue *v* dadlau.
argument *n* dadl *f*.
argumentative *adj* dadleugar.
arid *adj* cras.
aridity *n* craster *m*.
arise *v* cyfodi.
aristocracy *n* pendefigaeth *f*.
aristocrat *n* pendefig *m*.
arithmetic *n* rhifyddeg *f*.
arm *n* braich *f*. • *v* arfogi.
armament *n* arfogaeth *f*.
armchair *n* cadair freichiau *f*.
armed *adj* arfog.
armful *n* coflaid *f*.
armistice *n* cadoediad *m*.
armour *n* arfwisg *f*.
armpit *n* cesail *f*.
army *n* byddin *f*.
aroma *n* perarogl *m*.
aromatic *adj* persawrus.
around *prep* o gwmpas.
arouse *v* dihuno, codi.
arrange *v* trefnu.
arrangement *n* trefniant *m*.
array *n* rhestr *f*.
arrest *v* dal; arestio.
arrival *n* dyfodiad *m*.
arrive *v* cyrraedd.
arrogance *n* haerllugrwydd *m*.
arrogant *adj* haerllug.
arrow *n* saeth *f*.
arsenal *n* arfdy *m*.
art *n* celfyddyd *f*.
art gallery *n* oriel *f*.
artery *n* rhydweli *f*.
artful *adj* cyfrwys.
article *n* erthygl *f*.
articulate *v* ynganu.
articulation *n* ynganiad *m*.
artificial *adj* ffug, gosod.
artillery *n* magnelau *pl*.
artisan *n* crefftwr *m*.
artist *n* artist, arlunydd *m*.
artistic *adj* celfydd.
artistry *n* cywreinrwydd *m*.
as *conj* fel; mor, â.
ascend *v* dringo, esgyn.
ascension *n* esgyniad *m*.
ascent *n* esgyniad *m*.
ascertain *v* canfod.
ascetic *adj* meudwyaidd. • *n* asgetig *m/f*.
ash *n* onnen *f*; lludw *m*.
ashamed *adj* â chywilydd.
ashore *adv* ar y lan.
ashtray *n* blwch llwch *m*.
aside *adv* o'r neilltu.
ask *v* gofyn.
asleep *adv* yng nghwsg.
aspect *n* gwedd *f*.
aspersion *n* sen *f*.
asphyxiate *v* mygu.
asphyxiation *n* mogfa *f*.
aspirant *n* ymgeisydd *m*.
aspiration *n* dyhead *m*.
aspire *v* dyheu.
assail *v* ymosod.
assailant *n* ymosodwr *m*.
assassin *n* llofrudd *m*.
assassinate *v* llofruddio.
assault *n* ymosodiad *m*. • *v* ymosod.
assemble *v* crynhoi; cydosod.
assembly *n* cynulliad *m*; cymanfa *f*.
assent *n* cydsyniad *m*.

assert *v* mynnu.
assertion *n* honiad *m*.
assess *v* asesu, pwyso a mesur.
assessment *n* asesiad *m*.
assets *n* asedau *pl*.
assign *v* pennu.
assignment *n* gorchwyl *m*.
assimilate *v* cymathu.
assist *v* cynorthwyo.
assistance *n* cymorth *m*.
assistant *n* cynorthwyydd *m*.
associate *v* cysylltu.
association *n* cymdeithas *f*.
assortment *n* cymysgedd *m/f*.
assume *v* rhagdybio.
assumption *n* rhagdybiaeth *f*.
assurance *n* sicrwydd *m*.
assure *v* sicrhau.
asthma *n* y fogfa *f*; asthma *m*.
astonish *v* syfrdanu.
astonishment *n* syndod *m*.
astound *v* syfrdanu.
astrologer *n* sêr-ddewin *m*.
astrology *n* sêr-ddewiniaeth *f*.
astronaut *n* gofodwr *m*, gofodwraig *f*.
astronomer *n* seryddwr *m*, seryddwraig *f*.
astronomy *n* seryddiaeth.
astute *adj* craff.
asylum *n* noddfa *f*.
at *prep* am, ar, yn.
atheist *n* anffyddiwr *m*, anffyddwraig *f*.
athlete *n* mabolgampwr *m*, mabolgampwraig *f*.
athletic *adj* athletaidd.
atlas *n* atlas *m*.
atmosphere *n* awyrgylch; atmosffer *m*.
atom *n* atom *m/f*.
atomic *adj* atomig.
atrocious *adj* erchyll.
atrocity *n* erchylltra *m*.
attach *v* atodi.
attachment *n* atodyn; ymlyniad *m*.
attack *v* ymosod. • *n* ymosodiad *m*.
attacker *n* ymosodwr *m*, ymosodwraig *f*.
attain *v* cyrraedd, ennill.
attempt *v* ceisio; rhoi cynnig ar.
attend *v* mynychu; gweini.
attendance *n* presenoldeb *m*; gwasanaeth *m*.
attention *n* sylw *m*.
attentive *adj* astud, sylwgar.
attic *n* croglofft *f*.
attitude *n* agwedd *f*.
attract *v* denu.
attraction *n* atyniad *m*.
attractive *adj* atyniadol.
attribute *n* priodoledd *m*.
auction *n* arwerthiant *m*.
audacious *adj* beiddgar, haerllug.
audacity *n* beiddgarwch, haerllugrwydd *m*.
audible *adj* clywadwy.
audience *n* cynulleidfa *f*.
audit *n* archwiliad *m*. • *v* archwilio.
audition *n* clyweliad *m*.
auditor *n* archwilydd *m*.
augment *v* cynyddu.
August *n* Awst *m*.
aunt *n* modryb *f*.
auspicious *adj* addawol.
austere *adj* llym.

authentic *adj* dilys.
authenticity *n* dilysrwydd *m*.
author *n* awdur *m*; awdures *f*.
authoritarian *adj* awdurdodus.
authoritative *adj* awdurdodol.
authority *n* awdurdod *m*.
authorise *v* awdurdodi.
autobiography *n* hunangofiant *n*.
autocrat *n* teyrn *m*, unbennes *f*.
autocratic *adj* unbenaethol.
autograph *n* llofnod *m*.
automatic *adj* awtomatig.
autonomy *n* hunanlywodraeth *f*.
autopsy *n* awtopsi *m*.
autumn *n* hydref *m*.
auxiliary *adj* cynorthwyol, ategol.
available *adj* ar gael.
avalanche *n* eirlithriad *m*.
avarice *n* trachwant, cybydd-dod *m*.
avenge *v* dial.
avenue *n* coedlan *f*.
average *n* cyfartaledd *m*.
aversion *n* casbeth *m*.
avert *v* troi heibio.
avid *adj* awchus.
avoid *v* gochel.
await *v* aros, disgwyl.
awake *v* deffro, dihuno.
award *v* dyfarnu. • *n* dyfarniad *m*; gwobr *f*.
aware *adj* ymwybodol.
awareness *n* ymwybyddiaeth *f*.
away *adv* i ffwrdd, ymaith.
awe *n* parchedig ofn *m*.
awful *adj* ofnadwy.
awkward *adj* lletchwith, trwsgl.
axe *n* bwyall, bwyell *f*.
axis *n* echelin *f*.
axle *n* echel *f*.
azure *adj* asur.

B

babble *v* baldorddi.
babe, baby *n* baban *m*.
babyhood *n* babandod *m*.
babyish *adj* babïaidd.
bachelor *n* hen lanc *m*.
back *n* cefn *m*. • *adv* yn ôl. • *v* cefnogi.
backbone *n* asgwrn cefn *m*.
backdate *v* ôl-ddyddio.
backer *n* cefnogwr *m*, cefnogwraig *f*.
background *n* cefndir *m*.
back payment *n* ôl-daliad *m*.
backside *n* pen-ôl *m*.
backward *adj* araf. • *adv* yn ôl.
bacon *n* cig moch *m*.
bad *adj* drwg, sâl.
badge *n* bathodyn *m*.
badger *n* mochyn daear *m*.
badness *n* drygioni *m*.
baffle *v* drysu.
bag *n* bag, cwdyn *m*.
baggage *n* paciau *pl*.
bait *n* abwyd *m*.
bake *v* crasu, pobi.
baker *n* pobydd *m*.

bakery *n* popty *m*.
baking *n* pobiad *m*.
balance *n* cydbwysedd *m*; clorian *f*. • *v* cydbwyso.
balcony *n* balconi *m*.
bald *adj* moel.
baldness *n* moelni *m*.
bale *n* bwrn *m*.
ball *n* pêl, pelen *f*; dawns *f*.
ball bearing *n* pelferyn *f*.
ballad *n* baled *f*.
ballet *n* bale, ballet *m*.
balloon *n* balŵ *n m/f*.
ballot *n* pleidlais bapur *f*; balot *m*.
balm, balsam *n* balm *m*.
bamboo *n* bambŵ *m*.
ban *n* gwaharddiad *m*. • *v* gwahardd.
banal *adj* ystrydebol.
banana *n* banana *f*.
band *n* band *m*.
bandage *n* rhwymyn *m*. • *v* rhwymo.
bang *n* ergyd *m/f*. • *v* taro.
bangle *n* breichled *f*.
banish *v* alltudio.
banishment *n* alltudiaeth *f*.
bank *n* glan, torlan *f*; banc *m*.
banker *n* banciwr *m*.
banknote *n* arian papur.
bankrupt *n* methdalwr *m*.
bankruptcy *n* methdaliad *m*.
banquet *n* gwledd *f*.
banns *n* gostegion *pl*.
baptise *v* bedyddio.
baptism *n* bedydd *m*.
bar *n* bar *m*. • *v* bario.
barbarian *n* barbariad *m*.
barbarity *n* barbareiddiwch *m*.
barbecue *n* barbeciw *m*.
barbed wire *n* weiren bigog *f*.
barber *n* barbwr *m*.
bard *n* bardd *m*.
bare *adj* noeth. • *v* dinoethi.
barefoot(ed) *adj* troednoeth.
barely *adv* prin.
bareness *n* moelni *m*.
bargain *n* bargen *f*. • *v* bargeinio.
bark *n* rhisgl *m*; cyfarthiad *m*. • *v* cyfarth.
barn *n* ysgubor *f*.
barometer *n* baromedr *m*.
barracks *n* barics *pl*.
barrage *n* argae, cob *m*.
barrel *n* casgen *f*.
barren *adj* diffrwyth.
barricade *n* gwrthglawdd *m*.
barrier *n* rhwystr *m*.
barrister *n* bargyfreithiwr *m*, bargyfreithwraig *f*.
bartender *n* barmon *m*.
barter *v* ffeirio, trwco.
base *n* sylfaen *f*. • *v* sylfaenu.
basement *n* llawr isaf *m*.
bashful *adj* swil.
basic *adj* sylfaenol.
basin *n* basn, basin *m*.
basis *n* sail *f*.
basket *n* basged *f*; cawell *m*.
bass *n* (*mus*) bas *m*.
bastard *n* bastard *m*.
baste *v* brasbwytho.
bat *n* ystlum; bat *m*.
batch *n* ffyrnaid *f*; swp *m*.
bath *n* bath *m*.
bathe *v* ymdrochi.

bathing suit *n* gwisg nofio *f.*
bathroom *n* ystafell ymolchi *f.*
baths *n* pwll nofio *m.*
bathtub *n* twba *m.*
batter *v* pwyo. • *n* cytew *m.*
battery *n* batri *m.*
battle *n* brwydr *f.* • *v* brwydro.
battlefield *n* maes y gad *m.*
bawdy *adj* anweddus.
bawl *v* crochlefain.
bay *n* bae *m.*
bazaar *n* basâr *m.*
be *v* bod (*see* Appendix).
beach *n* traeth *m.*
beacon *n* coelcerth *f.*
bead *n* glain *m.*
beak *n* pig *f.*
beaker *n* bicer *m.*
beam *n* trawst; pelydryn *m.* • *v* tywynnu.
bean *n* ffeuen *f.*
bear[1] *n* arth *f.*
bear[2] *v* dwyn, goddef.
bearable *adj* goddefadwy.
beard *n* barf *m.*
bearded *adj* barfog.
bearer *n* cludwr *m.*
beast *n* bwystfil *m.*
beat *v* curo. • *n* curiad *m.*
beating *n* cosfa *f.*
beautiful *adj* prydferth.
beautify *v* harddu.
beauty *n* harddwch, tegwch *m.*
beaver *n* afanc *m.*
because *conj* oherwydd. • *prep* gan.
become *v* dod; gweddu.
becoming *adj* gweddus.
bed *n* gwely *m.*
bedclothes *n* dillad gwely *pl.*
bedridden *adj* gorweiddiog.
bedroom *n* ystafell wely *f.*
bedspread *n* cwrlid *m.*
bee *n* gwenynen *f.*
beef *n* cig eidion *m.*
beehive *n* cwch gwenyn *m.*
beer *n* cwrw *m.*
befit *v* gweddu.
before *adv* o'r blaen. • *prep* o flaen.
beforehand *adv* ymlaen llaw.
beg *v* ymbil; cardota.
beggar *n* cardotyn *m.*
begin *v* dechrau.
beginner *n* dechreuwr *m*, dechreuwraig *f.*
beginning *n* dechreuad *m.*
behave *v* ymddwyn.
behaviour *n* ymddygiad *m.*
behead *v* dienyddio.
behind *adv* ar ôl. • *prep* tu ôl, tu cefn.
behold *v* wele!
being *n* bod *m.*
belated *adj* diweddar.
belch *v* pecial, torri gwynt.
belie *v* gwrth-ddweud.
belief *n* cred *f.*
believable *adj* credadwy.
believe *v* credu, coelio.
believer *n* credwr *m*, credinwraig *f.*
belittle *v* bychanu.
bell *n* cloch *f.*
belligerent *adj* cwerylgar, rhyfelgar.
bellow *v* rhuo, bugunad.
belly *n* bol, bola *m.*

belong *v* perthyn.
beloved *adj* annwyl. • *n* cariad.
below *adv* oddi tanodd; islaw.
belt *n* gwregys *m*.
bench *n* mainc *f*.
bend *v* plygu. • *n* tro *m*.
beneath *adv*, *prep* oddi tanodd; tan.
benefactor *n* cymwynaswr *m*, cymwynaswraig *f*.
beneficent *adj* bendithiol.
beneficial *adj* buddiol, llesol.
benefit *n* budd, budd-dâl *m*.
benevolence *n* cymwynasgarwch *m*.
benevolent *adj* cymwynasgar.
benign *adj* tirion.
bequeath *v* cymynnu, ewyllysio.
bequest *n* cymynrodd *f*.
bereavement *n* profedigaeth *f*.
berries *n* aeron *pl*.
berserk *adj* gwyllt.
beseech *v* deisyf, erfyn.
beset *v* amgylchynu.
beside(s) *prep* gerllaw, yn ymyl.
besiege *v* gwarchae.
best *adj* gorau.
bestial *adj* ffiaidd, bwystfilaidd.
bestow *v* cyflwyno.
bet *n* bet *m*. • *v* betio.
betray *v* bradychu.
betrayal *n* brad, bradychiad *m*.
better *adj* gwell. • *adv* yn well.
between *prep* rhwng.
beverage *n* diod *f*.
bewilder *v* drysu, mwydro.
bewilderment *n* dryswch, penbleth *m*.
beyond *prep* tu hwnt.
bias *n* gogwydd *m*, rhagfarn *f*.
Bible *n* Beibl *m*.
bibliography *n* llyfryddiaeth *f*.
bicycle *n* beic, beisicl *m*.
bid *v* cynnig. • *n* ~*m*.
bide *v* aros, disgwyl.
biennial *adj* bob dwy flynedd, eilflwydd.
big *adj* mawr.
bigot *n* rhywun llawn rhagfarn.
bigoted *adj* cul.
bike *n* beic *m*.
bikini *n* bicini *m*.
bilberries *n* llus *pl*.
bile *n* bustl *m*.
bilingual *adj* dwyieithog.
bill *n* bil; mesur *m*.
billet *n* llety *m*.
billion *n* biliwn *f*.
billy-goat *n* bwch gafr.
bin *n* bin *m*.
bind *v* rhwymo.
binge *n* sbri *f*.
biochemistry *n* biocemeg *f*.
binoculars *n* gwydrau *pl*.
biographer *n* cofiannydd *m*.
biography *n* cofiant *m*.
biological *adj* biolegol.
biology *n* bioleg *f*.
birch *n* bedwen *f*.
bird *n* aderyn *m*.
birth *n* genedigaeth *f*.
birth certificate *n* tystysgrif geni *f*.
birth control *n* atal cenhedlu *vn*.
birthday *n* pen-blwydd *m*.
biscuit *n* bisgïen *f*.
bishop *n* esgob *m*.
bit *n* tamaid *m*; genfa *f*.

bitch *n* gast *f.*
bite *v* cnoi, brathu. • *n* cnoad, brathiad *m.*
bitter *adj* chwerw.
bitterness *n* chwerwder *m.*
bizarre *adj* od, rhyfedd.
black *adj* du.
blackberries *n* mwyar *pl.*
blackbird *n* aderyn du *m*, mwyalchen *f.*
blackboard *n* bwrdd du *m.*
blacken *v* duo, pardduo.
blackleg *n* bradwr *m.*
blackmail *n* blacmêl *m.*
blackness *n* düwch.
blacksmith *n* gof *m.*
bladder *n* pledren *f.*
blade *n* llafn *m.*
blame *v* beio. • *n* bai *m.*
blameless *adj* di-fai, difai.
bland *adj* mwyn; di-flas.
blank *adj* gwag. • *n* bwlch *m.*
blanket *n* carthen *f.*
blare *v* rhuo.
blaspheme *v* cablu.
blasphemy *n* cabledd *m.*
blast *n* ffrwydrad *m.* • *v* ffrwydro.
blatant *adj* eofn, haerllug.
blaze *n* tanllwyth *m.* • *v* fflamio.
bleach *n* cannydd. • *v* cannu.
bleak *adj* llwm.
bleakness *n* moelni *m.*
bleat *n* bref *f.* • *v* brefu, dolefain.
bleed *v* gwaedu.
blemish *v* llychwino. • *n* mefl *m.*
blend *v* ymdoddi; cyfuno.
bless *v* bendithio.
blessing *n* bendith *f.*
blight *v* difetha. • *n* malltod *m.*
blind *adj* dall. • *v* dallu.
blindfold *n* mwgwd *m.*
blindness *n* dallineb *m.*
bliss *n* gwynfyd *m.*
blissful *adj* dedwydd.
blister *n* chwysigen, pothell *f.*
blizzard *n* storm o eira *f.*
bloated *adj* chwyddedig.
blob *n* smotyn *m.*
block *n* bloc *m.*
blockade *v* gwarchae.
blond *adj* pryd golau.
blood *n* gwaed *m.*
blood donor *n* rhoddwr gwaed *m.*
blood group *n* grŵp gwaed *m.*
blood pressure *n* pwysedd gwaed *m.*
bloodstream *n* llif gwaed *m.*
blood transfusion *n* trallwysiad gwaed *m.*
blood vessel *n* pibell waed *f.*
bloody *adj* gwaedlyd.
bloom *v* blodeuo.
blossom *n* blodeuyn *m.*
blot *v* blotio. • *n* blotyn.
blouse *n* blows, blowsen *f.*
blow *v* chwythu. • *n* ergyd *m/f.*
blubber *n* bloneg morfil *m.*
blue *adj* glas.
blueprint *n* cynddelw *f.*
bluff *v* blyffio.
blunder *n* camgymeriad *m.*
blunt *adj* pŵl. • *v* pylu.
blur *n* aneglurder *m.*
blush *n* gwrid *m.* • *v* gwrido.
board *n* bwrdd *m*, bord *f.*
boarder *n* lletywr *m.*

boarding house *n* llety *m*.
boast *v* ymffrostio, brolio. • *n* ymffrost *m*; bost *f*.
boastful *adj* ymffrostgar.
boat *n* cwch, bad *m*.
bodily *adj* corfforol.
body *n* corff *m*.
bodywork *n* corff *m*.
bog *n* cors, siglen *f*.
bogus *adj* ffug.
boil *v* berwi. • *n* cornwyd *m*.
boiler *n* boeler *m*.
boisterous *adj* hoenus, swnllyd.
bold *adj* beiddgar, eofn.
boldness *n* beiddgarwch, ehofndra *m*.
bolt *n* bollt, bollten *f*. • *v* bolltio.
bomb *n* bom *m/f*.
bombard *v* bombardio, peledu.
bombastic *adj* chwyddedig, llawn gwynt.
bona fide *adj* dilys.
bond *n* rhwymyn *m*.
bone *n* asgwrn *m*.
bonfire *n* coelcerth *f*.
bonnet *n* boned *f*.
bonus *n* bonws *m*.
bony *adj* esgyrnog.
boo *v* bwio.
book *n* llyfr *m*.
bookcase *n* cwpwrdd llyfrau *m*.
bookkeeper *n* cyfrifydd *m*.
bookkeeping *n* cadw cyfrifon *vn*.
bookseller *n* llyfrwerthwr *m*, llyfrwerthwraig *f*.
bookstore *n* siop lyfrau *f*.
bookworm *n* llyfrbryf *m*.
boom *n* dwndwr *m*.
boot *n* esgid; cist *f*.
booth *n* bwth *m*, stondin *f*.
border *n* ffin *f*. • *v* ffinio.
bore *v* tyllu; llethu. • *n* bôr *m*.
boredom *n* diflastod *m*.
boring *adj* diflas, undonog.
born *adj* genedigol.
borrow *v* benthyca.
borrower *n* benthycwr *m*.
bosom *n* mynwes *f*.
boss *n* meistr, giaffer *m*.
botanic(al) *adj* botanegol.
botany *n* botaneg, llysieueg *f*.
botch *v* cawlio.
both *pron* y ddau, y ddwy.
bother *v* poeni, trafferthu.
bottle *n* potel *f*.
bottleneck *n* tagfa (draffig) *f*.
bottle-opener *n* teclyn agor poteli *m*.
bottom *n* gwaelod, pen ôl *m*.
bough *n* cangen *f*.
bounce *v* sboncio.
bound *v* llamu.
boundary *n* ffin *f*, terfyn *m*.
bout *n* gornest *f*; pwl *m*.
bow *v* moesymgrymu.
bow *n* bwa *m*.
bow tie *n* dici bô *m*.
bowels *n* perfedd, perfeddion *pl*.
bowl *n* dysgl, powlen *f*.
bowl *v* bowlio; powlio.
box *n* blwch *m*.
box office *n* swyddfa docynnau *f*.
boxer *n* paffiwr *m*, paffwraig *f*.
boy *n* bachgen *m*.
boycott *v* boicotio.
boyfriend *n* cariad, sboner *m*.

bra *n* bra, bronglwm *m.*
bracelet *n* breichled *f.*
bracket *n* bach *m.*
brag *v* brolio.
braid *n* pleth *f.* • *v* plethu.
brain *n* ymennydd *m.*
brainwave *n* fflach o weledigaeth *f.*
brainy *adj* peniog.
brake *n* brêc *m.* • *v* brecio.
bramble *n* drysïen *f.*
branch *n* cangen *f.*
brand *n* gwneuthuriad *m*; brand *m.*
brandy *n* brandi *m.*
brash *adj* hyf, digywilydd.
brat *n* crwtyn *m*; croten *f*; cythraul bach *m.*
brave *adj* dewr, gwrol.
bravery *n* dewrder, gwroldeb *m.*
brawl *n* ffrwgwd *m.* • *v* ffraeo, ymrafael.
bray *v* nadu.
braze *v* sodro â phres.
breach *n* adwy; tor (cyfraith) *f.*
bread *n* bara *m.*
breadth *n* lled *m.*
break *v* torri. • *n* toriad *m.*
breakdown *n* dosraniad *m*; gwaeledd nerfol *m.*
breakfast *n* brecwast *m.* • *v* brecwasta.
breast *n* bron, mynwes *f.*
breath *n* anadl *f.*
breathalyse *v* profi anadl.
breathe *v* anadlu.
breed *n* brid *m*, gwaedoliaeth *f.* • *v* bridio, magu.
breeder *n* bridiwr, magwr *m*; bridwraig, magwraig *f.*
breeze *n* awel *f.*
brevity *n* byrder, byrdra *m.*
brew *v* bragu, macsu; bwrw ffrwyth.
brewer *n* bragwr *m.*
brewery *n* bragdy *m.*
bribe *n* cildwrn *m.* • *v* llwgrwobrwyo.
brick *n* bricsen *f.*
bricklayer *n* briciwr *m.*
bride *n* priodferch, priodasferch *f.*
bridegroom *n* priodfab, priodasfab *m.*
bridge *n* pont *f.*
bridle *n* ffrwyn *f.*
brief *adj* byr, cwta.
brigand *n* gwylliad *m.*
bright *adj* disglair.
brighten *v* goleuo, gloywi.
brilliance *n* disgleirdeb, disgleirder *m.*
brilliant *adj* disglair, llachar.
brim *n* ymyl *m/f.*
bring *v* dod â, dwyn.
brisk *adj* sionc, heini.
bristle *n* gwrychyn *m.* • *v* codi gwrychyn.
brittle *adj* brau.
broad *adj* eang, llydan.
broadcast *n* darllediad *m.* • *v* darlledu.
broaden *v* ehangu, lledu.
broadness *n* ehangder, lled *m.*
broccoli *n* blodfresych gaeaf *f.*
brochure *n* pamffled, pamffledyn *m.*
broken *adj* wedi torri.
broker *n* brocer *m.*
bronze *n* efydd *m.*
brooch *n* broets *f*, tlws *m.*

brood *v* gori; pendroni. • *n* nythaid *f.*
brook *n* nant *f.*
broom *n* ysgub *f*; banadl *pl.*
brother *n* brawd *m.*
brother-in-law *n* brawd-yng-nghyfraith *m.*
brow *n* ael *f.*
brown *adj* brown.
browse *v* pori.
bruise *n* clais *m.*
brush *n* brwsh *m.*
brutal *adj* ciaidd.
brutality *n* creulondeb, creulonder *m.*
brute *n* bwystfil *m.*
bubble *n* cloch ddŵr *f.* • *v* byrlymu.
bucket *n* bwced *m.*
buckle *n* bwcl *m.*
budge *v* symud.
budget *n* cyllideb *f.*
buffet *n* pryd bys a bawd, bwffe *m.*
bug *n* lleuen *f*; byg *m.*
build *v* codi, adeiladu.
builder *n* adeiladydd *m.*
building *n* adeilad *m.*
bulb *n* bwlb *m.*
bulge *v* chwyddo. • *n* chwydd *m.*
bulk *n* crynswth, swmp *m.*
bulky *adj* swmpus.
bull *n* tarw *m.*
bulldozer *n* tarw dur *m.*
bullet *n* bwled *m/f.*
bulletproof *adj* atal bwledi.
bulletin *n* bwletin, hysbysiad *m.*
bully *n* bwli *m.* • *v* bwlio, gormesu.
bump *n* clonc. • *v* cnocio.
bun *n* bynen *f.*
bunch *n* cwlwm, tusw *m.*
bundle *n* bwndel, swp. • *v* sypynnu.
bungle *v* gwneud cawl.
bunk *n* gwely bach *m.*
buoy *n* bwi *m.*
buoyancy *n* hynofedd *m.*
buoyant *adj* hynawf, yn nofio.
burden *n* baich *m.*
bureau *n* biwro *m/f.*
bureaucrat *n* biwrocrat *m.*
burial *n* claddedigaeth *f.*
burly *adj* cydnerth.
burn *v* llosgi. • *n* llosgiad *m.*
burning *adj* tanbaid, llosg.
burst *v* byrstio.
bury *v* claddu.
bus *n* bws *m.*
bush *n* perth *f*; llwyn *m.*
business *n* busnes *m.*
businessman *n* dyn busnes *m.*
businesswoman *n* gwraig fusnes *f.*
bus-stop *n* arhosfan *f.*
busy *adj* prysur.
but *conj* ond.
butcher *n* cigydd *m.* • *v* bwtsiera.
butter *n* menyn, ymenyn *m.*
butterfly *n* glöyn byw, pilipala *m*, iâr fach yr haf *f.*
button *n* botwm *m.* • *v* botymu.
buy *v* prynu.
buyer *n* prynwr *m*, prynwraig *f.*
buzz *n* su *m/f.* • *v* suo.
by *prep* wrth; gan; erbyn.
by-election *n* isetholiad *m/f.*
by-law *n* is-deddf *f.*
bypass *n* ffordd osgoi *f.*
by-product *n* isgynnyrch *m.*
byte *n* talp *m.*

C

cabbage *n* bresychen *f.*
cabin *n* caban *m.*
cabinet *n* cabinet *m.*
cable *n* cebl *m.*
cache *n* celc *m.*
cackle *v* clochdar. • *n* clegar *m.*
caddie *n* cadi *m.*
cafe *n* caffe *m.*
cage *n* caets, cawell *m.*
cake *n* teisen *f.*
calamity *n* trychineb *m/f.*
calculate *v* bwrw cyfrif, clandro.
calculation *n* cyfrif *m.*
calendar *n* calendr *m.*
calf *n* llo *m/f.*
calibre *n* calibr *m.*
call *v* galw. • *n* galwad *f.*
calligraphy *n* caligraffi *m*, llythrennu'n gain.
calling *n* galwedigaeth *f.*
callous *adj* didrugaredd, dienaid.
calm *n* tawelwch *m.* • *adj* tawel. • *v* tawelu.
calorie *n* calori *m.*
camel *n* camel *m.*
camera *n* camera *m.*
camouflage *n* cuddliw *m.*
camp *n* gwersyll *m.* • *v* gwersylla, gwersyllu.
campaign *n* ymgyrch *m/f.*
camper *n* gwersyllwr *m*, gwersyllwraig *f.*
campsite *n* gwersyllfa.
campus *n* campws *m.*
can *v* gallu. • *n* bocs, can *m.*
can opener *n* agorwr caniau *m.*
canal *n* camlas *f.*
cancel *v* canslo, diddymu.
cancer *n* cancr, canser *m.*
candid *adj* agored, didwyll.
candidate *n* ymgeisydd *m.*
candle *n* cannwyll *f.*
candour *n* didwylledd *m.*
cane *n* corsen; gwialen *f.*
cannon *n* canon *m*, magnel *f.*
canoe *n* canŵ *m.*
canon *n* canon *m.*
canopy *n* canopi *m.*
cantankerous *adj* cecrus. cynhennus.
canteen *n* cantîn, ffreutur *m.*
canvas *n* cynfas *m/f.*
canvass *v* canfasio.
cap *n* cap, capan *m.*
capability *n* gallu *m.*
capable *adj* galluog.
capacity *n* maint; gallu *m.*
cape *n* mantell *f*; penrhyn *m.*
capital *adj* prif. • *n* cyfalaf *m.*
capital punishment *n* y gosb eithaf *f.*
capitalise *v* elwa.
capitalist *n* cyfalafwr *m*, cyfalafwraig *f.*
capitulate *v* ildio.
capricious *adj* mympwyol, oriog.

capsize *v* dymchwel.
capsule *n* capsiwl *m*.
captain *n* capten *m*.
captivate *v* swyno, cyfareddu.
captivation *n* cyfaredd *f*.
captive *n* carcharor *m*.
captivity *n* caethiwed *m*.
capture *v* dal.
car *n* car *m*.
caravan *n* carafán *f*.
carbohydrate *n* carbohydrad *m*.
carcass *n* celain *f*.
card *n* carden *f*.
cardboard *n* cardfwrdd *m*.
cardinal *adj* prif. • *n* cardinal *m*.
care *n* gofal *m*. • *v* poeni.
career *n* gyrfa *f*.
careful *adj* gofalus.
careless *adj* diofal, esgeulus.
carelessness *n* esgeulustod *m*.
caress *n* anwes *m*. • *v* anwesu.
caretaker *n* gofalwr *m*, gofalwraig *f*.
cargo *n* cargo; llwyth *m*.
caricature *n* gwawdlun *m*.
carnage *n* cyflafan *f*.
carnal *adj* cnawdol.
carnival *n* cárnifal *m*.
carnivorous *adj* cigysol.
carpenter *n* saer coed *m*.
carpentry *n* gwaith coed *m*.
carpet *n* carped *m*.
carriage *n* cerbyd *m*.
carrier *n* cludydd *m*.
carrion *n* celain *f*.
carrots *n* moron *pl*.
carry *v* cario, cludo, dwyn.
cart *n* trol *f*.
cartilage *n* madruddyn *m*.
cartoon *n* cartŵn *m*.
cartridge *n* cetrisen *f*.
carve *v* naddu, cerfio.
carving *n* cerfiad *m*.
case *n* achos; cas, casyn *m*.
cash *n* arian parod *m*.
cashier *n* ariannydd *m*.
casing *n* cragen *f*, casyn *m*.
casino *n* casino *m*.
cask *n* casgen *f*.
casket *n* blwch *m*.
casserole *n* caserol *m*.
cassette *n* casét *m*.
cassette player *n* chwaraewr casetiau *m*.
cast *v* bwrw.
caste *n* cast, dosbarth *m*.
castigate *v* cystwyo.
castle *n* castell *m*.
castrate *v* disbaddu, ysbaddu.
castration *n* disbaddiad *m*.
casual *adj* damweiniol, anffurfiol.
cat *n* cath *f*.
catalogue *n* catalog *m*, rhestr *f*.
catapult *n* blif, sling *m*.
cataract *n* rhaeadr; pilen *f*.
catastrophe *n* trychineb *m*.
catch *v* dal.
catchword *n* slogan *m/f*.
catechism *n* holwyddoreg *f*.
categorical *adj* pendant.
category *n* dosbarth, categori *m*.
cater *v* arlwyo.
catering *n* arlwyaeth *f*.
caterpillar *n* lindys *m*.
cathedral *n* eglwys gadeiriol *f*.
catholic *adj* catholig.

cattle *n* gwartheg *pl.*
cauliflower *n* blodfresychen *f.*
cause *n* achos *m.* • *v* achosi.
cauterise *v* serio.
caution *n* pwyll *m.* • *v* rhybuddio.
cautious *adj* gofalus, gwyliadwrus.
cavalry *n* gwŷr meirch *pl.*
cave *n* ogof *f.*
cavern *n* ceudwll *m.*
cavity *n* ceudod *m.*
cease *v* peidio, darfod.
ceaseless *adj* di-baid.
cede *v* ildio.
ceiling *n* nenfwd *m.*
celebrate *v* dathlu.
celebration *n* dathliad *m.*
celery *n* helogan *f.*
celibate *adj* diwair, dibriod.
cell *n* cell *f.*
cellar *n* seler *f.*
cement *n* sment *m.*
cemetery *n* mynwent *f.*
censor *n* sensor *m.*
censorship *n* sensoriaeth *f.*
censure *v* ceryddu.
census *n* cyfrifiad *m.*
centenary *n* canmlwyddiant *m.*
centigrade *adj* canradd.
centimetre *n* centimetr *m.*
central *adj* canolog.
centralise *v* canoli.
centre *n* canolfan *m/f*; canol *m.* • *v* canoli.
century *n* canrif *f.*
ceramic *adj* ceramig.
cereal *n* grawnfwyd *m.*
ceremonial *adj* defodol, seremonïol.
ceremony *n* defod, seremoni *f.*
certain *adj* sicr, diamau.
certainty *n* sicrwydd *m.*
certificate *n* tystysgrif *f.*
certification *n* ardystiad *m.*
certify *v* tystio, ardystio.
cessation *n* diwedd, terfyn *m.*
chafe *v* rhwbio.
chagrin *n* siom *m/f.*
chain *n* cadwyn *f.* • *v* cadwyno.
chair *n* cadair *f.* • *v* cadeirio.
chairman *n* cadeirydd *m.*
chalk *n* sialc *m.*
challenge *n* her *f.* • *v* herio.
chamber *n* siambr *f.*
champion *n* pencampwr *m*, pencampwraig *f.* • *v* amddiffyn.
championship *n* pencampwriaeth *f.*
chance *n* damwain, siawns *f.*
chancellor *n* canghellor *m.*
change *v* newid. • *n* newid *m.*
changeable *adj* cyfnewidiol.
channel *n* sianel *f.* • *v* sianelu.
chant *n* salm-dôn *f.* • *v* llafarganu.
chaos *n* anhrefn *f.*
chaotic *adj* anhrefnus, cawl gwyllt.
chapel *n* capel *m.*
chapter *n* pennod *f.*
character *n* cymeriad *m.*
characteristic *adj* nodweddiadol.
charcoal *n* golosg, sercol *m.*
charge *v* codi; hyrddio; siarsio. • *n* pris *m*; rhuthr *m*; cyhuddiad *m.*
charitable *adj* elusennol.
charity *n* elusen *f.*
charm *n* swyn *m.* • *v* swyno.
chart *n* siart *f.*
charter *n* siarter, breinlen *f.* • *v* llogi.

chase *v* hela, ymlid. • *n* helfa *f.*
chaste *adj* diwair.
chastise *v* cosbi, cystuddio.
chastisement *n* cosbedigaeth *f.*
chastity *n* diweirdeb *m.*
chat *v* sgwrsio. • *n* sgwrs *f.*
chatter *v* clebran; cogor.
chauffeur *n* gyrrwr *m.*
chauffeuse *n* gyrwraig *f.*
chauvinist *n* siofinydd *m.*
cheap *adj* rhad.
cheapen *v* gostwng (pris).
cheat *v* twyllo. • *n* twyllwr *m,* twyllwraig *f.*
check *v* gwirio. • *n* gwiriad *m.*
checkup *n* archwiliad *m.*
cheek *n* boch *f.*
cheer *n* bonllef *f.* • *v* bloeddio cymeradwyaeth.
cheerful *adj* siriol, llon.
cheerfulness *n* sirioldeb *m.*
cheese *n* caws *m.*
chef *n* pen-cogydd *m.*
chemist *n* cemegydd *m*; fferyllydd *m.*
chemistry *n* cemeg *f.*
cheque *n* siec *f.*
cherish *v* anwylo, coleddu.
cherry *n* ceiriosen *f.*
chess *n* gwyddbwyll *f.*
chest *n* brest *f*; cist *f.*
chew *v* cnoi.
chick *n* cyw *m.*
chicken *n* cyw iâr, ffowlyn *m.*
chief *adj* prif. • *n* pennaeth *m.*
chieftain *n* pennaeth *m.*
child *n* plentyn *m.*
childbirth *n* genedigaeth *f.*
childhood *n* plentyndod *m.*
childish *adj* plentynnaidd.
children *n* plant *pl.*
chill *n* annwyd *m.* • *v* oeri.
chilly *adj* oeraidd.
chimney *n* simdde, simnai *f.*
chin *n* gên *f.*
chip *v* naddu. • *n* sglodyn *m.*
chirp *v* trydar.
chisel *n* cŷn *m*, gaing *f.*
chivalry *n* sifalri *m.*
chocolate *n* siocled *m.*
choice *n* dewis *m.*
choir *n* côr *m.*
choke *v* tagu.
choose *v* dewis, dethol.
chop *v* torri. • *n* golwyth *m.*
chore *n* gorchwyl *m*, tasg *f.*
chorus *n* cytgan *f*; corws *m.*
christen *v* bedyddio.
christening *n* bedydd *m.*
Christian *adj* Cristnogol. • *n* Cristion *m.*
Christmas *n* Nadolig *m.*
Christmas Eve *n* Noswyl y Nadolig *f.*
chronic *adj* cronig, di-baid.
chronicle *n* cronicl *m.*
chronicler *n* croniclydd, cofiadur *m.*
chronological *adj* cronolegol.
chronology *n* cronoleg *f.*
chuckle *n* chwerthiniad *m.*
chum *n* mêt *m*, cyfaill mebyd.
church *n* eglwys *f.*
cider *n* seidr *m.*
cigar *n* sigâr *f.*
cigarette *n* sigarét *f.*

cinder *n* colsyn, marworyn *m*.
cinema *n* sinema *m*.
circle *n* cylch *m*. • *v* cylchu.
circuit *n* cylchdaith, cylched *f*.
circular *adj* crwn. • *n* cylchlythyr *m*.
circulate *v* cylchredeg.
circulation *n* cylchrediad *m*.
circumference *n* cylchedd *m*.
circumnavigation *n* mordaith (o gwmpas) *f*.
circumspect *adj* gochelgar.
circumspection *n* gochelgarwch, pwyll *m*.
circumstance *n* amgylchiad *m*.
circumvent *v* osgoi, twyllo.
circus *n* syrcas *f*.
cite *v* gwysio; dyfynnu.
citizen *n* dinesydd *m*.
city *n* dinas *f*.
civic *adj* dinesig.
civil *adj* sifil.
civilian *n* dinesydd (preifat) *m*.
civilisation *n* gwareiddiad *m*.
civilise *v* gwareiddio.
claim *v* hawlio; honni. • *n* cais; honiad *m*.
claimant *n* hawliwr, hawlydd *m*.
clamour *n* dadwrdd *m*.
clamp *n* clamp *m*. • *v* clampio.
clandestine *adj* dirgel.
clap *v* curo dwylo.
clarification *n* eglurhad *m*.
clarify *v* egluro; gloywi.
clarity *n* eglurder, gloywder *m*.
clash *v* gwrthdaro.
clasp *n* clesbyn *m*. • *v* gwasgu'n dynn.
class *n* dosbarth *m*.
classic(al) *adj* clasurol.
classification *n* dosbarthiad *m*.
classify *v* dosbarthu.
classroom *n* ystafell ddosbarth *f*.
clatter *v* clindarddach. • *n* twrw *m*.
claw *n* crafanc *f*.
clean *adj* glân. • *v* glanhau.
cleaning *n* glanhad, glanheuad *m*.
cleanliness *n* glanweithdra, glendid *m*.
clear *adj* clir, eglur. • *v* clirio.
cleft *n* hollt *f*.
clemency *n* trugaredd *f/m*.
clement *adj* tirion.
clergy *n* offeiriaid *pl*.
clergyman *n* clerigwr *m*.
clerical *adj* clerigol.
clerk *n* clerc *m*.
clever *adj* medrus, peniog.
click *v* clicio. • *n* clic *m*.
client *n* cwsmer *m*.
cliff *n* clogwyn *m*.
climate *n* hinsawdd *f*.
climatic *adj* hinsoddol.
climax *n* anterth, uchafbwynt *m*.
climb *v* dringo.
climber *n* dringwr *m*.
cling *v* glynu.
clinic *n* clinig *m*.
clip *v* tocio.
cloak *n* clogyn, mantell *f*. • *v* taflu mantell dros.
cloakroom *n* ystafell gotiau *f*.
clock *n* cloc *m*.
clog *n* clocsen *f*.
close *v* cau. • *n* diwedd *m*. • *adj* cyfagos; mwll.

closeness *n* agosrwydd *m.*
cloth *n* brethyn; lliain *m.*
clothe *v* dilladu.
clothes *n* dillad *pl.*
cloud *n* cwmwl *m.*
cloudy *adj* cymylog.
clover *n* meillionen *f.*
clown *n* clown *m.*
club *n* pastwn; clwb *m.*
clue *n* cliw *m.*
clumsiness *n* lletchwithdod *m.*
clumsy *adj* lletchwith, trwsgl.
cluster *n* clwstwr, clwm *m.* • *v* clystyru.
clutch *n* cydiwr, clyts *m.* • *v* gafael.
coach *n* coets *f,* hyfforddwr *m.* • *v* hy-fforddi.
coagulate *v* ceulo.
coal *n* glo *m.*
coalesce *v* ymdoddi.
coalition *n* clymblaid *f.*
coarse *adj* garw, aflednais.
coast *n* arfordir *m.*
coastal *adj* arfordirol.
coastguard *n* gwyliwr y glannau *m.*
coat *n* cot, côt *f.*
coating *n* cot, côt, haen *f.*
coax *v* perswadio.
cobweb *n* gwe pry copyn *f.*
cock *n* ceiliog *m.*
cockpit *n* talwrn *m.*
cocoa *n* coco *m.*
coconut *n* cneuen goco *f.*
cocoon *n* cocŵn *m.*
cod *n* penfras *m.*
code *n* cod *m.*
coercion *n* gorfodaeth *f.*
coexistence *n* cydfodolaeth *f.*
coffee *n* coffi *m.*
coffer *n* coffr *m/f.*
coffin *n* arch *f.*
cog *n* cocsyn *m,* cocsen *f.*
cogency *n* grym, argyhoeddiad *m.*
cogent *adj* grymus, cryf.
cognisance *n* gwybyddiaeth *f.*
cogwheel *n* olwyn gocos *f.*
cohabit *v* cyd-fyw, byw tali.
cohabitation *n* cyd-fyw *vn.*
cohere *v* cydlynu.
coherent *adj* yn dal dŵr, cydlynol.
cohesive *adj* ymlynol.
coil *n* torch *f.* • *v* torchi.
coin *n* darn arian *m.*
coincide *v* cyd-daro, cyd-ddigwydd.
coincidence *n* cyd-ddigwyddiad *m.*
colander *n* colandr *m,* hidl *f.*
cold *adj* oer. • *n* oerfel; annwyd *m.*
collaborate *v* cydweithio.
collaboration *n* cydweithrediad *m.*
collapse *v* dymchwelyd, syrthio. • *n* cwymp *m.*
collapsible *adj* plygu (cadair blygu).
collar *n* coler *f/m.*
collate *v* coladu.
collateral *adj* cyfochrog.
colleague *n* cyd-weithiwr *m,* cyd-weithwraig *f.*
collect *v* casglu, hel.
collection *n* casgliad *m.*
collector *n* casglwr, casglydd *m.*
college *n* coleg *m.*
collide *v* gwrthdaro.
collision *n* gwrthdrawiad *m.*

colloquial *adj* llafar.
colloquialism *n* ymadrodd llafar, gwerinair *m.*
collusion *n* cydgynllwyn *m.*
colonial *adj* trefedigaethol.
colonise *v* gwladychu.
colony *n* gwladfa, trefedigaeth *f.*
colour *n* lliw *m.* • *v* lliwio.
coloured *adj* lliw.
colourful *adj* lliwgar.
column *n* colofn *f.*
columnist *n* colofnydd *m.*
coma *n* côma *m.*
comatose *adj* swrth, mewn côma.
comb *n* crib *f/m.* • *v* cribo.
combat *n* gornest *f.* • *v* ymladd yn erbyn.
combatant *n* ymladdwr *m.*
combination *n* cyfuniad *m.*
combine *v* cyfuno.
combustion *n* hylosgiad *m.*
come *v* dod, dyfod (*see* Appendix).
comedian *n* digrifwr *m.*
comedienne *n* digrifwraig *f.*
comedy *n* comedi *f.*
comet *n* comed *f*, seren gynffon *f.*
comfort *n* cysur *m.* • *v* cysuro.
comfortable *adj* cyfforddus.
comic(al) *adj* digrif, smala.
command *v* gorchymyn. • *n* gorchymyn *m.*
commander *n* comander *m.*
commemorate *v* coffáu.
commemoration *n* coffâd *m.*
commence *v* cychwyn.
commencement *n* dechrau *m.*
commend *v* cyflwyno; cymeradwyo.
commendation *n* cymeradwyaeth *f.*
commensurate *adj* cymesur.
comment *n* sylw *m.* • *v* gwneud sylw.
commentary *n* sylwebaeth *f*; esboniad *m.*
commentator *n* sylwebydd *m.*
commerce *n* masnach *f.*
commercial *adj* masnachol.
commiserate *v* cydymdeimlo.
commiseration *n* cydymdeimlad.
commission *n* comisiwn *m.* • *v* comisiynu; dirprwyo.
commit *v* cyflawni; traddodi.
commitment *n* ymrwymiad *m.*
committee *n* pwyllgor *m.*
common *adj* cyffredin.
common sense *n* synnwyr cyffredin *m.*
commonly *adv* yn gyffredin.
commotion *n* cyffro, cynnwrf *m.*
communicable *adj* mynegadwy; heintus.
communicate *v* cyfathrebu.
communion *n* cymundeb *m.*
communist *n* comiwnydd *m.*
community *n* cymuned *f.*
commutable *adj* newidiadwy.
commute *v* cymudo.
compact *adj* cryno.
compact disc *n* cryno-ddisg *m.*
companion *n* cydymaith, cymar *m.*
company *n* cwmni *m.*
comparable *adj* hafal.
comparative *adj* cymharol.
compare *v* cymharu.
comparison *n* cymhariaeth *f.*
compass *n* cwmpas *m.*

compassion *n* tosturi *m.*
compassionate *adj* tosturiol, trugarog.
compatibility *n* cydnawsedd *m.*
compatible *adj* cydnaws.
compatriot *n* cyd-wladwr *m.*
compel *v* gorfodi, cymell.
compensate *v* digolledu.
compensation *n* iawndal *m.*
compete *v* cystadlu.
competence *n* cymhwysedd *m.*
competent *adj* cymwys.
competition *n* cystadleuaeth *f.*
competitive *adj* cystadleuol.
competitor *n* cystadleuydd *m.*
complacency *n* hunanfoddhad *m.*
complacent *adj* hunanfoddhaus; hunanfodlon.
complain *v* achwyn.
complaint *n* cwyn *f.*
complementary *adj* cyflenwol.
complete *adj* cyflawn. • *v* gorffen.
completion *n* cwblhad *m.*
complex *adj* cymhleth.
complexion *n* pryd *m*, gwedd *f.*
complexity *n* cymhlethdod *m.*
compliance *n* ufudd-dod; cydsyniad *m.*
complicate *v* cymhlethu.
complication *n* cymhlethdod *m.*
complicity *n* rhan *f.*
compliment *n* canmoliaeth *f.* • *v* canmol, llongyfarch.
comply *v* ufuddhau, cydsynio.
component *n* cydran *f.*
compose *v* cyfansoddi.
composer *n* cyfansoddwr *m*, cyfansoddwraig *f.*
composition *n* cyfansoddiad; traethawd *m.*
composure *n* hunanfeddiant *m.*
compound *adj* cyfansawdd. • *n* cyfansoddyn *m.*
comprehend *v* amgyffred.
comprehensible *adj* dealladwy.
comprehension *n* dirnadaeth *f.*
comprehensive *adj* cynhwysfawr; cyfun.
compress *v* gwasgu.
comprise *v* cynnwys.
compromise *n* cyfaddawd *m.* • *v* cyfaddawdu.
compulsion *n* gorfodaeth *f.*
compulsory *adj* gorfodol.
computer *n* cyfrifiadur *m.*
computerise *v* cyfrifiaduro.
computer science *n* cyfrifiadureg *f.*
comrade *n* cydymaith, cymrawd *m.*
comradeship *n* brawdoliaeth *f.*
conceal *v* cuddio.
concealment *n* cuddio, celu *vn.*
concede *v* ildio.
conceit *n* hunan-dyb *m/f*, balchder *m.*
conceive *v* beichiogi; dychmygu.
concentrate *v* canolbwyntio.
concentration *n* crynodiad *m.*
concept *n* cysyniad *m.*
conception *n* syniad; beichiogiad *m.*
concern *v* ymwneud â. • *n* gofal; busnes *m.*
concerning *prep* ynglŷn â.
concert *n* cyngerdd *m.*
conciliate *v* cymodi.
conciliation *n* cymod *m.*

concise *adj* cryno.
conclude *v* casglu; terfynu.
conclusion *n* casgliad; diweddglo *m*.
conclusive *adj* terfynol.
concoct *v* llunio, dyfeisio.
concord *n* cytgord *m*.
concordance *n* cytgord; mynegai *m*.
concrete *n* concrit *m*.
concur *v* cyd-weld.
concurrence *n* cydsyniad *m*.
concurrent *adj* cyfredol.
concussion *n* ysgytwad *m*.
condemn *v* condemnio, collfarnu.
condemnation *n* condemniad *m*; collfarn *f*.
condensation *n* cyddwysedd *m*.
condense *v* cywasgu; cyddwyso.
condescend *v* ymostwng.
condescending *adj* nawddogol, nawddoglyd.
condition *v* cyflyru. • *n* cyflwr *m*; amod *m/f*.
conditional *adj* amodol.
condolence *n* cydymdeimlad *m*.
condom *n* condom *m*.
conduct *n* ymddygiad, ymarweddiad *m*. • *v* arwain.
cone *n* côn *m*.
confectionery *n* melysion; teisennau *pl*.
confer *v* ymgynghori; cyflwyno.
conference *n* cynhadledd *f*.
confess *v* cyffesu, cyfaddef.
confession *n* cyfaddefiad *m*, cyffes *f*.
confidant *n* cyfaill mynwesol *m*.
confide *v* ymddiried.
confidence *n* hyder *m*; ymddiriedaeth *f*.
confident *adj* hyderus.
confidential *adj* cyfrinachol.
confine *v* cyfyngu.
confinement *n* caethiwed *m*.
confirm *v* cadarnhau.
confirmation *n* cadarnhad *m*.
confiscate *v* cymryd oddi ar.
conflict *n* gwrthdrawiad *m*.
conflicting *adj* anghyson.
conform *v* cydymffurfio.
conformity *n* cydymffurfiad *m*.
confront *v* wynebu, bod wyneb yn wyneb.
confrontation *n* gwrthdaro *vn*.
confuse *v* cymysgu, drysu.
confusion *n* dryswch *m*, anhrefn *f*.
congeal *v* fferru, ceulo.
congenial *adj* cydnaws.
congenital *adj* cynhenid.
congestion *n* caethder *m*; tagfa *f*.
congratulate *v* llongyfarch.
congratulations *n* llongyfarchiadau *pl*.
congregate *v* casglu, ymgynnull.
congregation *n* cynulleidfa *f*.
congress *n* cyngres *f*, cynulliad *m*.
congruity *n* cyfaddasrwydd *m*.
congruous *adj* addas.
conifer *n* coniffer *m/f*.
conjecture *v* tybio, dyfalu.
conjugal *adj* priodasol.
conjunction *n* cysylltiad; cysylltair *m*.
conjuncture *n* achlysur *m*.
connect *v* cysylltu, cydio.
connection *n* cysylltiad *m*.
connoisseur *n* arbenigwr *m*, arbenigwraig *f*.

conquer *v* gorchfygu, goresgyn.
conqueror *n* gorchfygwr, goresgynnwr *m*.
conquest *n* goresgyniad, gorchfygiad *m*.
conscience *n* cydwybod *f*.
conscientious *adj* cydwybodol.
conscious *adj* ymwybodol.
consciousness *n* ymwybyddiaeth *f*.
consecrate *v* cysegru.
consecration *n* cysegriad *m*.
consecutive *adj* olynol.
consensus *n* consensws *m*.
consent *n* caniatâd *m*. • *v* caniatáu, cydsynio.
consequence *n* canlyniad *m*.
consequent *adj* canlynol, dilynol.
conservation *n* cadwraeth, gwarchodaeth *f*.
conservative *adj* ceidwadol.
conserve *v* cadw, gwarchod.
consider *v* ystyried.
considerable *adj* sylweddol.
considerate *adj* ystyriol, meddylgar.
consideration *n* ystyriaeth *f*.
consign *v* anfon.
consignment *n* cyflenwad *m*.
consist *v* cynnwys.
consistency *n* cysondeb; ansawdd *m*.
consistent *adj* cyson.
consolation *n* cysur *m*.
console *v* cysuro.
consolidate *v* atgyfnerthu.
consolidation *n* cadarnhad, cyfnerthiad *m*.
conspicuous *adj* amlwg.
conspiracy *n* cynllwyn *m*.
conspire *v* cynllwynio.
constancy *n* sadrwydd *m*.
constant *adj* cyson.
constellation *n* cytser *m*.
consternation *n* syndod *m*.
constipation *n* rhwymedd *m*.
constitute *v* gwneud, creu.
constitution *n* cyfansoddiad *m*.
constitutional *adj* cyfansoddiadol.
constrain *v* gorfodi; cyfyngu.
constraint *n* cyfyngiad *m*.
constrict *v* cywasgu.
construct *v* adeiladu, llunio.
construction *n* adeilad, lluniad *m*.
consult *v* ymgynghori.
consultation *n* ymgynghoriad *m*.
consume *v* llyncu, difa.
consumer *n* prynwr, defnyddiwr *m*; prynwraig, defnyddwraig *f*.
consummate *v* cyflawni. • *adj* cyflawn.
consumption *n* traul *f*; darfodedigaeth *m*.
contact *n* cysylltiad *m*.
contagious *adj* heintus.
contain *v* cynnwys.
container *n* cynhwysydd *m*.
contaminate *v* llygru, heintio.
contamination *n* llygredd *m*.
contemplate *v* ystyried.
contemplation *n* myfyrdod *m*.
contemporary *adj* cyfoes.
contempt *n* dirmyg *m*.
contemptible *adj* gwarthus, cywilyddus.
contemptuous *adj* dirmygus.
contend *v* ymryson.

content *adj* bodlon. • *n* cynnwys *m*.
contention *n* cynnen *f*.
contentment *n* bodlonrwydd *m*.
contest *v* herio, ymryson. • *n* gornest *f*.
contestant *n* cystadleuydd *m*.
context *n* cyd-destun *m*.
continent *n* cyfandir *m*.
continental *adj* cyfandirol.
contingency *n* achlysur *m*.
contingent *n* mintai *f*.
continual *adj* parhaus.
continuation *n* parhad *m*.
continue *v* parhau.
continuous *adj* parhaol.
contort *v* ystumio.
contortion *n* dirdyniad *m*.
contour *n* cyfuchlinedd *m*.
contraception *n* atal cenhedlu *vn*.
contraceptive *n* dyfais atal cenhedlu *f*.
contract *v* cyfangu; cyfamodi. • *n* cyfamod *m*.
contradict *v* gwrth-ddweud.
contradiction *n* gwrthddywediad *m*.
contradictory *adj* yn gwrthddweud.
contraption *n* dyfais *f*.
contrary *adj* croes. • *n* gwrthwyneb *m*.
contrast *n* gwrthgyferbyniad *m*. • *v* cyferbynnu.
contravention *n* toriad *m*.
contribute *v* cyfrannu.
contribution *n* cyfraniad *m*.
contrite *adj* edifar.
contrivance *n* dichell *f*.
control *n* rheolaeth *f*. • *v* rheoli.
controversial *adj* dadleuol.
controversy *n* dadl *f*.
contusion *n* clais *m*.
conurbation *n* cytref *f*.
convalesce *v* cryfhau, gwella.
convalescent *adj* ymadfer.
convene *v* galw, cynnull.
convenience *n* cyfleustra *m*.
convenient *adj* cyfleus.
convention *n* confensiwn *m*; cynhadledd *f*.
conventional *adj* confensiynol.
converge *v* cydgyfarfod.
convergence *n* cydgyfeiriant *m*.
convergent *adj* cydgyfeiriol.
conversant *adj* hyddysg, cyfarwydd.
conversation *n* sgwrs, ymgom *f*.
converse *v* sgwrsio, ymddiddan.
conversion *n* tröedigaeth *f*.
convert *v* troi.
convey *v* trosglwyddo, cludo.
conveyance *n* cludiad *m*.
convict *n* carcharor *m*. • *v* dyfarnu'n euog.
conviction *n* argyhoeddiad *m*; collfarn *f*.
convince *v* argyhoeddi.
convivial *adj* llawen, siriol.
conviviality *n* miri *m*.
convoke *v* cydgynnull.
convoy *n* gosgordd *f*.
convulse *v* dirdynnu.
convulsion *n* dirdyniad *m*.
convulsive *adj* dirdynnol.
cook *n* cogydd *m*, -es *f*. • *v* coginio.
cooker *n* popty *m*, ffwrn *f*.

cookery *n* coginio *vn*.
cool *adj* oeraidd. • *v* oeri.
coolness *n* oerni *m*.
co-operate *v* cydweithio.
co-operation *n* cydweithrediad *m*.
co-operative *adj* cydweithredol.
co-ordinate *v* cydlynu.
coordination *n* cytgordiad *m*.
cope *v* ymdopi.
copious *adj* helaeth.
copy *n* copi *m*. • *v* copïo, dynwared.
copyright *n* hawlfraint *f*.
coral *n* cwrel *m*.
cord *n* corden *f*.
cordial *adj* calonnog.
core *n* calon *f*, craidd *m*.
cork *n* corcyn *m*.
corkscrew *n* corcsgriw *m*.
corn *n* llafur, ŷd *m*.
corner *n* cornel *f*.
cornerstone *n* conglfaen *m*.
cornflakes *n* creision ŷd *pl*.
coronation *n* coroni *vn*.
coroner *n* crwner *m*.
corporate *adj* corfforaethol.
corporation *n* corfforaeth *f*.
corps *n* corfflu *m*.
corpse *n* corff *m*, celain *f*.
corpulent *adj* tew, llond ei groen.
correct *v* cywiro. • *adj* cywir.
correction *n* cywiriad *m*.
correctness *n* cywirdeb *m*.
correlation *n* cydberthynas *f*.
correspond *v* gohebu; cyfateb.
correspondence *n* cyfatebiaeth; go-hebiaeth *f*.
correspondent *n* gohebydd *m*.
corridor *n* coridor *m*.
corroborate *v* cadarnhau, ategu.
corrode *v* cyrydu.
corrosion *n* cyrydiad *m*; traul *f*.
corrosive *adj* difaol.
corrupt *v* llygru. • *adj* llwgr, llygredig.
corruption *n* llygredd *m*.
cosmetic *adj* cosmetig.
cosmic *adj* cosmig.
cosmopolitan *adj* aml-hiliol.
cost *n* cost *f*. • *v* costio.
costly *adj* drud, drudfawr.
costume *n* gwisg *f*.
cottage *n* bwthyn *m*.
cotton *n* cotwm *m*.
cotton wool *n* gwlân cotwm *m*.
couch *n* soffa *f*.
cough *n* peswch *m*. • *v* peswch.
council *n* cyngor *m*.
counsel *n* cyngor *m*.
counsellor *n* cynghorydd *m*.
count *v* cyfrif. • *n* iarll *m*.
countenance *n* wynepryd *m*.
counter *n* cownter *m*.
counteract *v* gwrthweithio.
counterbalance *v* gwrthbwyso.
counterfeit *v* ffugio. • *adj* ffug.
counterpart *n* un sy'n cyfateb *m/f*.
countersign *v* cydlofnodi.
countrified *adj* gwladaidd.
country *n* gwlad *f*. • *adj* gwledig.
countryman *n* gwladwr, gwerinwr *m*.
county *n* sir, swydd *f*.
couple *n* cwpl *m*, deuddyn *f*. • *v* cyplysu, uno.
coupon *n* cwpon, tocyn *m*.
courage *n* dewrder, gwrhydri *m*.

courageous *adj* dewr, gwrol.
courier *n* negesydd; arweinydd *m.*
course *n* cwrs *m*; hynt *f.*
court *n* llys *m.* • *v* canlyn, caru.
courteous *adj* cwrtais, boneddigaidd.
courtesy *n* cwrteisi, boneddigeiddrwydd *m.*
courthouse *n* llys *m.*
courtroom *n* cwrt *m.*
cousin *n* cefnder *m*, cyfnither *f.*
cover *n* clawr, gorchudd *m.* • *v* gorchuddio.
covert *adj* cudd, dirgel.
cover-up *v* cuddio.
covet *v* chwennych, chwenychu.
cow *n* buwch *f.*
coward *n* llwfrgi *m.*
cowardice *n* llwfrdra *m.*
cowboy *n* cowboi *m.*
coy *adj* swil.
coyness *n* swildod *m.*
crab *n* cranc *m.*
crack *n* crac *m*, hollt *f.* • *v* cracio, hollti.
crackle *v* clecian.
cradle *n* crud *m.*
craft *n* crefft *f.*
craftsman *n* crefftwr *m.*
crafty *adj* cyfrwys.
cram *v* stwffio, gwthio.
cramp *n* cwlwm gwythi *m.* • *v* llesteirio.
crane *n* garan *f/m*; craen *m.*
crash *v* gwrthdaro. • *n* gwrthdrawiad, twrw *m.*
crate *n* crât, cawell *m.*
crater *n* crater, ceudwll *m.*
crawl *v* cropian.
crayon *n* creon *m.*
craze *n* chwilen, ffasiwn *f.*
craziness *n* gwallgofrwydd, ffolineb *m.*
crazy *adj* gwallgof, hurt.
creak *v* gwichian.
cream *n* hufen *m.*
crease *n* plygiad, crych *m.*
create *v* creu.
creation *n* cread *m*, creadigaeth *f.*
creature *n* creadur *m.*
credence *n* cred, coel *f.*
credibility *n* hygrededd *m.*
credible *adj* credadwy.
credit *n* coel *f*; clod *m/f.*
credit card *n* cerdyn credyd *m.*
creditable *adj* canmoladwy.
creditor *n* credydwr *m.*
creep *v* cropian, sleifio.
cremate *v* llosgi.
cremation *n* amlosgiad *m.*
crematorium *n* amlosgfa *f.*
cress *n* berwr *pl.*
crest *n* crib *m*; arfbais *f.*
crevice *n* agen, hollt *f.*
crew *n* criw *m.*
crib *n* preseb *m.*
crime *n* trosedd *m.*
criminal *adj* troseddol. • *n* troseddwr *m*, troseddwraig *f.*
cripple *n* crupl, efrydd *m.*
crisis *n* argyfwng *m.*
criterion *n* maen prawf *m.*
critic *n* beirniad *m.*
critical *adj* beirniadol.
criticise *v* beirniadu.
criticism *n* beirniadaeth *f.*

croak *v* crawcian.
crockery *n* llestri *pl*.
crocodile *n* crocodeil *m*.
crocus *n* saffrwm *m*.
crook *n* ffon fugail *f*.
crop *n* cnwd *m*.
cross *n* croes *f*. • *v* croesi. • *adj* croes, blin.
crossing *n* croesfan *f/m*.
cross-reference *n* croesgyfeiriad *m*.
crossroad *n* croesffordd *f*.
crouch *v* cyrcydu, cwtsio.
crow *n* brân *f*.
crowd *n* torf, tyrfa *f*.
crown *n* coron *f*. • *v* coroni.
crucial *adj* hanfodol.
crucifix *n* croes *f*.
crude *adj* amrwd.
cruel *adj* creulon, brwnt.
cruelty *n* creulondeb *m*.
crumb *n* briwsionyn *m*.
crumble *v* briwo, briwsioni.
crunch *v* crensian.
crush *v* gwasgu, mathru.
crust *n* crwstyn *m*; cramen *f*.
crutch *n* ffon fagl *f*.
crux *n* craidd *m*.
cry *v* llefain. • *n* cri, llef *f*.
crystal *n* grisial *m*.
crystalline *adj* grisialaidd.
crystallise *v* crisialu.
cube *n* ciwb *m*.
cuddle *v* cofleidio, anwesu.
cuff *n* torch llawes *f*.
culinary *adj* coginiol.
culminate *v* cyrraedd ei anterth.
culpable *adj* ar fai.
culprit *n* troseddwr *m*, troseddwraig *f*.
cult *n* cwlt *m*.
cultivate *v* meithrin, trin.
cultivation *n* trin tir *vn*.
culture *n* diwylliant *m*.
cumbersome *adj* trwsgl, afrosgo.
cumulative *adj* cynyddol.
cunning *adj* cyfrwys.
cup *n* cwpan *m/f*.
cupboard *n* cwpwrdd *m*.
curb *n* atalfa *f*. • *v* ffrwyno.
cure *n* iachâd *m*. • *v* gwella; halltu.
curiosity *n* chwilfrydedd *m*.
curious *adj* chwilfrydig.
curl *n* modrwy *f*. • *v* modrwyo, cyrlio.
curly *adj* cyrliog, modrwyog.
currency *n* arian treigl/breiniol *m*.
current *adj* cyfredol. • *n* cerrynt *m*.
current affairs *n* materion/pynciau'r dydd *pl*.
curriculum *n* cwricwlwm, maes lla-fur.
curse *v* melltithio.
curt *adj* cwta, swta.
curtain *n* llen *f*.
curve *v* gwyro, troi. • *n* tro *m*.
cushion *n* clustog *f*.
custodian *n* ceidwad *m*.
custom *n* arfer *m/f*.
customary *adj* arferol.
customer *n* cwsmer *m*.
customs *n* tollau *pl*.
customs officer *n* swyddog y tollau *m*.
cut *v* torri. • *n* toriad *m*.

cutlery *n* cyllyll a ffyrc *pl*.
cutting *n* toriad *m*.
cycle *n* cylch; beic *m*. • *v* seiclo.
cycling *n* beicio *vn*.
cyclist *n* beiciwr *m*, beicwraig *f*.
cygnet *n* cyw alarch *m*.
cylinder *n* silindr *m/f*.
cynic *n* sinig *m*.
cynical *adj* sinigaidd.
cynism *n* siniciaeth *f*.

D

dad(dy) *n* dad, dat, dada *m*.
daily *adj* beunyddiol, dyddiol.
daintiness *n* lledneisrwydd *m*.
dainty *adj* llednais, del.
dairy *n* llaethdy *m*.
dam *n* argae *m*, cronfa *f*. • *v* cronni.
damage *n* difrod, niwed *m*. • *v* niweidio.
damnation *n* damnedigaeth *f*.
damp *adj* llaith.
dampen *v* gwlychu.
dance *n* dawns *f*. • *v* dawnsio.
dancer *n* dawnsiwr *m*, dawnswraig *f*.
danger *n* perygl *m*.
dangerous *adj* peryglus.
dangle *v* hongian.
dare *v* meiddio, mentro.
daring *adj* beiddgar.
dark *adj* tywyll. • *n* tywyllwch *m*.
darken *v* tywyllu.
darkness *n* tywyllwch *m*.
darling *adj* annwyl. • *n* cariad *m*.
dart *n* dart *m*.
dash *v* rhuthro.
data *n* data *pl*.
data processing *n* prosesu data *vn*.
date *n* dyddiad *m*.
dated *adj* wedi dyddio; dyddiedig.
daughter *n* merch *f*; ~ **in-law** merch-yng-nghyfraith *f*.
dawn *n* gwawr *f*. • *v* gwawrio.
day *n* dydd, diwrnod *m*.
daylight *n* golau dydd *m*.
dazed *adj* syfrdan.
dazzle *v* dallu.
dead *adj* marw.
deaden *v* lladd.
deadline *n* dyddiad cau *m*.
deadly *adj* marwol, angheuol.
deaf *adj* byddar.
deafen *v* byddaru.
deafening *adj* byddarol.
deafness *n* byddardod *m*.
deal *n* bargen *f*. • *v* rhannu.
dealer *n* masnachwr *m*.
dear *adj* annwyl; drud.
dearness *n* anwyldeb *m*.
death *n* marwolaeth *f*.
death certificate *n* tystysgrif marwolaeth *f*.
death penalty *n* y gosb eithaf *f*.
debar *v* atal.
debase *v* diraddio, darostwng.
debasement *n* darostyngiad *m*.
debatable *adj* dadleuol.

debate *n* dadl *f*. • *v* dadlau.
debilitate *v* gwanhau, gwanio.
debit *n* debyd *m*.
debt *n* dyled *f*.
debtor *n* dyledwr *m*.
decade *n* degawd *m*.
decadence *n* dirywiad *m*, dirywiaeth *f*.
decaffeinated *adj* digaffein.
decay *v* dadfeilio. • *n* dirywiad *m*.
deceased *adj* ymadawedig, diweddar.
deceit *n* twyll *m*.
deceive *v* twyllo.
December *n* Rhagfyr *m*.
decency *n* gwedduster *m*.
decent *adj* gweddus, gweddaidd.
decide *v* penderfynu.
decimate *v* difrodi; degymu.
decipher *v* datrys.
decision *n* penderfyniad *m*.
decisive *adj* penderfynol.
deck *n* bwrdd *m*. • *v* addurno.
declaration *n* datganiad *m*.
declare *v* datgan.
decode *v* datrys, datgodio.
decorate *v* addurno.
decoration *n* addurn, addurniad *m*.
decorative *adj* addurniadol.
decoy *n* abwyd, llith *m*.
decrease *v* lleihau.
decree *n* gorchymyn *m*. • *v* gorchymyn.
decrepit *adj* musgrell.
dedicate *v* cysegru.
dedication *n* cysegriad; cyflwyniad; ymroddiad *m*.
deduce *v* casglu.
deduct *v* tynnu allan.
deed *n* gweithred *f*.
deep *adj* dwfn.
deepen *v* dyfnhau, dwysáu.
deepness *n* dyfnder *m*.
default *n* diffyg *m*.
defeat *n* gorchfygiad *m*. • *v* gorchfygu.
defect *n* nam, diffyg *m*.
defective *adj* diffygiol.
defence *n* amddiffyniad *m*.
defend *v* amddiffyn.
defendant *n* diffynnydd *m*.
defensive *adj* amddiffynnol.
defer *v* gohirio.
deference *n* parch *m*.
defiance *n* herio *vn*.
deficiency *n* diffyg *m*.
deficient *adj* diffygiol, yn eisiau.
define *v* diffinio.
definite *adj* pendant.
definition *n* diffiniad *m*.
definitive *adj* terfynol, diffiniol.
deflect *v* gwyro.
deform *v* anffurfio.
deformity *n* anffurfiad, hagrwch *m*.
defraud *v* twyllo.
deft *adj* deheuig.
degenerate *v* dirywio, dadfeilio. • *adj* dirywiedig.
degeneration *n* dirywiad *m*.
degradation *n* diraddiad *m*.
degrade *v* diraddio.
degree *n* gradd *f*.
dejected *adj* digalon.
dejection *n* digalondid *m*.
delay *v* oedi. • *n* oediad *m*.

delegate *v* dirprwyo. • *n* cynrychiol-ydd *m*.
delegation *n* dirprwyaeth *f*.
delete *v* dileu.
deliberate *v* ystyried. • *adj* pwyllog; bwriadol.
deliberation *n* ystyriaeth *f*.
delicacy *n* danteithfwyd; meinder *m*.
delicate *adj* cywrain, tyner.
delicious *adj* amheuthun.
delight *n* hyfrydwch *m*. • *v* swyno.
delighted *adj* wrth eich bodd.
delightful *adj* hyfryd.
delinquency *n* tramgwydd *m*.
delinquent *n* troseddwr *m*.
delirious *adj* gorffwyll.
deliver *v* dosbarthu, traddodi.
delivery *n* trosglwyddo; traddodi *vn*.
delude *v* twyllo.
delusion *n* twyll, camargraff *m*.
demand *n* galw *m*. • *v* galw ar, hawlio.
demean *v* ymddwyn.
demeanour *n* ymarweddiad *m*.
democracy *n* democratiaeth *f*.
democratic *adj* democrataidd.
demolish *v* dymchwel, dymchwelyd.
demolition *n* dymchweliad *m*.
demonstrate *v* arddangos.
demonstration *n* arddangosiad; gwrthdystiad *m*.
demonstrator *n* arddangoswr; gwrthdystiwr *m*, gwrthdystwraig *f*.
demoralise *v* digalonni, gwangalonni.
den *n* ffau, gwâl *f*.
denial *n* gwrthodiad, gwadiad *m*.
denims *n* dillad denim *pl*.
denomination *n* enwad *m*.
denote *v* dynodi.
denounce *v* lladd ar.
dense *adj* dwys, tew.
dentist *n* deintydd *m*, deintyddes *f*.
dentistry *n* deintyddiaeth *f*.
dentures *n* dannnedd gosod/dodi *m*.
denunciation *n* condemniad *m*.
deny *v* gwadu.
deodorant *n* diaroglydd *m*.
depart *v* ymadael.
department *n* adran *f*.
departure *n* ymadawiad *m*.
depend *v* dibynnu.
dependable *adj* dibynadwy, sad.
dependant *n* dibynnydd *m*.
dependent *adj* dibynnol.
depict *v* darlunio.
deplorable *adj* alaethus.
deplore *v* gresynu wrth.
depopulated *adj* wedi('i) d(d)iboblo-gi.
deport *v* alltudio.
deportation *n* caethglud, alltudiaeth *f*.
deportment *n* ymddygiad, ymarweddiad *m*.
deposit *v* dyddodi; gosod. • *n* adnau *m*.
deposition *n* diorseddiad, diswyddiad *m*.
depot *n* gorsaf, storfa *f*.
depreciate *v* dibrisio.
depreciation *n* dibrisiad *m*.

depress *v* gwasgu, dirwasgu.
depression *n* gostyngiad, diwasgedd *m.*
deprivation *n* amddifadiad; diffyg *m.*
deprive *v* amddifadu.
depth *n* dyfnder *m.*
deputation *n* dirprwyaeth *f.*
depute/deputise *v* dirprwyo.
deputy *n* dirprwy *m.*
deranged *adj* wedi drysu, gorffwyll.
derelict *adj* wedi'i esgeuluso.
deride *v* gwatwar, gwawdio.
derision *n* gwawd, dirmyg *m.*
derivative *adj* yn dynwared.
derive *v* deillio.
descend *v* disgyn.
descendant *n* disgynnydd *m.*
descent *n* disgyniad *m.*
describe *v* disgrifio.
description *n* disgrifiad *m.*
descriptive *adj* disgrifiadol.
desert[1] *n* anialwch, diffeithwch *m.* • *adj* anial, diffaith.
desert[2] *v* cefnu ar.
desertion *n* gwrthgiliad *m.*
deserve *v* haeddu, teilyngu.
design *v* cynllunio, dylunio.
designate *v* enwebu. • *adj* darpar.
desirable *adj* dymunol, dewisol.
desire *n* awydd *m.* • *v* dymuno.
desist *v* ymatal rhag.
desk *n* desg *f.*
desolate *adj* unig, anghyfannedd.
despair *n* anobaith *m.* • *v* anobeithio.
desperate *adj* enbyd; byrbwyll.
desperation *n* enbydrwydd, gwylltineb *m.*
despicable *adj* ffiaidd.
despise *v* dirmygu.
despite *prep* er gwaethaf.
despondency *n* digalondid *m.*
despondent *adj* digalon.
dessert *n* pwdin *m.*
destination *n* pen y daith *m.*
destine *v* arfaethu.
destiny *n* tynged, ffawd *f.*
destitute *adj* amddifad, ar y clwt.
destitution *n* tlodi, cyni *m.*
destroy *v* dinistrio, difa.
destruction *n* dinistr, distryw *m.*
detach *v* datod, gwahanu, datgysylltu.
detachable *adj* datodadwy.
detail *n* manylyn *m.* • *v* manylu.
detain *v* cadw.
detect *v* canfod, synhwyro.
detection *n* darganfyddiad *m.*
detective *n* detectif *m.*
detention *n* carchariad, ataliad *m.*
deteriorate *v* dirywio, gwaethygu.
deterioration *n* dirywiad *m.*
determination *n* penderfyniad *m.*
determine *v* penderfynu, pennu.
detest *v* casáu, ffieiddio.
detestable *adj* ffiaidd.
detour *n* dargyfeiriad *m.*
detriment *n* anfantais *f.*
devaluation *n* gostyngiad mewn gwerth *m.*
devastate *v* difrodi, anrheithio.
devastation *n* difrod, distryw *m.*
develop *v* datblygu.
development *n* cynnydd *m.*

deviate *v* gwyro, cyfeiliorni.
deviation *n* gwyriad *m.*
device *n* dyfais *f.*
devil *n* diafol *m.*
devise *v* dyfeisio.
devoid *adj* amddifad. • *prep* heb.
devote *v* cysegru, ymroi.
devoted *adj* ffyddlon.
devotion *n* ymroddiad *m.*
devour *v* traflyncu.
dew *n* gwlith *m.*
dexterity *n* deheurwydd *m.*
diagnosis *n* barn feddygol *f.*
diagram *n* diagram, darlun *m.*
dialect *n* tafodiaith *f.*
dialogue *n* ymddiddan *m.*
diamond *n* diemwnt *m.*
diary *n* dyddiadur *m.*
dictate *v* arddweud.
dictator *n* unben *m*, unbennes *f.*
dictionary *n* geiriadur *m.*
die *v* marw.
diet *n* diet *m.* • *v* colli pwysau.
differ *v* gwahaniaethu.
difference *n* gwahaniaeth *m.*
different *adj* gwahanol.
differentiate *v* gwahaniaethu.
difficult *adj* anodd.
difficulty *n* anhawster *m.*
dig *v* palu, cloddio.
digest *v* treulio.
digestion *n* traul *f.*
digestive *adj* treuliadol.
digit *n* bys, digid *m.*
digital *adj* digidol.
dignified *adj* urddasol.
dignity *n* urddas *f.*
digression *n* crwydrad *m.*
dilemma *n* penbleth *f/m*, cyfyng-gy-ngor *m.*
diligence *n* diwydrwydd, dycnwch *m.*
diligent *adj* diwyd, dygn.
dilute *v* glastwreiddio.
dim *adj* gwan, pŵl.
dimension *n* maintioli, dimensiwn *m.*
diminish *v* lleihau, gostwng.
diminutive *adj* bychan.
din *n* mwstwr *m.*
dine *v* ciniawa.
dinner *n* cinio *m.*
dip *v* trochi, dipio.
diploma *n* tystysgrif *f*, diploma *m/f.*
diplomat *n* diplomat *m.*
diplomatic *adj* diplomataidd, diplomyddol.
dire *adj* enbyd, dybryd.
direct *adj* uniongyrchol. • *v* cyfeirio.
direction *n* cyfarwyddyd; cyfeiriad *m.*
director *n* cyfarwyddwr *m*, cyfarwy-ddwraig *f.*
directory *n* cyfeirlyfr, cyfarwyd-diadur *m.*
dirt *n* baw, budreddi *m.*
dirty *adj* brwnt.
disability *n* anabledd *m.*
disabled *adj* anabl.
disadvantage *n* anfantais *f.* • *v* rhoi dan anfantais.
disagree *v* anghytuno, anghydweld.
disagreeable *adj* annymunol, annifyr.
disagreement *n* anghydfod, anghy-tundeb *m.*

disallow *v* gwrthod.
disappear *v* diflannu.
disappearance *n* diflaniad *m.*
disappoint *v* siomi.
disappointment *n* siom *f/m.*
disapproval *n* anghymeradwyaeth *f.*
disapprove *v* anghymeradwyo.
disarm *v* diarfogi.
disaster *n* trychineb *m/f.*
disastrous *adj* trychinebus.
disbelief *n* anghrediniaeth *f.*
discard *v* taflu, diosg.
discern *v* canfod, dirnad.
discerning *adj* craff.
disciple *n* disgybl *m.*
discipline *n* disgyblaeth *f.* • *v* disgyblu.
disclose *v* dadlennu, datgelu.
disclosure *n* dadleniad, datguddiad *m.*
disco *n* disgo *m.*
discomfort *n* anesmwythder, anesmwythyd *m.*
disconnect *v* datgysylltu.
disconsolate *adj* digysur.
discontent *n* anfodlonrwydd, anniddigrwydd *m.*
discontented *adj* anniddig, anfodlon.
discontinue *v* rhoi terfyn ar.
discord *n* anghytgord *m.*
discount *n* gostyngiad, disgownt *m.*
discourage *v* anghymeradwyo; digalonni.
discouragement *n* digalondid *m*; anghymeradwyaeth *f.*
discourse *n* ymddiddan *m*; trafodaeth *f.*
discourteous *adj* anghwrtais.
discover *v* darganfod.
discovery *n* darganfyddiad *m.*
discredit *v* difrïo, tanseilio.
discreet *adj* cynnil, pwyllog.
discrepancy *n* anghysondeb *m.*
discretion *n* barn *f*, synnwyr *m.*
discretionary *adj* diamod, dewisol.
discriminate *v* gwahaniaethu.
discrimination *n* anffafriaeth *f*; ffafriaeth *f*; chwaeth *f.*
discuss *v* trafod.
discussion *n* trafodaeth *f.*
disdain *v* dirmygu. • *n* dirmyg *m.*
disdainful *adj* dirmygus.
disease *n* clefyd *m.*
disembark *v* glanio.
disenchant *v* dadrithio.
disenchanted *adj* dadrithiedig.
disengage *v* rhyddhau, datgysylltu.
disfigure *v* anharddu, hagru.
disgrace *n* anfri, gwarth *m.* • *v* dwyn anfri ar.
disgraceful *adj* gwarthus.
disguise *v* cuddio. • *n* cuddwisg *f.*
disgust *n* ffieidd-dod, diflastod *m.* • *v* diflasu.
dish *n* dysgl *f.*
dishearten *v* digalonni.
dishonest *adj* anonest.
dishonesty *n* anonestrwydd *m.*
disillusion *v* dadrithio.
disillusioned *adj* dadrithiedig, siomedig.
disinfect *v* diheintio.
disinfectant *n* diheintydd *m.*

disinherit *v* diarddel.
disintegrate *v* chwalu.
disinterested *adj* difater; diduedd.
disk *n* disg *m.*
dislike *n* atgasedd *m.* • *v* casáu.
dislocate *v* datgymalu.
dislocation *n* datgymaliad *m.*
dislodge *v* symud, rhyddhau.
disloyal *adj* annheyrngar.
dismantle *v* dinoethi, datgymalu.
dismay *n* siom *m/f,* gofid *m.*
dismiss *v* diswyddo; wfftio.
dismissal *n* diswyddiad *m.*
disobedience *n* anufudd-dod *m.*
disobedient *adj* anufudd.
disobey *v* anufuddhau.
disorder *n* anhrefn *f.*
disorderly *adj* anhrefnus, afreolus.
disown *v* gwadu.
disparage *v* dibrisio, bychanu.
disparity *n* anghyfartaledd, gwahaniaeth *m.*
dispatch *v* anfon.
dispel *v* chwalu.
dispensary *n* fferyllfa *f.*
dispense *v* dosbarthu, gweinyddu.
disperse *v* chwalu, gwasgaru.
displace *v* disodli.
display *v* arddangos. • *n* arddangosfa *f.*
displease *v* digio.
displeased *adj* anfoddlon.
displeasure *n* anfodlonrwydd *m.*
dispose *v* cael gwared.
disposition *n* anian *m/f.*
disprove *v* gwrthbrofi.
dispute *n* cynnen, dadl *f.* • *v* dadlau.
disqualify *v* gwahardd, diarddel.
dissatisfaction *n* anfodlonrwydd *m.*
dissatisfied *adj* anfodlon.
disseminate *v* lledaenu.
dissension *n* anghytundeb, anghydfod *m.*
dissent *n* Anghydffurfiaeth, Ymneilltuaeth *f.*
dissertation *n* traethawd *m.*
dissident *n* gwrthwynebydd, anghydffurfiwr *m.*
dissimilar *adj* annhebyg.
dissimilarity *n* annhebygrwydd *m.*
dissipate *v* gwasgaru, chwalu.
dissipation *n* gwasgariad *m*; afradlonedd *m.*
dissolution *n* diddymiad *m.*
dissolve *v* toddi.
dissonance *n* anghytseinedd *m.*
dissuade *v* cymell, darbwyllo.
distance *n* pellter *m.*
distant *adj* pell.
distaste *n* diflastod *m.*
distasteful *adj* annymunol, dichwaeth.
distil *v* distyllu.
distinct *adj* eglur.
distinction *n* gwahaniaeth; anrhydedd *m.*
distinctive *adj* nodweddiadol.
distinguish *v* gwahaniaethu.
distort *v* ystumio, llurgunio.
distortion *n* gwyrdroad, llurguniad *m.*
distract *v* tynnu sylw.
distracted *adj* synfyfyriol, dryslyd.
distress *n* gofid *m.*
distribute *v* dosbarthu, rhannu.

distribution *n* dosraniad *m*.
district *n* ardal *f*.
disturb *v* tarfu, aflonyddu ar.
disturbance *n* cynnwrf *m*.
disturbed *adj* afreolaidd.
disturbing *adj* yn peri pryder.
disuse *n* diffyg defnydd *m*.
disused *adj* heb ei (d)defnyddio.
ditch *n* ffos *f*.
dive *v* plymio.
diver *n* deifiwr, trochiwr *m*.
diverge *v* ymwahanu.
divergent *adj* gwahanol, ymwahanol.
diverse *adj* gwahanol.
diversion *n* dargyfeiriad *m*.
diversity *n* amrywiaeth *f*.
divert *v* dargyfeirio.
divide *v* rhannu.
divine *adj* dwyfol.
divinity *n* duwdod *m*.
divisible *adj* rhanadwy.
division *n* rhaniad *m*.
divorce *n* ysgariad *m*. • *v* ysgaru.
divorced *adj* ysgar.
divulge *v* datgelu, dadlennu.
dizziness *n* pendro *f*.
dizzy *adj* penysgafn, penfeddw.
do *v* gwneud (*see* Appendix).
docile *adj* dof.
dock *n* doc *m*.
do-it-yourself *n* o'th waith dy hun, ymdopi *vn*.
doctor *n* meddyg, doethur *m*, doctores *f*.
doctrine *n* athrawiaeth, dysgeidiaeth *f*.
document *n* dogfen *f*.
documentary *adj* dogfennol.
dodge *v* ochrgamu.
dog *n* ci *m*.
dogmatic *adj* dogmataidd.
doll *n* dol, doli *f*.
dolphin *n* morhwch *m/f*.
dome *n* cromen *f*.
domestic *adj* teuluol, teuluaidd.
domesticate *v* hyweddu, cartrefoli.
domesticity *n* bywyd cartref *m*.
domicile *n* cartref *m*.
dominate *v* tra-arglwyddiaethu.
domination *n* tra-arglwyddiaeth *f*.
donate *v* rhoi, rhoddi.
donation *n* rhodd *f*.
donkey *n* asyn, mul *m*.
donor *n* rhoddwr *m*, rhoddwraig *f*.
door *n* drws *m*.
doorway *n* drws, porth *m*.
dormant *adj* ynghwsg.
dormitory *n* ystafell gysgu *f*.
dosage *n* dogn *m*.
dose *n* dogn *m*. • *v* dogni.
dossier *n* ffeil *f*.
dot *n* dot, dotyn *m*.
double *v* dyblu.
double room *n* ystafell ddwbl *f*.
double-dealing *n* chwarae'r ffon ddwybig *vn*.
doubt *n* amheuaeth *f*. • *v* amau.
doubtful *adj* amheus.
doughnut *n* toesen *f*.
douse *v* trochi, diffodd.
dove *n* colomen *f*.
down *n* manblu *pl*. • *prep* i lawr, i waered.
downfall *n* cwymp *m*.
downhearted *adj* digalon.

downhill *adv* goriwaered.
downstairs *adv* lawr llawr.
dowry *n* gwaddol *m.*
doze *v* hepian, pendwmpian.
dozen *n* dwsin *m.*
drab *adj* di-liw.
drag *v* llusgo.
drain *v* draenio, traenio. • *n* ffos *f.*
drama *n* drama *f.*
dramatic *adj* dramataidd, dramatig.
dramatist *n* dramodydd *m.*
draught *n* drafft *m.*
draw *v* tynnu.
drawback *n* anfantais *f.*
drawer *n* drâr, drôr *m/f.*
drawing *n* llun, lluniad *m.*
drawing room *n* parlwr *m.*
dread *n* arswyd *m.* • *v* arswydo, dychryn.
dreadful *adj* arswydus, erchyll.
dream *n* breuddwyd *m/f.* • *v* breuddwydio.
dreary *adj* diflas.
dress *v* gwisgo. • *n* gwisg, ffrog *f.*
dressy *adj* trwsiadus.
drift *v* drifftio; lluwchio.
drill *n* dril *m.* • *v* tyllu.
drink *v* yfed. • *n* diod *f.*
drinker *n* yfwr, llymeitiwr *m.*
drip *v* diferu. • *n* diferyn *m.*
drive *v* gyrru.
driver *n* gyrrwr *m*, gyrwraig *f.*
driving licence *n* trwydded yrru *f.*
drizzle *v* glaw mân *f.*
drop *n* dafn *m.* • *v* cwympo, gollwng.
drought *n* sychder, sychdwr *m.*
drown *v* boddi.
drowsiness *n* syrthni *m.*
drug *n* cyffur *m.* • *v* drygio.
drum *n* drwm *m.*
drunk *adj* meddw.
drunkard *n* meddwyn *m.*
drunkenness *n* medd-dod *m.*
dry *adj* sych. • *v* sychu.
dryness *n* sychder, crasder *m.*
dual *adj* deuol.
dub *v* urddo; trosleisio.
due *adj* dyladwy.
duel *n* gornest, cyfranc *f.*
dull *adj* twp; afloyw, pŵl.
dumb *adj* mud.
dump *n* tomen *f.*
duplicate *v* dyblygu.
duplicity *n* dichell *f.*
durability *n* gwydnwch, gwytnwch *m.*
durable *adj* gwydn, parhaol.
duration *n* parhad *m.*
during *prep* yn ystod, trwy gydol.
dusk *n* cyfnos, gwyll *m.*
dust *n* llwch *m.* • *v* tynnu llwch.
dutiful *adj* ufudd.
duty *n* dyletswydd *f.*
dwarf *n* corrach *m*, coraches *f.*
dwell *v* preswylio, trigo.
dwelling *n* anheddle *m*, preswylfa *f.*
dye *v* llifo, lliwio. • *n* llifyn, lliwur *m.*
dying *adj* yn marw, bron â marw.
dynamic *adj* deinamig, egnïol.
dynasty *n* llinach *f.*

E

each *pron* pob.
eager *adj* awyddus.
eagerness *n* awydd, awch *m.*
eagle *n* eryr *m.*
ear *n* clust *f.*
early *adj* cynnar.
earn *v* ennill.
earnest *adj* o ddifrif, taer.
earth *n* daear *f.*
earthquake *n* daeargryn *m/f.*
ease *v* lleddfu, esmwytho.
easiness *n* rhwyddineb *m.*
east *n* dwyrain *m.*
Easter *n* y Pasg *m.*
eastern *adj* dwyreiniol.
easy *adj* rhwydd, hawdd; esmwyth.
eat *v* bwyta.
ebb *v* treio.
eccentric *adj* ecsentrig, od.
eccentricity *n* hynodrwydd, odrwydd *m.*
echo *n* adlais *m*, atsain *f.*
eclipse *n* diffyg, eclips *m.*
ecology *n* ecoleg *f.*
economic *adj* economaidd.
economise *v* cynilo.
economist *n* economydd, economegydd *m.*
economy *n* economi *m/f.*
ecstasy *n* perlewyg *m.*
ecstatic *adj* llesmeiriol.
edge *n* min, awch *m.*
edible *adj* bwytadwy.
edifice *n* adeiladwaith *m.*
edit *v* golygu.
edition *n* argraffiad *m.*
editor *n* golygydd *m.*
educate *v* addysgu.
education *n* addysg *f.*
efface *v* dileu.
effect *n* effaith *f.*
effective *adj* effeithiol.
effectiveness *n* effeithiolrwydd *m.*
effectual *adj* mewn grym.
effeminate *adj* merchetaidd.
effervescence *n* bwrlwm *m.*
efficiency *n* effeithlonrwydd *m.*
efficient *adj* effeithlon.
effort *n* ymdrech *m/f.*
egg *n* wy *m.*
ego *n* yr hunan, ego *m.*
ego(t)istical *adj* myfïol.
eight *num* wyth.
eighteen *num* deunaw.
eighteenth *adj* deunawfed.
eighth *adj* wythfed.
eightieth *adj* pedwar ugeinfed.
eighty *num* pedwar ugain, wyth deg.
either *conj* naill ai, un ai. • *adv* ychwaith.
eject *v* bwrw/taflu allan, diarddel.
ejection *n* diarddeliad, tafliad allan *m.*
elaborate *v* manylu, ymhelaethu. • *adj* cymhleth.

elapse *v* mynd heibio.
elastic *adj* ystwyth, hydwyth.
elbow *n* penelin *m/f*.
elder *adj* hŷn.
eldest *adj* hynaf.
elect *v* ethol.
election *n* etholiad *m*.
electoral *adj* etholiadol.
electorate *n* etholaeth *f*, pleidleiswyr *pl*.
electric(al) *adj* trydanol.
electrician *n* trydanwr *m*.
electricity *n* trydan *m*.
electrify *v* trydanu, gwefreiddio.
electronic *adj* electronig, electronaidd.
elegance *n* ceinder, syberwyd.
elegant *adj* cain, syber.
element *n* elfen *f*.
elementary *adj* elfennol.
elephant *n* eliffant *m*.
elevate *v* dyrchafu.
elevation *n* dyrchafiad *m*.
eleven *num* un ar ddeg.
eleventh *adj* unfed ar ddeg.
eligibility *n* cymhwyster *m*.
eligible *adj* cymwys.
eliminate *v* dileu.
elocution *n* siarad cyhoeddus *vn*, areithyddiaeth *f*.
eloquence *n* huodledd *m*.
eloquent *adj* huawdl.
else *adv* arall, amgen.
elsewhere *adv* rhywle arall.
elude *v* osgoi.
emaciated *adj* llwglyd, esgyrnog.
emancipate *v* rhyddfreinio.
emancipation *n* rhyddfreiniad *m*.
embargo *n* embargo, gwaharddiad *m*.
embark *v* cychwyn, dechrau.
embarkation *n* esgyniad, dechreuad *m*.
embarrass *v* codi cywilydd, gwneud yn swil.
embarrassment *n* cywilydd *m*.
embassy *n* llysgenhadaeth *f*.
emblem *n* arwyddlun *m*.
embody *v* ymgorffori.
embrace *v* cofleidio, anwesu.
embryo *n* rhith, embryo *m*.
emerald *n* emrallt *m*.
emerge *v* ymddangos.
emergency *n* argyfwng *m*.
emergency exit *n* allanfa frys *f*.
emigrate *v* ymfudo.
emigration *n* ymfudiad *m*.
emission *n* lledaenu, gollwng *vn*.
emit *v* gollwng.
emotion *n* teimlad, emosiwn *m*.
emotional *adj* dan deimlad, emosiynol.
emphasise *v* pwysleisio.
emphatic *adj* pendant.
empire *n* ymerodraeth *f*.
employ *v* cyflogi.
employee *n* gweithiwr *m*, gweithwraig *f*.
employer *n* cyflogwr, cyflogydd *m*.
employment *n* cyflogaeth *f*.
emptiness *n* gwacter *m*.
empty *adj* gwag. • *v* gwagio.
emulate *v* efelychu.
enable *v* galluogi.
enamour *v* ennyn serch, swyno.
encamp *v* gwersyllu.

encampment *n* gwersyll *m*.
encase *v* cau mewn.
enchant *v* cyfareddu, hudo.
enchantment *n* hudoliaeth *f*.
encircle *v* amgylchynu.
enclose *v* amgáu.
enclosure *n* cae, lloc *m*.
encompass *v* cwmpasu, rhychwantu.
encounter *n* cyfarfod *m*. • *v* cyfarfod.
encourage *v* cefnogi, cymell.
encouragement *n* cefnogaeth *f*.
encyclopedia *n* gwyddoniadur *m*.
end *n* diwedd, terfyn *m*. • *v* diweddu, terfynu.
endanger *v* peryglu.
endeavour *v* ymdrechu. • *n* ymgais, ymdrech *m/f*.
endorse *v* ardystio; cymeradwyo.
endorsement *n* arnodiad *m*; cefnogaeth *f*.
endurable *adj* goddefadwy.
endurance *n* dycnwch, dygnwch *m*.
endure *v* dioddef, parhau.
enemy *n* gelyn *m*.
energetic *adj* egnïol, llawn egni.
energy *n* egni, ynni *m*.
enfold *v* lapio.
enforce *v* gorfodi.
engage *v* cyflogi, cysylltu.
engaged *adj* wedi dyweddïo.
engagement *n* dyweddïad *m*.
engender *v* peri, ennyn.
engine *n* peiriant *m*, injan *f*.
engineer *n* peiriannydd *m*.
engineering *n* peirianneg *f*.
enigma *n* dirgelwch *m*, enigma *f*.
enjoy *v* mwynhau, cael blas.
enjoyable *adj* dymunol, hyfryd.
enjoyment *n* mwynhad *m*.
enlarge *v* mwyhau, ehangu, chwyddo.
enlargement *n* mwyhad, estyniad *m*.
enlist *v* listio, ymrestru.
enliven *v* bywhau, bywiogi.
enmity *n* gelyniaeth *f*.
enormous *adj* anferth, enfawr.
enough *adv*, *n* digon *m*.
enrage *v* cynddeiriogi.
enrich *v* cyfoethogi.
enrol *v* cofrestru.
ensue *v* dilyn.
ensure *v* sicrhau.
entail *v* golygu.
enter *v* mynd/dod i mewn.
enterprise *n* menter *f*.
enterprising *adj* mentrus.
entertain *v* difyrru, diddanu.
entertaining *adj* difyr.
enthusiasm *n* brwdfrydedd *m*.
enthusiast *n* rhywun brwdfrydig *m*.
enthusiastic *adj* brwd, brwdfrydig.
entire *adj* cyfan, holl.
entitle *v* bod â hawl.
entity *n* endid *m*.
entrance *n* mynediad *m*; mynedfa *f*.
entrant *n* ymgeisydd, newyddian *m*.
entreat *v* ymbil, erfyn.
entrust *v* ymddiried.
entry *n* mynediad *m*.

enumerate *v* rhifo, cyfrif.
envelop *v* amgáu, gorchuddio.
envelope *n* amlen *f.*
envious *adj* eiddigeddus, cenfigennus.
environment *n* amgylchedd, amgylchfyd *m.*
environmental *adj* amgylcheddol.
envisage *v* gweld, dychmygu.
envy *n* cenfigen *f,* eiddigedd *m.* • *v* cenfigennu, eiddigeddu.
epidemic *n* haint *m/f.*
episode *n* pennod *f.*
epitomise *v* crynhoi, ymgorffori.
equable *adj* gwastad, cyfartal.
equal *adj* cydradd, cyfartal, hafal.
equalise *v* cydraddoli, dod yn gyfartal.
equality *n* cydraddoldeb, cyfartalwch *m.*
equanimity *n* pwyll, tawelwch meddwl *m.*
equate *v* hafalu, cymharu; cyfateb.
equator *n* cyhydedd *m.*
equilibrium *n* cydbwysedd *m.*
equip *v* cyfarparu.
equipment *n* cyfarpar *m.*
equivalent *adj* cyfwerth.
equivocal *adj* amwys, amhendant.
equivocate *v* anwadalu, bod yn amwys.
era *n* cyfnod *m.*
eradicate *v* cael gwared â.
eradication *n* dilead, difodiant *m.*
erase *v* dileu.
eraser *n* dilëwr.
erect *v* codi. • *adj* talsyth, union.
erode *v* erydu.
erotic *adj* erotig.
err *v* cyfeiliorni.
errand *n* neges *f.*
erratic *adj* afreolaidd, eratig.
erroneous *adj* anghywir.
error *n* gwall, camgymeriad *m.*
erudite *adj* dysgedig.
eruption *n* echdoriad, tarddiant *m.*
escalate *v* dwysáu, cynyddu.
escape *v* dianc. • *n* dihangfa *f.*
escort *n* gosgordd *f.* • *v* hebrwng.
especial *adj* arbennig.
essay *n* traethawd *m.*
essence *n* hanfod, craidd *m.*
essential *adj* hanfodol.
establish *v* sefydlu.
establishment *n* sefydliad *m.*
estate *n* stad, ystâd *f.*
esteem *v* edmygu, parchu. • *n* parch *m.*
esthetic *adj* esthetaidd, esthetig.
estimate *v* amcangyfrif.
estimation *n* barn *f,* tyb *m/f.*
estuary *n* aber *m/f,* moryd *f.*
eternal *adj* tragwyddol.
eternity *n* tragwyddoldeb *m.*
ethical *adj* moesol, ethegol.
ethics *n* moeseg *f.*
ethnic *adj* ethnig.
etiquette *n* cwrteisi *m,* safon ymddygiad *f.*
evacuate *v* gwacáu, gwagio.
evacuation *n* gwacâd *m.*
evade *v* osgoi.
evaluate *v* pwyso a mesur, gwerthuso.
evangelical *adj* efengylaidd.
evaporate *v* anweddu.

evaporation *n* anweddiad *m.*
evasion *n* gocheliad *m.*
evasive *adj* gochelgar.
eve *n* noswyl *f.*
even *adj* llyfn. • *adv* hyd yn oed.
evening *n* noswaith *f*, min nos *m.*
evenness *n* gwastadrwydd *m.*
event *n* digwyddiad *m.*
eventually *adv* ymhen hir a hwyr.
eventuality *n* digwyddiad posibl, posibilrwydd *m.*
ever *adv* byth, erioed.
everlasting *adj* bythol, tragwyddol.
every *adj* pob.
evict *v* troi allan.
evidence *n* tystiolaeth *f.*
evident *adj* amlwg.
evil *adj* drwg. • *n* drwg *m.*
evocative *adj* atgofus.
evoke *v* galw, dwyn (atgofion).
evolution *n* esblygiad *m.*
evolve *v* esblygu.
exacerbate *v* gwneud yn waeth, ffyr-nigo.
exact *adj* manwl gywir. • *v* hawlio.
exacting *adj* llym, gormesol.
exactness *n* manwl gywirdeb *m.*
exaggerate *v* gor-ddweud.
exalt *v* gorfoleddu.
examination *n* arholiad, archwiliad *m.*
examine *v* archwilio, arholi.
example *n* enghraifft *f.*
exasperate *v* gwaethygu; cynd-deiriogi.
exasperation *n* gwylltineb *m.*
excavate *v* cloddio, tyllu.
excavation *n* cloddfa *f.*
exceed *v* bod/mynd yn fwy na.
excel *v* rhagori.
excellence *n* rhagoriaeth *f*; godid-owgrwydd *m.*
excellent *adj* rhagorol, godidog.
except *prep* ac eithrio, heblaw.
exception *n* eithriad *m.*
exceptional *adj* eithriadol.
excess *n* gormodedd *m.*
excessive *adj* gormodol, eithafol.
exchange *v* cyfnewid. • *n* cyfnewidfa *f.*
exchange rate *n* cyfradd gyfnewid *f.*
excise *n* toll *f.*
excitable *adj* gwyllt.
excite *v* cynhyrfu.
excited *adj* cynhyrfus, llawn cynnwrf.
excitement *n* cyffro, cynnwrf *m.*
exciting *adj* cyffrous, cynhyrfus.
exclaim *v* ebychu.
exclamation *n* ebychiad *m.*
exclude *v* eithrio.
exclusion *n* gwaharddiad *m.*
exclusive *adj* cyfyngedig.
excommunicate *v* ysgymuno.
exculpate *v* esgusodi.
excursion *n* gwibdaith *f.*
excusable *adj* esgusadwy.
excuse *v* esgusodi. • *n* esgus *m.*
execute *v* dienyddio; cyflawni.
execution *n* dienyddiad; gweithre-diad *m.*
executive *adj* gweithredol. • *n* gweithredwr *m.*
exemplary *adj* canmoladwy, penigamp.

exemplify *v* bod yn enghraifft.
exempt *adj* rhydd, wedi'ch esgusodi.
exemption *n* rhyddhau, esgusodi *vn*.
exercise *n* arfer, ymarfer *m/f*. • *v* arfer, ymarfer.
exert *v* gweithredu, ymdrechu.
exertion *n* ymdrech *f*.
exhale *v* anadlu allan, gollwng.
exhaust *v* dihysbyddu, disbyddu.
exhausted *adj* lluddedig.
exhaustion *n* lludded *m*.
exhaustive *adj* trwyadl, trylwyr.
exhibit *v* arddangos.
exhibition *n* arddangosfa *f*.
exhilarating *adj* bywiocaol.
exhilaration *n* gorfoledd *m*, hoen *m/f*.
exhume *v* datgladdu.
exile *n* alltudiaeth *f*, alltud *m/f*. • *v* alltudio.
exist *v* bodoli.
existence *n* bodolaeth *f*.
existent *adj* sydd ohoni.
exit *n* allanfa *f*. • *v* ymadael.
exonerate *v* esgusodi.
exoneration *n* rhyddhad *m*.
exorbitant *adj* afresymol, gormodol.
exotic *adj* dieithr, lliwgar.
expand *v* ehangu, helaethu.
expanse *n* ehangder *m*.
expansion *n* ehangiad, twf *m*.
expect *v* disgwyl.
expectation *n* disgwyliad *m*.
expediency *n* hwylustod *m*.
expedient *adj* cyfleus.
expedite *v* hwyluso, prysuro.
expedition *n* ymgyrch *m/f*.
expel *v* diarddel.
expend *v* gwario, treulio.
expense *n* traul, cost *f*.
expensive *adj* drud, costus.
experience *n* profiad *m*. • *v* profi.
experienced *adj* profiadol.
experiment *n* arbrawf *m*. • *v* arbrofi.
experimental *adj* arbrofol.
expert *adj* arbenigol; medrus. • *n* arbenigwr *m*, arbenigwraig *f*.
expertise *n* gwybodaeth arbenigol; dawn arbennig *f*.
explain *v* egluro, esbonio.
explanation *n* eglurhad, esboniad *m*.
explanatory *adj* esboniadol.
explicit *adj* croyw, diamwys.
explode *v* ffrwydro.
exploit *v* defnyddio; camddefnyddio. • *n* camp, gorchest *f*.
exploration *n* archwiliad, ymchwiliad *m*.
explore *v* archwilio, fforio.
explorer *n* fforiwr *m*.
explosion *n* ffrwydrad *m*, tanchwa *f*.
explosive *adj* ffrwydrol, tanbaid.
export *v* allforio.
exportation *n* allforio *vn*.
exporter *n* allforiwr *m*.
expose *v* dinoethi, datguddio.
exposition *n* eglurhad, dehongliad *m*.
exposure *n* datguddiad, dinoethiad *m*.

expound *v* traethu.
express *v* mynegi. • *adj* unswydd. • *n* trên cyflym *m*.
expression *n* mynegiant *m*.
expressive *adj* llawn mynegiant, mynegiannol.
expropriate *v* difeddiannu.
expulsion *n* diarddel *vn*.
exquisite *adj* cain, cyfewin.
extemporise *v* siarad/chwarae yn ddifyfyr.
extend *v* estyn, ehangu, ymestyn.
extension *n* estyniad *m*.
extensive *adj* eang, helaeth.
extent *n* hyd a lled; graddau *pl*.
extenuate *v* lleddfu, lleihau.
exterior *adj* allanol.
exterminate *v* difodi, difa.
external *adj* allanol.
extinct *adj* wedi darfod.
extinction *n* diwedd, tranc *m*.
extinguish *v* diffodd.
extinguisher *n* diffoddydd *m*.
extort *v* cribddeilio.
extortion *n* cribddeiliaeth *f*.
extra *adj* ychwanegol.
extract *v* echdynnu, tynnu.
extraction *n* tyniad *m*; hil *f* (family).
extraneous *adj* allanol, estron.
extraordinary *adj* anarferol, arbennig.
extravagance *n* gormodedd, rhysedd *m*.
extravagant *adj* afradlon.
extreme *adj* eithaf, pellaf.
extremist *n* eithafwr *m*, eithafwraig *f*.
extricate *v* rhyddhau, datod.
extrovert *adj* allblyg.
exuberance *n* afiaith *m*, hwyl *f*.
exuberant *adj* afieithus.
eye *n* llygad *m*. • *v* llygadu.
eyebrow *n* ael *f*.
eyelash *n* blewyn (amrant) *m*.
eyelid *n* amrant, clawr llygad *m*.
eyesight *n* golwg *m*.

F

fabric *n* defnydd *m*.
fabricate *v* llunio, ffugio.
fabrication *n* ffugiad, anwiredd *m*.
fabulous *adj* chwedlonol; aruthrol.
face *n* wyneb *m*. • *v* wynebu.
facet *n* ochr, agwedd *f*.
facile *adj* arwynebol.
facilitate *v* hyrwyddo.
facility *n* rhwyddineb, cyfleuster *m*.
facing *adv* yn wynebu, gyferbyn â.
fact *n* ffaith *f*.
factory *n* ffatri *f*.
factual *adj* ffeithiol.
faculty *n* cynneddf; cyfadran *f*.
fail *v* methu.
failure *n* methiant *m*.
faint *v* llewygu. • *n* llewyg *m*. • *adj* gwan, aneglur.
fair *adj* teg, golau. • *n* ffair *f*.
fair play *n* chwarae teg.

fairness *n* tegwch *m*.
faith *n* ffydd *f*.
faithful *adj* ffyddlon.
fake *adj* ffug. • *v* ffugio.
fall *v* cwympo, syrthio. • *n* cwymp *m*.
fallacy *n* cam-dyb *m/f*.
fallibility *n* ffaeledigrwydd *m*.
fallible *adj* ffaeledig.
false *adj* ffug.
false alarm *n* braw di-sail *m*.
falsify *v* ffugio.
falter *v* petruso, pallu.
fame *n* enwogrwydd *m*.
familiar *adj* cyfarwydd, cynefin.
familiarise *v* cynefino.
familiarity *n* cynefindra *m*, adnabyddiaeth fanwl *f*.
family *n* teulu *m*.
famine *n* newyn *m*.
famous *adj* enwog.
fan *n* edmygydd *m*; gwyntyll *m*. • *v* gwyntyllu, megino.
fancy *n* dychymyg *m*. • *v* ffansïo.
fantastic *adj* ffantastig, anhygoel.
fantasy *n* dychymyg, ffantasi *m/f*.
far *adv* ymhell. • *adj* pell.
fare *n* pris, tâl *m*.
farewell *n* ffarwél *m/f*.
farm *n* fferm *f*. • *v* ffermio.
farmer *n* ffermwr *m*, ffermwraig *f*.
farming *n* amaethyddiaeth *f*, amaeth *m*.
fascinate *v* hudo, swyno.
fascination *n* cyfaredd *f*.
fashion *n* ffasiwn *m/f*.
fashionable *adj* ffasiynol.
fast *v* ymprydio. • *n* ympryd *m* • *adj* cyflym
fast food *n* bwyd parod *m*.
fasten *v* sicrhau, clymu.
fat *adj* tew, bras. • *n* saim, braster *m*.
fatal *adj* angheuol, marwol.
fatality *n* marwolaeth *f*.
fate *n* ffawd, tynged *f*.
father *n* tad *m*.
fatherhood *n* tadolaeth *f*.
fatigue *n* blinder, lludded *m*. • *v* blino, lluddedu.
fatuous *adj* gwirion, ffôl.
fault *n* bai, nam *m*.
faulty *adj* diffygiol, a nam arno.
favour *n* cymwynas *f*. • *v* ffafrio.
favourable *adj* ffafriol.
favourite *n* ffefryn *m*. • *adj* hoff.
fax *n* ffacs *m/f*. • *v* ffacsio.
fear *v* ofni. • *n* ofn *m*.
fearful *adj* ofnus.
fearless *adj* di-ofn.
feasibility *n* dichonoldeb *m*.
feasible *adj* posibl, dichonadwy.
feast *n* gwledd; gŵyl *f*.
feat *n* camp, gorchest *f*.
feather *n* pluen *f*.
feature *n* nodwedd *f*. • *v* dangos, amlygu.
February *n* Chwefror *m*.
fed-up *adj*: **to be** ~ syrffedu.
fee *n* ffi *f*, tâl *m*.
feeble *adj* gwan, eiddil.
feebleness *n* eiddilwch, gwendid *m*.
feed *v* bwydo.
feel *v* teimlo, clywed.
feeling *n* teimlad *m*.
feign *v* ffugio, esgus.
fellow *n* cymrawd *m*.

female *n* benyw *f.*
feminine *adj* benywaidd.
feminist *n* ffeminydd *m.*
fence *n* ffens *f.*
ferment *n* eples *m.* • *v* eplesu, gweithio.
ferocious *adj* ffyrnig.
ferocity *n* ffyrnigrwydd *m.*
ferry *n* fferi *f.*
fertile *adj* ffrwythlon, toreithiog.
fertility *n* ffrwythlondeb *m.*
fervent *adj* brwd, brwdfrydig.
fervour *n* brwdfrydedd *m*, sêl *f.*
festival *n* gŵyl *f.*
festive *adj* llawen, llawn hwyl.
fetch *v* ymofyn.
fetching *adj* deniadol.
feud *n* cynnen *f*, ymrafael *m.*
fever *n* twymyn *f.*
feverish *adj* a gwres arno.
few *adj* ychydig, ambell.
fibre *n* ffibr *m.*
fickle *adj* anwadal, oriog.
fiction *n* ffuglen *f.*
fictional *adj* mewn ffuglen.
fictitious *adj* dychmygol.
fidelity *n* ffyddlondeb *m.*
fidget *v* gwingo, bigitan.
fidgety *adj* aflonydd.
field *n* cae, maes *m.*
fiend *n* cythraul *m*, cythreules *f.*
fiendish *adj* cythreulig.
fierce *adj* ffyrnig, milain.
fierceness *n* ffyrnigrwydd *m.*
fifteen *num* pymtheg.
fifteenth *adj* pymthegfed.
fifth *adj* pumed.
fiftieth *adj* hanner canfed.
fifty *num* hanner cant, pum deg.
fight *v* ymladd, brwydro.
fighter *n* ymladdwr *m*, ymladdwraig *f.*
figure *n* ffurf *f*, ffigur *m.*
file *n* ffeil; rhathell *f.* • *v* ffeilio, llyfnhau.
fill *v* llanw, llenwi.
film *n* haen; ffilm *f.* • *v* ffilmio.
filter *n* hidlen *f.* • *v* hidlo.
filth *n* budreddi, mochyndra *m.*
filthy *adj* mochynnaidd.
fin *n* asgell *f.*
final *adj* olaf, terfynol.
finalise *v* cwblhau.
finance *n* cyllid *m.*
financial *adj* ariannol, cyllidol.
financier *n* cyllidwr *m*, cyllidwraig *f.*
find *v* darganfod. • *n* darganfyddiad *m.*
findings *n* casgliadau *pl.*
fine *adj* cain; mân. • *n* dirwy *f.*
finesse *n* cynildeb *m.*
finger *n* bys *m.* • *v* byseddu.
fingernail *n* ewin *m/f.*
finish *v* gorffen, cwblhau.
fir (tree) *n* ffynidwydden *f.*
fire *n* tân *m.* • *v* tanio.
fire engine *n* injan dân *f.*
fire extinguisher *n* diffoddydd tân *m.*
fire station *n* gorsaf dân *f.*
firearm *n* dryll *m.*
fireman *n* dyn tân *m.*
fireplace *n* lle tân *m.*
fireproof *adj* gwrthdan.
firework *n* tân gwyllt *m.*

firm *adj* cadarn, ffyrf. • *n* cwmni *m.*
firmness *n* cadernid *m.*
first *adj* cyntaf.
first aid *n* cymorth cyntaf *m.*
first name *n* enw cyntaf *m.*
first-class *adj* rhagorol, di-ail.
first-hand *adj* uniongyrchol.
first-rate *adj* o'r radd flaenaf.
fish *n* pysgodyn *m.* • *v* pysgota.
fisherman *n* pysgotwr *m.*
fisherwoman *n* pysgotwraig *f.*
fishing *n* pysgota *vn.*
fissure *n* hollt, agen *f.*
fist *n* dwrn *m.*
fit *n* ffit *f.* • *adj* ffit, heini. • *v* ffitio, gweddu.
fitness *n* ffitrwydd; addasrwydd *m.*
fitting *adj* addas, gweddus.
five *num* pump.
fix *v* sicrhau, gosod.
fixation *n* obsesiwn *m.*
fixed *adj* sefydlog.
fizz(le) *v* hisian.
fizzy *adj* byrlymog.
flabby *adj* llipa.
flag *n* baner *f.*
flagrant *adj* amlwg, eglur.
flair *n* dawn *f.*
flake *n* cen *pl*; pluen *f.* • *v* caenu; pluo.
flamboyant *adj* tanbaid, lliwgar.
flame *n* fflam *f.*
flammable *adj* hylosg.
flank *n* ystlys *f.*
flap *n* llabed *f.*
flare *v* ffaglu, fflachio. • *n* fflach *f.*
flash *n* fflach *f.* • *v* fflachio.
flask *n* fflasg *f.*
flat *adj* fflat, gwastad.
flatten *v* gwastatu.
flatter *v* gwenieithio.
flattery *n* sebon *m*, gweniaith *f.*
flaunt *v* gwneud yn fawr.
flavour *n* blas, sawr *m.* • *v* blasu.
flaw *n* nam *m*, mefl *f.*
fleck *n* smotyn, brychni *m.*
flee *v* dianc, ffoi.
fleece *n* cnu *m.*
fleet *n* llynges *f.* • *adj* chwim.
fleeting *adj* brysiog, diflanedig.
flesh *n* cnawd *m.*
flex *n* fflecs *m.* • *v* ystwytho.
flexibility *n* hyblygrwydd *m.*
flexible *adj* hyblyg, ystwyth.
flicker *v* neidio.
flight *n* ehediad, hediad *m.*
flimsy *adj* tila, bregus.
flinch *v* cilio, syflyd.
fling *v* taflu, lluchio.
flippant *adj* gwamal, ysgafala.
flipper *n* asgell *f.*
flirt *v* fflyrtian. • *n* merchetwr *m*, hoeden *f.*
flirtation *n* cyboli *vn.*
float *v* nofio, arnofio.
flock *n* praidd *m*, diadell *f.*
flood *n* llif, dilyw *m.* • *v* boddi.
floodlight *n* llifolau *m.*
floor *n* llawr *m.* • *v* llorio.
flop *n* methiant *m.*
floppy *adj* llipa. • ~ **disc** *n* disg hyblyg *m/f.*
flora *n* planhigion *pl.*
floral *adj* blodeuog.
florid *adj* blodeuog, gwritgoch.

florist *n* gwerthwr blodau *m*; siop flodau *f*.
flounder *v* ymdrybaeddu.
flour *n* blawd, fflŵr *m*.
flourish *v* ffynnu.
flourishing *adj* llewyrchus, ffyniannus.
flout *v* wfftio.
flow *v* llifo, ffrydio. • *n* llif; llanw *m*.
flower *n* blodyn, blodeuyn *m*. • *v* blodeuo.
flowery *adj* blodeuog.
fluctuate *v* amrywio.
fluctuation *n* amrywiad *m*.
fluency *n* llithrigrwydd *m*.
fluent *adj* rhugl, rhwydd.
fluff *n* blew, blewach *pl*.
fluid *n* hylif *m*.
fluke *n* lwc mwnci, lwc mul, ffliwcen *f*.
flurry *n* cwthwm, hwrdd *m*.
flush *v* gwrido; tynnu dŵr. • *n* gwrid *m*.
flushed *adj* gwridog.
fluster *v* drysu, hurtio.
flute *n* ffliwt, chwibanogl *f*.
flutter *v* ysgwyd, crynu.
fly *v* hedfan, ehedeg. • *n* cleren *f*, pryf *m*.
flyer *n* hedfanwr *m*, hedfanwraig *f*.
flying *n* hedfan *vn*.
foam *n* ewyn *m*. • *v* ewynnu.
foaming *adj* ewynnog.
focus *n* man canol, ffocws *m*.
foe *n* gelyn *m*.
fog *n* niwl *m*.
foggy *adj* niwlog.
fold *n* plyg, plygiad *m*. • *v* plygu.
folder *n* plygydd *m*.
foliage *n* dail, deiliach *pl*.
folio *n* ffolio *m*.
folk *n* pobl, gwerin *f*.
folklore *n* llên gwerin *f*.
follow *v* dilyn, canlyn.
follower *n* dilynwr, dilynydd *m*.
folly *n* ffolineb *m*.
fond *adj* hoff.
fondle *v* anwylo, anwesu.
fondness *n* hoffter *m*.
food *n* bwyd *m*.
food processor *n* prosesydd bwyd *m*.
foodstuffs *n* bwydydd *pl*.
fool *n* ffŵl, hurtyn *m*. • *v* twyllo.
foolhardy *adj* byrbwyll, rhyfygus.
foolish *adj* ffôl, gwirion.
foolproof *adj* di-feth.
foot *n* troed *f*.
football *n* pêl-droed *f*.
footballer *n* pêl-droediwr *m*.
footbridge *n* pompren *f*.
footnote *n* troednodyn *m*.
footpath *n* llwybr troed *m*.
footprint *n* ôl troed *m*.
footstep *n* cam *m*.
for *prep* am, ar gyfer. • *conj* gan, canys.
foray *n* cyrch, ymosodiad *m*.
forbid *v* gwahardd.
forbidding *adj* anghynnes, di-serch.
force *n* grym *m*. • *v* gorfodi.
forceful *adj* grymus, egnïol.
forceps *n* gefel (fain) *f*.
forcible *adj* trwy rym.
forearm *n* elin *f*.

foreboding *n* argoel *f.*
forecast *v* darogan. • *n* rhagolygon *pl.*
forefinger *n* bys blaen *m.*
foregone *adj* rhagweladwy, anochel.
foreground *n* tu blaen, blaendir *m.*
forehead *n* talcen *m.*
foreign *adj* estron.
foreigner *n* estron, tramorwr *m.*
foreman *n* fforman *m.*
foremost *adj* cyntaf, blaenaf.
forensic *adj* fforensig.
forerunner *n* rhagflaenydd *m.*
foresee *v* rhag-weld.
foresight *n* rhagwelediad *m.*
forest *n* coedwig, fforest *f.*
foretaste *n* rhagflas *m.*
foretell *v* darogan, proffwydo.
forever *adv* am byth.
forewarn *v* rhybuddio o flaen llaw.
foreword *n* rhagair *m.*
forfeit *v* fforffedu.
forge *n* gefail *f.* • *v* ffugio.
forger *n* ffugiwr *m.*
forgery *n* ffugiad *m.*
forget *v* anghofio.
forgetful *adj* anghofus.
forgive *v* maddau.
forgiveness *n* maddeuant *m.*
fork *n* fforc, fforch *f.* • *v* fforchio.
forked *adj* fforchog.
form *n* ffurf; ffurflen *f.* • *v* ffurfio.
formal *adj* ffurfiol.
formality *n* ffurfioldeb *m.*
format *n* diwyg *m.* • *v* fformatio.
formation *n* trefniant *m.*
formative *adj* ffurfiannol.
former *adj* blaenorol, cyn-.
formula *n* fformwla *f.*
forsake *v* gadael, cefnu ar.
fort *n* caer *f.*
forthcoming *adj* ar ddod, ar gyrraedd.
forthwith *adv* ar unwaith.
fortieth *adj* deugeinfed.
fortification *n* atgyfnerthiad *m.*
fortify *v* cryfhau, atgyfnerthu.
fortnight *n* pythefnos *m/f.*
fortuitous *adj* trwy hap a damwain.
fortunate *adj* ffodus.
fortune *n* ffawd *f*; golud *m.*
forty *num* deugain.
forward *adj* blaen; digywilydd. • *n* blaenwr *m.*
fossil *n* ffosil *m.*
foster *v* magu.
foster child *n* plentyn maeth *m.*
foster mother *n* mamfaeth *f.*
foul *adj* aflan. • *v* baeddu, difwyno.
found *v* sefydlu, sylfaenu.
foundation *n* sylfaen *m.*
foundry *n* ffowndri *f.*
fountain *n* ffynnon *f.*
four *num* pedwar *m*, pedair *f.*
fourfold *adj* yn bedwar cymaint.
fourteen *num* pedwar ar ddeg *m*, pedair ar ddeg *f.*
fourteenth *adj* pedwerydd *m*/pedwaredd *f* ar ddeg.
fourth *adj* pedwerydd *m*, pedwaredd *f.*
fowl *n* ffowlyn *m*, dofednod *pl.*
fox *n* cadno, llwynog *m.*
foyer *n* cyntedd *m.*
fracas *n* helynt *f.*

fraction *n* ffracsiwn *m.*
fracture *n* toriad *m.* • *v* torri.
fragile *adj* brau.
fragility *n* breuder, eiddilwch *m.*
fragment *n* darn, dryll *m.*
fragmentary *adj* darniog, drylliedig.
fragrance *n* peraroglau, persawr *m.*
fragrant *adj* persawrus.
frail *adj* brau, musgrell.
frailty *n* eiddilwch, llesgedd *m.*
frame *n* ffrâm *f*, fframwaith *m.* • *v* fframio.
franchise *n* rhyddfraint; masnachfraint *f.*
frank *adj* plaen, agored.
frankness *n* didwylledd *m.*
frantic *adj* gwyllt, gorffwyll.
fraternal *adj* brawdol.
fraternise *v* cyfeillachu.
fratricide *n* brawdladdiad *m.*
fraud *n* twyll *m.*
fraudulent *adj* twyllodrus.
free *adj* rhydd; rhad ac am ddim. • *v* rhyddhau.
freedom *n* rhyddid *m.*
freelance *adj* ar ei liwt ei hun.
freely *adv* yn rhydd.
freewheel *v* hwylio mynd.
free will *n* gwirfodd *m.*
freeze *v* rhewi.
freezer *n* rhewgell *f.*
freezing *adj* rhewllyd, iasoer.
freighter *n* llong gludo *f.*
French fries *n* sglodion tatws *pl.*
frenzied *adj* gorffwyll.
frenzy *n* gorffwylltra, gwylltineb *m.*
frequency *n* amlder, amledd *m.*
frequent *adj* aml, mynych. • *v* mynychu.
fresco *n* ffresgo *m.*
fresh *adj* newydd, croyw, iach.
freshly *adv* o'r newydd.
freshness *n* ffresni *m.*
freshwater *adj* dŵr croyw.
fret *v* poeni, pryderu.
friction *n* drwgdeimlad; ffrithiant *m.*
Friday *n* Gwener *m*: **Good** ~ Gwener y Groglith.
friend *n* cyfaill *m*, cyfeilles *f.*
friendliness *n* cyfeillgarwch *m.*
friendly *adj* cyfeillgar.
friendship *n* cyfeillgarwch *m.*
fright *n* ofn *m.*
frighten *v* codi ofn, dychryn.
frightened *adj* ofnus, wedi cael ofn.
frightful *adj* dychrynllyd.
frigid *adj* rhewllyd, oeraidd.
fringe *n* rhidens *pl*, cwr *m.*
frivolity *n* gwagedd, lol *m.*
frivolous *adj* gwamal, penchwiban.
frock *n* ffrog *f.*
frog *n* broga, llyffant (melyn) *m.*
frolic *v* prancio.
from *prep* o, oddi wrth.
front *n* blaen *m.* • *adj* ffrynt.
front door *n* drws ffrynt *m.*
frontier *n* ffin *f*, goror *m/f.*
front-wheel drive *n* blaenyriant *m.*
frost *n* rhew, barrug, llwydrew *m.*
frostbite *n* ewinrhew *m.*
frosty *adj* rhewllyd, barugog.
froth *n* ewyn *m.* • *v* ewynnnu.
frothy *adj* ewynnog.

frown *v* gwgu.
frozen *adj* wedi rhewi.
frugal *adj* cynnil, darbodus.
fruit *n* ffrwyth *m.*
fruiterer *n* gwerthwr ffrwythau *m.*
fruitful *adj* ffrwythlon.
fruition *n* dwyn ffrwyth *vn.*
fruitless *adj* diffrwyth.
frustrate *v* rhwystro.
frustrated *adj* rhwystredig.
frustration *n* rhwystredigaeth *f.*
fry *v* ffrio.
frying pan *n* padell ffrio *f.*
fudge *n* cyffug *m.*
fuel *n* tanwydd *m.*
fugitive *n* ffoadur *m.*
fulfil *v* cyflawni.
fulfilment *n* cwblhau *vn.*
full *adj* llawn, cyflawn.
full moon *n* lleuad lawn *f.*
fullness *n* llawnder *m.*
full-time *adj* llawn amser.
fully *adv* yn llawn, yn hollol.
fumble *v* ymbalfalu, dal yn lletchwith.
fume *v* berwi; mygu.
fumigate *v* mygdarthu.
fun *n* hwyl *f*, sbort *m/f.*
function *n* swyddogaeth *f*; ffwythiant *m.*
functional *adj* gweithrediadol.
fund *n* stôr, cronfa *f.* • *v* ariannu.
fundamental *adj* sylfaenol.
funeral *n* angladd, cynhebrwng *m.*
funnel *n* twmffat, twndis *m.*
funny *adj* doniol, digrif.
fur *n* ffwr *m.*
furious *adj* cynddeiriog, candryll.
furnace *n* ffwrnais, ffwrn *f.*
furnish *v* dodrefnu; rhoi.
furniture *n* dodrefn, celfi *pl.*
furrow *n* cwys *f.* • *v* aredig, torri cwys.
furry *adj* blewog.
further *adj* pellach. • *adv* ymhellach. • *v* hyrwyddo.
further education *n* addysg bellach *f.*
furthermore *adv* ar ben hynny.
furtive *adj* lladradaidd, llechwraidd.
fury *n* ffyrnigrwydd *m*, cynddaredd *f.*
fuse *v* ffiwsio; ymdoddi. • *n* ffiws *f.*
fuse box *n* blwch ffiwsiau *m.*
fusion *n* ymasiad *m.*
fuss *n* ffwdan *f.* • ffysan, ffwdanu.
fussy *adj* ffwdanus, trafferthus.
futile *adj* ofer, seithug.
futility *n* seithugrwydd *m.*
future *n* dyfodol *m.*
fuzzy *adj* crychiog; aneglur.

G

gabble *v* clebran, rwdlian.
gadget *n* dyfais *f*, teclyn *m*.
gaiety *n* sirioldeb, llonder *m*.
gain *n* ennill, cynnydd *m*. • *v* ennill, elwa.
gait *n* cerddediad, osgo *m*.
galaxy *n* galaeth *f*.
gale *n* tymestl *f*.
gallant *adj* dewr, gwrol.
gallery *n* oriel *f*.
gallop *n* carlam *m*. • *v* carlamu.
galore *adv* digonedd, llond gwlad.
galvanise *v* galfaneiddio.
gamble *v* gamblo, hapchwarae. • *n* menter *f*.
gambler *n* gamblwr *n*.
gambling *n* hapchwarae, gamblo *vn*.
game *n* gêm *f*, chwarae *m*.
gang *n* haid *f*, criw *m*.
gangway *n* eil, tramwyfa *f*.
gap *n* bwlch *m*, adwy *f*.
garage *n* garej *f*, modurdy *m*.
garbage *n* sbwriel *m*.
garbage can *n* bin sbwriel *m*.
garden *n* gardd *f*.
gardener *n* garddwr *m*, garddwraig *f*.
gardening *n* garddio *vn*.
garlic *n* garlleg *m*.
garment *n* dilledyn, pilyn *m*.
garnish *v* addurno, garnisio.
garret *n* croglofft *f*.
garrulous *adj* siaradus, tafodrydd.
garter *n* gardas *f/m*.
gas *n* nwy *m*.
gas cylinder *n* potel nwy *f*.
gaseous *adj* nwyol.
gash *n* archoll *f*. • *v* torri.
gasp *v* ebychu.
gassy *adj* nwyol.
gastronomic *adj* gastronomegol.
gate *n* clwyd *f*.
gather *v* crynhoi, ymgynnull.
gaudy *adj* gorliwgar.
gauge *n* medrydd, mesurydd *m*. • *v* mesur.
gaunt *adj* esgyrnog, main.
gay *adj* siriol; hoyw.
gaze *v* syllu. • *n* trem *f*.
gear *n* gêr *m/f*.
gearbox *n* gerbocs *m*.
gem *n* tlws *m*, gem *m/f*.
gender *n* cenedl; rhyw *f*.
gene *n* genyn *m*.
genealogical *adj* achyddol.
genealogy *n* achyddiaeth *f*.
general *adj* cyffredinol. • *n* cadfridog *m*.
generalisation *n* cyffredinoliad *m*.
generalise *v* cyffredinoli.
generation *n* cenhedlaeth *f*; cynhyrchiad *m*.
generator *n* generadur, cynhyrchydd *m*.
generosity *n* haelioni, haelfrydedd *m*.

generous *adj* hael.
genial *adj* hynaws, siriol.
genitals *n* organau cenhedlu *pl*.
genius *n* athrylith *f/m*..
gentle *adj* addfwyn, tirion.
gentleman *n* bonheddwr, gŵr bonheddig *m*.
gentleness *n* addfwynder *m*.
genuine *adj* dilys.
genus *n* math *m*, rhywogaeth *f*.
geographer *n* daearyddwr *m*, daearyddwraig *f*.
geography *n* daearyddiaeth *f*.
geologist *n* daearegydd *m*.
geology *n* daeareg *f*.
geometry *n* geometreg *f*.
germinate *v* egino.
gesticulate *v* gwneud ystumiau.
gesture *n* arwydd, ystum *m*.
get *v* cael, ymofyn.
geyser *n* ffynnon boeth, geiser *f*.
ghost *n* ysbryd *m*.
giant *n* cawr *m*, cawres *f*.
gibe *v* gwawdio, gwatwar. • *n* gwawd *m*.
giddiness *n* pendro *f*.
giddy *adj* chwil, penfeddw.
gift *n* anrheg, rhodd *f*.
gifted *adj* dawnus, galluog.
gigantic *adj* cawraidd.
gild *v* euro, goreuro.
gill *n* tagell *f*.
ginger *n* sinsir *m*. • *adj* coch.
ginger-haired person *n* cochyn *m*, cochen *f*.
girl *n* merch *f*.
girlfriend *n* cariad *m*.
gist *n* swm a sylwedd *m*.
give *v* rhoi.
gizzard *n* glasog *f*.
glacial *adj* rhewlifol.
glacier *n* rhewlif *m*, afon iâ *f*.
glad *adj* balch, llawen.
gladden *v* bodloni, sirioli.
glamorous *adj* hudolus, swynol.
glamour *n* swyngyfaredd, hudoliaeth *f*.
glance *v* bwrw cipolwg.
glare *n* disgleirdeb *m*. • *v* rhythu'n ddig.
glass *n* gwydr; gwydryn *m*.
glasses *n* sbectol *f*.
glaze *v* sgleinio; gosod gwydr mewn.
gleam *n* llygedyn, pelydryn *m*.
glee *n* afiaith *m*, hoen *f*.
glide *v* llithro.
glimmer *n* llygedyn *m*.
glimpse *n* cip *m*, cipolwg *m/f*. • *v* cael cipolwg.
glint *v* pefrio.
glitter *v* disgleirio, pelydru.
global *adj* byd-eang.
globe *n* cylch *m*, glob *f*, y byd *m*.
gloom *n* tywyllwch, gwyll *m*.
gloomy *adj* tywyll.
glorious *adj* gogoneddus, godidog.
glory *n* gogoniant *m*.
glove *n* maneg *f*.
glow *v* tywynnu, cochi. • *n* gwrid *m*, gwawr *f*.
glue *n* glud *m*. • *v* gludio, gludo.
glum *adj* digalon, prudd.
glutton *n* bolgi *m*.
gnome *n* dynan, pwca *m*.
go *v* mynd (*see* Appendix).

goal *n* gôl *f.*
goat *n* gafr *f.*
gobble *v* llowcio.
God *n* Duw *m.*
godfather *n* tad bedydd *m.*
godlike *adj* fel duw.
godmother *n* mam fedydd *f.*
gold *n* aur *m.*
golden *adj* aur, euraid.
goldsmith *n* eurych, gof aur *m.*
golf *n* golff *m.*
golfer *n* golffiwr *m*, golffwraig *f.*
gong *n* gong *f.*
good *adj* da.
goodbye *excl* da bo, hwyl.
good-looking *adj* golygus.
goodness *n* daioni *m.*
goodwill *n* ewyllys da *m.*
goose *n* gŵydd *f.*
gorge *n* ceunant *m.* • *v* bwyta llond bol.
gorgeous *adj* gwych, pert ofnadwy.
gory *adj* gwaedlyd.
gossip *n* hen geg *f*; clecs *pl.* • *v* hel clecs, cloncian.
govern *v* llywodraethu.
government *n* llywodraeth *f.*
governor *n* llywodraethwr *m*, llywodraethwraig *f.*
gown *n* gŵn *m.*
grab *v* cydio, gafael.
grace *n* gosgeiddrwydd *m*; bendith *f.* • *v* harddu.
graceful *adj* gosgeiddig.
gradation *n* graddoliad *m.*
grade *n* graddfa *f.*
gradual *adj* graddol, cynyddol.
graduate *v* graddio.
graft *n* impiad, impyn *m.* • *v* impio.
grain *n* gronyn *m.*
grammar *n* gramadeg *m/f.*
grammatical *adj* gramadegol.
grand *adj* crand, mawreddog.
grandchild *n* ŵyr *m*, wyres *f.*
grandad *n* tad-cu, taid *m.*
granddaughter *n* wyres *f.*
grandeur *n* gwychder, mawredd *m.*
grandfather *n* tad-cu, taid *m.*
grandma *n* mam-gu, nain *f.*
grandmother *n* mam-gu, nain *f.*
grandson *n* ŵyr *m.*
grandstand *n* prif safle *m.*
grant *v* caniatáu. • *n* grant, cymhorthdal *m.*
granulate *v* gronynnu.
granule *n* gronyn *m.*
grapes *n* grawnwin *pl.*
grapefruit *n* grawnffrwyth *m.*
graph *n* graff *m.*
graphic *adj* graffig.
grasp *v* cael gafael ar.
grass *n* porfa *f*, glaswellt *m.*
grasshopper *n* ceiliog y rhedyn, sioncyn y gwair *m.*
grassy *adj* gwelltog.
grate *n* grât *m/f.* • *v* rhygnu, merwino.
grateful *adj* diolchgar.
gratification *n* boddhad *m.*
gratify *v* boddhau, rhyngu bodd.
gratifying *adj* braf, boddhaus.
gratis *adv* am ddim.
gratitude *n* diolchgarwch *m.*
gratuitous *adj* di-alw-amdano, direswm.

gratuity *n* cildwrn *m*, rhodd *f*.
grave *n* bedd *m*. • *adj* difrifol.
graveyard *n* mynwent *f*.
gravity *n* disgyrchiant; difrifoldeb, dwyster *m*.
gravy *n* gwlych, grefi *m*.
graze *v* pori.
grease *n* saim *m*. • *v* iro.
great *adj* mawr.
greatness *n* mawredd *m*.
greed *n* trachwant, gwanc *m*.
greedy *adj* barus, gwancus.
green *adj* gwyrdd, glas.
greenery *n* glesni *m*.
greenhouse *n* tŷ gwydr *m*.
greenish *adj* gwyrddaidd.
greet *v* cyfarch.
greeting *n* cyfarchiad *m*.
grey *adj* llwyd, glas.
greyish *adj* llwydaidd.
grid *n* rhwyllwaith, gratin *m*.
grief *n* galar *m*.
grievance *n* cwyn *f*, achwyniad *m*.
grieve *v* galaru.
grievous *adj* difrifol.
grill *n* gridyll *m*. • *v* grilio.
grim *adj* didrugaredd.
grimace *n* ystum *m/f*, cuwch *m*.
grime *n* baw, parddu *m*.
grind *v* malu, llifanu.
grip *n* gafael *f*. • *v* gafael, gafaelyd.
groan *v* ochneidio, griddfan. • *n* ochenaid *f*, griddfan *m*.
grocer *n* groser *m*.
groom *n* gwas, gwastrawd *m*. • *v* gwastrodi, tacluso.
groove *n* rhigol *f*.
grope *v* ymbalfalu.
grotesque *adj* afluniaidd.
ground *n* daear *f*. • *v* tirio.
ground floor *n* llawr gwaelod *m*.
groundless *adj* di-sail.
group *n* twr, dyrnaid, grŵp *m*. • *v* casglu.
grove *n* llwyn *m*.
grovel *v* ymgreinio.
grow *v* tyfu.
grower *n* tyfwr *m*, tyfwraig *f*.
growl *v* chwyrnu, arthio.
growth *n* twf, tyfiant *m*.
grudge *n* dig *m*, cynnen *f*.
gruelling *adj* yn lladdfa.
gruesome *adj* erchyll.
grumble *v* cwyno, grwgnach.
guarantee *n* gwarant *f*. • *v* gwarantu.
guard *n* gard, giard, gwyliwr *m*. • *v* gwarchod.
guardian *n* gwarchodwr *m*, gwarchodwraig *f*.
guardianship *n* gwarchodaeth *f*.
guess *v* dyfalu. • *n* amcan, dyfaliad *m*.
guest *n* gwestai *m*.
guidance *n* arweiniad *m*.
guide *v* arwain, tywys. • *n* arweinydd, tywysydd *m*.
guidebook *n* arweinlyfr *m*.
guild *n* urdd *f*.
guile *n* dichell *f*, twyll *m*.
guilt *n* euogrwydd *m*.
guilty *adj* euog.
guise *n* rhith *m*.
guitar *n* gitâr *m*.
gull *n* gwylan *f*.
gullibility *n* gwiriondeb, diniweidrwydd *m*.

gullible *adj* hygoelus.
gulp *n* llwnc *m.* • *v* llyncu, llowcio.
gum *n* gwm *m.* • *v* gludio.
gun *n* dryll, gwn *m.*
gunpowder *n* powdwr gwn *m.*
gunshot *n* ergyd gwn *m/f.*
gurgle *v* byrlymu.
gush *v* ffrydio; parablu.
gust *n* hwrdd, cwthwm *m.*
gusto *n* awch, afiaith *m.*
gusty *adj* gwyntog.
gut *n* perfedd *m.* • *v* diberfeddu.
gutter *n* cafn *m*, landar *m/f.*
guzzle *v* llowcio.
gymnasium *n* campfa *f.*
gymnastics *n* gymnasteg *f.*
gynaecologist *n* gynecolegydd *m.*
gypsy *n* sipsi *m.*

H

habit *n* arfer *m/f*, arferiad *m.*
habitable *adj* y gellir byw ynddo, cyfannedd.
habitat *n* cynefin *m.*
habitual *adj* arferol, cyson.
haemorrhage *n* gwaedlif *m.*
haggard *adj* blinderus.
haggle *v* bargeinio.
hail *n* cenllysg, cesair *pl.* • *v* cyfarch; bwrw cenllysg/cesair.
hair *n* blewyn; gwallt *m.*
haircut *n* toriad gwallt *m.*
hairless *adj* di-wallt, moel.
hairstyle *n* ffasiwn gwallt *f.*
hairy *adj* blewog, gwalltog.
hale *adj* iach, sionc.
half *n* hanner *m.*
half-hearted *adj* llugoer, claear.
half-hour *n* hanner awr *m.*
half-moon *n* hanner lleuad *m.*
halfway *adv* hanner ffordd.
hall *n* neuadd *f.*
hallow *v* cysegru, sancteiddio.
hallucination *n* rhith *m.*
halt *v* aros, sefyll.
ham *n* cig mochyn *m.*
hammer *n* morthwyl, mwrthwl *m.* • *v* morthwylo.
hammock *n* gwely crog *m.*
hamper *n* basged, cawell *f.* • *v* rhwystro, atal.
hand *n* llaw *f.* • *v* estyn.
handbag *n* bag llaw *m.*
handbrake *n* brêc llaw *m.*
handful *n* llond llaw, dyrnaid *m.*
handicap *n* anfantais *f.*
handicapped *adj* dan anfantais.
handkerchief *n* hances, ffunen *f*, macyn *m.*
handle *n* carn, coes, dolen *m.* • *v* bodio, trafod.
handlebar *n* corn *m.*
handrail *n* canllaw *m/f.*
handsome *adj* golygus, hardd.
handwriting *n* ysgrifen *f.*
hang *v* crogi.
hangover *n* pen mawr *m.*
haphazard *adj* hap a damwain.

hapless *adj* anffodus.
happen *v* digwydd.
happening *n* digwyddiad *m.*
happily *adv* yn hapus.
happiness *n* hapusrwydd, dedwyddwch *m.*
happy *adj* hapus, dedwydd, llawen.
harass *v* blino, poeni.
harbour *n* porthladd *m.*
hard *adj* anodd, caled.
harden *v* caledu.
hardiness *n* caledwch, gwytnwch *m.*
hardly *adv* prin, o'r braidd.
hardness *n* caledwch *m.*
hard-up *adj* mae'n dynn/fain ar.
hardy *adj* caled, gwydn.
hare *n* ysgyfarnog *f.*
harm *n* drwg, niwed *m.* • *v* niweidio, gwneud drwg.
harmful *adj* niweidiol.
harmonious *adj* cytûn.
harmony *n* harmoni *m*, cynghanedd *f.*
harp *n* telyn *f.*
harsh *adj* garw, caled.
harshness *n* gerwinder, craster *m.*
harvest *n* cynhaeaf *m.* • *v* cynaeafu.
harvester *n* medelwr *m.*
haste *n* brys *m*, hast *f.*
hasten *v* brysio, cyflymu.
hasty *adj* brysiog, byrbwyll.
hat *n* het *f.*
hatch *v* deor.
hatchet *n* bwyell *f.*
hate *n* casineb, atgasedd *m.* • *v* casáu.
hatred *n* casineb, atgasedd *m.*
haughtiness *n* rhodres, trahauster *m.*
haughty *adj* ffroenuchel, trahaus.
haul *v* halio, llusgo.
haunt *v* aflonyddu ar.
have *v* bod gan, meddu ar (*see also* Appendix).
haversack *n* bag cefn *m*, ysgrepan *f.*
havoc *n* llanast *m.*
hay *n* gwair *m.*
hay fever *n* clefyd y gwair *m.*
hazard *n* perygl *m.* • *v* peryglu, mentro.
hazardous *adj* peryglus.
haze *n* tarth, tes *m.*
hazelnuts *n* cnau cyll *pl.*
hazy *adj* niwlog, tesog.
he *pron* ef, fe.
head *n* pen *m.*
headache *n* pen tost, cur pen *m.*
headland *n* penrhyn *m.*
headlight *n* lamp flaen *f.*
headline *n* pennawd *m.*
headlong *adv* pendramwnwgl; llwrw ei ben.
headstrong *adj* penstiff, gwrthnysig.
headwaiter *n* prif weinydd *m*, prif weinyddes *f.*
heady *adj* meddwol, llesmeiriol.
heal *v* gwella, iacháu.
health *n* iechyd *m.*
healthiness *n* iechyd da *m.*
healthy *adj* iach, iachus.
heap *n* pentwr *m*, tomen *f.* • *v* pentyrru.

hear *v* clywed.
hearing *n* clyw; gwrandawiad *m.*
heart *n* calon *f.*
heart failure *n* methiant y galon *m.*
hearth *n* aelwyd *f.*
heartless *adj* creulon, didostur.
hearty *adj* calonnog, twymgalon.
heat *n* gwres *m.* • *v* twymo.
heater *n* gwresogydd *m.*
heathen *n* pagan *m.*
heating *n* gwres *m.*
heatwave *n* gwres mawr *m.*
heave *v* codi, gwthio.
heaven *n* nefoedd, nef *f.*
heaviness *n* trymder *m.*
heavy *adj* trwm.
hectic *adj* fel ffair, prysur ofnadwy.
hedge *n* clawdd, gwrych *m.*
hedgehog *n* draenog *m.*
heed *v* talu sylw.
heedless *adj* di-hid, di-hidio.
heel *n* sawdl *m/f.*
hefty *adj* cadarn, glew.
height *n* taldra, uchder *m.*
heighten *v* codi'n uwch.
heinous *adj* ysgeler, anfad.
heir *n* etifedd, aer *m.*
helicopter *n* hofrenydd *m.*
hell *n* uffern *f.*
helmet *n* helm, helmed *f.*
help *v* cynorthwyo, helpu. • *n* cymorth *m.*
helper *n* cynorthwywr *m.*
helpful *adj* o gymorth, defnyddiol.
helpless *adj* diymgeledd, diymadferth.
hemisphere *n* hemisffer *m.*
hen *n* iâr *f.*
henceforward *adv* mwyach, o hyn ymlaen.
hen-house *n* cwt ieir *m.*
hepatitis *n* llid yr afu *m.*
her *pron* ei, hi.
herb *n* llysieuyn *m.*
herbalist *n* meddyg llysiau, perlysieuydd *m.*
herd *n* buches *f*, gyr *m*, haid *f.*
here *adv* yma.
hereby *adv* drwy hyn, gan hynny.
hereditary *adj* etifeddol.
heredity *n* etifeddeg *f.*
heritage *n* etifeddiaeth, treftadaeth *f.*
hermit *n* meudwy *m.*
hernia *n* torllengig *m.*
hero *n* arwr, gwron *m.*
heroic *adj* arwrol.
heroine *n* arwres *f.*
hers *pron* ei, 'w.
herself *pron* hi ei hun/hunan.
hesitate *v* petruso.
hesitation *n* petruster *m.*
heterogeneous *adj* cymysgryw, anghydryw.
heterosexual *adj* gwahanrywiol.
hiatus *n* bwlch *m*, adwy *f.*
hiccup *n* ig *f.* • *v* igian.
hide *v* cuddio. • *n* croen *m.*
hideaway *n* cuddfan *f.*
hideous *adj* erchyll, hyll.
hierarchy *n* hierarchaeth *f.*
hi-fi *n* hei-ffei *m.*
high *adj* uchel.
highlight *n* uchafbwynt *m.*
highness *n* uchder, uchelder *m.*
hike *v* heicio.

hilarious *adj* doniol iawn, digrif tu hwnt.
hill *n* bryn *m*, rhiw *f*.
hillside *n* llechwedd, llethr *f*.
hilly *adj* mynyddig, bryniog.
him *pron* ef, e, o, ei, 'i.
himself *pron* ei hun, hunan.
hinder *v* llesteirio, rhwystro.
hindrance *n* rhwystr, llestair *m*.
hindsight *n* synnwyr trannoeth *m*.
hint *n* awgrym, tinc *m*. • *v* lledawgrymu.
hip *n* clun *f*.
hire *v* llogi, cyflogi.
his *pron* ei, 'i.
hiss *v* poeri, hisian.
historian *n* hanesydd *m*.
historic(al) *adj* hanesyddol.
history *n* hanes *m*.
hit *v* bwrw, taro.
hitch-hike *v* bodio, ffawdheglu.
hoard *n* celc, casgliad *m*. • *v* casglu, cronni.
hoarse *adj* cryg, cryglyd.
hoarseness *n* crygni *m*.
hobby *n* diddordeb *m*, hobi *f*.
hoist *v* codi, halio.
hold *v* dal, gafael. • *n* howld *f*.
hold up *n* lladrad arfog *m*; tagfa *f*.
holder *n* deiliad *m*.
hole *n* twll *m*.
holiday *n* gŵyl *f*; **~s** gwyliau *pl*.
hollow *adj* gwag, cau.
holocaust *n* galanas, cyflafan *f*, holocawst *m*.
holy *adj* sanctaidd, cysegredig.
homage *n* gwrogaeth *f*.
home *n* cartref *m*, aelwyd *f*.
homeless *adj* di-gartref.
homely *adj* cartrefol.
homesick *adj* hiraethus.
homesickness *n* hiraeth *m*.
homework *n* gwaith cartref *m*.
homicide *n* dynleiddiad *m/f*.
homogeneous *adj* cydryw.
homosexual *adj* cyfunrhywiol. • *n* gwrywgydiwr *m*.
honest *adj* gonest, onest.
honesty *n* gonestrwydd, onestrwydd *m*.
honey *n* mêl *m*.
honorary *adj* mygedol, anrhydeddus.
honour *n* anrhydedd *m/f*, bri *m*. • *v* anrhydeddu.
honourable *adj* anrhydeddus.
hood *n* cwfl, cwcwll *m*.
hoof *n* carn *m*.
hook *n* bach, bachyn *m*. • *v* bachu.
hoop *n* cylchyn, cylch *m*.
hooter *n* corn *m*, hwter *f*.
hop *n* herc *m*, naid fach *f*. • *v* hercian.
hope *n* gobaith *m*. • *v* gobeithio.
hopeful *adj* gobeithiol.
horizon *n* gorwel *m*.
horizontal *adj* llorweddol.
hormone *n* hormon *m*.
horn *n* corn *m*.
horoscope *n* horosgop *m*.
horrible *adj* ofnadwy, erchyll.
horrific *adj* arswydus, dychrynllyd.
horrify *v* brawychu, arswydo.
horror *n* arswyd, dychryn *m*.
horse *n* ceffyl *m*.
horseback *adv*: **on ~** ar gefn ceffyl.

horseman *n* marchog *m.*
horsepower *n* marchnerth *m.*
horseshoe *n* pedol *f.*
horsewoman *n* marchoges *f.*
horticulture *n* garddwriaeth *f.*
horticulturist *n* garddwr *m*, garddwraig *f.*
hospitable *adj* croesawgar.
hospital *n* ysbyty *m.*
hospitality *n* croeso, lletygarwch *m.*
host *n* llu; gwesteiwr *m.*
hostage *n* gwystl *m.*
hostess *n* gwesteiwraig *f.*
hostile *adj* gelyniaethus.
hostility *n* gelyniaeth *f.*
hot *adj* twym, poeth.
hotel *n* gwesty *m.*
hotelier *n* gwestywr *m.*
hothead *n* penboethyn *m.*
hotplate *n* plât poeth *m.*
hour *n* awr *f.*
hour-glass *n* awrwydr *m.*
hourly *adv* o awr i awr, wrth yr awr.
house *n* tŷ *m.* • *v* lletya, cartrefu.
houseboat *n* cwch preswyl *m.*
household *n* teulu *m.*
householder *n* deiliad, penteulu *m.*
housekeeper *n* gwraig cadw tŷ *f.*
housewife *n* gwraig tŷ *f.*
housework *n* gwaith tŷ *m.*
hovel *n* hofel *f.*
hover *v* hofran.
how *adv* sut, fel; ~ **do you do!** sut mae, sut ydych chi.
however *adv* sut bynnag.
howl *v* udo. • *n* gwaedd *f.*
hub *n* both *f*, craidd *m.*
hue *n* arlliw *m*, gwawr *f.*
hug *v* cofleidio. • *n* cofleidiad *m.*
huge *adj* anferth, anferthol.
hull *n* cragen llong *f.*
hum *v* mwmian, mwmial, sïo, suo.
human *adj* dynol.
humane *adj* dyngarol.
humanist *n* dyneiddiwr *m.*
humanity *n* dynoliaeth, dynolryw *f.*
humanise *v* dynoli.
humble *adj* diymhongar, gostyngedig. • *v* darostwng.
humdrum *adj* undonog, diflas.
humid *adj* llaith.
humiliate *v* bychanu, torri crib.
humiliation *n* gwarth, cywilydd *m.*
humility *n* gostyngeiddrwydd, gwyleidd-dra *m.*
humorous *adj* doniol.
humour *n* doniolwch, hiwmor *m*; hwyliau *pl.*
hump *n* crwbi, crwb *m.*
hundred *num* can, cant.
hundredth *adj* canfed.
hunger *n* chwant bwyd, newyn *m.* • *v* newynu.
hungry *adj* newynog, ar fy nghythlwng.
hunt *v* hela. • *n* helfa *f.*
hunter *n* heliwr *m*, helwraig *f.*
hurdle *n* clwyd *f.*
hurl *v* lluchio, hyrddio.
hurricane *n* corwynt *m.*
hurry *v* brysio, prysuro. • *n* brys *m*, hast *m/f.*
hurt *v* brifo, niweidio. • *n* dolur *m*, gloes *f.*
hurtful *adj* niweidiol, cas.
husband *n* gŵr *m.*

hut *n* caban, cwt *m.*
hydrant *n* hydrant *m.*
hydraulic *adj* hydrolig.
hydroelectric *adj* hydro-electrig.
hygiene *n* hylendid, glanweithdra *m.*
hygienic *adj* hylan.
hypochondriac *n* claf diglefyd *m.*
hypocrisy *n* rhagrith *m.*
hypocritical *adj* rhagrithiol, dauwynebog.
hypothesis *n* damcaniaeth *f.*
hypothetical *adj* damcaniaethol.
hysterical *adj* hysteraidd, gorfwyll.
hysterics *n* sterics *pl.*

I

I *pron* fi, i, mi.
ice *n* iâ, rhew *m.*
ice cream *n* hufen iâ *m.*
ice rink *n* llawr sglefrio *m.*
ice skating *n* sglefrio *vn.*
icy *adj* rhewllyd.
idea *n* syniad *m.*
ideal *adj* delfrydol.
identical *adj* unfath.
identification *n* adnabyddiaeth *f.*
identify *v* adnabod, enwi.
identity *n* hunaniaeth *f.*
idiot *n* ynfytyn, hurtyn *m.*
idiotic *adj* ynfyd.
idle *adj* didoreth, segur.
idleness *n* segurdod *m.*
idler *n* diogyn *m.*
idol *n* eilun *m*, delw *f.*
idolise *v* addoli, dotio.
idyllic *adj* paradwysaidd.
if *conj* os, pe; ~ **not** oni.
ignite *v* cynnau, tanio.
ignoble *adj* israddol, taeogaidd.
ignominious *adj* gwarthus, cywilyddus.
ignorance *n* anwybodaeth *f.*
ignorant *adj* anwybodus.
ignore *v* anwybyddu, diystyru.
ill *adj* tost, sâl.
illegal *adj* anghyfreithlon.
illegality *n* anghyfreithlondeb *m.*
illegible *adj* annarllenadwy.
illegitimacy *n* anghyfreithlondeb *m.*
illegitimate *adj* anghyfreithlon.
illicit *adj* anghyfreithlon.
illiterate *adj* anllythrennog.
illness *n* salwch, afiechyd *m.*
illogical *adj* afresymegol.
illuminate *v* goleuo, addurno.
illusion *n* rhith *m.*
illusory *adj* lledrithiol.
illustrate *v* darlunio.
illustration *n* darlun *m.*
illustrious *adj* disglair, o fri.
image *n* delw, delwedd *f.*
imaginary *adj* dychmygol.
imagination *n* dychymyg *m.*
imagine *v* dychmygu.
imbecile *adj* ynfyd, gwan ei feddwl.

imitate *v* dynwared, efelychu.
imitation *n* dynwarediad, efelychiad *m.*
immaterial *adj* ansylweddol, dibwys.
immeasurable *adj* anfesuradwy, di-fesur.
immediate *adj* di-oed, syth.
immense *adj* anferth, enfawr.
immigrant *n* mewnfudwr *m*, mewnfudwraig *f.*
immigration *n* mewnfudiad *m.*
imminent *adj* ar ddigwydd, agos.
immobile *adj* disymud, diymod.
immobility *n* llonyddwch, ansymudoldeb *m.*
immoderate *adj* anghymedrol.
immoral *adj* anfoesol.
immorality *n* anfoesoldeb *m.*
immortal *adj* anfarwol.
immune *adj* rhydd rhag.
immunise *v* imwneiddio, gwrthheintio.
immutable *adj* digyfnewid.
impact *n* effaith *f*; trawiad *m.*
impalpable *adj* annheimladwy.
impart *v* rhoi, cyfrannu.
impartial *adj* diduedd.
impartiality *n* tegwch, amhleidioldeb *m.*
impassive *adj* didaro, digyffro.
impatience *n* diffyg amynedd *m.*
impatient *adj* diamynedd.
impeccable *adj* dilychwin, di-fai.
impede *v* rhwystro, atal.
impending *adj* agos, ar ddod.
impenetrable *adj* anhydraidd.
imperceptible *adj* anghanfyddadwy.
imperfect *adj* amherffaith.
imperfection *n* amherffeithrwydd *m.*
impermeable *adj* anhydraidd.
impersonal *adj* amhersonol.
impertinence *n* digywilydd-dra *m.*
impertinent *adj* digywilydd.
impetuosity *n* gwylltineb, byrbwylltra *m.*
impetuous *adj* byrbwyll.
implant *v* impio, mewnblannu.
implement *n* offeryn, erfyn *m.*
implicate *v* cysylltu rhywun â.
implication *n* goblygiad *m.*
implicit *adj* ymhlyg.
implore *v* crefu, deisyf, erfyn.
imply *v* awgrymu, golygu.
impolite *adj* anghwrtais, anfoesgar.
import *v* mewnforio.
importance *n* pwys, pwysigrwydd *m.*
important *adj* pwysig.
impose *v* gosod.
imposition *n* baich, bwrn *m.*
impossibility *n* amhosibilrwydd *m.*
impossible *adj* amhosibl.
impostor *n* twyllwr *m.*
impotence *n* anallu, diymadferthedd *m.*
impotent *adj* diymadferth, analluog.
impoverish *v* tlodi.
impoverishment *n* tlodi *vn.*
impracticable *adj* anymarferol.
imprecise *adj* amhenodol, heb fod yn fanwl.
impress *v* pwysleisio, pwyso.
impression *n* argraffiad *m.*

impressionable *adj* hawdd gwneud argraff arno.
impressive *adj* trawiadol.
imprint *n* argraffiad *m.*
imprison *v* carcharu.
imprisonment *n* carchariad *m.*
improbability *n* annhebygolrwydd *m.*
improbable *adj* annhebygol.
improper *adj* anghywir, anweddus.
improve *v* gwella.
improvement *n* gwelliant *m.*
improvise *v* cyfansoddi ar y pryd.
imprudent *adj* annoeth.
impudent *adj* digywilydd, haerllug.
impulse *n* ysgogiad *m.*
impulsive *adj* byrbwyll.
impunity *n* yn ddi-gosb.
in *prep* yn, mewn.
inability *n* anallu *m.*
inaccurate *adj* anghywir, anfanwl.
inactive *adj* diysgog, segur.
inadequate *adj* annigonol.
inadmissible *adj* annerbyniol.
inane *adj* hurt, gwirion.
inanimate *adj* difywyd.
inapplicable *adj* anaddas, anghymwys.
inaudible *adj* anghlywadwy, anhyglyw.
incalculable *adj* anfesuradwy, difesur.
incapable *adj* analluog.
incapacitate *v* analluogi.
incapacity *n* anallu, analluogrwydd *m.*
incarcerate *v* carcharu.
incautious *adj* difeddwl, diofal.
incentive *n* cymhelliad, symbyliad *m.*
inception *n* dechreuad, cychwyniad *m.*
incessant *adj* di-baid, di-dor.
incidence *n* trawiant, amlder *m.*
incident *n* digwyddiad *m.*
incidental *adj* achlysurol.
incisive *adj* miniog, treiddgar.
incite *v* annog, cymell.
inclination *n* gogwydd *m*, tuedd *f.*
incline *v* gogwyddo, tueddu.
include *v* cynnwys.
including *prep* yn cynnwys, gan gynnwys.
incognito *adv* heb wybod i neb.
incoherent *adj* digyswllt, dryslyd.
income *n* incwm *m.*
incomparable *adj* anghymarol, dihafal.
incompetence *n* analluogrwydd *m.*
incompetent *adj* anghymwys, anobeithiol.
incomplete *adj* anghyflawn, anorffenedig.
incomprehensible *adj* annealladwy.
inconceivable *adj* anhygoel,y tu hwnt i amgyffred.
incongruity *n* anghysondeb, anghymarusrwydd *m.*
incongruous *adj* anghymarus.
inconsiderate *adj* difeddwl, di-hid.
inconsistent *adj* anghyson.
inconspicuous *adj* disylw, anamlwg.
incontrovertible *adj* diamheuol, diymwad.

inconvenience *n* anghyfleustra, anhwylustod *m.*
inconvenient *adj* anghyfleus.
incorporate *v* corffori, ymgorffori.
incorporation *n* ymgorfforiad, corfforiad *m.*
incorrect *adj* anghywir.
increase *v* cynyddu. • *n* twf, cynnydd *m.*
increasing *adj* cynyddol.
incredible *adj* anghredadwy, anhygoel.
incredulous *adj* anghrediniol.
incriminate *v* taflu bai ar, cyhuddo.
incur *v* achosi.
incurable *adj* anwelladwy, na ellir ei wella.
incursion *n* cyrch *m.*
indebted *adj* dyledus.
indecent *adj* anweddus, aflednais.
indecision *n* petruster, amhendantrwydd *m.*
indecisive *adj* petrus, amhendant.
indefatigable *adj* diflino, dyfal.
indefinite *adj* amhendant.
indemnify *v* gwarantu, digolledu.
indemnity *n* sicrhad *m.*
independence *n* annibyniaeth *f.*
independent *adj* annibynnol.
indeterminate *adj* amhenodol, amheus.
index *n* mynegai *m.*
indicate *v* dynodi, mynegi.
indication *n* arwydd *m.*
indifference *n* difrawder, difaterwch *m.*
indifferent *adj* difater, dihidio.
indigenous *adj* brodorol, cynhenid.
indigent *adj* tlawd, anghenus.
indigestion *n* diffyg traul *m.*
indignant *adj* dig.
indignation *n* dicter, digofaint *m.*
indirect *adj* anuniongyrchol.
indiscreet *adj* annoeth, tafodrydd.
indiscretion *n* cam gwag; datgeliad cyfrinach *m.*
indispensable *adj* anhepgor, anhepgorol.
indisputable *adj* diamheuol.
indistinct *adj* aneglur.
indistinguishable *adj* diwahaniaeth, yr un ffunud.
individual *adj* unigol. • *n* unigolyn *m.*
individuality *n* hunaniaeth *f.*
indolence *n* diogi, syrthni *m.*
indolent *adj* dioglyd, didoreth.
indoors *adv* i mewn, gartref.
induce *v* cymell, darbwyllo.
inducement *n* cymhelliad, ysgogiad *m.*
indulge *v* boddio, maldodi.
indulgent *adj* goddefgar, maldodus.
industrial *adj* diwydiannol.
industrialise *v* diwydiannu.
industrious *adj* diwyd, gweithgar.
industry *n* diwydiant, gweithgarwch *m.*
inebriated *adj* meddw.
inedible *adj* anfwytadwy.
inefficiency *n* aneffeithlonrwydd *m.*
inefficient *adj* aneffeithlon.
ineligible *adj* anghymwys.
inept *adj* di-glem, lletchwith.

inequality *n* anghydraddoldeb, anghyfartaledd *m*.
inertia *n* syrthni, diffyg ynni *m*.
inestimable *adj* difesur, dirfawr.
inevitable *adj* anochel, anorfod.
inexhaustible *adj* dihysbydd.
inexpedient *adj* annoeth, anaddas.
inexpensive *adj* rhad.
inexplicable *adj* anesboniadwy, astrus.
infallible *adj* di-ffael, di-feth.
infamous *adj* gwarthus, cywilydd-dus.
infancy *n* babandod *m*.
infant *n* baban *m*.
infantile *adj* babanaidd, plentyn-naidd.
infatuated *adj* wedi gwirioni, wedi mopio.
infatuation *n* gwirioni, gwallgofi *vn*.
infect *v* heintio.
infectious *adj* heintus.
infer *v* casglu.
inference *n* casgliad *m*.
inferior *adj* israddol.
inferiority *n* israddoldeb *m*.
infernal *adj* uffernol.
infest *v* bod yn fyw o.
infidelity *n* anffyddlondeb *m*.
infiltrate *v* ymdreiddio.
infinite *adj* annherfynol.
infinity *n* anfeidroldeb, annherfynol-deb *m*.
infirm *adj* musgrell, methedig.
infirmity *n* gwendid, eiddilwch *m*.
inflame *v* cynnau, ennyn.
inflammation *n* llid, enyniad *m*.
inflatable *adj* pwmpiadwy.
inflate *v* chwythu gwynt i.
inflation *n* chwyddiant *m*.
inflict *v* peri.
influence *n* dylanwad *m*. • *v* dylan-wadu.
influential *adj* dylanwadol.
influenza *n* ffliw *f*.
inform *v* hysbysu.
informal *adj* anffurfiol.
informality *n* anffurfioldeb *m*.
information *n* gwybodaeth *f*, hys-bysrwydd *m*.
infrequent *adj* anaml, prin.
infringe *v* torri, troseddu.
infringement *n* trosedd *m*.
infuriate *v* cynddeiriogi.
ingenious *adj* dyfeisgar.
ingenuity *n* dyfeisgarwch *m*.
ingenuous *adj* diniwed, didwyll.
inglorious *adj* distadl, dinod.
ingratitude *n* anniolchgarwch *m*.
ingredient *n* elfen *f*; cynhwysyn *m*.
inhabit *v* byw, preswylio.
inhabitable *adj* preswyliadwy, ffit i fyw.
inhabitants *n* trigolion *pl*.
inhale *v* anadlu i mewn.
inherit *v* etifeddu.
inheritance *n* etifeddiaeth, tref-tadaeth *f*.
inhibit *v* rhwystro, atal.
inhibition *n* ataliaeth *f*.
inhospitable *adj* digroeso.
inhuman *adj* annynol.
inhumanity *n* creulondeb *m*.
inimical *adj* gelyniaethus.
inimitable *adj* dihafal, unigryw.

initial *adj* cychwynnol, dechreuol.
initiate *v* cychwyn, dechrau.
initiation *n* cychwyniad; derbyniad *m*.
initiative *n* cam cyntaf *m*; menter *f*.
inject *v* chwistrellu.
injection *n* chwystrelliad *m*.
injunction *n* gorchymyn *m*, gwaharddeb *f*.
injure *v* anafu, niweidio.
injury *n* anaf, niwed *m*.
injustice *n* anghyfiawnder, cam *m*.
ink *n* inc *m*.
inlet *n* cilfach *f*.
inn *n* tafarndy, gwesty *m*.
innate *adj* cynhenid.
inner *adj* mewnol.
innkeeper *n* tafarnwr *m*, tafarnwraig *f*.
innocence *n* diniweidrwydd; dieuo-grwydd *m*.
innocent *adj* diniwed, dieuog.
innocuous *adj* diniwed, diddrwg.
innovate *v* arloesi.
innuendo *n* ensyniad *m*.
innumerable *adj* dirifedi, aneirif.
inoculate *v* brechu.
inoffensive *adj* diniwed, difalais.
inopportune *adj* anghyfleus, annhymig.
inquest *n* cwest, cwêst *m*.
inquire *v* holi, gofyn.
inquiry *n* ymchwiliad, ymholiad *m*.
inquisition *n* chwil-lys *m*.
inquisitive *adj* chwilfrydig, busneslyd.
insane *adj* gwallgof, gorffwyll.
insanity *n* gwallgofrwydd *m*.
insatiable *adj* anniwall.
inscribe *v* llythrennu, arysgrifennu.
inscription *n* arysgrif *f*; cyflwyniad *m*.
inscrutable *adj* annirnad.
insect *n* trychfilyn *m*.
insecure *adj* llac, ansicr.
insecurity *n* ansicrwydd *m*.
insemination *n* ffrwythloniad *m*.
insensible *adj* anymwybodol.
insensitive *adj* ansensitif, croendew.
inseparable *adj* anwahanadwy.
insert *v* gosod, mewnosod.
insertion *n* mewnosodiad *m*, addalen *f*.
inside *n* tu mewn *m*.
inside out *adv* y tu chwith allan, tu mewn tu maes.
insidious *adj* llechwraidd.
insight *n* mewnwelediad *m*.
insignificant *adj* dinod, distadl.
insinuate *v* ensynio.
insinuation *n* ensyniad *m*.
insipid *adj* diflas, merfaidd.
insist *v* mynnu.
insistence *n* taerineb *m*.
insistent *adj* taer, penderfynol.
insolence *n* haerllugrwydd *m*.
insolent *adj* haerllug.
inspect *v* archwilio, arolygu.
inspection *n* archwiliad, arolygiad *m*.
inspector *n* arolygwr, arolygydd *m*.
instability *n* ansefydlogrwydd *m*.
install *v* sefydlu; gosod.
instalment *n* rhan *f*, rhandal *m*.
instance *n* enghraifft *f*.

instant *adj* parod, di-oed. • *n* eiliad *f/m*.
instead (of) *prep* yn lle.
instigate *v* symbylu, ysgogi.
instinct *n* greddf *f*.
instinctive *adj* greddfol.
institute *v* sefydlu, cychwyn.
institution *n* sefydliad *m*.
instruct *v* hyfforddi.
instrument *n* erfyn, offeryn *m*.
insufficiency *n* diffyg, prinder *m*.
insufficient *adj* annigonol, dim digon.
insular *adj* ynysig.
insulate *v* ynysu.
insulation *n* inswleiddio *vn*.
insult *v* sarhau. • *n* sarhad *m*.
insurance *n* yswiriant *m*.
insure *v* yswirio.
intact *adj* cyfan.
integrate *v* cyfannu, cymathu.
integration *n* integreiddio *vn*.
integrity *n* uniondeb, gonestrwydd *m*.
intellect *n* deall *m*.
intellectual *adj* deallusol.
intelligence *n* deallusrwydd *m*.
intelligent *adj* deallus, call.
intelligible *adj* dealladwy.
intend *v* bwriadu, amcanu.
intense *adj* dwys, angerddol.
intensify *v* dwysáu.
intensity *n* dwysedd, dwyster *m*.
intensive *adj* dwys.
intention *n* bwriad, amcan *m*.
intentional *adj* bwriadol.
intercede *v* eiriol.
intercept *v* rhyng-gipio.
interest *v* diddori. • *n* diddordeb; llog *m*.
interesting *adj* diddorol.
interfere *v* ymyrryd.
interior *adj* y tu mewn.
interlock *v* cyd-gloi.
interlude *n* egwyl *f*.
intermediary *n* canolwr, cyfryngwr *m*.
intermediate *adj* canolradd.
interminable *adj* di-ben-draw, diddiwedd.
intermingle *v* cydgymysgu.
intermittent *adj* ysbeidiol.
intern *v* carcharu.
internal *adj* mewnol.
international *adj* rhyngwladol, cydwladol.
interpret *v* dehongli.
interpretation *n* dehongliad *m*.
interpreter *n* lladmerydd, dehonglwr *m*.
interrogate *v* holi.
interrogation *n* holiad *m*.
interrupt *v* ymyrryd, torri ar draws.
interruption *n* ymyriad *m*.
intersect *v* croestorri.
intersection *n* croesffordd *f*.
intertwine *v* plethu.
interval *n* egwyl *f*; cyfwng *m*.
intervene *v* ymyrryd.
intervention *n* ymyrraeth *f*.
interview *n* cyfweliad *m*. • *v* cyfweld.
interviewer *n* holwr, cyfwelydd *m*.
intestine *n* coluddyn *m*.
intimacy *n* agosatrwydd *m*.
intimidate *v* dychryn.

into *prep* i mewn.
intolerable *adj* annioddefol.
intolerant *adj* anoddefgar.
intonation *n* goslef; cyweiriaeth *f.*
intoxicate *v* meddwi.
intoxication *n* meddwdod *m.*
intricacy *n* cymhlethdod *m.*
intricate *adj* cymhleth, cywrain.
intrigue *n* cynllwyn *m.* • *v* cyfareddu.
intriguing *adj* cyfareddol.
intrinsic *adj* hanfodol, cynhwynol.
introduce *v* cyflwyno.
introduction *n* cyflwyniad *m.*
introverted *adj* mewnblyg.
intruder *n* tresmaswr *m.*
intuition *n* greddf *f.*
intuitive *adj* greddfol.
inundate *v* gorlifo, boddi.
invade *v* goresgyn.
invader *n* gosresgynnydd *m.*
invalid *n* claf *m.*
invalidate *v* dirymu.
invaluable *adj* hynod werthfawr.
invasion *n* goresgyniad *m.*
invent *v* dyfeisio.
invention *n* dyfais *f.*
inventor *n* dyfeisydd *m.*
investigation *n* ymchwiliad *m.*
investigator *n* ymchwilydd *m.*
invincible *adj* anorchfygol.
inviolable *adj* dihalog.
invisible *adj* anweledig, anweladwy.
invitation *n* gwahoddiad *m.*
invite *v* gwahodd.
invoice *n* anfoneb *f.*
invoke *v* galw ar.
involuntary *adj* anfwriadol.
involve *v* tynnu mewn.
involvement *n* cysylltiad *m*, rhan *f.*
irascible *adj* piwis, pigog.
irate *adj* dig, dicllon.
iron *n* haearn *m.* • *v* smwddio.
ironic *adj* eironig.
irony *n* eironi *m.*
irrational *adj* afresymol.
irreconcilable *adj* anghymodadwy.
irregular *adj* afreolaidd.
irregularity *n* afreoleidd-dra *m.*
irreparable *adj* anadferadwy, na ellir ei drwsio.
irreplaceable *adj* na ellir ei debyg.
irresistible *adj* anorchfygol.
irresponsible *adj* anghyfrifol.
irreverence *n* amarch *m.*
irrigate *v* dyfrhau.
irrigation *n* dyfrhad *m.*
irritability *n* anniddigrwydd *m.*
irritable *adj* piwis, anniddig.
irritate *v* cythruddo, pryfocio.
irritation *n* dig *m*; cosi *vn.*
island *n* ynys *f.*
isle *n* ynys *f.*
isolate *v* ynysu.
isolation *n* ynysiad, arwahanrwydd *m.*
issue *n* rhifyn; testun *m.*
it *pron* ef; hi; ei.
itch *v* cosi.
item *n* eitem *f.*
itinerant *adj* crwydrol, teithiol.
itinerary *n* amserlen deithio *f.*
its *pron* ei.
itself *pron* ei hun, ei hunan.
ivory *n* ifori *m.*
ivy *n* iorwg, eiddew *m.*

J

jabber *v* clebran, baldorddi.
jack *n* jac; cnaf, gwalch (card) *m.*
jacket *n* siaced *f.*
jackpot *n* gwobr fawr *f.*
jagged *adj* danheddog.
jail *n* carchar *m*, dalfa *f.*
jailer *n* ceidwad/swyddog carchar *m.*
jam *n* jam *m.*
January *n* Ionawr *m.*
jar *n* jar *f.*
jargon *n* jargon *m/f.*
jaw *n* gên *f.*
jazz *n* jazz *m.*
jealous *adj* eiddigeddus, cenfigennus.
jealousy *n* cenfigen *f*, eiddigedd *m.*
jeans *n* jîns *pl.*
jeer *v* gwawdio, gwatwar.
jelly *n* jeli *m.*
jeopardise *v* peryglu.
jerk *n* plwc *m.*
jersey *n* siersi *f.*
jest *n* cellwair *m.*
jester *n* croesan, cellweiriwr *m.*
jet *n* ffrwd; jet *f*; muchudd *m.*
jettison *v* gollwng, taflu dros y bwrdd.
jewel *n* gem *f.*
jewellery *n* gemwaith *m.*
Jewish *adj* Iddewig.
jigsaw *n* jig-so *m.*
jinx *n* rhaib *m.*
job *n* gwaith *m.*
jockey *n* joci *m.*
jocular *adj* cellweirus.
jog *v* loncian.
join *v* cydio, uno; ymuno.
joint *n* cymal; uniad *m.*
joke *n* jôc *m.* • *v* jocan.
joker *n* digrifwr *m.*
jolly *adj* llawen, llon.
jostle *v* gwthio.
journal *n* cylchgrawn *m.*
journalism *n* newyddiaduraeth *f.*
journalist *n* newyddiadurwr *m.*
journey *n* taith *f.* • *v* teithio.
joy *n* llawenydd *m.*
joyful *adj* gorfoleddus.
jubilation *n* gorfoledd *m.*
jubilee *n* jiwbilî *f.*
Judaism *n* Iddewiaeth *f.*
judge *n* barnwr, beirniad *m.* • *v* barnu.
judgment *n* barn *f.*
judicious *adj* doeth.
judo *n* jiwdo *m.*
jug *n* j^{2}g *m/f.*
juggle *v* jyglo.
juice *n* sudd *m.*
juicy *adj* llawn sudd.
July *n* Gorffennaf *m.*
jumble *v* cymysgu, drysu.
jump *v* neidio. • *n* naid *f.*
June *n* Mehefin *m.*
jungle *n* jyngl *f.*

junior *adj* iau.
jurisdiction *n* awdurdod *m*.
juror *n* rheithiwr *m*.
jury *n* rheithgor *m*.
just *adj* teg, cyfiawn.
justice *n* cyfiawnder *m*.
justification *n* cyfiawnhad *m*.
justify *v* cyfiawnhau.
juvenile *adj* ifanc.
juxtaposition *n* cyfosodiad *m*.

K

kaleidoscope *n* caleidosgop *m*.
kangaroo *n* cangarŵ *m*.
keen *adj* craff; brwd.
keenness *n* brwdfrydedd; awch *m*.
keep *v* cadw.
kernel *n* cnewyllyn *m*.
kettle *n* tegell *m*.
key *n* allwedd *f*, cywair *m*.
keyboard *n* bysellfwrdd *m*, allweddell *f*.
key ring *n* cylch allweddi *m*.
keystone *n* maen clo *m*.
kick *v* cicio. • *n* cic *f*.
kidnap *v* herwgipio.
kidney *n* aren *f*.
killer *n* lleiddiad, lladdwr *m*.
killing *n* lladd *vn*.
kiln *n* odyn *f*.
kilo *n* kilo *m*.
kilogram *n* kilogram *m*.
kilometre *n* kilometr *m*.
kin *n* tylwyth *m*.
kind *adj* caredig. • *n* math *m/f*.
kindle *v* cynnau, ennyn.
kindliness *n* caredigrwydd *m*.
kindly *adj* twymgalon, hynaws.
kindness *n* caredigrwydd *m*.
king *n* brenin *m*.
kingdom *n* teyrnas *f*.
kiss *n* cusan *f/m*. • *v* cusanu.
kit *n* pac, gêr *m*.
kitchen *n* cegin *f*.
kitten *n* cath fach *f*.
knack *n* dawn *f*.
knead *v* tylino.
knee *n* pen-glin *m*.
kneel *v* penlinio, penglinio.
knife *n* cyllell *f*.
knight *n* marchog *m*.
knit *v* gwau, gweu.
knob *n* bwlyn, dwrn *m*.
knock *v* curo. • *n* cnoc *f*.
knot *n* cwlwm *m*. • *v* clymu.
know *v* gwybod, adnabod.
know-how *n* gallu, medr *m*.
knowledge *n* gwybodaeth, adnabyddiaeth *f*.
knowledgeable *adj* gwybodus, hyddysg.
knuckle *n* cwgn, migwrn *m*.

L

label *n* label *m/f.*
laboratory *n* labordy *m.*
labour *n* llafur *m.* • *v* llafurio.
labourer *n* llafurwr, gweithiwr *m.*
labourious *adj* llafurus.
lace *n* carrai; les *f.*
lacerate *v* rhwygo.
lack *v* bod heb. • *n* diffyg *m.*
lad *n* llanc *m.*
ladder *n* ysgol *f.*
lady *n* boneddiges; arglwyddes *f.*
lag *v* llusgo.
lagoon *n* lagŵn *m.*
lair *n* gwâl, ffau *f.*
lake *n* llyn *m.*
lame *adj* cloff.
lament *v* galaru. • *n* galarnad *f.*
lamentable *adj* truenus.
lamentation *n* galarnad *f.*
lamp *n* lamp, llusern *f.*
lance *n* gwaywffon *f.*
lancet *n* fflaim *f.*
land *n* tir *m*; gwlad *f.* • *v* glanio.
landlord *n* landlord *m.*
landmark *n* carreg derfyn *f*; nod tir *m.*
landscape *n* tirlun *m.*
landslide *n* tirlithriad *m.*
lane *n* lôn *f.*
language *n* iaith *f.*
languish *v* nychu, dihoeni.
lantern *n* llusern *f.*
lapel *n* llabed *f/m.*
lapse *n* esgeulustra, llithriad *m.* • *v* llithro.
larder *n* pantri *m.*
large *adj* mawr, bras.
larva *n* larfa *m/f.*
lascivious *adj* anllad, trythyll.
lash *n* llach *f.* • *v* chwipio, fflangellu.
last *adj* diwethaf, olaf. • *v* para, parhau.
last-minute *adj* munud olaf.
late *adj* hwyr, diweddar.
latent *adj* cudd, cêl.
lateral *adj* ochrol.
lather *n* ewyn *m*, trochion *pl.*
latitude *n* lledred; rhyddid *m.*
laudable *adj* clodwiw, canmoladwy.
laugh *v* chwerthin. • *n* chwerthiniad *m.*
laughter *n* chwerthin *vn.*
launch *v* lansio, gwthio cwch i'r dŵr.
laundry *n* golchdy *m.*
lava *n* lafa *m.*
lavatory *n* tŷ bach *m.*
lavish *adj* hael.
law *n* deddf, cyfraith *f.*
lawful *adj* cyfreithlon.
lawmaker *n* deddfwr *m.*
lawn *n* lawnt *f.*
lawyer *n* cyfreithiwr *m*, cyfreithwraig *f.*

lax *adj* llac.
laxative *n* moddion gweithio *m.*
lay *v* dodwy; gosod.
layer *n* haen, haenen *f.*
laziness *n* diogi *m.*
lazy *adj* diog.
lead *n* plwm *m.* • *v* arwain.
leader *n* arweinydd *m.*
leadership *n* arweinyddiaeth *f.*
leading *adj* blaenllaw.
leaf *n* deilen *f.*
leaflet *n* taflen *f.*
league *n* cynghrair *f/m.*
leak *n* gollyngiad *m.* • *v* gollwng.
lean *v* pwyso. • *adj* main.
leap *v* neidio. • *n* naid *f.*
learn *v* dysgu.
learning *n* dysg *f.*
lease *n* prydles *f.* • *v* prydlesu.
leash *n* tennyn *m.*
least *adj* lleiaf; **at** ~ o leiaf.
leather *n* lledr *m.*
leave *n* caniatâd *m.* • *v* gadael.
lecture *n* darlith *f.* • *v* darlithio.
lecturer *n* darlithydd *m.*
left *adj* chwith.
left-handed *adj* llaw chwith.
left-luggage office *n* storfa baciau *f.*
leftovers *n* gweddillion *pl.*
leg *n* coes *f.*
legal *adj* cyfreithlon, cyfreithiol.
legalise *v* cyfreithloni.
legality *n* cyfreithlondeb *m.*
legend *n* chwedl *f.*
legendary *adj* chwedlonol.
legible *adj* darllenadwy.
legion *n* lleng *f.*
legislate *v* deddfu.
legislation *n* deddfwriaeth *f.*
legislative *adj* deddfwriaethol.
legislature *n* corff deddfwriaethol *m.*
legitimacy *n* cyfreithlondeb *m.*
legitimate *adj* cyfreithlon.
leisure *n* hamdden *f.* • **~ly** *adj* hamddenol.
lemon *n* lemon *m.*
lemonade *n* lemonêd *m.*
lend *v* benthyca.
length *n* hyd *m.*
lengthen *v* hwyhau, estyn.
lengthy *adj* hir.
lenient *adj* tirion.
lens *n* lens *f.*
leotard *n* leotard *m/f.*
lesbian *n* lesbiad *f.*
less *adj* llai.
lessen *v* lleihau.
lesser *adj* llai, lleiaf.
lesson *n* gwers *f.*
let *v* gadael; gosod.
lethal *adj* marwol, angheuol.
lethargic *adj* cysglyd, swrth.
lethargy *n* syrthni *m.*
letter *n* llythyr *m*; llythyren *f.*
lettering *n* llythrennu *vn.*
lettuce *n* letysen.
level *adj* gwastad. • *n* lefel *f.* • *v* gwastatáu.
lever *n* trosol *m.*
levity *n* ysgafnder *m.*
liability *n* atebolrwydd *m*; **he's a** ~ mae'n fwrn.
liable *adj* tueddol; tebyg.
liaise *v* cysylltu.

liaison *n* cysylltiad *m*.
liar *n* celwyddgi *m*.
liberal *adj* rhyddfrydig, rhyddfrydol.
liberate *v* rhyddhau.
liberation *n* rhyddhad *m*, gwaredigaeth *f*.
liberty *n* rhyddid *m*.
librarian *n* llyfrgellydd *m*.
library *n* llyfrgell *f*.
licence *n* trwydded *f*.
lick *v* llyfu.
lid *n* caead, clawr *m*.
lie *n* celwydd *m*. • *v* dweud celwyddau; gorwedd.
lieu *n*: **in ~ of** yn lle.
life *n* bywyd *m*.
life jacket *n* siaced achub *f*.
life sentence *n* carchar am oes.
lifeless *adj* marw, difywyd.
life-sized *adj* o faintioli llawn.
lift *v* codi.
ligament *n* gewyn, tennyn *m*.
light *n* goleuni *m*. • *adj* ysgafn; golau. • *v* cynnau.
lighten *v* ysgafnhau; goleuo.
lighthouse *n* goleudy *m*.
lighting *n* goleuo, tanio *vn*.
lightning *n* mellt *pl*.
light year *n* blwyddyn oleuni *f*.
like *adj* tebyg. • *adv* fel. • *v* hoffi.
likelihood *n* tebyg, tebygolrwydd *m*.
likely *adj* tebygol, tebyg.
liken *v* tebygu, cymharu.
likeness *n* tebygrwydd *m*.
likewise *adv* hefyd, yn ogystal.
liking *n* hoffter *m*.
limb *n* aelod *m*.
limit *n* terfyn *m*. • *v* cyfyngu.
limitation *n* cyfyngiad *m*.
limp *v* hercian. • *n* cloffni *m*. • *adj* llipa.
line *n* llinell *f*; llinyn *m*.
liner *n* llong fawr, leiner *f*.
linger *v* oedi, sefyllian.
linguist *n* ieithydd *m*.
linguistic *adj* ieithyddol.
link *n* dolen gyswllt *f*. • *v* cyplysu.
lion *n* llew *m*.
lip *n* gwefus *f*, min *m*.
lip-read *v* darllen gwefusau.
lipstick *n* minlliw *m*.
liqueur *n* gwirod *m/f*.
liquid *n* hylif *m*.
liquidise *v* hylifo.
liquor *n* gwirod *m/f*.
lisp *v* siarad â thafod tew. • *n* tafod tew *m*.
list *n* rhestr *f*. • *v* rhestru.
listen *v* gwrando.
literal *adj* llythrennol.
literary *adj* llenyddol.
literature *n* llenyddiaeth *f*.
litigation *n* mynd i gyfraith *vn*.
litigious *adj* ymgyfreithgar, cynhennus.
litre *n* litr *m*.
litter *n* sbwriel *m*.
little *adj* bach, ychydig.
live *v* byw. • *adj* byw.
livelihood *n* bywoliaeth *f*.
liveliness *n* bywiogrwydd *m*.
lively *adj* bywiog.
liver *n* afu, iau *m*.
livid *adj* (yn) gandryll.

living *n* byw *m*.
living room *n* ystafell fyw *f*.
load *v* llwytho. • *n* llwyth *m*.
loaf *n* torth *f*.
loan *n* benthyciad *m*.
loathe *v* casáu.
loathing *n* atgasedd, casineb *m*.
lobster *n* cimwch *m*.
local *adj* lleol.
locate *v* lleoli.
location *n* lleoliad *m*.
lock *n* clo *m*. • *v* cloi.
locker *n* cwpwrdd bach *m*.
lockout *n* cloi allan *vn*.
locomotive *n* injan drên *f*.
lodge *v* lletya.
lodger *n* lletywr *m*, lletywraig *f*.
log *n* boncyff, plocyn *m*.
logic *n* rhesymeg *f*.
logical *adj* rhesymegol.
loiter *v* loetran, sefyllian.
lollipop *n* lolipop *m*.
lonely *adj* unig.
loneliness *n* unigrwydd, unigedd *m*.
long *adj* hir, maith. • *v* dyheu, hiraethu.
longevity *n* hirhoedledd *m*.
longing *n* dyhead, hiraeth *m*.
long-range *adj* pellgyrhaeddol.
long-term *adj* hirdymor.
look *v* edrych, disgwyl. • *n* golwg *f*.
loop *n* dolen *f*.
loose *adj* rhydd, llaes.
loosen *v* rhyddhau, llaesu.
loot *v* ysbeilio. • *n* ysbail *f*.
loquacious *adj* siaradus, huawdl.
loquacity *n* huodledd *m*.
lose *v* colli.
loss *n* colled *f*.
lot *n* coelbren *m*; **a** ~ llawer.
lotion *n* hufen, eli *m*.
lottery *n* lotri, loteri *f/m*.
loud *adj* uchel.
loudspeaker *n* uchelseinydd, corn siarad *m*.
lounge *n* lolfa *f*.
lovable *adj* hoffus, serchus.
love *n* cariad, serch *m*. • *v* caru, dwlu.
loveliness *n* prydferthwch *m*.
lovely *adj* hyfryd, prydferth.
lover *n* cariad, carwr *m*.
loving *adj* cariadus.
low *adj* isel. • *v* brefu.
lower *v* gostwng.
lowly *adj* gostyngedig.
loyal *adj* teyrngar, ffyddlon.
loyalty *n* teyrngarwch *m*.
lucid *adj* clir, eglur.
luck *n* lwc, ffawd *f*.
luckless *adj* anlwcus.
lucky *adj* lwcus, ffodus.
lucrative *adj* proffidiol.
ludricrous *adj* chwerthinllyd, hurt.
luggage *n* bagiau *pl*.
lukewarm *adj* claear, llugoer.
lull *v* gostegu. • *n* gosteg *m/f*.
luminous *adj* disglair, golau.
lump *n* lwmpyn, talp *m*.
lunch *n* cinio canol dydd *m*.
lungs *n* ysgyfaint *pl*.
lure *n* abwydyn, llith *m*. • *v* denu.
lurk *v* llechu.
lush *adj* toreithiog, iraidd.

lust *n* blys, trachwant *m.* • *v* chwennych.
lustre *n* llewyrch *m.*
luxuriance *n* helaethrwydd *m*, toreth *f.*
luxuriant *adj* toreithiog.
luxurious *adj* moethus.
luxury *n* moethusrwydd *m.*
lyrical *adj* telynegol.
lyrics *n* geiriau *pl.*

M

machination *n* cynllwyn *m.*
machine *n* peiriant *m.*
machinery *n* peirianwaith *m.*
mad *adj* gwallgof.
madam *n* madam, meistres *f.*
madden *v* gwylltio, cynddeiriogi.
madman *n* gwallgofddyn *m.*
madness *n* gwallgofrwydd *m.*
magazine *n* cylchgrawn *m.*
magic *n* hud a lledrith *m.* • *adj* lledrithiol.
magnanimous *adj* mawrfrydig, hael.
magnet *n* magned *m.*
magnetic *adj* magnetig.
magnetism *n* magneteg *f.*
magnificence *n* gwychder, ardderchowgrwydd *m.*
magnificent *adj* gwych, ardderchog.
magnify *v* chwyddo, mwyhau.
magnitude *n* maintioli *m.*
maid *n* morwyn *f.*
mail *n* post *m.*
mail train *n* trên post *m.*
maim *v* andwyo, llurgunio.
main *adj* prif.
main line *n* lein fawr *f.*
main road *n* priffordd, ffordd fawr *f.*
mainland *n* tir mawr *m.*
maintain *v* cynnal; maentumio.
maintenance *n* cynhaliaeth *f*; cynnal a chadw *vn.*
majestic *adj* urddasol.
majesty *n* urddas; mawrhydi *m.*
major *adj* prif, mwyaf.
majority *n* mwyafrif *m.*
make *v* gwneud.
makeshift *adj* dros dro.
make-up *n* colur *m.*
malady *n* anhwylder, clefyd *m.*
malaise *n* anniddigrwydd, anhwylder *m.*
malaria *n* malaria, y cryd *m.*
malcontent *adj* anfoddog, anfodlon.
male *adj* gwryw, gwrywaidd. • *n* gwryw *m.*
malevolence *n* malais, mileindra *m.*
malevolent *adj* maleisus, milain.
malice *n* malais *m.*
malicious *adj* maleisus.
malign *adj* niweidiol, milain. • *v* par-dduo.

malleable *adj* hydrin.
malnutrition *n* diffyg maeth *m.*
malpractice *n* camymddygiad, esgeulustod *m.*
maltreat *v* cam-drin.
mammal *n* mamolyn *m.*
man *n* dyn, gŵr *m.*
manage *v* rheoli, ymdopi.
management *n* rheolaeth *f.*
manager *n* rheolwr *m*, rheolwraig *f.*
managing director *n* rheolwr-gyfarwyddwr *m.*
mandatory *adj* gorfodol.
manhandle *v* trafod â nerth bôn braich.
maniac *n* gwallgofddyn *m.*
manic *adj* manig, lloerig.
manifest *adj* amlwg. • *v* datguddio.
manifestation *n* amlygiad, ymddangosiad *m.*
manipulate *v* trafod, trin.
mankind *n* dynolryw, dynoliaeth *f.*
manliness *n* gwroldeb, dewrder *m.*
manly *adj* gwrol.
man-made *adj* o waith llaw dyn.
manner *n* ffordd *f*, modd *m.*
manoeuvre *n* symudiad *m.*
manual *adj* llaw. • *n* llawlyfr *m.*
manufacture *v* gweithgynhyrchu.
manufacturer *n* gwneuthurwr *m.*
manuscript *n* llawysgrif *f.*
many *adj* llawer; **how ~?** pa faint, pa sawl.
map *n* map *m.*
mar *v* difetha, sbwylio.
marble *n* marmor *m.*
March *n* Mawrth *m.*
march *n* gorymdaith; ymdeithgan *f.* • *v* gorymdeithio.
margarine *n* margarîn *m.*
margin *n* ymyl *m/f*, godre *m.*
marginal *adj* ymylol.
marine *adj* morol.
marital *adj* priodasol.
maritime *adj* glan môr.
mark *n* marc, nod *m.* • *v* nodi, marcio.
market *n* marchnad *f.*
marketable *adj* gwerthadwy.
marmalade *n* marmalêd *m.*
marriage *n* priodas *f.*
married *adj* priod.
marry *v* priodi.
marsh *n* cors, mignen *f.*
marshy *adj* corsog.
martial *adj* milwrol.
martyr *n* merthyr *m*, merthyres *f.*
marvel *n* rhyfeddod *m.* • *v* rhyfeddu.
marvellous *adj* rhyfeddol.
masculine *adj* gwryw, gwrywaidd.
mask *n* mwgwd *m.* • *v* mygydu, cuddio.
mason *n* saer maen, masiwn *m.*
mass *n* offeren *f*; màs *m.*
massacre *n* cyflafan *f.* • *v* lladd.
massage *n* tylino'r corff *vn.*
massive *adj* anferth, enfawr.
mast *n* hwylbren, mast *m.*
master *n* meistr *m.* • *v* meistroli.
mastermind *v* cynllunio.
mastery *n* meistrolaeth *f.*
match *n* matsen; gêm *f.*
matchless *adj* digymar, digyffelyb.

mate *n* mêt, partner *m.* • *v* cyplu.
material *adj* materol; pwysig.
maternal *adj* mamol.
maternity hospital *n* ysbyty mamau *m.*
mathematical *adj* mathemategol.
mathematics *n* mathemateg *f.*
matrimonial *adj* priodasol.
matted *adj* yn glymau.
matter *n* sylwedd, mater *m.* • *v* bod yn bwysig.
mattress *n* matres *m/f.*
mature *adj* aeddfed. • *v* aeddfedu.
maturity *n* aeddfedrwydd *m.*
maximum *n* uchafswm *m.*
may *v* gallu.
May *n* Mai *m.*
mayor *n* maer *m*, maeres *f.*
maze *n* drysfa *f.*
me *pron* fi, fy, 'm, mi.
meadow *n* dôl *f.*
meagre *adj* prin, tenau.
meal *n* pryd *m.*
mean *adj* cybyddlyd. • *v* golygu.
meander *v* ymddolennu, dolennu.
meaning *n* ystyr *m/f.*
meanness *n* crintachrwydd, cybydd-dod *m.*
meantime *n* cyfamser.
measure *n* mesur *vn.*
measurement *n* mesur, mesuriad *m.*
meat *n* cig *m.*
mechanic *n* peiriannydd *m.*
mechanical *adj* peirianyddol, mecanyddol.
mechanism *n* peirianwaith *m.*
medal *n* medal *f.*
media *n* cyfryngau *pl.*
mediate *v* cyflafareddu.
mediator *n* eiriolwr, cyfryngydd *m.*
medical *adj* meddygol.
medicinal *adj* meddyginiaethol.
medicine *n* meddyginiaeth *f*, moddion *pl.*
mediocre *adj* gweddol, cyffredin.
meditate *v* myfyrio, synfyfyrio.
meditation *n* myfyrdod *m.*
meditative *adj* synfyfyriol.
medium *n* canol; cyfrwng *m.* • *adj* gweddol, cymedrol.
medium wave *n* y donfedd ganol *f.*
meek *adj* addfwyn, gostyngedig.
meekness *n* gostyngeiddrwydd, add-fwynder *m.*
meet *v* cyfarfod.
meeting *n* cyfarfod *m.*
melancholy *n* iselder ysbryd *m.* • *adj* pruddglwyfus.
mellow *adj* aeddfed, mwyn. • *v* aeddfedu.
melody *n* alaw *f.*
melon *n* melon *m.*
melt *v* toddi, ymdoddi.
member *n* aelod *m.*
memorable *adj* cofiadwy, byth-gofiadwy.
memorandum *n* memorandwm *m.*
memorise *v* dysgu ar gof.
memory *n* cof *m.*
menace *n* bygythiad *m.*
mend *v* cyweirio, trwsio.
menial *adj* isel, gwasaidd.
menstruation *n* mislif *m.*
mental *adj* meddyliol.
mentality *n* meddylfryd *m.*

mention *v* crybwyll, sôn.
menu *n* bwydlen *f.*
mercantile *adj* masnachol.
mercenary *n* milwr cyflog *m.*
merchandise *n* marsiandïaeth *f,* nwyddau *pl.*
merchant *n* masnachwr, gwerthwr *m*; masnachwraig, gwerthwraig *f.*
merciful *adj* trugarog.
mercy *n* trugaredd *m/f.*
mere *adj* dim ond, yn unig.
merge *v* cyfuno.
merger *n* cyfuniad *m.*
merit *n* haeddiant, teilyngdod *m.* • *v* haeddu, teilyngu.
merry *adj* llawen, llon.
mesh *n* rhwyll, masgl *f.*
mesmerise *v* mesmereiddio.
mess *n* llanastr *m*, smonach *f.*
message *n* neges *f.*
messenger *n* negesydd *m.*
metal *n* metel *m.*
metallic *adj* metelaidd.
meteorological *adj* meteorolegol.
meteorology *n* meteoroleg *f.*
meter *n* mesurydd *m.*
method *n* dull *m.*
methodical *adj* trefnus.
metropolitan *adj* prifddinasol.
mew *v* mewian.
microphone *n* microffon *m.*
microscope *n* microsgop *m.*
mid *adj* canol.
midday *n* canol dydd *m.*
middle *adj* canol. • *n* canol *m.*
middling *adj* canolig, gweddol.
midnight *n* hanner nos *m.*
midway *adv* hanner ffordd.
midwife *n* bydwraig *f.*
might *n* grym, nerth *m.*
mighty *adj* nerthol, aruthrol fawr.
migrate *v* mudo, ymfudo.
migration *n* ymfudiad *m.*
mild *adj* mwyn, tyner.
mildness *n* mwynder, tynerwch *m.*
mile *n* milltir *f.*
militant *adj* milwriaethus.
militate *v* milwrio.
milk *n* llaeth, llefrith *m.* • *v* godro.
milky *adj* llaethog.
mill *n* melin *f.* • *v* malu, melino.
millimetre *n* milimetr *m.*
million *n* miliwn *f.*
millionaire *n* miliwnydd *m.*
millionth *adj* miliynfed.
mime *n* meim *f.*
mimic *v* dynwared.
mimicry *n* dynwarediad *m.*
mince *v* briwo, briwsioni.
mind *n* meddwl *m.* • *v* gwarchod; malio.
mindful *adj* gofalus.
mine *pron* eiddof fi.
miner *n* glöwr, mwynwr *m.*
mineral *n* mwyn *m.*
mingle *v* cymysgu.
miniature *n* miniatur *m.*
minimise *v* lleihau.
minimum *n* isafbwynt, lleiafswm *m.*
minister *n* gweinidog *m.* • *v* bugeilio, gweinidogaethu.
ministry *n* gweinyddiaeth *f*; gweinidogaeth *f.*
minor *adj* lleiaf.

minority *n* lleiafrif *m*.
minus *n* minws *m*.
minute *adj* mân.
minute *n* munud *f/m*.
miracle *n* gwyrth *f*.
miraculous *adj* gwyrthiol.
mirage *n* rhith *m*.
mirror *n* drych *m*.
misadventure *n* anffawd *f*.
misbehave *v* camymddwyn.
misbehaviour *n* camymddygiad *m*.
miscarriage *n* camweinyddiad; erthy-liad *m*.
miscellaneous *adj* amrywiol.
miscellany *n* amrywiaeth *f*, cymys-gwch *m*.
mischief *n* drygioni, drwg *m*.
mischievous *adj* drygionus, maleisus.
misconception *n* camdybiaeth *f*, camsyniad *m*.
misconduct *n* camymddygiad, camweinyddiad *m*.
misdeed *n* trosedd, camwedd *m*.
misdemeanour *n* camymddygiad *m*.
miser *n* cybydd *m*.
miserable *adj* diflas, trist, digalon.
misery *n* diflastod, trueni *m*.
misfortune *n* anlwc, anffawd *f*.
misgovern *v* camreoli.
mishap *n* damwain *f*.
misjudge *v* camfarnu.
mislead *v* camarwain.
misogynist *n* casäwr gwragedd *m*.
misprint *n* gwall argraffu *m*.
Miss *n* Miss, Y Fns *f*.
miss *v* methu, colli.
missing *adj* coll, ar goll.
mission *n* perwyl *m*; cenhadaeth *f*.
mist *n* niwl *m*.
mistake *v* camgymryd. • *n* cam-gymeriad *m*.
Mister *n* Mister, bonwr *m*.
mistress *n* meistres *f*.
mistrust *v* drwgdybio. • *n* drwgdyb-iaeth *f*.
misty *adj* niwlog.
misunderstanding *n* camddealltwr-iaeth *f*.
misuse *v* camddefnyddio.
mitigate *v* lliniaru, lleddfu.
mitigation *n* lleddfiad, lliniariad *m*.
mix *v* cymysgu.
mixed *adj* cymysg.
mixture *n* cymysgedd *m/f*.
moan *n* ochenaid *f*. • *v* ocheneidio, griddfan.
moat *n* ffos *f*.
mob *n* ciwed, haid *f*.
mobile *adj* symudol.
mobilise *v* cynnull, byddino.
mobility *n* symudedd *m*.
mock *v* gwatwar, gwawdio.
mockery *n* gwatwar, gwawd *m*.
mode *n* dull, modd *m*.
model *n* model *m*. • *v* modelu.
moderate *adj* cymedrol, gweddol. • *v* cymedroli.
moderation *n* cymedroldeb *m*.
modern *adj* modern.
modernise *v* moderneiddio, diwed-daru.
modest *adj* diymhongar.
modesty *n* gwyleidd-dra *m*.

modification *n* newidiad, addasiad *m.*
modify *v* addasu, cyfaddasu.
moist *adj* llaith, gwlyb.
moisten *v* gwlychu.
moisture *n* lleithder *m.*
molest *v* aflonyddu, ymyrryd.
molten *adj* tawdd.
moment *n* moment *f.*
momentary *adj* dros dro.
monastery *n* mynachlog *f.*
monastic *adj* mynachaidd.
Monday *n* Llun *m.*
monetary *adj* ariannol.
money *n* arian *m.*
monk *n* mynach *m.*
monkey *n* mwnci *m.*
monopolise *v* monopoleiddio.
monopoly *n* monopoli *m.*
monotonous *adj* undonog.
monotony *n* undonedd *m.*
monster *n* anghenfil *m.*
monstrous *adj* anferthol; gwarthus.
month *n* mis *m.*
monthly *adj* misol.
mood *n* hwyl *f*, tymer *m/f.*
moon *n* lleuad, lloer *f.*
moonlight *n* golau lleuad *m.*
moral *adj* moesol. • **~s** *n* moesau *pl.*
morale *n* hyder, ysbryd *m.*
morality *n* moesoldeb *m.*
morbid *adj* afiach, morbid.
more *adj* mwy, ychwaneg; **~ and ~** mwyfwy.
moreover *adv* yn ogystal, at hynny.
morning *n* bore *m*; **good ~** bore da.
morsel *n* tamaid bach *m.*
mortal *adj* meidrol, marwol. • *n* meidrolyn *m.*
mortality *n* marwolaeth *f.*
mortgage *n* morgais *m.* • *v* morgeisio.
mortuary *n* marwdy, corffdy *m.*
mosque *n* mosg *m.*
most *adj* mwyaf.
mother *n* mam *f.*
mother tongue *n* mamiaith *f.*
motherhood *n* mamolaeth *f*, bod yn fam.
mother-in-law *n* mam-yng-nghyfraith *f.*
motherly *adj* mamol.
motif *n* nodwedd *m*, motiff *m.*
motion *n* symudiad; cynnig *m.*
motionless *adj* disymud, llonydd.
motivation *n* ysgogiad, cymhelliad *m.*
motive *n* cymhelliad *m.*
motor *n* motor *m.*
motor vehicle *n* modur *m.*
motorbike *n* beic modur *m.*
motto *n* arwyddair *m.*
mould *n* mowld *m.* • *v* mowldio.
mound *n* twmpath *m.*
mount *n* mynydd *m.* • *v* dringo, esgyn.
mountain *n* mynydd *m.*
mountaineer *n* mynyddwr *m*, mynydd-wraig *f.*
mountainous *adj* mynyddig.
mourn *v* galaru.
mourning *n* galar *m.*
mouse *n* llygoden *f.*
moustache *n* mwstas *m.*

mouth *n* ceg *f.*
mouthful *n* cegaid, llond ceg *m.*
movable *adj* symudol, symudadwy.
move *v* symud. • *n* symudiad *m.*
movement *n* symudiad *m.*
moving *adj* gwefreiddiol, cyffrous.
mow *v* lladd, torri.
Mrs *n* Bns *f.*
much *adj* llawer.
mud *n* llaid, mwd *m.*
muddy *adj* mwdlyd.
multiple *n* lluosrif *m.*
multiplication *n* lluosi *vn.*
multiply *v* lluosi.
multitude *n* lliaws *m*, tyrfa *f.*
mumble *v* mwmian, mwmial.
munch *v* cnoi.
mundane *adj* cyffredin, dinod.
municipal *adj* bwrdeistrefol, trefol.
mural *n* murlun *m.*
murder *n* llofruddiaeth *f.* • *v* llofruddio.
murderer *n* llofruddiaeth *f.*
murky *adj* tywyll, lleidiog.
murmur *n* murmur, su *m.* • *v* sibrwd, suo.
muscle *n* cyhyr *m.*
muscular *adj* cyhyrog.
museum *n* amgueddfa *f.*
music *n* cerddoriaeth *f.*
musical *adj* cerddorol.
musician *n* cerddor *m.*
must *v* rhaid.
musty *adj* wedi llwydo.
mutate *v* treiglo.
mutation *n* treiglad *m.*
mute *adj* mud.
mutilate *v* llurgunio, difrodi.
mutilation *n* llurguniad *m.*
mutter *v* mwmian, dweud dan eich dannedd.
mutual *adj* eich gilydd, y naill a'r llall.
my *pron* fy.
myriad *n* myrdd *m.*
myself *pron* myfi fy hun.
mysterious *adj* rhyfedd, dirgel.
mystery *n* dirgelwch *m.*
myth *n* myth *m.*
mythology *n* mytholeg *f.*

N

nag *v* swnian, cadw sŵn.
nail *n* hoelen *f*, ewin *m.* • *v* hoelio.
naive *adj* diniwed.
naked *adj* noeth.
name *n* enw *m.* • *v* enwi.
nap *n* cyntun *m.*
nape *n* gwar *m/f*, gwegil *m.*
napkin *n* napcyn *m.*
narrate *v* adrodd, traethu.
narrative *n* traethiad, naratif *m.*
narrow *adj* cul, main.
nasty *adj* cas, brwnt.
nation *n* cenedl *f.*
national *adj* cenedlaethol.

nationalist *n* cenedlaetholwr *m*, cenedlaetholwraig *f*.
nationality *n* cenedligrwydd *m*.
native *adj* brodorol. • *n* brodor *m*, brodores *f*.
natural *adj* naturiol.
naturalist *n* naturiaethwr *m*, naturiaethwraig *f*.
nature *n* natur, anian *f*.
naughty *adj* drwg.
nausea *n* cyfog *m*.
nauseous *adj* cyfoglyd.
navel *n* bogail *m*.
navigate *v* mordwyo.
navigation *n* mordwyaeth *f*.
navy *n* llynges *f*.
near *prep*, *adv* yn agos. • *adj* agos.
nearly *adv* bron.
neat *adj* taclus, twt.
necessary *adj* angenrheidiol.
necessitate *v* gwneud yn angenrheidiol.
necessity *n* anghenraid, rheidrwydd *m*.
neck *n* gwddf *m*.
necklace *n* cadwyn am y gwddf *f*.
need *n* angen, eisiau *m*. • *v* bod ag angen.
needle *n* nodwydd *f*.
needy *adj* anghenus.
negation *n* nacâd *m*.
negative *adj* negyddol. • *n* negydd *m*.
neglect *v* esgeuluso. • *n* esgeulustra *m*.
negligence *n* esgeulustod *m*.
negligent *adj* esgeulus.
negotiate *v* trafod.
negotiation *n* trafodaeth *f*.
neighbour *n* cymydog *m*, cymdoges *f*.
neighbouring *adj* cyfagos.
neither *conj* na, nac.
nephew *n* nai *m*.
nerve *n* nerf *f/m*.
nervous *adj* nerfus, ar binnau.
nest *n* nyth *m/f*.
net *n* rhwyd *f*.
netball *n* pêl-rwyd *f*.
nettle *n* danhadlen *f*.
network *n* rhwydwaith *m*.
neutral *adj* niwtral.
neutrality *n* niwtraliaeth *f*.
never *adv* byth, erioed.
nevertheless *adv* serch hynny.
new *adj* newydd.
newborn *adj* newydd-anedig.
news *n* newyddion *pl*.
newspaper *n* papur newydd *m*.
New Year *n* Blwyddyn Newydd *m*; **~'s Day** *n* Dydd Calan *m*; **~'s Eve** Nos Galan *f*.
next *adj* nesaf, wedyn.
nibble *v* deintio, cnoi.
nice *adj* dymunol, hyfryd.
niche *n* cilfach *f*.
nickname *n* llysenw *m*. • *v* llysenwi.
niece *n* nith *f*.
night *n* nos, noson *f*; **good** ~ nos da.
nightly *adv* beunos. • *adj* nosol.
nightmare *n* hunllef *f*.
nimble *adj* chwim, heini.
nine *num* naw.
nineteen *num* pedwar ar bymtheg *m*, pedair ar bymtheg *f*.

nineteenth *adj* pedwerydd (*m*)/pedwaredd (*f*) ar bymtheg.
ninetieth *adj* naw degfed.
ninety *num* naw deg.
ninth *adj* nawfed.
no *adv* na, ni. • *adj* dim.
noble *adj* bonheddig, urddasol.
nobody *pron* neb.
nocturnal *adj* nosol.
nod *n* amnaid *f*. • *v* amneidio.
noise *n* sŵn, twrw *m*.
noisiness *n* sŵn, twrw *m*.
nominal *adj* mewn enw.
nominate *v* enwebu, cynnig enw.
nomination *n* enwebiad *m*.
nonchalant *adj* didaro.
none *pron* dim un.
nonentity *n* neb o bwys *m*.
nonetheless *adv* serch hynny.
nonplussed *adj* syn, syfrdan.
nonsense *n* dwli *m*, lol *f*, ffwlbri *m*.
nonsensical *adj* gwirion, hurt.
nonstop *adj* dibaid, syth.
noon *n* canol dydd, hanner dydd *m*.
nor *conj* na, nac.
normal *adj* arferol, rheolaidd.
north *n* gogledd *m*.
northeast *n* gogledd-ddwyrain *m*.
northern *adj* gogleddol.
northwest *n* gogledd-orllewin *m*.
nose *n* trwyn *m*.
nostalgia *n* hiraeth *m*.
nostril *n* ffroen *f*.
not *adv* heb, na, nad, ni, nid.
notable *adj* nodedig, hynod.
note *n* nodyn *m*. • *v* nodi.
notebook *n* llyfr nodiadau *m*.
nothing *n* dim byd *m*.
notice *n* hysbysiad *m*. • *v* sylwi.
noticeable *adj* amlwg.
notify *v* hysbysu, rhoi gwybod.
notion *n* syniad, amcan *m*.
notoriety *n* enwogrwydd *m*.
notorious *adj* ag enw drwg.
nourish *v* meithrin.
nourishment *n* maeth *m*.
novel *n* nofel *f*.
novelty *n* newyddbeth *m*.
November *n* Tachwedd *m*.
novice *n* newyddian *m/f*.
now *adv* yn awr.
nowadays *adv* heddiw, y dyddiau hyn.
nowhere *adv* yn unman.
nuance *n* arlliw *m*.
nuclear *adj* niwclear.
nude *adj* noethlymun.
nudity *n* noethni *m*.
nuisance *n* digon o farn, poendod *m*.
numb *adj* dideimlad. • *v* merwino, fferru.
number *n* rhif *m*, nifer *m/f*. • *v* cyfrif, rhifo.
numbness *n* merwindod, diffyg teimlad *m*.
numeral *n* rhifol *m*.
numerical *adj* rhifol.
nurse *n* nyrs *f/m*. • *v* nyrsio.
nursery *n* meithrinfa *f*.
nurture *v* meithrin, magu.
nut *n* cneuen *f*.
nutritious *adj* maethlon.
nylon *n* neilon *m*.

O

oak *n* derwen *f.*
oar *n* rhwyf *f.*
oath *n* llw *m.*
obedience *n* ufudd-dod *m.*
obedient *adj* ufudd.
obese *adj* tew iawn.
obesity *n* tewdra *m.*
obey *v* ufuddhau.
object *n* gwrthrych *m.* • *v* gwrthwynebu.
objection *n* gwrthwynebiad *m.*
objective *adj* gwrthrychol.
obligation *n* gorfodaeth *f*, rheidrwydd *m.*
obligatory *adj* gorfodol.
oblige *v* gorfodi; gwneud tro da.
obliging *adj* cymwynasgar.
oblique *adj* lletraws, ar osgo.
oblivious *adj* heb sylwi.
obnoxious *adj* ffiaidd.
obscene *adj* anweddus.
obscure *adj* aneglur, tywyll. • *v* cuddio, tywyllu.
obscurity *n* dinodedd, tywyllwch *m.*
observant *adj* sylwgar.
observation *n* sylw *m.*
observatory *n* arsyllfa *f.*
observe *v* cadw; gwylio.
obsession *n* obsesiwn *n.*
obsessive *adj* obsesiynol.
obsolete *adj* wedi hen ddarfod.
obstacle *n* rhwystr *m.*
obstinate *adj* ystyfnig, pengaled.
obstruct *v* rhwystro, cau.
obstruction *n* rhwystr *m*, tagfa *f.*
obtain *v* cael, ennill.
obtainable *adj* ar gael.
obvious *adj* amlwg.
occasion *n* achlysur *m.* • *v* achosi.
occasional *adj* achlysurol.
occupant *n* deiliad *m.*
occupation *n* gwaith *m*; deiliadaeth *f.*
occupy *v* meddiannu.
occur *v* digwydd, taro.
occurrence *n* digwyddiad *m.*
ocean *n* cefnfor *m.*
oceanic *adj* cefnforol.
October *n* Hydref *m.*
odd *adj* od, rhyfedd.
odious *adj* ffiaidd, anghynnes.
odour *n* aroglau, oglau *m.*
of *prep* o.
off *adv* ymaith, i ffwrdd.
offence *n* trosedd *m/f.*
offend *v* pechu, tramgwyddo.
offensive *adj* ymosodol; sarhaus.
offer *v* cynnig. • *n* cynnig *m.*
office *n* swyddfa *f.*
officer *n* swyddog *m.*
official *adj* swyddogol.
officiate *v* gweinyddu, gweinidogaethu.
offset *v* gwrthbwyso.
offshore *adj* ar y môr.

offspring *n* epil *pl*, hil *f*.
oil *n* olew *m*. • *v* iro.
oil painting *n* darlun olew *m*.
oil tanker *n* tancer olew *m/f*.
ointment *n* eli *m*.
O.K. *excl* iawn, i'r dim.
old *adj* hen.
old age *n* henaint *m*.
olive *n* ffrwyth yr olewydd *m*.
olive oil *n* olew olewydd *m*.
omelette *n* omled *m/f*.
omission *n* hepgoriad, esgeulustod *m*.
omit *v* gadael allan.
on *prep* ar. • *adv* ymlaen.
once *adv* unwaith.
one *num* un.
onerous *adj* beichus, trwm.
one-sided *adj* unochrog.
onion *n* wynionyn *m*.
onlooker *n* gwyliwr *m*.
only *adj* unig. • *adv* dim ond, yn unig.
onus *n* cyfrifoldeb *m*.
opaque *adj* afloyw, didraidd.
open *adj* agored. • *v* agor.
opening *n* agoriad *m*.
openness *n* natur agored *f*.
opera *n* opera *f*.
operate *v* gweithio, gweithredu.
operation *n* llawdriniaeth *f*, gweithrediad *m*.
operator *n* gweithiwr, gweithredwr *m*.
opine *v* barnu, tybio.
opinion *n* barn *f*.
opinion poll *n* pôl piniwn, arolwg barn *m*.
opponent *n* gwrthwynebydd *m*.
opportune *adj* amserol, cyfleus.
opportunity *n* cyfle *m*.
oppose *v* gwrthwynebu.
opposing *adj* gwrthwynebus.
opposite *adj* cyferbyn.
opposition *n* gwrthwynebiad *m*.
oppress *v* gormesu.
oppressive *adj* gormesol.
optimist *n* optimydd *m*.
optimistic *adj* optimistaidd, ffyddiog.
optimum *adj* gorau posibl.
option *n* dewis *m*.
optional *adj* dewisol.
opulent *adj* cyfoethog, godidog.
or *conj* neu.
oral *adj* llafar, geneuol.
orange *n* oren *m*.
orbit *n* cylchdro *m*.
orchestra *n* cerddorfa *f*.
ordain *v* ordeinio.
order *n* gorchymyn *m*; trefn *f*. • *v* gorchymyn.
orderly *adj* trefnus.
ordinary *adj* cyffredin.
ore *n* mwyn *m*.
organ *n* organ *f*.
organic *adj* organaidd.
organisation *n* mudiad *m*; trefnu *vn*.
organise *v* trefnu.
organism *n* organedd *m*.
oriental *adj* dwyreiniol.
orifice *n* twll *m*.
origin *n* dechreuad, tarddiad *m*.
original *adj* gwreiddiol.
originality *n* gwreiddioldeb *m*.

ornament *n* addurn *m*.
ornate *adj* addurnedig.
orphan *adj* amddifad.
orthodox *adj* uniongred.
oscillate *v* pendilio.
other *pron* arall, llall, amgen.
otherwise *adv* fel arall.
our *pron* ein.
ourselves *pron* ein hunain.
out *adv* allan, maes.
outburst *n* ffrwydrad *m*.
outcome *n* canlyniad *m*.
outdo *v* rhagori ar.
outdoor *adj* awyr agored, allanol.
outer *adj* allanol.
outfit *n* dillad *pl*.
outgoing *adj* ymadawol; rhadlon.
outlay *n* gwariant *m*; traul *f*.
outline *n* amlinelliad, braslun *m*.
outlook *n* rhagolwg *m*.
output *n* allgynnyrch *m*.
outrage *n* gwarth *m*. • *v* gwylltio, cythruddo.
outright *adv* yn llwyr; yn syth. • *adj* llwyr.
outset *n* dechrau *m*.
outside *n adv* tu allan.
outstrip *v* trechu.
oval *adj* hirgrwn.
ovary *n* ofari *m/f*.
oven *n* ffwrn *f*, popty *m*.
over *prep* uwch, dros. • *adj* gor, rhy.
overall *adj* at ei gilydd.
overbalance *v* cwympo drososdd.
overcast *adj* cymylog.
overcharge *v* codi gormod.
overcoat *n* cot fawr *f*.
overcome *v* goresgyn, trechu.
overdo *v* gorwneud.
overdraft *n* gorddrafft *m*.
overdue *adj* hwyr.
overestimate *v* goramcangyfrif.
overflow *v* gorlifo. • *n* gorlifiad *m*.
overhaul *n* archwiliad *m*, atgyweirio *vn*.
overland *adj* traws gwlad.
overlap *v* gorgyffwrdd.
overlook *v* edrych dros; esgeuluso.
overnight *adv* dros nos.
overpower *v* trechu.
overrate *v* gorbrisio, gorganmol.
overrun *v* heidio.
overseas *adv* dramor.
oversee *v* goruchwylio.
oversight *n* amryfusedd *m*; arolygiaeth *f*.
oversleep *v* cysgu'n hwyr.
overtake *v* goddiweddyd.
overthrow *v* dymchwel.
overtime *n* goramser *m*, oriau ychwanegol *pl*.
overturn *v* dymchwel, moelyd.
overwhelm *v* llethu, sathru.
overwhelming *adj* llethol, anorthrech.
overwork *v* gorweithio.
owe *v* mae ar.
owing *adj* dyledus; oherwydd.
owl *n* tylluan *f*.
own *adj* hunan. • *v* meddu, piau.
owner *n* perchennog *m*.
ox *n* ych *m*.
oxygen *n* ocsygen *m*.
oyster *n* wystrysen *f*.
ozone *n* osôn *m*.

P

pace *n* cam *m.* • *v* camu.
pacific *adj* heddychlon, heddychol.
pacification *n* tawelu, llonyddu *vn.*
pacify *v* tawelu, gwastrodi.
pack *n* pecyn *m.* • *v* pacio.
package *n* pecyn *m.*
packet *n* paced *m.*
pact *n* cyfamod, cytundeb *m.*
pad *n* pad *m.*
paddle *v* padlo. • *n* padlen, rhodl *f.*
pagan *adj* paganaidd.
page *n* tudalen *m/f*; macwy *m.*
pail *n* bwced *m/f.*
pain *n* poen *m/f*, dolur *m.* • *v* brifo.
pained *adj* poenus, pryderus.
painful *adj* poenus.
painstaking *adj* gofalus, dyfal.
paint *v* peintio.
painter *n* peintiwr *m*, peintwraig *f.*
painting *n* peintiad, llun *m.*
pair *n* pâr *m.*
palatable *adj* blasus.
palate *n* taflod y genau *f.*
pale *adj* gwelw, llwyd.
palette *n* paled *m.*
pallet *n* gwely gwellt *m.*
pallid *adj* gwelw, llwyd.
palpable *adj* cyffyrddadwy; eglur.
palpitation *n* dychlamiad y galon *m.*
pamper *v* mwytho, maldodi.
pamphlet *n* pamffledyn, llyfryn *m.*
pan *n* padell *f.*
panache *n* steil *m.*
pane *n* cwarel, paen *m.*
panel *n* panel *m.*
pang *n* gwayw *f.*
panic *v* gwylltio, gwylltu.
pant *v* dyhefod, peuo.
panther *n* panther *m.*
pantry *n* pantri *m.*
pants *n* trôns *pl.*
paper *n* papur *m.* • *v* papuro.
paperweight *n* pwysau papur *m.*
par *n* cyfartaledd *m.* • *adj* cyfartal.
parachute *n* parasiwt *m.*
parade *n* sioe, gorymdaith *f.*
paradise *n* paradwys *f.*
paradox *n* paradocs *m.*
paragraph *n* paragraff *m.*
parallel *adj* cyfochrog . • *n* cyflin *f.*
paralyse *v* parlysu.
paralysis *n* parlys *m.*
paramount *adj* goruchaf, pennaf.
paranoid *adj* paranoiaidd.
parasite *n* parasit *m.*
parcel *n* parsel *m.* • *v* parselu.
parch *v* crasu, sychu.
pardon *n* maddeuant *m.* • *v* maddau.
parent *n* rhiant *m*; **~s** rhieni *pl.*
park *n* parc *m.* • *v* parcio.
parking lot *n* maes parcio *m.*
parliament *n* senedd *f.*
parody *n* parodi *m/f.* • *v* paraďïo.
parry *v* troi naill ochr.

part *n* rhan *f.* • *v* gwahanu, rhannu. • **~ly** *adv* yn rhannol.
partial *adj* rhannol; pleidiol.
participate *v* cyfranogi, cymryd rhan.
participation *n* cyfranogiad *m.*
particle *n* gronyn; geiryn *m.*
particular *adj* arbennig, neilltuol.
partition *n* pared, palis *m.* • *v* rhannu.
partner *n* cymar *m/f.*
party *n* plaid *f*; parti *m.*
pass *v* pasio. • *n* bwlch *m.*
passage *n* tramwyfa, rhodfa *f.*
passenger *n* teithiwr *m*, teithwraig *f.*
passer-by *n* un sy'n mynd heibio.
passion *n* angerdd *m*, nwyd *m/f.*
passionate *adj* angerddol.
passive *adj* goddefol.
passport *n* trwydded deithio *f*, pasport *m.*
past *adj* cynt. • *n* gorffennol *m.* • *prep* wedi.
paste *n* past *m.* • *v* pastio.
pastime *n* difyrrwch *m.*
pastry *n* toes *m.*
pasture *n* porfa *f.*
patch *n* clwt *m.* • *v* clytio.
patent *adj* amlwg. • *n* breinlen *f*, patent *m.* • *v* rhoi patent ar.
paternal *adj* tadol.
paternity *n* tadogaeth *f.*
path *n* llwybr *m.*
pathetic *adj* truenus, pathetig.
patience *n* amynedd *m/f.*
patient *adj* amyneddgar. • *n* claf *m.*
patrol *v* patrolio.
patron *n* noddwr *m*, noddwraig *f.*
patronise *v* noddi; bod yn nawddogol.
pattern *n* patrwm *m.*
pause *n* saib *m.* • *v* oedi, gorffwys.
pave *v* palmantu.
pavement *n* palmant, pafin *m.*
paw *n* pawen *f.* • *v* pawennu.
pay *n* cyflog *m.* • *v* talu; **to ~ back** ad-dalu.
payable *adj* taladwy, dyledus.
payment *n* tâl *m.*
pea *n* pysen *f.*
peace *n* heddwch *m*, tangnefedd *m/f.*
peaceful *adj* heddychol, heddychlon, distaw.
peak *n* pig *m/f*, brig *m.*
pear *n* gellygen, peren *f.*
pearl *n* perl *m.*
peasant *n* gwladwr *m.*
pebble *n* cerigyn *m.*
peculiar *adj* hynod.
peculiarity *n* hynodrwydd *m*; nodwedd *f.*
pedal *n* pedal *m.* • *v* pedlo.
pedestrian *n* cerddwr *m.* • *adj* ar draed, pedestraidd.
peel *v* crafu, plicio. • *n* croen, pil *m.*
peer *n* cymar *m.*
peerless *adj* digymar.
pelt *n* croen *m.*
pen *n* pin ysgrifennu *m*; corlan *f.*
penalty *n* cosb *f.*
pencil *n* pensel, pensil *f.*
pendulum *n* pendil *m.*
penetrate *v* treiddio.
peninsula *n* gorynys *f*, penrhyn *m.*

penitentiary *n* carchar *m*.
penknife *n* cyllell boced *f*.
penpal *n* cyfaill drwy'r post *m*.
pension *n* pensiwn *m*. • *v* pensiynu.
pensive *adj* meddylgar.
penultimate *adj* cynderfynol, olaf ond un.
people *n* pobl *f*. • *v* poblogi.
pepper *n* pupur *m*. • *v* pupro.
per annum *adv* y flwyddyn.
perceive *v* canfod.
percentage *n* canran *f*.
perception *n* dirnadaeth *f*.
perch *n* clwyd *f*.
percussion *n* taro *vn*; offerynnau taro *pl*.
perdition *n* colledigaeth *f*, difancoll *m*.
perennial *adj* lluosflwydd.
perfect *adj* perffaith. • *v* perffeithio.
perfection *n* perffeithrwydd *m*.
perform *v* perfformio, chwarae.
performance *n* perfformiad *m*.
performer *n* perfformiwr, chwaraewr *m*.
perfume *n* persawr *m*. • *v* perarogli.
perhaps *adv* efallai, hwyrach.
peril *n* perygl *m*.
perilous *adj* peryglus.
perimeter *n* perimedr; terfyn allanol *m*.
period *n* cyfnod *m*.
periodic *adj* cyfnodol.
perish *v* marw, trengi.
perishable *adj* darfodus, byrhoedlog.
permanent *adj* parhaol.
permissible *adj* caniataol, goddefadwy.
permission *n* caniatâd *m*.
permissive *adj* goddefgar.
permit *v* caniatáu. • *n* trwydded, haw-len *f*.
perpetrate *v* bod yn gyfrifol, cyflawni.
perpetual *adj* parhaol, parhaus.
perplex *v* drysu, mwydro.
persecute *v* erlid.
persecution *n* erledigaeth *f*.
persevere *v* dyfalbarhau, dal ati.
persist *v* dyfalbarhau, dal ati.
persistence *n* dyfalbarhad *m*.
persistent *adj* dyfal.
person *n* rhywun *m*.
personage *n* rhywun pwysig *m*.
personal *adv* personol.
personality *n* personoliaeth *f*.
personnel *n* personél *m*.
perspective *n* persbectif *m*.
perspiration *n* chwys *m*.
perspire *v* chwysu.
persuade *v* darbwyllo, perswadio.
persuasion *n* perswâd *m*.
persuasive *adj* yn dwyn perswâd.
pertaining: ~ **to** *prep* parthed, ynglŷn â.
pertinent *adj* perthnasol.
perturb *v* aflonyddu, tarfu.
peruse *v* darllen, craffu ar.
perverse *adj* gwrthnysig, croes.
pessimist *n* pesimist *m/f*.
pest *n* pla; poendod *m*.
pester *v* plagio, poeni.
pestilence *n* pla *m*, haint *m/f*.
pet *n* anifail anwes *m*.

petal *n* petal *m.*
petition *n* deiseb *f.*
petticoat *n* pais *f.*
pettiness *n* bychander, bychandra *m.*
petty *adj* mân, pitw.
phantom *n* drychiolaeth *f*, ysbryd *m.*
pharmacist *n* fferyllydd *m.*
pharmacy *n* fferyllfa *f.*
phase *n* cyfnod *m.*
phenomenal *adj* gwyrthiol.
phenomenon *n* ffenomen *f*, rhyfeddod *m.*
philosopher *n* athronydd *m.*
philosophical *adj* athronyddol.
philosophise *v* athronyddu.
philosophy *n* athroniaeth *f.*
phobia *n* ffobia *m.*
phone *n* ffôn *m.* • *v* ffonio.
phone book *n* llyfr ffôn *m.*
phone call *n* galwad ffôn *m.*
photograph *n* ffotograff *m.* • *v* tynnu llun.
photographer *n* tynnwr lluniau, ffotograffydd *m.*
photography *n* ffotograffiaeth *f.*
phrase *n* ymadrodd *m.* • *v* mynegi, geirio.
phrase book *n* llyfr ymadrodion *m.*
physical *adj* corfforol.
physician *n* meddyg *m.*
physicist *n* ffisegydd *m.*
physiotherapy *n* ffisiotherapi *m.*
physique *n* corffolaeth *f.*
pianist *n* pianydd *m.*
piano *n* piano *m.*
pick *v* pigo, dewis. • *n* y gorau *m.*
picnic *n* picnic *m.*
pictorial *adj* darluniadol.
picture *n* llun, darlun *m.* • *v* darlunio, dychmygu.
pie *n* pastai *f.*
piece *n* darn *m.*
pierce *v* gwanu, trywanu.
piercing *adj* treiddgar.
pig *n* mochyn *m.*
pigeon *n* colomen *f.*
pile *n* twmpath, pentwr *m.* • *v* pentyrru.
pilgrim *n* pererin *m.*
pill *n* pilsen *f.*
pillar *n* piler *m*, colofn *f.*
pillow *n* clustog *f*, gobennydd *m.*
pilot *n* peilot *m.* • *v* llywio.
pin *n* pin *m.* • *v* pinio.
pincers *n* pinsiwrn *m.*
pine *n* pinwydden *f.* • *v* hiraethu.
pineapple *n* pinafal *m.*
pink *adj* pinc.
pint *n* peint *m.*
pioneer *n* arloeswr *m*, arloeswraig *f.*
pious *adj* duwiol.
pipe *n* pibell *f*, pib *m.*
pipeline *n* piblin *m.*
piracy *n* môr-ladrad *m.*
pirate *n* môr-leidr *m.*
pistol *n* pistol *m.*
pitcher *n* piser *m.*
pitiable *adj* truenus, gresynus.
pitiful *adj* truenus.
pity *n* tosturi *m.* • *v* tosturio wrth.
placard *n* placard *m.*
placate *v* tawelu.
place *n* lle *m.* • *v* lleoli.

placid *adj* llonydd, tawel.
plague *n* pla *m*. • *v* plagio, poeni.
plain *adj* plaen, moel. • *n* gwastadedd *m*.
plait *n* pleth *f*, plethyn *m*. • *v* plethu.
plan *n* cynllun *m*. • *v* cynllunio.
plane *n* plân *m*. • *v* plaenio.
planet *n* planed *f*.
plank *n* astell, ystyllen *f*.
planner *n* cynlluniwr *m*.
plant *n* llysieuyn, planhigyn *m*. • *v* plannu.
plantation *n* planhigfa *f*.
plaster *n* plastr *m*. • *v* plastro.
plastic *adj* plastig.
plate *n* plât *m*.
platform *n* platfform *m*.
platter *n* dysgl *f*.
plausible *adj* credadwy.
play *n* drama *f*. • *v* chwarae.
player *n* chwaraewr *m*, chwaraewraig *f*.
playful *adj* chwareus.
playwright *n* dramodydd *m*.
plea *n* deisyfiad *m*, apêl *m/f*.
plead *v* pledio, erfyn.
pleasant *adj* hyfryd, dymunol.
please *v* rhyngu bodd, plesio.
pleased *adj* bodlon, balch.
pleasure *n* pleser, mwynhad *m*.
pledge *n* ernes *f*, addewid *m/f*. • *v* addo.
plentiful *adj* helaeth, toreithiog.
plenty *n* digon, digonedd *m*.
pliable *adj* hyblyg, ystwyth.
pliers *n* gefelen *f*.
plot *n* llain *f*, plot *m*. • *v* plotio.
plough *n* aradr *m/f*. • *v* aredig.
pluck *v* tynnu, plycio. • *n* dewrder, plwc *m*.
plug *n* plwg *m*. • *v* plwgio.
plumber *n* plymer *m*.
plump *adj* llond eich croen.
plunge *v* plymio.
plural *adj* lluosog.
plus *n* plws *m*.
pneumonia *n* llid yr ysgyfaint, niwmonia *m*.
poach *v* potsio, herwhela.
poacher *n* potsiwr *m*.
pocket *n* poced *f*. • *v* pocedu.
poem *n* cerdd *f*.
poet *n* bardd *m*.
poetry *n* barddoniaeth *f*.
poignant *adj* dwys, ingol.
point *n* pwynt *m*. • *v* pwyntio.
pointed *adj* miniog.
poise *n* ymarweddiad *m*.
poison *n* gwenwyn *m*. • *v* gwenwyno.
poisonous *adj* gwenwynig, gwenwyn-llyd.
poke *v* gwthio, procio.
poker-faced *adj* difynegiant.
pole *n* polyn; pegwn *m*.
police *n* heddlu *m*.
police officer *n* heddwas, plismon *m*, plismones *f*.
police station *n* swyddfa'r heddlu *f*.
policy *n* polisi *m*.
polish *v* gloywi, caboli.
polished *adj* caboledig, gloyw.
polite *adj* boneddigaidd.
politeness *n* boneddigeiddrwydd *m*.
political *adj* gwleidyddol.
politician *n* gwleidydd *m*.

politics *n* gwleidyddiaeth *f.*
pollute *v* llygru.
pollution *n* llygredd *m.*
pompous *adj* mawreddog.
pond *n* pwll *m.*
ponder *v* ystyried.
pony *n* merlyn *m*, poni *m/f.*
pool *n* pwll *m.*
poor *adj* tlawd, truan.
populace *n* poblogaeth *f.*
popular *adj* poblogaidd.
popularity *n* poblogrwydd *m.*
populate *v* poblogi.
population *n* poblogaeth *f.*
porch *n* porth, cyntedd *m.*
pork *n* porc, cig mochyn *m.*
port *n* porthladd *m.*
portable *adj* cludadwy.
portion *n* rhan, cyfran *f.*
portrait *n* portread, darlun *m.*
portray *v* portreadu, darlunio.
pose *n* ystum *m/f.*
position *n* ystum *m/f*, safle *m.*
positive *adj* cadarnhaol, pendant.
possess *v* meddu, perchenogi.
possession *n* meddiant *m*, perchenogaeth *f.*
possibility *n* posibilrwydd *m.*
possible *adj* posibl.
post *n* post *m.*
postage stamp *n* stamp post *m.*
postcard *n* cerdyn post *m.*
poster *n* poster *m.*
posterior *n* pen-ôl *m.*
posthumous *adj* ar ôl marwolaeth.
postman *n* postmon *m.*
post office *n* llythyrdy *m*, swyddfa bost *f.*
postpone *v* gohirio.
potion *n* dogn *m.*
pouch *n* cod *f*, cwdyn *m.*
poultry *n* dofednod *pl.*
pound *n* punt *f*; pwys *m.* • *v* pwyo, pwnio.
pour *v* arllwys, tywallt.
poverty *n* tlodi *m.*
powder *n* powdr, powdwr *m.* • *v* powdro.
powdery *adj* fel powdr mân.
power *n* gallu, grym *m.*
powerful *adj* grymus.
powerless *adj* di-rym.
practicable *adj* ymarferol, posibl.
practical *adj* ymarferol.
practicality *n* ymarferoldeb *m.*
practice *n* ymarfer, arfer *m/f.*
practise *v* ymarfer.
pragmatic *adj* pragmataidd.
praise *n* canmoliaeth *f.*
prance *v* prancio.
prattle *v* clebran, clepian.
prawn *n* corgimwch *m.*
pray *v* gweddïo.
prayer *n* gweddi *f.*
preach *v* pregethu.
preacher *n* pregethwr *m.*
precarious *adj* ansicr.
precaution *n* gofal, rhagofal *m.*
precede *v* rhagflaenu.
precedent *n* cynsail *m/f.*
precinct *n* canolfan siopa *m/f.*
precious *adj* gwerthfawr.
precipitate *v* ysgogi, bwrw. • *adj* brysiog.
precise *adj* manwl.
precision *n* manwl gywirdeb *m.*

precocious *adj* henaidd.
preconceive *v* rhagdybio.
preconception *n* rhagdybiaeth *f.*
predator *n* rheibiwr *m.*
predecessor *n* rhagflaenydd *m.*
predict *v* darogan, proffwydo.
predictable *adj* rhagweladwy.
prediction *n* proffwydoliaeth *f.*
predominant *adj* mwyaf, pennaf.
predominate *v* tra-arglwyddiaethu.
preface *n* rhagair *m.*
prefer *v* bod yn well gan, ffafrio.
preferable *adj* gwell.
preference *n* ffafriaeth *f.*
preferential *adj* ffafriol.
prefix *n* rhagddodiad *m.*
pregnancy *n* beichiogrwydd *m.*
pregnant *adj* beichiog.
prehistoric *adj* cynhanesyddol.
prejudice *n* rhagfarn *f.* • *v* niweidio.
prejudiced *adj* rhagfarnllyd.
prejudicial *adj* niweidiol.
preliminary *adj* rhagarweiniol.
premature *adj* cynamserol, annhymig.
premeditated *adj* bwriadol.
premises *n* adeilad *m/f*, tŷ *m.*
premium *n* premiwm *m.*
premonition *n* rhagrybudd *m.*
preparation *n* paratoad *m.*
preparatory *adj* rhagbaratoawl.
prepare *v* paratoi.
preposterous *adj* hurt, chwerthinllyd.
prerogative *n* braint *f.*
prescription *n* presgripsiwn *m.*
presence *n* presenoldeb *m.*
present *n* anrheg, rhodd *f.* • *adj* presennol. • *v* cyflwyno.
presentable *adj* cymeradwy, taclus.
presenter *n* cyflwynydd *m.*
preservation *n* cadwraeth *f.*
preservator *n* cadwriaethwr *m*, cadwriaethwraig *f.*
preserve *v* cadw; cyffeithio. • *n* cy-ffaith, jam *m.*
preside *v* llywyddu.
president *n* llywydd *m.*
press *v* gwasgu. • *n* gwasg *f.*
pressure *n* pwysau, pwysedd, gwasgedd *m.*
prestige *n* bri *m.*
presumable *adj* tebygol.
presume *v* tybio, rhagdybio.
presumption *n* tybiaeth *f.*
pretence *n* esgus *m.*
pretend *v* cymryd arnoch.
pretext *n* esgus *m.*
pretty *adj* pert, del.
prevail *v* darbwyllo.
prevalent *adj* cyffredin.
prevent *v* rhwystro, atal.
prevention *n* rhwystro, atal *vn.*
previous *adj* blaenorol, cynt.
prey *n* ysglyfaeth *f.*
price *n* pris *m.*
prick *v* pigo.
pride *n* balchder *m.*
priest *n* offeiriad *m.*
priesthood *n* offeiriadaeth *f.*
primacy *n* blaenoriaeth *f.*
primarily *adv* yn bennaf.
primary *adj* cynradd, cychwynnol.
primate *n* primat *m.*

prime *n* anterth *m.* • *adj* prif.
prime minister *n* prif weinidog *m.*
primitive *adj* cyntefig.
prince *n* tywysog *m.*
princess *n* tywysoges *f.*
principal *adj* prif. • *n* pennaeth *m.*
principle *n* egwyddor *m.*
print *v* argraffu. • *n* ôl; print *m.*
printer *n* argraffwr, argraffydd *m.*
prior *adj* cynharach, cynt.
priority *n* blaenoriaeth *f.*
prison *n* carchar *m.*
prisoner *n* carcharor *m.*
privacy *n* preifatrwydd *m.*
private *adj* preifat.
privilege *n* braint *f.*
prize *n* gwobr *f.* • *v* gwerthfawrogi.
pro *prep* o blaid.
probability *n* tebyg, tebygolrwydd *m.*
probable *adj* tebygol, tebyg.
probation *n* profiannaeth *f.*
probationary *adj* ar brawf.
probe *n* chwiliedydd *m.* • *v* chwilio.
problem *n* problem *f.*
problematical *adj* amheus, problematig.
procedure *n* trefn *f,* dull o weithredu *m.*
proceed *v* mynd ymlaen.
process *n* proses *f.*
procession *n* gorymdaith *f.*
proclaim *v* datgan, cyhoeddi.
proclamation *n* datganiad, cyhoeddiad *m.*
procure *v* cael, sicrhau.
procurement *n* caffaeliad *m.*
prod *v* procio.
prodigious *adj* aruthrol.
prodigy *n* rhyfeddod *m.*
produce *v* cynhyrchu.
producer *n* cynhyrchydd *m.*
product *n* cynnyrch *m.*
production *n* cynhyrchiad *m.*
productive *adj* cynhyrchiol.
profess *v* proffesu.
profession *n* galwedigaeth *f,* proffesiwn *m.*
professional *adj* proffesiynol.
professor *n* athro *m.*
proficiency *n* gallu, medr *m.*
proficient *adj* hyddysg; rhugl.
profile *n* amlinell *f,* proffil *m.*
profit *n* elw *m.* • *v* elwa.
profitability *n* proffidioldeb *m.*
profitable *adj* proffidiol.
profound *adj* dwfn.
program(me) *n* rhaglen *f.*
programmer *n* rhaglennwr, rhaglennydd *m.*
progress *n* hynt, cwrs *m.* • *v* mynd yn eich blaen.
progression *n* dilyniant, symudiad *m.*
progressive *adj* blaengar; cynyddol.
prohibit *v* gwahardd.
project *v* taflu, taflunio. • *n* cywaith *m.*
projection *n* tafluniad *m.*
prolific *adj* toreithiog.
prolong *v* hwyhau.
promenade *n* rhodfa *f.*
prominence *n* amlygrwydd *m.*
prominent *adj* amlwg.

promise *n* addewid *m/f.* • *v* addo.
promising *adj* addawol.
promote *v* dyrchafu; hyrwyddo.
promoter *n* hyrwyddwr *m.*
promotion *n* dyrchafiad *m.*
prompt *adj* prydlon, diymdroi. • *v* procio cof.
prone *adj* wyneb i waered; chwannog.
pronounce *v* datgan; ynganu.
pronounced *adj* pendant, amlwg.
pronouncement *n* datganiad *m.*
pronunciation *n* ynganiad, cynaniad *m.*
proof *n* prawf *m.*
prop *v* pwyso yn erbyn. • *n* prop *m,* ateg *f.*
propaganda *n* propaganda *m.*
propel *v* gyrru, gwthio ymlaen.
propeller *n* sgriw yrru *f.*
propensity *n* tuedd *f,* tueddiad *m.*
proper *adj* go iawn, priodol.
property *n* eiddo *m*; priodoledd *f.*
prophecy *n* proffwydoliaeth *f.*
prophet *n* proffwyd *m,* proffwydes *f.*
proportion *n* rhan, cyfran *f.*
proportional *adj* cyfrannol, cymesurol.
proposal *n* cynnig *m.*
propose *v* cynnig *m.*
proposition *n* cynnig, cynigiad *m.*
proprietor *n* perchen, perchennog *m.*
prosecute *v* erlyn.
prosecution *n* erlyniad *m.*
prospect *n* rhagolwg *m.* • *v* chwilota.
prospective *adj* arfaethedig.
prosper *v* ffynnu.
prosperity *n* ffyniant *m.*
prosperous *adj* ffyniannus, llewyrchus.
prostitute *n* putain *f.*
protagonist *n* prif gymeriad *m.*
protect *v* amddiffyn, gwarchod.
protection *n* amddiffyniad *m.*
protective *adj* amddiffynnol, gwarch-eidiol.
protein *n* protein *m.*
protest *v* gwrthdystio, protestio. • *n* gwrthdystiad *m,* protest *f.*
Protestant *n* Protestant *m.*
protester *n* gwrthdystiwr *m,* gwrthdystwraig *f.*
prototype *n* cynddelw *f.*
proud *adj* balch.
prove *v* profi.
proverb *n* dihareb *f.*
provide *v* darparu.
providence *n* rhagluniaeth *f.*
province *n* talaith *f.*
provincial *adj* taleithiol.
provision *n* darpariaeth *f.*
provisional *adj* dros dro.
provocation *n* cythrudd, achos.
provocative *adj* pryfoclyd.
provoke *v* cythruddo, pryfocio.
prowess *n* medrusrwydd *m.*
prowl *v* prowlan.
prowler *n* llerciwr *m.*
proximity *n* agosrwydd *m.*
prudence *n* pwyll, gofal *m.*
prudent *adj* darbodus, gofalus.
pry *v* busnesa.
pseudonym *n* ffugenw *m.*

psychiatric *adj* seiciatrig, seiciatraidd.
psychiatrist *n* seiciatrydd *m.*
psychic *adj* seicig.
psychoanalyst *n* seicdreiddiwr *m.*
psychologist *n* seicolegydd *m.*
psychology *n* seicoleg *f.*
puberty *n* oed aeddfedrwydd *m.*
public *adj* cyhoeddus. • *n* y cyhoedd *m.*
publication *n* cyhoeddiad *m.*
publicity *n* cyhoeddusrwydd *m.*
publish *v* cyhoeddi.
publisher *n* cyhoeddwr *m.*
publishing *n* cyhoeddi *vn.*
pudding *n* pwdin *m.*
puddle *n* pwll *m.*
puff *n* chwa *f.* • *v* chwythu, pwffian.
pull *v* tynnu. • *n* tynfa *f*, plwc *m.*
pulley *n* pwli *m*, chwerfan *f.*
pulsate *v* curo, dychlamu.
pulse *n* curiad y galon *m.*
pulverise *v* malurio.
pump *n* pwmp *m.* • *v* pwmpio.
punch *n* dyrnod *m/f.* • *v* dyrnu, pwnsio.
punctual *adj* prydlon.
punctuate *v* atalnodi.
punctuation *n* atalnodiad *m.*
punish *v* cosbi.
punishment *n* cosb *f.*
puny *adj* eiddil, pitw.
pupil *n* disgybl *m*; cannwyll y llygad *f.*
puppet *n* pyped *m.*
puppy *n* ci bach *m.*
purchase *v* prynu. • *n* pryniant *m.*
purchaser *n* prynwr *m*, prynwraig *f.*
pure *adj* pur.
purification *n* puro, pureiddio *vn.*
purify *v* puro, pureiddio.
purity *n* purdeb *m.*
purple *adj* porffor.
purpose *n* bwriad, pwrpas *m.*
purse *n* pwrs *m*, cod *f.*
pursue *v* ymlid, dilyn.
pursuit *n* ymlid *m.*
push *v* gwthio. • *n* gwthiad, hwb *m.*
put *v* rhoi, gosod.
putrid *adj* pwdr.
putty *n* pwti *m.*
puzzle *n* pos, pysl *m.*
puzzling *adj* astrus.
pyjamas *n* pyjamas *pl.*
pylon *n* peilon *m.*
pyramid *n* pyramid *m.*
python *n* peithon *m.*

Q

quack *v* cwacio. • *n* doctor bôn clawdd *m.*
quagmire *n* cors, mignen *f.*
quaint *adj* od, henffasiwn.
quake *v* dirgrynu.
qualification *n* cymhwyster *m.*
qualified *adj* trwyddedig.
qualify *v* bod yn gymwys; cymhwyso; goleddfu.
quality *n* ansawdd *m/f.*
qualm *n* pang *m*, petruso *vn.*
quantity *n* maint, swm *m.*
quarantine *n* cwarantin *m.*
quarrel *n* ffrae *f.* • *v* ffraeo, cecru.
quarrelsome *adj* cecrus.
quarry *n* cloddio.
quarter *n* chwarter *m.* • *v* rhannu'n bedair, chwarteru.
quarterly *adj* chwarterol.
quash *v* dileu, gwastrodi.
quay *n* cei *m.*
queen *n* brenhines *f.*
queer *adj* rhyfedd.
quell *v* tawelu, gostegu.
quench *v* diffodd, torri.
query *n* ymholiad *m.* • *v* holi; amau.
quest *n* cais *m.*
question *n* cwestiwn *m.* • *v* holi.
questionable *adj* amheus.
questioner *n* holwr *m*, holwraig *f.*
questionnaire *n* holiadur *m.*
quibble *v* hollti blew.
quick *adj* cyflym, buan.
quicken *v* cyflymu.
quiet *adj* tawel, distaw.
quietness *n* tawelwch, distawrwydd *m.*
quip *n* ateb parod *m.* • *v* cellwair.
quit *v* gadael, rhoi'r gorau i.
quite *adv* yn hollol.
quiver *v* crynu.
quiz *n* cwis *m*, cystadleuaeth *f.* • *v* holi.
quota *n* cwota *m.*
quotation *n* dyfyniad *m.*
quote *v* dyfynnu.

R

rabbit *n* cwningen *f.*
rabble *n* ciwed *f.*
rabies *n* y gynddaredd *f.*
race *n* ras; hil *f.* • *v* rhedeg ras, rasio.
racial *adj* hiliol.
rack *n* rhesel *f.*
racket *n* raced *f.*
radiant *adj* pelydrol, yn disgleirio.
radiate *v* tywynnu, disgleirio.

radiation *n* pelydriad *m*, ymbelydredd *m*.
radiator *n* rheiddiadur *m*.
radical *adj* radicalaidd.
radio *n* radio *m*.
radioactive *adj* ymbelydrol.
raft *n* rafft *f*.
rag *n* clwtyn, cadach *m*.
rage *n* cynddaredd *f*. • *v* cynddeiriogi.
ragged *adj* carpiog.
raging *adj* gwyllt, ffyrnig.
raid *n* cyrch, ymosodiad *m*. • *v* ymosod, dwyn cyrch.
rail *n* canllaw; cledren *f*.
railway *n* rheilffordd *f*.
rain *n* glaw *m*. • *v* bwrw glaw, glawio.
rainbow *n* enfys *f*.
rainy *adj* glawiog.
raise *v* codi.
raisin *n* rhesinen *f*.
rally *n* rali *f*.
ramble *v* crwydro.
ramp *n* esgynfa *f*.
ramshackle *adj* simsan.
rancid *adj* sur.
rancour *n* chwerwder, gwenwyn *m*.
random *adj* ar hap, damweiniol.
range *n* amrediad; paith *m*.
rank *n* rheng *f*.
ransack *v* chwilota; anrheithio.
ransom *n* pridwerth *m*.
rape *n* trais *m*. • *v* treisio.
rapid *adj* cyflym, buan.
rapidity *n* cyflymdra, buander *m*.
rapist *n* treisiwr *m*.
rapt *adj* wedi ymgolli.
rapture *n* perlewyg *m*.
rare *adj* prin.
rarity *n* prinder *m*.
rash *adj* byrbwyll, carlamus. • *n* brech *f*.
rashness *n* byrbwylltra, gwylltineb *m*.
rat *n* llygoden Ffrengig *f*.
rate *n* cyfradd, graddfa *f*.
rather *adv* yn hytrach.
ratification *n* cadarnhad *m*.
ratify *v* cadarnhau.
ration *n* dogn *m/f*.
rational *adj* rhesymol.
rattle *v* clecian, clindarddach. • *n* rygaryg *m*.
ravage *v* difrodi.
rave *v* rafio.
ravenous *adj* gwancus.
ravine *n* ceunant *m*.
raw *adj* amrwd, crai.
ray *n* pelydryn *m*.
raze *v* chwalu.
razor *n* rasel *f*.
reach *v* cyrraedd, estyn.
react *v* adweithio.
reaction *n* adwaith, ymateb *m*.
read *v* darllen.
reader *n* darllenydd *m*.
readily *adv* â chroeso; yn hawdd.
readiness *n* parodrwydd *m*.
reading *n* darlleniad *m*.
readjust *v* ailaddasu.
ready *adj* parod.
real *adj* go iawn, gwirioneddol.
realisation *n* cyflawniad *m*; sylweddoli *vn*.
realise *v* sylweddoli; cyflawni.

reality *n* gwirionedd *m.*
reappear *v* ailymddangos.
rear *n* y tu ôl *m.* • *v* codi.
reason *n* rheswm *m.* • *v* rhesymu.
reasonable *adj* rhesymol.
reasoning *n* ymresymiad *m.*
reassure *v* tawelu meddwl, codi calon.
rebel *n* gwrthryfelwr *m*, gwrthryfelwraig *f.* • *v* gwrthryfela.
rebellion *n* gwrthryfel *m.*
rebound *v* adlamu.
rebuild *v* ailadeiladu.
rebuke *v* ceryddu. • *n* cerydd *m.*
recall *v* galw yn ôl, cofio.
recapture *v* adennill, ailfeddiannu.
recede *v* cilio.
receipt *n* derbynneb *f.*
receivable *adj* derbyniadwy.
receive *v* derbyn.
recent *adj* diweddar.
receptacle *n* llestr *m.*
reception *n* derbyniad *m.*
recession *n* dirwasgiad *m.*
recipe *n* rysáit *f.*
recipient *n* derbynnydd *m.*
reciprocal *adj* o'r ddwy ochr.
recital *n* datganiad *m.*
recite *v* adrodd.
reckless *adj* dibris, dienaid.
reckon *v* cyfrif.
reclaim *v* adennill, adfer.
recline *v* gorwedd, gorweddian.
recognise *v* adnabod, cydnabod.
recognition *n* cydnabyddiaeth *f.*
recoil *v* adlamu.
recollect *v* dwyn i gof, cofio.
recollection *n* cof *m.*
recommend *v* argymell.
recompense *n* iawn, ad-daliad *m.* • *v* talu iawn.
reconcile *v* cymodi, cysoni.
reconciliation *n* cymod *m.*
reconsider *v* ailystyried.
record *v* cofnodi, recordio. • *n* cofnod *m.*
recount *v* adrodd, traethu.
recourse *n*: **to have ~ to** troi at.
recover *v* ailddarganfod; adennill; adfer.
recovery *n* adferiad *m.*
recreation *n* adloniant *m.*
recriminate *v* edliw, dannod.
recrimination *n* edliwiad *m.*
recruit *v* recriwtio.
rectangle *n* hirsgwar, petryal *m.*
rectification *n* cywiriad *m*, unioni *vn.*
rectify *v* unioni, cywiro.
recumbent *adj* ar eich gorwedd.
recur *v* digwydd eto, ailddigwydd.
recurrence *n* ail-ymddangosiad, ail-ddigwyddiad *m.*
recurrent *adj* drosodd a thro.
red *adj* coch. • *n* cochni *m.*
redden *v* cochi.
redeem *v* prynu; cyfnewid.
redemption *n* iachawdwriaeth *f.*
redness *n* cochni *m.*
redouble *v* dwysáu.
redress *v* unioni.
reduce *v* lleihau.
reduction *n* lleihad *m.*
redundancy *n* colli swydd *vn.*
redundant *adj* diangen, segur.
reel *n* ril, rilen *f.*

re-enter *v* ailddychwelyd.
re-establish *v* ailsefydlu.
refer *v* cyfeirio.
referee *n* dyfarnwr; canolwr *m.*
reference *n* cyfeiriad; tystlythyr *m.*
refine *v* puro, coethi.
refinement *n* coethder, cywreinrwydd *m.*
reflect *v* adlewyrchu; myfyrio.
reflection *n* adlewyrchiad; meddwl *m.*
reform *v* diwygio. • *n* diwygiad *m.*
reformer *n* diwygiwr *m.*
refrain *v*: **to ~ from** ymatal rhag.
refresh *v* adfywio.
refrigerator *n* cwpwrdd rhew *m.*
refuge *n* noddfa, lloches *f.*
refugee *n* ffoadur *m.*
refund *v* ad-dalu. • *n* ad-daliad *m.*
refusal *n* gwrthodiad *m.*
refuse *v* gwrthod. • *n* sbwriel, ysbwriel *m.*
regain *v* adennill, ailennill.
regal *adj* brenhinol.
regard *v* edrych ar.
regardless *adv* er hynny, er gwaethaf pawb a phopeth.
regenerate *v* aileni, adfywio.
regeneration *n* adfywiad *m.*
regime *n* cyfundrefn *f.*
region *n* rhanbarth *m.*
register *n* cofrestr *f.* • *v* cofrestru, cofnodi.
registration *n* cofrestru *vn.*
regressive *adj* atchweliadol.
regret *n* edifeirwch *m.* • *v* edifarhau, difaru.
regular *adj* cyson, rheolaidd. • **~s** *n* ffyddloniaid *pl.*
regularity *n* cysondeb *m.*
regulate *v* rheoli, rheoleiddio.
regulation *n* rheol *f.*
rehabilitate *v* adsefydlu; ymaddasu.
rehabilitation *n* ymaddasiad *m.*
reimburse *v* ad-dalu.
reimbursement *n* ad-daliad *m.*
reinforce *v* atgyfnerthu.
reiterate *v* ailadrodd.
reiteration *n* ailadrodd *vn.*
reject *v* gwrthod.
rejection *n* gwrthodiad *m.*
rejoice *v* gorfoleddu.
relapse *v* llithro'n ôl, cwympo'n ôl.
relate *v* adrodd; cydymdeimlo.
relation *n* perthynas *f.*
relationship *n* perthynas *f.*
relative *adj* perthynol. • *n* perthynas *m/f.*
relax *v* ymlacio.
relaxation *n* ymlaciad *m.*
relay *v* trosglwyddo.
release *v* rhyddhau.
relevant *adj* perthnasol.
reliable *adj* dibynadwy, sicr.
reliance *n* hyder *m*, ffydd *f.*
relief *n* rhyddhad *m.*
relieve *v* lleddfu, rhyddhau.
religion *n* crefydd *f.*
religious *adj* crefyddol.
relinquish *v* gollwng, rhoi'r gorau i.
reluctant *adj* anfodlon.
rely *v* dibynnu.
remain *v* aros.

remainder *n* gweddill, rhelyw *m.*
remark *n* sylw *m.* • *v* gwneud sylw, dweud.
remarkable *adj* hynod, nodedig.
remedy *n* meddyginiaeth *f.* • *v* gwella.
remember *v* cofio.
remind *v* atgoffa.
reminiscences *n* atgofion *pl.*
remit *v* maddau; anfon.
remnant *n* gweddill *m.*
remonstrate *v* protestio wrth.
remote *adj* diarffordd, anghysbell.
remoteness *n* pellenigrwydd *m.*
removable *adj* symudol.
remove *v* symud ymaith, dileu.
remunerate *v* talu, gwobrwyo.
renew *v* adnewyddu.
renewal *n* adnewyddiad *m.*
renounce *v* rhoi'r gorau i.
renovate *v* adnewyddu.
renown *n* enwogrwydd *m.*
rent *n* rhent *m.* • *v* gosod ar rent.
renunciation *n* ymwrthod, ymwadu â *vn.*
reorganisation *n* ad-drefnu *vn.*
reorganise *v* ad-drefnu.
repair *v* atgyweirio, trwsio. • *n* atgyweiriad *m.*
repatriate *v* dychwelyd i'w wlad ei hun.
repay *v* ad-dalu.
repayment *n* ad-daliad *m.*
repeal *v* diddymu. • *n* diddymiad *m.*
repeat *v* ailadrodd.
repent *v* edifarhau, edifaru.
repetition *n* ailadroddiad *m.*
replace *v* ailosod; amnewid.
replenish *v* ail-lenwi, adnewyddu.
replete *adj* llawn, cyforiog.
reply *n* ateb *m.* • *v* ateb.
report *v* adrodd. • *n* adroddiad *m.*
reporter *n* gohebydd *m.*
reprehend *v* ceryddu.
reprehensible *adj* gresynus, beius.
represent *v* cynrychioli.
representation *n* portread, darlun *m.*
representative *adj* cynrychiadol. • *n* cynrychiolydd *m.*
repress *v* gwastrodi, ffrwyno.
repression *n* gormes *m/f*, gorthrwm *f.*
reprieve *n* gohiriad *m.*
reprimand *v* ceryddu.
reprisal *n* dial, dialedd *m.*
reproach *n* cerydd *m.* • *v* ceryddu, edliw.
reproduce *v* atgynhyrchu.
reproduction *n* atgynhyrchiad, copi *m.*
republic *n* gweriniaeth *f.*
republican *adj* gweriniaethol.
repudiate *v* gwrthod arddel.
repulse *n* ôl-hyrddio *vn.*
repulsion *n* ffieidd-dra *m.*
repulsive *adj* ffiaidd, atgas.
reputation *n* enw, bri *m.*
request *n* cais *m.* • *v* gofyn am, ceisio.
require *v* gofyn, mynnu.
requirement *n* angen *m.*
requisite *adj* gofynnol, angenrheidiol.
rescue *v* achub.

research *v* ymchwilio. • *n* ymchwil *f/m*.
resemblance *n* tebygrwydd *m*.
resemble *v* bod yn debyg.
resent *v* bod yn ddig.
resentment *n* dig *m*.
reservation *n* gwarchodfa *f*.
reserve *v* cadw.
reside *v* byw.
residence *n* tŷ *m*, preswylfa *f*.
resident *n* preswylydd *m*.
resign *v* ymddiswyddo.
resignation *n* ymddiswyddiad *m*.
resist *v* gwrthsefyll.
resistance *n* gwrthsafiad *m*.
resolute *adj* di-droi'n-ôl, penderfynol.
resolution *n* adduned *f*, penderfyniad *m*.
resolve *v* penderfynu, torri (dadl).
resort *v* defnyddio. • *n* cyrchfan *m*.
resource *n* adnodd *m*.
respect *n* parch *m*. • *v* parchu.
respectability *n* parchusrwydd *m*.
respectable *adj* parchus.
respectful *adj* llawn parch.
respecting *prep* ynglŷn â.
respective *adj* priod, priodol.
respite *n* seibiant, saib *m*.
respond *v* ymateb.
response *n* ateb, ymateb *m*.
responsibility *n* cyfrifoldeb *m*.
responsible *adj* cyfrifol.
rest *n* saib, seibiant *m*. • *v* gorffwys.
restitution *n* adferiad *m*.
restive *adj* anhydrin.
restoration *n* adferiad *m*.
restore *v* adfer.
restrain *v* ffrwyno, dal yn ôl.
restrict *v* cyfyngu.
restriction *n* cyfyngiad *m*.
restrictive *adj* cyfyngol.
result *n* canlyniad *m*.
resume *v* ailgychwyn.
resuscitate *v* dadebru, adfywio.
retail *v* adwerthu, mân-werthu.
retain *v* cadw.
retaliate *v* talu'r pwyth yn ôl.
reticence *n* swildod *m*.
retire *v* ymddeol.
retired *adj* wedi ymddeol.
retirement *n* ymddeoliad *m*.
retort *n* ateb parod *m*.
retrace *v* olrhain.
retreat *v* cilio.
retribution *n* dial *m*, cosb *f*.
retrieve *v* adennill.
return *v* dychwelyd. • *n* dychweliad *m*.
reunion *n* aduniad *m*.
reunite *v* aduno.
reveal *v* datgelu.
revelation *n* datguddiad *m*.
revenge *n* dial, dialedd *m*.
revengeful *adj* dialgar.
revenue *n* cyllid, incwm *m*.
reverberate *v* atseinio, diasbedain.
reverberation *n* atsain *f*, dirgryniad *m*.
reversal *n* gwrthdroad *m*.
reverse *v* bacio.
reversible *adj* cildroadwy.
reversion *n* atchweliad *m*.
revert *v* dychwelyd.

review *v* adolygu. • *n* adolygiad *m.*
revise *v* diwygio, adolygu.
revision *n* adolygiad *m.*
revival *n* adfywiad, diwygiad *m.*
revive *v* adfywio, bywiogi.
revoke *v* diddymu.
revolt *v* gwrthryfela. • *n* gwrthryfel *m.*
revolution *n* chwyldro *m.*
revolutionary *adj* chwyldroadol.
revolve *v* cylchdroi.
revulsion *n* ffieidd-dod *m.*
reward *n* gwobr *f.* • *v* gwobrwyo.
rhetorical *adj* rhethregol.
rheumatism *n* gwynegon *pl*, cryd cymalau *m.*
rhyme *n* odl *f.* • *v* odli.
rhythm *n* rhythm *m.*
rhythmical *adj* rhythmig.
rib *n* asen *f.*
ribbon *n* rhuban *m.*
rice *n* reis *m.*
rich *adj* cyfoethog.
richness *n* cyfoeth *m.*
rid *v* cael gwared.
riddle *n* pos *m.*
ride *v* marchogaeth; teithio.
ridge *n* trum, crib *f.*
ridicule *n* gwawd, gwatwar *m.* • *v* gwawdio, gwatwar.
ridiculous *adj* chwerthinllyd.
rife *adj* rhemp.
rifle *n* reiffl *f.*
rig *v* rigio. • *n* llwyfan (olew) *m/f.*
right *adj* de, iawn. • *n* hawl *f.*
righteous *adj* cyfiawn.
rigid *adj* anhyblyg.
rigorous *adj* llym, llwyr.
rigour *n* llymder *m.*
rim *n* ymyl *m/f.*
ring *n* modrwy *f*, cylch *m.* • *v* canu.
rink *n* llawr *m.*
rinse *v* streulio, rinsio.
riot *n* terfysg *m.*
riotous *adj* terfysglyd.
rip *v* rhwygo.
ripe *adj* aeddfed.
ripen *v* aeddfedu.
ripple *n* crychiad *m.*
rise *v* esgyn. • *n* codiad, esgyniad *m.*
rising *adj* sy'n codi.
risk *n* perygl *m*, menter *f.* • *v* mentro.
risky *adj* peryglus, mentrus.
rite *n* defod *f.*
ritual *adj* defodol.
rival *n* cystadleuydd *m.* • *v* cystadlu â.
rivalry *n* cystadleuaeth *f.*
river *n* afon *f.*
road *n* ffordd, heol *f.*
roam *v* crwydro.
roar *v* rhuo. • *n* rhu, rhuad *m.*
roast *v* rhostio.
rob *v* dwyn, lladrata.
robber *n* lleidr *m.*
robbery *n* lladrad *m.*
robust *adj* cryf, cydnerth.
robustness *n* cryfder, cadernid *m.*
rock *n* craig *f.* • *v* siglo.
rocket *n* roced *f.*
rocking chair *n* cadair siglo *f.*
rocky *adj* creigiog.
rodent *n* cnofil *m.*
rogue *n* gwalch, cnaf *m.*

roll *v* treiglo, rholio.
roller *n* rowl *m/f*.
romance *n* rhamant *f*.
romantic *adj* rhamantaidd, rhamantus.
roof *n* to *m*. • *v* toi.
room *n* ystafell *f*.
root *n* gwraidd, gwreiddyn *m*.
rope *n* rhaff *f*.
rose *n* rhosyn *m*.
rosemary *n* rhosmari *m*.
rot *v* pydru. • *n* pydredd *m*.
rotate *v* cylchdroi.
rotation *n* cylchdro *m*.
rotund *adj* crwn.
rouge *n* powdwr coch *m*.
rough *adj* garw.
roughness *n* garwedd, gerwinder *m*.
round *adj* crwn. • *n* tôn gron *f*.
roundness *n* crynder *m*.
rouse *v* cynhyrfu, deffro.
route *n* ffordd *f*.
routine *n* arfer *m/f*, trefn arferol *f*.
rove *v* crwydro.
row *n* ffrae *f*, twrw *m*.
row *n* rhes *f*.
royal *adj* brenhinol.
royalty *n* brenhiniaeth *f*, breindal *m*.
rub *v* rhwbio.
rubber *n* rwber *m*.
rubbish *n* sbwriel *m*.
rudder *n* llyw *m*.
ruddiness *n* gwrid *m*, cochni *m*.
rude *adj* anghwrtais.
rudeness *n* anghwrteisi, haerllugrwydd *m*.
ruffle *v* crychu, chwalu, aflonyddu.
rug *n* rỳg, carthen *f*.
rugged *adj* garw, clogyrnog.
ruin *n* adfail, murddun *m*. • *v* llwyr ddifetha, distrywio.
ruinous *adj* dinistriol, andwyol.
rule *n* rheol *f*. • *v* rheoli, teyrnasu.
rumble *v* trystio, rymblan.
ruminate *v* cnoi cil.
rummage *v* chwilota, twrio.
rumour *n* si, sôn *m*.
run *v* rhedeg.
rung *n* ffon *f*, gris *m*.
runner *n* rhedwr *m*.
runway *n* llwybr glanio *m*.
rupture *n* torllengig *m*.
ruse *n* ystryw *m/f*.
rush *n* rhuthr *m*. • *v* rhuthro.
rust *n* rhwd *m*. • *v* rhydu.
rustic *adj* gwladaidd. • *n* gwerinwr, gwladwr *m*.
rustle *v* siffrwd.
rusty *adj* rhydlyd.
ruthless *adj* didostur.
rye *n* rhyg *m*.

S

sabotage *n* difrod bwriadol *m.*
sachet *n* bag bychan *m.*
sack *n* sach *m/f.*
sacrament *n* sagrafen *f*, y cymun *m.*
sacred *adj* cysegredig.
sacrifice *n* aberth *m/f.* • *v* aberthu.
sacrilege *n* halogiad *m.*
sad *adj* trist.
sadden *v* tristáu.
saddle *n* cyfrwy *m.* • *v* cyfrwyo.
sadness *n* tristwch *m.*
safe *adj* diogel.
safeguard *n* amddiffynfa *f.* • *v* diogelu.
safety *n* diogelwch *m.*
sage *n* saets *m.*
sail *n* hwyl *f.* • *v* hwylio.
sailor *n* morwr *m.*
saint *n* sant *m*, santes *f.*
sake *n*: **for the** ~ er mwyn.
salad *n* salad *m.*
salary *n* cyflog *m/f.*
sale *n* arwerthiant *m*, sêl *f.*
salesman *n* gwerthwr *m.*
saliva *n* poer *m.*
salmon *n* eog *m.*
saloon *n* salŵn *m/f.*
salt *n* halen *m.* • *v* halltu.
salt cellar *n* llestr halen *m.*
salubrious *adj* iachusol.
salubrity *n* iachusrwydd *m.*
salutary *adj* llesol.
salute *v* saliwtio. • *n* saliwt *f.*
salvation *n* achubiaeth, iachawdwriaeth *f.*
same *adj* yr un.
sameness *n* unffurfiaeth *f.*
sample *n* sampl *f.* • *v* samplo.
sanatorium *n* sanatoriwm *m.*
sanctify *v* sancteiddio, cysegru.
sanction *n* cosb *f*, sancsiwn *m.* • *v* cadarnhau.
sanctuary *n* seintwar *f*; cysegr *m.*
sand *n* tywod *m.*
sandal *n* sandal *f.*
sandwich *n* brechdan *f.*
sandy *adj* tywodlyd.
sane *adj* call.
sanguine *adj* hyderus.
sanity *n* pwyll, callineb *m.*
sapling *n* coeden ifanc *f.*
sarcasm *n* coegni *m.*
sarcastic *adj* coeglyd, sarcastig.
sardine *n* sardîn *m.*
satchel *n* bag ysgol *m.*
sate *v* digoni.
satellite *n* lloeren *f.*
satin *n* sidan gloyw *m.* • *adj* sidanaidd.
satire *n* dychan *m.*
satirical *adj* dychanol.
satisfaction *n* bodlonrwydd *m.*
satisfactory *adj* boddhaol.
satisfy *v* bodloni.
saturate *v* trwytho, mwydo.

Saturday *n* Sadwrn *m*.
sauce *n* saws *m*.
saucepan *n* sosban *f*.
saucer *n* soser *f*.
saunter *v* mynd ling-di-long, mynd o dow i dow.
sausage *n* selsigen, sosej *f*.
savage *adj* anwaraidd. • *n* anwariad *m/f*.
savagery *n* anwarineb *m*.
save *v* achub; cynilo.
saving *n* achubiaeth *f*.
savings bank *n* banc cynilo *m*.
savour *v* blasu, sawru.
saw *n* llif *f*. • *v* llifio.
say *v* dweud.
saying *n* dywediad *m*.
scaffolding *n* sgaffaldwaith *m*.
scald *v* sgaldian. • *n* llosgiad, sgaldiad *m*.
scale *n* graddfa *f*; cen *m*. • *v* dringo.
scan *v* sganio.
scandal *n* sgandal, gwarth *f*.
scandalise *v* pechu.
scandalous *adj* gwarthus, cywilyddus.
scant *adj* prin.
scantiness *n* prinder *m*.
scapegoat *n* bwch dihangol *m*.
scar *n* craith *f*.
scarce *adj* prin.
scare *v* dychryn, brawychu. • *n* dychryn, braw *m*.
scarf *n* sgarff *f*.
scarlet *n* ysgarlad, coch *m*.
scatter *v* chwalu, gwasgaru.
scene *n* golygfa *f*, lleoliad *m*.
scenery *n* golygfeydd *pl*.
scenic *adj* golygfaol.
scent *n* persawr, sawr *m*. • *v* synhwyro, ogleuo.
sceptic *n* amheuwr *m*.
sceptic(al) *adj* sgeptig.
schedule *n* rhestr; rhaglen *f*.
scheme *n* cynllun *m*. • *v* cynllwynio.
scholar *n* disgybl, ysgolhaig *m*.
school *n* ysgol *f*.
schoolboy *n* bachgen ysgol *m*.
schoolgirl *n* merch ysgol *f*.
schoolteacher *n* athro ysgol *m*, athrawes *f*.
science *n* gwyddoniaeth; gwyddor *f*.
scientific *adj* gwyddonol.
scientist *n* gwyddonydd *m*.
scintillate *v* pefrio, gwreichioni.
scissors *n* siswrn *m*.
scoff *v* gwawdio, chwerthin am ben.
scold *v* dwrdio, dweud y drefn.
scope *n* cwmpas, maes *m*.
scorch *v* rhuddo, deifio.
score *n* sgôr *f*. • *v* sgorio.
scorn *v* dirmygu, gwawdio. • *n* dirmyg *m*.
scornful *adj* dirmygus.
scoundrel *n* dihiryn *m*.
scour *v* sgwrio, ysgwrio.
scout *n* sgowt *m*.
scowl *v* gwgu, cuchio.
scramble *v* sgrialu, sgramblo.
scrap *n* darn; sgrap *m*.
scrape *v* crafu.
scratch *v* crafu. • *n* crafiad *m*.
scream *v* sgrechian. • *n* sgrech *f*.

screen *n* sgrin *f.*
screw *n* sgriw *f.* • *v* sgriwio.
screwdriver *n* sgriwdreifer *m.*
scribble *v* sgriblan. • *n* ysgrifen *f,* sgribl *m.*
script *n* sgript *f.*
Scripture *n* yr Ysgrythur *f.*
scrub *v* sgwrio. • *n* prysgwydd *pl.*
scruple *n* poen cydwybod *f.*
scrupulous *adj* gofalus, manwl gywir.
scuffle *n* ysgarmes *f.* • *v* ymgiprys.
sculptor *n* cerflunydd *m.*
sculpture *n* cerflun *m.*
scum *n* llysnafedd, ewyn *m.*
sea *n* môr *m.*
seafood *n* bwyd môr *m.*
seagull *n* gwylan *f.*
seal *n* morlo *m*; sêl *f.* • *v* selio.
seamy *adj* salw.
search *v* chwilio.
seashore *n* glan môr *f.*
seasickness *n* salwch môr *m.*
season *n* tymor *m.*
seasonable *adj* tymhorol.
seasoning *n* sesnin *m.*
seat *n* sedd *f.* • *v* eistedd.
seaweed *n* gwymon *m.*
seclude *v* o'r neilltu.
seclusion *n* neilltuaeth *f.*
second *adj* ail. • *n* eiliad *m/f.*
secondary *adj* uwchradd; eilaidd.
secrecy *n* cyfrinachedd *m.*
secret *adj* cyfrinachol. • *n* cyfrinach *f.*
secretary *n* ysgrifennydd *m,* ysgrifenyddes *f.*
secretive *adj* tawedog.
section *n* adran *f*; trychiad *m.*
sector *n* sector *m.*
secular *adj* seciwlar, lleyg.
secure *adj* diogel, sicr. • *v* sicrhau.
security *n* diogelwch *m.*
sedative *n* tawelydd *m.*
sediment *n* gwaddod *m.*
sedition *n* annog bradwriaeth *vn.*
seduce *v* hudo.
seductive *adj* hudol, hudolus.
see *v* gweld.
seed *n* hedyn, had *m.* • *v* hadu.
seek *v* ceisio, chwilio.
seem *v* ymddangos.
seemliness *n* gweddustier *m.*
seemly *adj* gweddus.
seesaw *n* si-so *m.*
segment *n* darn *m.*
seize *v* cydio, ymaflyd.
seizure *n* atafaeliad; trawiad *m.*
seldom *adv* anaml, prin.
select *v* dewis, dethol.
selection *n* detholiad *m.*
self *n* hunan *m.*
self-confident *adj* hunanhyder.
self-defence *n* hunanamddiffyn *m.*
self-employed *adj* hunangyflogedig.
self-interest *n* hunan-les *m.*
selfish *adj* hunanol.
selfishness *n* hunanoldeb *m.*
self-portrait *n* hunanbortread *m.*
self-respect *n* hunan-barch *m.*
self-service *adj* gweini arnoch eich hun.
self-styled *adj* hunanhonedig.
self-sufficient *adj* hunangynhaliol.
self-taught *adj* hunanaddysgedig.

sell *v* gwerthu.
seller *n* gwerthwr *m*, gwerthwraig *f*.
semblance *n* llun *m*, golwg *f*.
semicircle *n* hanner cylch *m*.
senate *n* senedd *f*.
senator *n* seneddwr *m*, seneddwraig *f*.
send *v* anfon.
senile *adj* hen a musgrell.
senility *n* musgrellni *m*.
senior *adj* hŷn, uwch.
sensation *n* teimlad, cynnwrf *m*.
sense *n* synnwyr *m*.
senseless *adj* disynnwyr; anymwybodol.
sensible *adj* synhwyrol.
sensitive *adj* sensitif, teimladwy.
sensual *adj* nwydus.
sensuality *n* trythyllwch *m*.
sentence *n* brawddeg; dedfryd *f*.
sentiment *n* teimlad *m*.
sentimental *adj* teimladwy.
sentinel *n* gwarchodwr *m*.
separable *adj* gwahanadwy.
separate *v* gwahanu. • *adj* ar wahân.
separation *n* gwahaniad *m*.
September *n* Medi *m*.
sepulchre *n* beddrod *m*.
sequel *n* dilyniant *m*.
sequence *n* trefn, olyniaeth *f*.
serenade *n* nosgan, serenâd *f*. • *v* canu serenâd.
serene *adj* tawel, digyffro.
serenity *n* tawelwch *m*.
sergeant *n* rhingyll *m*.
serial *n* cyfres *f*.
series *n* cyfres *f*.
serious *adj* difrifol.
sermon *n* pregeth *f*.
serpent *n* sarff *f*.
servant *n* gwas *m*.
serve *v* gwasanaethu.
service *n* gwasanaeth *m*.
serviceable *adj* defnyddiol.
servile *adj* gwasaidd.
servitude *n* caethwasanaeth *m*.
session *n* sesiwn *m/f*.
set *v* dodi, gosod. • *adj* sefydlog.
setting *n* gosodiad *m*; ~ **of the sun** machlud *m*.
settle *v* cartrefu; torri dadl.
settlement *n* cytundeb; anheddiad *m*.
seven *num* saith.
seventeen *num* dau/dwy ar bymtheg.
seventeenth *adj* ail ar bymtheg.
seventh *adj* seithfed.
seventieth *adj* saith degfed.
seventy *num* saith deg.
several *adj* sawl.
severe *adj* caled, llym.
severity *n* llymder, gerwinder *m*.
sew *v* gwnïo.
sewer *n* carthffos *f*.
sex *n* rhyw *m/f*.
sexist *adj* rhywiaethol.
sexual *adj* rhywiol.
shabby *adj* diraen.
shackle *v* llyffetheirio.
shade *n* cysgod *m*. • *v* cysgodi.
shadow *n* cysgod *m*.
shady *adj* cysgodol.
shaft *n* coes; siafft *f*.

shake *v* ysgwyd, siglo.
shallow *adj* bas.
sham *v* ffugio. • *n* twyll *m*.
shame *n* cywilydd, gwarth *m*. • *v* codi cywilydd.
shamefaced *adj* penisel.
shameful *adj* cywilyddus, gwarthus.
shampoo *n* siampŵ *m*.
shape *v* llunio. • *n* siâp *m*, ffurf *f*.
shapely *adj* lluniaidd, siapus.
share *n* cyfran *f*. • *v* rhannu.
shark *n* siarc *m*.
sharp *adj* miniog.
sharpen *v* rhoi min ar, miniogi.
sharpness *n* awch, min *m*.
shatter *v* dryllio.
shave *v* eillio.
shaver *n* rasel drydan *f*.
shawl *n* siôl *f*.
she *pron* hi.
sheaf *n* ysgub *f*.
shear *v* cneifio.
shed *n* cwt *m*, sièd *f*.
sheep *n* dafad *f*.
sheer *adj* serth.
sheet *n* cynfas *f*.
shelf *n* silff *f*.
shell *n* cragen *f*. • *v* bombardio; plisgo.
shelter *n* cysgodfan *m/f*. • *v* cysgodi.
shepherd *n* bugail *m*, bugeiles *f*.
sheriff *n* siryf *m*.
shield *n* tarian *f*. • *v* gwarchod.
shift *v* symud, newid. • *n* newid *m*; sifft *f*.
shine *v* disgleirio, tywynnu.
shining *adj* disglair, gloyw.
ship *n* llong *f*.
shipment *n* llwyth llong *m*.
shipwreck *n* llongdrylliad *m*.
shirt *n* crys *m*.
shiver *v* crynu, rhynnu.
shock *n* ysgytwad *m*, sioc *f*. • *v* rhoi ysgytwad, syfrdanu.
shoe *n* esgid *f*.
shoemaker *n* crydd *m*.
shoot *v* saethu. • *n* eginyn, blaguryn *m*.
shop *n* siop *f*.
shopper *n* siopwr *m*, siopwraig *f*.
shore *n* glan *f*.
short *adj* byr, cwta.
shortcoming *n* diffyg *m*.
shorten *v* byrhau, cwtogi.
short-sighted *adj* byr eich golwg.
shortwave *n* tonfedd fer *f*.
shot *n* ergyd *f/m*.
shotgun *n* dryll *m/f*.
shoulder *n* ysgwydd *f*.
shout *v* gweiddi. • *n* bloedd, gwaedd *f*.
shove *v* gwthio. • *n* gwthiad *m*.
shovel *n* rhaw *f*. • *v* rhofio.
show *v* dangos. • *n* arddangosfa, sioe *f*.
shower *n* cawod *f*.
shred *n* rhecsyn, darn *m*. • *v* rhwygo.
shrewd *adj* craff, hirben.
shriek *v* gwichian, sgrechian. • *n* sgrech *f*.
shrill *adj* main, treiddgar.
shrimp *n* berdysen *f*.
shrink *v* crebachu, mynd yn llai.

shrivel *v* crebachu, crychu.
shroud *n* amdo *m.*
shrub *n* prysgwydden *f.*
shudder *v* crynu. • *n* ias *f.*
shun *v* gochel, osgoi.
shut *v* cau.
shutter *n* caead *m.*
shy *adj* swil.
shyness *n* swildod *m.*
sick *adj* sâl, tost.
sicken *v* clafychu, gwneud yn sâl.
sickly *adj* gwanllyd.
sickness *n* gwaeledd *m.*
side *n* ochr *f.*
sideboard *n* seld *f.*
sidestep *v* ochrgamu.
siege *n* gwarchae *m.*
sieve *n* gogr, rhidyll *m.* • *v* rhidyllu.
sift *v* gogrwn, hidlo.
sigh *v* ochneidio. • *n* ochenaid *f.*
sight *n* golwg *m* (faculty); golygfa *f* (spectacle).
sightseeing *n* ymweld *vn.*
sign *n* arwydd *m.* • *v* arwyddo.
signal *n* arwydd; signal *m.*
signature *n* llofnod *m.*
significance *n* arwyddocâd *m.*
significant *adj* arwyddocaol.
signify *v* golygu, dynodi.
silence *n* tawelwch, distawrwydd *m.*
silent *adj* distaw, mud.
silicon chip *n* ysglodyn silicon *m.*
silk *n* sidan *m.*
silken *adj* sidanaidd.
sill *n* silff *f.*
silliness *n* ffolineb, hurtrwydd *m.*
silly *adj* ffôl, hurt.
silver *n* arian *m.*
silvery *adj* ariannaidd.
similar *adj* tebyg, fel.
similarity *n* tebygrwydd *m.*
simile *n* cyffelybiaeth, cymhariaeth *f.*
simmer *v* mudferwi.
simper *v* glaswenu.
simple *adj* syml; gwirion.
simplicity *n* symlrwydd, diniweidrwydd *m.*
simplification *n* symleiddio *vn.*
simplify *v* symleiddio.
simulate *v* dynwared.
simultaneous *adj* ar y pryd, cydamserol.
sin *n* pechod *m.* • *v* pechu.
since *adv, prep* ers, er. • *conj* gan.
sincere *adj* diffuant, didwyll. • **~ly** *adv* yn bur.
sincerity *n* didwylledd, diffuantrwydd *m.*
sinew *n* gewyn, giewyn *m.*
sing *v* canu.
singe *v* deifio, rhuddo.
singer *n* canwr *m*, cantores *f.*
single *adj* sengl.
singly *adv* fesul un; ar eich pen eich hun.
singular *adj* unigol.
sinister *adj* sinistr, anfad.
sink *v* suddo. • *n* sinc *f.*
sinner *n* pechadur *m*, perchadures *f.*
sinuous *adj* dolennog, troellog.
siphon *n* siffon, seiffon *m.*
sir *n* syr *m.*
sister *n* chwaer *f.*

sister-in-law *n* chwaer-yng-nghyfraith *f.*
sit *v* eistedd.
site *n* safle *m.*
sitting *n* eistedd, eisteddiad *m.*
sitting room *n* lolfa *f.*
situation *n* sefyllfa *f.*
six *num* chwe, chwech.
sixteen *num* un ar bymtheg.
sixteenth *adj* unfed ar bymtheg.
sixth *adj* chweched.
sixtieth *adj* trigeinfed.
sixty *num* trigain, chwe deg.
size *n* maint, maintioli *m.*
sizeable *adj* sylweddol.
skate *n* esgid sglefrio *f.* • *v* sglefrio.
skating rink *n* llawr sglefrio *m.*
skeleton *n* sgerbwd *m.*
sketch *n* braslun *m.*
skewer *n* gwäell *f.* • *v* gwaëllu.
ski *n* sgi *f.* • *v* sgio.
skid *n* sglefriad *m.* • *v* sglefrio, sgidio.
skier *n* sgïwr *m.*
skill *n* medr *m.*
skilful *adj* medrus, deheuig.
skim *v* sgimio.
skin *n* croen *m.* • *v* blingo.
skinny *adj* tenau, esgyrnog.
skip *v* sgipio.
skirmish *n* sgarmes *f.*
skirt *n* sgert *f.* • *v* mynd wrth odre.
skulk *v* llechu, stelcian.
skull *n* penglog *f.*
sky *n* awyr *f.*
skylight *n* ffenestr do *f.*
skyscraper *n* cwmwlgrafwr *m.*
slab *n* slabyn *m*, slaben *f.*
slack *adj* llac.
slack(en) *v* llacio, llaesu.
slackness *n* llacrwydd, diogi *m.*
slam *v* cau'n glep.
slander *v* athrodi. • *n* athrod *m.*
slanderous *adj* athrodus.
slang *n* bratiaith *f.*
slant *v* goleddfu, gogwyddo. • *n* goleddf, gogwydd *m.*
slap *n* slapen *f.* • *v* taro, slapian.
slaughter *n* lladdfa, cyflafan *f.* • *v* lladd.
slave *n* caethwas *m*, caethferch *f.*
slavery *n* caethwasiaeth *m.*
slay *v* lladd.
sleazy *adj* llwgr.
sledge *n* sled *f.*
sleep *v* cysgu. • *n* cwsg *m.*
sleeper *n* cysgadur, cysgwr *m.*
sleepiness *n* syrthni, awydd cysgu *m.*
sleepwalking *n* cerdded yn eich cwsg.
sleepy *adj* cysglyd.
sleet *n* eirlaw *m.*
sleeve *n* llawes *f.*
slender *adj* main.
slenderness *n* meinder *m.*
slice *n* tafell, sleisen *f.* • *v* torri'n dafelli.
slide *v* llithro. • *n* llithren *f*; tryloywder *m.*
slight *adj* bychan, eiddil. • *n* sarhad *m.*
slightness *n* bychander, eiddilwch *m.*
slim *adj* main. • *v* colli pwysau.
sling *n* ffon dafl *f.*

slip *v* llithro. • *n* llithrad *m*.
slipper *n* sliper *f*.
slippery *adj* llithrig.
slit *v* hollti, torri.
slogan *n* arwyddair *m*, slogan *m/f*.
slope *n* llechwedd *f*. • *v* goleddfu.
sloth *n* diogi *m*.
slovenliness *n* blerwch, anniben-dod *m*.
slovenly *adj* blêr, di-hid.
slow *adj* araf.
slowness *n* arafwch *m*.
slug *n* gwlithen *f*.
sluggish *adj* dioglyd, diegni.
sluice *n* llifddor *f*.
slum *n* slym *f*.
slump *n* cwymp *m*.
slur *v* llithro, llusgo. • *n* sarhad *m*, sen *f*.
slush *n* slwtsh *m*.
sly *adj* slei, dichellgar.
slyness *n* cyfrwyster, twyll *m*.
smack *n* clec *f*. • *v* taro, curo.
small *adj* bach, bychan, mân.
smallness *n* bychander, bychandra *m*.
smart *adj* taclus, twt; call. • *v* llosgi.
smartness *n* craffter; taclusrwydd *m*.
smash *v* malu, malurio. • *n* gwrth-drawiad *m*.
smear *v* iro; difwyno.
smell *v* arogleuo, gwynto. • *n* oglau, gwynt, arogl *m*.
smelt *v* toddi.
smile *v* gwenu. • *n* gwên *f*.
smite *v* taro.
smith *n* gof *m*.
smoke *n* mwg *m*. • *v* mygu.
smoker *n* ysmygwr *m*, ysmygwraig *f*.
smoky *adj* myglyd.
smooth *adj* llyfn. • *v* llyfnhau, llyfnu.
smoothness *n* llyfnder *m*.
smother *v* mogi, mygu.
smudge *v* llychwino, gadael ôl. • *n* ôl, staen *m*.
smuggle *v* smyglo.
smuggler *n* smyglwr *m*.
snack *n* byrbryd *m*.
snail *n* malwen, malwoden *f*.
snake *n* neidr *f*.
snap *v* clecian. • *n* clec, snap *m*.
snare *n* magl *f*.
snatch *v* cipio.
sneer *v* glaswenu.
sneeze *v* tisian.
sniff *v* ffroeni, sniffian.
snivel *v* snwffian, nadu.
snob *n* hen drwyn, snobyn *m*.
snobbish *adj* crachaidd, snoby-ddlyd.
snooze *n* cyntun *m*.
snore *v* chwyrnu.
snow *n* eira *m*. • *v* bwrw eira.
snowman *n* dyn eira *m*.
snowplough *n* swch eira *f*.
snowy *adj* o eira.
snub *adj* smwt.
snug *adj* diddos, clyd.
so *adv* felly; mor, cyn.
soak *v* mwydo, rhoi yng ngwlych.
soap *n* sebon *m*. • *v* seboni.
soar *v* hedfan.

sob *n* ochenaid *f.* • *v* beichio wylo.
sober *adj* sobr.
sobriety *n* sobrwydd *m.*
sociability *n* cymdeithasgarwch *m.*
sociable *adj* cymdeithasgar.
social *adj* cymdeithasol.
social worker *n* gweithiwr cymdeithasol *m.*
socialist *n* sosialydd *m.*
society *n* cymdeithas *f.*
sociologist *n* cymdeithasegydd *m.*
sock *n* hosan *f.*
socket *n* soced *m/f.*
sofa *n* soffa *f.*
soft *adj* meddal, distaw.
soften *v* meddalu, tyneru, distewi.
softness *n* meddalwch, tynerwch *m.*
software *n* meddalwedd *m/f.*
soil *v* baeddu. • *n* pridd *m.*
solace *v* cysuro. • *n* cysur, solas *m.*
solar *adj* (o)'r haul.
solder *v* sodro. • *n* sodr, sodor *m.*
soldier *n* milwr *m.*
sole *n* gwadn *f/m.* • *adj* unig.
solemn *adj* difrifol, dwys.
solemnity *n* difrifoldeb *m.*
solicit *v* deisyf, erfyn.
solicitor *n* cyfreithiwr *m.*
solid *adj* cydnerth, solet. • *n* solid *m.*
solidify *v* caledu.
solidity *n* cadernid *m.*
solitary *adj* unig, ar eich pen eich hun.
solitude *n* unigedd *m.*
solstice *n* heuldro *m.*
soluble *adj* toddadwy, hydawdd.
solution *n* toddiant *m.*
solve *v* datrys.
solvency *n* y gallu i dalu *m.*
solvent *adj* ag arian.
some *adj* peth, rhyw, rhai.
somebody *pron* rhywun.
somehow *adv* rhywsut.
something *pron* rhywbeth.
sometimes *adv* weithiau, ambell waith.
somewhat *adv* rhywfaint.
somewhere *adv* rhywle.
somnolence *n* syrthni *m.*
somnolent *adj* cysglyd, swrth.
son *n* mab *m.*
song *n* cân *f.*
son-in-law *n* mab-yng-nghyfraith *m.*
sonorous *adj* soniarus.
soon *adv* cyn bo hir, yn fuan.
soot *n* parddu, huddygl *m.*
soothe *v* lliniaru, lleddfu.
sophisticated *adj* soffistigedig.
soporific *adj* cysglyd.
sordid *adj* budr, gwael.
sore *n* briw, dolur *m.* • *adj* poenus, tost.
sorrow *n* galar, tristwch *m.* • *v* gofidio, tristáu.
sorrowful *adj* trist, gofidus.
sorry *adj* edifar.
sort *n* math *m.* • *v* didoli.
soul *n* enaid *m.*
sound *adj* iach, solet. • *n* sŵn *m.*
soundness *n* sadrwydd *m.*
soup *n* cawl *m.*
sour *adj* sur.
source *n* ffynhonnell *f.*

south *n* de *m*.
southern *adj* deheuol.
southward(s) *adv* tua'r de.
souvenir *n* swfenîr *m*.
sovereign *adj* goruchaf. • *n* sofren *f*.
sovereignty *n* sofraniaeth, penarglwyddiaeth *f*.
sow *v* hau.
space *n* gofod, lle *m*.
spacious *adj* helaeth, eang.
spade *n* pâl, rhaw *f*.
span *n* rhychwant *m*. • *v* rhychwantu.
spare *v* arbed, sbario. • *adj* cynnil, prin.
sparing *adj* cynnil, darbodus.
spark *n* gwreichionen *f*.
sparkle *n* fflach *f*. • *v* pefrio, serennu.
sparse *adj* tenau, prin.
spasm *n* pwl, plwc *m*.
spatter *v* ysgeintio, tasgu.
speak *v* siarad, llefaru.
speaker *n* siaradwr *m*, siaradwraig *f*; llefarydd *m*.
spear *n* gwaywffon *f*.
special *adj* arbennig.
speciality *n* arbenigedd *m*.
species *n* rhywogaeth *f*.
specific *adj* penodol.
specification *n* manyleb *f*.
specify *v* pennu.
specimen *n* esiampl *f*.
spectacle *n* golygfa *f*.
spectacles *n* sbectol *f*, gwydrau *pl*.
spectator *n* gwyliwr *m*.
spectre *n* drychiolaeth *f*, ysbryd *m*.
speculate *v* damcaniaethu; mentro.
speculation *n* dyfaliad *m*, menter *f*.
speculative *adj* damcaniaethol; mentrus.
speech *n* lleferydd *m*; araith *f*.
speed *n* cyflymder, buanedd *m*.
speed limit *n* cyfyngiad cyflymder *m*.
speediness *n* cyflymder, cyflymdra *m*.
speedy *adj* buan.
spell *n* swyn *m*. • *v* sillafu.
spelling *n* sillafiad *m*.
spend *v* gwario, treulio.
sphere *n* sffêr *m/f*, cronnell *f*.
spherical *adj* sfferaidd.
spice *n* sbeis *m*.
spicy *adj* sbeislyd.
spider *n* corryn, pryf copyn *m*.
spike *n* pigyn *m*.
spill *v* colli, sarnu.
spin *v* troelli; nyddu.
spinal *adj* y cefn.
spine *n* asgwrn cefn *m*.
spire *n* meindwr *m*.
spirit *n* ysbryd, enaid *m*; calon *f*; gwirod *m/f*.
spirited *adj* bywiog, nwyfus.
spiritless *adj* dieneiniad, merfaidd.
spiritual *adj* ysbrydol.
spirituality *n* ysbrydolrwydd *m*.
spit *n* poer *m*. • *v* poeri.
spite *n* sbeit *m*; **in ~ of** er gwaethaf.
spiteful *adj* mileinig, milain.
splash *v* tasgu, sblasio.
splendid *adj* ardderchog, campus.
splendour *n* gogoniant, ysblander *m*.

splinter *n* ysgyren *f.* • *v* torri'n ysgyrion.
split *n* hollt *f.* • *v* hollti.
spoil *v* difetha.
spokesman *n* llefarydd *m.*
sponge *n* sbwng *m.*
sponsor *n* noddwr *m.*
sponsorship *n* nawdd *m.*
spontaneity *n* natur ddigymell *f.*
spontaneous *adj* digymell.
spoon *n* llwy *f.*
sporadic(al) *adj* ysbeidiol, anfynych.
sport *n* sbort *m/f*; chwaraeon *pl.*
sportsman *n* chwaraewr *m.*
sportswoman *n* chwaraewraig *f.*
spot *n* man *m/f.* • *v* brychu; gweld.
spotless *adj* dilychwin, difrycheulyd.
spouse *n* priod *m/f.*
spout *v* pistyllio, ffrydio. • *n* ffrwd *f*; pig *m/f.*
sprain *v* ysigo.
spray *n* tusw *m*; ewyn *m.* • *v* chwistrellu.
spread *v* taenu, lledaenu.
spring *v* neidio. • *n* gwanwyn *m*; ffynnon *f.*
sprinkle *v* ysgeintio.
sprout *n* eginyn, blaguryn *m.*
spruce *adj* twt, testlus.
spur *n* sbardun *m/f.* • *v* sbarduno.
spurn *v* dirmygu.
sputter *v* ffrwtian.
spy *n* ysbïwr *m*, ysbïwraig *f.* • *v* ysbïo.
squabble *v* ffraeo. • *n* ffrae *f.*
squad *n* carfan *f.*
squadron *n* sgwadron *m/f.*
squalid *adj* brwnt, budr.
squall *n* hwrdd (o wynt) *m.*
squalor *n* budreddi, aflendid *m.*
square *n* sgwâr *f/m.*
squash *v* gwasgu.
squat *v* cyrcydu.
squeak *v* gwichian.
squeal *n* gwich *f.*
squeeze *v* gwasgu.
squint *v* ciledrych. • *n* tro (yn y) llygad *m.* • *adj* llygatgam.
squirt *v* chwistrellu.
stab *v* trywanu.
stability *n* sadrwydd, sefydlogrwydd *m.*
stable *n* stabl *f.* • *adj* sefydlog.
stack *n* pentwr *m.* • *v* pentyrru.
staff *n* staff *m*; ffon *f.*
stage *n* llwyfan *m/f.*
stagger *v* gwegian.
stagnation *n* marweidd-dra *m.*
stagnate *v* troi'n ferddwr.
stain *v* staenio. • *n* staen *m.*
stair *n* gris *m/f.*
stake *n* polyn *m.*
stale *adj* hen.
stalk *n* coes *f*, coesyn *m.*
stall *n* côr *m*; stondin *m.*
stamina *n* dyfalbarhad *m.*
stammer *v* bod ag atal dweud, cecian. • *n* atal dweud *m.*
stamp *v* curo traed, pystylad. • *n* stamp *m.*
stand *v* sefyll; goddef. • *n* safiad, eisteddle *m.*
standard *n* safon; baner *f.* • *adj* safonol.

standstill *n* sefyll (yn stond) *vn.*
staple *n* ystwffwl *m.* • *adj* prif.
star *n* seren *f.*
starch *n* startsh *m.*
stare *v* rhythu, syllu.
starry *adj* serennog, serog.
start *v* cychwyn, dechrau; neidio. • *n* dechreuad *m.*
starter *n* cychwynnwr *m.*
startle *v* dychryn.
starvation *n* newyn *m.*
starve *v* newynu, llwgu.
state *n* cyflwr *m*; gwladwriaeth *f.* • *v* datgan.
stately *adj* urddasol.
statement *n* datganiad, gosodiad *m.*
statesman *n* gwladweinydd *m.*
static *adj* statig; sefydlog.
station *n* gorsaf *f.*
stationary *adj* disymud, yn eich unfan.
stationery *n* papur ysgrifennu *m.*
statistical *adj* ystadegol.
statue *n* cerflun *m.*
stature *n* corffolaeth *f*, maintoli *m.*
statute *n* statud *f.*
stay *v* aros, sefyll.
steadfast *adj* cadarn, disyflyd.
steadiness *n* sadrwydd, sefydlogrwydd *m.*
steady *adj* sefydlog, cyson. • *v* sefydlogi.
steak *n* stêc, stecen *f.*
steal *v* lladrata, dwyn.
stealthy *adj* llechwraidd, lladradaidd.
steam *n* ager *m.* • *v* mygu.
steam engine *n* peiriant ager *m.*
steel *n* dur *m.*
steep *adj* serth.
steepness *n* pa mor serth yw.
steer *v* llywio, cyfeirio.
steering wheel *n* olwyn yrru *f.*
stem *n* coes *f.*
step *n* cam, gris *m.* • *v* camu.
stepbrother *n* llysfrawd *m.*
stepsister *n* llyschwaer *f.*
stereotype *n* ystrydeb *f.*
sterile *adj* di-haint.
sterilise *v* steryllu.
sterling *adj* dilys; sterling.
stern *adj* llym, caled.
stew *n* stiw *m.*
steward *n* stiward *m.*
stewardess *n* stiwardes *f.*
stick *n* ffon *f.*
sticky *adj* gludiog.
stiff *adj* anystwyth, anhyblyg.
stiffen *v* cryfhau; caledu, cyffio.
stiffness *n* anystwythder, stiffrwydd *f.*
stifle *v* mygu.
stifling *adj* llethol.
stigmatise *v* stigmateiddio.
still *v* tawelu. • *adj* llonydd. • *adv* o hyd.
stillness *n* llonyddwch *m.*
stimulate *v* symbylu, cyffroi.
stimulus *n* symbyliad *m.*
sting *v* pigo, brathu.
stinginess *n* crintachrwydd *m.*
stingy *adj* crintachlyd, cybyddlyd.
stink *v* drewi. • *n* drewdod.
stipulate *v* mynnu.
stipulation *n* amod *m/f.*

stir *v* troi, corddi.
stitch *v* pwytho. • *n* pwyth *m.*
stock *n* stoc; cyff *m.* • *v* stocio.
stock exchange *n* cyfnewidfa stoc *f.*
stockbroker *n* brocer stoc *m.*
stocking *n* hosan *f.*
stoical *adj* stoicaidd.
stomach *n* stumog *f,* bola *m.*
stone *n* carreg *f.* • *v* llabyddio.
stony *adj* caregog.
stool *n* stôl *f.*
stoop *v* gwargrymu, plygu.
stop *v* aros, atal.
stoppage *n* ataliad *m.*
storage *n* crynhoad *m,* storfa *f.*
store *n* storfa *f.* • *v* storio.
stork *n* storc *m.*
storm *n* storm, drycin *f.*
stormy *adj* stormus.
story *n* stori *f,* hanes *m.*
stout *adj* tew; glew.
stoutness *n* tewdra *m.*
stove *n* stôf *f.*
stow *v* rhoi i'w gadw.
straight *adj* syth, union.
straightaway *adv* ar unwaith, yn union.
straighten *v* unioni.
strain *v* straenio. • *n* straen *f.*
strait *n* culfor *m.*
strand *n* traethell *f,* marian *m.*
strange *adj* rhyfedd.
strangeness *n* dieithrwch *m.*
stranger *n* dieithryn *m.*
strangle *v* llindagu, tagu.
strap *n* strapen *f.*
stratagem *n* ystryw *m/f.*
strategic *adj* strategol.
strategy *n* strategaeth *f.*
straw *n* gwellt *m.*
strawberry *n* mefusen *f.*
stray *v* crwydro. • *adj* crwydrol, ar grwydr.
streak *n* strimyn *m.*
stream *n* nant, ffrwd *f.* • *v* llifo, ffrydio.
street *n* stryd, heol *f.*
strength *n* nerth, cryfder *m.*
strengthen *v* cryfhau, atgyfnerthu.
stress *n* pwysau *m.* • *v* pwysleisio.
stretch *v* estyn, ymestyn.
stretcher *n* cludwely *m.*
strew *v* gwasgaru.
strict *adj* llym, caeth.
strictness *n* llymder, cywirdeb *m.*
stride *n* cam bras *m.*
strife *n* cynnen *f,* ymryson *m.*
strike *v* taro, bwrw.
striker *n* streiciwr; saethwr *m.*
striking *adj* trawiadol.
string *n* llinyn, cortyn *m.*
stringent *adj* caeth, llym.
strip *v* tynnu dillad. • *n* stribed *m/f.*
stripe *n* rhesen, streipen *f.*
strive *v* ymdrechu, ymlafnio.
stroke *n* ergyd *m/f,* trawiad *m.* • *v* canmol, anwesu.
stroll *v* mynd am dro.
strong *adj* grymus, cryf, cadarn.
strongbox *n* coffr cryf *m.*
structure *n* adeiledd, strwythur *m.*
struggle *v* strancio. • *n* ymdrech, brwydr *f.*
strut *v* torsythu.

stubborn *adj* ystyfnig, cyndyn.
stubbornness *n* ystyfnigrwydd, cyndynrwydd *m.*
stud *n* styden *m.*
student *n* myfyriwr *m.*
studio *n* stiwdio *f.*
studious *adj* myfyrgar.
study *n* astudiaeth *f*; efrydiau *pl.* • *v* astudio.
stuff *n* defnydd, sylwedd *m.* • *v* stwffio.
stuffing *n* stwffin *m.*
stumble *v* baglu.
stump *n* bôn, bonyn *m.*
stun *v* syfrdanu, hurtio.
stunt *n* sbloet *f.*
stupefy *v* peri i gysgu; syfrdanu.
stupendous *adj* aruthrol.
stupid *adj* twp.
stupidity *n* twpdra *m.*
stupor *n* syrthni *m.*
sturdiness *n* cryfder, cadernid *m.*
sturdy *adj* cydnerth, praff.
stutter *v* cecian, cecial.
style *n* steil *m.*
stylish *adj* cain.
suave *adj* gwên-deg.
subdivide *v* isrannu.
subdue *v* darostwng, gostegu.
subject *n* testun, goddrych *m.*
subjective *adj* goddrychol.
subjugate *v* darostwng.
subjugation *n* darostyngiad *m.*
sublimate *v* sychdarthu.
sublime *adj* aruchel, dyrchafedig.
sublimity *n* arucheledd *m.*
submarine *n* llong danfor *f.*
submerge *v* suddo, ymsuddo.
submission *n* ymostyngiad; cyflwyniad *m.*
submissive *adj* ymostyngol.
submit *v* ymostwng; cyflwyno.
subordinate *adj* israddol.
subscribe *v* tanysgrifio.
subscriber *n* tanysgrifiwr *m.*
subscription *n* tanysgrifiad *m.*
subsequent *adj* dilynol.
subside *v* suddo, gostwng.
subsidence *n* ymsuddiant *m.*
subsidiary *adj* cynorthwyol, atodol.
subsidise *v* sybsideiddio.
subsidy *n* cymhorthdal *m.*
subsist *v* dal i fyw, bodoli.
subsistence *n* cynhaliaeth *f.*
substance *n* sylwedd *m.*
substantial *adj* sylweddol.
substantiate *v* cadarnhau, profi.
substitute *v* eilyddio, cyfnewid.
substitution *n* cyfnewidiad *m.*
subterranean *adj* tanddaearol.
subtitle *n* is-deitl *m.*
subtle *adj* cynnil, cyfrwys.
subtlety *n* cynildeb, cywreinrwydd *m.*
subtract *v* tynnu.
suburb *n* maestref *f.*
suburban *adj* maestrefol.
subversive *adj* yn tanseilio, chwyldroadol.
subvert *v* tanseilio.
succeed *v* llwyddo.
success *n* llwyddiant *m.*
successful *adj* llwyddiannus.
succession *n* olyniaeth *f.*
successive *adj* olynol.

successor *n* olynydd *m.*
succinct *adj* cryno, byr.
succumb *v* ildio.
such *adj* cyfryw, y fath.
suck *v* sugno.
suckle *v* sugno.
sudden *adj* annisgwyl, dirybudd.
suddenness *n* sydynrwydd *m.*
sue *v* erlyn, siwio.
suffer *v* dioddef.
suffering *n* dioddefaint *m.*
suffice *v* bod yn ddigon, digoni.
sufficient *adj* digon.
suffocate *v* mogi, mygu.
suffocation *n* mogfa *f.*
sugar *n* siwgwr *m.*
sugary *adj* siwgwraidd.
suggest *v* awgrymu.
suggestion *n* awgrym *m.*
suicidal *adj* hunanddinistriol.
suicide *n* hunanladdiad *m.*
suit *n* siwt *f.* • *v* addasu, bod yn addas.
suitable *adj* addas, cymwys.
suitcase *n* cês dillad *m.*
sulky *adj* pwdlyd.
sullen *adj* sarrug, swrth.
sultry *adj* mwll.
sum *n* cyfanswm *m.* • *v*: **to – up** crynhoi.
summary *n* crynodeb *m.*
summer *n* haf *m.*
summit *n* copa *f/m.*
summon *v* gwysio.
summons *n* gwŷs *f.*
sumptuous *adj* moethus.
sun *n* haul *m.*
sunbathe *v* bolaheulo, torheulo.
sunburn *n* llosg haul *m.*
Sunday *n* dydd Sul *m.*
sundry *adj* amryw, amrywiol.
sunflower *n* blodyn yr haul *m.*
sunny *adj* heulog, tesog.
sunrise *n* codiad haul *m.*
sunset *n* machlud haul *m.*
sunshade *n* cysgodlen *f.*
sunshine *n* heulwen *f,* golau haul *m.*
sunstroke *n* twymyn yr haul *f.*
suntan *n* lliw haul *m.*
super *adj* penigamp, rhagorol.
superb *adj* gwych.
supercilious *adj* ffroenuchel.
superficial *adj* arwynebol.
superfluity *n* toreth *f.*
superfluous *adj* dianghenraid.
superior *adj* uwch, uwchradd.
superiority *n* rhagoriaeth *f.*
superlative *adj* rhagorol, eithaf.
supermarket *n* uwchfarchnad *f.*
supernatural *n* goruwchnaturiol *m.*
supersede *v* disodli, cymryd lle.
supersonic *adj* uwchsonig.
superstition *n* ofergoel *f.*
superstitious *adj* ofergoelus.
supervene *v* digwydd, dilyn.
supervise *v* goruchwylio, arolygu.
supervision *n* goruchwyliaeth *f.*
supervisor *n* goruchwyliwr *m,* arolygydd *m.*
supper *n* cinio *m.*
supplant *v* disodli, cymryd lle.
supple *adj* ystwyth, hydwyth.
supplement *n* atodiad, ychwanegiad *m.*
supplementary *adj* atodol, ychwanegol.

suppleness *n* ystwythder, hyblygrwydd *m*.
supplicate *v* erfyn, deisyf.
supplication *n* erfyniad, deisyfiad *m*.
supplier *n* cyflenwr *m*.
supply *v* cyflenwi. • *n* cyflenwad *m*.
support *v* cynnal. • *n* cefnogaeth, cynhaliaeth *f*.
supporter *n* cefnogwr *m*.
suppose *v* tybio, a bwrw.
supposition *n* tybiaeth *f*.
suppress *v* atal, gostegu.
suppression *n* atal, gostegu *vn*.
supremacy *n* goruchafiaeth *f*.
supreme *adj* pennaf, goruchaf.
surcharge *v* codi ychwaneg. • *n* tâl ychwanegol *m*.
sure *adj* sicr.
sureness *n* sicrwydd *m*.
surf *n* ewyn *m*. • *v* beistonna.
surface *n* wyneb *m*. • *v* codi i'r wyneb.
surfboard *n* astell feiston *f*.
surge *n* ymchwydd, dygyfor *m*.
surgeon *n* llawfeddyg *m*.
surgery *n* meddygfa; triniaeth lawfeddygol *f*.
surgical *adj* llawfeddygol.
surly *adj* sarrug, swrth.
surmise *v* dyfalu, tybio.
surmount *v* gorchfygu.
surname *n* cyfenw *m*.
surpass *v* rhagori ar.
surplus *n* gweddill *m*, gwarged *m/f*.
surprise *v* synnu. • *n* peth annisgwyl, syndod *m*.
surrender *v* ildio.
surreptitious *adj* llechwraidd.
surrogate *adj* dirprwyol.
surround *v* amgylchynu.
survey *v* gwneud arolwg. • *n* arolwg *m*.
survive *v* goroesi.
survivor *n* goroeswr *m*.
susceptibility *n* chwanogrwydd; teimlad *m*.
susceptible *adj* tueddol, chwannog.
suspect *v* drwgdybio. • *n* rhywun dan amheuaeth *m*.
suspend *v* hongian; diarddel.
suspense *n* gwewyr meddwl *m*.
suspicion *n* amheuaeth, drwgdybiaeth *f*.
suspicious *adj* amheus, drwgdybus.
sustain *v* cynnal.
sustenance *n* cynhaliaeth *f*.
swagger *v* rhodresa, torsythu.
swallow *v* llyncu.
swamp *n* cors, mignen *f*.
swap *v* cyfnewid, ffeirio.
swarm *n* haid *f*. • *v* heidio.
swath *n* ystod *f*.
sway *v* gwegian, siglo.
swear *v* tyngu, rhegi.
sweat *n* chwys *m*. • *v* chwysu.
sweep *v* ysgubo.
sweet *adj* melys. • *n* losin, da-da, fferins *m/pl*.
sweeten *v* melysu.
sweetener *n* melysydd *m*.
sweetness *n* melyster, melystra *m*.
swell *v* chwyddo.

swelling *n* chwydd, ymchwydd *m*.
swerve *v* gwyro.
swift *adj* cyflym, buan.
swiftness *n* cyflymder, cyflymdra *m*.
swim *v* nofio. • *n* nofiad *m*.
swimming pool *n* pwll nofio *m*.
swimsuit *n* gwisg nofio *f*.
swindle *v* twyllo.
swing *v* siglo. • *n* siglen *f*.
swirl *n* chwyrlïad *m*.
switch *n* swits *m*. • *v* newid; **to ~ off** diffodd; **to ~ on** troi ymlaen.
swivel *v* troi ar ei echel.
swoon *v* llesmeirio. • *n* llesmair *m*.
swoop *v* disgyn.
sword *n* cleddyf *m*.
sycophant *n* cynffonnwr *m*.
syllabic *adj* sillafog.
syllable *n* sillaf *f*.
syllabus *n* maes llafur *m*.
symbol *n* symbol *m*.
symbolic(al) *adj* symbolaidd.
symbolise *v* symboleiddio.
symmetrical *adj* cymesur.
symmetry *n* cymesuredd *m*.
sympathetic *adj* llawn cydymdeimlad.
sympathise *v* cydymdeimlo.
sympathy *n* cydymdeimlad *m*.
symphony *n* symffoni *f*.
symptom *n* arwydd, symptom *m*.
synagogue *n* synagog *f*.
syndrome *n* syndrom *m*.
synonym *n* cyfystyr *m*.
synonymous *adj* cyfystyr.
synopsis *n* crynodeb *m*.
syntax *n* cystrawen *f*.
synthesis *n* cyfuniad, cyfosodiad *m*.
syringe *n* chwistrell *f*.
system *n* cyfundrefn, system *f*.
systematic *adj* trwyadl, systematig.

T

table *n* bwrdd *m*, bord *f*.
tablecloth *n* lliain bwrdd *m*.
tablet *n* tabled *f*.
tacit *adj* dealledig.
taciturn *adj* tawedog, di-ddweud.
tack *n* tac *f/m*. • *v* tacio.
tackle *n* gêr, tacl *m*.
tact *n* tact, pwyll *m*.
tactics *n* tacteg *f*.
tag *n* tag, tocyn *m*.
tail *n* cynffon, cwt *f*.
tailor *n* teiliwr *m*.
taint *v* llygru, halogi.
tainted *adj* llygredig, drwg.
take *v* cymryd.
takeoff *n* esgyniad *m*.
takeover *n* cymryd drosodd, cipio grym *vn*.
takings *n* derbyniadau *pl*.
talc *n* talc *m*.
talent *n* dawn, talent *f*.
talented *adj* dawnus, talentog.

talk *v* siarad. • *n* sgwrs *f*.
talkative *adj* siaradus.
tall *adj* tal.
tally *v* cyfateb.
tame *adj* dof. • *v* dofi, hyweddu.
tamper *v* ymyrryd â.
tan *v* cael lliw haul. • *n* lliw haul *m*.
tangible *adj* diriaethol, go iawn.
tangle *v* drysu.
tank *n* tanc *m*.
tanker *n* tancer *m/f*.
tantrum *n* strancio *vn*.
tap *v* tapio. • *n* tap *m*.
tape *n* tâp *m*. • *v* tapio.
tape recorder *n* recordydd tâp *m*.
target *n* targed *m*.
tariff *n* toll *f*.
tarnish *v* pylu.
tart *n* tarten *f*.
task *n* gorchwyl *m/f*, gwaith *m*.
taste *n* blas *m*, chwaeth *f*. • *v* blasu.
tasteful *adj* chwaethus.
tasty *adj* blasus.
tattoo *n* tatŵ *m*.
taunt *v* edliw, dannod. • *n* edliwiad *m*.
taut *adj* tyn.
tawdry *adj* tsiêp.
tax *n* treth *f*. • *v* trethu.
taxable *adj* trethadwy.
taxation *n* treth *f*, trethiad *m*.
taxi *n* tacsi *m*.
taxpayer *n* trethdalwr *m*.
tea *n* te *m*.
teach *v* dysgu, addysgu.
teacher *n* athro *m*, athrawes *f*.
teaching *n* dysgeidiaeth *f*.
team *n* tîm *m*.
teapot *n* tebot *m*.
tear[1] *v* rhwygo.
tear[2] *n* rhwyg; deigryn *m*.
tearful *adj* dagreuol.
tease *v* poeni, pryfocio.
teaspoon *n* llwy de *f*.
technical *adj* technegol.
technician *n* technegydd *m*.
technique *n* techneg *f*.
technological *adj* technolegol.
technology *n* technoleg *f*.
tedious *adj* diflas.
tedium *n* diflastod, undonedd *m*.
teenage *adj* yn eich arddegau. • **~r** *n* glaslanc *m*.
teethe *v* torri dannedd.
telepathy *n* telepathi *m*.
telephone *n* ffôn *m*.
telephone directory *n* llyfr ffôn *m*.
telephone number *n* rhif ffôn *m*.
telescope *n* telesgop *m*.
telescopic *adj* telesgopig.
televise *v* teledu.
television *n* teledu *m*.
television set *n* set deledu *f*.
tell *v* dweud, adrodd.
temper *v* tymheru. • *n* tymer *f*.
temperament *n* anian *f*.
temperate *adj* cymedrol.
temperature *n* tymheredd *m*.
tempest *n* tymestl *f*.
temple *n* teml; arlais *f*.
temporary *adj* dros dro.
tempt *v* temtio.
temptation *n* temtasiwn *m/f*.
ten *num* deg.
tenacious *adj* cyndyn.
tenacity *n* dycnwch *m*.

tenant *n* deiliad, tenant *m*.
tend *v* gogwyddo; tendio.
tendency *n* tuedd *f*.
tender *adj* tyner, brau.
tendon *n* gewyn, giewyn *m*.
tennis *n* tennis *m*.
tenor *n* tenor *m*.
tense *adj* tyn. • *n* amser *m*.
tension *n* tyndra *m*.
tent *n* pabell *f*.
tentative *adj* petrus.
tenth *adj* degfed.
tenuous *adj* tenau.
tepid *adj* claear, llugoer.
term *n* tymor *m*.
terminal *adj* terfynol. • *n* terfynell *f*.
terminate *v* terfynu, dibennu.
termination *n* terfyniad *m*.
terrace *n* teras *m/f*.
terrain *n* tir *m*.
terrestrial *adj* daearol.
terrible *adj* ofnadwy.
terrific *adj* aruthrol.
terrify *v* dychryn, brawychu.
territorial *adj* tiriogaethol.
territory *n* tiriogaeth *f*.
terror *n* arswyd, braw *m*.
terrorise *v* brawychu, dychryn.
terrorist *n* terfysgwr *m*.
terse *adj* byr, cryno.
test *n* prawf *m*. • *v* rhoi prawf ar, profi.
test tube *n* tiwb prawf *m*.
testify *v* tystio.
testimony *n* tystiolaeth *f*.
tether *n* tennyn *m*.
text *n* testun *m*.
textual *adj* testunol.
texture *n* gwead *m*.
than *adv* na, nag.
thank *v* diolch.
thankful *adj* diolchgar.
thanks *n* diolchiadau *pl*.
that *pron* hwnnw, honno, hynny. • *conj* mai.
thatch *n* gwellt *m*.
thaw *v* dadmer, meirioli.
the *art* y, yr, 'r.
theatre *n* theatr *f*.
theatrical *adj* theatraidd.
theft *n* lladrad *m*.
theirs *poss pron* eiddynt hwy.
them *pron* hwy, nhw.
theme *n* thema *f*.
themselves *pron* eu hunain.
then *adv, conj* yna.
theological *adj* diwinyddol.
theology *n* diwinyddiaeth *f*.
theorem *n* theorem *f*.
theoretic(al) *adj* damcaniaethol.
theory *n* damcaniaeth *f*.
therapist *n* therapydd *m*.
therapy *n* triniaeth *f*, therapi *m*.
there *adv* acw, yna.
thereafter *adv* wedyn, wedi hynny.
therefore *adv* felly.
thermal *adj* thermol.
thermometer *n* thermomedr *m*.
these *pron* y rhai hyn, rhain.
thesis *n* traethawd *m*.
they *pron* hwy, nhw.
thick *adj* trwchus, tew.
thicken *v* tewychu.
thickness *n* trwch, tewdra *m*.
thickset *adj* cydnerth.

thief *n* lleidr *m*.
thigh *n* clun, morddwyd *f*.
thin *adj* tenau, main.
thing *n* peth *m*.
think *v* meddwl.
thinker *n* meddyliwr *m*.
third *adj* trydydd *m*, trydedd *f*.
thirst *n* syched *m*.
thirsty *adj* sychedig.
thirteen *num* tri ar ddeg *m*, tair ~*f*.
thirteenth *adj* trydydd ar ddeg *m*, trydedd ~ *f*.
thirtieth *adj* degfed ar hugain.
thirty *num* deg ar hugain, tri deg.
this *adj*, *pron* hwn, hon, hyn.
thistle *n* ysgallen *f*.
thorn *n* draenen *f*.
thorough *adj* trylwyr, trwyadl.
thoroughfare *n* ffordd agored *f*.
those *pron*, *adj* y rhai hynny.
though *conj* er, pe, ped.
thought *n* meddwl *m*.
thoughtful *adj* meddylgar.
thoughtless *adj* difeddwl, anystyriol.
thousand *num* mil.
thousandth *adj* milfed.
thrash *v* dyrnu, colbio.
thread *n* edau *f*, edefyn *m*.
threat *n* bygythiad *m*.
threaten *v* bygwth.
three *num* tri *m*, tair *f*.
threshold *n* trothwy *m*.
thrifty *adj* cynnil, darbodus.
thrill *v* gwefreiddio. • *n* gwefr, ias *f*.
thrive *v* ffynnu.
throat *n* gwddf *m*.
throb *v* gwynio; dyrnu.
throne *n* gorsedd *f*.
throng *n* torf, tyrfa *f*.
throttle *n* sbardun *m/f*. • *v* tagu, llindagu.
through *prep* trwy, drwy.
throughout *prep* ledled, trwy gydol.
throw *v* taflu. • *n* tafliad *m*.
thrust *v* gwthio. • *n* gwthiad *m*.
thug *n* llabwst, dihiryn *m*.
thumb *n* bawd *f*.
thump *n* ergyd, cur *m/f*. • *v* colbio, taro.
thunder *n* taranau, tyrfau *pl*. • *v* taranu.
thunderclap *n* taraniad *m*.
thunderstorm *n* storm o fellt a tharanau.
Thursday *n* dydd Iau *m*.
thus *adv* felly.
thwart *v* atal, llesteirio.
tic *n* tic *m*.
tick *n* tipiad *m*. • *v* tipian.
ticket *n* tocyn *m*.
ticket office *n* swyddfa docynnau *f*.
tickle *v* gogleisio, cosi.
tidal wave *n* ton lanw *f*.
tide *n* llanw *m*.
tidy *adj* taclus, trefnus.
tie *v* clymu. • *n* tei *m/f*.
tier *n* rhes *f*.
tiger *n* teigr *m*.
tight *adj* tyn.
tighten *v* tynhau.
tile *n* teilsen *f*.
till *v* trin, braenaru.
tilt *v* gogwyddo, gwyro.
timber *n* coed, pren *m*.

time *n* amser *m.* • *v* amseru.
time lag *n* oedi *vn.*
time zone *n* cylchfa amser *f.*
timeless *adj* digyfnewid.
timely *adj* amserol.
timid *adj* swil, ofnus.
timidity *n* swildod, diffyg hyder *m.*
tin *n* alcam, tun *m.*
tinge *n* arlliw *m.*
tingle *v* gyrru ias trwy.
tinkle *v* tincial.
tint *n* arlliw *m*, gwawr *f.* • *v* lliwio.
tinted *adj* wedi'i lliwio.
tiny *adj* bychan, pitw.
tip *n* blaen; cildwrn; tip *m.* • *v* tipio; cynnig cildwrn.
tirade *n* pregeth *f.*
tire *v* blino, diffygio.
tireless *adj* diflino.
tiresome *adj* diflas, syrffedus.
tissue *n* meinwe *f.*
titbit *n* tamaid blasus *m.*
titillate *v* goglais.
title *n* teitl *m.*
titular *adj* mewn enw.
titular saint *n* nawddsant *m.*
to *prep* i, at, wrth.
toad *n* llyffant *m.*
toast *v* crasu; cynnig llwncdestun. • *n* tost; llwncdestun *m.*
toaster *n* tostiwr *m.*
tobacco *n* tybaco *m.*
toboggan *n* sled *f.*
today *adv* heddiw.
toe *n* bys troed *m.*
together *adv* gyda'ch gilydd, ynghyd.
toil *v* llafurio.
toilet *n* tŷ bach, toiled *m.*
toilet paper *n* papur tŷ bach *m.*
toiletries *n* pethau ymolchi *pl.*
token *n* arwydd; tocyn *m.*
tolerable *adj* goddefadwy, gweddol.
tolerant *adj* goddefgar.
tolerate *v* goddef.
toll *n* toll *f.* • *v* canu cnul.
tomato *n* tomato *m.*
tomb *n* bedd *m.*
tombstone *n* carreg fedd *f.*
tomorrow *adv* yfory.
ton *n* tunnell *f.*
tone *n* tôn; gwawr *f.*
tongs *n* gefel *f.*
tongue *n* tafod *m.*
tonight *adv* heno.
too *adv* rhy.
tool *n* arf, erfyn *m.*
tooth *n* dant *m.*
toothache *n* y ddannoedd *f.*
toothbrush *n* brws dannedd *m.*
toothpaste *n* past dannedd *m.*
top *n* pen, brig *m.*
topic *n* pwnc, testun *m.*
topical *adj* amserol.
topmost *adj* uchaf.
topographic(al) *adj* topograffaidd.
topography *n* topograffeg *f.*
topple *v* cwympo, disgyn.
torch *n* fflachlamp *f.*
torment *v* poenydio. • *n* artaith *f*, cystudd *m.*
tornado *n* corwynt *m.*
torrent *n* cenllif, llifeiriant *m.*
tortuous *adj* troellog, trofaus.
torture *n* artaith *f.* • *v* arteithio.

toss *v* taflu.
total *adj* holl, cyfan, llwyr.
totality *n* cyfanrwydd *m.*
totter *v* gwegian, simsanu.
touch *v* cyffwrdd. • *n* cyffyrddiad *m.*
touchdown *n* glaniad *m.*
touching *adj* teimladwy.
tough *adj* gwydn, caled.
toughen *v* caledu, cryfhau.
tour *n* cylchdaith *f*, tro *m.*
tourism *n* twristiaeth *f.*
tourist *n* ymwelydd *m.*
tournament *n* twrnamaint *m.*
tow *v* halio, tynnu.
toward(s) *prep* tua, tuag.
towel *n* lliain *m.*
tower *n* tŵr *m.*
town *n* tref *f.*
town hall *n* neuadd y dref *f.*
towrope *n* rhaff halio *f.*
toy *n* tegan *m.*
trace *n* ôl, arlliw *m.* • *v* olrhain, amlinellu.
track *n* trywydd *m.*
tract *n* ehangder; pamffledyn *m.*
traction *n* tyniant *m.*
trade *n* masnach; crefft *f.* • *v* masnachu.
trademark *n* nod masnach *m.*
trader *n* masnachwr *m.*
trade(s) union *n* undeb llafur *m.*
trade unionist *n* undebwr *m.*
trading *adj* masnachol.
tradition *n* traddodiad *m.*
traditional *adj* traddodiadol.
traffic *n* trafnidiaeth *f*, traffig *m.*
traffic jam *n* tagfa *f.*
tragedy *n* trasiedi *f.*
tragic *adj* alaethus, trist.
trail *n* ôl, trywydd *m.*
train *v* hyfforddi, ymarfer. • *n* trên *m.*
trainer *n* hyfforddwr *m.*
training *n* hyfforddiant *m.*
trait *n* nodwedd *f.*
traitor *n* bradwr *m.*
tramp *n* sŵn traed *m.* • *v* cerdded yn drwm.
trance *n* llesmair *m.*
tranquil *adj* tawel, llonydd.
transact *v* trafod, trin.
transactions *n* trafodion *pl.*
transcend *v* codi uwchlaw.
transcription *n* adysgrif *f.*
transfer *v* trosglwyddo, adleoli. • *n* trosglwyddiad, adleoliad *m.*
transform *v* gweddnewid, trawsnewid.
transfusion *n* trallwyso *vn.*
transition *n* trawsnewidiad *m.*
transitional *adj* trawsnewidiol.
translate *v* cyfieithu.
translation *n* cyfieithiad *m.*
translator *n* cyfieithydd *m.*
transmission *n* trosglwyddo *vn.*
transmit *v* anfon, trosglwyddo.
transparency *n* tryloywder *m.*
transparent *adj* tryloyw.
transplant *v* trawsblannu.
transport *v* cludo. • *n* cludiant *m.*
trap *n* magl *f*, trap *m.* • *v* maglu, dal.
travel *v* teithio. • *n* taith *f.*
traveller *n* teithiwr, trafaelwr *m.*
traveller's cheque *n* siec deithio *f.*
travesty *n* parodi *m.*

tray *n* hambwrdd *m.*
treacherous *adj* bradwrus, dichellgar.
treachery *n* brad *m*, bradwriaeth *f.*
tread *v* camu, troedio.
treason *n* bradwriaeth, teyrnfradwriaeth *f.*
treasure *n* trysor *m.*
treasurer *n* trysorydd *m.*
treat *v* trin, trafod. • *n* peth amheuthun *m.*
treatment *n* triniaeth *f.*
treaty *n* cytundeb *m.*
treble *v* treblu.
tree *n* coeden *f.*
trek *n* ymdaith *f.*
tremble *v* crynu.
tremendous *adj* aruthrol.
trend *n* tuedd *f*, cyfeiriad *m.*
trespass *v* tresmasu.
trial *n* achos llys, treial *m.*
triangle *n* triongl *m.*
tribal *adj* llwythol.
tribe *n* llwyth *m.*
tribunal *n* tribiwnlys *m.*
tributary *n* llednant *f.*
trick *n* ystryw *m/f*, tric *m.* • *v* twyllo.
tricky *adj* cyfrwys; anodd.
trifle *n* peth dibwys; treiffl *m.*
trifling *adj* dibwys, pitw.
trigger *n* clicied *f.*
trim *adj* trwsiadus, testlus. • *v* tocio, twtio.
trip *v* baglu. • *n* gwibdaith *f.*
triple *adj* triphlyg. • *v* treblu.
trite *adj* ystrydebol.
triumph *n* buddugoliaeth *f.* • *v* ennill buddugoliaeth.
triumphant *adj* buddugoliaethus.
trivia *n* pethau dibwys *pl.*
trivial *adj* pitw, dibwys.
triviality *n* dinodedd, distadledd *m.*
troop *n* mintai *f*, criw *m.*
tropical *adj* trofannol.
trouble *v* poeni. • *n* pryder, gofid *m.*
troublesome *adj* trafferthus.
trousers *n* trywser, trywsus *m.*
trout *n* brithyll *m.*
truck *n* tryc *m.*
truck driver *n* gyrrwr lorri *m.*
truculent *adj* ffyrnig, mileinig.
true *adj* gwir, cywir.
trump *n* trwmp *m.*
trumpet *n* trwmped *m.*
trunk *n* boncyff, trwnc *m.*
trust *n* ymddiriedaeth; ymddiriedolaeth *f.* • *v* ymddiried.
trustworthy *adj* dibynadwy.
trusty *adj* ffyddlon, dibynadwy.
truth *n* gwir, gwirionedd *m.*
truthful *adj* geirwir, gonest.
truthfulness *n* gwirionedd, geirwiredd *m.*
try *v* profi, ceisio. • *n* cais *m*, ymgais *m/f.*
tub *n* twb, twba *m.*
tube *n* tiwb *m.*
tuck *n* twc *m.* • *v* twcio.
Tuesday *n* dydd Mawrth *m.*
tug *v* tynnu, llusgo. • *n* tyniad. plwc *m.*
tuition *n* hyfforddiant *m.*
tulip *n* tiwlip *m.*
tumble *v* syrthio, cael codwm. • *n* codwm *m.*

tumbler *n* gwydryn *m.*
tumultuous *adj* cythryblus.
tune *n* alaw, tôn *f.*
tuneful *adj* persain.
tunnel *n* twnnel *m.*
turbulence *n* cynnwrf *m.*
turbulent *adj* cythryblus, aflonydd.
turf *n* tywarchen *f.*
turkey *n* twrci *m.*
turmoil *n* berw, cynnwrf *m.*
turn *v* troi. • *n* tro, troad *m.*
turning *n* tro *m.*
turnover *n* trosiant *m.*
turnstile *n* giât dro *f.*
turquoise *adj* gwyrddlas.
turtle *n* crwban y môr *m.*
tusk *n* ysgithr *m.*
tutor *n* tiwtor *m.*
tweezers *n* gefel *f.*
twelfth *adj* deuddegfed.
twelve *num* deuddeg.
twentieth *adj* ugeinfed.
twenty *num* ugain.
twice *adv* dwywaith.
twilight *n* cyfnos, gwyll *m.*
twin *n* gefell *m/f.*
twine *v* cordeddu, cyfrodeddu.
twinkle *v* pefrio, serennu.
twirl *v* chwyrlïad *m.*
twist *v* cyfrodeddu.
twitch *n* plwc *m.*
two *num* dau *m*, dwy *f.*
twofold *adj* deublyg.
tycoon *n* teicŵn *m.*
type *n* math; teip *m.* • *v* teipio.
typeface *n* wyneb teip *m.*
typewriter *n* teipiadur *m.*
typical *adj* nodweddiadol.
tyrannical *adj* gormesol.
tyrant *n* teyrn *m.*
tyre *n* teiar *m.*

U

ugliness *n* hagrwch *m.*
ugly *adj* hyll, hagr, salw.
ulcer *n* briw, dolur *m.*
ulterior *adj* cudd.
ultimate *adj* terfynol, olaf.
ultimatum *n* cynnig terfynol, rhybudd olaf *m.*
umbrella *n* ambarél, ymbarél *m/f.*
umpire *n* dyfarnwr *m.*
unable *adj* analluog, methu.
unaccomplished *adj* heb ei gyflawni; di-ddawn.
unaccountable *adj* anesboniadwy.
unaccustomed *adj* anarferol, anghyfarwydd.
unacknowledged *adj* anghydnabyddedig.
unadulterated *adj* pur, digymysg.
unaltered *adj* digyfnewid.
unanimity *n* unfrydedd *m.*
unanimous *adj* unfrydol.
unanswerable *adj* anatebadwy.
unapproachable *adj* anhygyrch, pell.

unarmed *adj* heb arfau, diarfog.
unattached *adj* heb fod ynghlwm, digyswllt.
unattainable *adj* anghyraeddadwy.
unavoidable *adj* anochel.
unaware *adj* anymwybodol.
unbalanced *adj* anghytbwys.
unbearable *adj* annioddefol.
unbelievable *adj* anghredadwy, anhygoel.
unbiased *adj* diduedd, cytbwys.
unbreakable *adj* anhydor, na ellir mo'i dorri.
unbroken *adj* di-dor.
unbutton *v* datod botymau.
unceasing *adj* di-baid, di-drai.
unceremonious *adj* diseremoni, di-lol.
uncertain *adj* ansicr.
uncertainty *n* ansicrwydd, amhendantrwydd *m.*
unchangeable *adj* digyfnewid.
uncharitable *adj* angharedig, didostur.
uncivil *adj* anghwrtais.
uncivilised *adj* anwaraidd.
uncle *n* ewythr *m.*
uncomfortable *adj* anghyfforddus, anghysurus.
uncommon *adj* anghyffredin, anarferol.
uncompromising *adj* digyfaddawd.
unconcern *n* difrawder, dihidrwydd *m.*
unconditional *adj* diamod, diamodol.
unconscious *adj* anymwybodol, diymwybod.
uncork *v* tynnu corcyn.
uncouth *adj* aflednais, anwaraidd.
uncover *v* dinoethi, datguddio.
uncultivated *adj* heb ei drin, anniwy-lliedig.
undecided *adj* ansicr.
undeniable *adj* anwadadwy, diymwad.
under *prep* tan, dan. • *adv* tanodd, danodd.
underclothing *n* dillad isaf *pl.*
undercover *adj* cudd, cuddiedig.
underdeveloped *adj* heb ei ddatblygu.
underestimate *v* meddwl yn rhy isel am.
undergo *v* cael.
undergraduate *n* myfyriwr *m.*
undergrowth *n* prysgwydd *pl.*
underhand *adj* dichellgar, twyllodrus.
underline *v* tanlinellu.
underneath *adv* oddi tanodd. • *prep* tan, dan.
underpaid *adj* ar gyflog gwael.
underprivileged *adj* difreintiedig.
underside *n* tu isaf *m,* tor *f.*
understand *v* deall, dirnad.
understandable *adj* dealladwy.
understanding *n* dealltwriaeth, dirnadaeth *f.*
undertake *v* ymgymryd.
undertaking *n* menter *f.*
undervalue *v* tanbrisio.
underwater *adj* tanddwr.
underwear *n* dillad isaf *pl.*
underwrite *v* gwarantu.
undeserved *adj* anhaeddiannol.

undetermined *adj* amhenodol, amhendant.
undisciplined *adj* annisgybledig.
undisputed *adj* diameuol, diddadl.
undivided *adj* diwahân.
undo *v* datod, dad-wneud.
undoing *n* diwedd, distryw *m.*
undoubted *adj* diamau, diamheuol.
undress *v* dadwisgo, ymddihatru.
undue *adj* gormodol, afraid.
uneasy *adj* anesmwyth, anniddig.
uneducated *adj* annysgedig.
unemployed *adj* di-waith, segur.
unemployment *n* diweithdra *m.*
unending *adj* diddiwedd, diderfyn.
unequal *adj* anghyfartal.
unequalled *adj* digymar, digyffelyb.
uneven *adj* anwastad.
unexpected *adj* annisgwyl.
unfailing *adj* di-feth, di-ffael.
unfair *adj* anghyfiawn.
unfaithful *adj* anffyddlon.
unfashionable *adj* anffasiynol.
unfasten *v* datod, agor.
unfavourable *adj* anffafriol.
unfeeling *adj* dideimlad, oeraidd.
unfinished *adj* anorffenedig.
unfit *adj* anaddas, anghymwys.
unfold *v* agor; mynd rhagddo.
unforeseen *adj* annisgwyl.
unforgettable *adj* bythgofiadwy, anfarwol.
unfortunate *adj* anffodus.
unfounded *adj* di-sail.
unfriendly *adj* di-groeso, anghyfeillgar.
ungrateful *adj* anniolchgar.
unhappiness *n* tristwch, anhapusrwydd *m.*
unhappy *adj* anhapus, trist.
unhealthy *adj* afiach.
unheeding *adj* didaro, dihidio.
unhook *v* dadfachu.
unhurt *adj* dianaf.
uniform *adj* unffurf.
uniformity *n* unffurfiaeth *f.*
unify *v* uno.
unimaginable *adj* anhygoel; y tu hwnt i'r dychymyg.
uninhabitable *adj* yn amhosibl byw ynddo.
uninhabited *adj* anghyfannedd.
uninjured *adj* dianaf.
unintelligible *adj* annealladwy.
unintentional *adj* anfwriadol.
uninterested *adj* difater, di-hid.
uninterrupted *adj* di-dor, di-baid.
union *n* uniad *m*, undeb *f.*
unique *adj* unigryw.
unison *n* unsain *f.*
unit *n* uned *f.*
unite *v* uno.
unity *n* undod *m.*
universal *adv* byd-eang.
universe *n* bydysawd *m.*
university *n* prifysgol *f.*
unjust *adj* anghyfiawn, annheg.
unknown *adj* anadnabyddus, anhysbys.
unlawful *adj* anghyfreithlon.
unlawfulness *n* anghyfreithlondeb *m.*
unleash *v* gollwng, rhyddhau.
unless *conj* oni, onid.
unlicensed *adj* annhrwyddedig.

unlikely *adj* annhebygol.
unlikelihood *n* annhebygolrwydd *m.*
unlimited *adj* diderfyn, di-ben-draw.
unload *v* dadlwytho.
unlucky *adj* anffodus, anlwcus.
unmask *v* dinoethi.
unmerited *adj* anhaeddiannol.
unmistakable *adj* digamsyniol.
unmoved *adj* diysgog, disyflyd.
unnecessary *adj* dianghenraid, afraid.
unnoticed *adj* disylw.
unobserved *adj* heb sylwi arno.
unoccupied *adj* gwag.
unoffending *adj* didramgwydd.
unpack *v* dadbacio.
unparalleled *adj* digyffelyb.
unpleasant *adj* annymunol.
unpopular *adj* amhoblogaidd.
unprecedented *adj* heb gynsail.
unpredictable *adj* anrhagweladwy.
unprejudiced *adj* diragfarn.
unprofitable *adj* dielw, di-fudd.
unpublished *adj* anghyhoeddedig.
unqualified *adj* anghymwys.
unquestionable *adj* diamheuol.
unreal *adj* afreal.
unreasonable *adv* afresymol.
unrelated *adj* digyswllt.
unrelenting *adj* diarbed, di-idio.
unreserved *adj* heb ei gadw.
unrest *n* aflonyddwch *m.*
unripe *adj* anaeddfed.
unroll *v* dadrolio.
unsafe *adj* anniogel, peryglus.
unsatisfactory *adj* anfoddhaol.
unscrew *v* dadsgriwio.
unseasonable *adj* annhymhorol.
unseemly *adj* anweddus.
unsettled *adj* ansefydlog.
unsociable *adj* anghymdeithasol.
unspeakable *adj* anhraethol.
unstable *adj* ansefydlog.
unsteady *adj* simsan.
untamed *adj* anystywallt, gwyllt.
untapped *adj* dihysbydd.
untenable *adj* anghynaladwy.
unthinkable *adj* y tu hwnt i amgyffred.
untidiness *n* annibendod, llanast *m.*
untidy *adj* anniben.
untie *v* datod.
until *prep, conj* hyd, nes, tan.
untimely *adj* annhymig, cynamserol.
untouched *adj* heb ei gyffwrdd.
untroubled *adj* digyffro.
untrue *adj* anghywir.
untrustworthy *adj* annibynadwy.
unused *adj* heb ei ddefnyddio.
unusual *adj* anarferol, anghyffredin.
unveil *v* dadlennu, dadorchuddio.
unwelcoming *adj* digroeso.
unwell *adj* gwael, anhwylus.
unwilling *adj* amharod, anfodlon.
unwind *v* dadweindio, datod.
unwise *adj* annoeth.
unwitting *adj* diarwybod.
unworkable *adj* anymarferol.
unworthy *adj* annheilwng.
up *adv, prep* i fyny, lan, i lan.
upbringing *n* magwraeth *f.*
update *v* diweddaru.
upheaval *n* cyffro, terfysg *m.*

uphold *v* cynnal, ategu.
upholstery *n* clustogwaith *m*.
upkeep *n* cynhaliaeth *f*.
upon *prep* ar, ar warthaf.
upper *adj* uwch, uchaf.
uppermost *adj* uchaf.
upright *adj* union, unionsyth.
uprising *n* terfysg, gwrthryfel *m*.
uproar *n* trwst, twrw *m*.
uproot *v* dadwreiddio.
upset *v* troi, dymchwelyd, gofidio.
upshot *n* canlyniad *m*.
upside-down *adv* wyneb i waered.
upstairs *adv* lan lofft, i fyny'r staer.
up-to-date *adj* hollol gyfoes.
upturn *n* ar i fyny.
urban *adj* trefol, dinesig.
urbane *adj* hynaws, moesgar.
urchin *n* crwt *m*.
urge *v* annog, cymell. • *n* cymhelliad, cynhyrfiad *m*.
urgency *n* brys *m*.
urgent *adj* o frys.
urinate *v* gwneud dŵr, pisio.
urn *n* wrn *m*.
us *pron* ni, ninnau.
usage *n* defnydd *m*, triniaeth *f*.
use *v* defnyddio.
useful *adj* defnyddiol.
usefulness *n* defnyddioldeb *m*.
useless *adj* da i ddim.
uselessness *n* anfuddioldeb *m*.
usher *n* tywysydd *m*.
usual *adj* arferol.
usurp *v* camfeddiannu.
utensil *n* llestr *m*.
uterus *n* croth *f*.
utility *n* defnyddioldeb *m*.
utmost *adj* eithaf, mwyaf.
utter *adj* llwyr, hollol. • *v* yngan, ynganu.
utterly *adv* yn llwyr.

V

vacancy *n* swydd wag *f*.
vacant *adj* gwag.
vacate *v* gadael.
vacation *n* gwyliau *pl*.
vaccinate *v* brechu.
vacuum *n* gwactod *m*.
vague *adj* annelwig, amhendant.
vain *adj* balch, ofer.
valiant *adj* dewr.
valid *adj* dilys.
valley *n* dyffryn, cwm, glyn *m*.
valuable *adj* gwerthfawr.
value *n* gwerth *m*. • *v* prisio.
valve *n* falf *f*.
van *n* fan *f*.
vandalise *v* fandaleiddio.
vanish *v* diflannu.
vanity *n* gwagedd, balchder *m*.
vanquish *v* gorchfygu, trechu.
vantage point *n* llecyn manteisiol *m*.
vapour *n* tarth *m*.
variable *adj* amrywiol, cyfnewidiol.
variation *n* amrywiad *m*.

variety *n* amrywiaeth *f.*
various *adj* gwahanol, amryfal.
vary *v* amrywio.
vase *n* llestr blodau *m.*
vast *adj* anferth, aruthrol.
vault *n* cromen *f.* • *v* neidio.
vegetable *adj* llysieuol. • *n* llysieuyn *m.*
vegetarian *n* llysieuwr, llysieuydd *m.*
vegetate *v* pydru byw.
vegetation *n* llystyfiant *m.*
vehemence *n* taerineb, angerdd *m.*
vehement *adj* chwyrn, angerddol.
vehicle *n* cerbyd *m.*
veil *n* llen *f.*
vein *n* gwythïen *f.*
velocity *n* cyflymder, cyflymdra *m.*
velvet *n* melfed *m.*
vendor *n* gwerthwr *m.*
venerate *v* parchu, anrhydeddu.
veneration *n* parch *m.*
vengeance *n* dial, dialedd *m.*
venom *n* gwenwyn *m.*
venomous *adj* gwenwynig.
ventilate *v* awyru, gwyntyllu.
ventilation *n* awyru *vn.*
venture *n* menter *f.* • *v* mentro.
verb *n* berf *f.*
verbal *adj* llafar.
verb-noun *n* berfenw *m.*
verification *n* gwiriad *m.*
verify *v* gwirio, cadarnhau.
versatile *adj* amryddawn.
verse *n* adnod *f*; pennill *m.*
version *n* fersiwn *m/f.*
versus *prep* yn erbyn.
vertical *adj* unionsyth, fertigol.
vertigo *n* y bendro *f.*
very *adv* iawn, dros ben.
vessel *n* llestr *m*; llong *f*, cwch *m.*
veteran *adj* profiadol.
veterinarian *n* milfeddyg *m.*
veterinary *adj* milfeddygol.
veto *n* pleidlais atal *f.*
vex *v* digio, codi gwrychyn; becsio.
vexed *adj* dadleuol.
via *prep* trwy law.
viaduct *n* traphont *f.*
vibrate *v* dirgrynu, crynu.
vibration *n* dirgryniad, cryndod *m.*
vice *n* drygioni *m*, llygredigaeth *f.*
vicinity *n* cyffiniau *pl.*
vicious *adj* mileinig, milain.
victim *n* ysglyfaeth *f.*
victor *n* buddugwr, gorchfygwr *m.*
victory *n* buddugoliaeth, gorchuchafiaeth *f.*
video *n* fideo *m/f.*
viewer *n* gwyliwr *m.*
vie *v* cystadlu, ymgiprys.
view *n* golygfa, golwg *f.* • *v* gwylio, bwrw golwg.
vigil *n* gwylnos *f.*
vigilance *n* gwyliadwriaeth *f.*
vigilant *adj* gwyliadwrus, effro.
vigour *n* egni, grym *m.*
vigorous *adj* egnïol, heini.
vile *adj* ffiaidd, brwnt.
village *n* pentref *m.*
vindicate *v* cyfiawnhau, achub cam.
vindication *n* cyfiawnhad *m.*
vindictive *adj* dialgar.
vine *n* gwinwydden *f.*
vinegar *n* finegr *m.*
vineyard *n* gwinllan *f.*

violate *v* treisio.
violation *n* toriad, trais *m*.
violence *n* trais, ffyrnigrwydd *m*.
violent *adj* treisgar, treisiol.
violin *n* feiolin, ffidl *f*.
virgin *n* gwyryf, morwyn *f*.
virile *adj* egnïol.
virility *n* gwrywdod; egni *m*.
virtual *adj* i bob pwrpas; dichonadwy.
virtue *n* rhinwedd *m/f*.
virtuous *adj* rhinweddol.
virulent *adj* gwenwynig; milain.
visa *n* fisa *f*.
vis-a-vis *prep* ynglŷn â.
visibility *n* amlygrwydd *m*, natur weladwy *f*.
visible *adj* gweladwy, gweledig.
vision *n* golwg *m*.
visit *v* ymweld â. • *n* ymweliad *m*.
visitor *n* ymwelydd *m*.
visual *adj* gweledol.
visualise *v* dychmygu.
vital *adj* hanfodol.
vitality *n* bywiogrwydd, bywyd *m*.
vitamin *n* fitamin *m*.
vivacious *adj* hoenus, nwyfus, llawn bywyd.
vivid *adj* llachar, tanbaid.
vocabulary *n* geirfa *f*.
vocal *adj* llafar, lleisiol.
vocation *n* galwedigaeth *f*.
voice *n* llais *m*. • *v* lleisio.
void *n* gwagle, gwacter *m*.
volatile *adj* gwamal, anwadal.
volcano *n* llosgfynydd, folcano *m*.
volition *n* ewyllys, gwirfodd *m*.
voltage *n* foltedd *m*.
voluble *adj* huawdl, siaradus.
volume *n* uchder; cyfaint *m*; cyfrol *f*.
voluntary *adj* gwirfoddol.
volunteer *n* gwirfoddolwr *m*.
voluptuous *adj* synhwyrus, nwydus.
vomit *v* cyfogi, chwydu.
voracious *adj* gwancus, barus.
vote *n* pleidlais *f*. • *v* pleidleisio.
voter *n* pleidleisiwr *m*, pleidleiswraig *f*.
voucher *n* taleb *f*, tocyn *m*.
vow *n* adduned *f*. • *v* addunedu.
voyage *n* mordaith *f*.
vulgar *adj* di-chwaeth; cyffredin.
vulnerable *adj* hawdd eich clwyfo, bregus.

W

wade *v* cerdded trwy ddŵr, bracso.
wafer *n* waffer; afrlladen *f*.
wag *v* siglo, ysgwyd.
wage *n* cyflog *m*.
wager *n* bet *f/m*. • *v* codi bet, betio.
wages *n* cyflog *m*.
wagon *n* wagen *f*.
wail *n* llef *f*. • *v* nadu, llefain.
waist *n* gwasg *m/f*.

wait *v* aros. • *n* arhosiad *m.*
waiter *n* gweinydd, gwas *m.*
waive *v* hepgor.
wake *v* dihuno, deffro.
walk *v* cerdded. • *n* tro *m.*
walker *n* cerddwr *m*, cerddwraig *f.*
walking stick *n* ffon *f.*
wall *n* mur *m.*
wallet *n* waled *f.*
wallow *v* ymdrochi, ymdrybaeddu.
wallpaper *n* papur wal *m.*
walnuts *n* cnau Ffrengig *pl.*
wander *v* crwydro.
wane *v* cilio.
want *n* eisiau *m.* • *v* ymofyn.
wanton *adj* trythyll, anllad.
war *n* rhyfel *m.*
wardrobe *n* cwpwrdd dillad *m.*
warehouse *n* warws *m/f.*
wariness *n* pwyll *m*, gwyliadwriaeth *f.*
warm *adj* cynnes, twym. • *v* cynhesu, twymo.
warm-hearted *adj* twymgalon.
warmth *n* gwres, cynhesrwydd *m.*
warn *v* rhybuddio.
warning *n* rhybudd *m.*
warp *v* camu, ystumio.
warrant *n* gwarant *f.*
warrior *n* rhyfelwr *m.*
wary *adj* gwyliadwrus, gochelgar.
wash *v* ymolchi, golchi.
washbowl *n* basn ymolchi *m*, powlen ymolchi *f.*
washing *n* golch, golchiad *m.*
washing machine *n* peiriant golchi *m.*
washing-up *n* golchi llestri *vn.*
wasps *n* cacwn, piffgwn *pl.*
wastage *n* gwastraff *m.*
waste *v* gwastraffu.
wasteful *adj* gwastraffus.
watch *n* oriawr; gwyliadwriaeth *f.* • *v* gwylio.
watchful *adj* gwyliadwrus.
water *n* dŵr *m.* • *v* dyfrhau, dyfrio.
water closet *n* tŷ bach *m.*
watercolour *n* dyfrlliw *m.*
waterfall *n* rhaeadr *f.*
watering-can *n* can dyfrio *m.*
watermark *n* dyfrnod *m.*
watershed *n* cefndeuddwr *m.*
watertight *adj* dwrglos.
wave *n* ton *f.* • *v* chwifio, codi llaw.
waver *v* gwamalu, simsanu.
wavy *adj* tonnog.
wax *n* cwyr, gwêr *m.*
way *n* ffordd *f.*
wayward *adj* anwadal; gwrthnysig.
we *pron* ni, ninnau.
weak *adj* gwan, eiddil.
weaken *v* gwanhau.
weakness *n* gwendid *m.*
wealth *n* cyfoeth *m.*
wealthy *adj* cyfoethog.
weapon *n* arf *m.*
wear *v* gwisgo, treulio. • *n* traul *f.*
weariness *n* blinder, diflastod *m.*
weary *adj* blinedig, wedi blino.
weather *n* tywydd *m*; ~ **forecast** *n* rhagolygon y tywydd *pl.*
weave *v* gwau, gweu; gwehyddu.
web *n* gwe *f.*
wed *v* priodi.
wedding *n* priodas *f.*

wedding ring *n* modrwy briodas *f.*
wedge *n* lletem *f.*
Wednesday *n* dydd Mercher *m.*
weed *n* chwyn *pl.* • *v* chwynnu.
week *n* wythnos *f.*
weekday *n* dydd/diwrnod gwaith *m.*
weekend *n* penwythnos; fwrw'r Sul.
weekly *adj* wythnosol.
weep *v* wylo.
weigh *v* pwyso.
weight *n* pwysau *m/pl.*
weighty *adj* trwm, o bwys.
welcome *n* croeso *m.* • *v* croesawu.
welfare *n* lles, budd *m.*
well *n* ffynnon *f.* • *adj* da.
well-being *n* lles *m.*
well-bred *adj* o dras.
well-deserved *adj* haeddiannol.
well-known *adj* adnabyddus.
well-off *adj* cefnog.
west *n* gorllewin.
westerly, western *adj* gorllewinol.
wet *adj* gwlyb. • *n* gwlybaniaeth *m.* • *v* gwlychu.
whale *n* morfil *m.*
wharf *n* cei *m*, glanfa *f.*
what *pron* beth, pa beth.
whatever *pron* beth bynnag.
wheat *n* gwenith *m.*
wheel *n* olwyn, rhod *f.*
wheelbarrow *n* berfa, whilber *f.*
wheelchair *n* cadair olwyn(ion) *f.*
when *adv conj* pryd, pan.
whenever *adv* bob tro, pa bryd bynnag.
where *adv* ym mha le; lle.
whereas *conj* tra.
whereby *pron* trwy'r hwn/hon/hyn.
whereupon *conj* gyda hyn/hynny.
wherever *adv* pa le bynnag.
whet *v* hogi.
whether *conj* a; p'un ai.
which *pron adj* pa.
while *n* ysbaid *m.* • *conj* tra.
whim *n* mympwy *m.*
whimsical *adj* mympwyol.
whip *n* chwip *f.* • *v* chwipio.
whirl *v* chwylïo, troelli.
whirlpool *n* trobwll *m.*
whirlwind *n* corwynt *m.*
whisper *v* sibrwd, sisial. • *n* sibrwd *m.*
whistle *v* chwibanu. • *n* chwiban *m/f.*
white *adj* gwyn.
whiten *v* gwynnu.
whiteness *n* gwynder *m.*
who *pron* pwy; a.
whoever *pron* pwy bynnag.
whole *adj* cyfan, holl.
wholesale *n* cyfanwerthu *vn.*
wholesome *adj* iachus, iachusol.
wholly *adv* yn llwyr.
whom *pron* a.
why *adv* paham, pam.
wicked *adj* drwg, ysgeler.
wickedness *n* drygioni *m.*
wide *adj* llydan.
widen *v* lledu.
widow *n* gweddw, gwraig weddw *f.*
widower *n* gŵr gweddw *m.*
width *n* lled *m.*
wield *v* trin, trafod.
wife *n* gwraig *f.*
wild *adj* gwyllt.

wild life *n* bywyd gwyllt *m.*
wilful *adj* ystyfnig.
wilfulness *n* ystyfnigrwydd *m.*
will *n* ewyllys *f* (document), *m* (spirit).
willing *adj* parod.
willpower *n* grym ewyllys *m.*
wily *adj* cyfrwys, castiog.
win *v* ennill.
wind *n* gwynt *m.*
wind *v* dolennu, weindio.
windmill *n* melin wynt *f.*
window *n* ffenestr *f.*
window pane *n* gwydr ffenestr *m.*
windpipe *n* pibell wynt *f.*
windscreen *n* ffenestr flaen *f.*
windy *adj* gwyntog.
wine *n* gwin *m.*
wine cellar *n* seler win *f.*
wing *n* adain, asgell *f.*
wink *n* amrantiad, chwinciad *m.*
winner *n* enillydd, buddugwr *m.*
winter *n* gaeaf *m.* • *v* hendrefu, gaeafu.
wintry *adj* gaeafol.
wipe *v* sychu.
wire *n* gwifr, gwifren *f.*
wisdom *n* doethineb *m.*
wise *adj* doeth.
wish *v* dymuno. • *n* awydd, dymuniad *m.*
wit *n* ffraethineb, arabedd *m.*
witch *n* gwrach *f.*
with *prep* â, ag, gyd, gydag, gan.
withdraw *v* tynnu yn ôl; encilio.
wither *v* gwywo, crino.
withhold *v* dal yn ôl, celu.
within *prep, adv* i mewn, o fewn.
without *prep* heb.
withstand *v* gwrthsefyll.
witness *n* tyst *m.* • *v* tystio.
wittingly *adv* yn fwriadol.
witty *adj* ffraeth.
woe *n* gwae *m/f*, trallod *m.*
woeful *adj* trist, athrist.
wolf *n* blaidd *m.*
woman *n* menyw, gwraig *f.*
womanly *adj* benywaidd.
womb *n* croth *f.*
wonder *n* rhyfeddod *m.* • *v* rhyfeddu.
wonderful *adj* rhagorol, rhyfeddol.
woo *v* canlyn.
wood *n* pren, coed *m*; coedwig *f.*
wooden *adj* pren, o bren.
woodwork *n* gwaith coed *m.*
wool *n* gwlân *m.*
woollen *adj* gwlanog.
word *n* gair *m.* • *v* geirio.
word processing *n* prosesu geiriau *vn.*
wording *n* geiriad *m.*
work *v* gweithio. • *n* gwaith *m.*
worker *n* gweithiwr *m.*
workforce *n* gweithlu *m.*
workshop *n* gweithdy *m.*
world *n* byd *m.*
worldly *adj* bydol.
worldwide *adj* byd-eang.
worn-out *adj* wedi treulio.
worry *v* pryderu, gofidio. • *n* pryder, gofid *m.*
worrying *adj* pryderus, gofidus.
worse *adj* gwaeth.
worship *n* addoliad *m.* • *v* addoli.
worst *adj* gwaethaf.

worth *n* gwerth *m*.
worthily *adv* yn deilwng.
worthless *adj* diwerth, da i ddim.
worthy *adj* teilwng.
wound *n* anaf, clwyf *m*. • *v* clwyfo, anafu.
wrap *v* lapio.
wreath *n* torch *f*.
wreck *n* llong wedi'i dryllio. • *v* dry-llio, malu.
wrench *v* rhwygo.
wrestle *v* ymaflyd codwm.
wretched *adj* truenus.
wrinkle *n* crych *m*. • *v* crychu.
wrist *n* arddwrn *m*.
write *v* ysgrifennu.
writer *n* ysgrifennwr, awdur *m*.
writing *n* ysgrifen *f*.
wrong *adj* anghywir. • *n* cam *m*. • *v* gwneud cam â.
wrongful *adj* ar gam, anghyfiawn.
wrongly *adv* ar gam.
wry *adj* mingam.

XYZ

xenophobe *n* un sy'n casáu estron-iaid.
xenophobic *adj* senoffobic, drwgdybus o estroniaid.
X-ray *n* pelydr X *m*.
xylophone *n* seiloffon *m*.
yacht *n* cwch hwylio *m*, llong bleser *f*.
yawn *v* dylyfu gên, ymagor. • *n* dylyfiad gên *m*.
year *n* blwyddyn *f*.
yearbook *n* blwyddlyfr *m*.
yearly *adj* blynyddol.
yearn *v* dyheu, hiraethu.
yeast *n* burum *m*.
yell *v* gweiddi, bloeddio. • *n* bloedd, gwaedd *f*.
yellow *adj* melyn (*m*), melen (f).
yes *adv* do, ie, ydywf.
yesterday *adv* ddoe, doe.
yet *conj*, *adv* eto, er hynny.
yield *v* ildio; cynhyrchu. • *n* cyn-nyrch *m*.
yoghurt *n* iogwrt *m*.
you *pron* chi, chwi, ti, di.
young *adj* ifanc, ieuanc.
youngster *n* plentyn, person ifanc *m*.
your *pron* eich, dy.
yours *pron* eiddoch chi, eiddot ti.
yourself *pron* eich hunain, dy hun.
youth *n* ieuenctid *m*.
zeal *n* brwdfrydedd *m*, sêl *f*.
zealous *adj* brwdfrydig, selog.
zenith *n* anterth, entrych *m*.
zero *n* sero, dim *m*.
zest *n* afiaith, arddeliad *m*.
zigzag *adj* igam-ogam.
zip *n* sip *m*.
zodiac *n* sidydd *m*.
zone *n* cylch *m*, cylchfa *f*.
zoo *n* sw *m*.
zoologist *n* sŵolegydd *m*.
zoology *n* sŵoleg *f*.

APPENDIX

Some of the more frequently encountered Welsh irregular verbs

bod to be

present tense

	singular	plural
1	wyf, ydwyf	ŷm, ydym
2	wyt, ydwyt	ych, ydych
3	mae, yw, oes	ŷnt, ydynt

impersonal ydys

imperfect tense

	singular	plural
1	oeddwn	oeddem
2	oeddit	oeddech
3	oedd	oeddynt

impersonal oeddid

future tense

	singular	plural
1	byddaf	byddwn
2	byddi	byddwch
3	bydd	byddant

impersonal byddir

habitual imperfect

	singular	plural
1	byddwn	byddem
2	byddet	byddech
3	byddai	byddent

impersonal byddid

past tense

	singular	plural
1	bûm	buom
2	buost	buoch
3	bu	buonr

impersonal buwyd

conditional imperfect

	singular	plural
1	bawn	baem
2	bait	baech
3	bai	baent

impersonal bid, byddid

cael to have

present tense

	singular	plural
1	caf	cawn
2	cei	cewch
3	caiff	cânt

impersonal ceir

past tense

	singular	plural
1	cefais	cawsom
2	cefaist	cawsoch
3	cafodd	cawsant

impersonal cafwyd

imperfect tense

	singular	*plural*
1	cawn	caem
2	caet	caech
3	câi	caent

impersonal ceid

imperative

	singular	*plural*
1	–	–
2	–	–
3	caffed	caffent

impersonal caffer

dod to come

present tense

	singular	*plural*
1	dof	down
2	doi	dewch
3	daw	dônt

impersonal deuir

past tense

	singular	*plural*
1	deuthum	daethom
2	daethost	daethoch
3	daeth	daethant

impersonal doed

imperfect tense

	singular	*plural*
1	deuwn/down	deuem
2	deuet	deuech
3	deuai/dôi	deuent

impersonal doid

imperative

	singular	*plural*
1	–	down
2	dere/tyrd	dewch
3	doed/deled	delent

impersonal deuer/deler

gwneud to do

present tense

	singular	*plural*
1	gwnaf	gwnawn
2	gwnei	gwnewch
3	gwna	gwnânt

impersonal gwneir

past tense

	singular	*plural*
1	gwneuthum	gwnaethom
2	gwnaethost	gwnaethoch
3	gwnaeth	gwnaethant

impersonal gwnaed, gwnaethpwyd

imperfect tense

	singular	*plural*
1	gwnawn	gwnaem
2	gwnaet	gwnaech
3	gwnâi	gwnaent

impersonal gwneid

imperative

	singular	*plural*
1	–	gwnawn
2	gwna	gwnewch
3	gwnaed	gwanaent

impersonal gwneler

mynd to go

present tense

	singular	plural
1	af	awn
2	ei	ewch
3	â	ânt

impersonal eir

past tense

	singular	plural
1	euthum	aethom
2	aethost	aethoch
3	aeth	aethant

impersonal aed

imperfect tense

	singular	plural
1	awn	aem
2	aet	aech
3	âi	aent

impersonal eid

imperative

	singular	plural
1	–	awn
2	dos, cer	ewch
3	aed	aent

impersonal eler

Welsh PHRASEBOOK

ABBREVIATIONS

f	–	feminine
m	–	masculine
NW	–	north Wales
SW	–	south Wales

KEY TO PRONUNCIATION

Vowels

As in English, the **vowels** can either be long or short:

a	a	short as in c*a*p, m*a*n
	ah	long as in f*a*ther, c*ar*
e	e	short as in m*e*n, w*e*nt
	eh	long as in g*a*me, p*a*le
i	i	short as in p*i*n, b*i*t
	ee	long as in mach*ine*, *fee*l
	y	(half consonant) as *y* in *y*es
o	o	short as in h*o*t, g*o*ne
	oh	long as in h*o*le, m*o*le
u	i	short as in b*i*n, tw*i*n (there is no exact English equivalent for the 'u', which is pronounced farther back in the mouth in north Wales; a gutteral vowel)
	ee	long as in b*ee*n, w*ee*k (again there is the guttural vowel in north Wales)
w	**oo**	short as in b*oo*k, t*oo*k
	oo	long as in f*oo*l, m*oo*n
	w	(half consonant) as *w* in week
y	i	short as in p*i*n, b*i*n
	ee	long as in b*ee*n, w*ee*k
	uh	as in f*u*n, h*o*ney

Consonants

Consonants have approximately the same sounds as in English, but note the following:

c	k	as in *c*all, *c*at
ch	ch	as in Scottish *loch*, German Ba*ch* (never as in *ch*ur*ch*)
dd	**th**	as in *th*at, *th*eir
f	v	as in *v*an, *v*olume
ff	ff	as in o*ff*, *f*ilm
ng	ng	as in wi*ng*, si*ng*
ll	ll	no English equivalent, but place the tongue in the *l* position (behind the front teeth) and blow voicelessly
r	rr	as in *r*un, *r*epair (trilled)
rh	rrh	r followed by h
th	th	as in *th*ing, *th*ink

Certain consonants are subject to change at the beginning of words, a phenomenon known as mutation that is common to all Celtic languages.

Nouns in Welsh are either masculine or feminine; the gender sometimes denoted by a different ending to the word. The stress or accent in Welsh usually falls on the penultimate syllable, that is the last syllable but one.

GETTING STARTED

Everyday words and phrases

Yes, I am / I do
Ydw
uh-d*oo*

Yes, she /he is – she /he does
Ydy
uh-di (i = short i as in in)

Yes, we are / we do
Ydyn
uh-din

Yes, you are /you do
Ydych
uh-dich

Yes, they are / they do
Ydyn
uh-din

Yes, please
Ydw, os gwelwch yn dda
uh-d*oo* os gwel-*oo*ch uhn *th*ah

No, I am not / do not
Nac ydw
nag uh-d*oo*

No, she/he isn't – she /he doesn't
Nac ydy
nag uh-di

No, we are not / do not
Nac ydyn
nag uh-din

No, you are not / do not
Nac ydych
nag uh-dich

No, they are not / do not
Nac ydyn
nag uh-din

No, thank you
Na, dim diolch
nah dim di-olch

OK
Iawn
yown

Please
Os gwelwch yn dda
os gwel-*oo*ch uhn *th*ah

Thank you
Diolch
di-olch

Excuse me
Esgusodwch fi
es-gis-od-*oo*ch vi

Very good
Da iawn
dah yown

I am very sorry
Mae'n ddrwg iawn 'da fi
m(eye)n ***th***roog yown da vi

Being understood

I don't speak Welsh
Dwi ddim yn siarad Cymraeg
dwee ***th***im uhn shar-ad kuhm-r(eye)g

I don't understand
Dwi ddim yn deall
dwee ***th***im uhn de-all

It doesn't matter
Does dim gwahaniaeth
doys dim gwa-han-y(eye)th

I don't mind
Dwi ddim yn hidio
dwee ***th***im uhn hid-yo

I'm learning Welsh
Dwi'n dysgu Cymraeg
dween duhsg-i kuhm-r(eye)g

Say that again
Dwedwch hy'na eto
dwed-***oo***ch huh-nah et-o

I am a learner
Dysgwr ydw i
duhs-g***oo***rr uh-d***oo*** i

I'm sorry
Mae'n ddrwg 'da fi
m(eye)n ***th***roog dah vi

Once again
Unwaith eto
een-w(eye)th et-o

Please say it again slowly
Dwedwch eto'n araf, os gwelwch yn dda
dwed-***oo***ch et-on a-rav os gwel-***oo***ch uhn ***th***ah

Slower, please
Yn arafach, os gwelwch yn dda
uhn a-rav-ach os gwel-***oo***ch uhn ***th***ah

Will you speak slowly, please?
Wnewch chi siarad yn araf, os gwelwch yn dda?
wne***oo***ch chi shar-ad uhn a-rav os gwel-***oo***ch uhn ***th***ah

Can you find someone who speaks English?
Allwch chi ffeindio rhywun sy'n siarad Saesneg?
all-ooch chi f(eye)nd-yo rhi***oo***-in seen shar-ad s(eye)s-neg

Can you find someone who speaks Welsh?
Allwch chi ffeindio rhywun sy'n siarad Cymraeg?
all-ooch chi f(eye)nd-yo rhi*oo*-in seen shar-ad kuhm-r(eye)g

Can you help me, please?
Allwch chi fy helpu, os gwelwch yn dda?
all-ooch chi vuh help-i, os gwel-*oo*ch uhn ***th***ah

Greetings and exchanges

Hello
Helô
hel-oh

Hi
Sut mae
sh*oo*d m(eye)

Good evening
Noswaith dda
nos-w(eye)th ***th***ah

Good morning
Bore da
bo-re dah

Good night
Nos da
nohss dah

Goodbye
Da boch chi
dah bohch chi

Bye
Pob hwyl
pohb h*oo*il (short oo as in look, followed closely by i [as in merry])

How are you?
Sut ych chi?
sh*oo*d eech chi

I am very well, thank you
Dwi'n dda iawn, diolch
dween ***th***ah yown di-olch

It is good to see you
Mae'n dda eich gweld chi
m(eye)n ***th***ah uhch gweld chi

It is nice to meet you
Mae'n braf cwrdd â chi
m(eye)n brahv k**oo**rr***th*** a chi

There are five of us
Mae pump ohonon ni
m(eye) pimp o-hon-on ni

Here is my son
Dyma fy mab
duh-ma vuh mahb

This is my daughter
Dyma fy merch
duh-ma vuh merrch

This is my husband
Dyma fy ngŵr
duh-ma vuhng-oor

Greetings and exchanges

This is my wife
Dyma fy ngwraig
duh-ma vuhng-wr(eye)g

My name is . . .
Fy enw yw . . .
vuh en-***oo*** i-***oo**** (*as yew)

What is your name?
Beth yw'ch enw chi?
beth i*oo*ch en-***oo*** chi

You are very kind
Ych chi'n garedig iawn
ich chin gar-e-dig yown

You are very welcome!
Croeso i chi!
croy-so i chi

See you soon
Gwela i chi'n fuan
gwel-(eye) chin vee-an

I am on holiday
Dwi ar fy ngwyliau
dwee arr vuhng-wil-y(eye)

I live in London
Dwi'n byw yn Llundain
dween bi-***oo*** uhn llin-d(eye)n

I'm a student (f)
Myfyrwraig ydw i
muh-vuhr-wr(eye)g uh-d***oo*** i

I'm a student (m)
Myfyriwr ydw i
muh-vuhr-y*oo*rr uh-d***oo*** i

I am from — America
Dwi'n dod o — America
dween dohd o — a-mer-i-ka

— Australia
— Awstralia
— ows-tral-ya

— Britain
— Brydain
— bruh-d(eye)n

— Canada
— Ganada
— gan-a-da

— England
— Loegr
— loy-gerr

— Ireland
— Iwerddon
— yoo-wer***th***-on

I am from — New Zealand
Dwi'n dod o — Seland Newydd
dween dohd o — se-land ne-wi***th***

— South Africa
— Dde Affrica
— ***th***ey af-rik-a

— Wales
— Gymru
— guhm-ri

I come from Scotland
Dwi'n dod o'r Alban
dween dohd orr al-ban

Useful words and phrases

Thanks
Diolch
di-olch

Happy Birthday
Pen-blwydd hapus
pen bl***ooith*** hap-is

Happy Christmas
Nadolig Llawen
nad-o-lig llow-en

Happy New Year
Blwyddyn Newydd Dda
bl***ooith***-in ne-wi***th*** ***th***ah

Welcome to Wales
Croeso i Gymru
kroy-so i guhm-ree

Good luck
Pob lwc
pohb l***oo***k

Congratulations
Llongyfarchiadau
llon-guh-varrch-yad-(eye)

Good health or Cheers
Iechyd da
ye-chid dah

No thank you
Dim diolch
dim di-olch

Alright or okay
O'r gorau
orr gor-(eye)

Excuse me
Esgusodwch fi
es-gis-od-***oo***ch vi

With pleasure
Gyda phleser
guh-da fless-err

Pardon?
Pardwn?
parr-d***oo***n

Of course
Wrth gwrs
oorrth g***oo***rrs

Exactly
Yn hollol
uhn holl-ol

Really, you can be sure
Yn wir (i chi)
uhn weerr i chi

Common questions

Where?
Ble?
ble

How?
Sut?
sh***oo***d

Common questions

Where is? / Where are?
Ble mae?
ble m(eye)

Who?
Pwy?
p*oo*i (short oo [as in look] followed by i [as in merry])

When?
Pryd?
preed

Why?
Pam?
pam

What?
Beth?
behth

Which?
Pa?
pah

How much?
Faint yw?
v(eye)nt i-*oo*

How long will it take?
Faint o amser gymer hi?
v(eye)nt o am-serr guh-merr hee

Do you know a good restaurant?
Ych chi'n gwybod lle mae bwyty da?
ich chin g*oo*i-bod lle m(eye) b*oo*i-ti dah

How can I contact American Express or Diners Club?
Sut alla i gysylltu â'r American Express/Diners Club?
sh*oo*d all-(eye) guh-suhll-ti arr a-merr-i-kan ex-press d(eye)n-ers kluhb

Do you mind if I . . . ?
Fyddech chi'n hidio taswn i'n . . . ?
vuh*th*-ech chin hid-yo ta-s*oo*n een

Have you got any change?
Oes newid 'da chi?
oyss ne-wid da chi

May I borrow your map?
Ga' i fenthyg eich map?
gah i ven-thig uhch map

What is the problem?
Beth yw'r broblem?
behth i*oo*rr brob-lem

What is this?
Beth yw hwn?
behth i*oo* h*oo*n

What is wrong?
Beth sy'n bod?
behth seen bohd

When do you close?
Pryd ych chi'n cau?
preed ich chin k(eye)

Where can I buy a postcard?
Ble ga' i brynu cerdyn post?
Ble gah i bruhn-i kerr-din post

Where can I change my clothes?
Ble ga' i newid fy nillad?
ble gah i ne-wid vuh ni-llad

Who did this?
Pwy wnaeth hyn?
p*oo*i wn(eye)th hin

Who should I see about this?
Pwy ddylwn ni weld am hyn?
p*oo*i *th*uhl-*oo*n ni weld am hin

Will you come?
Ddowch chi?
*th*owch chi

Asking the time

What time is it?
Faint o'r gloch yw hi?
v(eye)nt orr glohch i-*oo* hee

It is — five past ten
Mae'n — bum munud wedi deg
m(eye)n — bim min-id wed-i dehg

— ten o'clock
— ddeg o'r gloch
— *th*ehg orr glohch

— midnight
— ganol nos
— gan-ol nohss

— half past ten
— hanner awr wedi deg
— han-ner owrr wed-i dehg

— five to eleven
— bum munud i un ar ddeg
— bim min-id i een arr *th*ehg

— twenty-five past ten
— bum munud ar hugain wedi deg
— bim min-id arr hee-g(eye)n wed-i dehg

— eleven o'clock
— un ar ddeg o'r gloch
— een arr *th*ehg orr glohch

— after three o'clock
— ar ôl tri o'r gloch
— arr ohl tree orr glohch

— nearly five o'clock
— bron yn bump o'r gloch
— bron uhn bimp orr glohch

— quarter to eleven
— chwarter i un ar ddeg
— chwarr-terr i een arr *th*ehg

— quarter past ten
— chwarter wedi deg
— chwarr-terr wed-i dehg

— half past eight exactly
— hanner awr wedi wyth yn union
— han-nerr owrr wed-i *oo*ith uhn een-yon

— ten to eleven
— ddeg munud i un ar ddeg
— *th*ehg min-id i een arr *th*ehg

Asking the time

— **twenty to eleven**
— ugain munud i un ar ddeg
— ee-g(eye)n min-id i een arr *th*ehg

— **twenty past ten**
— ugain munud wedi deg
— ee-g(eye)n min-id wed-i dehg

— **twenty-five to eleven**
— bum munud ar hugain i un ar ddeg
— bim min-id arr hee-g(eye)n i een arr *th*ehg

before midnight
cyn hanner nos
kin han-nerr nohss

this morning
y bore 'ma
uh bo-re ma

tonight
heno
hen-o

this evening
'da'r nos
darr nohss

this afternoon
prynhawn 'ma
prin-hown ma

soon
toc *(or* cyn bo hir)
tock *(or* kin boh heerr)

in an hour's time
ymhen mewn awr
uhm-hen me*oo*n owrr

twelve o'clock (midday)
deuddeg o'r gloch (canol dydd)
d(eye)-*th*eg orr glohch kan-ol dee*th*

at night
yn ystod y nos
uhn uh-stod uh nohss

at half past six
am hanner awr wedi chwech
am han-nerr owrr wed-i chwech

at about one o'clock
am tua un o'r gloch
am tee-a een orr glohch

two hours ago
Ddwy awr yn ôl
*thoo*i owrr uhn ohl

in half an hour
Mewn hanner awr
meoon han-nerr owrr

late
hwyr
h*oo*ir (short oo [as in look] followed closely by short i)

early
gynnar
guhn-narr

Common problems

I am late
Dwi'n hwyr
dween h*oo*irr

I haven't enough money
Does dim digon o arian 'da fi
doys dim dig-on o ar-yan da vi

I have no currency
Does dim arian cyfredol 'da fi
doys dim ar-yan kuh-vredol da vi

My son is lost
Mae fy mab ar goll
m(eye) vuh mahb arr goll

I have lost my credit cards
Dwi wedi colli fy nghardiau credyd
dwee wed-i coll-i vuhng harrd-y(eye) kre-did

I have lost my — key
Dwi wedi colli fy — allwedd
dwee wed-i coll-i vuh — all-we*th*

— ticket
— nhocyn
— nho-kin

— traveller's cheques
— sieciau teithio
— shek-y(eye) t(eye)th-yo

My car has been stolen
Mae fy nghar wedi cael ei ddwyn
m(eye) vuhng harr wed-i k(eye)l (eye) ***thoo***in

My handbag has been stolen
Mae fy mag wedi cael ei ddwyn
m(eye) vuh mag wed-i k(eye)l (eye) ***thoo***in

My wallet has been stolen
Mae fy ngwaled wedi cael ei dwyn
m(eye) vuhng wal-ed wed-i k(eye)l (eye) d***oo***in

Arriving in Wales

By air

Wales is an extremely accessible country and Cardiff International Airport has a vital role to play in promoting that image. In fact, it is the only airport of any significance in Wales and is considered to be one of the busiest and most successful regional airports in the UK. Situated 12 miles from Cardiff city centre and 10 miles from the M4 motorway, Cardiff International Airport handles 1.5 million passengers a year.

In addition to an extensive range of leisure services throughout Europe, the Mediterranean and North America, daily schedule services operate direct from Cardiff to 13 key destinations across the UK and Europe. The airport houses one of the largest Tax and Duty Free shops of any UK regional airport, offering an extensive range of tax-free goods to all passengers, irrespective of destination.

There are direct flights from Amsterdam, Belfast, Brussels, Channel Islands, Dublin, Edinburgh, Glasgow, Isle of Man and Paris to Cardiff International Airport. There are many worldwide connections to Cardiff via Amsterdam, Brussels, Dublin and Paris. A rail or air link coach service runs from the airport to Cardiff 's central train and bus stations. Birmingham and Manchester Airports have also proved convenient for travel to Wales by car, bus or train. Car hire service is available at Cardiff International, Manchester and Birmingham Airports.

By ferry

Wales has four ferry ports, which provide direct sailings between Wales and Ireland. Ferries from Dublin, and both ferries and catamarans from Dun Laoghaire, which is situated 6 miles south of

Dublin, arrive at Holyhead on the north-west coast of Anglesey in north Wales. Rosslare is the departure point for ferries and catamarans to Fishguard and ferries to Pembroke Dock in south-west Wales. There is also a ferry from Cork to Swansea. The major ports in England are linked via the United Kingdom's road network to Wales. Portsmouth, Dover, Ramsgate and Folkestone provide convenient access to Wales from all parts of Europe and beyond.

By train

There are several ways to reach Wales from England and Scotland by train. The Great Western InterCity Service to Cardiff takes two hours from London Paddington and travels via Reading, Swindon, Bristol and Newport. This hourly service (every half hour at peak times) also runs to Swansea with onward connections to Carmarthen and stations in Pembrokeshire in west Wales. Fast and frequent Virgin Trains link London Euston with the north Wales coast to Holyhead.

Mid-Wales is served by Alphaline trains to Aberystwyth and other mid-Wales resorts from Birmingham via Shrewsbury. This service connects with Virgin Trains from London Euston at Birmingham New Street Station.

Wales and West Passenger Trains run Alphaline services direct from London Waterloo (via Woking and Basingstoke) to Cardiff. There are also trains direct to Cardiff (some running through to south-west Wales) from:

- Manchester/the north-west
- Brighton/Portsmouth/Salisbury/Southampton
- The west of England/Bristol
- Nottingham/Birmingham/Gloucester.

The North-West Express train services run direct via Chester from Manchester and Birmingham and serve most resorts on the north Wales coast via Chester.

The Heart of Wales runs approximately 4 times daily from Shrewsbury into Wales and travels through the picturesque countryside via Knighton, Llandrindod Wells, Llanwrtyd Wells, Llandovery, Llandeilo and a host of village halts as it makes it way south to Llanelli and Swansea. The Conwy Valley line from Llandudno Junction to Blaenau Ffestiniog is an ideal way of exploring parts of north Wales by train, and the Cambrian Coaster, which runs along the shoreline from Pwllheli on the Llŷn peninsula to Machynlleth and Aberystwyth, will give you a taste of the natural beauty of the Welsh countryside.

By coach

The biggest national operator is National Express, which provides a nationwide network of express coach services linking major cities and towns in Wales. The company's daily express services link Wales with the main UK airports and around 1,300 destinations around England, Wales and Scotland. Many services have been upgraded to Rapide specification.

Convenient services to Wales operate from London's Victoria Coach Station and from almost all other major towns and cities in England and Scotland. Towns and resorts throughout Wales are connected by a range of local and regional services. Those, however, who wish to travel from Llandudno to Cardiff via Bangor, Aberystwyth, Carmarthen and Swansea, may wish to take the Traws-Cambria 701 service.

By car

The M4 carriageway from London enters Wales across the River Severn Bridges. With the opening of the second Severn crossing, traffic for Cardiff and west Wales follows the revised route of the M4 across the new bridge. Travellers for Chepstow and the Wye Valley need to take the M48 across the original Severn Bridge.

In north Wales, the A55, a dual carriageway from Chester via Holywell, St Asaph and Colwyn Bay, passes through a tunnel under the Conway Estuary and goes on to Bangor, where it connects with the old trunk route, the A5. Mid-Wales is easily reached by the M54, which links with the M6, M5 and M1.

Arrival

Here is my passport
Dyma fy mhasport
duh-ma vuhm hass-porrt

I am attending a convention
Dwi'n mynd i gynhadledd
dween mind i guhn-had-le***th***

I am here on business
Dwi yma ar fusnes
dwee uh-ma arr viss-ness

I will be staying here for eight weeks
Bydda i'n aros yma am wyth wythnos
buh-***th***(eye)n arr-oss uh-ma am ***oo***ith ***oo***ith-noss

We are visiting friends
Dŷn ni'n ymweld â ffrindiau
deen nin uhm-weld a frind-y(eye)

We have a joint passport
Mae pasport ar y cyd 'da ni
m(eye) pass-porrt arr uh keed da ni

I have nothing to declare
Does dim byd 'da fi i'w ddatgan
doys dim beed da vi i***oo*** ***th***at-gan

I have the usual allowances
Mae'r lwfansau arferol 'da fi
m(eye)rr ***loo***v-ans-(eye) arr-ve-rol da vi

How long will this take?
Faint gymer hyn?
v(eye)nt guh-merr hin

How much will I have to pay?
Faint sy'n rhaid ifi dalu?
v(eye)nt seen rh(eye)d iv-i dal-i

This is for my own use
At fy nefnydd fy hun mae hwn
at vuh nev-ni***th*** vuh hee-nan m(eye) h***oo***n

Common problems and requests

Can I upgrade to first class?
Ga' i uwchraddio i ddosbarth cynta'?
gah i i-***oo***ch-ra***th***-yo i ***th***oss-barrth kuhn-ta

How long will the delay be?
Am faint fydd yr oedi?
am v(eye)nt vee***th*** uhrr oy-di

I am in a hurry
Dwi ar frys
dwee arr vreess

I have lost my ticket
Dwi wedi colli fy nhocyn
dwee wed-i coll-i vuhn ho-kin

I have missed my connection
Dwi wedi colli fy nghysylltiad
dwee wed-i coll-i vuhng huh-suhllt-yad

The people who were to meet me have not arrived
Dyw'r bobl oedd fod i gwrdd â fi ddim wedi cyrraedd
di***oo***rr bob-ol oy***th*** vohd i g***oo***rr***th*** a vi ***th***im wed-i kuhrr-(eye)***th***

Common problems and requests

Where is the — toilet?
Ble mae'r — toiled?
ble m(eye)rr — toy-led

— bar?
— bar?
— barr

— information desk?
— ddesg wybodaeth?
— ***th***esg wi-bod-(eye)th

— departure lounge?
— lolfa ymadael?
— lol-va uhm-ad-(eye)l

— transfer desk?
— ddesg drosglwyddo?
— ***th***esg dros-gl***ooith***-o

Where can I buy currency?
Ble galla i brynu arian cyfredol?
ble gall-(eye) bruhn-i ar-yan kuh-vre-dol

Where can I change traveller's cheques?
Ble galla i newid sieciau teithio?
ble gall-(eye) ne-wid shek-y(eye) t(eye)th-yo

Where can I get a taxi?
Ble galla i gael tacsi?
ble gall-(eye) g(eye)l tak-si

Where do I get the connection flight to Cologne?
Ble galla i gael cysylltiad y ffleit i Cologne?
ble gall-(eye) g(eye)l kuh-suhllt-yad uh fl(eye)t i kohl-ohn

Where will I find the airline representative?
Ble galla i ffeindio cynrychiolydd y cwmni hedfan?
ble gall-(eye) f(eye)nd-yo kuhn-rich-yol-i***th*** uh k***oo***m-ni hed-van

My flight was late
Roedd fy ffleit yn hwyr
roy***th*** vuh fl(eye)t uhn h***oo***irr

I was delayed at the airport
Ces i fy rhwystro yn y maes awyr
kess i vuh rh*oo*i-stro uhn uh m(eye)ss a-wirr

I was held up at immigration
Ces i fy nal yn ôl yn yr adran mewnfudo
kess i vuh nal uhn ohl uhn uhrr a-dran me*oo*n-vid-o

Luggage

Where is the baggage from flight number . . . ?
Ble mae'r bagiau ar gyfer ffleit rhif . . . ?
ble m(eye)rr bag-y(eye) arr guh-verr fl(eye)t rheev . . .

Are there any baggage trolleys?
Oes troli fagiau ar gael?
oyss trol-i fag-y(eye) arr g(eye)l

Can I have help with my bag?
Ga i help gyda fy mag?
gah i help guh-da vuh mag

Careful, the handle is broken
Byddwch yn ofalus, mae'r handlen wedi torri
buh*th*-*oo*ch uhn ov-al-iss m(eye)rr hand-len wed-i torr-i

I will carry that myself
Garia i hwnna fy hunan
garr-i-(eye) h*oo*n-a vuh hee-nan

Is there a left-luggage office?
Oes swyddfa i adael bagiau?
oyss s*oo*ith-va i ad-(eye)l bag-y(eye)

Is there any charge?
Oes 'na unrhyw dâl?
oyss nah een rhi*oo* dahl

Please take these bags to a taxi
Ewch â'r bagiau hyn i'r tacsi, os gwelwch yn dda
e*oo*ch arr bag-y(eye) hin irr tak-si os gwel-*oo*ch uhn ***th***ah

Where is my bag?
Ble mae fy mag?
ble m(eye) vuh mag

I have lost my bag
Dwi wedi colli fy mag
dwee wed-i coll-i vuh mag

My baggage has not arrived
Dyw fy magiau ddim wedi cyrraedd
di*oo* vuh mag-y(eye) ***th***im wed-i kuhrr-(eye)***th***

These bags are not mine
Nid fy magiau i yw'r rhain
nid vuh mag-y(eye) i i*oo*rr rh(eye)n

It is a large suitcase
Siwtces mawr yw e
soot-kehss mowrr i*oo* e

It is a rucksack
Sach deithio yw hi
sach d(eye)th-yo i*oo* hee

It is a small bag
Bag bach yw e
bag bahch i*oo* e

This package is fragile
Mae'r pecyn hwn yn frau
m(eye)rr pe-kin h*oo*n uhn vrr(eye)

No, do not put that on top
Na, peidiwch â rhoi hwnna ar y top
nah p(eye)d-y*oo*ch a rhoy h*oo*n-na arr uh top

At the Hotel

Types of hotel

The general standard of hotels in Wales is very high. At the luxury end of the market there are sumptuously converted castles and mansions. At the other end of the scale are basic guesthouses with limited facilities that charge very reasonable rates.

The Wales Tourist Board operates a grading system for all kinds of accommodation, hotels, guesthouses and farmhouses included. All are graded from the simple 1-star category to the luxury 5-star. Places that score highly will have an especially welcoming atmosphere and pleasing ambience, high levels of comfort and guest care. They will also have attractive surroundings enhanced by thoughtful design and attention to detail.

It is important to bear in mind when organising accommodation in Wales that the star grade awarded by the Wales Tourist Board takes into account the nature of the property and expectation of the guests. In fact, a farmhouse is just as entitled to 5 stars as a country hotel, as long as what it offers is of the highest quality.

For grading purposes, the Wales Tourist Board has divided the accommodation into various categories, for example: hotel, bed and breakfast, farm and hostel.

Self-catering accommodation

Many visitors prefer the freedom and flexibility of a self-catering holiday. There is a good choice of accommodation available, for example from purpose built chalets by the seaside, to well appointed country cottages that provide a haven of peace and seclusion.

The Wales Tourist Board has also introduced a new star grading system to assess the quality of self-catering accommodation. It ranges from 1 star (simple and reasonable) to 5 star (excellent quality). The grades reflect the overall quality of furnishings and decoration, not the range of facilities on offer.

Caravan holiday home parks

The Wales Tourist Board has also introduced a star grading scheme to cover caravan holiday home parks (including touring caravan and camping parks). The star grade reflects the overall quality of the park.

Choosing accommodation

All the accommodation listed by the Wales Tourist Board will have been inspected and verified by one of the quality advisers, who will have awarded a star rating on a scale of 1 to 5. A great choice of accommodation is included in their guides, ranging from seaside guesthouses and farmhouses deep in the country to historic inns and small, family-run hotels.

Brochures and listings can be obtained from:

Wales Tourist Board
Brunel House
2 Fitzalan Road
Cardiff
CF24 OUY

Reservations and enquiries

I am sorry I am late
Mae'n ddrwg 'da fi mod i'n hwyr
m(eye)n ***th***roog da vi mohd een h***oo***irr

I have a reservation
Dwi wedi llogi stafell
dwee wed-i llog-i stav-ell

I shall be staying until July 4th
Bydda i'n aros tan y pedwerydd o Orffennaf
buh-***th***(eye)n arr-oss tan uh ped-werr-i***th*** o orr-fen-av

I want to stay for 5 nights
Hoffwn i aros am bum noson
hoff-***oo***n i arr-oss am bim noss-on

Do you have a double room with a bath?
Oes stafell ddwbl â bàth 'da chi?
oyss stav-ell ***thoo***b-l a bath da chi

Do you have a room with twin beds and a shower?
Oes stafell â phâr o welyau a chawod 'da chi?
oyss stav-ell a fahr o wel-i-(eye) a cha-wod da chi

Do you have a single room?
Oes stafell sengl 'da chi?
oyss stav-ell seng-uhl da chi

I need a double room with a bed for a child
Dwi angen stafell ddwbl â gwely i blentyn
Dwee ang-en stav-ell ***thoo***b-l a gwel-i i blen-tin

I need — a single room with a shower or bath
Dwi angen — stafell sengl â chawod neu fàth
Dwee ang-en — stav-ell seng-uhl a cha-wod n(eye) vath

— a room with a double bed
— stafell â gwely dwbl
— stav-ell a gwel-i d***oo***b-l

Reservations and enquiries

— a room with twin beds and bath
— stafell â phâr o welyau a bàth
— stav-ell a fahr o wel-i-(eye) a bath

I need — a single room
Dwi angen — stafell sengl
Dwee ang-en — stav-ell seng-uhl

How much is — full board?
Faint yw — llety llawn?
v(eye)nt i-*oo* — llet-i llown

— half-board?
— hanner darpariaeth?
— han-ner darr-parr-y(eye)th

— it per night?
— e, y noson?
— e uh noss-on

— the room per night?
— stafell y noson?
— stav-ell uh noss-on

Do you take traveller's cheques?
Ych chi'n cymryd sieciau teithio?
ich chin kuhm-rid shek-y(eye) t(eye)th-yo

Does the price include — room and breakfast?
Ydy'r pris yn cynnwys — stafell a brecwast?
uh-dirr preess uhn kuhn-wiss — stav-ell a brek-wast

— room and all meals?
— stafell a phob pryd bwyd?
— stav-ell a phohb preed b*oo*id

— room and dinner?
— stafell a chinio?
— stav-ell a chin-yo

Can we have adjoining rooms?
Gawn ni stafelloedd drws nesa' i'n gilydd?
gown ni sta-vell-oy*th* drooss ness-a een gil-i*th*

Reservations and enquiries

Do you have a car park?
Oes maes parcio 'da chi?
oyss m(eye)ss parrk-yo da chi

Do you have a cot for my baby?
Oes cot 'da chi i fy mabi?
oyss kot da chi i vuh mab-i

Are there supervised activities for the children?
Oes yna weithgareddau sy'n cael eu goruchwylio i blant?
oyss uh-na wehth-garr-***eth***-(eye) seen k(eye)l (eye) gorr-ich-wil-yo i blant

Can my son sleep in our room?
All fy mab gysgu yn ein stafell?
all vuh mahb guhs-gi uhn (eye)n stav-ell

Are there other children staying at the hotel?
Oes plant eraill yn aros yn y gwesty?
oyss plant err-(eye)ll uhn arr-oss uhn uh gwest-i

Do you have a fax machine?
Oes peiriant ffacs 'da chi?
oyss p(eye)-rr-yant faks da chi

Do you have a laundry service?
Oes gwasanaeth golchi 'da chi?
oyss gwa-ssan-(eye)th gol-chi da chi

Do you have a safe for valuables?
Oes seff 'da chi i gadw pethau gwerthfawr?
oyss sehff da chi i gad-***oo*** peth-(eye) gwerrth-vowrr

Do you have any English newspapers?
Oes unrhyw bapurau newydd Saesneg 'da chi?
oyss een-rhi***oo*** bap-irr-(eye) ne-wi***th*** s(eye)s-neg da chi

Do you have any Welsh newspapers?
Oes unrhyw bapurau newydd Cymraeg 'da chi?
oyss een-rhi***oo*** bap-irr-(eye) ne-wi***th*** kuhm-r(eye)g da chi

Do you have satellite TV?
Oes teledu lloeren 'da chi?
oyss tel-e-di lloy-ren da chi

Which floor is my room on?
Ar ba lawr mae fy stafell?
arr bah lowrr m(eye) vuh stav-ell

Is there a casino?
Oes yna gasino?
oyss uhn-a gas-een-o

Is there a hairdryer?
Oes yna sychwr gwallt?
oyss uhn-a suhch-*oo*r gwallt

Is there a lift?
Oes yna lifft?
oyss uhn-a lift

Is there a minibar?
Oes yna far yn fy stafell?
oyss uhn-a varr uhn vuh stav-ell

Is there a sauna?
Oes yna sauna?
oyss uhn-a sauna (sauna as in English)

Is there a swimming pool?
Oes yna bwll nofio?
oyss uhn-a b*oo*ll nov-yo

Is there a telephone?
Oes yna ffôn?
oyss uhn-a fohn

Is there a television?
Oes yna deledu?
oyss uhn-a del-e-di

Is there a trouser press?
Oes yna wasg trywsus?
oyss uhn-a wask trow-siss

Where is the socket for my razor?
Ble mae'r soced i fy raser?
ble m(eye)rr sok-ed i vuh rass-err

Reservations and enquiries

What is the voltage here?
Beth yw'r foltedd 'ma?
behth i-*oo*rr vol-te*th* ma

Is the voltage 220 or 110?
Ai dau gant ac ugain neu gant a deg yw'r foltedd?
(eye) d(eye) gant ag ee-g(eye)n n(eye) gant a dehg i-*oo*rr vol-te*th*

Is this a safe area?
Ydy hon yn ardal ddiogel?
uh-di hon uhn arr-dal *th*i-o-gel

Is there a market in the town?
Oes yna farchnad yn y dre?
oyss uhn-a varrch-nad uhn uh dre

Can you recommend a good local restaurant?
Allwch chi argymell bwyty lleol da?
all-*oo*ch chi arr-guh-mell b*oo*i-ti lle-ol dah

Is there a Chinese restaurant?
Oes yna fwyty Tsieineaidd?
oyss uhn-a v*oo*i-ti sh(eye)n-e-(eye)*th*

Is there an Indian restaurant?
Oes yna fwyty Indiaidd?
oyss uhn-a v*oo*i-ti in-de-(eye)*th*

Can I use traveller's cheques?
Ga' i ddefnyddio sieciau teithio?
gah i *th*ev-nuh*th*-yo shek-y(eye) t(eye)th-yo

Has my colleague arrived yet?
Ydy fy nghydweithiwr wedi cyrraedd eto?
uh-di vuhng heed-wehth-y*oo*r wed-i kuhrr-(eye)*th* et-o

What time does the restaurant close?
Pryd mae'r bwyty'n cau?
preed m(eye)rr b*oo*i-teen k(eye)

When does the bar open?
Pryd mae'r bar yn agor?
preed m(eye)rr barr uhn ag-orr

What time does the hotel close?
Pryd mae'r gwesty'n cau?
preed m(eye)rr gwest-een k(eye)

What time is breakfast?
Pryd mae brecwast?
preed m(eye) brek-wast

What time is dinner?
Pryd mae cinio?
preed m(eye) kin-yo

What time is lunch?
Pryd mae cinio canol dydd?
preed m(eye) kin-yo kan-ol dee***th***

Service

Can I make a telephone call from here?
Ga' i wneud galwad ffôn o'r fan 'ma?
gah i wnehd gal-wad fohn orr van ma

Can I dial direct from my room?
Ga' i ddeialu'n uniongyrchol o fy stafell?
gah i ***th***(eye)-al-een een-yon-guhrrch-ol o vuh stav-ell

Can I have an outside line?
Ga' i linell allan?
gah i lin-ell all-an

Can I charge this to my room?
Ga' i dalu am hwn 'da fy stafell?
gah i dal-i am h***oo***n da vuh sta-vell

Can I have my key, please?
Ga' i fy allwedd, os gwelwch yn dda?
gah i vuh all-we***th*** os gwel-***oo***ch uhn ***th***ah

Can I have a newspaper?
Ga' i bapur newydd?
gah i bap-irr ne-wi***th***

Service

Can I have an ashtray?
Ga' i soser lwch?
gah i soss-err l*oo*ch

Can I have another blanket?
Ga' i flanced arall?
gah i vlan-ked arr-all

Can I have another pillow?
Ga' i obennydd arall?
gah i o-ben-ni***th*** arr-all

Can I have my wallet from the safe?
Ga' i fy waled o'r seff?
gah i vuh wal-ed orr sehff

Can I hire a portable telephone?
Ga' i logi ffôn cludadwy?
Gah i log-i fohn kleed-ad-wi

Can I send this by courier?
Ga' i anfon hwn 'da chludydd?
gah i an-von h*oo*n da chlid-i***th***

Can I use my credit card?
Ga' i ddefnyddio fy ngherdyn credyd?
gah i ***th***ev-nuh***th***-yo vuhn herr-din kre-did

Can I use my personal computer here?
Ga' i ddefnyddio fy nghyfrifiadur personol 'ma?
gah i ***th***ev-nuh***th***-yo vuhng huhv-riv-yad-eerr perr-son-ol ma

Can we have breakfast in our room, please?
Gawn ni frecwast yn ein stafell, os gwelwch yn dda?
gown ni frek-wast uhn (eye)n stav-ell os gwel-*oo*ch uhn ***th***ah

Is there a room service menu?
Oes bwydlen ar gyfer gwasanaeth stafell?
oyss b*oo*id-len arr guh-verr gwa-ssan-(eye)th stav-ell

I need an early morning call
Dwi angen galwad ben bore
dwee ang-en gal-wad ben bo-re

Is there a trouser press I can use?
Oes yna wasg trywsus alla i ddefnyddio?
oyss uhn-a wasg trow-siss all-(eye) ***th***ev-nuh***th***-yo

I am expecting a fax
Dwi'n disgwyl ffacs
dween diss-gw***oo***il faks

Where can I send a fax?
Ble ga' i anfon ffacs?
ble gah i an-von faks

I need to charge these batteries
Rhaid ifi tshiarjo'r batris hyn
rh(eye)d iv-i shiarr-jorr ba-trees hin

I want to press these clothes
Hoffwn i bresio'r dillad 'ma
hoff-***oo***n i bress-yorr di-llad ma

I want to clean these shoes
Hoffwn i lanhau'r 'sgidiau 'ma
hoff-***oo***n i lan-h(eye)rr sgid-y(eye) ma

Please can I leave a message?
Ga' i adael neges, os gwelwch yn dda?
gah i ad-(eye)l neg-ess os gwel-***oo***ch uhn ***th***ah

My room number is 22
Rhif fy stafell yw dau ddeg dau
rheev vuh stav-ell i-***oo*** d(eye) ***th***eg d(eye)

Please fill the minibar
Wnewch chi lenwi'r bar yn fy stafell
wne***oo***ch chi len-wirr barr uhn vuh stav-ell

I need a razor
Dwi angen raser
dwee ang-en rass-err

I need some soap
Dwi angen sebon
dwee ang-en se-bon

Service

I need some toilet paper
Dwi angenpapur tŷ bach
dwee ang-en pap-irr tee-bahch

I need some towels
Dwi angen tywelion
dwee ang-en tuh-wel-yon

I need some coat hangers
Dwi angen prennau hongian dillad
dwee ang-en pren-n(eye) hong-yan di-llad

I need some writing paper
Dwi angen papur sgrifennu
dwee ang-en pap-irr sgri-ven-ni

Can I have writing paper?
Ga' i bapur sgrifennu?
gah i bap-irr sgri-ven-ni

My room is cold. Please turn the heating up
Mae fy stafell yn oer. Wnewch chi droi'r gwres lan, os gwelwch yn dda
m(eye) vuh stav-ell yn oyrr wne*oo*ch chi droyrr gwress lan os gwel-*oo*ch uhn *th*ah

Please wake me at 7 o'clock in the morning
Dihunwch fi am saith o'r gloch yn y bore, os gwelwch yn dda
di-heen-*oo*ch vi am s(eye)th orr glohch uhn uh bo-re os gwel-*oo*ch uhn *th*ah

Please turn the heating off
Wnewch chi droi'r gwres i ffwrdd, os gwelwch yn dda
wne*oo*ch chi droyrr gwress i f*oo*rr*th* os gwel-*oo*ch uhn *th*ah

Please send this fax for me
Anfonwch y ffacs hwn ifi, os gwelwch yn dda
an-von-*oo*ch y faks h*oo*n iv-i os gwel-*oo*ch yn *th*ah

Where is the manager?
Ble mae'r rheolwr?
ble m(eye)rr rheh-ol-*oo*r

Can I speak to the manager?
Ga' i siarad â'r rheolwr?
gah i shar-ad arr rheh-ol-***oo***r

Hello, this is the manager
Helô, y rheolwr sy 'ma
hel-oh uh rheh-ol-***oo***r see ma

Problems

I cannot close the window
Fedra i ddim cau'r ffenest
ve-dr(eye) ***th***im k(eye)rr fen-est

I cannot open the window
Fedra i ddim agor y ffenest
ve-dr(eye) ***th***im ag-orr uh fen-est

The air conditioning is not working
Dyw'r tymherwr awyr ddim yn gweithio
di***oo***rr tuhm-herr-***oo***rr a-wirr ***th***im uhn gw(eye)th-yo

The bathroom is dirty
Mae'r stafell 'molchi'n frwnt
m(eye)rr stav-ell molch-een vr***oo***nt

The heating is not working
Dyw'r gwresogydd ddim yn gweithio
di***oo***rr gwress-og-i***th*** ***th***im uhn gw(eye)th-yo

The light is not working
Dyw'r golau ddim yn gweithio
di***oo***rr gol-(eye) ***th***im uhn gw(eye)th-yo

The room is not serviced
Dyw'r stafell ddim wedi ei gwasanaethu
di***oo***rr stav-ell ***th***im wed-i (eye) gwass-an-(eye)th-i

The room is too noisy
Mae'r stafell yn rhy swnllyd
m(eye)rr stav-ell uhn rhee s***oo***n-llid

The room key does not work
Dyw allwedd y stafell ddim yn gweithio
di*oo* all-we*th* uh stav-ell *th*im uhn gw(eye)th-yo

There are no towels in the room
Does dim tywelion yn y stafell
doys dim tuh-wel-yon uhn uh stav-ell

There is no hot water
Does dim dŵr poeth
doys dim doorr poyth

There is no plug for the washbasin
Does dim plwg i'r basn 'molchi
doys dim pluhg irr bass-in mol-chi

Checking out

We will be leaving early tomorrow
Byddwn ni'n gadael yn gynnar bore 'fory
buh*th*-*oo*n een gad-(eye)l uhn guhn-narr bo-re vorr-i

I have to leave tomorrow
Mae'n rhaid ifi adael 'fory
m(eye)n rh(eye)d iv-i ad-(eye)l vorr-i

Can I have the bill please?
Ga' i'r bil, os gwelwch yn dda?
gah eerr bil os gwel-*oo*ch uhn *th*ah

I want to stay an extra night
Dwi eisiau aros am noson ychwanegol
dwee (eye)sh-y(eye) arr-oss am noss-on uhch-wan-eg-ol

Do I have to change rooms?
Oes rhaid ifi newid stafelloedd?
oyss rh(eye)d iv-i ne-wid sta-vell-oy*th*

Could you have my bags brought down?
Allwch chi drefnu dod â fy magiau i lawr?
all-*oo*ch chi drev-ni dohd a vuh mag-y(eye) i lowrr

Please leave the bags in the lobby
Gadewch y bagiau yn y cyntedd, os gwelwch yn dda
gad-e*oo*ch uh bag-y(eye) uhn uh kuhn-te***th*** os gwel-***oo***ch uhn ***th***ah

Could you order me a taxi?
Allech chi archebu tacsi i fi?
all-ech chi arrch-eb-i tak-si i vi

Thank you, we enjoyed our stay
Diolch, dŷn ni wedi mwynhau ein arhosiad
di-olch deen ni wed-i m***oo***in-h(eye) (eye)n arr-hoss-yad

Other Accomodation

Renting a house

We have rented this house
Dŷn ni wedi rhentu'r tŷ 'ma
deen ni wed-i rhen-tirr tee ma

We have rented this cottage
Dŷn ni wedi rhentu'r bwthyn 'ma
deen ni wed-i rhen-tirr b*oo*-thin ma

Here is our booking form
Dyma'n ffurflen fwcio
duh-man firrv-len v*oo*k-yo

We need 2 sets of keys
Dŵn ni eisiau dwy set o allweddi
deen ni (eye)sh-y(eye) d*oo*i set o all-we*th*-i

When does the cleaner come?
Pryd mae'r glanhawr yn dod?
preed m(eye)rr glan-howrr uhn dohd

Where is the bathroom?
Ble mae'r stafell 'molchi?
ble m(eye)rr stav-ell mol-chi

Can I contact you on this number?
Alla i gysylltu â chi ar y rhif hwn?
all-(eye) guh-suhll-ti a chi arr uh rheev h*oo*n

Can you send someone to repair this?
Allwch chi anfon rhywun i drwsio hwn?
all-*oo*ch chi an-von rhi*oo*-in i dr*oo*sh-o h*oo*n

How does this work?
Sut mae hwn yn gweithio?
sh*oo*d m(eye) h*oo*n uhn gw(eye)th-yo

I cannot open the window
Fedra i ddim agor y ffenest
ved-rr(eye) ***th***im ag-orr uh fen-est

Is the water heater working?
Ydy'r gwresogydd dŵr yn gweithio?
uh-dirr gwress-og-i***th*** doorr uhn gw(eye)th-yo

Is the water safe to drink?
Ydy'r dŵr yn ddiogel i'w yfed?
uh-dirr doorr uhn ***th***i-o-gel yoo uh-ved

Is there any spare bedding?
Oes yna ddillad gwely sbâr?
oyss uhn-a ***th***i-llad gwel-i sbahrr

The cooker does not work
Dyw'r cwcer ddim yn gweithio
di***oo***rr k***oo***-kerr ***th***im uhn gw(eye)th-yo

The refrigerator does not work
Dyw'r oergell ddim yn gweithio
di***oo***rr oyrr-gell ***th***im uhn gw(eye)th-yo

The toilet is blocked
Mae'r toiled wedi blocio
m(eye)rr toy-led wed-i blok-yo

There is a leak
Mae'r dŵr yn diferu
m(eye)rr doorr uhn di-verr-i

We do not have any water
Does dim dŵr 'da ni
doys dim doorr da ni

Where is the fuse box?
Ble mae'r blwch ffiwsiau?
ble m(eye)rr bl***oo***ch fi***oo***s-y(eye)

Where is the key for this door?
Ble mae allwedd y drws 'ma?
ble m(eye) all-we***th*** uh drooss ma

Where is the socket for my razor?
Ble mae soced i fy raser?
ble m(eye) so-ked i vuh rass-err

Around the house

bath
bàth
bath

cooker
cwcer
k*oo*-kerr

bathroom
stafell 'molchi
stav-ell mol-chi

corkscrew
tynnwr corcyn
tuhn-*oo*rr korr-kin

bed
gwely
gwel-i

cup
cwpan
c*oo*p-an

brush
brwsh
br*oo*sh

fork
fforc
forrk

tin opener
agorwr tuniau
agor-*oo*rr tin-y(eye)

glass
gwydryn
gwi-drin

chair
cadair
kad-(eye)rr

kitchen
cegin
keg-in

knife
cyllell
kuhll-ell

spoon
llwy
ll*oo*i

mirror
drych
dreech

stove
stof
stohv

pan
padell
pad-ell

table
bwrdd
b*oo*rr*th*

plate
plât
plaht

tap
tap
tap

refrigerator
oergell
oyrr-gell

toilet
toiled
toy-led

sheet
cynfasen
kuhn-vass-en

vacuum cleaner
sugnydd llwch
sig-ni***th*** llooch

sink
sinc
sink

washbasin
basn 'molchi
bass-in mol-chi

kettle
tegell
teg-ell

toaster
tostiwr
tost-y***oo***r

rubbish
sbwriel
sb***oo***rr-yel

dustbin
bin sbwriel
bin sb***oo***r-yel

Camping

There are hundreds of campsites in Wales, with the main concentration along the coasts and lakeshores. For confidence in booking camping accommodation, look for the Welsh Tourist Board Star Grading System. The star grade reflects the overall quality of the park: 5 star – exceptional quality; 1 star – fair to good quality. The best sites will have amenities such as laundries, public telephone, shops and sports facilities. In addition to the official sites, farmers may offer pitches for a small fee. It should be remembered, however, that permission is required from the landowner before setting up a tent. Camping rough is illegal in national parks and nature reserves.

The Wales Tourist Board produces self-catering and camping directories, which are available free from the following address:

Wales Tourist Board
Brunel House
2 Fitzalan Road
Cardiff
CF24 OUY

Camping questions

Can we camp in your field?
Gawn ni wersylla yn eich cae?
gown ni wehrr-suhll-a uhn uhch k(eye)

Can we camp near here?
Gawn ni wersylla'n agos i'r fan hyn?
gown ni wehrr-suhll-an ag-oss irr van hin

Can we park our caravan here?
Gawn ni barcio ein carafán 'ma?
gown ni barrk-yo (eye)n kar-a-van ma

Do I pay in advance?
Oes rhaid talu ymlaen llaw?
oyss rh(eye)d tal-i uhm-l(eye)n llow *(*ow as in how*)*

Do I pay when I leave?
Wrth adael yr hoffech chi ifi dalu?
oorrth ad-(eye)l uhrr hoff-ech chi iv-i dal-i

Is there a more sheltered site?
Oes yna safle mwy cysgodol?
oyss uhn-a sav-leh m***oo***i kuhs-god-ol

Is there a restaurant or a shop on the site?
Oes yna fwyty neu siop ar y safle?
oyss uhn-a v***oo***i-ti n(eye) shop arr uh sav-leh

Is there another campsite near there?
Oes yna safle gwersylla arall ar bwys?
oyss uhn-ah sav-leh gwehrr-suhll-a arr-all arr b*oo*iss

Is this the drinking water?
Ai hwn yw'r dŵr yfed?
(eye) h*oo*n i-*oo*rr doorr uh-ved

Please can we pitch our tent here?
Gawn ni godi ein pabell yma, os gwelwch yn dda?
Gown ni god-i (eye)n pab-ell uh-ma, os gwel-*oo*ch uhn *th*ah

The site is very wet and muddy
Mae'r safle'n wlyb ac yn lleidiog
m(eye)rr sav-len wleeb ak uhn ll(eye)d-yog

Where are the toilets?
Ble mae'r toiledau?
ble m(eye)rr toy-led-(eye)

Where can I have a shower?
Ble ga' i gawod?
ble gah i ga-wod

Where can we wash our dishes?
Ble gawn ni olchi'r llestri?
ble gown ni ol-chirr lless-tri

Around the campsite

air mattress
matras awyr
mat-rass a-wirr

camp chair
cadair gynfas
kad-(eye)rr guhn-vass

bottle-opener
peth agor poteli
pehth ag-orr pot-el-i

can opener
agorwr tuniau
agor-*oo*rr tin-y(eye)

bucket
bwced
b*oo*-ked

candle
cannwyll
kan-*oo*ill

Around the campsite

camp bed
gwely cynfas
gwel-i kuhn-vass

cup
cwpan
k*oo*p-an

fire
tân
tahn

matches
matsis
match-es

fly sheet
rhyddlen
rhuh*th*-len

penknife
cyllell boced
kuhll-ell bok-ed

fork
fforc
forrk

plate
plât
plaht

frying pan
padell ffrio
pad-ell free-o

rucksack
sach deithio
sahch d(eye)th-yo

ground sheet
cynfas lawr
kuhn-vass lowrr

sleeping bag
sach gysgu
sahch guhs-gi

guy line
rhaff dynhau
rhahf duhn-h(eye)

spoon
llwy
ll*oo*i

knife
cyllell
kuhll-ell

stove
ffwrn
f*oo*rrn

mallet
gordd bren
gorr*th* bren

tent peg
peg pabell
peg pab-ell

tent pole
polyn pabell
pol-in pab-ell

thermos flask
fflasg thermos
flasg therr-moss

tent
pabell
pab-ell

torch
fflachlamp
flach-lamp

Hostelling

The Youth Hostels Association has 37 properties in Wales offering bunk-bed accommodation in single-sex dormitories or smaller rooms. There are clusters of youth hostels in each of the contrasting national parks in Wales – Snowdonia, the Brecon Beacons, and the Pembrokeshire Coast.

The landscape in each of these lends itself to a range of recreational activities, and available at or near many of the hostels, are opportunities to enjoy horse riding, pony trekking, hill walking, climbing, caving, water sports or even dry stone walling and spinning.

Youth hostels in Wales have been classified under the Wales Tourist Board's star quality grading scheme, which rates hostel and hostel-type accommodation from 1 to 5 stars according to the quality and condition of the facilities and the service provided.

If you don't want to plan your visit in advance, you can just turn up at your chosen youth hostel on the day. Alternatively, try calling the hostel *en route* to check availability. Hostels are often full; it is therefore advisable to book your bed in advance.

For full details, contact:

YHA (England and Wales) Ltd
8 St Stephen's Hill,
St Albans
AL1 2DY

or

Youth Hostels Association
1 Cathedral Road,
Cardiff
CF11 9HA

Hostelling

Are you open during the day?
Ych chi ar agor yn ystod y dydd?
ich chi arr ag-orr uhn uh-stod uh dee***th***

Can I join here?
Ga' i ymuno 'ma?
gah i uh-meen-o ma

Can I use the kitchen?
Ga' i ddefnyddio'r gegin?
gah i ***th***ev-nuh***dd***-yorr geg-in

Can we stay 5 nights here?
Gawn ni aros pum noson 'ma?
gown ni arr-oss pim noss-on ma

Can we stay until Sunday?
Gawn ni aros tan ddydd Sul?
gown ni arr-oss tan ***thee******th*** seel

Do you serve meals?
Ych chi'n darparu bwyd?
ich chin dar-par-ri b***oo***id

to take away?
i fynd allan?
i vind all-an

Here is my membership card
Dyma fy ngherdyn aelodaeth
duh-ma vuhng herr-din (eye)-lod-(eye)th

I do not have my card
Dyw fy ngherdyn ddim 'da fi
di-***oo*** vuhng herr-din ***th***im da vi

Is there a youth hostel near here?
Oes yna hostel ieuenctid ar bwys?
oyss uhn-a hoss-tel y(eye)-enk-tid arr b***oo***is?

What time do you close?
Pryd ych chi'n cau?
preed ich chin k(eye)

Childcare

Can you warm this milk for me?
Allwch chi dwymo'r llaeth / llefrith hwn i fi?
(1) all-*oo*ch chi d*oo*i-morr ll(eye)th h*oo*n i vi
(2) all-*oo*ch chi d*oo*i-morr lle-vrrith h*oo*n i vi (NW)

Do you have a high chair?
Oes cadair uchel 'da chi?
oyss kad-(eye)rr i-chel da chi

How old is your daughter?
Beth yw oedran eich merch?
behth i-*oo* oy-dran uhch merrch

My daugher is 7 years old
Mae fy merch yn saith mlwydd oed
m(eye) vuh merrch uhn s(eye)th ml*ooith* oyd

My son is 10 years old
Mae fy mab yn ddeng mlwydd oed
m(eye) vuh mahb uhn *th*eng ml*ooith* oyd

I am very sorry. That was very naughty of him.
Mae'n ddrwg 'da fi. 'Na fachgen drygionus yw e *(m)*
m(eye)n *th*roog da vi nah vach-gen druhg-yon-is i-*oo* e

I am very sorry. That was very naughty of her.
Mae'n ddrwg 'da fi. 'Na ferch ddrygionus yw hi *(f)*
m(eye)n *th*roog da vi nah verrch *th*ruhg-yon-is i*oo* hee

It will not happen again
Wnaiff e ddim digwydd eto
wn(eye)f e *th*im dig-wi*th* et-o

Is there a babysitter?
Oes yna warchodwr plant?
oyss uhn-a warr-chod-*oo*rr plant

Childcare

Is there a cot for our baby?
Oes yna got i'n babi ni?
oyss uhn-a got in bab-i ni

Is there a paddling pool?
Oes yna bwll padlo?
oyss uhn-ah b*oo*ll pad-lo

Is there a swimming pool?
Oes yna bwll nofio?
oyss uhn-a b*oo*ll nov-yo

Is there a swing park?
Oes yna le chwarae?
oyss uhn-a le chwarr-(eye)

She goes to bed at 9 o'clock
Mae hi'n mynd i'r gwely am naw o'r gloch
m(eye) heen mind irr gwel-i am now orr glohch

He goes to bed at 10 o'clock
Mae e'n mynd i'r gwely am ddeg o'r gloch
m(eye) en mind irr gwel-i am ***th***ehg orr glohch

We will be back in 2 hours
Byddwn ni 'nôl mewn dwy awr
buh***th***-*oo*n ni nohl me*oo*n d*oo*i owrr

Where can I buy some disposable nappies?
Ble galla i brynu cewynnau papur?
ble gall-(eye) bruhn-i ke-wuhn-n(eye) pap-irr

Where can I change the baby?
Ble ga' i newid y babi?
ble gah i ne-wid uh bab-i

Where can I feed my baby?
Ble ga' i fwydo fy mabi?
ble gah i v*oo*id-o vuh mab-i

Where can I breastfeed my baby?
Ble ga' i fwydo fy mabi o'r fron?
ble gah i v*oo*id-o vuh mab-i orr vron

GETTING AROUND

Getting around

Tourist Information Centres are normally open daily between 10.00 and 17.00. Some of the centres are open all year whilst the remainder are, in the main, open between Easter and October.

Post offices are generally open from 09.00 until 17.30 Monday to Friday and main post offices are open 09.00–12.30 on Saturday. Stamps are available from most newsagents and some large supermarkets.

Banks are open Monday to Friday from 09.30 to 16.30, but a few banks open earlier and/or close later. Some banks in the busy shopping centres are open on Saturdays and some are open on Sundays for a few hours. British currency can also be obtained at large travel agents. Many branches of banks have 24-hour banking lobbies where a range of services can be obtained through machines.

Public houses (pubs) are permitted to open for the sale of alcoholic drinks throughout the day, from 11.00 to 23.00 on weekdays. On Sundays, the licensing hours are 12.00 to 22.30.

Shops and departmental stores are generally open Monday to Saturday 09.00 to 17.30 or 18.00. However, most towns and some villages have at least one supermarket that is open until about 22.00. These supermarkets tend also to open on Sunday from 10.00 to 16.00. In some of the larger towns and cities an increasing number of supermarkets are open Monday to Saturday for 24 hours.

Most offices and shops are closed on public holidays.

Asking for directions

Where is the art gallery?
Ble mae'r oriel gelfyddyd?
ble m(eye)rr or-yel gel-vuh***th***-id

Where is the post office?
Ble mae Swyddfa'r Post?
ble m(eye) s***ooith***-varr post

Where is the Tourist Information Service?
Ble mae'r Ganolfan Groeso?
ble m(eye)rr gan-ol-van groy-so

Can you show me on the map?
Allwch chi ddangos ifi ar y map?
all-***oo***ch chi ***th***an-goss iv-i arr uh map

Can you tell me the way to the station?
Allwch chi ddweud wrtha i'r ffordd i'r orsaf?
all-***oo***ch chi ***th***wehd ***oo***rrtha irr forr***th*** irr orss-av

Can you walk there?
Allwch chi gerdded yno?
all-***oo***ch chi gerr-***th***ed uhn-o

I am looking for the Tourist Information Office
Dwi'n edrych am y Ganolfan Groeso
dween e-drich am uh gan-ol-van groy-so

Where are the toilets?
Ble mae'r toiledau?
ble m(eye)rr toy-led-(eye)

I am lost
Dwi ar goll
dwee arr goll

I am lost. How do I get to the Cambrian Hotel?
Dwi ar goll. Sut ych chi'n mynd i Westy'r Cambrian?
dwee arr goll sh***oo***d ich chin mind i west-irr kam-bri-an

I am trying to get to the market
Dwi'n ceisio mynd i'r farchnad
dween k(eye)ss-yo mind irr varrch-nad

I want to go to the theatre
Dwi eisiau mynd i'r theatr
dwee (eye)sh-y(eye) mind irr thee-et-uhrr

Is it far?
Ydy hi 'mhell?
uh-di hee mhell

Is there a bus that goes there?
Oes yna fws sy'n mynd 'na?
oyss uhn-a v*oo*ss seen mind na

Is there a train that goes there?
Oes yna drên sy'n mynd 'na?
oyss uhn-a drehn seen mind na

Is this the right way to the supermarket?
Ai dyma'r ffordd gywir i'r archfarchnad?
(eye) duhm-arr forr***th*** guh-wirr irr arrch-varrch-nad

We are looking for a restaurant
Dŷn ni'n edrych am fwyty
deen nin e-drich am v*oo*i-ti

Where do I get a bus for the city centre?
Ble galla i ddal bws i ganol y ddinas?
ble gall-(eye) ***th***ahl b*oo*ss i gan-ol uh ***th***ee-nass

Directions – by road

Do I turn here for Blue Street?
Ych chi'n troi yma am Blue Street?
ich chin troy uh-ma am bloo street

How far is it to Cardiff?
Pa mor bell yw Caerdydd?
pah morr bell i*oo* k(eye)rr-dee***th***

How long will it take to get there?
Faint gymer hi i fynd 'na?
v(eye)nt guh-merr hee i vind na

Is there a filling station near here?
Oes yna orsaf betrol ar bwys?
oyss uhn-a orss-av bet-rol arr b*oo*is

I am looking for the next exit
Dwi'n edrych am yr allanfa nesa'
dween e-drich am uhrr all-an-va ness-a

Where does this road go to?
Ble mae'r ffordd hon yn mynd?
ble m(eye)rr forr***th*** hon uhn mind

How do I get onto the motorway?
Ble dwi'n gallu ymuno â'r draffordd?
ble dween gall-i uh-meen-o arr dra-forr***th***

Which is the best route to Swansea?
Pa un yw'r ffordd orau i Abertawe?
pah een i*oo*rr forr***th*** orr-(eye) i a-berr-tow-e

Which road do I take to Aberystwyth?
Pa ffordd ddylwn i gymryd i Aberystwyth?
pah forr**th** ***th***uh-l*oo*n i guhm-rid i a-berr-uhst-with

Which is the fastest route?
Pa un yw'r ffordd gyflyma?
pah een i*oo*rr forr***th*** guhv-luhm-a

Will we arrive in time for dinner?
Wnawn ni gyrraedd mewn pryd i swper?
wnown ni guh-rr(eye)***th*** me*oo*n preed i s*oo*-perr

Directions – what you may hear

Ych chi'n mynd — cyn belled â . . .
Ich chin mind — kin bell-ed a . . .
You go — as far as . . .

Directions – what you may hear

— **i'r chwith**
— irr chweeth
— left

— **i'r dde**
— irr ***th**eh*
— right

— **tua . . .**
— tee-a . . .
— towards . . .

Mae e — **ger y groesffordd**
m(eye) e — gerr uh groyss-forr***th***
It is — at the crossroads

— **dan y bont**
— dan uh bont
— under the bridge

— **ar ôl y goleuadau traffig**
— arr ohl uh gol-(eye)-ad-(eye) traff-ig
— after the traffic lights

— **rownd y gornel**
— rohnd uh gorrn-el
— around the corner

— **nesa i'r sinema**
— ness-a irr sin-e-ma
— next to the cinema

Mae e — **ar y llawr nesa'**
m(eye) e — arr uh llowrr ness-a
It is — on the next floor

— **gyferbyn â'r orsaf reilffordd**
— guh-verr-bin arr orss-av rehl-forr***th***
— opposite the railway station

— **draw fan 'na**
— drow (ow as in how) van na
— over there

Directions – what you may hear

Croeswch y stryd
kroyss-***oo***ch uh streed
Cross the street

Trowch i'r chwith
trowch irr chweeth
Turn left

Trowch i'r dde
trowch irr ***th***eh
Turn right

Dilynwch yr arwyddion — i'r draffordd
dil-uhn-***oo***ch uhrr arr-wi***th***-yon — irr dra-forr***th***
Follow the signs — for the motorway

— i'r gyffordd nesa'
— irr guh-forr***th*** nesa
— for the next junction

— i'r sgwâr
— irr sgwahrr
— for the square

Daliwch i fynd yn syth ymlaen
dal-y***oo***ch i vind uhn seeth uhm-l(eye)n
Keep going straight ahead

Cymerwch y ffordd gynta' ar y dde
kuhm-err-***oo***ch uh forr***th*** guhn-ta arr uh ***th***eh
Take the first road on the right

Rhaid i chi fynd 'nôl
rh(eye)d i chi vind nohl
You have to go back

Cymerwch y ffordd i Fangor
kuhm-err-***oo***ch uh forr***th*** i vang-or
Take the road for Bangor

Cymerwch yr ail ffordd ar y chwith
kuhm-err-***oo***ch uhrr (eye)l forr***th*** arr uh chweeth
Take the second road on the left

Rhaid i chi dalu'r doll
rh(eye)d i chi dal-irr doll
You have to pay the toll

Hiring a car

Major car hire agencies all operate in Wales and there is a wide range of cars available at different prices. To rent a car, you will need to produce your driving licence and have at least 1 year's driving experience. Most will only rent to people between 21 and 70 years of age. It is often worth arranging car hire well in advance through one of the multinational chains, or opting for a fly-drive deal.

Can I hire a car?
Ga' i logi car?
gah i log-i karr

Can I hire a car with an automatic gearbox?
Ga' i logi car â gerbocs awtomatig?
gah i log-i karr a gehrr-boks aw-tom-a-tig

I want to hire a car
Dwi eisiau llogi car
dwee (eye)sh-y(eye) llog-i karr

I need it for 2 weeks
Dwi angen e am bythefnos
dwee ang-en e am buhth-ev-noss

We will both be driving
Byddwn ni'n dau yn gyrru
buh***th-oo***n nin d(eye) uhn guh-ri

Do you have a large car?
Oes car mawr 'da chi?
oyss karr mowrr da chi

Do you have a smaller car?
Oes car yn llai 'da chi?
oyss karr uhn ll(eye) da chi

Do you have an automatic?
Oes un awtomatig 'da chi?
oyss een aw-tom-a-tig da chi

Do you have an estate car?
Oes car stad 'da chi?
oyss karr stahd da chi

I would like to leave the car at the airport
Hoffwn i adael y car yn y maes awyr
hoff-***oo***n i ad-(eye)l uh karr uhn uh m(eye)ss a-wirr

I want to leave the car at the airport
Dwi eisiau gadael y car yn y maes awyr
dwee (eye)sh-y(eye) gad-(eye)l uh karr uhn uh m(eye)ss a-wirr

Is there a charge per mile?
Oes yna dâl am bob milltir?
oyss uhn-a dahl am bohb mill-tirr

Must I return the car here?
Oes rhaid ifi ddychwelyd y car 'ma?
oyss rh(eye)d iv-i ***th***uhch-wel-id uh karr ma

Please explain the documents
Wnewch chi esbonio'r dogfennau, os gwelwch yn dda
wne***oo***ch chi ess-bon-yorr dog-ven-n(eye) os gwel-***oo***ch uhn ***th***ah

How much is it per mile?
Faint yw e'r filltir?
v(eye)nt i***oo*** ehrr vill-tirr

Can I pay for insurance?
Ga' i dalu am yr yswiriant?
gah i dal-i am uhrr uhss-wirr-yant

Do I have to pay a deposit?
Oes rhaid ifi dalu blaendal?
oyss rh(eye)d iv-i dal-i bl(eye)n-dal

I would like a spare set of keys
Hoffwn i set o allweddi sbâr
hoff-***oo***n i set o all-we***th***-i sbahrr

How does the steering lock work?
Sut mae clo'r llyw'n gweithio?
sh*oo*d m(eye) klohrr lli*oo*n gw(eye)th-yo

Please show me how
Wnewch chi ddangos ifi, os gwelwch yn dda
wne*oo*ch chi *th*an-goss iv-i os gwel-*oo*ch uhn *th*ah

—to operate the lights
—sut mae gweithio'r goleuadau
—sh*oo*d m(eye) gw(eye)th-yorr gol-(eye)-ad-(eye)

—to operate the windscreen wipers
—sut mae gweithio'r sychwyr ffenestri
—sh*oo*d m(eye) gw(eye)th-yorr suhch-wirr ffen-ess-tri

Where is reverse gear?
Ble mae'r gêr bacio?
ble m(eye)rr gehrr bak-yo

Where is the tool kit?
Ble mae'r taclau trwsio?
ble m(eye)rr tak-l(eye) tr*oo*sh-o

By taxi

Taxis are readily available in main towns and cities throughout Wales. Distinguished by the taxi sign on the roof of the vehicle, they are usually black- or white-coloured saloon cars, which can be hailed at stations, taxi ranks or in the streets. In the country, there are also private hire firms with cars displaying the taxi sign and/or phone numbers. Rates are reasonable and normally metered.

Please show us around the town
Wnewch chi ddangos i ni o gwmpas y dre', os gwelwch yn dda
wne*oo*ch chi *th*an-goss i ni o g*oo*m-pass uh dre os gwel-*oo*ch uhn *th*ah

Please take me to this address
Wnewch chi fynd â fi i'r cyfeiriad 'ma, os gwelwch yn dda
wne*oo*ch chi vind a vi irr kuh-v(eye)rr-yad ma os gwel-*oo*ch uhn *th*ah

By taxi

Take me to the airport, please
Ewch â fi i'r maes awyr, os gwelwch yn dda
e***oo***ch a vi irr m(eye)ss a-wirr os gwel-***oo***ch uhn ***th***ah

The bus station, please
Yr orsaf bysiau, os gwelwch yn dda
uhrr orss-av buhss-y(eye) os gwel-***oo***ch uhn ***th***ah

Turn left, please
Trowch i'r chwith, os gwelwch yn dda
trowch irr chweeth os gwel-***oo***ch ***th***ah

Turn right, please
Trowch i'r dde, os gwelwch yn dda
trowch irr ***th***eh os gwel-***oo***ch uhn ***th***ah

Will you put the bags in the boot?
Wnewch chi roi'r bagiau yn y bŵt?
wne***oo***ch chi royrr bag-y(eye) uhn uh b***oo***t

Please wait here for a few minutes
Arhoswch 'ma am ychydig funudau, os gwelwch yn dda
arr-hoss-***oo***ch ma am uh-chuh-dig vin-i-d(eye) os gwel-***oo***ch uhn ***th***ah

I am in a hurry
Dwi ar frys
dwee arr vreess

Please hurry, I am late
Brysiwch, os gwelwch yn dda, dwi'n hwyr
bruhss-y***oo***ch os gwel-***oo***ch uhn ***th***ah dween h***oo***irr

Can you come back in one hour?
Allwch chi ddod nôl mewn awr?
all-ooch chi ***th***ohd nohl me***oo***n owrr

Please, stop at the corner
Stopiwch wrth y gornel, os gwelwch yn dda
stop-y***oo***ch ***oo***rrth uh gorrn-el os gwel-***oo***ch uhn ***th***ah

Please, wait here
Arhoswch 'ma, os gwelwch yn dda
arr-hoss-***oo***ch ma os gwel-***oo***ch uhn ***th***ah

Wait for me, please
Arhoswch amdana i, os gwelwch yn dda
arr-hoss-***oo***ch am-dan-a i os gwel-***oo***ch uhn ***th***ah

How much is that, please
Faint yw e, os gwelwch yn dda?
v(eye)nt i***oo*** e os gwel-***oo***ch uhn ***th***ah

Keep the change
Cadwch y newid
kad-***oo***ch uh ne-wid

By bus or coach

Due to the absence of a railway in many regions of Wales, buses are very much part of everyday life for those who live in rural areas. There are some inter-town buses or coaches run by National Express whose network covers England, Scotland and parts of Wales. Its main routes are as follows:

- London to Cardiff, Swansea and on through Carmarthen to Pembroke and Milford Haven in west Wales
- Bristol to Swansea
- Bradford to Cardiff
- Scarborough to Cardiff
- London to Wrexham
- London to Aberystwyth
- London, Chester along the north Wales coast to Bangor, Caernarfon and Pwllheli
- Hull, Leeds, Manchester, Liverpool, Rhyl, Llandudno, Bangor, Caernarfon and Pwllheli
- Edinburgh, Newcastle, Leeds, Bradford, Manchester, Chester and Wrexham.

For travelling within Wales, it will be necessary to use the local bus services run by a number of different companies. Very few places are without a bus service, although services are less frequent in the most rural areas of north and mid-Wales.

Arriva Cymru runs most of the local services in north Wales and also in parts of west Wales. This company has bases in Llandudno, Bangor and in Aberystwyth. It also provides a Traws-Cambrian 701 service between Llandudno and Cardiff.

Services west of Cardiff and west Wales are mostly run by the Swansea-based company, First Cymru, and Bws Caerdydd serves Cardiff and the Vale of Glamorgan.

The best way of getting around Snowdonia without a car is on the Snowdon Sherpa network of buses (including special park-and-ride services), which operates from June to October. There is also a limited winter service. The network runs into and around the most popular parts of Snowdonia in north Wales, and also links with main rail and bus services.

In south Wales, Brecons Bus operates a similar service in the Brecon Beacons National Park.

Does this bus go to the castle?
Ydy'r bws hwn yn mynd i'r castell?
uh-dirr b*oo*ss h*oo*n uhn mind irr kass-tell

How frequent is the service?
Pa mor aml yw'r gwasanaeth?
pah morr am-al i*oo*rr gwa-ssan-(eye)th

How long does it take to get to the park?
Faint o amser gymer hi i fynd i'r parc?
v(eye)nt o am-serr guh-merr hee i vind irr parrk

Is there a bus into town?
Oes yna fws i'r dre'?
oyss uhn-a v*oo*ss irr dre

What is the fare to the city centre?
Faint yw'r pris i ganol y ddinas?
v(eye)nt i*oo*rr preess i gan-ol uh ***th***ee-nass

When is the last bus?
Pryd mae'r bws ola'?
preed m(eye)rr b*oo*ss ol-a

Where do I get the bus for the airport?
Ble galla i ddal y bws i'r maes awyr?
ble gall-(eye) ***th***ahl uh b*oo*ss irr m(eye)ss a-wirr

Where should I change?
Ble dylwn i newid?
ble duh-l*oo*n i ne-wid

Which bus do I take for the football stadium?
Pa fws ddylwn i ddal i'r stadiwm pêl-droed?
pah v*oo*ss ***th***uh-l*oo*n i ***th***ahl irr stad-y*oo*m pehl droyd

Which bus do I take for the station?
Pa fws ddylwn i ddal i'r orsaf?
pah v*oo*ss ***th***uh-l*oo*n i ***th***ahl irr orss-av

Will you tell me when to get off the bus?
Wnewch chi ddweud wrtha i pryd i fynd oddi ar y bws?
wne*oo*ch chi ***th***wehd *oo*rrth-a i preed i vind o***th***-i arr uh b*oo*ss

By train

The rail network within Wales serves all the main holiday areas. Should anyone wish to explore all parts of Wales by public transport, then it will be necessary to make use of both rail and bus services. Combined rail/bus unlimited travel tickets make it easier for travellers to make use of both forms of transport.

The two main lines at opposite ends of the country connect Wales with the England and Scotland network and the rest of Europe. In the north, the system runs from London Euston, via Milton Keynes, Crewe, Chester, Rhyl, Llandudno Junction, Bangor and on to Holyhead for the Irish ferries. Along the south coast, a frequent and fast service extends from London Paddington via Reading, Bristol Parkway, Newport, Cardiff, Port Talbot to Fishguard in Pembrokeshire where it is also possible to catch ferries to Ireland. It is also possible to travel from the north-east of England to Swansea via Newcastle, Durham, Darlington, York, Sheffield, Derby, Bristol Parkway, Newport (where a change of train is usually necessary) and on to Cardiff and Swansea. From London Euston there is a train service via Birmingham or Wolverhampton with connections at both to Shrewsbury, Welshpool, Newtown, Machynlleth and Aberystwyth in mid-Wales. The Heart of Wales line extends 120 miles from Shrewsbury to Swansea. It crosses the border into Wales at Knighton and the whole journey takes approximately 4 hours. The Cambrian Coast line runs along the Cardigan Bay, a 70-mile route, from Aberystwyth to Pwllheli. Local services around Cardiff are run by Valley Lines.

The Freedom of Wales Flexi Pass offers unlimited travel in all mainline rail services in Wales, plus most scheduled bus services. The north and mid-Wales Rover ticket gives much the same unlimited travel benefits by train/bus as the Flexi Pass, though on a regional basis.

With the BritRail Pass, overseas visitors can get unlimited travel over the whole of the United Kingdom rail network without restrictions. Passes are available in both first and standard (economy) class. Visitors can choose from a range of tickets to suit their travel needs. The Flexi Pass is valid for 4, 8, or 15 days within a period of 2 months. Consecutive Day Passes give continuous travel over a period of 8, 15, 22 days or 1 month. Passes must be purchased overseas through either Rail Europe offices abroad, major travel agents abroad or appointed sales agents.

Special prices in standard class are available for senior citizens aged 60 and over, and for young people aged between 16 and 25.

At the railway station

A return (ticket) to Fishguard, please
Tocyn dwyffordd i Abergwaun, os gwelwch yn dda
tok-in d*oo*i-forr***th*** i a-berr-gw(eye)n os gwel-*oo*ch uhn ***th***ah

At the railway station

A return to London, first-class, please
Tocyn dwyffordd i Lundain, dosbarth cynta', os gwelwch yn dda
tok-in d*oo*i-forr*th* i lin-d(eye)n dos-barrth kuhnt-a os gwel-*oo*ch uhn *th*ah

A single (one-way ticket) to Shrewsbury
Tocyn sengl i'r Amwythig
tok-in seng-uhl irr am-*oo*ith-ig

Can I buy a return ticket?
Ga' i brynu tocyn dwyffordd?
gah i bruhn-i tok-in d*oo*i-forr*th*

I want to book a seat on the sleeper to Edinburgh
Dwi eisiau bwcio sedd ar y trên cysgu i Gaeredin
dwee (eye)sh-y(eye) b*oo*k-yo seh*th* arr uh trehn kuhss-gi i g(eye)rr-e-din

Second class. A window seat, please
Ail ddosbarth. Sedd ger y ffenest, os gwelwch yn dda
(eye)l *th*oss-barth seh*th* gerr uh fen-est os gwel-*oo*ch uhn *th*ah

What are the times of the trains to Chester?
Am faint o'r gloch mae'r trenau'n mynd i Gaer?
am v(eye)nt orr glohch m(eye)rr tren-(eye)n mind i g(eye)rr

Where can I buy a ticket?
Ble galla i brynu tocyn?
ble gall-(eye) bruhn-i tok-in

A smoking compartment, first-class
Adran smygu, dosbarth cynta'
ad-ran smuh-gi doss-barrth kuhn-ta

A non-smoking compartment, please
Adran dim smygu, os gwelwch yn dda
ad-ran dim smuh-gi os gwel-*oo*ch uhn *th*ah

When is the next train to Brecon?
Pryd mae'r trên nesa' i Aberhonddu?
preed m(eye)rr trehn ness-a i a-berr-hon-*th*i

When is the next train to Holyhead?
Pryd mae'r trên nesa' i Gaergybi?
preed m(eye)rr trehn ness-a i g(eye)rr-guh-bi

At the railway station

How long do I have before my next train leaves?
Faint o amser sy 'da fi tan bydd fy nhrên nesa'n gadael?
v(eye)nt o am-serr see da vi tahn bee***th*** vuh nrehn ness-an gad-(eye)l

Do I have time to go shopping?
Oes amser 'da fi i fynd i siopa?
oyss am-serr da vi i vind i shop-a

Can I take my bicycle?
Ga' i fynd â fy meic?
gah i vind a vuh m(eye)k

What time does the train leave?
Pryd mae'r trên yn gadael?
preed m(eye)rr trehn uhn gad-(eye)l

When is the last train?
Pryd mae'r trên ola'?
preed m(eye)rr trehn ol-a

Where do I have to change?
Ble mae eisiau ifi newid?
ble m(eye) (eye)sh-y(eye) iv-i ne-wid

I want to leave these bags in the left-luggage
Dwi eisiau gadael fy magiau yn y storfa baciau
dwee (eye)sh-y(eye) gad-(eye)l vuh mag-y(eye) uhn uh storr-va bak-y(eye)

Can I check in my bags?
Ga' i gofnodi fy magiau?
gah i gov-nod-i vuh mag-y(eye)

How much is it per bag?
Faint yw e fesul bag?
v(eye)nt i***oo*** e vess-il bag

I shall pick them up this evening
Bydda i'n eu casglu nhw heno
buh-***th***(eye)n i kass-gli nhoo hen-o

Where do I pick up my bags?
Ble dwi'n casglu fy magiau?
ble dween kass-gli vuh mag-y(eye)

On the train

Is there a buffet car or club car?
Oes yna gerbyd bwffe / gerbyd lolfa?
oyss uhn-a gerr-bid b*oo*-fe / gerr-bid lol-va

Is there a dining car?
Oes yna gerbyd bwyta?
oyss uhn-a gerr-bid b*oo*i-ta

Is there a restaurant on the train?
Oes yna fwyty ar y trên?
oyss uhn-a v*oo*i-ti arr uh trehn

Where is the departure board (listing)?
Ble mae'r bwrdd ymadael?
ble m(eye)rr b*oorrth* uhm-ad-(eye)l

Which platform do I go to?
I ba blatfform y dylwn i fynd?
i bah blat-forrm uh duh-l*oo*n i vind

Is this the platform for Chester?
Ai hwn yw'r platfform i Gaer?
(eye) h*oo*n i*oo*rr plat-forrm i g(eye)rr

Is this a through train?
Ydy'r trên yn mynd yn syth?
uh-dirr trehn uhn mind uhn seeth

Is this the Llanelli train?
Ai hwn yw trên Llanelli?
(eye) h*oo*n i*oo* trehn llan-ell-i

Do we stop at Carmarthen?
Ydyn ni'n stopio yng Nghaerfyrddin?
uh-di nin stop-yo uhng h(eye)rr-vuhrr-*th*in

What time do we get to Shrewsbury?
Pryd fyddwn ni'n cyrraedd Amwythig?
preed vuh-*thoo*n nin kuhrr-(eye)*th* am-*oo*ith-ig

Are we at Rhyl yet?
Ydyn ni wedi cyrraedd y Rhyl eto?
uh-di ni wed-i kuhrr-(eye)***th*** y rhil et-o

Are we on time?
Ydyn ni ar amser?
uh-di ni arr am-serr

Can you help me with my bags?
Allwch chi helpu fi gyda fy magiau?
all-***oo***ch chi help-i vi guh-da vuh mag-y(eye)

I have lost my ticket
Dwi wedi colli fy nhocyn
dwee wed-i coll-i vuh nho-kin

My wife has my ticket
Mae fy nhocyn gyda fy ngwraig
m(eye) vuh nho-kin guh-da vuhng wr(eye)g

Is this seat taken?
Oes rhywun yn eistedd 'ma?
oyss rhi***oo***-in uhn (eye)-ste***th*** ma

May I open the window?
Ga' i agor y ffenest?
gah i ag-orr uh fen-est

This is a non-smoking compartment
Mae hon yn adran dim smygu
m(eye) hon uhn ad-ran dim smuh-gi

This is my seat
Fy sedd i yw hon
vuh seh***th*** ee i-***oo*** hon

Where is the toilet?
Ble mae'r toiled?
ble m(eye)rr toy-led

Why have we stopped?
Pam dŷn ni wedi stopio?
pam deen ni wed-i stop-yo

Driving

Driving in Wales is a rewarding experience and although the country is, in the main, rural in character, it has excellent motorway links with the rest of the United Kingdom. Journeys on some of the country roads may take a little longer, but the scenery and the charm of the uncrowded and remote countryside more than compensate for the lost time on the roads.

Wales has just the one M4 motorway. This is the main westbound route from London, which links the major towns of south Wales. Its route enters Wales across the new Severn Bridge and bypassing Newport, Cardiff, Bridgend, Swansea, it stops short of Carmarthen in south-west Wales. It is also possible to enter Wales on the M48 across the original Severn Bridge. Both bridges carry a toll on the westbound journey only. In north Wales, the A55 coastal expressway connects Snowdonia and the coast with Manchester Airport and the UK motorway network. The M54, which links with the M6, M5 and M1, provides easy access to mid-Wales and also connects the Heart of Wales with Birmingham Airport and central England.

Road regulations

In Wales, as in the UK in general, you drive on the left-hand side of the road and overtake on the right. Speed limits are 30–40 mph (48–65 kmh) in built-up areas, 70 mph (113 kmh) on motorways and dual carriageways. Road regulations are given in the Highway Code, obtainable from most bookshops and from the offices of the AA (Automobile Association) or the RAC (Royal Automobile Club). Traffic signs in the majority conform to international standards. In Wales, on our main roads in particular, place names on road signs appear in both English and Welsh. For example, *Caerdydd* and *Cardiff*, *Abertawe* and *Swansea*. The wearing of seat belts is compulsory for driver and front-seat passenger, and rear-seat passengers where seat belts are fitted. Fines for drunken driving are heavy, therefore all drivers are strongly advised not to drink and drive.

Driving licence

You are permitted to use your own driving licence to drive in Britain for up to 12 months from the date of your last entry into the country. It is also possible to supplement this with an International Driving Permit.

Traffic and weather conditions

Are there any hold-ups?
Oes yna unrhyw rwystrau?
oyss uhn-a een-rhi*oo* *roo*is-tr(eye)

Is there a different way to the stadium?
Oes yna ffordd wahanol i'r stadiwm?
oyss uhn-a forr***th*** wa-han-ol irr stad-y*oo*m

Is there a toll on this motorway?
Oes yna doll ar y draffordd 'ma?
oyss uh-na doll arr uh dra-forr***th*** ma

What is causing this traffic jam?
Beth sy'n achosi'r dagfa draffig?
behth seen a-choss-irr dag-va draff-ig

What is the speed limit?
Beth yw'r cyfyngiad cyflymder?
behth i-***oo***rr kuh-fuhng-yad kuh-vluhm-derr

When is the rush hour?
Pryd mae'r adeg brysura'?
preed m(eye)rr ad-eg bruh-seerr-a

Is the traffic heavy?
Ydy'r traffig yn drwm?
uh-dirr traff-ig uhn dr*oo*m

Is the traffic one-way?
Ydy'r traffig yn unffordd?
uh-dirr traff-ig uhn in-forr*th*

When will the road be clear?
Pryd bydd y ffordd yn glir?
preed bee*th* uh forr*th* uhn gleerr

Do I need snow chains?
Oes angen cadwyni eira?
oyss ang-en kad-*oo*in-i (eye)rr-a

Is the road open?
Ydy'r ffordd ar agor?
uh-dirr forr*th* arr ag-orr

Is the road to Builth Wells snowed up?
Ydy'r ffordd i Lanfair-ym-Muallt wedi cau gan eira?
uh-dirr forr*th* i Lan-v(eye)rr-uhm-Mee-allt wed-i k(eye) gan (eye)rr-a

Parking

No parking is allowed where you see yellow lines along the kerbs. Parking regulations are also indicated on road signs. Roadside parking in built-up areas is usually restricted to half an hour. In car parks that are designated for the public, or in designated parking areas in towns, parking tickets can be purchased by inserting coins into a meter.

Where is there a car park?
Ble mae maes parcio?
ble m(eye) m(eye)ss parrk-yo

Can I park here?
Ga' i barcio 'ma?
gah i barrk-yo ma

Do I need a parking ticket?
Oes angen tocyn parcio arna i?
oyss ang-en tok-in parrk-yo arr-na i

Where can I get a parking ticket?
Ble ga' i docyn parcio?
ble gah i dok-in parrk-yo

How long can I stay here?
Pa mor hir ga' i aros 'ma?
pah morr heerr gah i arr-oss ma

Is it safe to park here?
Ydy hi'n ddiogel / saff i fi barcio 'ma?
uh-di hin ***th***i-o-gel / sahff i vi barrk-yo ma

What time does the car park / multi-storey car park close?
Pryd mae'r maes parcio / maes parcio amrylawr yn cau?
preed m(eye)rr m(eye)ss parrk-yo / m(eye)ss parrk-yo am-ruh-lowrr uhn k(eye)

Where do I pay?
Ble dwi'n talu?
ble dween tal-i

Do I need coins for the meter?
Oes angen darnau arian ar gyfer y mesurydd?
oyss ang-en darrn-(eye) ar-yan arr guh-verr uh mess-i-ri***th***

Do I need parking lights?
Oes angen golau parcio?
oyss ang-en gol-(eye) parrk-yo

At the service station

Fuel is sold in litres. Most cars in the UK now run on lead-free petrol. Alternative fuel for cars that used to run on 4-star petrol, and diesel fuel are also available. Prices are generally lowest in the suburbs of cities and larger towns.

At the service station

Do you take credit cards?
Ych chi'n cymryd cardiau credyd?
ich chin kuhm-rid karrd-y(eye) kre-did

Fill the tank please
Llenwch y tanc, os gwelwch yn dda
llen-*oo*ch uh tank os gwel-*oo*ch uhn ***th***ah

25 litres of — unleaded petrol
dau ddeg pump litr o — betrol di-blwm
d(eye) ***th***eg pimp leet-rr o — bet-trol dee bl*oo*m

— diesel
— ddisel
— ***th***ee-sel

Can you clean the windscreen?
Wnewch chi lanhau'r sgrîn wynt?
wne*oo*ch chi lan-h(eye)rr sgreen wint

Will you check the oil?
Wnewch chi siecio'r olew?
wne*oo*ch chi shek-yorr ol-e*oo*

Will you check the water?
Wnewch chi siecio'r dŵr?
wne*oo*ch chi shek-yorr doorr

Check the tyre pressure please
Sieciwch wynt y teiars, os gwelwch yn dda
shek-y*oo*ch wint uh teh-arrss os gwel-*oo*ch uhn ***th***ah

The pressure should be 2.3 at the front and 2.5 at the rear
Dylai'r gwynt fod yn ddau bwynt tri yn y ffrynt ac yn ddau bwynt pump yn y cefn
duh-l(eye)rr gwint vohd uhn ***th***(eye) b*oo*int tree uhn uh fruhnt ak uhn ***th***(eye) b*oo*int pimp uhn uh kev-n

I need some distilled water
Dwi angen dŵr distyll
dwee ang-en doorr diss-till

Breakdown and repairs

The Royal Automobile Club (RAC), the Automobile Association (AA) and the Green Flag National Breakdown all operate a 24-hour emergency breakdown service.

In cases of breakdown on motorways you should find emergency telephones situated at 1-mile intervals, connected to an emergency service.

Elsewhere, ring any motoring organisation, and if you are not a member you will be charged a call out fee:

Royal Automobile Club
Breakdown
RAC House
1 Forest Road
Feltham
Middlesex TW13 7RR

Green Flag National
Green Flag House
Cote Lane
Leeds LS28 5GF

Automobile Association
Norfolk House
Priestly Road
Basingstoke
Hants RG24 9NZ

At the garage / At the roadside

Is there a telephone nearby?
Oes ffôn ar bwys?
oyss fohn arr b*oo*is

Can you send a recovery truck?
Allwch chi anfon lorri adfer?
all-*oo*ch chi an-von lorr-i ad-verr

At the garage / At the roadside

Can you take me to the nearest garage?
Allwch chi fynd â fi i'r modurdy / garej agosa'?
all-*oo*ch chi vind a vi irr mo-dirr-di / gar-edge ag-oss-a

I have run out of petrol
Dwi wedi rhedeg allan o betrol
dwee wed-i rhed-eg all-an o bet-rol

Can you give me a can of petrol, please?
Ga' i gan o betrol, os gwelwch yn dda?
gah i gan o bet-rol os gwel-*oo*ch uhn *th*ah

Can you give me a push?
Allwch chi roi gwthiad i fi?
all-*oo*ch chi roy g*oo*th-yad i vi

Can you give me a tow?
Allwch chi roi tow i fi? / Allwch chi fy llusgo i?
all-*oo*ch chi roy tow i vi / all-*oo*ch chi vuh lliss-go i

Is there a mechanic here?
Oes mecanig 'ma?
oyss mek-an-ig ma

Do you have an emergency fan belt?
Oes ffanbelt brys 'da chi?
oyss fan-belt breess da chi

Do you have jump leads?
Oes gwifrau cyswllt 'da chi?
oyss gwi-vr(eye) kuh-ss*oo*llt da chi

Can you find out what the trouble is?
Allwch chi gael gweld beth yw'r drafferth?
all-*oo*ch chi g(eye)l gweld behth i*oo*rr dra-ferrth

There is something wrong
Mae rhywbeth yn bod
m(eye) rhi*oo*-beth uhn bohd

There is something wrong with the car
Mae rhywbeth yn bod ar y car
m(eye) rhi*oo*-beth uhn bohd arr uh karr

At the garage / At the roadside

Will it take long to repair it?
Gymer hi'n hir i'w drwsio?
guh-merr heen heerr yoo dr*oo*sh-o

Is it serious?
Ydy e'n ddifrifol?
uh-di en *th*i-vreev-ol

Can you repair it for the time being?
Allwch chi ei drwsio dros dro?
all-*oo*ch chi (eye) dr*oo*sh-o dross dro

Can you replace the windscreen wiper blades?
Allwch chi newid llafnau weipar y sgrîn wynt?
all-*oo*ch chi ne-wid llav-n(eye) w(eye)-parr uh sgreen wint

Can you repair a flat tyre?
Allwch chi drwsio teiar fflat?
all-*oo*ch chi dr*oo*sh-o teh-arr flat

Do you have the spare parts?
Ydy'r darnau sbâr 'da chi?
uh-dirr darrn-(eye) sbahrr da chi

I have a flat tyre
Mae teiar fflat 'da fi
m(eye) teh-arr flat da vi

I have locked myself out of the car
Dwi wedi 'nghloi fy hunan allan o'r car
dwee wed-i ung-hloy vuh hee-nan all-an orr karr

I have locked the ignition key inside the car
Dwi wedi cloi'r allwedd danio tu mewn i'r car
dwee wed-i kloyrr all-we*th* dan-yo tee me*oo*n irr karr

I need a new fan belt
Dwi angen ffanbelt newydd
dwee ang-en fan-belt ne-wi*th*

I think there is a bad connection
Dwi'n meddwl bod cysylltiad gwael
dween me*th*-*oo*l bohd kuh-suhllt-yad gw(eye)l

At the garage / At the roadside

My car has been towed away
Mae fy nghar wedi ei dowio / lusgo i ffwrdd
m(eye) vuhng harr wed-i (eye) dow-yo / lis-go i f***oo***rth

My car has broken down
Mae fy nghar wedi torri lawr
m(eye) vuhng harr wed-i torr-i lowrr

My car will not start
Wnaiff fy nghar ddim dechrau / cychwyn (NW)
wn(eye)ff vuhng harr ***th***im dech-r(eye)/kuhch-win

My windscreen has cracked
Mae fy sgrîn wynt wedi cracio
m(eye) vuh sgreen wint wed-i krak-yo

The air-conditioning does not work
Dyw'r system dymheru ddim yn gweithio
di***oo***rr siss-tem duhm-herri ***th***im uhn gw(eye)th-yo

The battery is flat
Mae'r batri'n fflat
m(eye)rr bat-reen flat

The engine has broken down
Mae'r peiriant wedi torri lawr
m(eye)rr p(eye)-rr-yant wed-i torr-i lowrr

The engine is overheating
Mae'r peiriant yn gorboethi
m (eye)rr p(eye)-rr-yant uhn gorr-boy-thi

The lights are not working
Dyw'r goleuadau ddim yn gweithio
di***oo***rr gol-(eye)-ad-(eye) ***th***im uhn gw(eye)th-yo

The brake lights are not working
Dyw'r goleuadau brecio ddim yn gweithio
di***oo***rr gol-(eye)-ad-(eye) brehk-yo ***th***im uhn gw(eye)th-yo

The exhaust pipe has fallen off
Mae'r biben fwg wedi syrthio
m(eye)rr bib-en v***oo***g wed-i suhrrth-yo

There is a leak in the radiator
Mae'r rheiddiadur yn gollwng
m(eye)rr rh(eye)***th***-yad-irr uhn goll-***oo***ng

Accidents and the police

In an emergency dial 999 from any phone to obtain the services of the Police, Fire Brigade, Ambulance, and in certain areas Mountain Rescue or Coastguard. In phone boxes you do not need to insert a coin first.

There has been an accident
Mae damwain wedi bod
m(eye) dam-w(eye)n wed-i bohd

We must call an ambulance
Rhaid inni alw'r ambiwlans
rh(eye)d in-ni al-***oo***rr am-bi***oo***-lanss

We must call the police
Rhaid inni alw'r heddlu
rh(eye)d in-ni al-***oo***rr he***th***-li

What is your name and address?
Beth yw'ch enw a'ch cyfeiriad?
behth i***oo***ch en-***oo*** ach kuh-v(eye)rr-yad

You must not move
Peidiwch â symud
p(eye)d-y***oo***ch a suh-mid

I could not stop in time
Fedrwn i ddim stopio mewn pryd
ved-r***oo***n i ***th***im stop-yo me***oo***n preed

I did not know about the speed limit
Doeddwn i ddim yn gwybod am y cyfyngiad cyflymder
doy***th***-***oo***n i ***th***im uhn g***oo***i-bod am uh kuh-fuhng-yad kuh-vluhm-derr

I did not see the bicycle
Welais i ddim o'r beic
wel-(eye)ss i ***th***im orr b(eye)k

Accidents and the police

He did not stop
Wnaeth e ddim stopio
wn(eye)th e ***th***im stop-yo

He is a witness
Mae e'n dyst
m(eye) en deest

He overtook on a bend
Aeth e heibio ar y tro
(eye)th e hehb-yo arr uh tro

He ran into the back of my car
Gwnaeth e fwrw yn erbyn cefn fy nghar
gwn(eye)th e f*oo*rr*oo* uhn err-bin kev-n vuhng harr

He stopped suddenly
Stopiodd e'n sydyn
stop-yo***th*** en suh-din

He was moving too fast
Roedd e'n symud yn rhy gyflym
roy***th*** en suh-mid uhn rhee guhv-lim

I did not see the sign
Welais i ddim o'r arwydd
wel-(eye)ss i ***th***im orr arr-wi***th***

Here are my insurance documents
Dyma fy nogfennau yswiriant
duh-ma vuh nog-ven-n(eye) uhss-wirr-yant

Here is my driving licence
Dyma fy nhrwydded yrru
duh-ma vuhn hr*oo*i***th***-ed uh-ri

I cannot find my driving licence
Dwi ddim yn gallu ffeindio fy nhrwydded yrru
dwee ***th***im uhn gall-i f(eye)nd-yo vuhn hr*oo*i***th***-ed uh-ri

Do you want my credit card?
Ych chi eisiau fy ngherdyn credyd?
ich chi (eye)sh-y(eye) vuhng herr-din kre-did

Do you want my passport?
Ych chi eisiau fy mhasport?
ich chi (eye)sh-y(eye) vuhm hass-porrt

I am very sorry. I am a visitor
Mae'n ddrwg 'da fi. Ymwelydd 'dw i
m(eye)n ***thr**oo*g da vi uhm-wel-i***th*** d*oo* i

I did not understand the sign
Wnes i ddim deall yr arwydd
wness i ***th***im de-all uhrr arr-wi***th***

How much is the fine?
Faint yw'r ddirwy?
v(eye)nt i*oo*rr ***th***i-r*oo*i

I have not got enough money. Can I pay at the police station?
Does dim digon o arian 'da fi. Alla i dalu yng ngorsaf yr heddlu?
doys dim dig-on o ar-yan da vi all-(eye) dal-i uhng orr-ssav uhrr he***th***-li

I was only driving 40 miles an hour
Do'n i ddim ond yn gyrru pedwar deg milltir yr awr
dohn i ***th***im ond uhn guh-ri ped-warr dehg mill-tirr uhrr owrr

I have not had anything to drink
Dwi ddim wedi cael dim byd i'w yfed
dwee ***th***im wed-i k(eye)l dim beed yoo uh-ved

I was overtaking
Ro'n i'n mynd heibio
rohn een mind hehb-yo

I was parking
Ro'n i'n parcio
rohn een parrk-yo

That car was too close
Roedd y car 'na'n rhy agos
roy***th*** uh karr nan rhee ag-oss

The brakes failed
Methodd y breciau
meth-o***th*** uh brehk-y(eye)

The car number was
Rhif y car oedd
rheev uh karr oy***th***

The car skidded
Llithrodd y car
llith-ro***th*** uh karr

The car swerved
Swerfiodd y car
swer-vi-o***th*** uh karr

The road was icy
Roedd y ffordd yn rhewllyd
roy***th*** uh forr***th*** uhn rhe***oo***-llid

The tyre burst
Byrstiodd y teiar
buhrrst-yo***th*** uh teh-arr

The car turned right without signalling
Trodd y car i'r dde heb arwyddo
tro***th*** uh karr irr ***th***eh heb arr-***oo***i-***th***o

Car parts

accelerator
cyflymydd / 'sbardun
kuhv-luhm-i***th*** / sbarr-din

aerial
erial
eh-rri-al

air filter
hidlydd aer
hid-li***th*** (eye)rr

brake fluid
hylif brêc
huh-liv brehk

alternator
eiliadur
(eye)l-yad-irr

brake light
golau brêc
gol-(eye) brehk

antifreeze
gwrthrewydd
g***oo***rrth-re-wi***th***

brakes
breciau
brek-y(eye)

Car parts

automatic gearbox
gerbocs awtomatig
gehrr-boks aw-tom-a-tig

bulb
bylb
buhlb

axle
echel
ech-el

bumper
bympar
buhm-parr

battery
batri
bat-ri

car-phone
ffôn y car
fohn uh karr

bonnet
boned
bon-ed

carburettor
carbwradur
karr-b*oo*-rad-irr

boot
cwt car / bŵt
c*oo*t karr / boot

child seat
sedd plentyn
seh*th* plen-tin

choke
tagydd
tag-i*th*

electrical system
system drydanol
siss-tem druh-dan-ol

clutch
clytsh / cydiwr
kluhtsh / kuhd-y*oo*r

engine
peiriant
p(eye)-rr-yant

cooling system
system oeri
siss-tem oy-ri

exhaust system
system wagio / wacáu
siss-tem wag-yo / wak-(eye)

cylinder
silindr
sil-ind-rr

fan belt
ffan belt
fan-belt

disc brake
brêc disg
brehk disg

foot pump
pwmp troed
p*oo*mp troyd

distributor
dosbarthydd
dos-barrth-i*th*

Car parts

fuel guage
mesurydd tanwydd
mess-i-ri*th* tan-*ooith*

door
drws
droos

fuel pump
pwmp tanwydd
p*oo*mp tan-*ooith*

dynamo
deinamo
d(eye)n-am-o

fuse
ffiws
fi*oo*ss

gear box
gerbocs
gehrr-boks

hood
to
toh

gear lever
lifer gêr
lee-verr gehrr

horn
corn
korrn

generator
generadur
g(en)-err-a-dirr

hose
pibell / piben
pib-ell / pib-en

hammer
morthwyl
morrth-*oo*il

ignition key
allwedd danio
all-we*th* dan-yo

hand brake
brêc llaw
brehk llow (as in how)

ignition
tanio
tan-yo

hazard lights
goleuadau rhybudd
gol-(eye)-ad-(eye) rhuh-bi*th*

indicator
cyfeiriwr / cyfeirydd
kuh-v(eye)rr-y*oo*rr / kuh-v(eye)rr-i*th*

headlights
prif lampau / prif olau
preev-lamp-(eye) / preev ol-(eye)

jack
jac
jak

heating system
system wresogi
siss-tem wress-og-i

Car parts

lights
goleuadau
gol-(eye)-ad-(eye)

lock
clo
kloh

rear view mirror
drych ôl
dreech ohl

oil filter
hidlydd olew
hid-li***th*** ol-***eoo***

reflectors
gwydrau cochion
gwi-dr(eye) koch-yon

oil
olew
ol-***eoo***

reversing light
golau bacio
gol-(eye) bak-yo

oil pressure
pwysedd olew
p***oo***i-se***th*** ol-***eoo***

roof-rack
rhesel ben to
rhess-el ben toh

petrol
petrol
pet-rol

screwdriver
sgriwdreifer
sgr***oo***-dr(eye)v-err

points
pwyntiau
p***oo***int-y(eye)

seat belt
gwregys diogelwch
gwreg-iss di-o-gel-***oo***ch

pump
pwmp
p***oo***mp

seat
sedd
seh***th***

radiator
rheiddiadur
rh(eye)***th***-yad-irr

shock absorber
siocleddfwr
shok-le***th***-v***oo***rr

silencer
tawelydd
ta-wel-i***th***

steering wheel
olwyn lywio
ol-win li***oo***-yo

socket set
set o socedi
set o so-ked-i

Car parts

sun roof
to haul
toh h(eye)l

spanner
sbaner
sban-err

suspension
hongiad
hong-yad

spare part
darn sbâr
darrn sbahrr

tools
offer / tŵls
off-err / tools

spark plug
plwg tanio
pluhg tan-yo

towbar
bar halio
barr hal-yo

speedometer
sbidomedr
sbeed-om-ed-err

transmission
trawsyriant
trowss-uhrr-yant

starter motor
peiriant tanio
p(eye)-rr-yant tan-yo

tyre pressure
gwynt teiars
gwint teh-arrss

steering
llyw
lli*oo*

tyre
teiar
teh-arr

warning light
golau rhybudd
gol-(eye) rhuh-bi***th***

windscreen
sgrîn wynt
sgreen wint

water
dŵr
doorr

windshield
ffenest flaen
fen-est vl(eye)n

wheel
olwyn
ol-win

wipers
weipars
w(eye)-parrss

Road signs

Keep to the right
Cadwch i'r dde
kad-***oo***ch irr ***th***eh

Private road
Ffordd breifat
forr***th*** br(eye)v-at

No thoroughfare
Dim ffordd drwodd
dim forr***th*** dr***oo***-o***th***

Parking for residents only
Parcio ar gyfer preswylwyr yn unig
parrk-yo arr guh-verr press-***oo***il-wirr uhn een-ig

No entry
Dim mynediad
dim muhn-ed-yad

Diversion
Dargyfeiriad / gwyriad
darr-guh-v(eye)rr-yad / g***oo***irr-yad

EATING OUT

Where to eat

There are eating places to suit all tastes and pockets in Wales, from humble cafés in small villages and towns to elegant restaurants in larger towns and cities. Eating out is fast becoming a favourite pastime among the Welsh people and very often you will find families going out for lunch on Sundays and public holidays. In fact, dining in Wales is a social event as much as it is a matter of gastronomic indulgence.

Traditionally, there are three main categories of places to eat in Wales: cafés, pubs and restaurants. In addition to those, you have fish and chip shops, bistros, brasseries, burger bars, pizza parlours and so on.

In cafés, which are plentiful in all parts of Wales, you can order any meal of the day: a hearty breakfast, a full meal for lunch or a light snack, and in some instances, an evening meal as well. Breakfasts are served from 09.00 onwards, lunch is mostly taken from about 12.00 to 14.00 and evening meal any time after about 19.00. Most cafés remain open from 09.00 to 17.30 and longer in the summer months.

Foods in public houses (pubs) vary according to the size and location of the hostelry. Many pubs in Wales now offer quite imaginative dishes rather than the standard fish and chips or microwaved snack. Most places serve food at lunchtime and in the evening, usually until 21.00. Prices are generally inexpensive for simple straightforward food.

If you consider dining in a restaurant, you can expect to pay more for your meal than you would normally pay in a café or a pub. Restaurants offer a plethora of choice to their customers and Wales' increasing sophistication in the food industry is reflected in its cuisine. The Welsh culinary art is now on a par with that of the other countries of the UK. The indigenous Welsh cuisine of meats, fish, pies, cheeses and puddings, is still on offer everywhere in the principality and certain native Welsh dishes are becoming very popular again in some restaurants in Wales.

An eclectic range of international options is on offer in most towns and cities, from Chinese, Japanese and Portuguese to Indian, Italian, Greek and French. A number of fast food chains also exist all over Wales to cater for every need.

Reservations

Should we reserve a table?
Ddylen ni fwcio bwrdd?
*th*uh-len ni v*oo*k-yo b*oo*rr*th*

Can I book a table for four at 8 o'clock?
Ga i fwcio bwrdd i bedwar ar gyfer wyth o'r gloch?
gah i v*oo*k-yo b*oo*rr*th* i bed-warr arr guh-verr *oo*ith orr glohch

Can we have a table for four?
Gawn ni fwrdd i bedwar?
gown ni v*oo*rr*th* i bed-warr

I am a vegetarian
Dwi'n llysieuwr
dween lluh-sheh-*oo*r

We would like a table by the window
Hoffen ni fwrdd ar bwys y ffenest
hoff-en ni v*oo*rr*th* arr b*oo*is uh fen-est

We would like a table on the terrace
Hoffen ni fwrdd ar y teras
hoff-en ni v*oo*rr*th* arr uh ter-ass

Useful questions

Do you have a local speciality?
Oes 'da chi bryd lleol arbennig?
oyss da chi breed lle-ol arr-ben-nig

Useful questions

Do you have a set menu?
Oes 'da chi fwydlen osod?
oyss da chi v*oo*id-len oss-od

What do you recommend?
Beth ych chi'n ei argymell?
behth ich chin (eye) arr-guh-mell

What is the dish of the day?
Beth yw saig osod y dydd?
behth i*oo* s(eye)g oss-od uh dee*th*

What is this called?
Beth ych chi'n galw hwn?
behth ich chin gal-*oo* h*oo*n

What is this dish like?
Sut mae'r saig hon yn blasu?
sh*oo*d m(eye)rr s(eye)g hon uhn blass-i

Which Welsh wine do you recommend?
Pa win Cymreig ych chi'n ei argymell?
pah ween kuhm-rehg ich chin (eye) arr-guh-mell

Are vegetables included?
Ydy'r llysiau'n gynwysedig?
uh-dirr lluhss-y(eye)n guhn-*oo*iss-ed-ig

Is the local Welsh wine good?
Ydy'r gwin lleol Cymreig yn dda?
uh-dirr gween lle-ol kuhm-rehg uhn *th*ah

Is this cheese very strong?
Ydy'r caws yn gryf iawn?
uh-dirr kowss uhn greev yown

Is this good?
Ydy hwn yn dda?
uh-di h*oo*n uhn *th*ah

Do you have yoghurt?
Oes iogwrt 'da chi?
oyss yog-*oo*rrt da chi

How do I eat this?
Sut dwi'n bwyta hwn?
sh*oo*d dween b*oo*i-ta h*oo*n

What is the soup of the day?
Beth yw cawl y dydd?
behth i*oo* kowl uh dee*th*

Ordering your meal

I will take the set menu
Gymra i'r fwydlen osod
guhm-r(eye)rr v*oo*id-len oss-od

The menu, please
Y fwydlen, os gwelwch yn dda
uh v*oo*id-len os gwel-*oo*ch uhn *th*ah

Could we have some more bread, please?
Gawn ni ragor o fara, os gwelwch yn dda?
gown ni rag-orr o far-ra os gwel-*oo*ch uhn *th*ah

Can I see the menu again, please
Ga i olwg eto ar y fwydlen, os gwelwch yn dda?
gah i ol-*oo*g et-o arr uh v*oo*id-len os gwel-*oo*ch uhn *th*ah

Can we have some bread?
Gawn ni fara?
gown ni fa-ra

I will take that
Gymra i hwnna
guhm-r(eye) h*oo*n-na

That is for me
Mae hwnna i fi
m(eye) h*oo*n-na i vi

Can we start with soup?
Gawn ni ddechrau â chawl?
gown ni *th*ech-r(eye) a chowl

I will have salad
Gymra i salad
guhm-r(eye) sal-ad

Could we have some butter?
Gawn ni fenyn?
gown ni ven-in

I like my steak — very rare
Dwi'n hoffi fy stêc — yn waedlyd iawn
dween hoff-i vuh stehk — uhn w(eye)d-lid yown

— medium rare
— yn weddol waedlyd
— uhn we***th***-ol w(eye)d-lid

— rare
— yn waedlyd
— uhn w(eye)d-lid

— well done
— wedi ei rostio'n dda
— wed-i (eye) rost-yon ***th***ah

Ordering drinks

The wine list, please
Y rhestr winoedd, os gwelwch yn dda
uh rhest-rr win-oy***th*** os gwel-***oo***ch uhn ***th***ah

We will take the Riesling
Gymerwn ni y Riesling
guh-merr-***oo***n ni uhrr rees-ling

A bottle of house red wine, please
Potelaid o win coch y tŷ, os gwelwch yn dda
pot-el-(eye)d o ween kohch uh tee os gwel-***oo***ch uhn ***th***ah

A glass of dry white wine, please
Gwydraid o win gwyn sych, os gwelwch yn dda
gwi-dr(eye)d o ween gwin seech os gwel-***oo***ch uhn ***th***ah

Another bottle of red wine, please
Potelaid arall o win coch, os gwelwch yn dda
pot-el-(eye)d arr-all o ween kohch os gwel-***oo***ch uhn ***th***ah

Another glass, please
Gwydryn arall, os gwelwch yn dda
gwi-drin arr-all os gwel-***oo***ch uhn ***th***ah

Black coffee, please
Coffi du, os gwelwch yn dda
koff-i dee os gwel-***oo***ch uhn ***th***ah

Coffee with milk, please
Coffi gyda llaeth, os gwelwch yn dda
koff-i guh-da ll(eye)th os gwel-***oo***ch uhn ***th***ah

Some plain water, please
Dŵr plaen, os gwelwch yn dda
doorr pl(eye)n os gwel-***oo***ch uhn ***th***ah

Can we have some mineral water?
Gawn ni ddŵr mwynol?
gown ni ***th***oorr m***oo***in-ol

Two beers, please
Dau gwrw, os gwelwch yn dda
d(eye) g***oo***-r***oo*** os gwel-***oo***ch uhn ***th***ah

Paying the bill

Welsh restaurateurs are very accommodating when it comes to splitting the bill for people who want to pay separately for a meal. In fact, waiters and waitresses in small establishments often add up individual bills at the table. Tipping in Wales, as in the rest of the UK, is purely voluntary, but it indicates your particular satisfaction with the service you have received. It is usually recommended that a tip of around 10 per cent be made, unless the service was unsatisfactory. Some restaurants include a service charge in the bill, in which case a gratuity is unnecessary.

Paying the bill

Can we have the bill, please?
Gawn ni'r bil, os gwelwch yn dda?
gown neerr bil os gwel-*oo*ch uhn ***th***ah

Can I have an itemized bill?
Ga' i fil wedi ei restru'n fanwl / wedi ei eitemeiddio, os gwelwch yn dda?
gah i vil wed-i (eye) ress-treen van-*oo*l / wed-i (eye) (eye)-tem-(eye)***th***-yo os gwel-*oo*ch uhn ***th***ah

Do you accept traveller's cheques?
Ych chi'n derbyn sieciau teithio?
ich chin derr-bin shek-y(eye) t(eye)th-yo

Is service included?
Ydy'r gwasanaeth yn gynwysedig?
uh-dirr gwa-ssan-(eye)th uhn guhn-*oo*iss-ed-ig

Is tax included?
Ydy'r dreth yn gynwysedig?
uh-dirr drehth uhn guhn-*oo*iss-ed-ig

Is there any extra charge?
Oes unrhyw gostau ychwanegol?
oyss een-rhi*oo* gost-(eye) uhch-wan-eg-ol

Can I have a receipt?
Ga' i dderbynneb?
gah i ***th***err-buhn-neb

I would like to pay with my credit card
Hoffwn i dalu â fy nghherdyn credyd
Hoff-*oo*n i dal-i a vuhng herr-din kre-did

I do not have enough currency
Does dim digon o arian cyfredol 'da fi
Doys dim dig-on o ar-yan kuh-vred-ol da vi

This is not correct
Dyw hwn ddim yn gywir
di*oo* h*oo*n ***th***im uhn guh-wirr

This is not my bill
Nid fy mil i yw hwn
nid vuh mil ee i-*oo* h*oo*n

You have given me the wrong change
Ych chi wedi rhoi'r newid anghywir i fi
ich chi wed-i rhoyrr ne-wid ang-huh-wirr i vi

Complaints and compliments

This is cold
Mae hwn yn oer
m(eye) h*oo*n uhn oyrr

This is not what I ordered
Nid dymaarchebais i
nid duh-ma arr-cheb-(eye)ss i

Waiter! We have been waiting for a long time
Wetar! Dŷn ni wedi bod yn disgwyl am amser hir
weht-arr deen ni wed-i bohd uhn diss-gw*oo*il am am-serr heerr

The meal was excellent
Roedd y pryd yn rhagorol
roy*th* uh preed uhn rhag-o-rol

This is excellent
Mae hwn yn rhagorol
m(eye) h*oo*n uhn rhag-o-rol

Can I have the recipe?
Ga' i'r rysáit?
Gah irr ruhss-(eye)t

Food

Wales has a well-earned reputation for producing some of the finest food in the world. For centuries it has been exporting beef, lamb, pork and other foods to England, with the market expanding in comparatively recent times to include Europe. Before the advent of modern transport, drovers walked herds of animals across the border, using the ancient pathways over the mountains and moors.

Meat produced in Wales from animals grazed on the mountains

or the lush valley meadows, is renowned for its sweet flavour and wholesome additive-free quality. Welsh lamb and Welsh Black beef are just two of the many kinds of home-produced meat that are available in shops and restaurants. In addition, many small outlets use traditional methods to produce speciality meats such as home-cured bacon and sausages. These provide an alternative to the mass-produced food supplied by the large manufacturing chains. Local organic foods, including fresh vegetables and fruit, are now also more widely available in the supermarkets as well as the smaller shops.

With its good pastureland, Wales is famed for its milk products. In addition to the big creameries, numerous small producers use cows', sheep and goats' milk to make a wonderfully varied range of cheeses, as well as fruit-flavoured yoghurt, butter and clotted cream, sometimes from organically produced milk.

Sea and river fish from Wales also have a well-deserved reputation for flavour and quality. Oyster, cockle and mussel beds have been re-seeded in north and south Wales and yield tons of sea food for the markets both at home and on the continent. Shellfish, including crabs and lobster, are also exported from the south coast and Cardigan Bay, together with other sea fish such as bass, cod, hake, whiting and plaice. Mackerel are plentiful in the summer months and can also be purchased fresh from stalls at the seaside. Salmon, the king of freshwater fish, and flavoursome sewin, both sadly dwindling in numbers, come from the rivers of Wales. But to compensate there are many fish farms where you can buy fresh trout.

Most of these home-produced foods can be found in supermarkets in the larger towns and cities, and in smaller shops or delicatessens throughout Wales, and there are some that can be purchased directly from the farmer or producer. Meat, in particular, will be clearly labelled on the supermarket shelf assuring the customer of its Welsh origin.

On your journey through Wales you will often see a roadside notice advertising local produce for sale direct from the farmer or producer, including free-range eggs, honey, sacks of potatoes etc. There's no doubt that visiting a farm in beautiful scenery to buy a unique product from the people who made it, can add a special dimension to its enjoyment after the visitor has returned home.

Many traditional Welsh dishes are still prepared in the home by the housewife. They will also appear for sale in the local weekly markets (often on the Women's Institute stall) or in cafés and restaurants, and in shops, such as the baker, butcher, delicatessen etc. If you are out having tea, for example, the menu will probably include a kind of tea loaf called *bara brith* (pronounced ba-ra breeth) meaning literally 'speckled bread' and the famous Welsh cake – a type of griddle-baked fruit scone.

Cawl (pronounced kowl), a popular, lunchtime meal, is a hearty soup made from lamb or other meat and vegetables that can be served with bread and cheese. Traditionally *cawl* is eaten as part of the St David's Day celebrations that take place throughout Wales, on or around 1st March.

Laverbread, from a very old recipe, is made from seaweed and is eaten at breakfast time with bacon and can be purchased in local weekly markets in south Wales.

There is so much choice for the visitor to Wales. For more information on Welsh food products and where to obtain local specialities contact:

Welsh Development Agency
Food Directorate
Cardiff Business Technology Centre
Senghennydd Road
Cardiff CF24 4AY

Drinks

Ever since the industrial revolution, beer has been the staple drink in Wales and, as a result, every large town once had its own brewery. Centralisation of the brewing industry has reduced the number of breweries but the contemporary beverage remains very popular, especially among the male population of Wales. Today, many of the pubs in Wales are owned by large United Kingdom breweries that sell their own brands of beers, including the most popular drinks such as bitter, lager, mild and Irish stout.

In south-east Wales, you will find brews produced by the long-established Cardiff-based company, Brains. In particular, their bitter is reputed to be one of the finest in the country. Also, in south Wales the produce of Felinfoel is found, a Llanelli-based company that was the first company to can beer in Europe. Its pioneering work in beer canning, which was to have a lasting impact on the industry, and its early connections, give a strong hint of its later enterprise. Crown Buckley is another company based in Llanelli, which produces three bitters and a mild beer, all of which are distinctive and of good quality. More recently, small brewers in the Towy and Wye valleys have been particularly successful, but many connoisseurs have their own favourites, such as Buckley's bitter and Brains SA.

Welsh gin and Taffski vodka made in Penderyn in south-east Wales, can also be found in some stores should you want to taste the local produce. In the past, only one whisky distillery, based at Bala, existed in Wales but it ceased production early last century. However, the industry has begun distilling again following a break of a hundred years, with the production of new blends of whisky such as *Sŵn y Môr* and also liqueurs that are 'mountain inspired', including the brand Welsh Whisky Liqueur made by Celtic Spirit, a company based in Abergavenny in south-east Wales.

Wines

Almost all the vineyards are found in the south, where the Romans planted one of the largest vineyards in Britain in the Vale of Glamorgan. Today, there are fifteen vineyards in Wales, situated in sheltered pockets of land that suit certain grape varieties. These produce in the main fruity, light, dry white wines, some red and rosé wines and *méthode traditionnelle* sparkling wines. Some of the names to look out for are:

- Glyndŵr
- Pant Teg
- Wyecliffe
- Monnow Valley
- Sugar Loaf
- Cariad
- Cwm Deri
- Ffynnon Las
- Brecon Court
- Offa

Mead is the oldest alcoholic beverage still produced in Wales, with a variety of fruit-flavoured meads available.

Non-alcoholic beverages

One of Wales' great natural assets is its abundance of water. The climate and wholesome environment produce sufficient water to supply cities throughout Britain via numerous reservoirs. Also, in recent years the mineral water industry has grown in Wales with water bottled from natural springs and sold worldwide.

Over the last few hundred years tea has become the most popular hot beverage of all, and the Celtic countries consume more tea than others. Various blends of teas have been created and brands sold in Wales such as Welsh Brew and Glengettie are very popular for Welsh afternoon tea.

The influence of Welsh-Italians in the valleys made coffee the second most popular drink to tea, and a good variety of speciality coffees is available in cafés and shops in towns and cities.

Menu reader

apple cake
teisen afalau
t(eye)ss-en av-al-(eye)

apple dumpling
twmplen afalau
*too*mp-len av-al-(eye)

apple sauce
saws afalau
sowss av-al-(eye)

apple tart
tarten afalau
tarr-ten av-al-(eye)

Menu reader

apples
afalau
av-al-(eye)

apricots
bricyll
bri-kill

artichoke
artisiog
arrt-ish-yog

asparagus
asbaragws
as-bar-a-g*oo*s

aubergine
planhigyn wy
plan-hig-in *oo*i

avocado
afocado
av-o-kad-o

bacon egg and chips
bacwn, wy a 'sglodion
bak-*oo*n *oo*i a sglod-yon

bacon sandwich
brechdan gig moch
brech-dan geeg mohch

baked apple
afal pob
av-al pohb

baked beans
ffa pob
fah pohb

baked potato
taten bob
tat-en bohb

bananas
bananas
ba-nan-as

basil
basil
bass-il

beef broth
cawl biff
kowl beef

beef stew
stiw biff
sti*oo* beef

beetroot
betys coch
bet-iss kohch

biscuits
bisgedi
biss-ged-i

black pudding
pwdin gwaed
p*oo*d-in gw(eye)d

blackberry tart
tarten fwyar duon
tarr-ten f*oo*i-arr dee-on

blackcurrants
cyrens duon
kuhrr-ens dee-on

brawn
brôn
brawn

bread and butter
bara 'menyn
ba-ra men-in

bread and butter pudding
pwdin bara 'menyn
p*oo*d-in ba-ra men-in

bread roll
rholyn bara
rhol-in ba-ra

Menu reader

bread rolls
rholiau bara
rhol-y(eye) ba-ra

broad beans
ffa
fah

Brussels sprouts
ysgewyll
uhss-ge-will

butter
menyn
men-in

cabbage
bresych / cabets
bress-ich / cab-etsh

cake
teisen (NW) / cacen (SW)
t(eye)ss-en (NW) / kak-en (SW)

carrots
moron
mor-on

cauliflower
blodfresych
blod-vress-ich

cauliflower cheese
blodfresych a chaws
blod-vress-ich a chows

celery
seleri / helogan
sel-er-i / he-log-an

cheese and salad sandwich
brechdan gaws a salad
brech-dan gowss a sal-ad

cheesecake
cacen gaws (SW) / teisen gaws (NW)
kak-en gowss (SW)
t(eye)ss-en gowss (NW)

cheese roll
rholyn caws
rhol-in kawss

cherries
ceirios
k(eye)rr-yoss

chicken broth
cawl cyw iâr
kowl ki*oo* yahrr

chives
cennin syfi
ken-nin suh-vi

chocolate mousse
mws siocled
mooss shok-led

corned beef
corn-biff
korrn beef

crayfish
cimwch coch
kim-*oo*ch kohch

cream of mushroom soup
cawl madarch hufennog
kowl mad-arrch heev-en-nog

cream of tomato soup
cawl tomato hufennog
kowl tom-a-to heev-en-nog

Menu reader

cream of vegetable soup
cawl llysiau hufennog
kowl lluhss-y(eye) heev-en-nog

crème caramel
caramel hufennog
karr-a-mel heev-en-nog

cucumber
ciwcymbr / cucumer
ki***oo***-kumb-rr / ki-ki-merr

cucumber salad
salad ciwcymbr / cucumer
sal-ad ki***oo***-kumb-rr / ki-ki-merr

cured ham
ham wedi'i halltu
ham wed-i hall-ti

currant bread
bara cyrens
ba-ra kuhrr-ens

custard
cwstard
k***oo***ss-tarrd

dates
dêts / datys
dehtss / dat-iss

doughnuts
toesennau
toyss-en-(eye)

drop scone
sgon gytew
sgon guh-te***oo***

duck
hwyaden
h***oo***i-ad-en

dumplings
twmplenni
t***oo***mp-len-ni

egg and bacon
wy a bacwn
ooi a bak-***oo***n

egg and sausages
wy a sosejys / selsig
ooi a soss-edges / sel-sig

egg and tomato sandwich
brechdan wy a thomato
brech-dan ***oo***i a thom-a-to

egg custard
cwstard wy
k***oo***ss-tarrd ***oo***i

egg sandwich
brechdan wy
brech-dan ***oo***i

fillet steak
stecen ffiled
stek-en fil-ed

fish
pysgod
puhs-god

fish and chips
pysgod a 'sglodion
puhs-god a sglod-yon

French beans
ffa Ffrengig
fah fren-gig

French bread
bara Ffrengig
ba-ra fren-gig

French fries
'sglodion tatws
sglod-yon tat-***oo***ss

fried chicken
cyw iâr wedi'i ffrio
ki***oo*** yahrr wed-i free-o

fried eggs
wyau wedi'u ffrio
*oo*i-(eye) wed-i free-o

fried trout
brithyll wedi'i ffrio
brith-ill wed-i free-o

fruit cake
teisen lap
t(eye)ss-en lap

fruit salad
salad ffrwythau
sal-ad fr*oo*ith-(eye)

fruit with whipped cream
ffrwythau gyda hufen wedi'i chwipio
fr*oo*ith-(eye) guh-da hee-ven wed-i chwip-yo

garlic
garlleg
garr-lleg

garlic bread
bara garlleg
bar-ra garr-lleg

goose
gŵydd
g*ooith*

grapefruit
grawnffrwyth
grown-fr*oo*ith

grapes
grawnwin
grown-win

gravy
grefi
grev-i

green pepper (spice)
pupur gwyrdd (sbeis)
pip-irr gwirr*th* sb(eye)ss

green pepper (vegetable)
pupryn gwyrdd (llysieuyn)
pip-rin gwirrth lluh-sh(eye)-in

greengages
eirin gwyrdd
(eye)rr-in gwirr*th*

grilled meat
cig wedi'i grilio
keeg wed-i gril-yo

hake fillet
ffiled o gegddu
fil-ed o gehg-*th*ee

ham sandwich
brechdan ham
brech-dan ham

ham, eggs and chips
ham, wy a 'sglodion
ham *oo*i a sglod-yon

ice cream
hufen iâ
hee-ven yah

jacket potato
taten trwy'i chroen
tat-en tr*oo*i chroyn

jam
jam
jam

jelly
jeli
jel-i

kidney beans
ffa Ffrengig
fah fren-gig

Menu reader

lamb cutlet
cytled oen
kuht-led oyn

leek soup
cawl cennin
kowl ken-nin

leeks
cennin
ken-nin

leg of lamb
coes oen
koyss oyn

lemon
lemon
lem-on

lemon meringue
meringue lemon
merr-ang lem-on

lettuce
letys
let-iss

lettuce sandwich
brechdan letys
brech-dan let-iss

liver
afu (SW) / iau (NW)
av-i (SW) / y(eye) (NW)

liver sausage
sosej iau / selsigen iau
soss-edge y(eye) / sel-sig-en iau

lobster
cimwch
kim-*oo*ch

mackerel
macrell
mak-rell

marinated mackerel
macrell wedi'i farinadu
mak-rell wed-i var-in-ad-i

marrow
pwmpen
p*oo*mp-en

mashed potato
tatws stwnsh (NW) / tato pwtsh / potsh / stwmp (SW)
tat-*oo*ss st*oo*nsh (NW)
tat-o p*oo*tsh / potsh / st*oo*mp (SW)

meat
cig
keeg

meat pie
pastai gig
past-(eye) geeg

melon
melon
mel-on

mint
mintys
min-tiss

mixed salad
salad cymysg
sal-ad kuhm-isg

mushrooms
madarch
mad-arrch

mushrooms in sauce
madarch mewn saws
mad-arrch me*oo*n sowss

mushrooms with garlic
madarch gyda garlleg
mad-arrch guh-da garr-lleg

mussels
cregin gleision
kreg-in gl(eye)-shon

mustard
mwstard
m*oo*s-tard

oil
olew
ol-e*oo*

olives
ffrwythau'r olewydd / olifau
fr*oo*ith-(eye)rr ol-e-wi*th* / ol-iv-(eye)

onion
nionyn (NW) / winwnsyn (SW)
nee-on-in (NW) / win-*oo*n-sin (SW)

onion sauce
saws nionod / winwns
sowss nee-on-od / win-*oo*ns

oranges
orennau
orr-en-n(eye)

oysters
wystrys
*oo*iss-triss

pancakes
crempogau (NW) / ffrois / pancos (SW)
krem-pog-(eye) (NW)
froyss / pan-koss (SW)

parsley
persli
perrss-li

parsnips
panas
pan-ass

pasta
pasta
past-a

pea soup
cawl pys
kowl peess

peach
eirinen wlanog
(eye)rr-in-en wlan-og

pear
peren (NW) / persen (SW)
per-en (NW) / perr-sen (SW)

peas
pys
peess

pepper and salt
pupur a halen
pip-irr a hal-en

pheasant
ffesant
fes-ant

pie
pastai
past-(eye)

pineapple
pin-afal
peen av-al

Menu reader

plums
eirin
(eye)rr-in

pork
porc / cig moch
porrk / keeg mohch

pork cutlet
cytled porc / cytled cig moch
kuht-led porrk / kuht-led keeg mohch

potato salad
salad tatws
sal-ad tat-***oo***ss

pudding
pwdin
p***oo***d-in

radishes
radisys / rhuddygl
rad-i-siss / rhi***th***-i-gil

raspberries
mafon
mav-on

red pepper
pupryn coch
pip-rin kohch

rhubarb
rhiwbob
rhi***oo***-bob

rice pudding
pwdin reis
p***oo***d-in r(eye)ss

roast beef
biff rhost
beef rhosst

roast chicken
cyw iâr wedi'i rostio
ki***oo*** yahrr wed-i rosst-yo

roast pork
porc / cig moch wedi'i rostio
porrk / keeg mohch wed-i rosst-yo

roast potatoes
tatws rhost
tat-***oo***ss rhosst

rosemary
rhosmari
rhoss-mar-i

rump steak
stecen balfais
stek-en bal-v(eye)ss

runner beans
ffa dringo
fah drin-go

Russian salad
salad Rwsiaidd
sal-ad r***oo***sh-y(eye)***th***

sage
saets
s(eye)tss

salad cream
hufen salad
hee-ven sal-ad

salad dressing
dresin salad
dress-in sal-ad

salad sandwich
brechdan salad
brech-dan sal-ad

sandwich
brechdan
brech-dan

sardines
sardîns
sarr-deenss

sausage roll
rholyn sosej / selsigen
rhol-in soss-edge / sel-sig-en

sausage, egg and chips
sosej / selsigen, wy a 'sglodion
soss-edge / sel-sig-en ***oo***i a sglod-yon

scampi
sgampi
sgamp-i

scone
sgonsen
sgon-sen

Scotch egg
wy mewn sosej / wy cig selsig
ooi me***oo***n soss-edge / ***oo***i keeg sel-sig

scrambled eggs
wyau wedi'u sgramblo
ooi-(eye) wed-i sgram-blo

shallots
shibwns (SW) / sialóts (NW)
shib-***oo***ns (SW) / sha-lots (NW)

sirloin steak
stecen syrlwyn
stek-en suhrr-l***oo***in

soft boiled egg
wy wedi'i led-ferwi
ooi wed-i lehd verr-wi

soft egg
wy meddal
ooi me***th***-al

soup
cawl
kowl

spaghetti on toast
sbageti ar dost
sbag-et-i arr dost

spinach
pigoglys
pig-og-liss

sponge cake
teisen sbwnj
t(eye)ss-en sp***oo***nge

sponge pudding
pwdin sbwnj
p***oo***d-in sp***oo***nge

steak
stecen
stek-en

steak and kidney pie
pastai stêc ac arennau
past-(eye) stehk ag aren-n(eye)

stewed apples
stiw afalau
sti***oo*** av-al-(eye)

strawberries
mefus
mev-iss

Menu reader

strawberries with cream
mefus gyda hufen
mev-iss guh-da hee-ven

swede
swejen (SW) / rwden (NW)
swedge-en (SW) / r*oo*-den (NW)

sweetcorn
india-corn
ind-ya korrn

sweetcorn on the cob
india-corn ar y cobyn
ind-ya korrn arr uh kob-in

tarragon
taragon
tar-a-gon

thyme
teim
t(eye)m

toast
tost
tost

tomato salad
salad tomato
sal-ad tom-a-to

tomato sauce
saws tomato / sos coch
sowss tom-a-to / sohs kohch

tomato soup
cawl tomato
kowl tom-a-to

tomatoes
tomatos
tom-a-toss

tongue
tafod
tav-od

trifle
treiffl
tr(eye)f-l

trout
brithyll
brith-ill

tuna
tiwna
ti*oo*n-a

tuna sandwich
brechdan diwna
brech-dan di-*oo*-na

turkey
twrci
t*oo*rr-ki

turnips
erfin (SW) / maip (NW)
err-vin (SW) / m(eye)p (NW)

veal cutlet
cytled cig llo
kuht-led keeg lloh

vegetables
llysiau
lluh-sh(eye)

vinegar
finegr
vin-eg-rr

watermelon
melon dŵr
mel-on doorr

watercress
berwr y dŵr
berr-*oo*rr uh doorr

Welsh cake
pice ar y maen (SW) / cacen gri / teisen gri (NW)
pik-e arr uh m(eye)n / kak-en gree (SW) / t(eye)ss-en gree (NW)

Welsh rarebit
caws ar dost
kawss arr dost

white bread
bara gwyn
ba-ra gwin

wholemeal bread
bara gwenith cyflawn
ba-ra gwen-ith kuhv-lown

wine sauce
saws gwin
sowss gween

—with chocolate
—gyda siocled
—guh-da shok-led

—with jam
—gyda jam
—guh-da jam

—with lemon
—gyda lemon
—guh-da lem-on

yoghurt
iogwrt
yog-*oo*rrt

Drinks reader

a brandy
brandi
brand-i

a cup of coffee
cwpanaid o goffi
k*oo*-pan-(eye)d o goff-i

a glass of red wine
gwydraid o win coch
gwi-dr(eye)d o ween kohch

a glass of white wine
gwydraid o win gwyn
gwi-dr(eye)d o ween gwin

a large beer
gwydraid mawr o gwrw
gwi-dr(eye)d mowrr o g*oo*-r*oo*

a pint of beer
peint o gwrw
pehnt o g*oo*-r*oo*

apple brandy
brandi afalau
brand-i av-al-(eye)

apple juice
sudd afal
see*th* av-al

Drinks reader

banana milkshake
ysgytlaeth banana
uhss-guht-l(eye)th ba-nan-a

beer
cwrw
k*oo*-r*oo*

bitter
chwerw
chwe-r*oo*

bottled beer
cwrw potel
k*oo*-r*oo* pot-el

camomile tea
te camri
teh kam-ri

canned beer
cwrw mewn can
k*oo*-r*oo* me*oo*n kan

champagne
siampaen / siampên
sham-p(eye)n / sham-pehn

cider
seidr
s(eye)d-rr

coffee
coffi
koff-i

coffee with cream
coffi gyda hufen
koff-i guh-da hee-ven

coffee with full cream milk
coffi gyda llaeth cyflawn
koff-i guh-da ll(eye)th kuhv-lown

coffee with milk
coffi gyda llaeth / llefrith (NW)
koff-i guh-da ll(eye)th / lle-vrith (NW)

coffee with skimmed milk
coffi gyda llaeth sgìm
koff-i guh-da ll(eye)th sgim

coke
côc
kohk

decaffeinated coffee
coffi digaffin
koff-i di-gaff-in

gin
jin
jin

grape juice
sudd grawnwin
see*th* grown-win

ground coffee
coffi powdwr
koff-i powd-*oo*r

iced coffee
coffi iâ
koff-i yah

iced water
dŵr a rhew / iâ
doorr a rhe*oo* / yah

instant coffee
coffi parod
koff-i par-od

lager
lager
lah-gerr

Drinks reader

lemon tea
te lemon
teh lem-on

lemonade
lemonêd
lem-on-ehd

liqueur
gwirodlyn
gwirr-od-lin

mineral water
dŵr mwynol
doorr m*oo*in-ol

orange drink
diod oren
di-od or-en

orange juice
sudd oren
see*th* or-en

peach juice
sudd eirin gwlanog
see*th* (eye)rr-in gwlan-og

pineapple juice
sudd pin-afal
see*th* peen av-al

port
port
porrt

rose wine
gwin rhosliw
gween rhos-li-*oo*

rum
rym
ruhm

sherry
sieri
sherr-i

small pot of coffee
potaid bach o goffi
pot-(eye)d bahch o goff-i

soda
soda
so-da

stout
stowt
stowt

strong tea
te cryf
teh kreev

tea
te
teh

tea with milk
te gyda llaeth
teh guh-da ll(eye)th

tonic water
dŵr tonig
doorr ton-ig

vermouth
fermwth
verr-m*oo*th

vodka
fodca
vod-ka

weak tea
te gwan
teh gwan

whisky
wisgi
wis-gi

white coffee
coffi gwyn
koff-i gwin

Out and About

The weather

Wales' climate is predominantly mild and temperate but often variable. Along the coastal areas, however, the weather can get very warm in the summer. Cold snaps in the winter can plunge the temperatures well below freezing particularly in the middle and north areas of the country. Seasonal temperature differences are more pronounced in places like Snowdonia in north Wales and the Brecon Beacons in the rural heartland of mid-Wales.

Average summer temperatures range from 16°C–18°C (61°–65°F). The average winter temperature fluctuates from 3°C–7°C (37°–45° F).[1] In the inland areas of north Wales the temperatures in January and February can fall to 1°C or less but with a decrease of about 0.5°C for each 100-metre increase in altitude.

The average monthly rainfall during the summer months varies between 69 mm and 85 mm (2.7 in and 3 in). This increases to 107 mm to 111 mm (4 in to 4.5 in) during the winter months.[2] Wales' rainfall is highest in the western mountains. Not surprisingly, the wettest place is the summit of Snowdon, with an annual average of 4,500 mm (180 in). The east of Wales and coastal regions have less than 1,000 mm (39 in) a year.

The sea reaches its lowest temperature in late February or early March so that around the coasts February is normally the coldest month. Away from the coast there is very little to choose between January and February as the coldest month.

The sunniest part of Wales is the south-western coastal strip of Pembrokeshire with an annual average of over 1,700 hours. The least sunny parts are the mountainous areas, which have less than 1,200 hours sunshine a year on average. These figures compare with values of less than 1,100 hours a year in the Shetlands to over 1,750 hours along the south coast of England.

In summer, rainfall is often of a showery nature falling over short periods and is normally more intense than winter rainfall, which tends to be more frontal in character with falls occurring over long periods.

(1) Source: National Assembly of Wales
(2) Source: National Assembly of Wales

Is it going to get any warmer?
Ydy hi'n mynd i gynhesu?
uh-di heen mind i guhn-hess-i

Is it going to stay like this?
Ydy hi'n mynd i aros fel hyn?
uh-di heen mind i arr-oss vel hin

Is there going to be a thunderstorm?
Oes yna storm o daranau yn mynd i fod?
oyss uhn-a storr-m o dar-an-(eye) uhn mind i vohd

Isn't it a lovely day?
On'd dyw hi'n ddiwrnod braf?
ond di-*oo* heen *th*i-*oo*rr-nod brahv

It has stopped snowing
Mae hi wedi stopio bwrw eira
m(eye) hee wed-i stop-yo b*oo*-r*oo* (eye)rr-a

It is a very clear night
Mae'n noson glir iawn
m(eye)n noss-on gleerr yown

It is far too hot
Mae'n llawer rhy boeth
m(eye)n llow-err rhee boyth

It is foggy
Mae'n niwlog
m(eye)n ni*oo*-log

It is going to be fine
Mae'n mynd i fod yn braf
m(eye)n mind i vohd uhn brahv

The weather

It is going to be windy
Mae'n mynd i fod yn wyntog
m(eye)n mind i vohd uhn win-tog

It is going to rain
Mae'n mynd i fwrw glaw
m(eye)n mind i f***oo***-r***oo*** glow (as in how)

It is going to snow
Mae'n mynd i fwrw eira
m(eye)n mind i f***oo***-r***oo*** (eye)rr-a

It is raining again
Mae'n bwrw glaw eto / Mae'n glawio eto (NW)
m(eye)n b***oo***-r***oo*** glow et-o / m(eye)n glow-yo et-o (NW)

It is very cold
Mae'n oer iawn
m(eye)n oyrr yown

It is very windy
Mae'n wyntog iawn
m(eye)n win-tog yown

There is a cool breeze
Mae awel oerllyd 'da hi
m(eye) a-wel oyrr-llid da hee

What is the temperature?
Beth yw'r tymheredd?
behth i***oo***rr tuhm-herr-e***th***

Will it be cold tonight?
Fydd hi'n heno oer?
vee***th*** heen hen-o oyrr

Will the weather improve?
Fydd y tywydd yn gwella?
vee***th*** uh tuh-wi***th*** uhn gwell-a

Will the wind die down?
Fydd y gwynt yn gostegu?
vee***th*** uh gwint uhn gos-teg-i

On the beach

Twelve beaches in Wales were recently awarded the European Blue Flag, which is Europe's highest accolade for beaches. There is much choice along Wales' 750-mile seashore. Small resorts and fishing villages in north Wales have beaches of outstanding beauty. The Isle of Anglesey has a 125-mile coastline of sandy bays and cliffs and most of its beaches are award winning. Cardigan Bay has a wonderful 75-mile coastline dotted with picturesque villages and towns.

Pembrokeshire in west Wales is another area where every visitor is spoilt for choice with over 50 beaches from which to choose. This is a 180-mile coastline with some of the best beaches in Britain. In fact, 4 of its beaches have Blue Flag awards, 8 Green Coast awards and another 30 Seaside Awards.

You could also head for the Gower Peninsula, which in 1956 was the first place in Britain to be designated an Area of Outstanding Natural Beauty. With an area of 70 square miles, it has spectacular scenery and is easily accessible. Another popular area is Cardigan Bay between Pembrokeshire and Gower. Easily accessible by car, its beaches tend to be crowded in peak season.

Is the sea calm?
Ydy'r môr yn dawel?
uh-dirr mohrr uhn da-wel

When is low tide?
Pryd mae'r trai?
preed m(eye) tr(eye)

Can you recommend a quiet beach?
Allwch chi argymell traeth tawel?
all-*oo*ch chi arr-guh-mell tr(eye)th ta-wel

Is the current strong?
Ydy'r cerrynt yn gryf?
uh-dirr kerr-uhnt uhn greev

Is the water warm?
Ydy'r dŵr yn gynnes?
uh-dirr doorr uhn guhn-ness

Is there a lifeguard here?
Oes yna achubwr (bywydau) 'ma?
oyss uhn-a ach-i-b*oo*rr buh-wuh-d(eye) ma

Can we change here?
Gawn ni newid 'ma?
gown ni ne-wid ma

When is high tide?
Pryd mae'r penllanw?
preed m(eye)rr pen-llan-*oo*

Is it possible to go surfing?
Ydy hi'n bosib mynd i frigdonni?
uh-di heen boss-ib mind i vrig-don-ni

Is it possible to go water skiing?
Ydy hi'n bosib mynd i sgïo dŵr?
uh-di heen boss-ib mind i sgee-o doorr

Is it possible to go wind surfing?
Ydy hi'n bosib mynd i fordhwylio?
uh-di heen boss-ib mind i vorrd-h*oo*il-yo

Is this beach private?
Ydy'r traeth hwn yn breifat?
uh-dirr tr(eye)th h*oo*n uhn br(eye)v-at

Is it possible to go sailing?
Ydy hi'n bosib mynd i hwylio?
uh-di heen boss-ib mind i h*oo*il-yo

Is it safe to swim here?
Ydy hi'n ddiogel i nofio 'ma?
uh-di heen ***th***i-o-gel i nov-yo ma

Sport and recreation

More than a million adults in Wales play sport on a regular basis and 55 per cent of the population are involved in some form of sport.

Over the last 30 years the number of built sports facilities in the country has trebled: for example, in 1972 Wales had 44 swimming pools, in 2001 it had 140. Again, there were 11 sports halls in Wales in 1972, and by 2001 that number had increased to 187. In addition, the country has 202 golf courses at 184 different locations, 404 squash courts, 15 synthetic athletics tracks, 9 indoor tennis centres, 88 artificial grass pitches, 27 indoor bowls centres and 2 ice rinks.[1] It is hardly surprising that twice as many people participate now in sport in Wales compared to 1977, and there are also more than 3 times as many sporting occasions in Wales as there were in the 1970s.

The new £7 million National Indoor Athletics Centre at UWIC in Cardiff is one of Wales' more modern sporting assets and so is the Millennium Stadium, which was completed in time to host the 1999 Rugby World Cup. The stadium, a £126-million development in the centre of Cardiff, has seating for 72,500. The facility's distinctive feature is its acoustically insulated retractable roof, which enables the Welsh Rugby Union to hold events throughout the year.

Welsh rugby experienced its glory days back in the 1970s when Wales had one of its finest teams in the Five Nations Championship, winning six out of the ten championships – three of them Grand Slams. Wales has never regained the splendour of that era. Victories seldom came their way in the 1980s and the 1990s and supporters and players alike became disillusioned with the continued ill-fated performances of the Welsh team on the international scene. With the appointment of a new coach in 1998, the Welsh team achieved a level of success in the sport, but they still battle to regain their former glory. Away from the international arena, rugby is still enjoyed by a multitude of supporters on Saturdays, and more than 50,000 players participate every year from September to just after Easter in what is still held to be the national game.

Traditionally, the support for rugby in Wales has always been strongest in industrial south Wales, whereas in north Wales football has also been dominant with many on Saturday crossing the border to see teams such as Manchester United and Liverpool playing. There are three top football sides in Wales: Cardiff City, Swansea City and Wrexham, all of which play in the English Football League.

Wales' sportsmen and women perform well in sports at the highest level. The number of Welsh performers achieving British representation or equivalent and those winning British Championships has shown significant increases in recent years. The only major international games where Wales competes as a nation are the Commonwealth Games. In the 1998 Commonwealth Games, Wales won 15 medals (3 gold, 4 silver and 8 bronze). Although this placed Wales 10th in the overall medal table, in terms of medals per capita Wales finished 3rd. More recently, in the 2006 Commonwealth Games, Wales was placed 13th in the overall medal table with a total of 19 medals (3 gold, 5 silver and 11 bronze). Wales also produces many outstanding disabled sportsmen and women. Welsh performers were particularly successful at the Sydney Paralympics winning 26 medals, including 11 gold.

Wales has always vigorously promoted itself as a place for activity-based holidays and these have become increasingly popular with holidaymakers in recent years. The country has long enjoyed a strong reputation for mountaineering, climbing, walking, fishing and horse riding, while the clean waters and attractive coastline around Wales now lure many watersport enthusiasts with opportunities for surfing, windsurfing, diving and sailing.

(1) Source: Sports Council for Wales

Is there a heated swimming pool?
Oes yna bwll nofio twym?
oyss uhn-a b*oo*ll nov-yo t*oo*im

Can I hire a sailing boat?
Ga' i logi cwch hwyliau?
gah i log-i c*oo*ch h*oo*il-y(eye)

Can I hire a rowing boat?
Ga' i logi cwch rhwyfo?
gah i log-i *coo*ch rh*oo*i-vo

Can I hire the equipment?
Ga' i logi'r offer / cyfarpar?
gah i log-irr off-err / kuh-varr-parr

Can we play tennis?
Gawn ni chwarae tennis?
gown ni chwarr-(eye) ten-niss

Can we play golf?
Gawn ni chwarae golff?
gown ni chwarr-(eye) golf

Can we play volleyball?
Gawn ni chwarae pêl foli?
gown ni chwarr-(eye) pehl vol-i

Can we go riding?
Gawn ni fynd i farchogaeth?
gown ni vind i varrch-o-g(eye)th

Where can we fish?
Ble gawn ni bysgota?
ble gown ni buhss-got-a

Do we need a permit?
Oes angen trwydded?
oyss ang-en tr*ooith*-ed

Entertainment

Wales has a reputation of being a land of song and that projected image is deeply rooted in tradition. The singing of the works of the poets to the accompaniment of the harp was a regular feature in the courts in medieval Wales. Latterly, Dylan Thomas proclaimed in the last century that the Welsh are a musical nation. As in other Celtic countries, folk music has always had its appeal in Wales and has a wider meaning than its English counterpart.

In a folk festival in Wales, you would be just as likely to meet a rock band as you would a traditional folk group. Both rock and folk music are bastions of the Welsh language and its culture. Although folk songs have remained an integral part of popular culture in Wales, the modern messages contained in the songs themselves are often political and controversial, reflecting the present condition of the language and the Welsh people. In fact, some have the quality of topical ballads and are widely known for their patriotic stance and satirical quality.

The Welsh male voice choir is widely recognised as an institution associated with the coalmining communities of south Wales and the quarries of north Wales. Their repertoires are particularly strong on hymns, and although those industries have declined considerably the choral tradition remains very much alive and flourishing.

In 1964, the Welsh language had its first rock group and this gave rise to a host of imitators who purposely expounded their strong national identity. As a result, a thriving Welsh-language rock scene has emerged over the years. Groups working through the medium of the English language have also achieved great commercial success. Many bands choose to sing in both English and Welsh, which allows them to take Welsh contemporary music to an international audience without compromising any of their lyrical dexterity and contemporary lyrics.

Wales has also made an impact on the international scene by exporting leading singers to opera houses throughout the world. The National Orchestra, which was formed in 1928 and revived in 1935, has also made a valuable contribution to music in Wales.

The National Eisteddfod is the country's foremost cultural institution, incorporating music (rock to choirs), theatre, dance, ceremonies, competitions and exhibitions. Its tradition dates from 1176 when it was held in Cardigan under the patronage of Lord Rhys ap Gruffudd. It is held annually in August and lasts for 8 days. It attracts over 160,000 visitors and some 6,000 competitors. It is the largest popular festival of competitive music-making and poetry-writing in Europe. Its main aims are to promote the Welsh language, to encourage popular participation in artistic and cultural activities and to provide entertainment. There are also numerous other minor and regional *eisteddfodau* held throughout Wales, which make a significant contribution to Welsh culture. The first Llangollen International Musical Eisteddfod was held in July 1947, and since then this week-long event has been held annually in the small town of Llangollen in north-east Wales. Since its inception, this eisteddfod has become internationally renowned, attracting each year nearly 2,500 foreign and around 1,000 British competitors to take part in folk singing, folk dancing and instrumentalist competitions, as well as professional artistes of international repute, from more than 40 countries. Some 67,000 to 100,000 visitors attend every year to enjoy its colourful and multilingual competitions and concerts.

The *Urdd Gobaith Cymru* (Welsh League of Youth), founded in 1922, holds its annual eisteddfod in late May to early June. This six-day event is the largest youth festival in Europe and is attended by about 100,000 annually and at least 18,000 competitors. It is held alternately, as indeed is the National Eisteddfod, in north and south Wales.

Over the last 40 years, important contributions have been made to literary drama in Wales. At the same time a number of gifted Welsh actors have made their names on the London stage and in the cinema.

Central to the promotion and advancement of drama and popular entertainment in Wales, in general, have been television and radio. The tradition of the eisteddfod was fostered by the radio back in the 1950s, but the increasing appeal of television in the early 1960s and the launching of BBC Wales Television in 1964 caused a decline in public interest in radio, which was only arrested with the advent of Radio Wales in 1978 and Radio Cymru in 1979. Although a limited number of television programmes were transmitted by 1952, it was not until 1962 that approximately a dozen Welsh-language programmes were produced by the BBC and independent companies. The year 1982 saw the advent of Wales' own Welsh-language channel, *Sianel Pedwar Cymru*, known as S4C (pronounced ess ped-warr eck). The channel is subsidised by the government and its programmes supplied by the BBC, HTV and a number of minor independent companies. Over 70 per cent of its programmes are subtitled in English on the Teletext system. Weekly broadcasting hours were originally set at 23 hours, mainly in peak-time viewing, but have now been increased to an average of 34 hours per week. Two channels are operated by the BBC in Wales, namely BBC 1 Wales and BBC 2 Wales, but the majority of the programmes are intended for the UK-wide audience, and programmes for Welsh viewers, principally news and sport, are slotted into the regular schedules. This is also true of HTV, the holder in Wales of the licence to broadcast on the commercial ITV network.

Opportunities abound for an evening's entertainment in Wales and most towns and cities have lots to offer, whether it's a pub, cinema, theatre, concert, disco or something entirely different. The large hotels run regular dinner dances and cabarets. Make use of the Tourist Information Centres to find out what's on.

Is there a disco?
Oes yna ddisgo?
oyss uhn-a ***th***is-go

Is there a casino?
Oes yna gasino?
oyss uhn-a gas-een-o

Is there a theatre?
Oes yna theatr?
oyss uhn-a thee-et-uhrr

Is there a good nightclub?
Oes yna glwb nos da?
oyss uhn-a gl***oo***b nohss dah

Are there any films in Welsh?
Oes yna ffilmiau yn y Gymraeg?
oyss uhn-a ffilm-y(eye) uhn uh guhm-r(eye)g

How much is it per person?
Faint yw e'r un?
v(eye)nt i*oo* err een

How much is it to get in?
Faint yw e i fynd mewn?
v(eye)nt i*oo* e i vind me*oo*n

Is there a reduction for children?
Oes yna ostyngiad i blant?
oyss uhn-a ost-uhn-gyad i blant

Two tickets, please
Dau docyn, os gwelwch yn dda
d(eye) dok-in os gwel-*oo*ch uhn *th*ah

Four stall tickets, please
Pedwar tocyn i'r seddau blaen, os gwelwch yn dda
ped-warr tok-in irr se*th*-(eye) bl(eye)n os gwel-*oo*ch uhn *th*ah

Sightseeing

The landscape of Wales is essentially rural. In terms of land use, 80 per cent is used for agriculture, 12 per cent is covered in woodland, and 8 per cent is categorised as urban.(1) The Welsh landscape has an abundance of historic sites, which vividly illustrate the nation's history and development over some 250,000 years. Open countryside, valleys, deep gorges and mountains and shorelines provide a legendary backdrop to some of these historical features, most notably the castles of Wales dating from Norman times. Wales had no castles before the Norman Conquest but within the space of 2 centuries many hundreds were established and they remain impregnable symbols of oppression and conquest.

The landscape in north and south-east Wales is scarred by quarries and slag heaps, although the recent 'greening' of old tips has transformed the valleys of the south-east. Many of the old collieries and quarries have become museums. The Preseli Mountains in south-west Wales are dotted with Neolithic remains, as is the 19-mile expanse of the Gower peninsula.

The border country around Monmouth and Abergavenny and the Wye Valley consists of hills and fertile farmlands. The central region of Wales is also farming country, with small market towns and traditional villages. Forestry is an important feature of mid-Wales' high country, and other significant man-made features are the reservoirs, built to take advantage of the higher rainfall in Wales' western mountains. Dominating the north Wales landscape to the west is the Snowdonia mountain range, which has been attracting visitors since Victorian times. Exploring this area of mountains, lakes and river valleys is quite a thrill on foot or in the comfort of a car. Further east, the rugged landscape softens to a patchwork of forests, open moorlands, hills and wooded valleys.

At least 14 steam railways operate in Wales and are run primarily as tourist attractions. There are 9 members of Wales' narrow-gauge 'Great Little Trains'. The majority of these are situated in north and west Wales.

Wales' scenic, traffic-free highways and byways are ideal for cycling. Walkers will find that Wales has beautiful woodlands, highland hikes, family trails and some challenging mountains. The long-distance footpaths along the Pembrokeshire coast are extremely popular as is the Offa's Dyke border country. There are special 'ride and walk' bus services operated in the country's three national parks. In north-east Wales, the town of Llangollen is much famed for its steam railway and horse-drawn canal boats. Down in south Wales you will find the Monmouthshire Canal, extending for 33 miles from Brecon to Pontypool. It is considered to be one of the most beautiful and peaceful waterways of Britain. A large stretch of the canal is within the Brecon Beacons and weaves its way through a varied and spectacular patchwork of landscapes.

(1) Source: Wales Tourist Board

Are there any boat trips on the river?
Oes yna deithiau cychod ar yr afon?
yss uhn-a d(eye)th-y(eye) kuhch-od arr uhrr av-on

Are there any guided tours of the castle?
Oes yna deithiau tywysedig o amgylch y castell?
oyss uhn-a d(eye)th-y(eye) tuh-wuhss-ed-ig o am-gilch uh kass-tell

Are there any guided tours?
Oes yna unrhyw deithiau tywysedig?
oyss uhn-a een-rhi*oo* d(eye)th-y(eye) tuh-wuhss-ed-ig

Is there a tour of the cathedral?
Oes yna daith o gwmpas yr eglwys gadeiriol?
oyss uhn-a d(eye)th o g*oo*m-pass uhrr eg-l*oo*iss gad-(eye)rr-yol

Is there an English-speaking guide?
Oes yna arweinydd sy'n siarad Saesneg?
oyss uhn-a arr-weh-ni***th*** seen shar-ad s(eye)s-neg

Is there an Welsh-speaking guide?
Oes yna arweinydd sy'n siarad Cymraeg?
oyss uhn-a arr-weh-ni***th*** seen shar-ad kuhm-r(eye)g

How long does the tour take?
Faint gymer y daith?
v(eye)nt guh-merr uh d(eye)th

When is the bus tour?
Pryd mae'r daith fws?
preed m(eye)rr d(eye)th v*oo*ss

What is there to see here?
Beth sy' i'w weld 'ma?
behth see yoo weld ma

What is this building?
Beth yw'r adeilad 'ma?
behth i-*oo*rr a-deh-lad ma

When was it built?
Pryd adeiladwyd e?
preed a-deh-lad-*oo*id e

Can we go in?
Gawn ni fynd i mewn?
gown ni vind-i me*oo*n

Is it open to the public?
Ydy e ar agor i'r cyhoedd?
uh-di e arr ag-orr irr kuh-hoy***th***

Is there a guidebook?
Oes yna arweinlyfr?
oyss uhn-a ar-w(eye)n-luhv-rr

What is the admission charge?
Beth yw'r pris mynediad?
behth i*oo*rr preess muhn-ed-yad

How much is it for a child?
Faint yw hi i blentyn?
v(eye)nt i*oo* hee i blen-tin

Can we go up to the top?
Gawn ni i fynd fyny i'r top / lan i'r top? (SW)
gown ni vind-i vuhn-i irr top / lan irr top (SW)

Is this the best view?
Ai dyma'r olygfa orau?
(eye) duhm-arr o-luhg-va orr-(eye)

What time does the gallery open?
Pryd mae'r oriel yn agor?
preed m(eye)rr or-i-el uhn ag-orr

Can I take photos?
Ga' i dynnu lluniau?
gah i duhn-i llin-y(eye)

Can I use flash?
Ga' i ddefnyddio fflach?
gah i ***th***ev-nuh***th***-yo flach

Souvenirs

Where can I buy postcards?
Ble galla i brynu cardiau post?
ble gall-(eye) bruhn-i karrd-y(eye) post

Where can we buy souvenirs?
Ble gallwn ni brynu cofroddion / swfenîrs?
ble gall-***oo***n ni bruhn-i kov-ro***th***-yon / s***oo***-ven-eerrs

Have you got an English guidebook?
Oes 'da chi arweinlyfr Saesneg?
oyss da chi ar-w(eye)n-luhv-rr s(eye)s-neg

Have you got a Welsh guidebook?
Oes 'da chi arweinlyfr Cymraeg?
oyss da chi ar-w(eye)n-luhv-rr kuhm-r(eye)g

Have you got any colour slides?
Oes 'da chi sleidiau lliw?
oyss da chi sl(eye)d-y(eye) lli***oo***

Going to church

The Nonconformist movement in Wales grew from John Penry, the first Welsh dissenter, who was martyred in 1593 at the age of 30. As the movement developed, Methodist and other denominations were formed and from the late 19th century until the middle of the 20th century, the culture in Wales was the culture of Nonconformity. Chapels were built in every hamlet in rural Wales to accommodate the various denominations and as their influence increased, the chapels became by default centres of vigorous Welsh language activity. During the period from 1905 to 1910, the attendance figure for community services held by all the Nonconformist denominations was 550,280. If the number of church communicants is added to this figure, then the total attendance during that period reached 743,361. With a total population of 1,864,696, it is clear that 2 out of every 5 persons in Wales at that time attended chapel or church on a regular basis. (1)

This vitality of organised religion generated many charismatic preachers as well as an enormous wealth of religious literature including published sermons, biblical commentaries and Welsh hymn books. Religion and the Welsh language were inextricably linked and any cultural activity of value was grounded deeply in religion.

It is evident, therefore, that religious decline is one of the most striking aspects of Welsh history following the Second World War. By the end of the 20th century, only 14 per cent of the inhabitants of Wales were members of a Christian church. This is in comparison with 20 per cent in 1980 and 16 per cent in 1990.(2)

The result of a survey produced in 1995 revealed that an estimated

8.7 per cent of the population attended churches in Wales. Of that number, the Church in Wales recorded the highest attendance with 28 per cent, followed by the Roman Catholic Church with 21 per cent and the Presbyterian Church with 10 per cent. The other groups – Welsh Independents, Baptist Union of Wales and Methodist – achieved around 6 per cent only. At least 67 per cent of those who attend churches are women aged 45 or over, and around 25 per cent of the churches in Wales have no minister. As one historian commented in 1991: 'The fire now burns on Cambria's altars only with a smoky and fitful flame' (Glanmor Williams).[3]

It would be impossible to claim any longer that the Welsh are a Christian nation. Recent estimates suggest that churchgoing is declining more rapidly in Wales than elsewhere in the United Kingdom. According to demographic figures produced by Christian Research, Presbyterian congregations have been falling by 3.5 per cent each year, Baptist by 2.7 per cent, Methodist by 2.5 per cent and Congregationalist by 2.3 per cent. The rate of decline for the Anglican Church in Wales is estimated to be 2 per cent. Only the Roman Catholic Church appears to be holding its own, although even in their case the numbers of churchgoers are falling by around 1 per cent a year.

All this suggests that the Welsh are rapidly abandoning their allegiance to organised religion and, in particular, that the young and the middle classes in Wales have defected from Christianity. However, the sale of empty chapels for conversion into businesses or residential premises is still a cause of sadness even among those who never attend a place of worship.

(1) D Gareth Evans, *A History of Wales 1906–2000* (Cardiff, 2000)
(2) Christian Research – *Religious Trends* 1998/99
(3) Glanmor Williams, *The Welsh and Their Religion*, (Cardiff, 1991)

I would like to see a priest
Hoffwn i weld offeiriad
hoff-*oo*n i weld off-(eye)rr-yad

I would like to see a minister
Hoffwn i weld gweinidog
hoff-***oo***n i weld gweh-nee-dog

I would like to see a rabbi
Hoffwn i weld rabi
hoff-***oo***n i weld rab-i

Where is the Catholic church?
Ble mae'r eglwys Gatholig?
ble m(eye)rr eg-l***oo***iss gath-ol-ig

Where is the Baptist church?
Ble mae eglwys y Bedyddwyr?
ble m(eye) eg-l***oo***iss uh bed-uh***th***-wirr

Where is the mosque?
Ble mae'r mosg?
ble m(eye)rr mosg

Where is the Protestant church?
Ble mae'r eglwys Brotestannaidd?
ble m(eye)rr eg-l***oo***iss brot-ess-tan-n(eye)***th***

Where is the synagogue?
Ble mae'r synagog?
ble m(eye)rr sin-a-gog

Where is the Methodist chapel?
Ble mae capel y Methodistiaid?
ble m(eye) kap-el uh meth-o-dist-i-(eye)d

What time is the service?
Pryd mae'r gwasanaeth?
preed m(eye)rr gwa-ssan-(eye)th

What time is the Welsh service?
Pryd mae'r gwasanaeth Cymraeg?
preed m(eye)rr gwa-ssan-(eye)th kuhm-r(eye)g

SHOPPING

Department stores are generally open from 09.00 to 17.30, 6 days a week. On Sunday most shops are closed, apart from supermarkets, DIY stores and some corner shops, which are open from 10.00 to 16.00. Newsagents and petrol stations are open for most of Sunday. The vast majority of shops are closed on public holidays.

Much of the shopping in Wales is done in superstores, the number of which has quadrupled in recent years. Fifty years ago, more than half the groceries were bought at local stores. By the end of the 20th century that figure had fallen to less than 14 per cent. Supermarkets, in fact, take 75 per cent of the current trade in Wales. Choice is of the essence and is fundamental to the Welsh way of life. Supermarkets have raised the art of acquisition to a more intense level and shoppers are encouraged to be adventurous by the sheer diversity of goods that are available.

Most towns and city centres have their pedestrian shopping precincts with departmental stores, boutiques, hairdressers, pharmacies, florists, butchers, bakers, cafés and specialist shops. Outside the centres, there are supermarkets, DIY stores, car showrooms, carpet warehouses and petrol stations.

General phrases and requests

How much is this?
Faint yw hwn?
v(eye)nt i*oo* h*oo*n

How much does that cost?
Faint mae hwnna'n ei gostio?
v(eye)nt m(eye) h***oo***n-an (eye) gost-yo

How much is it, per kilo?
Faint yw e, y cilo?
v(eye)nt i***oo*** e uh keel-o

How much is it, per metre?
Faint yw e, y medr?
v(eye)nt i*oo* e uh med-rr

I like this one
Dwi'n hoffi 'run 'ma
dween hoff-i reen ma

I do not like it
Dwi ddim yn 'i hoffi e (m) / hi (f)
dwee ***th***im uhn i hoff-i e (m) / hee (f)

I will take that one
Gymra i hwnna (m) / honna (f)
guhm-r(eye) h*oo*n-na (m) / hon-na (f)

I will take the other one
Gymra i'r un arall
guhm-r(eye)rr een arr-all

I will take this one
Gymra i hwn (m) / hon (f)
guhm-r(eye) h*oo*n (m) / hon (f)

No, the other one
Na, yr un arall
nah uhrr een arr-all

Have you got anything cheaper?
Oes rhywbeth rhatach 'da chi?
oyss rhi*oo*-beth rhat-ach da chi

Can I have a carrier bag?
Ga' i fag plastig?
gah i vag plass-tig

Can I pay for air insurance?
Ga' i dalu am yswiriant awyr?
gah i dal-i am uhss-wirr-yant a-wirr

Can I see that one over there?
Ga i weld hwnna (m) / honna (f) fan draw?
gah i weld h*oo*n-a (m) / hon-na (f) van drow (as in how)

General phrases and requests

Can I see that umbrella?
Ga i weld yr ymbarél 'na?
gah i weld uhrr uhm-barr-el na

Can you deliver to my hotel?
Allwch chi ddanfon pethau i fy ngwesty?
all-*oo*ch chi ***th***an-von peth-(eye) i vuhng west-i

Do you sell sunglasses?
Ych chi'n gwerthu sbectol haul?
ich chin gwerrth-i sbek-tol h(eye)l

I am looking for a souvenir
Dwi'n edrych am gofrodd / swfenîr
dween e-drich am gov-ro***th*** / s*oo*-ven-eerr

I do not have enough money
Does dim digon o arian 'da fi
doys dim dig-on o ar-yan da vi

Please forward a receipt to this address
Wnewch chi anfon derbynneb i'r cyfeiriad 'ma, os gwelwch yn dda
wne*oo*ch chi an-von derr-buhn-neb irr kuh-v(eye)rr-yad ma os gwel-*oo*ch uhn ***th***ah

Will you send it by air freight?
Wnewch chi ei anfon e trwy gludiant awyr?
wne*oo*ch chi (eye) an-von e tr*oo*i gleed-yant a-wirr

Please pack it for shipment
Wnewch chi ei bacio e i'w ddanfon, os gwelwch yn dda?
wne*oo*ch chi (eye) bak-yo i*oo* ***th***an-von os gwel-*oo*ch uhn ***th***ah

Please wrap it up for me
Lapiwch e ifi, os gwelwch yn dda
lap-y*oo*ch e iv-i os gwel-*oo*ch uhn ***th***ah

There is no need to wrap it
Does dim eisiau ei lapio
doys dim (eye)sh-y(eye) (eye) lap-yo

We need to buy some food
Mae angen arnon ni brynu bwyd
m(eye) ang-en arr-non ni bruhn-i b*oo*id

What is the total?
Beth yw'r cyfanswm?
behth i*oo*rr kuh-van-s*oo*m

Where can I buy some clothes?
Ble galla i brynu dillad?
ble gall-(eye) bruhn-i dill-ad

Where can I buy cassette tapes and compact discs?
Ble galla i brynu tapiau casét a chrynoddisgiau?
ble gall-(eye) bruhn-i tap-y(eye) kass-et a chruhn-o-***th***issg-y(eye)

Where can I buy tapes for my camcorder?
Ble galla i brynu tapiau i fy nghamcorder?
ble gall-(eye) bruhn-i tap-y(eye) i vuhng ham-korrd-err

Where can I get my camcorder repaired?
Ble galla i gael fy nghamcorder wedi ei drwsio?
ble gall-(eye) g(eye)l vuhng ham-korrd-err wed-i (eye) dr*oo*sh-o

Where is the children's department?
Ble mae adran y plant?
ble m(eye) ad-ran uh plant

Where is the food department?
Ble mae'r adran fwyd?
ble m(eye)rr ad-ran v*oo*id

Buying groceries

Supermarkets proliferate in Wales, but some people prefer the friendlier atmospheres of smaller shops.

Most cities and major centres have markets and the produce there will usually reflect the regional cuisine. On sale in Swansea market, for example, you will find the local delicacies such as laverbread, a savoury made from seaweed, as well as cockles trawled from the nearby Loughor estuary. The prices of fresh fruit, vegetables and meat are likely to be lower in these markets than in the shops.

Buying groceries

Can I please have some sugar?
Ga' i siwgr, os gwelwch yn dda?
Gah i sh*oo*g-*oo*rr os gwel-*oo*ch uhn ***th***ah

Can I have a bottle of wine, please?
Ga' i botelaid o win, os gwelwch yn dda?
Gah i bot-el-(eye)d o ween os gwel-*oo*ch uhn ***th***ah

Can I have a kilo of sausages, please?
Ga' i gilo o sosejis / selsig, os gwelwch yn dda?
Gah i geel-o o soss-e-jis / sel-sig os gwel-*oo*ch uhn ***th***ah

Can I have a leg of lamb, please?
Ga' i goes oen, os gwelwch yn dda?
Gah i goyss oyn os gwel-*oo*ch uhn ***th***ah

Can I have a pound of bacon, please?
Ga' i bwys o gig moch, os gwelwch yn dda?
Gah i b*oo*is o geeg mohch os gwel-*oo*ch uhn ***th***ah

Can I have a litre of milk, please?
Ga' i litr o laeth / lefrith (NW), os gwelwch yn dda?
gah i leet-rr o l(eye)th / lev-rith (NW) os gwel-*oo*ch uhn ***th***ah

Can I have two pints of skimmed milk, please?
Ga' i ddau beint o laeth sgìm / lefrith (NW) sgìm, os gwelwch yn dda?
gah i ***th***(eye) b(eye)nt o l(eye)th / lev-rith (NW) sgim os gwel-*oo*ch uhn ***th***ah

Can I have two steaks, please?
Ga' i ddwy stecen, os gwelwch yn dda?
Gah i ***thoo***i stek-en os gwel-*oo*ch uhn ***th***ah

Can I have a kilo of potatoes, please?
Ga' i gilo o datws, os gwelwch yn dda?
Gah i geel-o o dat-*oo*s os gwel-*oo*ch uhn ***th***ah

Can I have a bar of chocolate, please?
Ga' i far o siocled, os gwelwch yn dda?
Gah i varr o shok-led os gwel-*oo*ch uhn ***th***ah

Can I have five slices of ham, please?
Ga' i bum tafell o ham, os gwelwch yn dda?
Gah i bim tav-ell o ham os gwel-*oo*ch uhn ***th***ah

Can I have 100 grams of ground coffee, please?
Ga' i gan gram o goffi powdwr, os gwelwch yn dda?
Gah i gan gram o goff-i powd-***oo***r os gwel-***oo***ch uhn ***th***ah

Can I have a brown loaf, please?
Ga' i dorth frown, os gwelwch yn dda?
Gah i dorrth vrown (as in own) os gwel-***oo***ch uhn ***th***ah

Can I have half a dozen eggs, please?
Ga' i hanner dwsin o wyau, os gwelwch yn dda?
Gah i han-ner d***oo***ss-in o ***oo***i-(eye) os gwel-***oo***ch uhn ***th***ah

Can I have half a pound of butter, please?
Ga' i hanner pwys o fenyn, os gwelwch yn dda?
Gah i han-ner p***oo***is o fen-in os gwel-***oo***ch uhn ***th***ah

Groceries

baby food
bwyd i'r babi
b***oo***id irr bab-i

biscuits
bisgedi
biss-ged-i

bread
bara
ba-ra

butter
menyn
men-in

cake
teisen (NW) / cacen (SW)
t(eye)ss-en (NW) / kak-en (SW)

cereal
grawnfwyd
grown-v***oo***id

cheese
caws
kowss

coffee
coffi
koff-i

cornflakes
creision ŷd
kr(eye)-shon eed

cream
hufen
hee-ven

crisps
creision
kr(eye)-shon

current loaf
bara brith
ba-ra breeth

Groceries

eggs
wyau
*oo*i-(eye)

flour
fflŵr (SW) / blawd
floorr (SW) / blowd (as in how)

groceries
bwydydd
b*oo*id-i*th*

honey
mêl
mehl

jam
jam
jam

jelly
jeli
jel-i

margarine
margarîn
marr-jarr-een

marmalade
marmalêd
marr-ma-lehd

milk
llaeth / llefrith (NW)
ll(eye)th / lle-vrith (NW)

mustard
mwstard
m*oo*s-tarrd

oil
olew
ol-e*oo*

pasta
pasta
past-a

pepper
pupur
pip-irr

potatoes
tatws
tat-*oo*ss

rice
reis
r(eye)ss

rolls
rholiau
rhol-y(eye)

salt
halen
hal-en

soup
cawl
kowl

sugar
siwgr
sh*oo*g-*oo*rr

sweets
da-da (NW) / losin (SW)
dah-dah (NW) / losh-in (SW)

tea
te
teh

tomatoes
tomatos
tom-a-toss

vinegar
finegr
vin-eg-rr

yoghurt
iogwrt
yog-*oo*rrt

Fruit

apple
afal
av-al

apricots
bricyll
bri-kill

berries
aeron
(eye)-ron

bilberries
llus
llees

blackberries
mwyar duon
m*oo*i-arr dee-on

blackcurrants
cyrens duon
kuh-rens dee-on

cherries
ceirios
k(eye)rr-yoss

currants
cyrens
kuh-rens

damsons
eirin duon
(eye)rr-in dee-on

figs
ffigys
fig-iss

gooseberries
gwsberys / eirin mair
g*oo*s-ber-iss / (eye)rr-in m(eye)rr

grapes
grawnwin
grown-win

lemon
lemon
lem-on

linseed
had llin
hahd lleen

marrow
pwmpen
p*oo*mp-en

nuts
cnau
k-n(eye)

orange
oren
orr-en

peaches
eirin gwlanog
(eye)rr-in gwlan-og

pear
peren
per-en

plums
eirin
(eye)rr-in

raspberries
mafon
mav-on

strawberries
mefus
mev-iss

Meat and fish

bacon
bacwn
bak-*oo*n

beef
biff (NW) / cig eidion
beef (NW) / keeg (eye)d-yon

chicken
cyw iâr
ki*oo* yahrr

cod
penfras
pen-vrass

fish
pysgod
puhs-god

hake
cegddu
keg-***th***ee

ham
ham
ham

herring
ysgadenyn
uhs-ga-den-in

kidneys
arennau
aren-n(eye)

lamb
cig oen
keeg oyn

liver
iau (NW) / afu (SW)
y(eye) (NW) / av-i (SW)

meat
cig
keeg

mussels
cregyn gleision
kreg-in gl(eye)-shon

pork
porc / cig moch
porrk / keeg mohch

sole
lleden chwithig
lled-en chwith-ig

tuna
tiwna
ti*oo*n-a

veal
cig llo
keeg lloh

At the newsagent's

Newsagents usually sell tobacco, confectionery, soft drinks, stationery, snacks etc., as well as newspapers and magazines.

The Welsh are avid newspaper readers and virtually every county in Wales has its own weekly newspaper. Unlike Scotland and the Republic of Ireland, however, Wales doesn't have a significant 'national' press, i.e. papers that tackle a Wales-wide agenda rather than purely local or regional issues. The *Western Mail* in the south and the *Daily Post* in the north come closest, with *Wales on Sunday* trying to corner the weekend market. The *Daily Mirror* is sold in Wales as the *Welsh Mirror* and incorporates a significant amount of Welsh news and sport in its pages. *The Sun* has the highest level of household penetration in Wales with 22.5 per cent of the market, while the *Western Mail* and *Daily Post* each have 6 per cent. Circulation of the evening titles, *South Wales Echo* (80,000 copies) and *South Wales Evening Post* (69,000), is confined to the southern urban areas.

What Wales does possess is a highly developed local Welsh-language press with some 53 titles across Wales to choose from, generally containing a mix of local news, parish gossip and events listings. Many of these have deep market penetration and most householders take a newspaper produced in Wales at least once a week. For those proficient in the Welsh language, the weekly news digest *Y Cymro* contains a decent spectrum of news and features. Also in Welsh is the weekly news file *Golwg* that carries a profusion of articles and reviews on the arts, politics and social issues in Wales.

Do you have a Welsh newspaper?
Oes papur newydd Cymraeg 'da chi?
oyss pap-irr ne-wi***th*** kuhm-r(eye)g da chi

Do you have any postcards?
Oes cardiau post 'da chi?
oyss karrd-y(eye) post da chi

At the newsagent's

Do you have any Welsh books?
Oes llyfrau Cymraeg 'da chi?
oyss lluh-vr(eye) kuhm-r(eye)g da chi

Do you sell — Welsh paperbacks?
Ych chi'n gwerthu — llyfrau Cymraeg clawr papur?
ich chin gwerrth-i — lluh-vr(eye) kuhm-r(eye)g klowrr pap-irr

— coloured pencils?
— pensiliau lliw?
— pen-sil-y(eye) lli*oo*

— drawing paper?
— papur tynnu lluniau?
— pap-irr tuhn-i llin-y(eye)

— felt pens?
— pennau ffelt?
— pen-n(eye) felt

— street maps?
— mapiau stryd?
— map-y(eye) streed

I would like — some postage stamps
Hoffwn i — stampiau post
hoff-*oo*n i — stamp-y(eye) post

— a bottle of ink
— botelaid o inc
— bot-el-(eye)d o ink

I would like — a pen
Hoffwn i — ben
hoff-*oo*n i — ben

— a pencil
— bensel
— ben-sel

— adhesive tape
— dâp glynu
— dahp gluh-ni

— some envelopes
— amlenni
— am-len-i

I need — some writing paper
Dwi angen — papur sgrifennu
dwee ang-en — pap-irr sgri-ven-ni

— a local map
— map lleol
— map lle-ol

— a road map
— map ffordd
— map forr***th***

At the tobacconist's

I would like — a box of matches
Hoffwn i — focsaid o fatsis
hoff-***oo***n i — foks-(eye)d o vatch-ess

— a cigar
— sigâr
— sig-ahrr

I would like — a cigarette lighter
Hoffwn i — daniwr sigaréts
hoff-***oo***n i — dan-y***oo***rr sig-a-rets

— a gas (butane) refill
— ail-lenwad o nwy biwtan
— (eye)l len-wad o n***oo***i bi-***oo***-tan

— a pipe
— bibell
— bib-ell

— a pouch of pipe tobacco
— becyn o faco pibell
— bek-in o fak-o pib-ell

— some pipe cleaners
— lanhawyr pibelli
— lan-ha-wirr pib-ell-i

Do you have cigarette papers?
Oes papurau sigaréts 'da chi?
oyss pap-irr-(eye) sig-a-rets da chi

Do you have rolling tobacco?
Oes baco rolio 'da chi?
oyss bak-o rol-yo da chi

Have you got any other brands?
Oes unrhyw frandiau eraill 'da chi?
oyss een-rhi***oo*** vrand-y(eye) err-(eye)ll da chi

Have you got any foreign brands?
Oes unrhyw frandiau tramor 'da chi?
oyss een-rhi***oo*** vrand-y(eye) tra-mor da chi

A packet of . . . please
Paced o . . . os gwelwch yn dda
pak-ed o . . . os gwel-***oo***ch uhn ***th***ah

—with filter tips
—â blaenau hidlo
—a bl(eye)n-(eye) hid-lo

—without filters
—heb flaenau hidlo
—heb vl(eye)n-(eye) hid-lo

At the chemist's

You can buy medicines and take a doctor's prescription to a chemist (*fferyllfa*–pronounced ferr-uhll-va) during shopping hours. Rotas of chemists open at other times are posted in their shop windows and also published in the local press.

I need some high-protection suntan cream
Dwi eisiau hufen lliw haul amddiffyniad uchel
dwee (eye)sh-y(eye) hee-ven lli***oo*** h(eye)l am-***th***i-fuhn-yad i-chel

I need some antibiotics
Dwi eisiau gwrthfiotigau
dwee (eye)sh-y(eye) g*oo*rth-vyot-i-g(eye)

Can you give me something for a headache?
Allwch chi roi rhywbeth ifi at ben tost (SW) / gur pen (NW)?
all-*oo*ch chi roy rhi*oo*-beth iv-i at ben tost (SW) / geerr pen (NW)

Can you give me something for a cold?
Allwch chi roi rhywbeth ifi at annwyd?
all-*oo*ch chi roy rhi*oo*-beth iv-i at an-wid

Can you give me something for a cough?
Allwch chi roi rhywbeth ifi at beswch?
all-*oo*ch chi roy rhi*oo*-beth iv-i at bess-*oo*ch

Can you give me something for a sore throat?
Allwch chi roi rhywbeth ifi at wddwg tost (SW) / ddolur gwddw (NW)?
all-*oo*ch chi roy rhi*oo*-beth iv-i at ***ooth-oo***g tost (SW) / ***th***ol-irr g***ooth-oo*** (NW)

Can you give me something for an upset stomach?
Allwch chi roi rhywbeth ifi at ddiffyg traul?
all-*oo*ch chi roy rhi*oo*-beth iv-i at ***th***iff-ig tr(eye)l

Can you give me something for sunburn?
Allwch chi roi rhywbeth ifi at losg haul?
all-*oo*ch chi roy rhi*oo*-beth iv-i at losg h(eye)l

Can you give me something for chapped lips?
Allwch chi roi rhywbeth ifi at wefusau craciog?
all-*oo*ch chi roy rhi*oo*-beth iv-i at we-viss-(eye) krak-yog

Can you give me something for swollen feet?
Allwch chi roi rhywbeth ifi at draed wedi chwyddo?
all-*oo*ch chi roy rhi*oo*-beth iv-i at dr(eye)d wed-i chwi***th***-o

Can you give me something for blisters on my feet?
Allwch chi roi rhywbeth ifi at bothelli ar fy nhraed?
all-*oo*ch chi roy rhi*oo*-beth iv-i at both-ell-i arr vuhn hr(eye)d

Can you give me something for toothache?
Allwch chi roi rhywbeth ifi at y ddannoedd?
all-*oo*ch chi roy rhi*oo*-beth iv-i at uh ***th***an-oy***th***

Can you give me something for insect bites?
Allwch chi roi rhywbeth ifi at bigiad pryfyn?
all-*oo*ch chi roy rhi*oo*-beth iv-i at big-yad pruh-vin

Do I need a prescription?
Oes angen presgripsiwn arna i?
oyss ang-en pres-grip-sh*oo*n arr-na i

How many do I take?
Sawl un dylwn i gymryd?
sowl een duh-l*oo*n i guhm-rid

How often do I take them?
Pa mor aml dylwn i eu cymryd nhw?
pah morr am-al duh-l*oo*n i (eye) kuhm-rid nh*oo*

Are they safe for children to take?
Ydyn nhw'n ddiogel i blant eu cymryd?
uh-di nh*oo*n *th*i-o-gel i blant (eye) kuhm-rid

Do you have toothpaste?
Oes pâst dannedd 'da chi?
oyss pahst dan-*eth* da chi

Medicines and toiletries

aftershave
persawr eillio
perr-s(ow)rr (eye)ll-yo

antiseptic
antiseptig
an-ti-sep-tig

aspirin
aspirin
asp-rin

bandage
rhwymyn
rh*oo*i-min

cleansing milk
llaeth glanhau
ll(eye)th glan-h(eye)

contraceptive
offer atal cenhedlu
off-err at-al ken-hed-li

cotton wool
wadin
wad-in

deodorant
diaroglydd
di-arr-og-li*th*

disinfectant
diheintydd
di-h(eye)n-ti***th***

eau de Cologne
dŵr persawrus
doorr perr-sowrr-iss

eye shadow
colur llygaid
kol-irr lluh-g(eye)d

hair spray
chwistrell wallt
chwiss-trell wallt

hand cream
hufen dwylo
hee-ven d***oo***i-lo

hay fever
clefyd y gwair
kle-vid uh gw(eye)rr

insect repellent
peth ymlid pryfed
pehth uhm-lid pruh-ved

laxative
moddion gweithio
mo***th***-yon gw(eye)th-yo

lipstick
minlliw
min-lli***oo***

mascara
masgara
mass-gar-ra

mouthwash
cegolch
keg-olch

nail brush
brwsh ewinedd
br***oo***sh e-win-e***th***

nail file
ffeil ewinedd
f(eye)l e-win-e***th***

nail varnish
farnis ewinedd
varr-nish e-win-e***th***

nail varnish remover
toddwr farnis ewinedd
to***th-oo***rr varr-nish e-win-e***th***

perfume
persawr
perr-sowrr

perfumed soap
sebon sent
seb-on sent

plaster
plastar
plas-tarr

powder
powdwr
powd-***oo***r

razor blades
llafnau rasel
llav-n(eye) rass-el

sanitary towels
tyweli misglwyf
tuh-wel-i mis-gl***oo***iv

shampoo
siampŵ
sham-poo

shaving cream
ewyn eillio (NW) / sebon siafio (SW)
e-win (eye)ll-yo (NW) seb-on shav-yo (SW)

skin moisturiser
lleithydd croen
llehth-i***th*** kroyn

suntan oil
olew lliw haul
ol-e***oo*** lli***oo*** h(eye)l

talc
powdwr talc
powd-***oo***r talk

tissue
hances bapur
han-kess bap-irr

toilet water
dŵr pêr
doorr pehrr

toothpaste
pâst dannedd
pahst dan-e***th***

Shopping for clothes

I am just looking, thank you
Dwi ddim ond yn cael golwg, diolch
dwee *th*im ond uhn k(eye)l gol-*oo*g di-olch

I like it
Dwi'n yn ei hoffi e (m) / hi (f)
dween uhn (eye) hoff-i e (m) / hee (f)

I do not like it
Dwi ddim yn ei hoffi e (m) / hi (f)
dwee ***th***im uhn (eye) hoff-i e (m) / hee (f)

I would like this hat
Hoffwn i'r het 'ma
hoff-***oo***n irr het ma

I would like this suit
Hoffwn i'r siwt 'ma
hoff-***oo***n irr si***oo***t ma

I like this one
Dwi'n hoffi hon (f) / hwn (m)
dween hoff-i hon (f) / h*oo*n (m)

I like that one there
Dwi'n hoffi honna (f) / hwnna (m) fan'na
dween hoff-i hon-na (f) / h*oo*n-na (m) van-na

I like the one in the window
Dwi'n hoffi'r un yn y ffenest
dween hoff-irr een uhn uh fen-est

I will take it
Gymera i hi (f) / e (m)
guh-merr-(eye) hee (f) / e (m)

Can I change it if it does not fit?
Ga' i newid e os na fydd e'n ffitio? (m) / Ga' i newid hi os na fydd hi'n ffitio? (f)
gah i ne-wid e os nah vee***th*** en fit-yo (m)
gah i ne-wid hee os nah vee***th*** heen fit-yo (f)

Can you please measure me?
Allwch chi fy mesur i, os gwelwch yn dda?
all-*oo*ch chi vuh mess-irr i os gwel-*oo*ch uhn ***th***ah

I wear a size 12
Dwi'n gwisgo seis deuddeg
dween gwiss-go s(eye)s d(eye)-***th***eg

Have you got a large size?
Oes 'da chi seis / faint mawr?
oyss da chi s(eye)s / v(eye)nt mowrr

Have you got a smaller size?
Oes 'da chi seis / faint llai?
oyss da chi s(eye)s / v(eye)nt ll(eye)

Have you got this in other colours?
Ydy hon 'da chi mewn lliwiau eraill?
uh-di hon da chi me*oo*n lli*oo*-y(eye) err-(eye)ll

Shopping for clothes

Where are the changing rooms?
Ble mae'r stafelloedd newid?
ble m(eye)rr sta-vell-oy*th* ne-wid

Where can I try it on?
Ble galla i ei thrio hi 'mlaen?
ble gall-(eye) i three-o hee ml(eye)n

Is there a full length mirror?
Oes yna ddrych llawn hyd 'ma?
oyss uhn-a *th*reech llown heed ma

May I see it in daylight?
Ga i ei gweld (f) / weld (m) yng ngolau dydd?
gah i (eye) gweld uhng ol-(eye) dee*th* (f)
gah i (eye) weld uhng ol-(eye) dee*th* (m)

It does not fit
Dyw hi (f) / e (m) ddim yn ffitio
di*oo* hee (f) / e (m) *th*im uhn fit-yo

Is it too long?
Ydy hi'n (f) / e'n (m) rhy hir?
uh-di heen (f) / en (m) rhee heerr

Is it too short?
Ydy hi'n (f) / e'n (m) rhy fyr?
uh-di heen (f) / en (m) rhee virr

Is this all you have?
Dyma'r cyfan sy 'da chi?
duhm-arr kuh-van see da chi

It does not suit me
Dyw hi ddim yn gweddu ifi
di*oo* hee *th*im uhn gwe*th*-i iv-i

I would like one with a zip
Hoffwn i un â sip
hoff-*oo*n i een a sip

I would like one without a belt
Hoffwn i un heb wregys
hoff-*oo*n i een heb wreg-iss

Is it guaranteed?
Ydy hi (f) / e (m) dan warant?
uh-di hee (f) / e (m) dan warr-ant

What is it made of?
O beth mae hi wedi ei gwneud? (f) / O beth mae e wedi ei wneud? (m)
o behth m(eye) hee wed-i (eye) gwnehd (f) / o behth m(eye) e wed-i (eye) wnehd (m)

Is it drip-dry?
Ydy e'n ddripsych? (m) Ydy hi'n ddripsych? (f)
uh-di en ***th***rip-sich (m) / uh-di heen ***th***rip-sich (f)

Is it dry-clean only?
Ai ar gyfer ei sychlanhau yn unig mae e? (m) Ai ar gyfer ei sychlanhau yn unig mae hi? (f)
(eye) arr guh-verr (eye) seech-lan-h(eye) uhn een-ig m(eye) e (m)
(eye) arr guh-verr (eye) seech-lan-h(eye) uhn een-ig m(eye) hee (f)

Is it machine-washable?
Allwch chi ei olchi e yn y peiriant? (m) Allwch chi ei golchi hi yn y peiriant? (f)
all-***oo***ch chi (eye) ol-chi e uhn uh p(eye)-rr-yant (m)
all-***oo***ch chi (eye) gol-chi hee uhn uh p(eye)-rr-yant (f)

Will it shrink?
Wnaiff e dynnu ato? (m) Wnaiff hi dynnu ati? (f)
wn(eye)ff e duhn-ni at-o (m)
wn(eye)ff hee duhn-ni at-i (f)

Clothes and accessories

acrylic
acrylig
a-kruhl-ig

apron
ffedog
fed-og

belt
gwregys
gwreg-iss

blouse
blows
blowss

Clothes and accessories

bra
bronglwm
bron-gl*oo*m

bracelet
breichled
br(eye)ch-led

brooch
tlws
tlooss

button
botwm
bot-*oo*m

cap
cap
kap

cardigan
cardigan
karr-di-gan

casual wear
dillad hamdden
dill-ad ham-*th*en

coat
côt
koht

collar
coler
kol-err

corduroy
melfaréd
mel-va-red

denim
denim
den-im

dress
ffrog
frog

dressing gown
coban nos
kob-an nohss

dungarees
dyngarîs
duhn-garr-eess

earrings
clustdlysau
cleest-dluh-s(eye)

fur
ffwr
f*oo*rr

gloves
menig
men-ig

handbag
bag llaw
bag llow (as in how)

handkerchief
cadach poced / macyn (SW) / hances (NW)
kad-ach pok-ed / mak-in (SW) han-kess (NW)

hat
het
het

jacket
siaced
sha-ked

Clothes and accessories

jeans
jîns
jeens

jersey
jersi
jerr-si

jumper
jymper
juhm-perr

lace
les
lehss

leather
lledr
lled-rr

linen
lliain
lli-(eye)n

necklace
cadwyn wddw / mwclis (NW)
kad-win ***ooth-oo*** / m*oo*k-liss (NW)

night-dress
gwn-nos
g*oo*n-nohss

nylon
neilon
neh-lon

panties
pantis
pan-tiss

pendant
tlws crog
tlooss krohg

petticoat
pais
p(eye)ss

polyester
polyester
pol-i-est-err

poplin
poplin
pop-lin

pullover
pwlofer
p*oo*-lov-err

purse
pwrs
p*oo*rrss

pyjamas
pyjamas
puh-jahm-ass

raincoat
côt law
koht low (as in how)

rayon
reion
reh-on

ring
modrwy
mod-r*oo*i

sandals
sandalau
san-dal-au

scarf
sgarff
sgarrf

Clothes and accessories

shirt
crys
kreess

shoes
esgidiau
es-gid-y(eye)

shorts
trywsus byr
trow-siss birr

silk
sidan
sid-an

skirt
sgert
sgerrt

slip
pais
p(eye)ss

socks
hosanau / socs
ho-ssan-(eye) / sokss

stockings
hosanau
ho-ssan-(eye)

suede
swêd
swehd

suit (men's)
siwt
si*oo*t

suit (women's)
gwisg / siwt
gwisg / si*oo*t

sweater
sweter
swet-err

swimming trunks
trôns nofio
trohns nov-yo

swimsuit
siwt nofio
si-*oo*t nov-yo

terylene
terylen
ter-uh-len

tie
tei
t(eye)

tights
teits
t(eye)ts

towel
tywel
tuh-wel

trousers
trywsus
trow-siss

T-shirt
crys-T
kreess tee

umbrella
ymbarél
uhm-barr-el

underpants
trôns
trohns

velvet
melfed
mel-ved

vest
fest
vest

wallet
waled
wal-ed

watch
wats
watss

waistcoat
gwasgod
gwas-god

wool
gwlân
gwlahn

zip
sip
sip

Photography

Can you develop this film, please?
Allwch chi ddatblygu'r ffilm hon, os gwelwch yn dda?
all-*oo*ch chi *th*at-bluhg-irr film hon os gwel-*oo*ch uhn ***th***ah

I would like this photo enlarged
Hoffwn i'r llun hwn gael ei chwyddo
hoff-***oo***n irr lleen h***oo***n g(eye)l (eye) chwi***th***-o

I would like two prints of this one
Hoffwn i ddau brint o hwn
hoff-***oo***n i ***th***(eye) brint o h***oo***n

When will the photos be ready?
Pryd bydd y lluniau'n barod?
preed bee***th*** uh llin-y(eye)n bar-od

I need a film — for this camera
Dwi eisiau ffilm — ar gyfer y camera hwn
dwee (eye)sh-y(eye) film — arr guh-verr uh kam-ra h***oo***n

— for this camcorder
— ar gyfer y camcorder hwn
— arr guh-verr uh kam-korrd-err h***oo***n

— for this cine camera
— ar gyfer y sine-camera hwn
— arr guh-verr uh sin-e-kam-ra h***oo***n

— for this video camera
— ar gyfer y camera fideo hwn
— arr guh-verr uh kam-ra vid-yo h***oo***n

I want — a black and white film
Dwi eisiau — ffilm ddu a gwyn
dwee (eye)sh-y(eye) — film ***th***ee a gwin

I want — a colour print film
Dwi eisiau — ffilm printiau lliw
dwee (eye)sh-y(eye) — film print-y(eye) lli***oo***

— a colour slide film
— ffilm sleidiau lliw
— film sl(eye)d-y(eye) lli***oo***

— batteries for the flash
— batris i'r fflach
— ba-tris irr flach

Camera repairs

I am having trouble with my camera
Dwi'n cael trafferth gyda fy nghamera
dween k(eye)l traff-errth guh-da vuhng ham-ra

The film is jammed
Mae'r ffilm yn sownd
m(eye)rr film uhn sownd

There is something wrong with my camera
Mae rhywbeth yn bod ar fy nghamera
m(eye) rhi***oo***-beth uhn bohd arr vuhng ham-ra

Can you repair it?
Allwch chi ei drwsio e?
all-***oo***ch chi (eye) dr***oo***sh-o e

Where can I get my camera repaired?
Ble galla i gael fy nghamera wedi ei drwsio?
ble gall-(eye) g(eye)l vuhng ham-ra wed-i (eye) dr*oo*sh-o

Cameras and photography

accessory
ategolyn
at-e-gol-in

blue filter
hidlydd glas
hid-li*th* glahss

camcorder
camcorder
kam-korrd-err

cartridge
cetrisen
ke-triss-en

cassette
casét
kass-et

ciné camera
sine-camera
sin-e-kam-ra

distance
pellter
pell-terr

enlargement
mwyhad / llun wedi ei chwyddo
m*oo*i-had / lleen wed-i (eye) chwi*th*-o

exposure
datguddiad
dat-gu*th*-yad

exposure meter
mesurydd datguddio
mess-i-ri*th* dat-gu*th*-yo

flash
fflach
flach

flash bulb
bylb fflach
buhlb flach

flash cube
ciwb fflach
ki*oo*b flach

focal distance
pellter ffocal
pell-terr fok-al

focus
ffocws
fohk-*oo*ss

image
delwedd / dwysäwr
del-we*th* / d*oo*i-sah-*oo*r

Cameras and photography

in focus
mewn ffocws
me*oo*n fohk-*oo*ss

lens
lens
lenss

lens cover
gorchudd lens
gorr-chi*th* lenss

negative
negydd
neg-i*th*

out of focus
allan o ffocws
all-an o fohk-*oo*ss

over-exposed
rhy olau
rhee ol-(eye)

picture
llun
lleen

print
print
print

projector
taflunydd
tav-lin-i*th*

red filter
hidlydd coch
hid-li*th* kohch

reel
ril
reel

rewind mechanism
mecanwaith ailddirwyn
me-kan-w(eye)th (eye)l-*th*irr-*oo*in

shade
cysgod
kuhs-god

shutter
caead
k(eye)-ad

shutter speed
cyflymder caead
kuh-vluhm-derr k(eye)-ad

slide
sleid
sl(eye)d

transparency
tryloywlun / sleid
truh-loy*oo*-lin / sl(eye)d

tripod
trybedd
truh-be*th*

under-exposed
rhy dywyll
rhee duh-will

viewfinder
ffenest
fen-est

wide-angle lens
lens ongl lydan
lenss ong-l luh-dan

yellow filter
hidlydd melyn
hid-li*th* mel-in

At the hairdresser's

I would like to make an appointment
Hoffwn i wneud apwyntiad
hoff-***oo***n i wnehd a-p***oo***int-yad

I would like — a perm
Hoffwn i gael — pyrm
hoff-***oo***n i g(eye)l — puhrrm

— a blow dry
— fy ngwallt wedi ei chwythu'n sych
— vuhng wallt wed-i (eye) chwuhth-een seech

— my hair dyed
— fy ngwallt wedi ei liwio
— vuhng wallt wed-i (eye) li***oo***-yo

— my hair streaked
— fy ngwallt wedi ei fritho
— vuhng wallt wed-i (eye) vrith-o

— shampoo and cut
— fy ngwallt wedi ei siampŵo a'i dorri
— vuhng wallt wed-i (eye) sham-p***oo***-o (eye) dorr-i

— shampoo and set
— fy ngwallt wedi ei siampŵo a'i setio
— vuhng wallt wed-i (eye) sham-p***oo***-o (eye) set-yo

I want a haircut
Dwi eisiau fy ngwallt wedi ei dorri
dwee (eye)sh-(eye) vuhng wallt wed-i (eye) dorr-i

I want a trim
Dwi eisiau trim
dwee (eye)sh-(eye) trim

Please cut my hair — short
Torrwch fy ngwallt, os gwelwch yn dda — yn fyr
torr-***oo***ch vuhng wallt os gwel-***oo***ch uhn ***th***ah — uhn virr

At the hairdresser's

— fairly short
— yn gymharol fyr
— uhn guhm-harr-ol virr

— in a fringe
— yn rhimyn
— uhn rhi-min

Take a little more off at the back
Torrwch ychydig yn fwy o'r cefn
torr-*oo*ch uh-chuh-dig uhn f*oo*i orr kev-n

Not too much off
Ddim gormod i ffwrdd
thim gorr-mod i f***oo***rr***th***

I would like — a conditioner
Hoffwn i — gyflyrydd
hoff-***oo***n i — guh-vluh-ri***th***

— hair spray
— chwistrell wallt
— chwiss-trell wallt

That is fine, thank you
Iawn, diolch
yown di-olch

The dryer is too hot
Mae'r sychwr yn rhy boeth
m(eye)rr suhch-***oo***r uhn rhee boyth

The water is too hot
Mae'r dŵr yn rhy boeth
m(eye)rr doorr uhn rhee boyth

Laundry

Is there a launderette nearby?
Oes yna olchdy ar bwys?
oyss uhn-a olch-di arr b*oo*is

How does the machine work?
Sut mae'r peiriant yn gweithio?
sh*oo*d m(ye)rr p(eye)-rr-yant uhn gw(eye)th-yo

How long will it take?
Faint gymer hi?
v(eye)nt guh-merr hee

I will come back in an hour
Bydda i'n dod 'nôl mewn awr
buh-***th***(eye)n dohd nohl me*oo*n owrr

What time do you close?
Pryd ych chi'n cau?
preed ich chin k(eye)

Can you — clean this skirt?
Allwch chi — lanhau'r sgert hon?
all-*oo*ch chi — lan-h(eye)rr sgerrt hon

— clean and press these shirts?
— lanhau a phresio'r crysau hyn?
— lan-h(eye)rr a fress-yorr kruhs-(eye) hin

— wash these clothes?
— olchi'r dillad hyn?
— ol-chirr dill-ad hin

This stain is oil
Staen olew yw hwn
st(eye)n ol-e*oo* i*oo* h*oo*n

This stain is blood
Staen gwaed yw hwn
st(eye)n gw(eye)d i*oo* h*oo*n

This stain is coffee
Staen coffi yw hwn
st(eye)n koff-i i*oo* h*oo*n

This stain is ink
Staen inc yw hwn
st(eye)n ink i*oo* h*oo*n

I will come back later
Bydda i'n dod 'nôl yn nes ymlaen
buh*th*(eye)n dohd nohl uhn nehss uhm-l(eye)n

When should I come back?
Pryd dylwn i ddod 'nôl?
preed duh-l*oo*n i *th*ohd nohl

When will my things be ready?
Pryd bydd fy mhethau yn barod?
preed bee*th* vuhm heth-(eye) uhn bar-od

Can you do it quickly?
Allwch chi ei wneud ar frys?
all-*oo*ch chi (eye) wnehd arr vreess

Please send it to this address
Wnewch chi ei ddanfon e i'r cyfeiriad hwn
wne*oo*ch chi (eye) *th*an-von e irr kuh-v(eye)rr-yad h*oo*n

General repairs

This is — broken
Mae hwn — wedi torri
m(eye) h*oo*n — wed-i torr-i

— damaged
— wedi cael niwed
— wed-i k(eye)l ni*oo*-ed

— torn
— wedi rhwygo
— wed-i rh*oo*i-go

Can you repair it?
Allwch chi ei drwsio e?
all-***oo***ch chi (eye) dr***oo***sh-yo e

Have you got a spare part for this?
Oes darn sbâr 'da chi i hwn?
oyss darrn sbahrr da chi i h***oo***n

Would you have a look at this please?
Fyddech chi'n fodlon cael golwg ar hwn, os gwelwch yn dda?
vuh***th***-ech chin vod-lon k(eye)l gol-***oo***g arr h***oo***n os gwel-***oo***ch uhn ***th***ah

Here is the guarantee
Dyma'r warant
duhm-arr warr-ant

I need new heels on these shoes
Mae angen sodlau newydd ar yr esgidiau hyn
m(eye) an-gen sod-l(eye) ne-wi***th*** arr uhr ess-gid-y(eye) hin

At the post office

Virtually all post offices (*swyddfa'r post* – pronounced s***ooith***-varr post) are open Monday to Friday, 09.00 to 17.30, and on Saturday from 09.00 to 12.30 (with some open all day). In rural areas, you will find sub-post offices operating out of a shop or house, but these open only for a limited number of hours. Postage stamps can be purchased at post office counters, from vending machines outside, or from a large number of newsagents, supermarkets and other shops. Stamps are sold as first or second class, with first class post normally arriving at UK destinations the day after posting. Post boxes are painted red and are usually situated near post offices.

12 stamps please
Deuddeg stamp, os gwelwch yn dda
d(eye)-***th***eg stamp os gwel-***oo***ch uhn ***th***ah

I need to send this by courier
Dwi angen anfon hwn 'da chludydd
dwee ang-en an-von h*oo*n da chlid-i*th*

I want to send this by registered post
Dwi eisiau anfon hwn 'da'r post cofrestredig
dwee (eye)sh-y(eye) an-von h*oo*n darr post kov-res-tred-ig

I want to send this parcel
Dwi eisiau anfon y parsel 'ma
dwee (eye)sh-y(eye) an-von uh parr-sel ma

When will it arrive?
Pryd wnaiff e gyrraedd?
preed wn(eye)ff e guh-rr(eye)*th*

How much is a letter — to Germany?
Faint yw llythyr — i'r Almaen?
v(eye)nt i*oo* lluhth-irr — irr al-m(eye)n

How much is a letter — to the United States?
Faint yw llythyr — i'r Unol Daleithiau?
v(eye)nt i-*oo* lluhth-irr — irr een-ol dal-(eye)th-y(eye)

Can I have 6 first class stamps, please?
Ga' i chwe stamp dosbarth cynta', os gwelwch yn dda?
gah i chwe stamp doss-barrth kuhn-ta os gwel-*oo*ch uhn *th*ah

Can I have 6 stamps for postcards to France, please?
Ga' i chwe stamp i gardiau post i Ffrainc, os gwelwch yn dda?
gah i chwe stamp i garrd-y(eye) post i fr(eye)nk os gwel-*oo*ch uhn *th*ah

Can I have 2 second class stamps, please?
Ga' i ddau stamp ail ddosbarth, os gwelwch yn dda?
Gah i *th*(eye) stamp (eye)l *th*oss-barth os gwel-*oo*ch uhn *th*ah

Using the telephone

In the UK, telephone numbers have 6 or 7 digits that are preceded by an area code of 4 or 5 digits, the first of which is always 0.

The area code must be used when calling from one area to another.

To call Wales from outside the UK, dial the international access code followed by 44, then the area code minus its initial zero, and finally the number.

To call overseas from Wales, all you need to do is dial the international network access code – 00 – then the appropriate country code, the area code and then the number of the person you want to call.

Some payphones (*teleffon* – pronounced tel-e-fon) accept only coins but an increasing number accept phone cards, available from post offices and newsagents displaying British Telecom's logo, and credit cards. Inland and international calls are cheapest during reduced rate periods: 18.00 to 08.00 on weekdays and all day at weekends and on Bank Holidays.

Can I use the telephone, please?
Ga' i ddefnyddio'r ffôn, os gwelwch yn dda?
gah i ***th***ev-nuh***th***-yorr fohn os gwel-***oo***ch uhn ***th***ah

Can you connect me with the international operator?
Allwch chi fy nghysylltu â theleffonydd rhyngwladol?
all-***oo***ch chi vuhng huh-suhll-ti a thel-e-fon-i***th*** rhuhng-wlad-ol

Can I dial direct?
Alla i ddeialu'n uniongyrchol?
all-(eye) ***th***(eye)-al-in een-yon-guhrrch-ol

How do I use the telephone?
Sut mae defnyddio'r ffôn?
sh***oo***d m(eye) dev-nuh***th***-yorr fohn

I must make a phone call to Argentina
Rhaid ifi wneud galwad ffôn i'r Ariannin
rh(eye)d iv-i wnehd gal-wad fohn irr Ar-yan-in

I need to make a phone call
Dwi angen gwneud galwad ffôn
dwee ang-en gwnehd gal-wad fohn

What you may hear

The number I need is . . .
Y rhif dwi angen yw . . .
uh rheev dwee ang-en i*oo* . . .

What is the charge?
Beth yw'r pris?
behth i*oo*rr preess

What is the code for Glasgow?
Beth yw'r cod i Glasgow?
behth i*oo*rr kohd i glas-go

How much is it to phone to Belfast?
Faint yw galwad ffôn i Belfast?
v(eye)nt i*oo* gal-wad fohn i Bel-fast

Please call me back
Galwch fi yn ôl, os gwelwch yn dda
gal-*oo*ch vi uhn ohl os gwel-*oo*ch uhn *th*ah

I am sorry. We were cut off
Mae'n ddrwg 'da fi. Fe gawson ni'n torri i ffwrdd
m(eye)n *th*roog da vi ve gow-son nin torr-i i f*oorrth*

I would like to make a reversed charge call
Hoffwn i wneud galwad wrthdal
hoff-*oo*n i wnehd gal-wad *oo*rth-dal

What you may hear

Ewch yn eich blaen, os gwelwch yn dda
e*oo*ch uhn uhch bl(eye)n os gwel-*oo*ch uhn *th*ah
Please go ahead

Dyw'r rhif ddim yn gweithio
di*oo*rr rheev *th*im uhn gw(eye)th-yo
The number is out of order

Mae'r llinell yn brysur
m(eye)rr llin-ell uhn bruhss-irr
The line is engaged

Alla i ddim cael y rhif 'ma
all-(eye) ***th***im k(eye)l uh rheev ma
I cannot obtain this number

Dwi'n eich cysylltu chi â Mr Smith
dween uhch kuh-sullt-i chi a mis-terr smith
I am putting you through to Mr Smith

Dwi'n ceisio eich cysylltu chi
dween k(eye)ss-yo uhch kuh-sullt-i chi
I am trying to connect you

Changing money

Most people prefer the banks (*banciau* – pronounced bank-y(eye)) to change money and cheques, and in most towns in Wales you will find a branch of at least one or two of the major banks: Lloyds TSB, HSBC, NatWest, Barclays. Most banks are open on Monday to Friday 09.30 to 15.30, though branches in larger towns and cities are often open until late in the afternoons and on Saturday mornings. A bureau de change is found in most city centres and also in major train stations and airports.

Most hotels, shops and restaurants in Wales readily accept credit cards, although some smaller establishments still prefer to use cash. In case your credit cards are not accepted, it is advisable to carry money in traveller's cheques available for a small commission from any bank.

Can I contact my bank to arrange for a transfer?
Ga' i gysylltu â fy manc i drefnu trosglwyddiad?
gah i guh-suhllt-i a vuh mank i drev-ni tros-gl***oo***ith-yad

I would like to obtain a cash advance with my credit card
Hoffwn i gael benthyciad â fy ngherdyn credyd
hoff-***oo***n i g(eye)l ben-thuhk-yad a vuhng herr-din kre-did

Changing money

Has my cash arrived?
Ydy fy arian wedi cyrraedd?
uh-di vuh ar-yan wed-i kuhrr-(eye)***th***

Here is my passport
Dyma fy mhasport
duh-ma vuhm hass-porrt

This is the name and address of my bank
Dyma enw a chyfeiriad fy manc
duh-ma en-***oo*** a chuh-v(eye)rr-yad vuh mank

What is the rate of exchange?
Beth yw'r gyfradd gyfnewid?
behth i***oo***rr guh-vra***th*** guhv-ne-wid

What is your commission?
Beth yw'ch comisiwn?
behth i***oo***ch kom-i-sh***oo***n

Can I change — these traveller's cheques?
Ga' i newid — y sieciau teithio hyn?
gah i ne-wid — uh shek-y(eye) t(eye)th-yo hin

— these notes?
— yr arian papur hyn?
— uhrr ar-yan pap-irr hin

What is the rate for — sterling?
Beth yw cyfradd — sterling?
behth i***oo*** kuh-vra***th*** — sterr-ling

— dollars?
— doleri?
— dol-e-ri

HEALTH

If you are travelling to Wales from outside the United Kingdom, it is advisable to take out travel insurance before you begin of your visit against the cost of any medical and dental treatment. Citizens of all European Union countries should bring their European Health Insurance Card (Cerdyn Yswiriant Iechyd Ewrop (EHIC). They are entitled to free medical treatment at NHS hospitals. Citizens of other countries are charged for all medical services except those administered by accident and emergency units at NHS hospitals.

Medicines can be obtained from a chemist during shopping hours. Rotas of chemists open at other times are posted in their shop windows and published in local newspapers. Doctors' surgeries are normally open from about 09.00 to midday on weekdays and some are open for a few hours in the evenings. A Saturday morning surgery is available for urgent cases. In an emergency or accident, call 999 for an ambulance.

What's wrong?

I need a doctor
Dwi angen doctor
dwee ang-en dok-torr

Can I see a doctor?
Ga' i weld doctor?
gah i weld dok-torr

He has been badly injured
Mae e wedi cael ei anafu'n wael
m(eye) e wed-i k(eye)l (eye) an-a-vin w(eye)l

He is unconscious
Mae e'n anymwybodol
m(eye) en an-uhm-wi-bod-ol

What's wrong?

He has burnt himself
Mae e wedi ei losgi'i hunan
m(eye) e wed-i (eye) loss-gi-(eye) hee-nan

He has dislocated his shoulder
Mae e wedi tynnu'i ysgwydd o'i lle
m(eye) e wed-i tuhn-i-(eye) uhsg-wi***th*** oy lle

He is hurt
Mae e wedi cael dolur
m(eye) e wed-i k(eye)l dol-irr

My son is ill
Mae fy mab yn sâl
m(eye) vuh mahb uhn sahl

I am a diabetic
Dwi'n ddiabetig / Mae clefyd siwgr arna i
dween ***th***(eye)-a-bet-ig / m(eye) kle-vid sh***oo***g-***oo***rr arr-na i

I am allergic to penicillin
Mae 'da fi alergedd i benisilin
m(eye) da vi al-err-ge***th*** i ben-i-ssil-in

I am badly sunburnt
Mae llosg haul drwg 'da fi
m(eye) llosg h(eye)l droog da vi

I am constipated
Dwi'n rhwym
dween rh***oo***i-m

I cannot sleep
Dwi ddim yn gallu cysgu
dwee ***th***im uhn gall-i kuhss-gi

I feel dizzy
Mae'r bendro arna i
m(eye)rr ben-dro arr-na i

I feel faint
Mae fy mhen i'n troi
m(eye) vuhm hen een troy

I feel nauseous
Dwi'n teimlo'n gyfoglyd
dween t(eye)m-lon guh-vog-lid

I fell
Syrthiais / cwympais i (NW)
suhrrth-y(eye)ss / k*oo*im-p(eye)ss i

I have a pain here
Mae poen 'da fi fan hyn
m(eye) poyn da vi van hin

I have a rash here
Mae brech 'da fi fan hyn
m(eye) brehch da vi van hin

I have been sick
Dwi wedi bod yn sâl
dwee wed-i bohd uhn sahl

I have been stung
Dwi wedi cael fy mhigo
dwee wed-i k(eye)l vuhm hig-o

I have cut myself
Dwi wedi fy nhorri fy hunan
dwee wed-i vuhn horr-i vuh hee-nan

I have diarrhoea
Mae dolur rhydd arna i
m(eye) dol-irr rhee*th* arna i

I have pulled a muscle
Dwi wedi tynnu cyhyr
dwee wed-i tuhn-i kuh-hirr

What's wrong?

I have sunstroke
Dwi wedi cael trawiad haul
dwee wed-i k(eye)l trow-yad h(eye)l

I suffer from high blood pressure
Dwi'n dioddef gan bwysedd gwaed uchel
dween di-o***th***-e gan b***oo***i-se***th*** gw(eye)d i-chel

I think I have food poisoning
Dwi'n meddwl fy mod yn dioddef o wenwyn bwyd
dween me***th-oo***l vuh mohd uhn di-o***th***-e o wen-win b***oo***id

It is inflamed here
Mae'n llidus 'ma
m(eye)n llid-iss ma

My arm is broken
Dwi wedi torri fy mraich
dwee wed-i torr-i vuhm r(eye)ch

My stomach is upset
Dwi'n cael anhwylder ar y stumog
dween k(eye)l an-h***oo***il-derr arr uh stim-og

My tongue is coated
Mae tafod blewog 'da fi
m(eye) tav-od ble-wog da vi

She has a temperature
Mae tymheredd uchel 'da hi
m(eye) tuhm-herr-e***th*** i-chel da hee

She has been bitten
Mae hi wedi cael ei chnoi
m(eye) hee wed-i k(eye)l (eye) chnoy

She has sprained her ankle
Mae hi wedi 'sigo ei migwrn / ffêr (NW)
m(eye) hee wed-i sig-o (eye) mig-***oo***rrn / fehrr (NW)

There is a swelling here
Mae chwyddi 'ma
m(eye) chwuh***th***-i ma

I have hurt — my arm
Dwi wedi anafu — fy mraich
dwee wed-i an-av-i — vuhm r(eye)ch

— my leg
— fy nghoes
— vuhng hoyss

It is painful — to walk
Mae'n boenus — cerdded
m(eye)n boy-niss — kerr-***th***ed

— to breathe
— anadlu
— a-nad-li

— to swallow
— llyncu
— lluhn-ki

I have a headache
Mae gen i gur pen (NW) / Mae pen tost 'da fi (SW)
m(eye) gen i geerr pen (NW) / m(eye) pen tost da vi (SW)

I have a sore throat
Mae dolur gwddw gen i (NW) / Mae gwddwg tost 'da fi (SW)
m(eye) dol-irr g***ooth-oo*** gen i (NW) / m(eye) g***ooth-oo***g tost da vi (SW)

I have earache
Mae pigyn clust gen i (NW) / Mae clust tost 'da fi (SW)
m(eye) pig-in clist gen i (NW) / m(eye) clist tost da vi (SW)

I have cramp
Mae cramp 'da fi
m(eye) kramp da vi

What's wrong?

I am taking these drugs
Dwi'n cymryd y cyffuriau 'ma
dween kuhm-rid uh kuh-firr-y(eye) ma

Can you give me a prescription for them?
Allwch chi roi presgripsiwn ifi eu cael nhw?
all-*oo*ch chi roy pres-grip-sh*oo*n iv-i (eye) k(eye)l nh*oo*

Do I have to go into hospital?
Oes rhaid ifi fynd i'r ysbyty?
oyss rh(eye)d iv-i vind irr uhs-buh-ti

Do I need an operation?
Oes angen llawdriniaeth?
oyss ang-en llow-drin-y(eye)th

I am ill
Dwi'n sâl
dween sahl

I am on the pill
Dwi ar y bilsen
dwee arr uh bil-sen

I am pregnant
Dwi'n feichiog
dween v(eye)ch-yog

My blood group is
Fy ngrŵp gwaed yw
vuhng roop gw(eye)d i*oo*

I do not know my blood group
Dwi ddim yn gwybod fy ngrŵp gwaed
dwee *th*im uhn g*oo*i-bod vuhng roop gw(eye)d

At the hospital

Here is my European Health Insurance Card
Dyma fy Cerdyn Yswiriant Iechyd Ewrop
duh-ma vuh kerr-din uhss-wirr-yant ye-chid eh-oo-roh-p

How do I get reimbursed?
Sut ydw i'n cael ad-daliad?
sh*oo*d uh-d*oo* een k(eye)l ad-dal-yad

Must I stay in bed?
Oes rhaid ifi aros yn y gwely?
oyss rh(eye)d iv-i arr-oss uhn uh gwel-i

When will I be able to travel?
Pryd fydda i'n gallu teithio?
preed vuh***th***-(eye)n gall-i t(eye)th-yo

Will I be able to go out tomorrow?
Fydda i'n gallu gadael 'fory?
vuh***th***-(eye)n gall-i gad-(eye)l vorr-i

Parts of the body

ankle
ffêr (NW) / migwrn (SW)
fehrr (NW) / mig-***oo***rrn (SW)

arm
braich
br(eye)ch

back
cefn
kev-n

bone
asgwrn
ass-g*oo*rrn

breast
bron
bron

cheek
boch
bohch

chest
brest
brest

ear
clust
clist

Parts of the body

elbow
penelin
pen-e-lin

face
wyneb
ooi-neb

finger
bys
beess

foot
troed
troyd

hand
llaw
llow (as in how)

heart
calon
kal-on

kidney
aren
arr-en

knee
pen-glin
pen gleen

leg
coes
koyss

liver
afu (SW) / iau (NW)
av-i / y(eye)

lungs
ysgyfaint
uhs-guh-v(eye)nt

mouth
ceg
kehg

neck
gwar
gwarr

nose
trwyn
tr***oo***in

skin
croen
kroyn

stomach
stumog
stim-og

throat
gwddw
g***ooth-oo***

wrist
arddwrn
arr-***thoo***rrn

At the dentist

I have toothache
Mae'r ddannoedd arna i
m(eye)rr ***th***an-oy***th*** arr-na i

I have to see the dentist
Mae'n rhaid ifi weld y deintydd
m(eye)n rh(eye)d iv-i weld uh dehnt-i***th***

My false teeth are broken
Mae fy nannedd gosod wedi torri
m(eye) vuh nan-e***th*** goss-od wed-i torr-i

Can you repair them?
Allwch chi eu trwsio nhw?
all-***oo***ch chi (eye) tr***oo***sh-o nh***oo***

My gums are sore
Mae cig fy nannedd yn ddolurus
m(eye) keeg vuh nan-ne***th*** uhn ***th***ol-irr-is

Please give me an injection
Rhowch bigiad ifi, os gwelwch yn dda
rhohch big-yad iv-i os gwel-***oo***ch uhn ***th***ah

The filling has come out
Mae'r llenwad wedi dod allan
m(eye)rr llen-wad wed-i dohd all-an

I have broken a tooth
Dwi wedi torri dant
dwee wed-i torr-i dant

At the dentist

That hurts
Mae hwnna'n brifo
m(eye) h*oo*n-an breev-o

This one hurts
Mae hwn yn brifo
m(eye) h*oo*n uhn breev-o

Are you going to fill it?
Ych chi'n mynd i'w lenwi?
ich chin mind yoo len-wi

For Your Information

Cardinal numbers

(m) masculine (f) feminine

Traditional numerals that are mainly used (1) to tell the time, (2) to tell one's age	*The more usual way of counting for other purposes*
0 dim dim	**0** dim dim
1 un een	**1** un een
2 dau (m) dwy (f) d(eye) (m) d*oo*i (f)	**2** dau (m) dwy (f) d(eye) (m) d*oo*i (f)
3 tri (m) tair (f) tree (m) t(eye)rr (f)	**3** tri (m) tair (f) tree (m) t(eye)rr (f)
4 pedwar (m) pedair (f) ped-warr (m) ped-(eye)rr (f)	**4** pedwar (m) pedair (f) ped-warr (m) ped-(eye)rr (f)
5 pump / pum (+ noun) pimp / pim	**5** pump / pum (+ noun) pimp / pim

Cardinal numbers

Traditional numerals that are mainly used (1) to tell the time, (2) to tell one's age	*The more usual way of counting for other purposes*
6 chwech / chwe (+ noun) chwech / chwe	**6** chwech / chwe (+ noun) chwech / chwe
7 saith s(eye)th	**7** saith s(eye)th
8 wyth ***oo***ith	**8** wyth ***oo***ith
9 naw now	**9** naw now
10 deg dehg	**10** deg dehg
11 un ar ddeg een arr ***th***ehg	**11** un deg un een dehg een
12 deuddeg d(eye)-***th***eg	**12** un deg dau (m) un deg dwy (f) een dehg d(eye) (m) een dehg d***oo***i (f)
13 tri ar ddeg (m) tair ar ddeg (f) tree arr ***th***ehg (m) t(eye)rr arr ***th***ehg (f)	**13** un deg tri (m) un deg tair (f) een dehg tree (m) een dehg tair (f)

Traditional numerals that are mainly used (1) to tell the time, (2) to tell one's age	*The more usual way of counting for other purposes*
14 pedwar ar ddeg (m) pedair ar ddeg (f) ped-warr arr ***th***ehg (m) ped-(eye)rr arr ***th***ehg (f)	**14** un deg pedwar (m) un deg pedair (f) een dehg pedwarr (m) een dehg ped(eye)rr (f)
15 pymtheg puhm-theg	**15** un deg pump een dehg pimp
16 un ar bymtheg een arr buhm-theg	**16** un deg chwech een dehg chwech
17 dau ar bymtheg (m) dwy ar bymtheg (f) d(eye) arr buhm-theg (m) d***oo***i arr buhm-theg (f)	**17** un deg saith een dehg s(eye)th
18 deunaw d(eye)-now	**18** un deg wyth een dehg ***oo***ith
19 pedwar ar bymtheg (m) pedair ar bymtheg (f) ped-warr arr buhm-theg (m) ped-(eye)rr arr buhm-theg (f)	**19** un deg naw een dehg now
20 ugain ee-g(eye)n	**20** dau ddeg d(eye) ***th***ehg

Cardinal numbers

Traditional numerals that are mainly used (1) to tell the time, (2) to tell one's age	*The more usual way of counting for other purposes*
21 un ar hugain een arr hee-g(eye)n	**21** dau ddeg un d(eye) ***th***ehg een
22 dau ar hugain (m) dwy ar hugain (f) d(eye) arr hee-g(eye)n (m) d***oo***i arr hee-g(eye)n (f)	**22** dau ddeg dau (m) dau ddeg dwy (f) d(eye) ***th***eg d(eye) (m) d(eye) ***th***ehg d***oo***i (f)
23 tri ar hugain (m) tair ar hugain (f) tree arr hee-g(eye)n (m) t(eye)rr arr hee-g(eye)n (f)	**23** dau ddeg tri (m) dau ddeg tair (f) d(eye) ***th***ehg tree (m) d(eye) ***th***ehg t(eye)rr (f)
24 pedwar ar hugain (m) pedair ar hugain (f) ped-warr arr hee-g(eye)n (m) ped-(eye)rr arr hee-g(eye)n (f)	**24** dau ddeg pedwar (m) dau ddeg pedair (f) d(eye) ***th***ehg ped-warr (m) d(eye) ***th***ehg ped-(eye)rr (f)
25 pump ar hugain pimp arr hee-g(eye)n	**25** dau ddeg pump d(eye) ***th***ehg pimp
26 chwech ar hugain chwech arr hee-g(eye)n	**26** dau ddeg chwech d(eye) ***th***ehg chwech
27 saith ar hugain s(eye)th arr hee-g(eye)n	**27** dau ddeg saith d(eye) ***th***ehg s(eye)th
28 wyth ar hugain ***oo***ith arr hee-g(eye)n	**28** dau ddeg wyth d(eye) ***th***ehg ***oo***ith

Cardinal numbers

Traditional numerals that are mainly used (1) to tell the time, (2) to tell one's age	*The more usual way of counting for other purposes*
29 naw ar hugain now arr hee-g(eye)n	**29** dau ddeg naw d(eye) ***th***ehg now
30 deg ar hugain dehg arr hee-g(eye)n	**30** tri deg tree dehg
40 deugain deh-g(eye)n	**40** pedwar deg ped-warr dehg
50 deg a deugain / hanner cant dehg ah deh-g(eye)n / han-ner cant	**50** pum deg pim dehg
60 trigain tree-g(eye)n	**60** chwe deg chwe dehg
70 deg a thrigain dehg ah three-g(eye)n	**70** saith deg s(eye)th dehg
80 pedwar ugain ped-warr ee-g(eye)n	**80** wyth deg ***oo***ith dehg
90 deg a phedwar ugain dehg ah fed-warr ee-g(eye)n	**90** naw deg naw dehg
100 cant cant	**100** cant cant

Cardinal numbers

Traditional numerals that are mainly used (1) to tell the time, (2) to tell one's age	*The more usual way of counting for other purposes*
200 dau gant d(eye) gant	**200** dau gant d(eye) gant
300 tri chant tree chant	**300** tri chant tree chant
400 pedwar cant ped-warr cant	**400** pedwar cant ped-warr cant
500 pum cant pim cant	**500** pum cant pim cant
600 chwe chant chwe chant	**600** chwe chant chwe chant
700 saith cant s(eye)th cant	**700** saith cant s(eye)th cant
800 wyth cant ***oo***ith cant	**800** wyth cant ***oo***ith cant
900 naw cant now cant	**900** naw cant now cant
1000 mil meel	**1000** mil mil

Traditional numerals that are mainly used (1) to tell the time, (2) to tell one's age	*The more usual way of counting for other purposes*
2000 dwy fil d*oo*i veel	**2000** dwy fil d*oo*i vil
3000 tair mil t(eye)rr meel	**3000** tair mil t(eye)rr mil
4000 pedair mil ped-(eye)rr meel	**4000** pedair mil ped-(eye)rr mil
1000000 miliwn mil-y*oo*n	**1000000** miliwn mil-y*oo*n

Ordinal numbers

first
cynta'
kuhnt-a

second
ail
(eye)l

third
trydydd (m) trydedd (f)
truhd-i***th*** (m) truhd-e***th*** (f)

fourth
pedwerydd (m) pedwaredd (f)
ped-werr-i***th*** (m) ped-wa-rre***th*** (f)

fifth
pumed
pim-ed

tenth
degfed
deg-ved

Fractions and percentages

a half
hanner
han-nerr

a quarter
chwarter
chwarr-terr

a third
traean / un rhan o dair
tr(eye)an / een rhan o d(eye)rr

two thirds
dau draean / dwy ran o dair
d(eye) dr(eye)-an / d*oo*i ran o d(eye)rr

10 per cent
deg y cant
dehg uh kant

Days

Sunday
Dydd Sul
dee*th* seel

Monday
Dydd Llun
dee*th* lleen

Tuesday
Dydd Mawrth
dee*th* mowrrth

Wednesday
Dydd Mercher
dee*th* merr-cherr

Thursday
Dydd Iau
dee*th* y(eye)

Friday
Dydd Gwener
dee*th* gwen-err

Saturday
Dydd Sadwrn
dee*th* sad-*oo*rrn

Dates

on Friday
ar ddydd Gwener
arr *theeth* gwen-err

next Thursday
dydd Iau nesa'
dee*th* y(eye) ness-a

last Tuesday
dydd Mawrth diwetha'
dee***th*** mowrrth di-weth-a

yesterday
ddoe
thoy

today
heddiw
he***th***-y***oo***

tomorrow
'fory
vorr-i

in June
ym Mehefin
uhm me-hev-in

7th July / 7 July
seithfed Gorffennaf
s(eye)th-ved gorr-fen-av

next week
wythnos nesa'
ooith-noss ness-a

last month
mis diwetha'
meess di-weth-a

The seasons

spring
gwanwyn
gwan-win

summer
haf
hahv

autumn
hydre'
huh-dre

winter
gaea'
g(eye)-a

Times of the year

in spring
yn y gwanwyn
uhn uh gwan-win

in summer
yn yr haf
uhn uhrr hahv

in autumn
yn yr hydre'
uhn uhrr huh-dre

in winter
yn y gaea'
uhn uh g(eye)-a

Months

January
Ionawr
yon-owrr

February
Chwefror
chwe-vrorr

March
Mawrth
mowrrth

April
Ebrill
e-brill

May
Mai
m(eye)

June
Mehefin
me-hev-in

July
Gorffennaf
gorr-fen-av

August
Awst
owst

September
Medi
med-i

October
Hydref
huh-drev

November
Tachwedd
tach-we***th***

December
Rhagfyr
rhag-firr

Public holidays

New Year's Day
Dydd Calan
dee***th*** kal-an

Good Friday
Dydd Gwener y Groglith
dee***th*** gwen-err uh grog-lith

Easter Monday
Dydd Llun y Pasg
dee***th*** lleen uh pask

May Day (early May)
Calan Mai
kal-an m(eye)

Whit Monday (late)
Y Llungwyn
uh llin-gwin

August Bank Holiday (late)
Gŵyl Banc Awst
g***oo***il bank owst

Christmas Day
Dydd Nadolig
dee***th*** nad-ol-ig

Boxing Day
Gŵyl San Steffan
g***oo***eel san stef-an

Festivals

25 January
St Dwynwen's Day (the Welsh equivalent of St Valentine's Day)
Dydd Santes Dwynwen
dee***th*** san-tess d***oo***in-wen

1 March
St David's Day (the Patron Saint of Wales)
Dydd Gŵyl Ddewi
dee***th*** g***oo***il ***th***e-wi

End of May / Beginning of June
The League of Youth National Eisteddfod (the largest youth festival in Europe)
Eisteddfod Genedlaethol yr Urdd
(eye)s-te***th***-vod gen-ed-l(eye)th-ol uhrr irr***th***

July
The Royal Welsh Agricultural Show in Builth Wells
Sioe Amaethyddol Frenhinol Cymru yn Llanfair-ym-Muallt
shoy am-(eye)-thu***th***-ol vren-heen-ol kuhm-ri uhn llan-v(eye)rr–uhm-mee-allt

Llangollen International Eisteddfod (with around 3,000 competitors from all over the world)
Eisteddfod Ryngwladol Llangollen
(eye)s-te***th***-vod ruhng-wlad-ol llan-goll-en

Cnapan Folk Festival (the name Cnapan is derived from an old ball game popular in south-west Wales played on Sundays and feast days by men of neighbouring parishes)
Gŵyl Werin y Cnapan
g***oo***il wer-in uh k-nap-an

First week in August
The National Eisteddfod (the most important and biggest annual event held in Wales)
Yr Eisteddfod Genedlaethol
uhrr (eye)s-te***th***-fod gen-ed-l(eye)th-ol

16 September
Owain Glyndŵr's Day (Owain Glyndŵr *c.*1354–1416, a national hero and outstanding military leader who led a rebellion against English sovereignty over Wales)
Dydd Owain Glyndŵr
dee***th*** o-w(eye)n glin-doorr

11 December
Llewelyn II's Day (Llewelyn ap Gruffudd *c.*1225–1282, known as the last Prince of Wales, who was killed by invading English troops at Cilmeri, near Builth Wells)
Dydd Llywelyn yr Ail
dee***th*** lluh-wel-in uhrr (eye)l

Colours

beige
llwydfelyn
ll***oo***id-vel-in

black
du
dee

blue
glas
glahss

brown
brown
brown (as in own)

cream
hufen
hee-ven

fawn
melyn llwyd
mel-in ll***oo***id

gold
aur
(eye)rr

green
gwyrdd
gwirr***th***

grey
llwyd
ll*oo*id

mauve
porffor golau
porr-forr gol-(eye)

orange
oren
or-en

pink
pinc
pink

purple
porffor
porr-forr

red
coch
kohch

silver
arian
ar-yan

tan
melyn
mel-in

white
gwyn
gwin

yellow
melyn
mel-in

Common adjectives

bad
drwg
droog

beautiful
hardd
harr*th*

big
mawr
mowrr

cold
oer
oyrr

difficult
anodd
an-o*th*

easy
rhwydd / hawdd
rh*ooith* / how*th*

expensive
drud
dreed

fast
cyflym
kuh-vlim

good
da
dah

high
uchel
i-chel

hot
poeth
poyth

little
ychydig
uh-chuh-dig

long
hir
heerr

new
newydd
ne-wi***th***

old
hen
hehn

short
byr
birr

slow
araf
a-rav

small
bach
bahch

tall
tal
tal

ugly
hyll
hill

Signs and notices

Acommodation
Llety
llet-i

Allowed Only For . . .
Caniateir i . . . yn unig
kan-ya-t(eye)rr ee uhn een-ig

Ambulance
Ambiwlans
am-bi***oo***-lanss

Arrivals
Cyraeddiadau
kuhrr-(eye)***th***-yad-(eye)

Baggage
Bagiau
bag-y(eye)

Bed and breakfast
Gwely a brecwast
gwel-i a brek-wast

Beware of the dog
Gochelwch y ci
go-chel-***oo***ch uh kee

Car park
Maes parcio
m(eye)ss parrk-yo

Car park for visitors only
Maes parcio i ymwelwyr yn unig
m(eye)ss parrk-yo i uhm-wel-wirr
uhn een-ig

Cashier
Derbynnydd arian
derr-buhn-i***th*** ar-yan

Caution
Rhybudd
rhuh-bi*th*

Closed in the afternoon
Ar gau yn y prynhawn
arr g(eye) uhn uh prin-hown

Closed
Ar gau
arr g(eye)

Closing down sale
Sêl cau i lawr
sehl k(eye) i lowrr

Cold
Oer
oyrr

Communication cord (rail)
Cordyn cyswllt
korrd-in kuh-ss*oo*llt

Customs
Tollau
toll-(eye)

Cycle path
Llwybr beiciau
ll*oo*ib-rr b(eye)k-y(eye)

Danger of fire
Perygl tân
perr-ig-l tahn

Danger
Perygl
perr-ig-l

Departures
Ymadawiadau
uhm-ad-ow-yad-(eye)

Disabled
Anabl
an-ab-al

Diversion
Dargyfeiriad / Gwyriad
darr-guh-v(eye)rr-yad / g*oo*irr-yad

Do not lean out
Peidiwch â phwyso allan
p(eye)d-y*oo*ch a f*oo*iss-o all-an

Do not touch
Peidiwch â chyffwrdd
p(eye)d-y*oo*ch a chuh-f*oo*rr*th*

Down
I lawr
i lowrr

Drinking water
Dŵr yfed
doorr uh-ved

Fire doors
Drysau tân
druhs-(eye) tahn

Emergency exit
Allanfa argyfwng
all-an-va arr-guh-v*oo*ng

Emergency exit
Ffordd allan mewn argyfwng
forr*th* all-an me*oo*n arr-guh-v*oo*ng

Emergency lay-by
Cilfan argyfwng
kil-van arr-guh-v*oo*ng

Emergency
Argyfwng
arr-guh-v*oo*ng

Signs and notices

Employees only
Staff yn unig
staff uhn een-ig

Enquiries
Ymholiadau
uhm-hol-yad-(eye)

Entrance
Mynediad
muhn-ed-yad

Exit
Allan / Allanfa
all-an / all-an-va

Fire alarm
Larwm tân
larr-*oo*m tahn

Fire brigade
Brigâd dân
bri-gahd dahn

Fire escape
Dihangfa dân
di-hang-va dahn

Fire extinguisher
Diffoddwr tân
di-fo*th*-*oo*r tahn

Fire station
Gorsaf dân
gorr-sav dahn

First aid
Cymorth cyntaf
kuh-morrth kuhn-tav

Floods
Llifogydd
lli-vog-i*th*

Footpath only
Llwybr troed yn unig
ll*oo*ib-rr troyd uhn een-ig

For sale
Ar werth
arr werrth

For external use only
I'w ddefnyddio o'r tu allan yn unig
yoo thev-nuh*th*-yo orr tee all-an uhn een-ig

Free parking
Parcio di-dâl
parrk-yo di dahl

Full
Yn llawn
uhn llown

Garage
Modurdy
mo-dirr-di

General office
Swyddfa gyffredinol
s*oo*i*th*-va guh-fre-deen-ol

Gentlemen
Dynion
duhn-yon

Give Way
Arhoswch
arr-hoss-***oo***ch

Have you paid and displayed?
A ydych wedi talu ac arddangos?
ah uh-dich wed-i tal-i ak arr-***th***an-goss

Hospital
Ysbyty
uhs-buh-ti

Hot
Poeth
poyth

Hotel
Gwesty
gwest-i

Information
Gwybodaeth
gwi-bod-(eye)th

Keep clear
Cadwch yn glir
kad-***oo***ch uhn gleerr

Keep crossing clear
Cadwch y groesfan yn glir
kad-***oo***ch uh groyss-van uhn gleerr

Keep dogs on a lead
Cadwch gŵn ar dennyn
kad-***oo***ch goon arr den-in

Keep in low gear
Cadwch mewn gêr isel
kad-***oo***ch me***oo***n gehrr iss-el

Keep off the grass
Na cherddwch ar y glaswellt
nah cherr-th***oo***ch arr uh glas-wellt

Keep to the right
Cadwch i'r dde
kad-***oo***ch irr ***th***eh

Ladies
Merched
merr-ched

Library
Llyfrgell
lluhv-rr-gell

Lift
Lifft
lift

Litter
Ysbwriel
uhs-b***oo***rr-yel

Long-term parking
Parcio cyfnod hir
parrk-yo kuhv-nod heerr

Lost property office
Swyddfa eiddo coll
s***ooith***-va (eye)***th***-o koll

Low gear for 2.5 miles
Gêr isel am ddwy filltir a hanner
gehrr iss-el am ***thoo***i vill-tirr a han-ner

Main building
Prif adeilad
preev a-deh-lad

Signs and notices

Main entrance
Prif fynedfa
preev vuhn-ed-va

Moved to . . .
Wedi symud i . . .
wed-i suh-mid i

No admission charge
Dim tâl mynediad
dim tahl muhn-ed-yad

No dogs
Dim cŵn
dim koon

No entrance for vehicles
Dim mynediad i gerbydau
dim muhn-ed-yad i gerr-buh-d(eye)

No entry
Dim mynediad
dim muhn-ed-yad

No parking allowed
Ni chaniateir parcio
nee chan-yat-(eye)rr parrk-yo

No parking
Dim parcio
dim parrk-yo

No picture taking
Gwaherddir tynnu lluniau
gwa-herr-***th***irr tuhn-i llin-y(eye)

No rubbish
Dim ysbwriel
dim uhs-b***oo***rr-yel

No smoking
Dim ysmygu
dim uhs-muh-gi

No thoroughfare
Dim ffordd trwodd
dim forr***th*** tr***oo***-o***th***

No trespassing
Dim tresmasu
dim tres-mass-i

No unauthorised entrance
Dim mynediad heb awdurdod
dim muhn-ed-yad heb ow-dirr-dod

No way out
Dim ffordd allan
dim forr***th*** all-an

Occupied
Prysur
pruhss-irr

Office
Swyddfa
s***ooith***-va

One way
Unffordd
in-forr***th***

Open
Ar agor
arr ag-orr

Pay and display
Talu a dangos
tal-i a dan-goss

Parking for more than 30 minutes prohibited
Gwaherddir parcio am fwy na hanner awr
gwa-herr-***th***irr parrk-yo am f***oo***i nah han-ner owrr

Pay here
Talwch yma
tal-***oo***ch uh-ma

Please ring
Canwch y gloch
kan-***oo***ch uh glohch

Poison
Gwenwyn
gwen-win

Police
Heddlu
he***th***-li

Price list
Rhestr brisiau
rhest-rr brish-(eye)

Private road
Ffordd breifat
forr***th*** br(eye)v-at

Private
Preifat
pr(eye)-vat

Public conveniences
Cyfleusterau cyhoeddus
kuhv-le-ster-(eye) kuh-hoy***th***-iss

Public footpath
Llwybr cyhoeddus
ll***oo***ib-rr kuh-hoy***th***-iss

Pull
Tynnwch
tuhn-***oo***ch

Push bar to open
Gwthiwch y bar i agor
g***oo***th-y***oo***ch uh barr i ag-orr

Push
Gwthiwch
g***oo***th-y***oo***ch

Reception
Derbynfa
derr-buhn-va

Refectory
Ffreutur
freh-tirr

Reserved
Ar gadw
arr gad-***oo***

Ring
Canwch
kan-***oo***ch

Ring bell for attention
Canwch y gloch i gael sylw
kan-***oo***ch uh glohch i g(eye)l suh-l***oo***

Sale
sêl
sehl

School
Ysgol
uhs-gol

Signs and notices

Short-term parking
Parcio cyfnod byr
parrk-yo kuhv-nod birr

Shut the gate
Caewch y glwyd
k(eye)-*oo*ch uh gl*oo*id

Side entrance
Mynedfa o'r ochr
muhn-ed-va orr och-rr

Slow down now
Arafwch nawr
ar-av-*oo*ch nowrr

Smoking area
Rhan ysmygu
rhan uhs-muh-gi

Smoking compartment
Cerbyd ysmygu
kerr-bid uhs-muh-gi

Sold out
Wedi ei werthu allan
wed-i (eye) werrth-i all-an

Ticket office
Swyddfa docynnau
sooith-va dok-uhn-(eye)

Souvenirs
Cofroddion / swfenîrs
kov-ro*th*-yon / s*oo*-ven-eerrs

Special offer
Cynnig arbennig
kuhn-ig arr-ben-nig

Stop
Stopiwch
stop-y*oo*ch

Taxi
Tacsi
tak-si

Telephone
Teleffon
tel-e-fon

Timetable
Amserlen
am-serr-len

To Let / For Hire
Ar osod
arr oss-od

Toilets
Toiledau / (more familiarly) Tŷ bach
toy-led-(eye) / tee bahch

Travel Agency
Swyddfa deithio
sooith-va d(eye)th-yo

Up
I fyny
i vuhn-i

Vacant
Gwag
gwahg

Visitors' car park
Maes parcio ymwelwyr
m(eye)ss parrk-yo uhm-wel-wirr

Visitors
Ymwelwyr
uhm-wel-wirr

Waiting room
Ystafell aros
uh-stav-ell arr-oss

Way out
Ffordd allan
forr***th*** all-an

Welcome
Croeso
kroy-so

In An Emergency

If you witness an accident or crime, you should phone the emergency services on 999. The call is free from anywhere, including public phone boxes. Should you be involved in an incident that requires reporting, you should go to the local police station. The 999 number should be used in emergencies only. Non-EU visitors who become ill while in Wales, as in any other part of the UK, are only eligible for free emergency treatment in the Accident and Emergency (A & E) departments of NHS hospitals. If you are admitted to hospital as an inpatient, even from an A & E department, or referred to an outpatient clinic, you will be asked to pay unless you are a national of the European Economic Area.

Pharmacies generally have the same opening times as shops. In major towns and cities some may remain open until about 22.00. Lists of late-night pharmacies are published in local newspapers.

Call — the fire brigade
Galwch — y frigâd dân
gal-*oo*ch — uh vri-gahd dahn

— the police
— yr heddlu
— uhrr he*th*-li

— an ambulance
— yr ambiwlans
— uhrr am-bi-*oo*-lanss

Get a doctor
Ewch i nôl meddyg / doctor
e*oo*ch i nohl me*th*-ig / dok-torr

There is a fire
Tân
tahn

Where is the police station?
Ble mae gorsaf yr heddlu?
ble m(eye) gorr-sav uhrr he*th*-li

SELECT BIBLIOGRAPHY

John Aitchison and Harold Carter, *A Geography of the Welsh Language 1961–1991* (Cardiff, 1994)

John Aitchison and Harold Carter, *The Welsh Language 1961–1981: An Interpretative Atlas* (Cardiff, 1985)

John Aitchison and Harold Carter, *Language, Economy and Society: The Changing Fortunes of the Welsh Language in the Twentieth Century* (Cardiff, 2000)

Colin Baker and Sylvia Prys Jones, *Encyclopaedia of Bilingualism and Bilingual Education* (Clevedon, 1998)

Martin J Ball and James Fife (eds.), *The Celtic Languages* (London, 1993)

Denis Balsom (ed.), *HTV Wales Yearbook 2000* (Cardiff, 2001)

David Cole (ed.), *The New Wales* (Cardiff, 1990)

Janet Davies, *The Welsh Language* (Cardiff, 1993)

John Davies, *A History of Wales* (London, 1993)

D Gareth Evans, *A History of Wales 1906–2000* (Cardiff, 2000)

Christopher Harris and Richard Startup, *The Church in Wales: The Sociology of a Traditional Institution* (Cardiff, 1999)

Trevor Herbert and Gareth Elwyn Jones (eds.), *Wales 1880–1914* (Cardiff, 1988)

Trevor Herbert and Gareth Elwyn Jones (eds.), *Post-War Wales* (Cardiff, 1995)

Ian Hume and W T R Pryce (eds.), *The Welsh and their Country* (Llandysul, 1986)

Geraint H Jenkins and Mari A Williams (eds.), *'Let's Do Our Best for the Ancient Tongue': The Welsh Language in the Twentieth Century* (Cardiff, 2000)

Philip Jenkins, *A History of Modern Wales 1536–1990* (London, 1992)

Gareth Elwyn Jones, *Modern Wales: A Concise History* (Cambridge, 1994)

D Densil Morgan, *The Span of the Cross; Christian Religion and Society in Wales 1914–2000* (Cardiff, 1999)

Kenneth O Morgan, *Rebirth of a Nation: Wales 1880–1980* (Oxford, 1981)

Kenneth O Morgan, *Modern Wales: Politics, Places and People* (Cardiff, 1995)

Meic Stephens (ed.), *The New Companion to the Literature of Wales* (Cardiff, 1998)

Glanmor Williams, *The Welsh and their Religion* (Cardiff, 1991) Gwyn A Williams, *When Was Wales? A History of the Welsh* (London, 1985)

ACKNOWLEDGEMENTS

I wish to acknowledge with gratitude the assistance and guidance given by the following during the writing of this book:

BBC
Countryside Council for Wales
Plaid Cymru – The Party of Wales
S4C
Sports Council for Wales
Wales Tourist Board
Welsh Development Agency
Welsh Language Board

A sincere debt of gratitude is owed to Dr Rhisiart Hincks and Ms Rose Jarmal whose generous assistance I have relied on to get this book published within the confines of the dates given by the publishers. I owe a special debt also to the late Mr T J L Edwards, Miss Megan Jenkins and Mr Arwyn Edwards who have assisted in many ways over the years.

D Islwyn Edwards